The Prentice-Hall Series in Marketing

PHILIP KOTLER, Series Editor

Abell/Hammond	*Strategic Market Planning*
Green/Tull	*Research for Marketing Decisions,* 4th ed.
Kleppner	*Advertising Procedure,* 7th ed.
Kotler	*Marketing Management,* 4th ed.
Kotler	*Marketing for Nonprofit Organizations,* 2nd ed.
Kotler	*Principles of Marketing*
Myers/Massy/Greyser	*Marketing Research and Knowledge Development*
Stern/El-Ansary	*Marketing Channels,* 2nd ed.
Urban/Hauser	*Design and Marketing of New Products*

PRENTICE-HALL INTERNATIONAL SERIES IN MANAGEMENT

SECOND EDITION

MARKETING
CHANNELS

LOUIS W. STERN

A. Montgomery Ward Professor of Marketing
Northwestern University

ADEL I. EL-ANSARY

Professor of Business Administration
Marketing Faculty Program Director
The George Washington University

PRENTICE-HALL, INC., *Englewood Cliffs, New Jersey 07632*

Library of Congress Cataloging in Publication Data

STERN, LOUIS W. (date)
  Marketing channels.

  (Prentice-Hall series in marketing)
  Includes bibliographical references and
indexes.
  1. Marketing, channels. I. Ansary, Adel I.
II. Title. III. Series.
HF5415.129.S75 1981   658.8′4   81-19217
ISBN 0-13-557173-1   AACR2

Editorial/production supervision and interior design by Maureen Wilson
Cover design by Tony Ferrara Studio
Manufacturing buyer: Ed O'Dougherty

Printed in the United States of America

10 9 8 7 6 5

ISBN 0-13-557173-1

PRENTICE-HALL INTERNATIONAL, INC., *London*
PRENTICE-HALL OF AUSTRALIA PTY. LIMITED, *Sydney*
PRENTICE-HALL OF CANADA, LTD., *Toronto*
PRENTICE-HALL OF INDIA PRIVATE LIMITED, *New Delhi*
PRENTICE-HALL OF JAPAN, INC., *Tokyo*
PRENTICE-HALL OF SOUTHEAST ASIA PTE. LTD., *Singapore*
WHITEHALL BOOKS LIMITED, *Wellington, New Zealand*

To
RUTH
and
NAWAL
with love

Contents

ELEVEN

PART FOUR

CHANNEL MANAGEMENT IN OTHER CONTEXTS

TWELVE

THIRTEEN

Preface

This edition of *Marketing Channels* adopts a *managerial* frame of reference. Emphasis is on how to *plan, organize,* and *control* the relationships among the institutions and agencies involved in the process of making certain that products and services are available for consumption by industrial, commercial, and household consumers. The end result of effective marketing channel management is the assurance of adequate levels of time, place, and possession utilities in all items of value to consumers. Therefore, the focus of the text is on channel *performance*.

Channel members can achieve high yield performance primarily through their demand stimulation and delivery activities. But performance requirements at one level of the marketing channel imply performance requirements and expectations at other levels. Retailers, for example, often measure their productivity by employing such criteria as sales per square foot, sales per employee, and sales per transaction. Generation of a high level of sales per square foot may necessitate heavy advertising by manufacturers and the maintenance of high inventory levels by wholesalers. These large promotion and storage burdens may, in turn, reduce the return on investment available to manufacturers and wholesalers. The interface among the various performance requirements, policies, and practices at different levels of marketing channels dictate the need for systemwide communication and coordination.

While the major thrust of the text is centered on developing means for securing systemwide coordination and, thereby, satisfactory marketing channel performance, we have spent the first two Parts of the text laying the groundwork for the managerial processes introduced later. Thus, Part I explores theories that describe why channels have emerged and why they assume the various structures that they do. It provides an essential backdrop to any discussion of channel management. Introduced in Part I are such concepts as service output levels and marketing flows on which we rely heavily in the remainder of the book. Part II is devoted to a strategic analysis of retailing, wholesaling, and physical distribution management. Because retailers, wholesalers, and logistic institutions comprise some of the foremost "actors" in channel networks, we believe that it is imperative that the reader have more than a nodding acquaintance with their orientations so that when the discussion turns to the question of interrelationships among channel members, everyone can be on an equal footing relative to the degree of knowledge about how the "actors" operate. We have not devoted a separate chapter to manufacturers because we assume that most readers have some knowledge of how manufacturers market their products, especially via previous course work or readings in marketing management.

Part III comprises the "core" of the text. It contains seven chapters in total. Chapter 5, the first chapter in Part III, deals with the planning and designing of channels. Chapter 6 focuses on how to organize and coordinate channel member behavior generally. Chapter 7 provides examples of specific ways in which channels have been organized, building on the principles laid out in Chapters 1 and 6. Chapter 8 indicates the various constraints present in federal U. S. law on the coordination and control of channel activities. Chapter 9 examines channel management strategies practiced by institutions located on different levels in the channel. The specific focus is on the question of channel leadership and a discussion of which institutions are likely to be in the best positions to allocate resources within channels. In Chapter 10, we examine communications problems and the development of information systems, given the critical nature of effective communications within channels. The final chapter in Part III, Chapter 11, is devoted to an assessment of the performance of channels and the institutions comprising them. It incorporates a broad, social viewpoint, but its main focus, like the previous chapters, is on managerial issues in marketing channels. It is in this chapter that instruments for monitoring performance—such as the strategic profit model, the channel audit, and distribution cost analysis—are described.

Part IV of the text deals with channel management in other contexts, i.e., in the international arena and in service industries. Exploring marketing channels in other countries enriches the analysis. It underscores the generalizability of channel management processes while recognizing the importance of cultural factors in adjusting the process. Because services constitute over 60 percent of the GNP in the U.S. and because the marketing of services is not always clearly understood, the final chapter in the text looks at marketing channels in the service sector. As with the international arena, the channel management process appears to be generic but in need of adjustments from time to time because of the significant nuances apparent in the marketing of services.

Because case analysis is frequently used as a pedagogical tool in courses dealing with marketing channels, we have included at the close of this preface a list of over 80 cases of varying length and orientation suitable for use with this text. The list has been keyed to the four separate parts of the text described above.

Although this edition bears a resemblance to the first edition, a great deal has been changed. The first chapter is a much revised version of the original Chapter 5 ("Channel Structure and Institutional Change"). We made the switch because a number of people informed us that the original Chapter 5 provided an excellent overview explaining why channels emerge and are structured as they are and that the original Chapter 1 ("Marketing Channels as Interorganization Systems") was just too difficult, in terms of its content, to be an effective leadoff. Chapter 2 on retailing has been totally rewritten. The emphasis has been placed on strategy. The chapter has been shortened, and most of the complex and/or mechanistic material of the original (e.g., the choice models and the merchandise budgeting procedures) has been placed in the appendix. Chapter 3 on wholesaling also has a much more strategic overtone. It has a great deal of new material, including a new, detailed section evaluating wholesalers as potential channel members. Chapter 4 has been updated and shortened. The complex appendix on warehousing location models has been eliminated and replaced by the material on forecasting that appeared in the first edition.

Individuals very familiar with the first edition will recognize Chapter 5 as the original Chapter 9 ("Marketing Channel Organization and Design: Policies"). A significant amount of new material, including many more examples, has been added, and the emphasis has been placed on how to plan and design a channel network. Chapter 6 is the old Chapter 7 ("The Interorganization Management of Marketing Channels: An Overview"). The material has been organized so that it conforms to a process for coordinating channel activities. It is much more managerially focused, although the basic theoretical framework remains intact. It also incorporates some of the material from the original Chapter 1 ("Marketing Channels as Interorganization Systems"). Chapter 7 is the old Chapter 10 ("Channel Organization and Design: Vertical Marketing Systems"). It logically follows the theoretical framework laid out in Chapter 6 and draws heavily upon it. Chapter 8 is the old Chapter 8 ("Legal Constraints . . ."), but it has been updated. Of special concern is a discussion of the importance to marketing channel management of the *Continental TV, Inc., et al. v. GTE Sylvania, Inc.,* decision. Chapter 9 is the original Chapter 11 ("Channel Management by Channel Participants"). It has been improved considerably by updating research evidence and by incorporating leadership frameworks at the outset of the discussion. Chapter 12 ("Channel Communications and Information Systems") from the first edition has become Chapter 10 in the new edition. We have, however, moved the discussion of distribution cost accounting to the chapter on performance (Chapter 11). In fact, the performance chapter (which was originally Chapter 6, entitled "Assessing the Performance of Channel Institutions and Structures") has been substantially updated and reorganized. It provides an assessment of performance as well as mechanisms by which performance might be evaluated.

The last two chapters of this edition (Chapters 12 and 13) are the old Chapters 13 ("International Marketing Channels") and 14 ("Marketing Channels for Services"). Although they have been updated and some new material has been added, they are basically the same as the original chapters. In all, there is one less chapter in the second edition than there was in the first.

ACKNOWLEDGMENTS   There are three sets of individuals who have deeply influenced the structure and content of this book. Although there is some overlap in the sets, one group has operated primarily in support and encouragement of the first author, another has aided the second author, and the third has been important to both authors.

The first author is deeply indebted to his marvelous colleagues at Northwestern University for their stimulation and interest. Being in the scholarly but warm and friendly atmosphere provided by them has been a source of considerable inspiration and pleasure. Most particularly, he is thankful and appreciative for the contributions to his thinking made by the doctoral students he has come in contact with over the years. Although they are too numerous to mention here by name, special thanks for their unique contributions to this and the previous edition of this text must go to Lynn W. Phillips, Torger Reve, Ravi Singh, Robert Becker, and C. M. Sashi. And the patience, pleasantness, thoroughness, and speed of Marion Davis, Peggy Ruhl, and most especially, Phyllis Van Hooser in typing the manuscript were significant factors in its preparation. All of these people, and many more, are owed a great deal for their contributions. Deep and affectionate appreciation go to his family for their continuous and unwavering advocacy.

The second author would like to acknowledge the encouragement and support of his colleagues at The George Washington University. Special thanks go to Chairman Ben Burdetsky, Robert Dyer, Salvatore Divita, and Dean Norma M. Loeser. This book could not have been possible without the inspiring work and contributions of a number of marketing scholars. Many thanks to all, particularly those who have been personally supportive and encouraging over a number of years. A special debt is owed to William R. Davidson, Bert C. McCammon, Jr., and Robert F. Lusch. The contributions of Mustafa Razian and others to the first edition have not been forgotten. The second edition would not have been possible without the capable research, typing, and editorial assistance of Elizabeth MacKillop. Her dedication, attention to detail, and patience could not have been surpassed. Special thanks to Anna Gunnarsson, who collected data from a number of federal agencies and associations. The long hours and support she provided toward the conclusion of the project when Elizabeth MacKillop became suddenly ill will not be forgotten. It is with deep affection that the support, encouragement, and love of his wife, Nawal, is acknowledged. The exciting personal growth and excellent academic performance of his son, Waleed, have been inspirational. The deep affection, artistic touches, and the prospects of a bright future of his son, Tarik, have provided the source of renewed energy and enthusiasm at difficult times.

Finally, both authors owe a great deal to Orville Walker, Robert Lusch, Brian Harris, James R. Brown, and John Nevin, who reviewed either one or both editions of the text. We are especially indebted to the large number of authors whose work we cite throughout the text. Without their efforts, we could not have written this book.

LIST OF CASES KEYED TO THE TEXT Listed below are a number of recommended cases with which the authors are familiar. Many of the cases come from the published casebooks at the end of this list. When individual cases rather than an entire book are used, users of the cases from casebooks should seek appropriate permissions and consent according to copyright laws. Where cases are available from the Intercollegiate Case Clearinghouse (ICH), the only reference given is the ICH number. These latter cases may be ordered from ICH by writing to the Intercollegiate Case Clearinghouse, c/o Harvard University, Graduate School of Business Administration, Soldiers Field, Boston, Mass. 02163.

Part I. The Emergence of Marketing Channels

- The Bonnie Norman Corporation ICH 9-573-013. Private label vs. branded production in the garment industry.
- Champions of Breakfast in Adler, Robinson, and Carlson, pp. 301-312. Formulation of a public relations program for the cereal industry.
- The Garfield Tire Company ICH 9-511-052. Which retail outlets to cultivate for the marketing of replacement passenger tires.
- Grantree Furniture Rental (B) in Davis, Boyd, and Webster, pp. 363-373. Adjusting channel structure and strategy of a changing environment.
- The Hindman Stores in DeLozier and Woodside, pp. 365-376. The addition of a customer service and consideration of who is going to perform it.
- Regulus Clock Company (A) ICH 9-506-081. Selection of distribution channels to reach a variety of retail outlets.
- The Sherwin-Williams Company ICH 9-576-207, Rev. 10/76. Determining which type of retail outlet is best for the sale of home decorating items.*
- Thetford Corporation (A) ICH 9-574-030, Rev. 8/74. How to reach the recreational vehicle market regarding the sale of portable toilets.

Part II. Components of Marketing Channels

- Ace Supermarkets, Inc. (B) ICH 9-507-062. Should a retail cooperative admit a new member?
- Affiliated Druggists ICH 9-574-854. The formation of a cooperative and the wholesaler's role.

*Cases for which industry and/or teacher's notes are available from Intercollegiate Case Clearinghouse.

- The Belfast and Moosehead Lake Railroad in Jain and Mather, pp. 233–244. Physical distribution strategy and the regulatory environment.
- The Cleveland Oil and Gas Company in Jain and Mather, pp. 261–273. Evaluation of an inventory control system.
- Crinshaw Company in Greer, pp. 151–156. An evaluation of retailing strategy.
- Federal Express (A) ICH 9–577–042, Rev. 9/78. Marketing an innovative delivery service.
- Fisher-Price Toys, Inc., ICH 14M61. Selecting strategies for motivating wholesalers and servicing retailers in a competitive environment.*
- Gladstone Industries, Inc., in Greer, pp. 160–162. Consideration of physical distribution decisions, particularly location.
- The Handyman ICH 9–595–196, Rev. 7/79. A major home improvement chain faces difficulties in being profitable in Chicago.
- Hill Industrial Supply ICH 9–573–693. A wholesaler is deciding whether to enter into systems selling arrangements.*
- Hills Department Stores ICH 9–577–024, Rev. 3/77. A discount department store is considering altering its prototype store.
- T. C. Javitts Company in Jain and Mather, pp. 245–260. Shopping center location and layout.
- Kibarian Brothers Oriental Rugs in Greer, pp. 341–347. Advising the brothers on retailing strategy involving relations with suppliers and target markets.
- Landau & Heyman, Inc. ICH 9–579–089, Rev. 3/79. A shopping center developer ponders the mix of stores for inclusion in a planned shopping center.
- Macy's in Greer, pp. 323–335. An evaluation of the strategy of a major retailer.
- Mason's Hardware in DeLozier and Woodside, pp. 330–338. Retail store location.
- Prime Cut Steakhouses in Dalrymple and Parsons, pp. 447–481. Site selection for a regional chain of steakhouse restaurants.
- Ryder System, Inc. ICH 9–510–052. The marketing of leased equipment to industrial accounts.
- Selmer's Department Store in DeLozier and Woodside, pp. 339–364. Store location decision.
- Steinberg's Limited ICH 9–572–066. Consideration of the expansion of a supermarket chain in France.
- Stonyridge Merchants' Association in Greer, pp. 156–159. An evaluation of retailing strategy.
- Westwood Furniture ICH 9–572–069. A warehouse furniture operation considers expansion.*

*Cases for which industry and/or teacher's notes are available from Intercollegiate Case Clearinghouse.

Part III. Channel Management:
Planning, Coordinating, Organizing, and Controlling

- Alpine Products, Inc. in Tootelian, Gaedeke, and Thompson, pp. 291–297. Channel organization decisions for a sporting goods manufacturer and implications for channel coordination.
- Amway Corporation in DeLozier and Woodside, pp. 376–388. An evaluation of a direct marketing system.
- Belmont Paint Corporation ICH 9–571–048, Rev. 3/74. The use of franchising to supplement a branch network.
- The Brockman Company, Inc. in DeLozier and Woodside, pp. 407–418. An evaluation of the performance of a wholesaling company in health care products field.
- Bulova Watch Company, Inc. (C) 9–513–073, Rev. 6/75. The need to assess a change in strategy due to competition from low-priced watches.
- Buttoneer ICH 9–513–154, Rev. 6/75. Marketing strategy for a notions product which is ready for national introduction.
- Carapace, Inc. in Kerin and Peterson, pp. 351–359. A producer of plastic bandages faced with a decision to select distributors.
- The Catawba Electric Motor Company in Weilbacher, pp. 327–353. Should Catawba rely solely on its own sales organization to reach target markets?
- Cessna Aircraft Company (C) ICH 9–514–051. The motivation and realignment of a dealer network.
- Cessna Aircraft Company: The Citation in Kerin and Peterson, pp. 386–396. Cessna is considering new channel organization and policies for the Citation.
- The Diego Martino Cigar Company in Weilbacher, pp. 290–311. Distribution channel planning and policies for a cigar manufacturer.
- Dirt Road, Inc. in Davis, pp. 429–438. A small firm manufacturing folding furniture is reconsidering its distribution strategy.
- Electronic Control, Inc. in Jain and Mather, pp. 217–231. Distribution planning and organization.
- Estes Industries (C) 9–576–714, Rev. 11/79. Reevaluation of channel policy in the face of a new product introduction.
- Estes Rockets in Dalrymple and Parsons, pp. 458–467. Channel planning and organization decisions for a model rockets manufacturer.
- Ever Clean Manufacturers in Greer, pp. 148–151. An examination of channel policies, particularly credit extension.
- FTC v. Levi Strauss ICH 9–579–081, Rev. 11/78. A major corporation is charged with violating the antitrust laws.
- GTE Sylvania ICH 9–578–155. The Supreme Court's decision overturning the Schwinn decision regarding territorial and customer restrictions.
- Gulf Oil Separation in Adler, Robinson, and Carlson, pp. 313–328. Responding to a lawsuit from a disgruntled franchisee.

- Toron Corporation in Jain and Mather, pp. 209–215. Channel planning and organization.
- U.S. Pioneer Electronics Corporation ICH 9-579-079. The management of conflict in the marketing channels for high fidelity equipment.
- Volkswagen of America, Inc. ICH 9-509-094, Rev. 2/74. Selecting new dealers.
- Yates Manufacturing Company in K. Davis, pp. 438–442. A manufacturer of a broad line of hand drills, large drilling machines, and air compressors is considering channel planning and organization decisions.

Part IV. Channel Management in Other Contexts

- Alaska Native Arts and Crafts Cooperative, Inc. in Tootelian, Gaedeke, and Thompson, pp. 307–313. A nonprofit cooperative organization considering the distribution of native arts and crafts through retail stores.
- Caterpillar Towmotor ICH 9-513-093. Assessment of alternative methods of distribution for a new acquisition in Europe.
- Choufont-Salva, Inc. ICH 9-513-009. Developing a marketing plan for an oral contraceptive in the Philippines.
- Colon Free Trade Zone in Greer, pp. 162–171. An evaluation of the physical distribution advantages and disadvantages of this trade zone for international marketers; an analysis of zone marketing strategy to reach target users.
- Department of the Treasury: Reissue of the $2 Bill (A) ICH 9-576-102, Rev. 5/78. The reintroduction and redistribution of an old product.
- Educational Tools in Dalrymple and Parsons, pp. 467–476, and in Bernhardt and Kinnear, pp. 336–348. Considering entry into the Japanese market and evaluating distribution alternatives.
- North Star Shipping Company in Davis, Boyd, and Webster, pp. 421–431. Consideration of a new channel organization and dealing with potential conflict and coordination problems resulting from the new organization.
- Northrop Corporation in Adler, Robinson, and Carlson, pp. 329–351. Northrop is considering a policy on international sales commissions.
- Premier Title Insurance Company in Tootelian, Gaedeke, and Thompson, pp. 284–290. Consideration of new services and new markets for a franchise dry cleaning company.
- Samahaiku Electronics in Bernhardt and Kinnear, pp. 289–296. A Japanese television producer is considering alternative distribution channels in U.S. markets.
- Smith's Potato Crisps Ltd. ICH 9-513-099. The marketing of snack items in the U.K. and other Western European countries.
- Steinberg's Limited ICH 9-572-066. Consideration of the expansion of a supermarket chain in France.
- A. B. Volvo in Davis, Boyd, and Webster, pp. 405–420. Integrating distribu-

tion policy decisions in European markets for Volvo and its newly acquired DAF Dutch automobile manufacturer.

Casebooks Containing
Marketing Channels Cases

ADLER, ROY D., LARRY M. ROBINSON, and JAN E. CARLSON. *Marketing and Society.* Englewood Cliffs, NJ: Prentice-Hall, Inc., 1981.

BERNHARDT, KENNETH L., and THOMAS C. KINNEAR. *Cases in Marketing Management,* revised ed. Dallas, TX: Business Publications, Inc., 1981.

DALRYMPLE, DOUGLAS J., and LEONARD J. PARSONS. *Marketing Management: Text and Cases,* 2nd ed. New York: John Wiley and Sons, 1980.

DAVIS, KENNETH R. *Marketing Management,* 4th ed. New York: Ronald Press, 1981.

DAVIS, ROBERT T., HARPER W. BOYD, and FREDERICK E. WEBSTER, JR. *Marketing Management Casebook,* 3rd ed. Homewood, IL: Richard D. Irwin, Inc., 1980.

DELOZIER, WAYNE A., and ARCH WOODSIDE. *Marketing Management Strategies and Cases.* Columbus, OH: Merrill Publishing Company, 1978.

FOSTER, J. ROBERT, ARCH G. WOODSIDE, and J. TAYLOR SIMS. *Cases in Marketing Channel Strategy.* New York: Harper & Row, 1977.

GREER, THOMAS V. *Cases in Marketing.* New York: Macmillan Publishing Co., 1979.

JAIN, SUBHASH C., and IGBAL MATHER. *Cases in Marketing Management.* Columbus, OH: Grid Publishing, Inc., 1978.

KERIN, ROGER A., and ROBERT A. PETERSON. *Strategic Marketing Problems,* 2nd ed. Boston, MA: Allyn and Bacon, 1981.

TOOTELIAN, DENNIS H., RALPH M. GAEDEKE, and LEETE A. THOMPSON (eds.). *Marketing Management: Cases and Readings.* Santa Monica, CA: Goodyear Publishing Co., 1980.

WEILBACHER, WILLIAM M. *Marketing Management Cases.* New York: Macmillan Publishing Co., 1980.

PART ONE

THE EMERGENCE
OF
MARKETING CHANNELS

When a consumer walks into a local furniture store to purchase a new sofa, armchair, or bedroom suite, it is unlikely that he or she has been forewarned, prior to his/her visit, that delivery on the furniture will take an average of ten weeks and, in not atypical cases, as much as four to five months. If the consumer were to seek out a reason as to why this lengthy waiting time exists, the response would be very predictable. Depending upon to whom in the marketing channel the question was directed, the answer would likely entail placing the blame for delayed delivery on the "other parties" involved in the product's distribution. In actuality, the answer is relatively complex, and at its core are systemic issues relating to the management of the distribution channels for household furniture.[1] Specifically, furniture manufacturers face strained production capability due to (1) increases in demand that are not accurately projected, (2) long lead times (two to six months) needed to obtain upholstery materials from fabric mills, and (3) labor shortages in North Carolina and Virginia, where many of the major furniture production centers are located. On the other hand, the traditional furniture retailer believes that the manufacturer is giving preferential treatment to the large furniture "warehouse" dealers, such as Levitz and Wickes, and therefore indirectly is discriminating against his customers. Differences in treatment would not be unjustified, however, because the traditional furniture retailer has generally shied away from assuming any risk or financial burden associated with holding inventory. Rather, he places orders with the manufacturers when he has an order in hand from his customer.

The scenario in the furniture industry is reenacted countless times in different settings every day. Distribution channels for the delivery of such essentials as health

[1] Stanley H. Slom, "Need Some Furniture? Better Plan Sitting on the Floor Awhile," *Wall Street Journal,* Vol. 50, No. 87 (November 2, 1972), p. 1.

services, automobiles, food, governmental services (e.g., garbage collection, mass transit), and financial services (e.g., mortgage loans) are often managed ineffectively and inefficiently, a situation resulting in not only an enormous loss of resources but in a disgruntled and disaffected consumer who seemingly is caught up and put upon by forces which he/she cannot control. The solution lies, it appears, not only in adopting consumer-oriented objectives and programs but in managing the systems responsible for the delivery of the objectives and programs in a more satisfactory manner.

The need for effective distribution systems management is especially crucial as economies move into periods of stunted growth. As new market opportunities decrease for many industries, numerous companies shift their marketing strategies away from expanding total market demand and toward building market share within their existing markets.[2] Such a situation forces, in turn, a reassessment of many corporate functions, particularly distribution. Although marketing strategies and tactics have traditionally been developed by management on the basis of a study of ultimate consumer or end-user needs, environmental contingencies are likely to compel deeper attention to distribution problems. For example, it has been predicted that, in periods of low economic growth, there is likely to be "a shift away from what the consumer wants and more critical emphasis on establishing a relationship with the jobber, wholesaler, and retailer . . . Instead of asking what kind of toothbrushes the consumer wants, one must go to Kresge, Sears, and the drug stores and find out what kind of packaging, display cases, delivery, pay terms, and buying incentives they need."[3]

Managerial analyses of marketing channels are required to find solutions to these and other types of problems. These analyses dissect and examine the past, present, and prospective efforts that channel members make to organize, coordinate, influence, direct, and control relationships within the entire channel. Specifically, channel management seeks to improve overall distribution system performance through forging more effective and efficient linkages among the organizations responsible for the delivery of a particular product or service to its predetermined points of consumption. The linkages or relationships among channel members are, however, greatly influenced by the basic structure of the channel itself. That is, it is important to know why certain types of structures emerge before we can turn to an in-depth analysis of channel member relations, because the relations take place within a specific structure, not apart from it. Therefore, Part I of this text deals with the emergence of channel structures.

[2] "Marketing When the Growth Slows," *Business Week* (April 14, 1975), pp. 44–50.
[3] *Ibid.,* p. 48.

ONE

Marketing Channels: Structure and Functions

Consumers are aware that literally thousands of goods and services are available through a very large number of diverse retail outlets. What consumers may not be as well aware of is the fact that the *channel structure,* or the set of institutions, agencies, and establishments through which the product must move to get to them, can be amazingly complex. To illustrate, the marketing channel structure for Clairol, Inc., a major marketer of personal care items, is shown in Fig. 1–1. Clairol's channel structure is fairly typical of its industry. It includes Clairol's own *internal* marketing organization (e.g., district sales managers) and independent *external* organizations, (e.g., distributors and retailers). Some of the members of the channel are large organizations, such as chain retail stores and wholesale distributors who carry a number of rival brands; others are small one-or-two-person operations.[1] The success of Clairol's marketing effort depends to a large extent upon the coordination of the effort of the internal and external marketing organizations which comprise the structure of its channel.

Usually, combinations of institutions specializing in manufacturing, wholesaling, retailing, and many other areas join forces in marketing channel arrangements to make possible the delivery of goods to industrial users or customers and to final consumers. The same is true for the marketing of services. For example, in health care delivery, hospitals, ambulance services, physicians, laboratories, insurance companies, and drug stores combine efforts in an organized channel arrangement to ensure the delivery of a critical service. All these institutions depend on each other to cater effectively to consumer demand. Therefore, marketing channels can be viewed as *sets of interdependent organizations involved in the process of making*

[1] Benson P. Shapiro, "Improve Distribution with Your Promotional Mix," *Harvard Business Review* (March-April 1977), p. 116.

FIGURE 1–1
Clairol's Appliance Division Distribution System

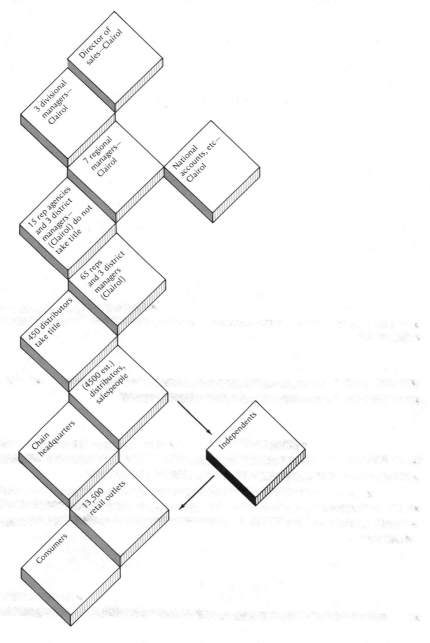

Source: Benson P. Shapiro, "Improve Distribution with your Promotional Mix," *Harvard Business Review* (March–April 1977), p. 11.

a product or service available for use or consumption. From the outset, it should be recognized that not only do marketing channels *satisfy demand* by supplying goods and services at the right place, quantity, quality, and price, but they also *stimulate demand* through the promotional activities of the units (e.g., retailers, manufacturers' representatives, sales offices, wholesalers, etc.) comprising them. Therefore, the channel should be viewed as an orchestrated network that creates value for the user or consumer through the generation of form, possession, time, and place utilities.[2]

A major focus of marketing channel management is on *delivery*. It is only through distribution that public and private goods[3] can be made available for consumption. Producers of such goods (including manufacturers of industrial and consumer goods, legislators framing laws, educational administrators conceiving new means for achieving quality education, and insurance companies developing unique health insurance coverage, among many others) are individually capable of generating only form or structural utility for their "products." They can organize their production capabilities in such a way that the products that they have developed can, in fact, be seen, analyzed, debated, and, by a select few perhaps, digested. But the actual large-scale delivery of the products to the consuming public demands different types of efforts which create time, place, and possession utilities. In other words, the consumer cannot obtain a finished product unless the product is transported to where he[4] can gain access to it, stored until he is ready for it, and eventually exchanged for money or other goods or services so that he can gain possession of it. In fact, the four types of utility (form, time, place, and possession) are inseparable; there can be no "complete" product without incorporating all four into any given object, idea, or service.

THE EMERGENCE OF MARKETING CHANNEL STRUCTURES

In order to provide an appropriate base for understanding the marketing channel, it is important to understand at the outset the underlying reasons for the emergence of channel structures. Here, emphasis is placed on the economic rationale for the existence of channels, because economic reasons are the foremost determinants of channel structures. Later, it is possible to introduce other determinants, including key technological, political, and social factors, and to examine how these factors influence the makeup of channel systems.

The emergence and arrangement of the wide variety of distribution-oriented institutions and agencies, typically called *intermediaries* because they stand in be-

---

[2] Robert F. Lusch, "Erase Distribution Channel from Your Vocabulary and Add Marketing Channels," *Marketing News* (July 27, 1979), p. 12.

[3] The term "goods" is being used in its broadest sense to encompass all things of value. For an enlightening discussion of the distinction between public and private goods (broadly defined), see Mancur Olson, Jr., *The Logic of Collective Action* (Cambridge, Mass.: Harvard University Press, 1965).

[4] We of course acknowledge the equal status of the female. However, we continue to use the traditional "he" to avoid unwieldy construction.

tween production, on the one hand, and consumption on the other, can be explained in terms of four logically related steps in an economic process, as follows:[5]

1. Intermediaries arise in the process of exchange because they can increase the efficiency of the process.

2. Channel intermediaries arise to adjust the discrepancy of assortments through the performance of the sorting processes.

3. Marketing agencies hang together in channel arrangements to provide for the routinization of transactions.

4. Also, channels exist to facilitate the searching process as well as the sorting process.

Each of these steps is examined below.

The Rationale for Intermediaries

In primitive cultures, most household needs are *produced* within the household. However, at an early stage in the development of economic activities, *exchange* replaced production as a means of satisfying individual needs. The development of exchange is facilitated when there is a surplus in production over current household requirements and when this surplus cannot be held for future consumption because of either the perishable nature of the products or the lack of storage facilities. Thus, if numerous households are able to affect small surpluses of different products, a basis for exchange is developed.

Alderson and Martin formulated the following law of exchange which specifies the conditions under which an exchange will take place:[6]

Given that x is an element of the assortment A_1 and y is an element of the assortment A_2, x is exchangeable for y if, and only if, these three conditions hold:

(a) x is different from y.
(b) The potency of the assortment A_1 is increased by dropping x and adding y.
(c) The potency of the assortment A_2 is increased by adding x and dropping y.

These conditions of exchange are more easily met when production becomes specialized and the assortment of goods is broadened. As households find their needs satisfied by an increased quantity and variety of goods, the mechanism of exchange increases in importance.

However, as the importance of exchange increases, so does the difficulty in maintaining *mutual* interactions between *all* households. For example, a small

---

[5] The following discussion is based on Wroe Alderson, "Factors Governing the Development of Marketing Channels," in R. M. Clewett (ed.), *Marketing Channels for Manufactured Products* (Homewood, Ill.: Richard D. Irwin, 1954), pp. 5–22.

[6] Wroe Alderson and Miles W. Martin, "Toward a Formal Theory of Transactions and Transvections," in Bruce E. Mallen (ed.), *The Marketing Channel: A Conceptual Viewpoint* (New York: John Wiley & Sons, 1967), pp. 50–51.

village of only five specialized households would require 10 transactions to carry out *decentralized* exchanges (i.e., exchanges at each production point). In order to reduce the complexity of this exchange system and thus facilitate transactions, intermediaries appear in the process. Through the operation of a central market, one dealer can considerably reduce the number of transactions. In the preceding example, only five transactions would be required to carry out a *centralized* exchange. This conception of decentralized versus centralized exchange is illustrated in Fig. 1–2.

FIGURE 1–2
Decentralized versus Centralized Exchange

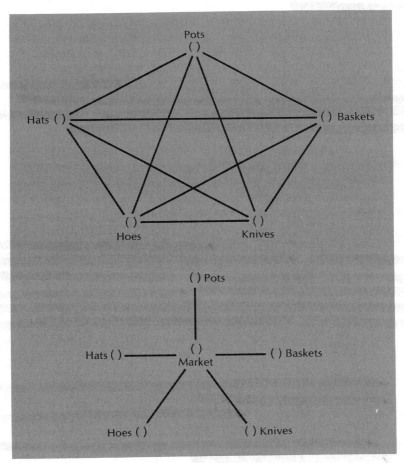

Source: Wroe Alderson, "Factors Governing the Development of Marketing Channels," in Richard M. Clewett (ed.), *Marketing Channels for Manufactured Products* (Homewood, Ill.: Richard D. Irwin, 1954), p. 7.

Implicit in the above example is the notion that a decentralized system of exchange is less efficient than a centralized network employing intermediaries. The same rationale can be applied to direct selling from manufacturers to retailers relative to selling through wholesalers. Figure 1-3 shows that, given four manufacturers and ten retailers who buy goods from each manufacturer, the number of contact lines amounts to 40. If the manufacturers sell to these retailers through one wholesaler, the number of necessary contacts is reduced to 14.

However, the number of necessary contacts increases dramatically as more wholesalers are added. For example, if the four manufacturers in the example above used two wholesalers, the number of contacts rises from 14 to 28, and if four wholesalers are used, the number of contacts will be 64. Thus, employing more and more intermediaries is subject to diminishing returns simply from a *contactual* efficiency perspective.

It should also be noted that, in this simple illustration, the cost of any two contact lines of transaction, i.e., manufacturer-wholesaler, wholesaler-retailer, manufacturer-retailer, is assumed to be the same. Also, it is assumed that whenever more than one wholesaler is employed by a manufacturer, each retailer will avail himself of the services of each of these wholesalers. Obviously, accounting must be made for differences between direct and indirect communication costs, in the effectiveness and efficiency of the institutions involved in the transaction, and in the quality of the contact between the various channel members.

The Discrepancy of Assortment and Sorting

In addition to increasing the efficiency of transactions, intermediaries smooth the flow of goods and services by creating possession, place, and time utilities. These utilities enhance the potency of the consumer's assortment. One aspect of this "smoothing" process requires that intermediaries engage in the performance of a "sorting" function. This procedure is necessary in order to bridge the *discrepancy* between the assortment of goods and services generated by the producer and the assortment demanded by the consumer. The discrepancy results from the fact that manufacturers typically produce a large quantity of a limited variety of goods, whereas consumers usually desire only a limited quantity of a wide variety of goods.

The sorting function performed by intermediaries includes the following activities:

1. *Sorting out.* Breaking down a heterogeneous supply into separate stocks which are relatively homogeneous. (Sorting out is typified by the grading of agricultural products, such as grading eggs according to size and grading beef as either choice or prime).

2. *Accumulation.* Bringing similar stocks from a number of sources together into a larger homogeneous supply.

3. *Allocation.* Breaking a homogeneous supply down into smaller and smaller lots. (Allocating at the wholesale level is referred to as "breaking bulk.")

FIGURE 1–3
Rationale for Intermediaries

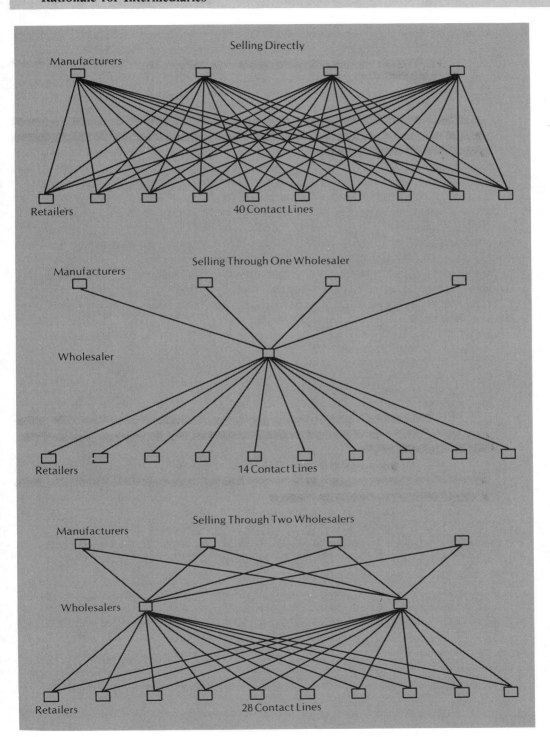

Goods received in carloads are sold in case lots. A buyer of case lots in turn sells individual units. The allocation processes generally coincide with geographical dispersal and successive movement of products from origin to end consumer.

4. *Assorting.* Building up the assortment of products for use in association with each other. (Wholesalers build assortments of goods for retailers, and retailers build assortments for their customers.)[7]

While sorting out and accumulation predominate in the marketing of agricultural and extractive products, allocation and sorting predominate in the marketing of finished manufactured goods. It should be noted that the discrepancy of assortment induces specialization in the exchange process, and the need for such specialization may impede the vertical integration of marketing agencies. For example, a manufacturer of a limited line of hardware items could open his own retail outlets only if he were willing to accumulate the wide variety of items generally sold through those outlets. In general, hardware wholesalers can perform such services more efficiently than can individual manufacturers. Assortment discrepancy also explains why Bethlehem Steel has told its small-volume customers not to buy from it directly but rather to obtain the assortments of the wide variety of steel products they require from wholesalers. On the other hand, large volume buyers who need homogeneous supplies of steel in large lots have been urged to deal with Bethlehem's steel mills on a direct basis.[8]

Routinization

Each transaction involves ordering of, valuation of, and payment for goods and services. The buyer and seller must agree to the amount, mode, and timing of payment. The cost of distribution can be minimized if the transactions are routinized; otherwise, every transaction would be subject to bargaining with a concomitant loss of efficiency.

Moreover, routinization facilitates the development of the exchange system. It leads to standardization of goods and services whose performance characteristics can be easily compared and assessed. It encourages production of items that are more highly valued. In fact, exchange relationships between buyers and sellers are standardized so that lot size, frequency of delivery and payment, and communication are routinized. Because of routinization, a sequence of marketing agencies is able to hang together in a channel arrangement or structure.

[7] Other authors have described the "sorting" processes alternatively as "concentration, equalization, and dispersion" and "collecting, sorting, and dispersing." See Rayburn D. Tousley, Eugene Clark, and Fred E. Clark, *Principles of Marketing* (New York: The Macmillan Company, 1962), pp. 7 and 8; and Roland S. Vaile, E. T. Grether, and Reavis Cox, *Marketing in the American Economy* (New York: The Ronald Press, 1952), pp. 134–150, respectively.

[8] Robert E. Weigand, "Fit Your Products to Your Markets," *Harvard Business Review* (January-February 1977), p. 102.

Automatic ordering is a prime illustration of the routinization that results in the elimination of the cost of placing orders when retail inventory levels reach the reordering point. For example, supplies of cereal and canned goods items at Safeway and A & P supermarkets are automatically replenished from distribution warehouses. These distribution warehouses have direct on-line computers to communicate orders to manufacturers and other suppliers. Kellogg has direct on-line communication capabilities with the distribution warehouses of major retail supermarket chains. Similar ordering systems have been established in the marketing channels for medical supplies and industrial abrasives by American Hospital Supply and Carborundum, respectively. Thus, hospitals and manufacturing firms who deal with these companies are able to achieve high transactional efficiency in their purchasing of medical supplies and abrasives. Without routinization activities, the cost of distribution can increase dramatically.

Searching

Buyers and sellers are engaged in a double search process in the marketplace. The process of search involves uncertainty because producers are not certain of consumers' needs, and consumers are not certain that they will be able to find what they are looking for. Marketing channels facilitate the process of searching as when, for example:

- Wholesale and retail institutions are organized by separate lines of trade, such as drug, hardware, and grocery.
- Products such as over-the-counter drugs are widely available through thousands of drug stores, supermarkets, convenience stores, and even gasoline stations.
- Hundreds of thousands of parts are supplied to automotive repair facilities from local jobbers within hours after the orders are placed.

COMPOSITION OF MARKETING CHANNELS

A marketing or distribution channel is comprised of a set of interdependent institutions and agencies involved with the task of moving anything of value from its point of conception, extraction, or production to points of consumption. As an example, some of the institutions and agencies involved in the distribution of air conditioning equipment are portrayed in Fig. 1-4. Included in Fig. 1-4 are the business firms that are primarily responsible for the flow of title to the merchandise from manufacturer to end (industrial or residential) user. Although excluded from Fig. 1-4 are the numerous agencies and institutions that *facilitate* the passage of title and the physical movement of the goods, such as common carriers, financial institutions, advertising agencies, and the like, they, too, are members of the channel for this particular product.

Even though it is incomplete, Fig. 1-4 permits at least a beginning conceptualization of the various channels of distribution for air conditioning equipment.

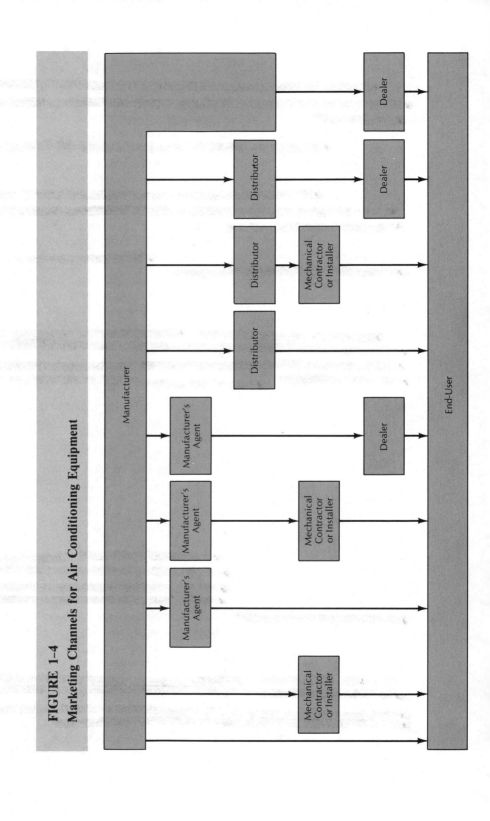

FIGURE 1-4
Marketing Channels for Air Conditioning Equipment

12

Thus, depicted in Fig. 1–4 are *nine* different channels of distribution for such equipment. Each of these channels may be designed to cater to the needs of different market segments and/or the operational requirements of the distributors, contractors, and/or dealers involved. For example, it is more efficient for large volume dealers to deal directly with the manufacturer, while limited volume dealers will have to order through distributors.

Functions and Flows in Marketing Channels

Manufacturers, wholesalers, and retailers as well as other channel members exist in channel arrangements to perform certain functions. For example, in the medical instrument industry, distributors perform four functions: (1) carrying inventory and physical distribution, (2) selling, (3) after-sale service, and (4) extending credit to their customers. If a manufacturer in the industry opts to sell directly to dealers and other customers, he will have to either assume all functions performed by his distributors or shift part of them to his dealers and other customers.[9]

The above discussion underscores important principles in the structure of marketing channels. They are:

1. One can eliminate or substitute institutions in the channel arrangement.

2. However, the functions which these institutions perform cannot be eliminated.

3. When institutions are eliminated, their functions are shifted either forward or backward in the channel and, therefore, are assumed by other members.

It is a truism that "You can eliminate the middleman but you cannot eliminate his functions."

To the extent that the same function is performed at more than one level of the marketing channel, the work load for the function is shared by members at these levels. For example, manufacturers, wholesalers, and retailers may all carry inventory. This duplication may increase distribution cost. However, the increase in cost is justifiable to the extent that it may be necessary to provide goods to customers at the right quantity, quality, time, and place.

In this text, we will refer frequently to "flows" in channels. A "flow" is *identical* to a "function." However, the term "flow" is somewhat more descriptive of movement, and, therefore, we tend to prefer it. Figure 1–5 depicts eight universal flows or functions. Physical possession, ownership, and promotion are typically forward flows from producer to consumer. Each of these moves "down" the distribution channel—a manufacturer promotes his product to a wholesaler, who in turn promotes it to a retailer, and so on. The negotiation, financing, and risking flows move in both directions, whereas ordering and payment are backward flows.

It is interesting and useful to note that any time inventories are held by one

---

[9] Benson P. Shapiro, *op. cit,* pp. 116–117.

FIGURE 1-5

Marketing Flows in Channels

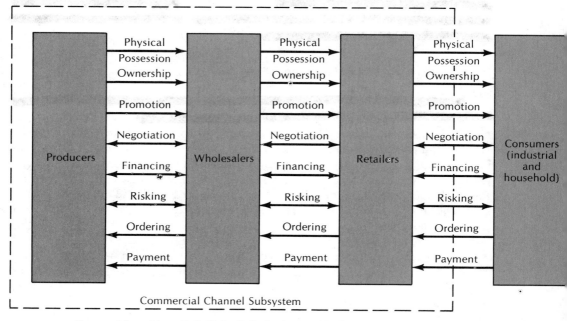

Source: Adapted from R. S. Vaile, E. T. Grether, and R. Cox, *Marketing in the American Economy* (New York: The Ronald Press, 1952), p. 113.

member of the channel system, a financing operation is underway. Thus, when a wholesaler takes title and assumes physical possession of a portion of the output of a manufacturer, the wholesaler is financing the manufacturer. Such a notion is made clear when one examines the carrying costs of inventory. The largest component of carrying cost is the cost of the capital tied up when inventories are held in a dormant state. (Other carrying costs are obsolescence, depreciation, pilferage, breakage, storage, insurance, and taxes.) The reason for the significance of capital costs is relatively obvious—if money were not tied up in inventory, a firm would be able to invest those funds elsewhere. In effect, capital costs are opportunity costs of holding inventory. Thus, when one member of a channel has been "freed" from holding inventory—when his inventories have been exchanged for cash—he may reinvest these funds. In the furniture industry, traditional furniture retailers operating on a sold-order basis choose not to participate in the backward financing flow. On the other hand, "warehouse" furniture retailers do participate in this flow directly and thereby receive benefits from manufacturers in the form of lower prices and preferential treatment.

Many other examples of the backward flow of financing can be found beyond those associated with the holding of inventory. Thus, when a department store buyer commits himself to purchasing a large volume of a particular fashion good prior to the mass production and shipment of the item, the commitment may be factored and the funds used by the garment manufacturer to finance his production process. Prepayment for merchandise is also another example of the backward financing flow.

The forward flow of financing is even more common. General Motors Acceptance Corporation is a specific institution established by the manufacturer to finance not only ultimate consumers of its automobiles but also inventories held by dealers. In fact, all terms of sale, with the exception of cash on delivery and prepayment, may be viewed as elements of the forward flow of financing.

Channel Member Specialization

All of the flows or functions are indispensable—at least one institution or agency within the system must assume responsibility for each of them if the channel is to operate at all. But it is not necessary that every institution participate in the furtherance of all of the flows. In fact, it is for this reason that the channel of distribution is an example of a division of labor on a macro scale. Certain institutions and agencies specialize in one or more of the flows, as is indicated in Fig. 1-6. The use of these and other intermediaries largely boils down to their superior efficiency in the performance of basic marketing tasks and functions. Marketing intermediaries, through their experience, their specialization, their contacts, and their scale, offer other channel members more than they can usually achieve on their own.[10]

In reality, channel member participation in different flows renders them members of a number of different channels, i.e., an ownership or title channel, a negotiations channel, a physical distribution channel, a financing channel, and a promotional channel. The task of channel member coordination should be extended to the coordination of these different channels. Often, new product introduction by manufacturers fails as a result of lack of synchronization of physical and promotional flows or channels. While national promotion may vigorously proceed on schedule, delays in transportation and lack of distribution warehouse space may delay the availability of the product at retail outlets.

ANALYZING MARKETING CHANNEL STRUCTURES

Although the basic economic rationale for the emergence of channel intermediaries and institutional arrangements can be understood in terms of the need for exchange and exchange efficiency, minimization of assortment discrepancies, routinization, and the facilitation of search procedures, such a rationale provides little information as to why channels, such as the one for heavy durable goods depicted in Fig. 1-7, are structured one way or another to satisfy this need. More specifically, how can one account for the

---

[10] Philip Kotler, *Marketing Management: Analysis, Planning, and Control,* 4th ed. (Englewood Cliffs, N.J.: Prentice-Hall, 1980), pp. 417–418.

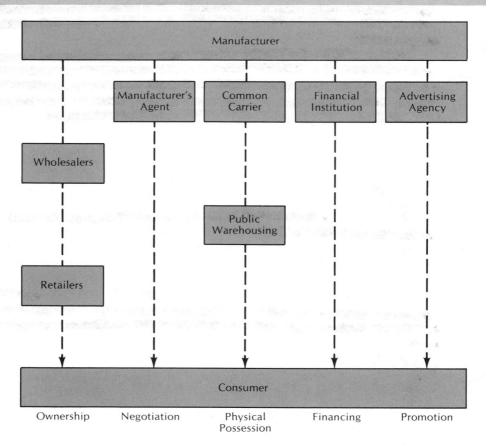

variations in channel structures in terms of the number of levels and the extent of specialization of functions or flows?

Channels As a Network of Systems

Perhaps most important to the analysis of channel structure is an understanding that channels consist of *interdependent* institutions and agencies; in other words, that there is interdependency among their members relative to task performance. A channel can be viewed as a system because of this interdependency—it is a set of *interrelated* and *interdependent* components engaged in producing an output. A distribution channel is comprised of two major subsystems or sectors: *commercial* and *consumer*. The commercial subsystem (to which major attention is given in this text) includes a set of vertically aligned marketing institutions and

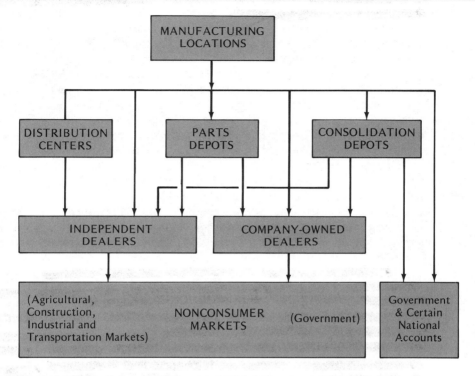

FIGURE 1–7
Company J—Distribution Channels

MANUFACTURING
LOCATIONS

DISTRIBUTION
CENTERS

PARTS
DEPOTS

CONSOLIDATION
DEPOTS

INDEPENDENT
DEALERS

COMPANY-OWNED
DEALERS

(Agricultural, Construction, Industrial and Transportation Markets)

NONCONSUMER
MARKETS

(Government)

Government & Certain National Accounts

Scenario

Company J sells a wide assortment of heavy durable goods to five nonconsumer markets. The primary channel of distribution utilizes independent dealers as a sales intermediary, although in one product area company-owned dealers are used along with independents. Dealers generally are limited to one of the company's product lines, but there are cases of combination product line dealers. Dealers are geographically spaced in order to assure sufficient market coverage and potential. The company within the franchise agreement reserves the right to sell direct to governments and to certain national accounts. In such cases the company makes the delivery and pays a predelivery service fee to a dealer in the area. If the dealer has a good relationship with a governmental unit then the dealer would handle the business.

Products are transported to dealers for predelivery preparation in virtually all cases. To a large extent, product is shipped direct from plant to dealers. However, in some product lines, consolidation depots or distribution centers are used as warehousing locations. Most products are shipped via truck, but rail is used to some extent.

The company also uses three parts depots.

Source: Douglas M. Lambert, *The Distribution Channels Decision* (New York: National Association of Accountants, 1978), pp. 166-67.

agencies, such as manufacturers, wholesalers, and retailers. The consumer (industrial and household) subsystem is incorporated in the *task environment* of the commercial channel. Each commercial channel member is dependent on other institutions for achieving its goal(s). For example, a producer (manufacturer, physician, welfare agency) is dependent on others (retailers, hospitals, day care centers) in getting his product to the consumer and, thereby, in gaining its objectives (profits, improved health care, a reduction in the welfare rolls).

Perhaps the most glaring example of the recognition of this interdependency in recent years was the effort expended by the Credit Committee of the Toy Manufacturers Association to save Toys R Us. This major retailer of toys was threatened with bankruptcy because of the weak financial condition of its parent company, Interstate Stores, Inc. The TMA Credit Committee worked directly with banks in devising a plan that not only kept Toys R Us healthy but also prevented toy manufacturers, in the aggregate, from losing $80 million in sales. The decision of the banks to grant credit to Toys R Us was, to a large extent, based on the fact that six of the largest toy manufacturers were willing to extend credit to Toys R Us on their own.[11] Clearly, the six manufacturers and the members of the TMA Credit Committee realized the importance of adopting a systems perspective in the marketing channel for toys. As a result of these and other actions, Toys R Us has become an even more significant and successful force in toy retailing.

The marketing channel has boundaries, as all systems do. These include geographic (market area), economic (capability to handle a certain volume of goods or services), and human (capability to interact) boundaries. Furthermore, a channel, like other systems, is part of a larger system which provides it with inputs and which imposes restrictions on its operation. A channel exists as part of an economy's distribution structure that encompasses other channels. The economy's distribution structure is a subsystem of the national environment, which is a subsystem of the international environment. Both the national and international environments encompass physical, economic, social, cultural, and political subsystems that influence the development of and impose constraints on the focal channel system. The configuration of systems is portrayed in Fig 1–8. The impact of these environments on individual channel members and on channel organization and design is discussed throughout later chapters.

It is important here to recognize that marketing channels evolve and function in dynamic environments. Channel structures are determined in part by the environment in which the channel operates. For example:

- As a result of high domestic labor cost, many U.S. footware manufacturers were displaced by international competitors from Brazil, Italy, and Spain.
- Direct "to consumer" marketing channels have become more popular in the 1970s as a result of the use of mass media, proliferation of toll-free telephone service, increased acceptance and popularity of bank credit cards, quick delivery through United Parcel Service, and the institution of trial periods, satisfaction guarantees, and return privileges.

---

[11] "How the TMA Saves Toys 'R' Us," *Toys* (May 1975), pp. 45–47.

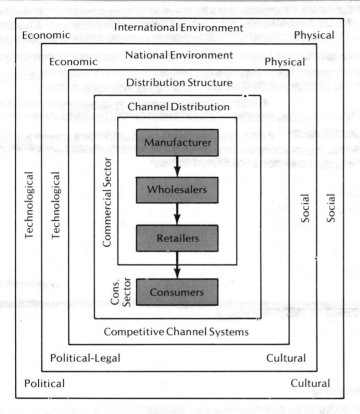

- Changing consumer life styles in the 1970s, including the increased emphasis on leisure time, sports, and convenience, have resulted in the emergence and/or growth of specialty sporting goods, supermarkets, health spas, and convenience 24-hour grocery stores.
- Dramatic increases in transportation cost have led the brewing industry to the establishment of more regional brewing plants closer to the points of consumption.

Channel Structures and Channel Outputs

To explain the key elements determining how channels are structured, Bucklin has developed a rather elaborate theory, the rudiments of which are outlined briefly here.[12] In essence, Bucklin argues that the separation of production from consump-

---

[12] Louis P. Bucklin, *A Theory of Distribution Channel Structure* (Berkeley, Calif.: IBER Special Publications, 1966). Much of the paraphrasing of Bucklin's model has been drawn from Michael Etgar, *An Empirical Analysis of the Motivations for the Development of Centrally Coordinated Vertical*

tion, because of the economic rules of specialization, necessitates the performance of the various marketing functions or flows. These are operationally expressed through a series of service outputs. Industrial or household consumers can provide these service outputs themselves, or they can buy them from commercial channel members. Consequently, marketing channels that provide higher levels of service outputs reduce consumers' search, waiting time, storage, and other costs by lessening their involvement with the actual accomplishment of these necessary activities. Other things being equal (especially price), consumers will prefer to deal with a marketing channel that provides a higher level of service outputs.

Bucklin has specified four service outputs: (1) spatial convenience (or market decentralization), (2) lot size, (3) waiting or delivery time, and (4) product variety (or assortment breadth).[13] Spatial convenience provided by market decentralization of wholesale and/or retail outlets increases consumers' satisfaction by reducing transportation requirements and search costs. Community shopping centers and neighborhood supermarkets, convenience stores, vending machines, and gas stations are but a few examples of satisfying consumers' spatial convenience. Similarly, the number of units to be purchased at each transaction can obviously affect the industrial or household consumer's welfare. When the marketing channel system allows consumers to buy in small units, purchases may move directly into the consumption process. If, however, consumers must purchase in larger lots, some disparity between purchasing and consumption patterns will emerge, burdening consumers with product storage and maintenance costs. Consequently, the smaller the lot size allowed by a channel, the higher the channel's output and, normally, the price to the consumer. For example, when food prices increased dramatically in 1973, price-conscious consumers rushed to food wholesale terminals, where they paid prices 20 to 40 percent below supermarket prices. However, in order to receive these lower prices, consumers had to purchase groceries in the larger lot sizes (e.g., cases or crates) typically available in food terminals.

"Waiting time," the third service output isolated by Bucklin, is defined as the period that the industrial or household consumer must wait after ordering until he receives his goods. Again, the longer the waiting time, the more inconvenient it is for the consumer, who is required to plan his/her consumption far in advance.

Marketing Systems: The Case of the Property and Casualty Insurance Industry, an unpublished Ph.D. dissertation, The University of California at Berkeley, 1974, pp. 95–97.

[13] Bucklin, *op. cit.,* pp. 7–10; and Louis P. Bucklin, *Competition and Evolution in the Distributive Trades* (Englewood Cliffs, N.J.: Prentice-Hall, 1972), pp. 18–31. Clearly, the list of service outputs provided to consumers by a channel can be expanded to include provision of credit, maintenance of product quality, availability of information, stability of supply, availability of personal service and attention, and risk reduction, among others. For exposition purposes, however, the discussion here is limited to the four major service outputs suggested by Bucklin in the monograph and book listed above. For further elaboration on this subject, see Louis P. Bucklin and James M. Carman, "Vertical Market Structure Theory and the Health Care Delivery System," in Jagdish N. Sheth and Peter L. Wright (eds.), *Marketing Analysis for Societal Problems* (Urbana, Ill.: University of Illinois Bureau of Economic and Business Research, 1974), pp. 7–21; Lee E. Preston and Norman R. Collins, *Studies in a Simulated Market* (Berkeley, Calif.: University of California Institute of Business and Economic Research, 1966); and Christina Fulop, *Competition for Consumers* (London: Allen and Unwin, Ltd., 1964), Chapter 2.

Usually, when customers are willing to wait, they are compensated in terms of lower prices, such as when ordering through a Sears catalog. Finally, the wider the breadth of assortment—the greater the product variety—available to the consumer, the higher the output of the marketing channel and the higher the distribution cost, since greater assortment entails carrying more inventory.

These service outputs are achieved through the performance of the marketing functions or flows. Various channel institutions pool their resources and produce outputs for consumers by allocating their resources in specific ways. The decisions on the amount of output to be delivered by channel members are obviously directly influenced by the amount of service desired by consumers. The result of the interaction between channel member decisions and consumer requirements is a channel structure or arrangement that is capable of satisfying the needs of both groups. Under reasonably competitive conditions and low barriers to entry, the channel structure that evolves over the long run should be comprised of a group of institutions so well adjusted to its task and environment that no type of arrangement could create greater returns (e.g., profits or other goals) or more consumer satisfaction per dollar of product cost.[14] This arrangement is called the "normative structure." The determination of channel structure by service outputs is illustrated in Fig. 1–9.

The more service outputs are required by consumers, the more likely it is that intermediaries will be included in the channel structure. Thus, if consumers wish to purchase in small lot sizes, then there are likely to be numerous middlemen performing sorting operations between mass producers and the final user level. If waiting time is to be reduced, then decentralization of outlets must follow, and, therefore, more middlemen will be included in the channel structure. The same type of reasoning can be applied to all of the service outputs. However, as service out-

FIGURE 1-9
The Determination of Channel Structure

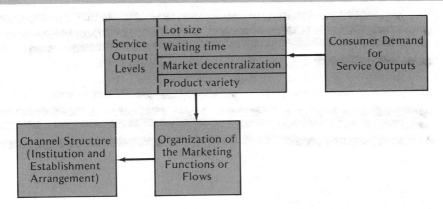

puts increase, costs will undoubtedly increase, and these higher costs will tend to be reflected in higher prices to consumers. Consumers are usually faced with the choice of dealing with channel structures in which few service outputs are provided but where prices are relatively low or with those structures where both service outputs and prices are high. The more the consumer or end-user participates in the marketing flows, the greater the costs he/she incurs (in terms of search, physical possession, financing, and the like), and, therefore, the more he should be compensated for his efforts. In cases where channel service outputs are low, consumers are supposedly compensated for their additional efforts through the lower relative prices which are provided by such channel structures. Thus, when construction machinery manufacturers, such as Caterpillar or J. I. Case, purchase brake parts in carload quantities from firms like Bendix or Gould and are willing to wait several months for delivery from distant plants, they can expect to pay lower prices than if they were to order the same parts from a local warehouse distributor who is willing to ship in smaller quantities and to deliver the parts much more quickly. The lower the level of service outputs provided, the greater are the economies of scale that can be achieved by channel members, and vice versa. The final structure that emerges is, therefore, a function of the desire of channel members to achieve scale economies relative to each of the marketing flows and the demand of consumers for service outputs of varying kinds. An optimal structure is one that minimizes the total costs of the system (both commercial and consumer) by the appropriate adjustment of the level of the service outputs.[15] Within a channel, members can attempt to shift the degree of participation relative to each flow in order to provide the greatest possible service output at the lowest possible cost. But such shifting calls for a tremendous amount of coordination and cooperation. This is one reason why the management of channel systems is so critical.

Postponement-Speculation and Channel Structure

The way in which channels are structured is, to a significant extent, determined by where inventories should best be held in order to provide appropriate service levels, fulfill the required sorting processes, and still deliver an adequate return to channel members. To explain the process involved in the determination of inventory locations, Bucklin, using Alderson's original scheme,[16] developed the principle of *postponement-speculation.*[17] According to Bucklin, efficiency in marketing channels is promoted by the postponement of changes in (a) the form and identity of a product to the latest possible point in the marketing process and (b) inventory location to the latest possible point in time. Risk and uncertainty costs increase as

[15] Bucklin and Carman, *op. cit.,* p. 12.

[16] Wroe Alderson, "Marketing Efficiency and the Principle of Postponement," *Cost and Profit Outlook,* Vol. 3 (September 1950).

[17] Louis P. Bucklin, "Postponement, Speculation and the Structure of Distribution Channels," in Mallen, *op. cit.,* pp. 67–74.

the product becomes more differentiated. Postponement promotes efficiency by moving differentiation nearer to the time of purchase when demand is more certain thus reducing risk and uncertainty costs. Also, the cost of physical distribution of goods is reduced by sorting products in large lots and in relatively undifferentiated states.

Postponement is a tool used by a channel member to shift the risk of owning goods to another channel member. For example:

- Manufacturers of special industrial machinery postpone by refusing to produce except upon receipt of orders.
- Middlemen postpone by buying from sellers who offer faster delivery, thus shifting inventory backward.
- Consumers postpone by buying from retail outlets where goods are available directly from the store shelf.

Speculation is the *opposite* of postponement. The speculation concept holds that "changes in form, and the movement of goods to forward inventories, should be made at the earliest possible time in the marketing process in order to reduce the costs of the marketing system."[18] Thus risk is shifted to or assumed by a channel institution rather than shifted away from it. Speculation makes possible cost reductions through (a) economies of large scale production, which are the result of changing form at the earliest point; (b) the elimination of frequent orders, which increase the costs of order processing and transportation; and (c) the reduction of stockouts and their attendant cost of consumer dissatisfaction and possible subsequent brand switching. An accurate sales forecast is essential in marketing channels for consumer goods, most of which are dominated by speculation.

The character of variables involved in the postponement-speculation theory are shown in Fig. 1–10. The vertical axis represents the average cost of performing some function, or set of functions, for one unit of any given commodity. The horizontal axis measures the time required to deliver the commodity to the buyer after an order has been placed. If these two elements are taken together, the coordinates measure the cost of certain marketing functions or flows performed in a channel with respect to delivery time.

Three basic sets of flows are shown in Fig. 1–10. The curve labelled C represents the costs incurred by the buyer in holding an inventory. The curve AD' shows the costs of those flows necessary to supply the buyer directly from a manufacturing point some specified distance away. Curve DB reveals the costs incurred by flows utilized to ship the commodity from this same production point through a speculative inventory (e.g., a stocking intermediary, such as a manufacturer's distribution center, public warehouse, merchant wholesaler, or retailer) to the buyer.

The postponement-speculation theory holds that channel structure is deter-

[18] *Ibid.*, p. 68.

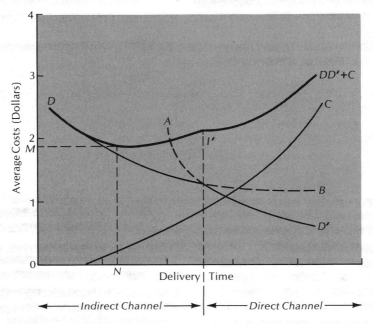

Source: Reprinted from Louis P. Bucklin and Leslie Halpert, "Exploring Channels of Distribution for Cement with the Principle of Postponement-Speculation," in Peter D. Bennett (ed.), *Marketing and Economic Development,* (Chicago: American Marketing Association, 1965), p. 698.

mined by the interrelationships of the three sets of curves, *C, AD'*, and *DB,* as follows:

1. The minimal cost of supplying the buyer for every possible delivery time is derived from curves *AD'* and *DB*. As may be seen in Fig. 1-10, especially fast delivery service can be provided only by the indirect channel (i.e., by using a stocking intermediary). However, at some delivery time, *I'*, the cost of serving the consumer directly from the producer will intersect and fall below the cost of indirect shipment. The minimal costs derived from both curves are designated *DD'*. From the perspective of channel cost, it will be cheaper to service the buyer from a speculative inventory if delivery times shorter than *I'* are demanded. If the consumer is willing to accept delivery times longer than *I'*, then direct shipment will be the least expensive.

2. The minimal *total* cost curve for the channel with respect to delivery time is derived by summing the cost of moving goods to the buyer, *DD'*, and the buyer's costs of holding inventory, *C*. The curve is represented in Fig. 1-10 by *DD'* + *C*. Total channel costs initially fall as delivery time lengthens, because increased buyer expenses are more than made up for by savings in other parts of the channel. Gradually, however, the savings from these sources diminish and buyer costs begin to rise more rapidly. A minimal cost point is reached and expenses for the channel rise thereafter. *Channel structure is controlled by the location of this minimum point.* If, as in the present case, it falls to the left of I', then goods would be expected to flow through the speculative inventory (i.e., an intermediary). If, on the other hand, the savings of the buyer from postponement had not been as great as those depicted, the minimum point would have fallen to the right of I' and shipments would be made directly from producer to the consumer.[19]

In the situation portrayed in Fig. 1–10, the costs of postponement are minimized by the use of a speculative inventory, because the minimal cost point M falls to the left of I'. If, however, the risk costs to the customer had been less, or the general cost of holding inventories at the customer's home (or warehouse, as the case may be) had been lower, then C would be farther to the right. Point M would also shift to the right. With a sufficient reduction in consumer cost, M would appear to the right of I', indicating that direct shipment in the channel would be the means to minimize postponement cost.

The theory of postponement-speculation provides a useful basis for understanding channel structure. It is possible to assert that speculative inventories create the opportunity for new institutions to hold title in the channel. The existence of speculative inventories leads to the use of indirect channels; the economic need to have such inventories opens the door to middlemen to demonstrate whether they are capable of reducing the cost of inventory risk-taking (that is, the costs associated with participating in the flows of physical possession and ownership). On the other hand, postponement creates an opportunity for different types of institutions in the channel. The latter are freight forwarders, drop shippers, and agent middlemen who do not take title to merchandise but who, in the absence of speculative inventories, facilitate the use of more direct channels of distribution.

It is also possible to apply the principle of postponement-speculation to an understanding of the differences between household and industrial buying. Much household buying is generally fragmented, involves small lots, and is undertaken frequently, especially with regard to convenience and some shopping goods. The costs of holding large inventories on the part of households tend to be relatively high. Thus, longer and more indirect channels often exist for convenience goods. Speculation is an important determinant of the channel structure for such goods, because there are more points in the channel where inventory may be held. In in-

[19] Louis P. Bucklin and Leslie Halpert, "Exploring Channels of Distribution for Cement with the Principle of Postponement-Speculation," in Peter D. Bennett (ed.), *Marketing and Economic Development* (Chicago: American Marketing Association, 1965), p. 699. It should be noted that the type of cost behavior discussed above and depicted in Fig. 1-10 excludes from consideration any potential savings from sorting in the channel. Such savings, derived from the possibility of economies in large-scale transport to the speculative inventory point, are, as mentioned in the preceding section, a fundamental characteristic of channels and must be introduced into the analysis before a final structure can be determined.

dustrial purchasing, however, the opposite factors generally operate, and thus the desire to postpone has led to the development of a different type of institutional arrangement where there are more direct, shorter channels.

As mentioned earlier, the accuracy of sales forecasting is a critical feature of speculation. This fact was underscored during 1979 by the troubles which plagued Chrysler Corporation. In order to achieve economies of scale in production, Chrysler amassed enormous speculative inventories of large, gas-guzzling cars. It had forecasted that United States consumers were wedded to large cars, and therefore would continue to demand them, even though sales of foreign imports of smaller cars were increasing. Its forecast was dead wrong, and the corporation was left with thousands of automobiles which it had produced but could not sell. General Motors, on the other hand, has always followed the postponement principle; GM produces an automobile only when it has received a specific order from its dealers. Thus, in accordance with its policy of postponement, it makes changes in the form and identity of the automobiles it produces only at the latest possible point in time in the marketing process.

Channel Structure and Functional Spinoff

Beyond consideration of physical possession, ownership, and risk-taking, it is possible to expand the analysis supplied by Bucklin to other flows associated with marketing channels. In fact, each marketing flow may be thought to have a differently shaped cost curve, which may include increasing, decreasing, or constant returns. Thus, savings can be affected if the activities or flows subject to increasing returns are performed at a higher output level. A firm with limited resources in a competitive industry will normally delegate these increasing return activities to enterprises that specialize in them. Through such delegation (or shifting of the flows), the firm is able, as Stigler observes,[20] to lower its average and marginal costs and thereby to improve its competitive position. In essence, specialized channel intermediaries provide external economies to firms employing them. Eventually, however, reintegration of the delegated flows may be warranted as a firm's output expands or as technology changes, because the firm may then find itself capable of performing them at an optimum scale.[21]

Such a pattern of vertical disintegration followed by vertical reintegration can be observed in the case of small manufacturers who rely heavily on agent middlemen to represent them in the market and on specialized storage, transportation, and financing institutions to perform the respective functions in their channels. As these small manufacturers expand, they tend to develop their own sales forces, perform their own storage, transportation, and financing, and thus dispense with the services of agent middlemen and other specialized institutions. Similar analyses can be applied to wholesalers and retailers. For example, Sears started as a mail-order

[20] George J. Stigler, "The Division of Labor Is Limited by the Extent of the Market," *Journal of Political Economy,* Vol. 59 (June 1951), pp. 185–193.

[21] Control as well as economic considerations are crucial here. In fact, control may override economics in many situations. This factor is discussed in detail in later chapters.

retailer and expanded horizontally. As its operations grew larger and larger, Sears integrated backward in terms of operating its own warehousing and other wholesaling facilities and then in terms of owning or controlling manufacturing facilities. Thus, when a firm's output and its market are limited, it will likely find itself shifting flows onto others in its channel, if it can, in fact, convince others to accept responsibility for these flows.[22] As market size expands, it becomes increasingly economical to vertically integrate, which is a pattern of behavior fully evident among the largest manufacturing and distributive organizations.[23]

It is important to note that there may be considerable problems associated with shifting flows or, as Mallen has put it, "spinning off" functions.[24] It may be exceedingly difficult to separate the joint costs associated with the performance of many marketing flows (e.g., physical possession and ownership). Furthermore, most companies deal with multiple products and services for which costs are shared. There is also a time horizon involved as well as a host of noneconomic considerations. Nevertheless, the concept of shifting flows is a viable one; like so many management decisions, it demands appropriate accounting procedures to be implemented correctly.

Additional Factors Determining Channel Structure

Added to these economics-oriented explanations about why channels take on certain structural properties must be considerations of technological, cultural, physical, social, and political factors.[25] For example, the emergence of the supermarket in the structure of food distribution was contingent upon the availability of technologies such as the mass media and mass communications, the cash register, packaging and refrigeration, and the automobile. However, the introduction of the supermarket in developing countries is impeded by cultural variables, such as the high rates of illiteracy, the habit of tasting food products before buying, and the delegation of buying to maids and domestic help. The employment of vending and dollar change machines provides another example of technological and cultural influences on the distribution structure of candy, snack foods, beverages, and other items. Thus, in affluent societies with convenience-oriented cultures, consumers are

[22] This is not always a foregone conclusion. Very small firms often find it difficult to secure needed services from agents, advertising agencies, and financial institutions, for example, and therefore, must integrate these flows, even though it would be more economical to pass them along to someone else.

[23] For a useful analytical perspective on this issue, see Stanley F. Stasch, *A Method of Dynamically Analyzing the Stability of the Economic Structure of Channels of Distribution,* an unpublished Ph.D. dissertation, School of Business, Northwestern University, 1964.

[24] Bruce E. Mallen, "Functional Spin-Off: A Key to Anticipating Change in Distribution Structure," *Journal of Marketing* Vol. 37 (July 1973), pp. 18–25. Also see William P. Dommermuth and R. Clifton Andersen, "Distribution Systems—Firms, Functions and Efficiencies," *MSU Business Topics,* Vol. 17 (Spring 1969), pp. 51–56.

[25] For example, Preston believes that channel structure is a function of population density and cluster, per capita income, geographic setting and resource endowment, volume and variety of goods, and managerial capabilities. See Lee E. Preston, "Marketing Organization and Economic Development: Structure, Products, and Management," in Louis P. Bucklin (ed.), *Vertical Marketing Systems* (Glenview, Ill.: Scott, Foresman and Co., 1970), pp. 116–133.

willing to pay the extra cost associated with buying from vending machines. And the advent and continuous development of electronic data processing systems have enabled manufacturers and middlemen to accurately assess their distribution costs and redesign their respective channels.

Geography, size of market area, location of production centers, and concentration of population, among other physical factors, also play important roles in determining the structure of channels. Distribution channels tend to be longer (i.e., include more intermediaries) when production is concentrated and population and markets are dispersed. Furthermore, we find that urban areas are served by a wide variety of retail outlets, including department stores, discount houses, and supermarkets, while rural areas may be served solely by a general store.

In addition, local, state, and federal laws can influence channel structure in both direct and indirect ways. There are laws that circumscribe territorial restrictions in distribution, price discrimination, full-line forcing, and unfair sales practices. There are also laws that protect channel members from the competition of larger, more efficient rivals or that penalize "bigness" in distribution. And there are licensing boards that screen entrants to particular channels.

Social and behavioral variables can also influence the makeup of a channel. For example, Galbraith has advanced the concept of countervailing power as a tentative explanation of channel structure and practices.[26] His theory emphasizes that: (a) private economic power is held in check by the countervailing power of those who are subject to it; (b) economic power begets countervailing power; (c) countervailing power is a self-generating force that complements competition as a regulatory force in the economy; and (d) countervailing power can take many forms, the most important of which is threatened or actual vertical integration. Manifestations of the effect of countervailing power on distribution channel structure are provided by the following examples:

- The emergence of the mass retailer to countervail the power of large manufacturers.
- Vertical integration by mass retailers, such as Sears' and Montgomery Ward's ownership of manufacturing facilities.
- The utilization of private brands by chain retailers to countervail the power of large manufacturers with popular national brands.
- The emergence of voluntary and retailer cooperative chains to countervail the power of the large corporate chains.
- Trade association activities by small retailers (pharmacies, independent service stations, and independent grocery stores) in an attempt to countervail the power of chains and manufacturers.

Admittedly, more could be said about each of the various factors mentioned above; it is to be hoped that the reader will be able to develop additional examples of their influence on the structure of channels with which he is familiar. The main

[26] John K. Galbraith, *American Capitalism,* rev. ed. (Boston: Houghton Mifflin Co., 1956), pp. 110–114, 117–123.

point to be remembered here, however, is that explanations of channel structure in terms of economic variables alone are obviously insufficient, even though such economic models provide an appropriate starting point for understanding why specific structures emerge. The necessity for going beyond economic variables is made especially clear when one attempts to find an answer to the question: why do uneconomic channel structures persist over time? In other words, why is it that all channels do not gravitate to or obtain the normative structure specified by Bucklin? The answer comes from examining a myriad of social, cultural, and political as well as economic variables. As McCammon points out, uneconomic channels may persist for the following reasons:[27]

1. *Reseller solidarity.* Channel participants organize and function as groups that tend to support traditional trade practices and long-established institutional relationships. Trade association actions, attempts by independent retailers to outlaw chain stores, and department store operators' efforts to block discount store operations attest to the role of reseller solidarity in determining channel structure.

2. *Entrepreneurial values.* Large resellers are growth-oriented, tend to adopt economic criteria for decision-making purposes, and use new efficient technologies. On the contrary, small resellers have limited expectations, tend to maintain the status quo, view their demand curve as relatively fixed, and resist growth beyond their limited growth expectations.

3. *Organizational rigidity.* Firms respond incrementally to innovations because of organizational rigidities. Thus, the process of change takes a long time.

4. *The firm's channel position.* Kriesberg grouped channel intermediaries into insiders, who are members of the dominant channel; strivers, who want to become members of the channel; complementors, who perform functions complementary to functions performed by insiders; and transients, who take advantage of temporary opportunities and are not interested in becoming members.[28] While transients usually disrupt the status quo by engaging in deviant competitive behavior, insiders, strivers, and complementors are more interested in maintaining the status quo. Thus, firms completely outside the channel are most likely to introduce basic and enduring innovations in the channel structure.

5. *Market segmentation.* New institutions do not appeal to all market segments. Traditional institutions seem to have loyal segments that they appeal to. Thus, these institutions are not compelled to change.

Indeed, to have a goal of moving towards a "normative channel structure," the assumptions of low barriers to entry and competitive conditions must be met. In many of the above examples, entry is purposively inhibited through group action,

---

[27] Bert C. McCammon, Jr., "Alternative Explanations of Institutional Change and Change Evolution," in William G. Moller, Jr., and David L. Wilemon (eds.), *Marketing Channels* (Homewood, Ill.: Richard D. Irwin, 1971), pp. 136–141.

[28] Louis Kriesberg, "Occupational Controls Among Steel Distributors," in Louis W. Stern (ed.), *Distribution Channels: Behavioral Dimensions* (Boston: Houghton Mifflin Co., 1969), pp. 50–60.

product differentiation, industrial norms, and the like. In addition, the concept of a normative channel structure is long-run in nature; in a dynamic environment, such a structure cannot be reached at any one point in time. Change must always take place according to an assessment of future requirements, and thus there will always be a gap between the actual and ideal. In fact, it is probably best to adopt an evolutionary view of structure, because what exists always seems to be a compromise between past structure, present requirements, and predictions about the future.

CHANNEL MANAGEMENT AND COMPETITION

Economic battles involving producers versus producers or middlemen versus middlemen will not, in the long run, determine the ultimate victors in the marketplace. Rather, the relevant unit of competition is an entire distribution system comprised of the entire network of interrelated institutions and agencies. For example, in the passenger tire industry, Firestone's system of distributors and dealers is in competition with Goodyear's entire system, and the long-term standing of either company will depend in large measure on how well each company manages the relations among the institutions and agencies involved in the distribution task so as best to satisfy the needs of the end-users of tires.

Exactly the same point applies to industrial goods as well. In the farm equipment and construction machinery markets, for instance, both Deere & Co. and Caterpillar have achieved market dominance by fine-tuning their marketing channels so that farmers, contractors, and other customers are served in highly effective and efficient ways. In the case of Deere, it has been noted that:

> Deere's marketing prowess . . . enhances the chances of succeeding with its strategy for thriving during a several-year stretch of slowing growth. Its vaunted marketing network—3,400 farm equipment dealers and a recently beefed-up corps of several hundred construction machinery vendors—is known for backing its products with extensive repair and parts-supply services, considered an important selling point for increasingly expensive and sophisticated equipment. One competitor observes: "The strength of Deere's dealer network is a very big influence in the success of that company."[29]

Viewing channels as competitive units is significant for all companies, including those that market their products through a number of different channels and those that develop assortments of goods and services by purchasing from a variety of suppliers. The way that the individual manufacturers coordinate their activities with the various intermediaries with whom they deal and vice versa will determine the viability of one type of channel alignment versus other channel alignments made up of different institutions and agencies handling similar or substitutable merchandise.

[29] "Deere: A Counter-Cyclical Expansion to Grab Market Share," *Business Week* (November 19, 1979), p. 80.

If, within a given marketing channel, an institution or agency does not see fit to coordinate effectively and efficiently with other members of the same network, but rather pursues its own goals in an independent self-serving manner, it is possible to predict the eventual demise of the channel alignment of which it is a part as a strong competitive force. Ideally, then, a channel member should attempt to coordinate his objectives, plans, and programs with other members in such a way that the performance of the total distribution system to which he belongs is enhanced. However, it has been argued that such integrated action up and down a marketing channel is actually a rarity. The following comments by a consumer goods marketer are illustrative:

> If I could gain more help from my distribution channels, we could substantially increase volume and have even greater impact on profits. But when I press the button which says, "Get the distributors to increase sales of product A immediately," all too often I get a push on product C in three months. Our channels are so long and complex that we have little effect on them.[30]

Fortunately, there are exceptions to this attitude. For example, the virtually snowless winter in the Northeast and Midwest of the U.S. in 1979 left retailers loaded with 1979 models of ski equipment, snowmobiles, and snowblowers. Traditionally, manufacturers of ski equipment encouraged retailers to place large orders early in the first quarter of a calendar year by offering discounts of 15 percent or more. Deliveries were made in the late summer or early fall, and retailers were required to pay for the shipments by December 10, with extra discounts given for payment made a month or two earlier. However, because of the lessons learned during the winter of 1979, manufacturers revised their marketing methods. Salomon/North America Inc., which holds about a 40 percent share of the ski bindings market, extended its early order period—during which large discounts are available—until June 1 and now permits retailers to receive partial shipments throughout the winter, with payment due within 60 days after delivery. Another bindings manufacturer, Geze, Boster & Co., is now offering retailers "no-snow insurance," which involves extending the payment time according to a formula that compares each season's snowfall with the average over the last 10 years.[31]

Channel participants are often not concerned with all the transactions that occur between each of the various links in the channel, however. Middlemen, in particular, are most concerned about the dealings that take place with those channel members immediately adjacent to them from whom they buy and to whom they sell.[32] In this sense, channel intermediaries are not, in fact, functioning as enlisted member components of a distribution system, but rather are acting individually as independent markets, with each one choosing those products and suppliers that best

---

[30] Benson P. Shapiro, *op. cit.,* p. 115.

[31] "Struggling to Cope Without Snow," *Business Week* (February 18, 1980), p. 66.

[32] Philip McVey, "Are Channels of Distribution What the Textbooks Say?" *Journal of Marketing,* Vol. 24 (January 1961), pp. 61–65.

help him serve the target groups for whom he acts as a purchasing agent. From this perspective, the middleman's method of operation—the functions he performs, the clients he serves, and the objectives, policies, and programs he adopts—is the result of his own independently made decisions.

This notion of each channel intermediary acting as an independent market must be qualified and analyzed with regard to total channel performance. Although an "independent" orientation on the part of any channel member may indeed be operational at times, it is put into effect only at the risk of sacrificing the levels of coordination necessary for overall channel effectiveness, efficiency, growth, and long-run survival. Thus, a high degree of independent, suboptimizing behavior on the part of individual channel participants serves as a detriment to the viability of the total channel network. The problem for actors within any distribution network is, therefore, to cooperate in developing an interorganization system that will minimize suboptimization so that a high degree of channel coordination is still attainable.

APPROACH OF THE TEXT

The above discussion underscores the critical nature of channel member coordination to ensure channel system viability. The *approach* of this text is *managerial*. It *focuses on planning, organizing, coordinating, directing, and controlling the efforts of channel members*.

The task of channel management is complex and taxing. Most businesses sell a number of products under different labels, and operate in a number of different markets. Products and services are marketed through several channels to a wide range of customers. Channel intermediaries differ in type, in volume purchased, in location, and many other operating characteristics. This "multimarketing"[33] phenomenon poses difficult channel management issues which will be dealt with in the remainder of this text.

ORGANIZATION OF THE TEXT

The organization of this text emanates from the framework for understanding channel management as shown in Fig. 1–11. The framework specifies channel management systems in terms of interrelated sets of structural and managerial variables. The various chapters in the text relate to these sets of variables as denoted in Fig. 1–11. The remainder of this section is devoted to an explanation of the organization of the text as outlined in the framework.

A necessary prerequisite to the effective management of marketing channels is a knowledge of why channels exist, the functions they perform, and the factors that account for the way they are structured. In this first chapter, key theoretical concepts have been examined, which explain why specialized institutions and agencies

[33] See Robert Weigand, "Fit Products to Your Markets," *Harvard Business Review* (January-February 1977), pp. 95–105.

FIGURE 1-11
A Framework for Understanding Channel Management[a]

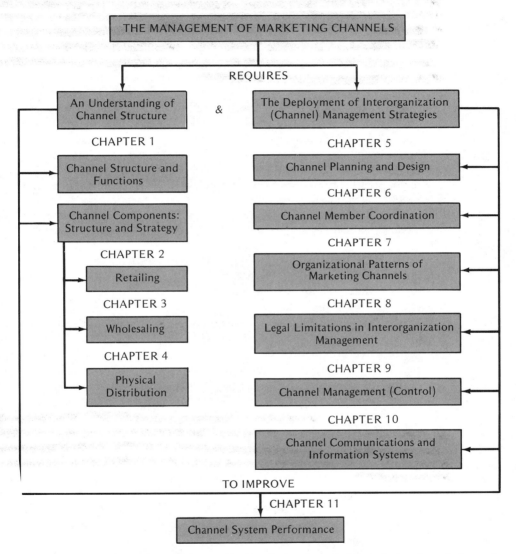

[a] Chapters 12 and 13 dealing with international marketing channels and marketing channels for services are not noted here. These chapters deal with channel management in special contexts. Therefore, they incorporate all variables in the framework.

have emerged to assist in the task of making goods and services available to industrial, institutional, and household consumers. The need for efficient exchange via sorting processes, routinization of marketing activities, and reasonably rapid search procedures compels the existence of a large variety of different types of intermediaries. The way in which these intermediaries are linked together depends on the service outputs demanded by consumers. The higher the output demanded, the greater the number of institutions and agencies that will likely be required to bridge the gap between production and consumption. The means by which service outputs are generated is through the organization of the marketing functions or flows—physical possession, ownership, promotion, negotiation, financing, risking, ordering, and payment. The actual levels of performance of these functions depend, in turn, on the *economics* of distribution, which requires balancing the needs of channel members to achieve profitability and manage risk, on the one hand, and the desires of consumers to receive the highest possible amount of service output at the lowest possible price, on the other hand. Therefore, there are pressures on channel members to both postpone and to speculate. In addition to these pressures, there are a host of social, political, and cultural factors impinging on channel members which influence and, in some cases, dictate how the channel will be structured.

All of the concepts introduced in this chapter provide relevant background information which can be employed in the management of marketing channels. Without an understanding of each of them and their interaction with one another, any attempts at channel management are likely to be short-sighted and superficial.

Against this backdrop, it is now possible to proceed to uncovering some of the specific attributes of the intermediaries comprising marketing channels in order to gain a deeper comprehension of their roles within channels and their potential for meeting the needs of the customers whom they serve. Part II of this text provides a description of some of the key components of marketing channels—retailers, wholesalers, transportation agencies, public and private warehouse facilities, and distribution centers. Each of these institutions and agencies has its own structure, performance requirements, and management styles. Because channel members tend to focus on their own goals and performance, these features must be understood before any attempts are made to plan, organize, coordinate, and control the channel as a system. In essence, it is imperative to develop an understanding of the internal management of these component institutions before trying to manage the relationships among them. Therefore, Chapters 2, 3, and 4 deal with the structure, management, and performance requirements of retailing, wholesaling, and physical distribution institutions, respectively.

It should be clearly noted at the outset that manufacturers and consumers are also significant components of marketing channels. However, specific chapters on manufacturer marketing strategy and on consumer behavior are not included in this text because these are extensively covered in almost all basic marketing and marketing management texts. In contrast, retailer, wholesaler, and physical distribution agency strategies are subjects of a special nature. Not many readers have had experience and/or training in these areas. Those who have an adequate background in them may wish to proceed directly from this chapter to Part III.

Part III of the text focuses on the management of the marketing channel, i.e., planning, organizing, coordinating, and controlling. Careful selection of channel members and planning of channel arrangements are essential if firms are to endure severe competition in the marketplace. Therefore, Chapter 5 is devoted to an examination of channel design strategies and considers different policies necessary for the orderly functioning of channels.

Marketing channels can be organized differently to reach similar or different market segments. Forms of channel organization vary. Channels may be organized as loose coalitions of independently owned manufacturers, wholesalers, retailers, and other institutions. Alternatively, the channel may be organized as a closely aligned marketing system. In the latter instance, channels may be fully integrated corporate vertical marketing systems, contractual systems, or administered systems. Also, channels may be simple (direct to the consumer) or complex (involving a number of levels and engaging a large number of intermediaries). The marketing channel is a complex technical and behavioral system. Different forms of channel organization and management necessitate an understanding of channel member behavior. Chapter 6 examines the marketing channel as a behavioral system. It focuses on the development of an understanding of channel member behavioral tendencies and responses to attempts to manage and coordinate the system. In turn, Chapter 7 discusses organizational patterns of marketing channels in the light of the behavioral tendencies and responses described in Chapter 6.

Naturally, marketers are not free to organize channels and deploy measures of channel management without any restrictions. The design, organization, and specification of policies guiding organizational relationships between channel members are governed by legal restrictions and constraints, which are the subject of Chapter 8.

The implementation of channel planning and organization cannot be effectively achieved without instituting channel coordination through (a) the exercise of leadership, (b) the application of various motivational methods to induce channel members to cooperate, and (c) the development of an appropriate network for communication and exchange of vital information among channel members. Chapter 9 deals with issues related to channel leadership and directing channel member effort through appropriate motivation. It incorporates discussions of channel management by manufacturers, wholesalers, and retailers, explores the methods for dominance and motivation deployed by each, and, finally, engages in a discussion of who should lead the channel.

Chapter 10 examines channel communication problems and the institution of effective channel information systems. Manufacturers, wholesalers, retailers, transportation agencies, and other participants in the marketing channel system need to communicate and share information in order to function effectively. Forecasting sales, controlling and managing inventories, tracking orders and shipments, launching cooperative advertising campaigns, introducing new products, and putting into effect price changes all require information sharing through a carefully planned and designed communication and information system.

The process of managing a channel system is incomplete without the design and activation of a performance control and audit system. Systematic assessment of channel member and channel system performance, the provision of feedback, and the institution of corrective action mechanisms are necessary to maintain channel control. The final chapter of Part III, Chapter 11, deals with the assessment of the performance of channel institutions and the channel system. Performance can be assessed from a macro and micro viewpoint. Both views are considered in Chapter 11. Performance issues such as system output, profitability, growth, distribution cost analysis, and equity in serving various markets are examined.

Part IV of the text examines channel management in other contexts—the international arena and the marketing of services. Exploring distribution channels in other countries enriches our managerial analysis. It enables us to examine the impact of different environments and managerial problems on channel system performance. Chapter 12 deals with international marketing channels.

Whether marketing channels for services are drastically different from marketing channels for goods is debatable. Some contend that they are structurally different and require different analyses and sets of strategies. Others indicate that although different in form and type, the structures for the distribution of goods and services encompass the same technical, behavioral, and managerial variables. Therefore, analysis and strategies for management of marketing channels for goods are adaptable and applicable to marketing channels for services. We subscribe to this viewpoint. But because services constitute over 40 percent of total consumer expenditures in the U.S., they warrant special attention. Furthermore, marketing channels for services are less understood. A discussion of such channels is, therefore, presented in Chapter 13.

DISCUSSION QUESTIONS

1. What are some alternative approaches to the study of distribution channels besides channel management?

2. In a low-growth economy, many strategists are emphasizing "demand management" rather than "demand stimulation." How might this affect a firm's marketing mix, particularly as it relates to distribution? If there is a continued deemphasis of demand stimulation in the future, will the role of channel management in marketing become more or less important as an influence on overall corporate performance?

3. Peter F. Drucker, a well-known management scholar, recently described the distribution function as the "economy's dark continent," implying that this aspect of organizational activity has long been ignored as a potential area for strategic development. Why, do you feel, was there such neglect for so long a period of time?

4. Consider these examples of contemporary marketing channels:

Avon's distribution system delivering cosmetics direct from manufacturer to consumer through a sales force of 400,000 saleswomen.

Levitz' warehouse-showroom method of furniture distribution, which stocks large quantities of furniture delivered to each warehouse-showroom at considerable savings, thus enabling Levitz to pass lower prices on to the consumer.

Hanes Corporation's consignment marketing channel for its L'eggs pantyhose, wherein the retailer takes no title for the goods, makes no financial investment, and performs no delivery service or display maintenance, but receives only a certain percentage of the pantyhose sales for his allocation of space to the L'eggs display.

(a) Select one of the above channels and speculate who the other channel participants are and to what extent each member participates in the eight universal marketing flows.

(b) How might these flows be shifted either among the members now in the channel or to different agencies or institutions not presently included in the system? What do you think would be the implications of such shifts?

(c) Within each of these distribution systems, specify what the consumer's role is from a flow-absorption perspective. How, in turn, does this affect the consumer's level of "compensation"?

5. Do you think a channel management approach is useful and applicable to all types of distribution channel systems? Which types of distribution channels would seemingly need it the most? Which would find it the least applicable?

6. Should advertising agencies and financial institutions be considered as channel members? Why? Why not?

7. Is it more useful, from a managerial perspective, to think of consumers (end-users) as members of a channel or as elements in the task environment of the channel? Can consumers be "manipulated" and/or incorporated by channel management?

8. Are "sorting" and "searching" marketing flows?

9. According to Alderson, "the number of intervening marketing agencies tends to go up as distance increases." Distance, in his conception, is measured in terms of "the time and cost involved in communication and transportaton." What factors, then, would tend to increase (or decrease) distance?

10. What does Alderson mean when he says that a product is viewed by a consumer as possibly increasing the "potency of his assortment?" Does this concept have any inherent managerial usefulness?

11. What is meant by the phrase "discrepancy of assortments?" What value does it have in explaining the factors governing the development of distribution channels?

12. Is routinization a restriction on economic freedom in marketing channels? How are the concepts of routinization and search interrelated?

13. Explain the tradeoffs between the number of available product alternatives *and* search and information costs; between spatial convenience *and* seller costs. Apply your answer to the health care delivery system and to the distribution channel for stainless steel.

14. Bucklin and Carman state that "An optimal structure is one which minimizes the total cost (both commercial and consumer) of the system by the appropriate adjustment of the level of . . . service outputs." Can you apply this statement to each of the marketing flows?

15. In what way does Adam Smith's tenet—"the division of labor is limited by the extent of the market"—relate to channel structure?

16. Is it likely that vertical disintegration is typical in growing industries while vertical integration is typical in declining industries?

17. Develop at least three examples of situations in which transient firms or organizations have disrupted the status quo in channels of distribution.

18. McCammon has argued that "large firms can overcome their tendency to maintain the status quo by underwriting *elite* activities." What do you think he means?

PART TWO

COMPONENTS OF MARKETING CHANNELS

Marketing channels are comprised of a whole host of different types of institutions and agencies. Among the most prominent of these are retailers, wholesalers, common and contract carriers, distribution centers, and public warehouses. In order to gain a perspective on how all of these various institutions might best be put together to form channels, it is necessary to start first with some fundamentals by examining what is going on in each of these various aspects of the so-called distributive trades. Without the fundamentals, it is impossible to design, select, and motivate a "winning" combination.

To some readers of this text, the material in the next three chapters will be "old hat." After all, previous work experience or course work in retailing, wholesaling, and/or physical distribution activities should be sufficient grounding for going on directly to a discussion of the planning, organizing, and controlling of channels. We quite agree. Therefore, the already educated might wish to skim the next several chapters and selectively read parts of them. For others, and for even those who merely will undertake a healthy skimming, here is a brief preview of coming attractions.

Chapter 2 deals with retailing, mainly from a stategic perspective. That is, after a very brief look at the structure of retailing, attention is turned to the operational orientations that retailers adopt in differentiating their offerings from those of their competitors. The dimensions addressed are margins and turnover, assortments, location, and customer services. Then, the strategic environment of retailing is examined. Specifically, the impact on retailing of changes in consumer and resource markets as well as among competitors are explored in some detail. The basic reason for all of the attention being given to environmental factors is quite simple—the environment of retailing is the environment for all consumer goods marketing channels, because retailers are the gatekeepers to the market. If manufacturers or wholesalers are going to deal with retailers, they had better have a thorough knowledge of the factors which impinge on retailing, both operationally and environmentally. For example, some of Sears' massive problems in the late 1970s and early 1980s can be traced to operational factors, such as the move to shopping mall anchor stores (malls have an intense fashion orientation; Sears is not known as a fashion merchant), the costs of developing a consumer franchise in private brands, the continued dependence on salespeople, and internal power struggles between field territories and headquarters merchandisers, *and* to environmental factors, such as the demise of vendor price-fixing (the umbrella under which Sears priced its private label merchandise), the developing force of specialist chains, and the social upheavals of the 1960s which affected shopping patterns into the 1970s and beyond.[1] Suppliers to Sears who did not watch these developments very closely were hurt very badly as Sears' sales started to stagnate.

The chapter on wholesaling (Chapter 3) takes a slightly different tack. A great deal of time is spent getting the reader to understand the structure of wholesaling—the kinds of agencies and institutions that make up this often misunderstood and confusing line of trade. Then the discussion turns to an examination of just what it is that wholesalers can be expected to accomplish for their customers and their suppliers. The examination is more or less what one might expect to find in most textbooks that have dealt with wholesaling. It is followed, however, by a critical (what we call "hard-nosed") assessment of what wholesalers *actually do* accomplish for others. Finally, we discuss some of the managerial concerns of wholesalers. These revolve mainly around asset management, because inventories and accounts receivable make up an enormous percentage of the total assets of any wholesaler's operation. We have devoted a whole chapter to the discussion of wholesaling, because wholesalers play very important roles in many lines of trade, especially those involved with the distribution of industrial goods.

Whether one is talking about retailing, wholesaling, or manufacturing, it is impossible to ignore the critical physical distribution functions involved with moving products from points of production to points of consumption. In fact, opportunities and problems associated with the management of physical distribution are, to some, what the marketing channel is all about. While there is no doubt that dealing effectively with issues surrounding the marketing flows of physical possession (storage and transportation) and ownership (inventory) is essential to the successful management of channels, it is probably better to think of marketing channels as encompassing *both* transaction and physical distribution channels.[2] As Bowersox, et al., state:

[1] See the excellent article entitled "Sears is so big. Until you've been in a huge institution like Sears—or, I suppose, G.M., or the Defense Department—you cannot understand how big it is," *Chain Store Age,* General Merchandise Edition (January 1980), pp. 93–116.

[2] Donald J. Bowersox, *Logistical Management,* rev. ed. (New York: The Macmillan Company, 1978), pp. 36–40.

The *transaction channel* consists of specialized intermediaries such as manufacturing agents, sales personnel, jobbers, wholesalers, and retailers engaged in negotiation, contracting, and post-transaction administration of sales on a continuing basis. The *physical distribution* channel contains a network of intermediaries engaged in the functions of physical movement. Participants are physical distribution specialists concerned with solving problems involved in product transfer.[3]

Chapter 4 explores physical distribution management, in general, and provides a description of physical distribution specialists, in particular. The latter are concerned with meeting customer service objectives of availability, speed and consistency, and quality.

All told, the next three chapters provide the foundation for the construction of marketing channels. Any attempt to manage a channel would be futile without at least a rudimentary knowledge of their contents.

[3] Donald J. Bowersox, M. Bixby Cooper, Douglas M. Lambert, and Donald A. Taylor, *Management in Marketing Channels* (New York: McGraw-Hill Book Company, 1980), p. 199.

TWO

Retailing:
Structure
and Strategy

Modern retailing has emerged as a fiercely competitive and innovation-oriented industry populated by an ever-growing variety of institutions and constantly buffeted by a highly fluid environment. The purpose of this chapter is to describe the complex phenomena impacting at the retail end of the marketing channel so that managers can more fully account for "bottom up" pressures when forming distribution strategies and designing channel systems.

THE STRUCTURE OF RETAILING

Retailing deals with the activities involved in selling goods and services to ultimate consumers. Thus, a retail sale is one in which the buyer is an ultimate consumer, as opposed to a business or institutional purchaser. In contrast to purchases for resale or for business, industrial, or institutional use, the buying motive for a retail sale is always personal or family satisfaction stemming from the final consumption of the item being purchased.[1]

Retailing is one of the major industries in the U.S. It consists of over 1½ million single-unit and over 330 thousand multiunit establishments and accounts for approximately 18 percent of all business in the country.[2] Transacted sales were $884 billion in 1979.[3]

---

[1] Theodore N. Beckman, William R. Davidson, and W. Wayne Talarzyk, *Marketing,* 9th ed. (New York: The Ronald Press Co., 1973), p. 234.

[2] The 330,000 multiunit establishments (defined as two or more units) were owned by 43,700 firms in 1977. U.S. Bureau of Census, *1977 Census of Retail Trade, Establishment and Firm Size,* RC77-S-1 (March 1980), pp. 1–62.

[3] U.S. Bureau of the Census, *Monthly Retail Trade* (December 1979), BR-79-12, (February 1980), p. 4. The $884 billion excludes sales of the service institutions shown in Table 2–1, but includes nonstore retailing.

While the commonly accepted conduits of retailing are stores, the mail, house-to-house salesmen, and automatic vending machines, it is logical to include under the retailing rubric all "outlets" that seek to serve ultimate consumers. These would include service establishments such as motels and hotels, as shown in Table 2-1. Under the broadened concept of marketing, such "outlets" as hospitals, day-care centers, churches, and perhaps even public schools might also be included. These latter institutions, as well as banks and financial institutions (the "retailers" of money), have been omitted from Table 2-1 for a simple reason—it is difficult to quantify their output in terms of dollar sales volume.

Over the past 50 years, retail sales have grown approximately nine times as fast as population and at about the same rate as income. Contrasted to the phenomenal growth in sales, the total number of retail outlets has increased only marginally from about 1½ million to 2 million during this time period, reflecting the increased importance of large-scale, high-volume operations in all fields of retailing and the significant application of managerial expertise that accompanied expansion.

Of the various categories of retailing institutions listed in Table 2-1, store retailing is by far the most significant, accounting for 90 percent of total retail sales volume. Within the store retailing category, food stores obtain the greatest share, accounting for 22 percent of total retail sales in 1979. If one adds eating and drinking place receipts to the food store sales, then food-oriented purchases would consume almost one-third of retail expenditures, giving some notion of the emphasis Americans place on eating and drinking. The automotive group (auto dealers, gas stations) transacted about 28 percent of all sales, while general merchandise stores accounted for approximately 13 percent.[4]

To a significant extent, however, statistics do not reveal the underlying dynamics of the exciting developments that have occurred over the past century. There has been a veritable revolution in retailing, even though small shopkeepers are still local "landmarks" in every community. Specific details of the revolution which highlight broad, secular trends can be found in the writings of Bucklin[5] and

---

[4] It is important to note that there are significant problems in using and analyzing Census of Business data in order to portray movements and shifts over time. As Dalrymple and Thompson point out, merchandise groupings are not necessarily descriptive of the type of merchandise sold, due, in large part, to the existence of scrambled merchandising. Three religious goods stores studied by Dalrymple and Thompson reported sales of packaged alcoholic beverages, cigars, cigarettes, curtains, draperies, hardware, footwear, furniture, and major appliances. In addition, there are changes in Census classifications from one enumeration to another, as well as reclassifications of establishments to reflect changes in the character of their operations. Also, each merchandise group encompasses several components, and changes in one or several of these are masked by the aggregation process. Thus, the category "food stores" includes grocery stores, meat markets, fish markets, fruit and vegetable markets, and candy, nut, and confectionery stores. Within the "food store" category, only grocery stores have fared remarkably well over time. Finally, the Census defines a retail establishment as one that makes at least 51 percent of its sales to retail customers. Under such a system, up to 49 percent of a store's sales could be misclassified. Although such misclassification might not affect drug store sales significantly, since most sales are made to the consumer in such outlets, they might have an important effect on sales of lumber yards. See Douglas J. Dalrymple and Donald L. Thompson, *Retailing: An Economic View* (New York: The Free Press, 1969), p. 17.

[5] See Louis P. Bucklin's careful study entitled *Competition and Evolution in the Distributive Trades* (Englewood Cliffs, N.J.: Prentice-Hall, 1972).

TABLE 2-1   Retail sales of store, nonstore, and service institutions

	1963 (billions of dollars)	1979 [a] (billions of dollars)	Average Annual Increase 1963-1979
Store Retailing			
Food stores	$57.1	$194.7	15.1%
Automobile dealers	45.4	172.2	17.5%
General merchandise group stores [b]	20.5	115.7	29.0%
Eating and drinking places	18.4	76.3	19.7%
Gasoline service stations	17.8	73.7	19.6%
Apparel stores	14.0	41.2	12.1%
Lumber and building material stores	14.6	50.0	15.2%
Drug stores	8.5	28.1	14.4%
Furniture and home furnishing stores	10.9	42.3	18.0%
Liquor stores	5.2	15.3	
Nonstore Retailing [c]	6.3	21.1	14.7%
Services			
Hotels, motels, tourist courts, camps	5.1	23.5	22.5%
Personal services (laundry, dry cleaning, beauty shops, barber shops, photographic, shoe repair, funeral, alteration, etc.)	9.2	22.2	8.8%
Automobile repair and other automotive services	5.4	29.3	27.7%
Miscellaneous repair services (electrical, watch, jewelry, furniture, etc.)	3.0	15.8	26.7%
Amusement, recreation services, motion pictures (dance halls, theatrical presentations, bowling, billiards, commercial sports, etc.)	6.7	25.7	17.7%

[a] Unadjusted for inflation. The total for store and nonstore retailing does not add to $884 billion, the figure cited in the text, because the sales of certain kinds of retailers, such as fuel oil dealers and used merchandise stores, are included in the total but are not included in any of the classifications shown in the table. For reconciliation to the total, see *Monthly Retail Trade*, cited below, pp. 46-51.

[b] Includes department stores, discount department stores, miscellaneous general merchandise stores, variety stores, and jewelry stores.

[c] Includes sales made by mail-order catalog desks located within department stores of some mail-order firms, sales of automatic merchandising machine operators (vending machines), and sales of direct selling establishments (house-to-house canvass, party plan, telephone selling, etc.).

Sources: U.S. Bureau of the Census, *Monthly Retail Trade, December 1979*, BR-79-12 (February 1980), p. 4; and U.S. Bureau of the Census, *Monthly Selected Services Receipts, December 1979*, BS-79-12 (February 1980), p. 2.

McNair and May.[6] The strategic changes which have occurred over the past decade have been cataloged by McCammon and Bates.[7] In this chapter, attention is given to current trends. The focus is on the implications of recent environmental changes for strategic planning in retailing. Without such knowledge on the part of individuals concerned with the marketing of consumer goods, channel management is destined to be shortsighted and ineffective.

Before examining the environment of retailing and its impact on strategy, it is first essential to gain an understanding of the operating dimensions common to all retailing institutions. It is these dimensions that management can manipulate in response to environmental change. From a strategic perspective, retail management can attempt to secure a differential advantage relative to competition by combining the dimensions in different ways. Therefore, we now turn to a discussion of the generic dimensions. Then we shall explore the strategic environment of retailing, carrying these dimensions along in our analytical kit.

THE OPERATIONAL DIMENSIONS OF RETAIL INSTITUTIONS

The character of almost all retail institutions is determined by the choices management makes, in light of marketplace pressures, relative to margin and inventory goals, assortments of merchandise to be carried, location of outlets, and customer services to be offered.[8] Thus, the typical definitions of a number of highly familiar retail institutions shown in Exhibit 2-1 are generally couched in terms reflecting these dimensions. The ultimate operating dimensions adopted by management are the resultant of two major forces: (1) consumer demand for service outputs[9] and (2) internal financial requirements. The latter directly affect the margin and turnover dimensions, while the former directly impact the assortment, location, and customer services dimensions. Each operating dimension is discussed briefly below.

"Margin" and "Turnover" Dimensions

The fundamental point of departure between traditional and modern retailing systems might best be conceptualized by contrasting institutions characterized by high-margin, low-turnover, and numerous personal services with those characterized by low-margin, high-turnover, and minimum services. Both sets of institutions

---

[6] Malcolm P. McNair and Eleanor G. May, *The Evolution of Retail Institutions in the United States* (Cambridge, Mass.: Marketing Science Institute, 1976).

[7] Bert C. McCammon, Jr., and Albert D. Bates, "Reseller Strategies and the Financial Performance of the Firm," in Hans B. Thorelli (ed.), *Strategy + Structure = Performance* (Bloomington, Ind.: Indiana University Press, 1977), pp. 146–178.

[8] The discussion of major operational concepts found here is based on Ronald R. Gist, *Retailing: Concepts and Decisions* (New York: John Wiley & Sons, 1968), pp. 37–79. It is possible to expand the list considerably by subdividing the various concepts, thereby explicitly highlighting such variables as layout, atmospherics, and promotion.

[9] The concept of service outputs was introduced in Chapter 1.

Department Stores are retail organizations that (1) sell a wide variety of merchandise, including piece goods, home furnishings, and furniture; (2) are organized by departments; (3) have large sales; (4) sell mainly to women; (5) are located typically in downtown shopping districts or in newer shopping centers; (6) frequently establish branch operations; and (7) usually offer a large amount of "free" service.

Specialty Stores retail a broad selection of a restricted class of goods. While there are departmentalized specialty stores of considerable size (e.g., Filene's and I. Magnin), the term "specialty store" is most commonly applied to small and medium-sized establishments or boutiques handling limited lines of soft (clothing, linens, etc.) or hard (kitchen utensils, appliances, etc.) goods.

Chain Store Systems are characterized by: (1) central ownership or control; (2) central management; (3) similarity of stores; and (4) two or more units. (Recent Census classification has expanded the number of stores comprising a chain to eleven or more.) Buying power combined with managerial efficiencies characterize effective chain store system operations.

Supermarkets are generally low-margin, high-turnover retail organizations. In the food industry, a supermarket can be defined as a large, departmentalized retail establishment offering a relatively broad and complete stock of dry groceries, fresh meat, perishable produce, and dairy products, supplemented by a variety of convenience, nonfood merchandise and operated on a self-serve basis.

Planned Shopping Centers are integrated developments, under single ownership, with coordinated and complete shopping facilities, and with adequate parking space. The stores in the centers are leased to various retailers. Frequently, the stores in the centers engage in joint advertising, promotional, and public relations programs.

Discount Houses are retail establishments which generally have the following features: (1) a broad merchandise assortment, including both soft and hard goods; (2) price as the main sales appeal; (3) relatively low operating cost ratios; (4) relatively inexpensive buildings, equipment, and fixtures; (5) an emphasis on self-service operations; (6) limited customer services; (7) emphasis on rapid turnover of merchandise; (8) large stores and parking areas; (9) carnival-like atmospheres; and (10) frequent use of leased departments.

Nonstore Retailers are typified by three general types of organizations:

1. *Automatic merchandisers* utilize vending machines. The assortment offered is limited to stable products of low unit value and certain other convenience goods. Costs of operations are usually high due to the use of expensive machines that re-

quire considerable stocking time and repair labor. Thus, both prices and margins are typically high.

2. *Mail order houses* are establishments that receive their orders by mail and make their sales (deliveries) by mail, parcel post, express, truck, or freight. Retail mail order houses are of three main types: the department store merchandise house (Alden's; Montgomery Ward; Sears, Roebuck; and Spiegel); the smaller general merchandise firm which carries lines that are far less broad than would be found in a department store; and the specialty house (e.g., Franklin Mint Corporation). Generally, installment credit is used extensively and other commonly offered services include telephone ordering, convenient pickup depots, catalog stores, strong guarantees, and liberal return policies. Prices are supposedly lower than at conventional retailers' outlets, although postal and delivery charges tend to bring their prices closer to those existing elsewhere.

3. *House-to-house selling* is typified by organizations, such as Avon and Stanley Home Products, that engage in direct sales to ultimate consumers in the latter's homes. Demonstration and return after trial are among the various services offered by house-to-house sellers, while cash, rather than credit, is the usual mode of transaction. In general, overhead costs are relatively low for these operations, with the major expense items being travel costs and salesperson turnover.

Source: Many of the definitions and descriptions provided above can be found in greater detail in James M. Carman and Kenneth P. Uhl, *Phillips and Duncan's Marketing: Principles and Methods*, 7th ed. (Homewood, Ill.: Richard D. Irwin, 1973), pp. 175-225.

continue to exist, but in the twentieth century, the spotlight has focused on the revolutionary volume efficiencies flowing out of the latter style of operation. This has been especially true in grocery retailing, where such mass merchandising outlets as limited item stores, warehouse stores, and combination stores (see Exhibit 2-2) continue to evolve.

Essentially, the low-margin/high-turnover model is oriented towards generating maximal operational efficiency and passing on the savings generated to the customer. However, many of the savings "passed on to the customer" must be seen as involving a *transfer* of cost (opportunity cost as well as actual "effort" cost) rather than a clear elimination of it. Thus, reductions in service output levels, such as those associated with product selection opportunity, convenience of location, "atmosphere," personal services, financial and delivery accommodations, and the like, accompany the typical retail "package" offered by the low-margin/high-turnover operation. In essence, then, this operational philosophy is founded on the costs (represented by marketing functions or flows) which certain segments of consumers are willing to absorb in certain classes of purchasing behavior.

What this means in terms of comparative, visible characteristics of the two polar prototypes is indicated in Exhibit 2-3. Exhibit 2-4 illustrates how specific stores may be positioned along these dimensions. Clearly, real world retailing organizations may fall anywhere in the space described by the two axes. Sometimes

EXHIBIT 2-2
New Alternatives in Grocery Retailing

Limited Item Store Characteristics	Combination Store Characteristics	Warehouse Store Characteristics
Normally less than 1000 items	Generally range from 35,000 to 60,000 square feet	Reduced gross margins, running as low as 11-12%.
Limited number of national brands and sporadic brand/item availability	Full food mix including perishables	Reduced labor costs, usually under 4% of sales or one half to one third that of a conventional supermarket.
Generally one brand and one size per item	Features a pharmacy, health and beauty aids, toiletries, and all general merchandise normally carried by a super drug store	High unit sales; individual store tapes run as high as five times the supermarket average.
Store hours limited		
Items displayed in cut cartons	Ratio of food to drug usually 60-40	Limited item selection; brands, sizes, and varieties carried by warehouse markets vary, but range from 1,000 to 8,000 items.
No individual item pricing	Average annual volume $13 million with some reaching $20 million or more	
Little or no perishables	25% to 30% of sales attributed to general merchandise	Erratic brand/item availability.
Customers do their own bagging		
Generally 5,000-14,000 sq. ft. of selling area	Common checkout area for food, drug, and general merchandise items	Special deal items; different brands will appear and disappear as manufacturer deals come and go.
No check cashing	Average 13 checkouts with average weekly sales of $19,000 per checkout	
Little advertising		Limited perishables; some warehouse markets carry fresh meat and push big cuts or large orders. Many carry frozen meat only—or none at all. Produce may be limited or in bulk only if available at all.
		Varied locations; warehouse stores emerged in fringe market areas drawing blue-collar workers, but many are now opening in large cities and drawing a cross section of the population.
		Low construction costs; preexisting buildings or simple concrete block construction with minimum decor are generally preferred.

Source: "Continuing Evolution in Grocery Retailing," *The Nielsen Researcher,* No. 2 (1980), pp. 4, 5, and 8.

EXHIBIT 2–3

**Characteristics of Low-Margin/High-Turnover Retailing Strategies
Vs. High-Margin/Low-Turnover Strategies**

Low Margin High Turnover	High Margin Low Turnover
(a) National advertised "presold" or "self-sold" merchandise—customers "buy," as distinct from being "sold" by store personnel.	(a) Merchandise "sold" in-store.
(b) Assumes low prices are the most important patronage determinant.	(b) Assumes service, distinctive merchandise, and sales skill are the most important patronage determinants.
(c) Few, if any, "free" services are offered: a separate or "optional" charge may be involved for these.	(c) Many services—besides sales help, credit, delivery, many subsidiary services also; e.g., baby-sitting, cooking classes, amusement rooms for children.
(d) Tends toward isolated or "low rent" locations.	(d) Downtown or shopping center "cluster" locations.
(e) Simplified organizational structures— few staff specialists, supervisory and administrative positions.	(e) Complex organization, relatively large number of specialists, supervisors, and administrators.

Source: Adapted from Ronald R. Gist, *Retailing Concepts and Decisions* (New York: John Wiley & Sons, 1968), pp. 39-40.

EXHIBIT 2–4

The Margin-Turnover Classification

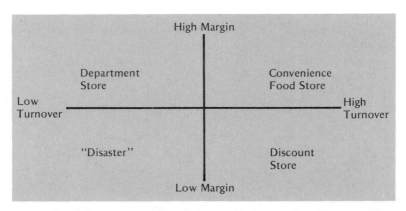

Source: Joseph B. Mason and Morris L. Mayer, *Modern Retailing: Theory and Practice* (Dallas: Business Publications, Inc., 1978), p. 27.

an outlet has, as Mason and Mayer point out, been forced by price competition to maintain low margins, but because of a poor location, incompetent management, or undercapitalization, it is unable to generate a sufficient volume of business.[10] Such an outlet might be described as operating in the low-margin/low-turnover quadrant. Obviously, this quadrant does not represent an institutional prototype in the sense of a class of organizations demonstrating a unique functional viability.

Of critical importance in determining which path to follow—low margin/high turnover vs. high margin/low turnover—are management's perceptions of the organization's financial requirements. The appropriate pathway can be highlighted by using the strategic profit model (SPM). The specifics of this model are spelled out in detail in Chapter 11. However, a brief description of the SPM is introduced here, so that the reader can gain some appreciation of its influence on the margin and turnover dimensions of retail strategy.

Basically, the SPM can be laid out as follows:

$$\frac{\frac{\text{Net profit}}{\text{Net sales}}}{\times} \quad = \quad \frac{\text{Net profit}}{\text{Total assets}} \quad \times \quad \frac{\text{Total assets}}{\text{Net worth}} \quad = \quad \frac{\text{Net profit}}{\text{Net worth}}$$

$$\frac{\text{Net sales}}{\text{Total assets}}$$

Management can pursue margin management (net profit/net sales), asset turnover (net sales/total assets), *and/or* financial management via financial leverage (total assets/net worth) in order to secure a target return on net worth. If there is tremendous downward pressure on margins, due to competitive forces and economic conditions generally, then a likely path for management to pursue is asset turnover, especially in "tight" money situations where interest rates are extremely high and leveraging is difficult. Clearly, these sets of conditions have, in recent years, led management to emphasize such criteria as sales per square foot (which reflects space and location productivity), sales per employee (which reflects labor productivity), and sales per transaction (which reflects merchandising program productivity).

Increasingly, retailers have turned to an evaluation of the gross margin return on inventory (GMROI) in line with their desire to improve asset turnover, specifically, and overall profitability, generally.[11] The components of GMROI are as follows:

$$\frac{\text{Gross margin}}{\text{Net sales}} \quad \times \quad \frac{\text{Net sales}}{\text{Average inventory}} \quad = \quad \frac{\text{Gross margin}}{\text{Average inventory}}$$
$$\text{(at cost)} \qquad\qquad\qquad \text{(at cost)}$$

[10] Joseph B. Mason and Morris L. Mayer, *Modern Retailing: Theory and Practice* (Dallas: Business Publications, Inc., 1978), p. 29.

[11] See Daniel J. Sweeney, "Improving the Profitability of Retail Merchandising Decisions," *Journal of Marketing,* Vol. 37 (January 1973), pp. 60–68.

GMROI allows the retailer to evaluate inventory on the return on investment it produces and not just on the gross margin percentage. As Bates observes, this means that GMROI often considers items with widely varying gross margin percentages as equally profitable, as in the following example:[12]

Item	Gross margin	×	Sales to inventory	=	GMROI
A	50%		3		150%
B	30%		5		150%
C	25%		6		150%

According to Bates:

> By using GMROI approaches the firm expands its alternatives in exploring methods for improving inventory results. There are many product categories where price competition prevents raising the gross margin. In this instance, improved inventory performance can be used to raise GMROI. If the firm were just using gross margin percentage, this flexibility would not be so obvious.
>
> GMROI also allows the firm to consciously consider the tradeoff between gross margin and inventory utilization. There might be instances in which the firm would knowingly lower its gross margin in an effort to produce a higher sales to inventory ratio and a higher GMROI. Only a concept such as GMROI can provide a basis for making such a decision.[13]

Another major criterion used by retailers, especially supermarkets, to select items which enhance asset turnover while at the same time providing an adequate return is gross margin dollars generated per linear or cubic foot of shelf space assigned to the item, as calculated by the following formula:

$$\frac{\text{Gross margin per unit (\$)} \times \text{Number of units sold}}{\text{Linear (cubic) feet of shelf space assigned to the unit}}$$

Such a measure permits assessment of performance as well as serves as a guide for determining which merchandise items to add or delete. The use of measures such as this one and GMROI by retailers places pressures on suppliers. Not only do the gross margins offered by suppliers have to be adequate, but the suppliers are often forced to engage in extensive promotion of the items in order to generate the sales volume (in units) required by the retailers. In addition, suppliers are forced to give more attention to the amount of shelf or floor space consumed by their items. Furthermore, any systems designed by suppliers to speed up the replenishment of inventory on the shelf can be helpful in generating the numbers for adequate perfor-

---

[12] Albert D. Bates, *Retailing and Its Environment* (New York: D. Van Nostrand Company, 1979), p. 155.

[13] *Ibid.*, pp. 155–156.

mance. Faster replenishment rates mean less need for shelf space and less inventory investment, thereby reducing the denominator in the formulae.

In order to secure consistent approaches in the margin and turnover dimensions and thus achieve targeted rates of return, some retailers, such as Radio Shack, Petrie Stores, and Target Stores, are adopting totally rationalized programs. These involve a high degree of centralized management control combined with the establishment of rigorous operating procedures for each phase of the retail operation.[14] In this way, every aspect of the company's operation is performed in an identical manner in every store. The implications for suppliers to such retailers are, again, profound:

> For manufacturers, rationalized retailing could lead to more formalized relationships with retail accounts as retailers develop sophisticated supplier evaluation programs, make greater use of buying committees and other centralized management techniques, and purchase a greater share of their requirements on a contractual, programmed basis.[15]

"Assortment" Dimensions

The three terms "general," "variety," and "specialty" are commonly used to describe retail stores based on the *extent* of product lines carried, i.e., the extent of consumer selection offered. However, while the specialty store has demonstrated a remarkable upswing in the last two decades, the concepts of general and variety stores have been so drastically overhauled that they have little defining power in the modern world of U.S. retailing. With the bankruptcy of W. T. Grant in 1975, Woolworth is the last *national* variety store chain. The strategic problem for variety chains is that supermarkets and drugstore chains are selling more and more variety-store-type merchandise. Traditional trade distinctions are rapidly evaporating in a very fluid market.

Therefore, rather than cling to old-hat definitions, it is better to use the term "variety" to describe generically different classes of goods making up the product offer, i.e., the *breadth* of product lines. The term "assortment," on the other hand, refers to the *depth* of product brands or models offered within each generic product category. Typically, a discount department store like K-Mart would have a limited assortment of fast-moving, low-priced items across a wide variety of household goods, ready-to-wear, cosmetics, sporting goods, electric appliances, auto accessories, and the like. In contrast, a specialty store dealing only, or primarily, in home audio-visual electronic goods, such as Radio Shack or Palmer Electronics, would have a very large and complete line of radios, tape recorders, and high fidelity equipment, offering the deepest selection of models, styles, sizes, prices, etc.

With many modern retail operations diversifying their traditional lines of generically "related" products into unrelated lines and with traditional concepts of what constitutes a retail line of trade being freely trampled upon, it may be more

[14] Albert D. Bates, "The Troubled Future of Retailing," *Business Horizons* (August 1976), p. 27.
[15] *Ibid.,* p. 28.

appropriate to focus most attention here on the practice of general merchandising and to discuss the principles that underlie "generalization" as a strategy. For example, from a strategic perspective, there is a major tradeoff between providing one-stop shopping convenience and offering locational convenience. The size of operations required to carry a wide variety of products which permit one-stop shopping militates against locational convenience. On the other hand, there is also a direct, and equally vital, tradeoff between selection convenience and delivered price. Carrying slower-moving models to complete the product assortment militates against price discounting. Consumer markets comprise numerous segments with differing sets of shopping needs. Normatively speaking, retailing institutions design and evolve their product-mix strategies to suit changing shopping patterns.

At the macro level, generalization takes the form of substantial integration of whole lines of trade. The strategic opportunity here lies in enhancing one-stop shopping convenience and, as a spillover, increasing exposure of the store's entire offer to impulse purchasing. Taken to its extreme, generalization can result in institutional diversification. All of these strategies are highly visible in today's fluid retail markets.

Across the board diversification by many leading retail chains has led to the emergence of what some authors describe as the *conglomerchant*,[16] and the trade literature continuously reports numerous takeover bids, acquisitions, and mergers. For example, at the close of 1979, Dayton Hudson, one of the nation's fastest growing and most profitable retailing giants, was operating 661 stores in 44 states, the District of Columbia, and Puerto Rico. Included in its holdings are Hudson's, Dayton's, Diamonds, and John A. Brown department stores, Target and Lechmere discount stores, B. Dalton Bookseller, several regional jewelry store chains, and Mervyn's, a softlines retail company with stores in California, Arizona, New Mexico, Nevada, and Oregon.

Two tactical concepts related to variety and assortment strategies are "creaming" and "scrambling." The "creaming" approach incorporates largely presold, fast-moving items picked out from some other line of retailing. For example, a specialty store adding some lines of impulse goods, such as candy bars, would typically offer only a small number of the fastest selling brands out of the scores of brands available for display. Creaming is a low-risk ("small but sure") profits tactic, because brands with strong consumer preferences typically allow only small retail margins.[17] Generalization strategies of supermarkets and drug chains have the appearance of "creaming" when compared to the more systematic departmentalization of discounter product mixes. Drug stores are carrying *selected* cameras, auto accessories, and even camping equipment and lawn furniture, but they certainly are not setting up whole departments in these lines.

Retailers generalizing with an eye to larger profit contributions tend to turn to

[16] See, for example, Rollie Tillman, "Rise of the Conglomerchant," *Harvard Business Review,* Vol. 49 (November-December 1971), pp. 44–51. Also see Richard Miller, "Strategic Pathways to Growth in Retailing," *The Journal of Business Strategy,* Vol. 1 (Winter 1981), pp. 16–29.

[17] Ronald R. Gist, *op. cit.,* p. 102.

"scrambling." Scrambling would typically carry the retailer into a much more diverse and unrelated mix of product lines. The brands involved offer higher margins, are slower moving, and do not have as strong consumer preferences. Scrambling is a "large but unsure" profit tactic with a greater measure of risk. It will likely involve the retailer in promotional activity to support the line. Scrambling is a widely practiced growth and profit strategy of mass retailers, and its impact on the structure of retailing has been far-reaching. As Gist observes, "The logic of 'scrambling' is such that we might expect the types of institutions that operate [exclusively] on a high-margin, low-stock-turnover philosophy to fall prey through 'scrambling' to the institutions that feature the low-margin, high-stock-turnover philosophy."[18] Nonprescription drugs and watches were among the first products to fall prey to scrambling by the new high-volume retailers.

The "assortment" dimension of retailing operations is clearly a matter which demands the attention of top management, for decisions in this area will "color" the entire character of the enterprise. However, once the general strategy is established for the organization, the tactical task of choosing specific products or brands usually falls to functionaries called "buyers." Buyers play a central role in retailing; unlike their counterparts in manufacturing concerns, their status within their "home" organizations is very high. Because buying is such a critical aspect of retailing, it is important to understand the evaluative processes and procedures that take place in vendor selection. Therefore, Appendix 2A contains a discussion of the choice strategies employed by retail buyers; Appendix 2B includes a glossary of pricing and buying terms commonly used by retailers; and Appendix 2C contains a brief description of some of their merchandise planning and control procedures.

"Location" Dimensions

In a general sense, products are classified on the basis of consumer purchasing patterns. That is, they are thought of as being convenience, shopping, or specialty goods. Implicit in this conceptualization is the extent of *search-shopping* activity the consumer is willing to expend. Consequently, there are strategic "location" implications in the product line variety and assortment strategies the retailer pursues. In addition, there are extremely critical environmental impacts deriving from shifts and trends in intracity and interregional residence patterns.

As discussed in Chapter 5, which deals with marketing channel strategy and design, Bucklin has suggested a matrix classification of convenience, shopping, and specialty *stores* against convenience, shopping, and specialty *goods*.[19] With such a cross-classification scheme to guide him, a retailer can first select his target markets

---

[18] *Ibid.,* p. 103. For some excellent analyses of these and related issues, see Edgar A. Pessemier, *Retail Assortments* (Cambridge, Mass.: Marketing Science Institute, Report No. 80–111, December 1980).

[19] Louis P. Bucklin, "Retail Strategy and the Classification of Consumer Goods," *Journal of Marketing,* Vol. 27 (January 1963), pp. 50–55. For an extension of Bucklin's scheme, see Morris L. Mayer, J. Barry Mason, and Morris Gee, "A Reconceptualization of Store Classification as Related to Retail Strategy Formulation," *Journal of Retailing,* Vol. 47 (Fall 1971), p. 35.

and then develop appropriate strategies to reach those segments. For example, to appeal to the convenience store-specialty good segment, two important elements in the retailer's marketing mix would be (1) a highly accessible location and (2) a good selection of widely accepted brands.[20] Depth of assortment, price, store promotion, facilities, and personal selling are less important when specialty goods are sold through convenience stores.

Consumer search-shopping behavior varies between consumer segments as well as between product categories. It also varies over time as demographic and lifestyle changes occur across market segments. For example, the tendency in recent times has been toward decreased search-shopping patterns. Research has indicated that the typical consumer may visit only one store and rarely more than two.[21] Significantly, such patterns seem to be true even for a variety of *shopping* goods.[22] As the section of this chapter devoted to a discussion of environmental change will develop more fully, time saved is becoming as important as money saved. This factor, along with widespread access and exposure to mass media, is reducing both shopping frequency as well as information "search" necessity.

The implications of these observations are profound, because they mean that location decisions are becoming even more critical to retailer viability. Once a retailer has selected a specific region of the country that he wishes to enter (e.g., the southwest) and a specific metropolitan or rural market within that region that he wishes to serve (e.g., Austin), he must delineate the relevant trading area for the type of retailing establishment he wishes to erect and then pick a specific location within the trading area as a store site. Because these decisions are so crucial, we now turn to a brief discussion of the major factors involved with each.

TRADING AREA MEASUREMENT AND EVALUATION. A trading area is the area from which a retailer draws or expects to draw the vast majority of his customers. Retailing is a localized activity, and the bulk of any establishment's sales may be traced to persons within the immediately surrounding area. Basically, the extent of a trading area is determined by two factors: (1) the nature of the product(s) or service(s) being offered, including price, availability from other sources, and the extent to which the merchandise or service reflects the user's taste; and (2) the consumer's perception of the shopping task or attitude toward the buying process. (Some consumers consider shopping a pleasure, while others see it as a chore. Obviously, the greater the number in the former category, the larger the trading area is likely to be.)

In operational terms, a *trading area* can be defined from a buyer's, seller's, and/or sales volume standpoint.

[20] William J. Stanton, *Fundamentals of Marketing,* 4th ed. (New York: McGraw-Hill Book Co., 1975), p. 134.

[21] William P. Dommermuth and Edward W. Cundiff, "Shopping Goods, Shopping Centers, and Selling Strategies," *Journal of Marketing,* Vol. 31 (October 1961), p. 33.

[22] Joseph B. Mason and Morris L. Mayer, "Empirical Observations of Consumer Behavior in the Marketplace: Implications for a Classification of Goods System and Retail Strategy Formulation," *Journal of Retailing,* Vol. 48 (Fall 1972), pp. 22–23.

- From a *buyer's standpoint,* a trading area is the region inside which the buyer may reasonably expect to find goods and services at competitive and prevailing prices.
- From a *seller's standpoint,* a trading area is a district whose size is usually determined by boundaries within which it is economical in terms of volume and cost for a marketing unit or group to sell and/or deliver a good or service.
- From a *sales volume standpoint,* a trading area is the area surrounding the community from which a retailer secures approximately 90 percent of his sales of a representative group of commodities. Sometimes the trading area is classified in terms of primary and secondary areas. The primary area includes 75 percent of the customers, and the secondary area includes 15 percent. The remaining 10 percent represents the fringe or tertiary trading area.

Trading area determination is a complex process, since an area's size is a function of the individual store character and mode of operation as well as the cluster or grouping of stores surrounding the individual store. For example, if the store sells unique and exclusive merchandise, its trading area definitely becomes larger. A case in point is Neiman Marcus in Dallas; because of its novel assortments, its trading area encompasses cities well outside Dallas' limits. Furthermore, because Neiman Marcus uses mail order extensively for some items during Christmas, its trading area is considerably broader than other department stores.[23] In fact, with the increased popularity of mail-order selling and, concomitantly, in-home purchasing, trading areas for a wide variety of organizations have increased markedly in recent years.[24]

Dalrymple and Thompson have observed that trading areas result from the collective responses people make in balancing the attractiveness of near and distant retail outlets against the cost, time, and energy that must be spent in overcoming distance.[25] Studies have shown that style and fashion goods produce significantly greater consumer travel and search activity than low-value, bulky items such as lumber, or convenience items such as food.[26] For existing stores and shopping centers, the geographic extent of trading areas can be established through the use of automobile license checks, charge account records, mail-order lists, check clearings, automobile traffic flow, and newspaper circulation. For example, Sears uses an optical scanner to read customer addresses off credit records; the addresses are then plotted by the computer on maps.[27] An analysis of the customer's demographic

---

[23] For an interesting discussion and empirical investigation concerning the problems and assumptions involved in estimating the economic potential for retail establishments, see Joseph B. Mason and Charles T. More, ''Traditional Assumptions in Trading Area and Economic Potential Studies: A Dissenting View,'' *Land Economics,* Vol. 46 (May 1970), pp. 199–201.

[24] See Rita Reif, ''Mail Order: Old Road to New Sales,'' *New York Times,* Section 3, August 24, 1975, p. 1. See also ''Happiness is Retailing without Stores,'' *Forbes* (January 15, 1977), p. 55.

[25] Dalrymple and Thompson, *op. cit.,* p. 98.

[26] *Ibid.*

[27] Computer graphics are becoming extremely useful in trading area and site location analysis. See ''The Spurt in Computer Graphics,'' *Business Week* (June 16, 1980), pp. 104–106.

characteristics can be obtained from these same records in order to develop a profile of each store's trading area within the Sears organization.

SELECTING A SPECIFIC SITE.   Once potential trading areas are defined, a description of several specifically proposed sites within each is developed with respect to such factors as accessibility and traffic flow, extent of trading area, population and its distribution, income, economic stability, and competition.[28] Evidence that can be used as a first approximation of the value of a site includes: (1) consumer preference for an existing store or cluster of stores, and (2) natural or man-made barriers to the free movement of customers in the direction of the proposed site. Even though retail location analysis is still a field characterized by its experts as an art rather than a science,[29] it is possible to go well beyond this first approximation in assessing a potential site. For example, Victory Markets, a chain comprised of over 90 supermarkets operating out of Norwich, N.Y., uses a computerized evaluation model to predict the weekly retail sales of a potential site. The predictions generated by Victory have been within 2 percent of the actual sales generated.[30]

Over the years, a number of attempts have been made to bring more rigorous approaches to retail site selection problem solving, including the development of checklist methods,[31] analog methods,[32] gravity models,[33] environmental models,[34]

[28] See Saul B. Cohen and William Applebaum, "Evaluating Store Sites and Determining Store Rents," *Economic Geography,* Vol. 36 (January 1960), pp. 1–35.

[29] See William Applebaum, "Methods for Determining Store Trade Areas, Market Penetration and Potential Sales," *Journal of Marketing Research,* Vol. 3 (May 1966), pp. 127–141.

[30] "Site Selection by Computer Model," *op. cit.,* p. E77. For another example of computerized site selection, see the approach that the Rayco Company has employed with considerable success in "Can a Computer Tell You Where to Locate Stores?" *Chain Store Age—Executive Edition* (December 1964), p. E28.

[31] See, for example, Kotler's modification of the traditional check-list approach in Philip Kotler, *Marketing Management: Analysis, Planning, and Control,* 2nd ed. (Englewood Cliffs, N.J.: Prentice-Hall, 1972), pp. 617–619.

[32] See William Applebaum, "The Analog Method for Estimating Potential Store Sales," in Curt Kornblau (ed.), *Guide to Store Location Research with Emphasis on Supermarkets* (Reading, Mass.: Addison Wesley, 1968), pp. 232–243.

[33] See, for example, David L. Huff, "Ecological Characteristics of Consumer Behavior," *Papers and Proceedings of the Regional Science Association,* Vol. 7 (1961), pp. 19–21; "Defining and Estimating a Trading Area," *Journal of Marketing,* Vol. 28 (July 1964), pp. 34–38; and "A Probabilistic Analysis of Consumer Spatial Behavior," in William S. Decker (ed.), *Emerging Concepts in Marketing* (Chicago: American Marketing Association, 1963), pp. 443–461. Huff's gravitation model appears to be the most widely quoted site selection approach in marketing textbooks. Unfortunately, the model suffers from severe operational and practical difficulties. For a discussion of these difficulties, see David B. MacKay, *Consumer Movement and Store Location Analysis,* unpublished Ph.D. dissertation, Northwestern University, June 19, 1971, pp. 40–43.

A useful extension of the gravitational models suggested by Huff is the Multiplicative Competitive Interactive (MCI) model. The MCI model explicitly incorporates the competitive environment in the evaluation of store sites. Furthermore, it has been demonstrated that the MCI model can be calibrated using least squares and simulation procedures. See Arun K. Jain and Vijay Mahajan, "Evaluating the Competitive Environment in Retailing Using Multiplicative Competitive Interactive Model," in Jagdish N. Sheth, *Research in Marketing,* Vol. 2 (Greenwich, Conn.: JAI Press, Inc., 1979), pp. 217–235.

[34] See William R. Kinney, Jr., "Separating Environmental Factor Effects for Location and Facility Decisions," *Journal of Retailing,* Vol. 48 (Spring 1972), pp. 67–75.

regression analysis,[35] sectogram techniques,[36] and microanalytic modeling.[37] A brief descriptive summary of each of these methods is provided in Exhibit 2–5. Most of these methods are, however, plagued with theoretical, operational, or practical difficulties[38] such that, irrespective of the approach taken in the store-location decision process, the retailer's qualitative judgment must enter into the final analysis. This is so because of the great many variables which affect the utility of a location beyond those employed in the various models or techniques, as specified in Exhibit 2–5. It would be essential to evaluate factors related to the nature and strength of competition, the socioeconomic pattern of the area, trading area growth potential, the availability of the site, and the existence of facilitating agencies (e.g., mass transit) before a decision is made.[39] For example, in many cases, retailers evaluate current demand and ignore future demand, even though the economic growth potential of an area is critical. In fact, the location decision is a dynamic one because of shifts in population concentration and the continuous development of the structure of retailing.

"Customer Service" Dimensions

Virtually all major retail innovations of the twentieth century have relied to greater or lesser degrees on manipulating the "services" variable to contribute to their strategic operational "offer." The principle is easy to appreciate when we consider such services as in-store sales help. When retailers drop the "friendly" behind-the-counter sales assistant who personally helps customers locate and compare merchandise and is available for "expert" advice, the whole locate-compare-selection process is being functionally shifted to the consumer.

Retailing is one of the few remaining industries that is highly labor intensive. Labor costs are estimated to exceed 50 to 60 percent of a store's total expenses and are even higher than this for a "full-service" organization.[40] Hence, the economies that can be passed on to the consumer by eliminating certain in-store assistance are usually substantial. The same is true for delivery functions, but the principle is not immediately apparent for services like customer credit. The fact is that, besides the cost of risk and the cost of administering credit plans, the retailer also assumes the

---

[35] See, for example, G. I. Heald, "Application of the Automatic Interaction Detector (AID) Programme and Multiple Regression Technique to the Assessment of Store Performance and Site Selection," *Operations Research Quarterly,* Vol. 23 (December 1972), pp. 445–457.

[36] See Schneider, *op. cit.*

[37] See David B. MacKay, "A Microanalytic Approach to Store Location Analysis," *Journal of Marketing Research,* Vol. 9 (May 1972), pp. 134–140.

[38] For a summary of the difficulties associated with many of these methods and models, see MacKay, *Consumer Movement . . ., op. cit.,* pp. 29–67. Also see Willard R. Bishop, Jr., *An Application of the Intra-Urban Gravity Model to Store Location Research,* unpublished Ph.D. dissertation, Cornell University, 1969.

[39] Robert F. Zaloudek, "Practical Location Analysis in New Market Areas," *Stores,* Vol. 53 (November 1971), pp. 15, 40–41.

[40] Larry D. Redinbaugh, *Retailing Management: A Planning Approach* (New York: McGraw-Hill Book Co., 1976), pp. 12 and 14.

EXHIBIT 2-5

Several Quantitative Approaches to Retail Store Location Analysis

Type of Technique/Approach	Technique/Approach Description
Checklist methods	Lists all factors that must be considered in site selection. Factors are given subjective weights by the retailer, and each potential site is rated on each factor. Numerical ratings result for each site on each factor and factor rankings for each site are then combined to yield an overall evaluation for each location.
Analog models	Sales or volume projections of new stores are based directly on the sales or volume estimates of existing stores.
Gravity models	Sales of proposed retail development are estimated on the basis of a potential site's size and its spatial relationship to the market it serves.
Environmental models	The performance of a retail outlet is described as the sum of the effects of various quantifiable location and facility factors (such as local population characteristics—income, ages, occupational class—competition, nature and condition of outlet facilities), and the effect of managerial actions. A linear statistical model scans the proposed locations and computes the expected contributions of all facility combinations of these locations.
Regression analysis	Annual store sales are predicted on the basis of a set of independent variables that record the demographic and physical characteristics of stores and their neighborhoods.
Sectogram techniques	The spatial relationship between a set of retail facilities and the consumers who utilize them is analyzed on a metropolis-wide basis. Determines how well the spatial pattern of retail outlets and population are matched, identifying those underserved areas as high potential locations.
Microanalytic modeling	Recognizes the multistop facet of shopping behavior. Evaluates potential retail locations using a spatial model defined by means of discriminant analysis and Monte Carlo simulation.

customer's inventory holding investment function in extending credit. It takes little imagination to visualize the considerable savings it would mean for operations like Sears to be able to reduce inventory "time" by a month, the usual period for which credit is allowed without charge. However, successful operations are not built on transferring "savings" for the sake of savings, but on being able to identify the functions that customers are willing to assume and the cost in time, money, effort, and convenience at which the assumption becomes attractive to them.

Because customers and products differ in their service requirements, successful retail operations can be designed around different levels of "service" offers. Thus, self-service outlets, such as warehouse retailers, supermarkets, and discount stores, provide very few services, emphasize price appeals, and generally focus on staple goods. Full-service outlets, such as specialty stores and department stores, provide a wide variety of services and tend to be oriented towards merchandising fashion or specialty merchandise. The most dramatic innovations in retailing over the past 40 years have hinged primarily on reducing customer services, though for certain services, like credit cards, competitive pressures have often made the innovators backtrack a little. Institutions that fall under descriptions of discount houses, warehouse retailers, and catalog showrooms belong to this group. But, on the other hand, mail-order selling, numerous specialty stores (e.g., The Limited, The Gap, Crate & Barrel), and retailing through vending machines have also demonstrated robust growth. These latter institutions represent situations where services have been maintained or increased.[41]

THE STRATEGIC ENVIRONMENT OF RETAILING

Retailers are the gatekeepers to the market for all other members of consumer goods marketing channels. In fact, retailers are the only channel members who come face-to-face *on a regular basis* with the most important elements of a commercial channel's environment—consumers. Due to their strategic position, it is not surprising that retailers are most immediately and acutely affected by changes and shifts in the interface between the commercial channel and the marketplace. The forces impinging on retailers will directly and significantly impact the performance of the entire channel system. Therefore, it is imperative to examine, in some detail, the various components of the environment.[42]

The Consumer Environment of Retailing

POPULATION SHIFTS. Among the most widely documented impacts on the structure of retailing has been the so-called "flight to the suburbs" which was made possible by the growth of automobile usage, road-building programs, and the deterioration of public transportation services to downtown central business districts. The suburban flight initially dealt a severe blow to "downtown" retailing centers, in general, and departments stores, in particular. On the other hand, the emergence and increasing viability of planned regional shopping centers and "malls" were prime factors in the recovery of department stores. In 1954, depart-

[41] Despite the fact that vending machines rely on self-service, such operations are not low in service. Except for in-home shopping, "automatic" retailers offer the highest delivery and convenience service of all institutions.

[42] The conceptualization of the retailing environment used here follows the excellent discussion found in Albert D. Bates, *Retailing and Its Environment* (New York: D. Van Nostrand Company, 1979).

ment store sales as a percentage of retail sales dipped to 6.2, down from 8.9 percent in 1929. However, by 1978, the department stores' share had risen to 10 percent.[43] In the mid-1970s, 74.3 percent of department stores' sales came from non-downtown units compared to 50.9 percent a decade earlier.[44]

The same forces that crippled the downtown central business districts were responsible for nurturing the shopping centers, viz., suburbanization and traffic congestion, parking headaches, and increasing crime in downtown areas. In addition, the shopping center provided more convenient and longer shopping hours and highly integrated one-stop shopping. Nevertheless, after years of unprecedented growth, the shopping center industry has been slowing down, with little hope of enjoying a quick recovery.[45] Stricter zoning laws, Environmental Protection Agency (EPA) regulations, escalating land value, capital and construction costs, over-stored markets, slower population growth, and less abundant energy sources are among the factors contributing to the industry's problems. As more and more regional centers were built, the maximum draw, or primary trading area, fell to three or four miles by the late 1960s. Although population growth counterbalanced the decline in trading areas for a while, predictions for the future growth of these centers (and especially the new "superregionals") are not bright. In fact, there is considerable vacant space available in the newer centers.[46] Some developers have speculated that increases in the number of neighborhood and multiuse centers (such as The Citadel in Colorado Springs) will be witnessed,[47] while others are foretelling an emphasis on improving, modernizing, and expanding existing centers, rather than on building new ones, especially if mortgage money remains difficult to obtain and if the number of promising sites available for development remains small.[48] Some shopping center owners have begun pruning unproductive shops from their centers, creating excitement by organizing spectator activities within the centers (such as tennis matches and orchestra concerts), and attempting to reposition their centers to serve the youth market.[49] However, despite a slower growth rate in the 1970s, the nation's estimated 19,300 shopping centers accounted for 62 percent of retail store sales by the end of 1979.[50]

[43] See "Department Stores Fight for Their Life," *Chicago Tribune,* Section 4, September 17, 1979, p. 11.

[44] Jay Scher, *The Financial and Operating Results of Department and Specialty Stores* (New York: National Retail Merchants Association, 1975). There is, however, a new threat on the horizon—discount shopping malls. See "The Discount Twist in Suburban Shopping Malls," *Business Week* (July 7, 1980), p. 94.

[45] See, for example, "Shopping Centers: What's Ahead?" *Chain Store Age—Executive Edition* (May, 1975), p. 23; and Donald M. Schwartz, "End of Era? Shopping Centers," *Chicago Sun-Times,* Real Estate Section, September 14, 1975, p. 15.

[46] See Schwartz, *op. cit.*

[47] "Is the Big Regional Dead?" *Chain Store Age—Executive Edition* (May 1975), p. 25.

[48] See Jeffrey H. Birnbaum, "Building of Shopping Centers is Curbed by Mortgage Problems, Scarcity of Sites," *Wall Street Journal,* August 13, 1980, p. 46; and Jerry C. Davis, "Need a Cure for All Ills? Try a Shopping Center," *Chicago Sun-Times,* Real Estate Section, September 14, 1975, p. 16.

[49] Jerry C. Davis, *op. cit.,* p. 16. See also "Shopping Centers Will Be America's Towns of Tomorrow," *Marketing News,* Vol. 14 (November 28, 1980), pp. 1, 10, and 11.

[50] Jeffrey H. Birnbaum, *op. cit.,* p. 46.

There are two important developments which are likely to have much to do with the future of shopping centers and their department store anchors. The first is the significant trend towards specialty shopping in many lines. The shopping malls provide a means of convenient shopping to customers, but as department stores turn more and more to soft goods and fashion-quality merchandising, they are likely to find that, instead of a supplementing synergy between the anchor and the specialty shops, the latter will begin to bleed the former in direct competition. Second, major efforts to revive and reconstruct downtown business and residential areas are underway in many cities. With spiraling transportation costs, there might be a new residential pattern emerging for the future, although, at present, any patterns of movement back to the city center are insignificant. Mall developers, city authorities, and top department store retailers seem to have placed their faith in a major revival of the central business district and are pouring millions (and, in some cases, billions) of dollars into renovation and construction. Massive projects are now underway or have been completed in such cities as Boston, Washington, Philadelphia, Detroit, Chicago, Los Angeles, and Miami.[51] Downtown revival is occurring not only in the big cities but also in others like Lexington, Kentucky; Lincoln, Nebraska; and Flint, Michigan. Nevertheless, suburban and neighborhood centers are likely to account for a major share of retail sales for the foreseeable future.[52]

Another major population trend has been the pronounced migration to the "sunbelt," i.e., southern and western states such as Florida, California, and Arizona. Among national retail chains, a very large portion of new construction money is being funneled in this direction. For example, in 1978 and 1979, K-Mart, the country's leading discount department store and number two general merchandise retailer (after Sears), opened one-third of its 329 new stores in small towns or in rural fringes of metropolitan markets in the sunbelt.[53]

Positioning stores in smaller towns and in metropolitan fringe communities (i.e., exurbia) reflects another important demographic development. It appears that such small towns, usually not more than four hours away from major cities, are enjoying explosive growth because of changes in lifestyles and values, especially the search for simplicity, lower crime rates, cleaner environments, less congestion, and

[51] See "The Big Stores Vote for Downtown Again, *Business Week* (September 20, 1976), p. 38; and "Woodward & Lothrop: Flourishing in the Face of Glossy Competition," *Business Week* (March 19, 1979), p. 156, for examples of efforts in major cities. See also Frederick C. Klein, "Chicago Pins Hopes of Revival on Big Shopping Mall," *Wall Street Journal,* March 11, 1980, p. 1, and Gurney Breckenfeld, "The Rouse Show Goes National," *Fortune* (July 17, 1981), pp. 49-54.

[52] From 1950 to 1977, the nation's shopping centers mushroomed from a scant 100 to 19,400, and in the decade 1965–1975 alone, the share of retail business carried by them boomed from 15 percent to a staggering 50 percent. C. Winston Borgen, *Learning Experiences in Retailing: Text and Cases* (Pacific Palisades, Calif.: Goodyear Publishing Co., 1976), pp. 55–63.

[53] See "Wal-Mart: A Discounter Sinks Deep Roots in Small Town, U.S.A.," *Business Week* (November 5, 1979), p. 146; and "Where K-Mart Goes Next Now That It's No. 2," *Business Week* (June 2, 1980), pp. 109–114. It should be noted, however, that K-Mart's new store orientation has tended to mask low growth rates for existing stores. See Charles W. Stevens, "K-Mart Stores Try New Look To Invite More Spending," *Wall Street Journal,* November 26, 1980, p. 21.

lower costs of living.[54] The future of such trends is uncertain because of the energy crisis, but, significantly, some top corporate forecasters optimistically anticipate that the energy crisis will stabilize in the 1980s.[55]

A discounter that has become very successful by positioning itself in smaller communities is Wal-Mart. Conventional retail yardsticks have generally based the minimum population for sustaining a full-line discount store at 100,000. Wal-Mart, with more than 80 percent of its units in towns of fewer than 15,000 residents, has exploded this myth. Founded in 1962, the chain consisted of 330 stores achieving $1.6 billion in sales by 1980.[56] Other chains, such as Bi-Lo (discount supermarkets) and Pamida (discount stores), in addition to Wal-Mart, have been able to achieve positions of competitive dominance at a relatively low cost by focusing on secondary markets.

Mobility is another important population variable. About 20 percent of the population moves every year, although two-thirds of these moves are within the same county. The high mobility rate means that most retail outlets turn over their customer base and must constantly attract new customers. It also means that multiple outlet firms have a decided advantage in the marketplace.

THE NEW AMERICAN FAMILY.   The American household is undergoing a major transformation. Less marriage, later marriage, fewer children, more divorce, one-parent families, and a dramatic increase in working-wife households are the new social realities. The average American home is now estimated at 2.8 persons, down from 3.3 in 1960, and expected to be 2.4 by 1990.[57] The divorce and marriage trends coupled with a significant gap in life expectancy of men and women are the principal factors behind the increase in single-person households, which now account for about 25 percent of all households.[58]

The most widely discussed phenomenon impacting the American family and its life style is the "working wife." Women's participation in the labor force has risen from 25 percent to almost 50 percent in the last three decades.[59] The total implications of the working wife are yet to be experienced, because, so far, much of female employment has been in traditional low-pay jobs. But barriers are crumbling, and less sex discrimination, combined with more education and professionalism, are increasingly changing the nature of jobs women are receiving. In general, the working-wife phenomenon has been largely responsible for what has been termed a growing "poverty of time."[60] Together with other changes in cultural

[54] Leonard L. Berry, "The New Consumer," in Ronald W. Stampfl and Elizabeth C. Hirschman (eds.), *Competitive Structure in Retail Markets: The Department Store Perspective* (Chicago: The American Marketing Association, 1980), p. 1. See also Steve Weiner, "With Many Cities Full of Stores, Chains Open Outlets in Small Towns," *Wall Street Journal,* May 28, 1981, p. 1.

[55] "The *U.S. News* Washington Letter," *U.S. News & World Report* (February 9, 1979), p. 3.

[56] Lynda Schuster, "Wal-Mart Chief's Approach Infects Employees; Keeps Retailer Growing," *Wall Street Journal,* April 20, 1981, p. 19.

[57] Fabian Linden, "Demographically, 1980's Look Bright," *Marketing News* (March 7, 1980), p. 2.

[58] Leonard L. Berry, *op. cit.,* p. 2.

[59] Fabian Linden, *op. cit.,* p. 2.

[60] William Lazer and John E. Smallwood, "Consumer Environments and Life Styles of the Seventies," *MSU Business Topics,* Vol. 20 (Spring 1972).

values, notably a remarkable increase in leisure time pursuits and physical fitness activities, it has radically reduced the amount of time households are willing to devote to "running the home" or shopping.

The impact of these trends has been far-reaching. On the one hand, they represent the opportunity behind the boom in convenience store retailing for "fill-in" purchases. On the other hand, they are fueling the ever-increasing demand for fast food outlets, prepared meals, and faster kitchen appliances, while cutting into the traditional supermarket business. For example, in 1957, there were 500 convenience stores; in 1977, there were 27,500 doing $7.4 billion in business.[61]

The delivery of convenience is likely to become highly sophisticated in the future, especially via in-home shopping through interactive telecommunication systems.[62] The forerunners of such systems are already in existence. For example, the 1.5 million members of Comp-U-Card, a buyers' club, can purchase name brand appliances, furniture, fine china, silver, and even automobiles at prices 20 to 40 percent below retail by simply calling a toll-free telephone number. Members provide basic product requirement information to operators who scan their electronic listings (which are updated daily) and quote the best available prices, delivery times, etc. Comp-U-Card has no showrooms, warehouses, or catalogs, but deals with over 100 vendors around the country.[63] At some point in the future, the data supplied by such buying services will be available to members over their own television sets, thus eliminating the need for intermediary information points.

An equally dramatic consequence of the "poverty of time" phenomenon is that Americans are, in record numbers, eating away from home. Eighteen percent of their meals are coming from restaurants, and 36 percent of their food dollars are going to this industry.[64] It is estimated that the latter figure will rise to 50 percent by 1987.[65] Of the $57 billion spent on eating out in 1978, 31 percent went to fast food franchise outlets like McDonald's, Kentucky Fried Chicken, and Pizza Hut, and one source expects this share to rise to 50 percent.[66] However, the impact of eating out as a sociological factor should not be underestimated or characterized as a purely "time" and "labor-saving" expedient of a "time" conscious society, because there appears to be a discernable *preference* pattern, especially for the type of foods available through fast-food outlets.[67]

AGE, INCOME, AND EDUCATION.   During the 1980s the overall population of the U.S. is expected to expand by about 10 percent, while the age category 24–44

[61] "Convenience Stores: A $7.4 Billion Mushroom," *Business Week* (March 21, 1977), p. 61.

[62] See, for example, F. Kelley Shuptrine, "The Distribution/Retailing Institute of Tomorrow," *Journal of Retailing,* Vol. 51 (Spring 1975), p. 20; Eleanor G. May, "Nontraditional Retailing," in Stampfl and Hirschman (eds.) *op. cit.,* pp. 124–131; and Larry J. Rosenberg and Elizabeth C. Hirschman, "Retailing Without Stores," *Harvard Business Review,* Vol. 58 (July-August 1980), pp. 103–112.

[63] "Comp-U-Card Helps 1.5 Million Shop by Phone," *Business Week* (September 10, 1979), p. 58.

[64] "Supermarkets Realize that Usual Food Items Won't Sustain Profits," *Wall Street Journal,* July 18, 1977, p. 1.

[65] "America Out to Eat," *Newsweek* (October 3, 1977), p. 86.

[66] "Maxwell: Fast-Food Sales May Grow 20% in '79," *Advertising Age* (September 10, 1979), p. 46.

[67] See "Want to Cook Meals Just Like Mother Used to Take Out?" *Wall Street Journal,* October 12, 1978, p. 1.

will increase 2½ times as fast.[68] Forty-three percent of all growth from 1980 to 1995 will be in the 35 to 64 group. As recently as 1978, the over-60 population was already comprised of 31 million people, representing an estimated $175 billion market.[69] What this strongly suggests is a growing mood of conservatism resulting from a waning youth culture and a generally more mature population, proportionately. To date, however, few manufacturers and fewer retailers seem to be taking full cognizance of the potential "graying of America." There is, in fact, some evidence that the elderly are not a homogeneous market segment; studies have shown that they exhibit unique shopping, credit, and media habits.[70]

In terms of income, the general expectation is that affluence will continue to spread but at a slower rate.[71] Predictions of real income increases are, at best, tentative in a double-digit inflation period. Irrespective of the specific impact of inflation on real dollars available to individuals or households, a "permanent inflation" frame of mind exists and is having profound influences on the American consumer.[72] An inflation psychology has the effect of sharpening value consciousness. This does not mean simply a low-price market sentiment. In fact, the trend is towards polarization favoring *both* the price and quality segments of all markets.

The emphasis on value is bound to be spurred by the "working wife" phenomenon. Combining the "poverty of time" with the dual incomes available to numerous households, the amount of "frivolous," time-consuming purchasing will be reduced, but the ability to purchase higher-quality goods and services may be enhanced. Because neither wife nor husband will wish to be saddled with the service problems which may attend questionable but inexpensive merchandise, both will insist on buying highly scrutinized brands, particularly in durables, from "reputable" merchants. Thus, the time spent shopping will continue to go down while the amount spent per shopping trip will increase. The actual number of items purchased may decline, but the amount spent per item should increase, inflation aside.

In terms of education, 60 percent of the 18-year-old population were high school graduates in 1950; by 1978, the percentage had risen to 74 and is projected to remain at this figure throughout the 1980s.[73] By the late 1970s, approximately 42

[68] Fabian Linden, *op. cit.,* p. 2.

[69] "The New Consumer," *Mart* (September 15, 1978), p. 6.

[70] William O. Bearden and J. Barry Mason, "Elderly Use of In-Store Information Sources and Dimensions of Product Satisfaction/Dissatisfaction," *Journal of Retailing* (Spring 1979), p. 80. For an excellent review of studies, see Lynn W. Phillips and Brian Sternthal, "Age Differences in Information Processing: A Perspective on the Aged Consumer," *Journal of Marketing Research,* Vol. 74 (November 1977), pp. 444–457.

[71] "The New Consumer," *op. cit.,* p. 6.

[72] One study reports that "the preoccupation of Americans (with inflation) is by far the most significant economic force with regard to the future of consumer markets." See " 'Permanent Inflation' is Key Factor in Future of Marketing," *Marketing News* (September 7, 1979), p. 3. See also Everett C. Ladd, "What the Voters Really Want," *Fortune* (December 18, 1978), p. 44.

[73] The 1950 percentage was obtained from U.S. Bureau of the Census, *Statistical Abstract of the United States, 1979* (100th edition) (Washington, D.C.: Government Printing Office, 1979). The 1978 percentage and the projections were obtained from Nancy B. Dearman and Valena White Plisko, *The Condition of Education, 1980 Edition* (Washington, D.C.: U.S. Government Printing Office, 1980), p. 80.

percent of the *under 30* population had attended college. Supposedly, educated consumers are more rational in consumption behavior, less susceptible to emotional appeals and brand-institutional loyalties, and place greater demands for product information.[74]

While the foregoing factors are likely to have highly diverse impacts on individuals and segments, two broad developments can be traced to the joint effect of the trends in income (inflation), dominant age groups, and education. On the one hand, there seems to be a trend away from frills, flash, and planned obsolescence. The booming discount industry and the rapid growth of "generic" brands in both the food and drug markets are indicative of the consumer's willingness to absorb some service functions, shop in austere surroundings, and deflate advertisers' claims in order to secure better prices.[75] On the other hand, while there are many indications that the new mood of the American consumer is more utilitarian and that consumers are willing to sacrifice some quality when the increment in quality is not worth the addition to price, it does not follow that there is a general mood of "price" consciousness. As mentioned above, it is a "value" consciousness. For example, in fields other than foods and drugs, there is a dramatic swing towards more expensive, higher-quality goods. The attitude seems to be that if a brand costs $20 or $30 more than a cheaper one but will last twice as long, the premium is well spent. Consumers are spending more, even splurging on quality, even if it means that they have to scrimp on other purchases.[76]

The demographic shifts enumerated above—particularly those creating the "poverty of time" and the inflation "psychology"—simply underscore the significance of retailing in marketing. Retailing is the final link in the commercial sector of marketing channels. Since retailers are in direct and constant contact with final consumers, they are more sensitive and respond more quickly to shifting market segments and consumers' changing demands for service outputs. Because of the multitude of market segments and the need to consider nontraditional bases for market segmentation, retailers have had to continually adjust their offerings and the ways in which they make their offerings available. For example, to serve segments characterized by the "poverty of time," mail-order houses, direct marketing schemes, and in-home and in-office selling emerge and flourish. In 1978, mail-order sales alone amounted to over $26 billion, an increase of more than 13

---

[74] Albert D. Bates, *op. cit.,* p. 13.

[75] See "Plain Labels Challenge the Supermarket Establishment," *Fortune* (March 26, 1979), p. 70. By the fall of 1979, generics had captured 10 percent market shares or greater in such product categories as peanut butter, salad and cooking oils, fabric softeners, liquid detergents, paper towels, and toilet tissue in stores handling generics in 1978 and 1979: "A Source of Generic Share Changes," *The Nielsen Researcher,* No. 2 (1980), p. 13. Excellent discussions of the impact of generics and limited-service stores can be found in "No-Frills Food: New Power for the Supermarkets," *Business Week* (March 23, 1981), pp. 70–80; Meg Cox, "Food Stores with Few Services Spring Up to Lure Increasingly Frugal Consumers," *Wall Street Journal,* January 23, 1981, p. 36; and Steve Weiner, "Many Stores Abandon 'Service with a Smile,' Rely on Signs, Displays," *Wall Street Journal,* March 16, 1981, p. 1. But also see Bill Abrams, "Reports of Generics' Success May be Greatly Exaggerated," *Wall Street Journal,* May 7, 1981, p. 27.

[76] "Buyers Swing to Quality," *Time* (December 3, 1979), p. 82. See also "Dual Incomes Will Lift More Families to Middle-Class Affluence in the Decade," *Wall Street Journal,* June 27, 1980, p. 21.

percent over the previous year.[77] Specialty retailers such as The Limited, The Gap, and Crate & Barrel cater to the same time-poor segment as these consumers look for broader assortments within a merchandise classification and require depth in lines carried. These specialty shopping attractions are designed to reduce search time. Simultaneously, discount houses, catalog showrooms, limited assortment grocery stores, and other institutions emerge to satisfy the needs of market segments anxious over the declining value of money. These segments are willing to trade off service outputs for lower prices, and the retailing sector has adapted accordingly.

CONSUMER VALUES.   There appears to have emerged a new set of consumer values which emphasizes "people-first, things-second" as opposed to the "things-first, people-second" culture which has basically dominated the U.S. since the end of World War II. Studies show that 80 percent of consumers are concerned with "being good to myself" and "improving myself."[78] The ramifications of the new values are many, including less pressure to conform, tolerance of diversity, personalization, customization, permissiveness, instant gratification, a need for more enjoyment, concern for ecology, and an emphasis on "doing" rather than "having." As Berry and Wilson observe:

> . . . more and more people are deciding that the quality of life is more important than the quantity of life, that human beings are more important than things.
> Significantly, the new values are not a refutation of money and the possessions and services that money can buy. Rather, what is occurring is a reordering of priorities, a growing awareness that a big income can't necessarily be equated with personal happiness, and that a fast-increasing GNP doesn't necessarily reflect a sound and healthy society.[79]

It is obvious that behavioral trends impinge heavily on consumer shopping habits and patronage patterns. However, as Bates points out, behavioral analysis is particularly useful for detailed studies of specific stores but is difficult to generalize to more global statements.[80] To illustrate how consumer attitudes affect retail opportunity, the implications of six widely held consumer values, as charted out by Bates, have been laid out in Exhibit 2-6.

In line with the emerging demographics, new values, economics of inflation, and the growing poverty of time, some major department stores are actually remodeling parts of their stores into mall-like clusters of specialty shops. Macy's (New York) was the first to make a success with such a plan in 1976. More recently, similar changes have been implemented by such stores as Bloomingdales, Gimbels,

[77] Maxwell Sroge Company, *News Release* (November 27, 1979).

[78] Roger D. Blackwell, "Successful Retailers of 80's Will Cater to Specific Lifestyle Segments," *Marketing News* (March 7, 1980), p. 3.

[79] Leonard L. Berry and Ian H. Wilson, "Retailing: The Next Ten Years," *Journal of Retailing,* Vol. 53 (Fall 1977), p. 10.

[80] Albert D. Bates, *op. cit.,* p. 14.

EXHIBIT 2-6

Six Widely Held Consumer Attitudes and Their Implications for Retailers

Consumer Attitude	Examples of Retailer Implications	Examples of Retailers Capitalizing on the Attitude
More Casual Life Styles—A desire to live in a more relaxed, informal style with regard to dress, home environment, etc.	• Need to maintain a current assortment of life style oriented merchandise • Construction of less formalized stores/displays	• Jeans West—Casual Apparel • Pier 1—Casual home furnishings
Instant Gratification—Desire for immediate access to goods and services	• Need for easier credit availability to facilitate purchasing • Reduction of in-store waiting time	• Levitz—Availability of furniture on an instant, take-with basis
Life Simplification—Reducing confusion in decision processes and reducing the difficulties of performing mundane tasks	• Simplifaction of warranties and service programs, such as using extended warranties • Explore opportunities in the sale of services as well as products	• Sears—aggressive extended warranty program on major appliances
Naturalism—A revolt against artificial, "plastic," mass produced characteristics of society in favor of more natural characteristics	• More natural product displays using wood, brick, etc. • Adding non-mass produced items to the assortment, possibly through special arrangements with local artisans	• Numerous firms that have shifted towards natural décor • Natural food stores
Creativity—A desire to achieve self-expression through crafts such as wood-working, sewing, macrame, etc.	• Aggressive merchansdising of craft products • Adding do-it-yourself instructional programs as a revenue-generating service	• Lee Wards—A chain specializing in a complete line of crafts and featuring instruction programs
Consumerism—A new feeling of power in dealing with business and an insistence on full quality for the price paid	• Need to identify consumer feelings precisely • Improve quality of complaint department • Establish consumer ombudsperson	• Giant Food—A food retailer with a complete package of consumerism services and an excellent reputation as a pro-consumer firm

Source: Albert D. Bates, *Retailing and Its Environment* (New York: D. Van Nostrand, 1979), p. 15, and Management Horizons, Inc.

and Jordan Marsh.[81] The "specialty" clustering is not simply a question of better defined departments. The major opportunity in clustering is that, instead of offering a single image for the whole store, a life-style type of segmentation within the store might evolve.

Mass merchandisers are increasingly faced with the problems of "image" projection and "positioning" in the market. K-Mart, known for its low prices, has been stressing quality. Sears, known for its quality, has been stressing price; and Penney's, a retailer with a solid but conservative "bargain basement" image, is stressing a fashion image.[82] The rapidly changing demographic and sociocultural composition of middle America is responsible for the traditional mass merchandiser's dilemma. Image positioning is increasingly becoming the crux of retail strategy. Pure demographics are becoming less accurate as segment definers, and "life-style" indicators are becoming more appropriate.[83] The increased emphasis on positioning in retailing is significant for manufacturers as well as for retailers:

> For retailers it could mean a strong increase in nonprice competition which will be difficult if not impossible for unpositioned firms to counter. In particular, firms with very broad target markets, such as conventional department stores and discount stores, will have great difficulty in competing with positioned firms. For manufacturers, positioning could necessitate the use of multiple market programs to meet the buying requirements of retail firms positioned in a variety of different ways.[84]

The Competitive Environment of Retailing

Broadly speaking, the structure of competition in retailing is described in Table 2–2. The nature of competition deriving from each of the sources listed in Table 2–2 is qualitatively different and poses different strategic implications. Furthermore, in recent years the competitive environment of retailing has become more difficult to decipher. A slowing economy, high inflation, and escalating costs of capital, construction, energy, and labor are squeezing profits on the one side while, on the other, increasingly saturated markets, new aggressive forms of innovative retailing, and generally more sophisticated management approaches are placing margins under continuous assault in most product categories. Average retail profits during the mid to late 1970s were at their lowest in over two decades.[85] Most retailers operate fairly close to their break-even volumes; therefore, they are ex-

---

[81] See "Department Stores Fight for Their Life," *op. cit.,* p. 11; and "Many Department Stores are Converting Open Floors into Varied Specialty Shops," *Wall Street Journal,* October 10, 1978, p. 40.

[82] "Dressing Up an Image," *Wall Street Journal,* January 16, 1979, p. 40.

[83] See Melvin R. Crask, "Department Stores vs. Discount Stores," in Stampfl and Hirschman (eds.), *op. cit.,* pp. 33–42. With regard to specific positioning methodologies, see Lawrence J. Ring, Charles W. King, and Douglas J. Tigert, "Market Structure and Retail Position," in *ibid.,* pp. 149–160. The multiattribute decision models or choice strategies discussed in Appendix 2A of this chapter are appropriate to employ as a starting point for perceptual mapping purposes.

[84] Albert D. Bates, "The Troubled Future of Retailing," *Business Horizons* (August 1976), p. 28.

[85] Albert D. Bates, *Retailing and Its Environment, op. cit.,* p. 31.

TABLE 2-2   Competition in the retailing sector

Type of Competition	Scope of Competition	Corporate Illustrations
Intratype competition	Competition between the *same* type of outlets	Thrifty vs. Walgreen
Intertype competition	Competition between *different* types of outlets	Kroger vs. K-Mart
Systems competition	Competition between *different* types of vertically integrated systems, including voluntary groups, co-operative groups, franchise networks, and corporate chains	A&P vs. IGA
Free-form competition	Competition between free-form corporations, each of which operates multiple types of outlets to serve multiple market segments	Carter, Hawley, Hale vs. Dayton-Hudson

Source: Bert C. McCammon, Jr., "Future Shock and the Practice of Management," a paper presented at the Fifth Annual Attitude Research Conference of the American Marketing Association, Madrid, Spain, 1973, p. 8.

ceedingly vulnerable to new entrants siphoning off even a modest part of their sales.[86] Given this picture, it is important to concentrate on understanding where the greatest threats seem to be coming from—increasing intertype competition, the growth of vertical marketing systems, including "free form" corporations, and the acceleration of institutional life cycles.

INCREASING INTERTYPE COMPETITION.   While some decades ago it might have been reasonable to think of supermarkets competing primarily with supermarkets, department stores with department stores, and so on, in the modern world of distribution, the fastest growing form of competition is intertype. Supermarkets compete against convenience stores, limited assortment ("box") stores, combination food and drug stores, and restaurants (especially fast food outlets) for the consumer's food dollar. Likewise, in many lines of general merchandise and apparel, the struggle for patronage is increasingly between specialty store chains, department stores, discount department stores, and family centers.[87] An idea of the extent of intertype competition emerges when the sales for three product categories—health and beauty aids, hardware, and machine-made glassware—are tracked. At one time, each of these was virtually the exclusive domain of a single

[86] Supermarkets have a break-even point that ranges between 94 and 96 percent of their current sales, while general merchandise retailers' break-even points approach 85 to 92 percent of their current sales. Bert C. McCammon, Jr., Jack J. Kasulis, and Jack A. Lesser, "The New Parameters of Retail Competition: The Intensified Struggle for Market Share," in Stampfl and Hirschman (eds.), *op. cit.,* p. 110.

[87] For some useful insights into the structure of retail markets, see Elizabeth C. Hirschman, "A Descriptive Theory of Retail Market Structure," *Journal of Retailing,* Vol. 54 (Winter 1978), pp. 29–48.

72 COMPONENTS OF MARKETING CHANNELS

type of outlet. Now, as shown in Exhibit 2–7, sales come from a wide spectrum of retailing establishments.

The intensity of intertype competition has been heightened by the appearance of specialty store chains like The Limited, Toys R Us, and Radio Shack. The profitability and growth of a number of these chains is shown in Table 2–3. Carrying extremely deep and broad assortments (like Toys R Us) and sharply focused on well-defined segments (like The Limited, which aims directly at the 18-to-35 year old style-and-fashion-conscious woman), these specialty chains have been highly successful and have posed an especially significant threat to traditional department stores.

The intensity of intertype competition has also been heightened by the appearance of new mass merchandisers, particularly the catalog showroom retailers

EXHIBIT 2–7
Sales of Health and Beauty Aids, Hardware Products, and Machine-made Glassware by Type of Outlet

Health and Beauty Aids		Hardware Products		Machine-Made Glassware	
Type of Outlet	Percent of Total Sales	Type of Outlet	Percent of Total Sales	Type of Outlet	Percent of Total Sales
Grocery stores	32.2%	Hardware and building material store	31.0%	Discount stores	27.8%
Drug stores	32.1	General merchandise and variety stores	23.8	General merchandise and variety stores	24.6
Discount stores	12.0	Discount stores	17.7	Department stores	18.2
General merchandise and variety stores	8.4	Home improvement centers	16.4	Grocery stores	11.8
Nonstore retailers	8.2	Department store	4.9	Specialty stores	7.9
Department stores	5.7	Non-Store retailers	2.0	Drug stores	4.3
All other	1.4	Grocery stores	2.0	All other	5.4
		All other	2.2		
Total	100.0%	Total	100.0%	Total	100.0%

Source: Albert D. Bates, *Retailing and Its Environment* (New York: D. Van Nostrand, 1979), p. 25.

like Best Products and Service Merchandise. As shown in Table 2–3, a number of these merchants have been extremely successful as well.

According to McCammon, Kasulis, and Lesser, all of the organizations depicted in Table 2–3 are particularly well positioned for the 1980s because of two factors.[88] First, their high profitability will permit them to finance their growth internally—a powerful advantage in a capital-scarce and high-interest environment. Second, they enjoy unusually strong consumer franchises, being perceived as places where a purchaser can receive "good value for money expended."

TABLE 2–3   Profitability and growth profile of leading specialty chains and catalog showroom chains, 1977

Company	Net Profits/ Net Sales (Percent)	Net Profits/ Total Assets (Percent)	Net Profits/ Net Worth (Percent)	Compound Annual Growth Rates (1973-1977)	
				Net Sales	Net Profits
Brooks Fashion	9.4%	22.8%	36.5%	41.5%	62.9%
The Gap	4.7	14.1	26.4	52.5	48.9
The Limited	7.1	18.0	43.1	61.1	71.8
Mervyn's	4.9	13.1	24.0	41.4	51.9
Miller-Wohl	9.3	18.5	33.9	23.3	52.4
Paul Harris	3.8	10.8	21.1	31.0	32.8
Best Products	4.3	9.4	26.0	34.7	75.3
Modern Merchandising	3.1	5.5	20.2	32.5	45.9
Service Merchandise	4.7	13.6	28.0	44.3	66.8
H.J. Wilson	4.6	5.9	19.3	32.4	25.2
Handy Dan	3.4	11.8	21.0	21.8	27.4
Hickory Farms	10.4	17.6	30.3	37.1	26.0
Radio Shack	6.2	12.0	47.6	26.7	34.1
Tandycrafts	4.5	9.9	18.3	18.9	18.4
Toys "R" Us	4.9	10.0	25.1	—	—
Pic 'N Save	10.2	18.2	24.5	28.2	44.4
RB Industries	5.0	11.9	28.5	16.5	21.6
Edison Brothers	5.7	12.4	22.4	14.6	27.8
Melville	5.0	13.3	24.4	20.0	24.4
Median (All Companies)	4.9	12.4	25.1	31.0	34.1

Source: Bert C. McCammon, Jr., Jack J. Kasulis, and Jack A. Lesser, "The New Parameters of Retail Competition: The Intensified Struggle for Market Share," in Ronald W. Stampfl and Elizabeth Hirschman (eds.), *Competitive Structure in Retail Markets: The Department Store Perspective* (Chicago: American Marketing Association, 1980), p. 112.

[88] McCammon, Kasulis, and Lesser, *op. cit.*, p. 111.

Another factor affecting the level of intertype competition has been the strong showing of super drug stores and combination food and drug stores. Their appeal has been essentially to the one-stop shopper and primarily in product lines like stationary, cosmetics, and housewares.

THE GROWTH OF VERTICAL MARKETING SYSTEMS AND "FREE-FORM" CORPORATIONS.   The significance of this fact of retailing life is evidenced by the attention it is given in this text—an entire chapter (Chapter 7) is devoted to examining vertical marketing systems. A highly dynamic environment is placing enormous demands for increasingly sophisticated management of manufacturer-wholesaler-retailer relations. The new technologies, the need for fine-tuning assortments, controlling inventories, and monitoring and adapting the retailer's position in the market require specialized and skilled staffs. Larger and more complex organizations are necessary to house the specialists who will take responsibility for managing the marketing channel all the way from point of production to point of consumption. Thus, the McDonald's, Super Valu's, Safeway's, Sear's, K-Mart's, and Federated's of this world will continue to dominate the retailing scene because, in large part, they administer, through franchising, vertical integration, or simply the use of their massive power, the marketing channels in which they are found so that the end result is a strong and positive impact on the ultimate consumer.

To a large extent, the growth of vertical marketing systems has spawned the growth of "free-form" corporations or, as discussed earlier, "conglomerchants." One way of looking at the growth of such companies as Dayton-Hudson; Edison Brothers; Carter, Hawley, Hale; and the Jewel Companies is to think of them as differentiating themselves to serve increasingly fragmented market segments. Another, complementary, way to look at their growth is to portray their acquisitions and internal developments as a strategic hedge against increasingly shorter retail life cycles and intensifying intertype competition. With the pace of innovation seeming always to accelerate, it makes a lot of sense to be into a variety of distributive modes rather than invested in a single type.

The end result of the growth of vertical market systems and free-form corporations is that the fully independent small store is likely to be squeezed even further. Also, market penetration of new forms of retailing and their maturing will occur much faster, as the larger organizations will be quick to spot potential ideas (e.g., generic brands) and bring their huge resources to bear in developing them. Finally, the larger organizations will be less vulnerable to attack, because they will be serving a wide number of market segments with a variety of different store types (e.g., department, discount, and specialty).[89] Stores will be tailored in image, size, location, merchandise, and services to fit specific consumer segments and will be deliberately managed to retain this fit for as long as the segments remain opportune. Indeed, future changes in patterns of distribution and retailing form are likely

[89] See Dillard B. Tinsley, John R. Brooks, Jr., and Michael d'Amico, "Will the Wheel of Retailing Stop Turning?" *Akron Business and Economic Review* (Summer 1978), p. 26.

to involve a more prominent element of managerial *intervention* rather than just environmental *determinism*.

THE ACCELERATION OF INSTITUTIONAL LIFE CYCLES. There are a number of theoretical schemes which have been suggested as descriptive of the process of institutional evolution in retailing. The best-known theory is the Wheel of Retailing. It hypothesizes that retail innovations emerge as low-cost, low-price, high-volume operations because of the void in the marketplace which exists as older institutions trade up. But, like the innovations before them, the new institutions profilerate, and, in order to differentiate themselves from one another, they also find themselves trading up in facilities, assortments, customer services, promotions, and the like. The vast majority of retail innovations in this century fit the low-cost "entry" principle, and most of these have been dogged by the trading up phenomenon.[90] But there are exceptions: automatic vending, suburban shopping centers, and specialty chains do not conform to the low-cost principle.

Ronald Gist, drawing on Hegel's philosophy of dialectical evolution, suggests that a pattern synthesis emerges when the "thesis" (the original institution) is challenged by the inevitable "antithesis" (the innovator), leading to a synthetical merging of the two.[91] The warehouse grocery store might be viewed as a synthesis of the supermarket and the discount food store modes of retailing, for example. Fast-food outlets are described as a combination of the early drive-ins (which had extensive menus and order-prepared food) and the later take-out operations featuring precooked food and very limited menus.[92]

Another popular descriptive model is the general-specific-general cycle or the retail "accordian" theory.[93] The theory describes discernible cycles of alternation between "general" wide-assortment merchandising and "specialty" narrow-line operations. A number of other theories exist, including the crisis-change model introduced in Chapter 5, which provide a reasonable "fit" to some of the evolutionary phenomena in retailing. However, none of the theories, including those mentioned above, generalize across all situations or provide any predictive leverage.[94] Despite their weaknesses, though, the theories do have a very useful role to play, because they focus attention on the fact that change is a way of life in retailing and provide speculative frameworks for trying to interpret (if not predict) the direction of change implied by current events.

One of the more intriguing theories of institutional change to emerge in recent

[90] Malcolm P. McNair and Eleanor G. May, *The Evolution of Retail Institutions in the United States* (Cambridge, Mass.: Marketing Science Institute, 1976). See also McNair and May, "The Next Revolution of the Retailing Wheel," *Harvard Business Review,* Vol. 56 (September-October 1978), pp. 81–91.

[91] Ronald E. Gist, *Retailing: Concepts and Decisions* (New York: John Wiley & Sons, 1968), p. 106.

[92] Joseph P. Mason and Morris L. Mayer, *Modern Retailing: Theory and Practice, op. cit.,* pp. 45 and 52.

[93] Stanley C. Hollander, "Notes on the Retail Accordian," *Journal of Retailing,* Vol. 42 (Summer 1966), pp. 29–40.

[94] For a critique, see Stanley C. Hollander, "Oddities, Nostalgia, Wheels and Other Patterns in Retail Evolution," in Stampfl and Hirschman (eds.), *op. cit.,* pp. 78–87.

years is the concept of the institutional life cycle.[95] Like the product life cycle concept, the argument here is that retail institutions go through anthropomorphic life cycles which can be partitioned into stages of *early growth, accelerated development, maturity,* and *decline.* As illustrated in Fig. 2–1, new retail institutions generate high rates of growth and attractive profitability ratios during their initial stages of development. Illustrative of institutions that achieved extraordinary results during their formative years are the department store in the late 1800s, the supermarket in the 1930s, and the discount department store in the late 1950s and early 1960s. However, as retail institutions mature, they are increasingly confronted by new forms of competition and forced to compete in overstored or saturated markets.[96] As a result, price competition for these institutions intensifies, accompanied by declines in market share and profitability. Ultimately, mature institutions enter the decline stage of their life cycle, wherein they invariably become disadvantaged participants in the marketplace. Thus, from this perspective, department stores, variety stores, and supermarkets are already mature and/or declining retail institutions. That is, they represent methods of doing business that no longer regularly produce high rates of growth or rates of return on investment.[97]

FIGURE 2–1
The Institutional Life Cycle in Retailing

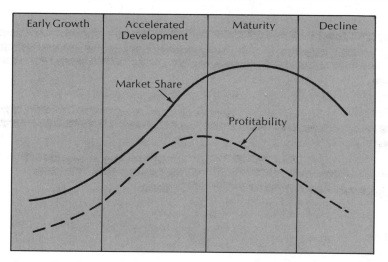

Source: Bert C. McCammon, Jr., "The Future of Catalog Showrooms: Growth and Its Challenges to Management," Marketing Science Institute Working Paper, April 1973, p. 2.

[95] William R. Davidson, Albert D. Bates, and Stephen J. Bass, "The Retail Lifecycle," *Harvard Business Review* (November-December 1976), pp. 89–96.
[96] See Bert C. McCammon, Jr., "The Future of Catalog Showrooms: Growth and Its Challenges to Management," Marketing Science Institute Working Paper, April 1973, pp. 2–3.
[97] *Ibid.,* p. 3. As indicated in Table 2–4, catalog showrooms are also entering maturity. See "No Christmas Cheer for Catalog Showrooms," *Business Week* (November 24, 1980), pp. 137 and 141.

More important, however, for managers is the knowledge that institutional life cycles within retailing have accelerated over the years. For example, it has been estimated that the time to reach maturity has declined from approximately 100 years, in the case of department stores, to approximately 10 years, in the case of catalog showrooms (see Table 2–4). Implicit is the point that those contemporary institutions that are now in their initial stages of development will soon be faced with problems and challenges that confront department stores and supermarkets today. Indeed, an accelerating technological environment, more fluid consumer behavioral patterns (e.g., falling brand loyalties), crumbling "line-of-trade" barriers, a more acute appreciation of change as a way of life among managements, and a high level of "awareness" served by the booming "trade journals" industry are all contributing to the pace of the life cycle and to the tensely charged competitive environment of retailing.

In a detailed elaboration of the life cycle concept, Davidson. Bates, and Bass have highlighted some of the management activities that become important in different stages (see Table 2–5). They have pointed out that, given the inevitability of the life cycle, management's responsibility in any one company is to anticipate

TABLE 2–4   Illustration of the accelerating pace of institutional life cycles

Institutional type	Period of fastest growth	Period from inception to maturity (years)	Stage of life cycle	Representative firms[a]
General store	1800–40	100	Declining	A local institution
Single-line/specialty store	1820–40	100	Mature	Hickory Farms
Department store	1860–1940	80	Mature	Zayre
Variety store	1870–1930	50	Declining	Morgan-Lindsay
Mail-order house	1915–50	50	Mature	Sears
Corporate chain	1920–30	50	Mature	Safeway
Discount store	1955–75	20	Mature	K-Mart
Supermarket	1935–65	35	Mature	A&P
Shopping center	1950–65	40	Mature	Paramus
Cooperative	1930–50	40	Mature	Ace Hardware
Gasoline station	1930–50	45	Mature	Texaco
Convenience store	1965–75	20	Mature	7-11
Fast-food operation	1960–75	15	Mature	Shoney's
Hypermarket	1973–?	?	Early growth	Laval (France)
Home development center	1965–80	15	Late growth	Lowes
Boutique	1965–75	10	Late growth	House of Nine
Warehouse retailing	1970–80	10	Late growth	Levitz
Catalog-showroom	1970–80	10	Late growth	Best Products

[a] These firms are representative of institutional types and are not necessarily in the stage of the life cycle specified for the institutional group as a whole.

Source: Joseph B. Mason and Morris L. Mayer, *Modern Retailing: Theory and Practice* (Dallas: Business Publications, Inc., 1978), p. 58.

TABLE 2-5   Management activities in the life cycle

	Area or subject of concern	Stage of life cycle development			
		1. Innovation	2. Accelerated development	3. Maturity	4. Decline
Market characteristics	Number of competitors	Very few	Moderate	Many direct competitors Moderate indirect competition	Moderate direct competition Many indirect competitors
	Rate of sales growth	Very rapid	Rapid	Moderate to slow	Slow or negative
	Level of profitability	Low to moderate	High	Moderate	Very low
	Duration of new innovations	3 to 5 years	5 to 6 years	Indefinite	Indefinite
Appropriate retailer actions	Investment/growth/ risk decisions	Investment minimiza- tion—high risks accepted	High levels of investment to sustain growth	Tightly controlled growth in untapped markets	Minimal capital ex- penditures and only when essential
	Central management concerns	Concept refinement through adjustment and experimentation	Establishing a pre- emptive market position	Excess capacity and "overstoring" Prolonging maturity and revising the retail concept	Engaging in a "run- out" strategy

78

	Minimal	Moderate	Extensive	Moderate
Use of management control techniques	Minimal	Moderate	Extensive	Moderate
Most successful management style	Entrepreneurial	Centralized	"Professional"	Caretaker
Appropriate supplier actions — Channel strategy	Develop a preemptive market position	Hold market position	Maintain profitable sales	Avoid excessive costs
Channel problems	Possible antagonism of other accounts	Possible antagonism of other accounts	Dealing with more scientific retailers	Servicing accounts at a profit
Channel research	Identification of key innovations	Identification of other retailers adopting the innovation	Initial screening of new innovation opportunities	Active search for new innovation opportunities
Trade incentives	Direct financial support	Price concessions	New price incentives	None

Source: William Davidson, Albert Bates, and Stephen Bass, "The Retail Life Cycle," *Harvard Business Review* (November–December 1976), p. 92.

changes in the stages and to adapt the organization to them as effectively as possible.[98] Furthermore, the concept has been extended to apply to individual *stores* (in addition to institutional types) through the development of a consumer segment/profile interface along the time horizon, as shown in Fig. 2–2. Applying much the same theory as is applicable to the diffusion of product innovations, it might be argued that the composition of a store's consumer segment will undergo natural change as the store matures.[99] In fact, as implied in Fig. 2–2, the same reasoning could be used to explain changes in consumer segments for products,

FIGURE 2–2
Life Cycle Analysis for Consumer Focus

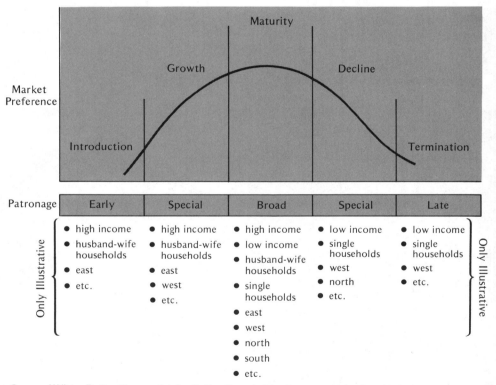

Source: William R. Davidson and John E. Smallwood, "An Overview of the Retail Life Cycle," in Ronald W. Stampfl and Elizabeth C. Hirschman (eds.), *Competitive Structure in Retail Markets: The Department Store Perspective* (Chicago: American Marketing Association, 1980), p. 56.

[98] William R. Davidson, Albert D. Bates, and Stephen J. Bass, "The Retail Life Cycle," *Harvard Business Review* (November-December 1976), p. 93.

[99] William R. Davidson and John E. Smallwood, "An Overview of the Retail Life Cycle," in Stampfl and Hirschman (eds.), *op. cit.*, p. 56.

brands, firms, and enterprises as well as for stores, locations, and institutions. From a strategic perspective, retailers must, in order to ensure their success, make adaptations in the operating dimensions (margins, assortments, services, etc.) to best suit their shifting consumer bases. And it may be necessary for firms to radically reposition themselves at appropriate times to continue to stay in touch with a chosen segment. Such retailers as Montgomery Ward and A&P have been very slow to learn this lesson. Unfortunately, W.T. Grant never did.

The Resource Environment of Retailing [100]

The economic bonanza of the post-World War II years, which demonstrated a remarkable degree of continuity between 1947 and 1973, is being replaced by a more sobering set of realities: higher unemployment and underemployment, higher inflation, higher cost of energy, lower real growth in GNP, erosion of consumer confidence, growing entanglement of resource availabilities with international politics, uncertain capital availability, and a growing ethic of resource conservation and environmental protection.[101] Bates has identified five major sources of resource turbulence that underlie the productivity and profitability squeeze on retailers that has become increasingly apparent during the late 1970s and early 1980s.[102] Each of these sources—capital costs, labor productivitiy, construction costs, merchandise availability, and the new technologies—is discussed briefly below.

CAPITAL COSTS.   Capital acquisition is an extremely critical strategic dimension for large-scale retailers. With the vast majority operating on relatively thin profit margins, even a small increase in interest rates can spell disaster for the balance sheet. This stark reality is compounded by the fact that retailing is not considered a very desirable investment field in financial circles. Analyzing 163 large-scale retailers and 746 similar-sized manufacturers, Bates found that between 1970 and 1976, the retailers faced effective interest rates about 0.5 percentage points above those charged the manufacturers.[103] Future capital availability does not look very promising, either. In a 1975 report, the Institute of Life Insurance Trend Analysis Program predicted:

> The biggest economic problem may not even be the twin blight of inflation with recession. It may be the now widely predicted shortfall of all forms of capital.[104]

However, such predictions are highly controversial. What is widely accepted, though, is that available capital will cost well above the long-run historical trend.

[100] This section is based largely on Albert D. Bates, *op. cit.,* pp. 14–20 and Chapter 2.
[101] Leonard L. Berry and Ian H. Wilson, *op. cit.,* p. 11.
[102] See Chapter 11 of this text for a discussion of performance by retailing institutions.
[103] Albert D. Bates, *op. cit.,* p. 16.
[104] Quoted in Leonard L. Berry and Ian H. Wilson, *op. cit.,* p. 12.

LABOR PRODUCTIVITY.   Retailing suffers from a strange paradox. Historically, the industry has had the lowest wage rates while simultaneously being among the most sensitive to wage increases. Although retail wages average $1.10 per hour below those in manufacturing, retailing is still one of the few remaining labor intensive industries. Even in self-service operations, payroll is over half the expense account, and for conventional department stores, payroll is almost two-thirds of it.[105]

CONSTRUCTION COSTS.   "Rentals" account for the second largest chunk of operating expenses. For example, sharply rising construction costs pushed rental charges in new regional shopping malls from $5.00 per square foot in 1970 to over $15 per square foot in 1980. Indeed, many retailers, like K-Mart, actually prefer to use free-standing locations rather than shopping centers and malls. Another resulting trend has been towards recycling of existing facilities, such as abandoned supermarkets, variety stores, discount department stores, warehouses, and even train stations. Others are experimenting with new low-cost construction techniques as well as with less elaborate interior designs and modular construction which allows rapid dismantling and rearrangement of display spaces. Given the pressures they face, retailers can increasingly be expected to turn to their suppliers for more direct investment assistance. In particular, the financing of inventory and fixtures could become integral parts of some suppliers' marketing programs.

MERCHANDISE AVAILABILITY.   Peacetime product shortages were phenomena largely unknown to U.S. retailers until the 1970s. The oil embargo of 1974 had a widespread impact on retailing far beyond the effect it had on retail service stations. Petroleum-based industries, particularly plastics, and high energy-dependent industries witnessed acute supply problems and rapidly escalating prices. Other shortages, such as the coffee shortage of 1976–77, affected profits in other industries.[106] While these specific instances are things of the past, the future of raw material resources in general remains highly uncertain, and their availability is increasingly tangled with international politics. Retailers may have to increase the length of their contracts with suppliers or even reduce the number of suppliers with whom they deal so as to assure themselves of needed goods. Clearly, this will increase retailers' dependency on their suppliers and thus alter relationships within the marketing channel. The importance of such dependencies within the channel is examined in detail in Chapter 6.

THE NEW TECHNOLOGIES.   Recent technological innovations have created a dilemma for retailers. On the one hand, they provide a major opportunity for improved operational and managerial efficiency. On the other, they involve major investments at a time when the short-run return picture is grim, and the long-run cost-benefit opportunity is very difficult to gauge.

---

[105] Albert D. Bates, *op. cit.,* p. 17. Labor productivity is discussed more fully in Chapter 11 where attention is turned to the performance of retailing institutions.

[106] See, for example, "Fast Food Chains Take a Beating on Breakfast," *Business Week* (February 21, 1977), p. 30.

Two general areas of technological innovation have been particularly impactful over the past decade. One is totally automated warehousing, applications of which at the retail level have resulted in the emergence of hybrid retail-warehouse institutions like catalog showrooms and home furnishings "warehouse" retailers (e.g., Levitz, Wickes) as well as the hypermarche in Europe. Another is the use of electronic point-of-sale (POS) machinery. The new POS electronic cash registers are often tied to sophisticated computerized information and inventory control systems. The "front-end" of a store is responsible for the bulk of labor expenses for many forms of retailing. When the adoption of the Universal Product Code (UPC) for packaged groceries and other codes for general merchandise (such as the Standard Merchandise Classification) is combined with the automation of the checkout procedure and detailed inventory monitoring, opportunities for increased efficiency are enhanced.[107] In addition, the impact on the relations between retailers and their suppliers, due to the significance of the data generated by such systems, is likely to be enormous, as discussed in Chapter 10.

On the horizon are electronic funds transfer systems (EFTS). These, integrated with the POS systems, allow for speedy credit authorization, credit card transactions, check verification, and funds transfer. Such systems are operational on a limited basis, but full-scale adoption has been moving somewhat slowly. The primary "gray areas" are high investment, uncertain effect on checkout time, negative effect on retailers' own credit cards (such as Sears and Wards), the technology itself, mandatory sharing of systems, and government regulation (i.e., it is still not certain whether EFTS falls under the purview of state branch banking laws).[108]

Despite the apparent efficiency promise of all the above systems, installation is expensive enough to make their true economics difficult to calculate. Plagued with a tight payback situation and prospects of a very difficult capital market, many retailers may find it difficult to justify the switchover, even considering their almost desperate need for improved labor productivity. As Bates points out:

> The difficulty is that technological improvements have never had a measurable impact on retailer profitability and probably never will. . . . The difficulty in the supermarket field and in other areas of retailing is that technology is open to all and produces very little in the way of a lasting differential advantage.[109]
>
> . . . .
>
> In addition, executives aren't totally convinced their employees can really utilize the information the systems produce since most retail managers don't have time to analyze the information they already receive. Further complicating the decision is the worry of rapid technological obsolescence given the speed with which both the electronics and data processing industries are moving.[110]

[107] See "Scanning Gains More Ground," *Chain Store Age Executive Edition* (Feburary 1977), p. 21.

[108] Joseph B. Mason and Morris L. Mayer, *Modern Retailing, op. cit.,* p. 304. For a more complete discussion of the impact of such systems on marketing channels, see J. Barry Mason and Morris L. Mayer, "Retail Merchandise Information Systems for the 1980's," *Journal of Retailing,* Vol. 56 (Spring 1980), pp. 56–76.

[109] Albert D. Bates, *op. cit.,* p. 20.

[110] *Ibid.,* p. 25.

When all of these developments on the technological front are put together with all of the other environmental shifts specified above, the problems *and* the opportunities confronting retailers seem overwhelming. The need for increasingly sophisticated marketing management in retailing has never been more acute.

CONSEQUENCES FOR MARKETING CHANNEL RELATIONSHIPS

The consequences of the various environmental factors facing retailers for marketing channel relationships are profound and far-reaching. Many of the consequences have already been enumerated, explicitly or implicitly, at different points throughout this chapter. Others will become evident in later chapters as issues relevant to marketing channel management are examined and analyzed. Rather than talk in abstractions, we provide here three brief examples of how some of the factors we have already discussed are having important effects on channel relations. The first example concerns the food industry generally. The second and third pertain to specific companies retailing general merchandise—Korvettes and Levitz.

The Food Industry [111]

Inflation is changing the balance of power in the food industry. Food retailers who once relied mainly on customer service and wide assortments to secure differential advantages are now struggling to maintain profits while attempting to price below their competitors. Supermarket advertisements and in-store displays increasingly tend to feature generic or private-label products as opposed to name brands. The result of these pressures on food retailers is that supermarket operators are assuming more responsibility for marketing while trying to get manufacturers to absorb more of their costs.

Specifically, food chains are becoming more selective when it comes to choosing new products, especially size and flavor variations. They are also becoming more selective about the manufacturer promotions they will support with advertising and special displays. And they are pressuring suppliers to improve credit terms and distribution methods in order to reduce expenses.

Manufacturers once held the balance of power in the food industry because of the tremendous advertising and promotion budgets they deployed to "pull" consumers into stores. Supermarkets deferred to suppliers' merchandising suggestions and relied on their data to determine what products to stock. Now supermarkets are collecting their own data and are resisting suppliers' efforts to "force" distribution. To a significant extent, generic brands have awakened food retailers to their power. Because of the availability of these brands, companies like General Foods and Car-

---

[111] Example drawn from Bill Abrams, "Food Chains Pressure Suppliers, Altering Industry Balance of Power," *Wall Street Journal*, August 21, 1980, p. 25. See also "No-Frills Food: New Power for the Supermarkets," *Business Week* (March 23, 1981), pp. 70–80; and Bill Abrams, "New Worry for Manufacturers: Growth of Warehouse Outlets," *Wall Street Journal*, May 28, 1981, p. 23.

nation now find themselves competing with their own customers for shelf space and promotional support.

Nevertheless, even though manufacturers have lost some of their power, they still have a considerable amount left over. When they "blitz" products with advertisements and promotion, retailers find themselves under an enormous pressure to carry the items. But even if they are forced to carry new products, supermarkets are more likely than ever to remove those that do not sell. And vigilance on sales performance will increase as more retailers install electronic checkout scanners that provide quick, detailed sales information.

Another major issue for food retailers facing high interest and labor costs is the expense of holding and handling inventory. Many stores are urging their suppliers to liberalize the typical 2 percent discount for bills paid within 10 days. To reduce their inventories, some supermarkets also ask for faster delivery from supplier warehouses.

Retailer demands are starting to get a response from manufacturers. Pillsbury and its Green Giant subsidiary frequently are praised for their efforts. They hold "rap sessions" with stores, sometimes preprice merchandise, and "tray-pack" canned goods that can go to store aisles without much handling. Pillsbury's sales force helps stores build displays and plan advertisements. Price changes are sent to stores by Mailgram. Pillsbury also provides a rack (which it developed at its own expense but which does not bear its name) that retailers use to organize their refrigerated dough cases. Even Procter & Gamble, a company not known for its retailer-oriented perspective, has made a major response. In 1980, it led the food industry when it raised to seven cents from five cents the fee paid to stores for handling cents-off coupons. P & G is also experimenting with payment of allowances to stores before they complete promotions. While other manufacturers follow this practice, P & G historically made stores wait until specials had ended, thus slowing supermarket cash flow.

Ironically, retailers might not benefit from the change in balance of power. Many industry experts believe that the stores will likely pass the savings along to consumers in the form of lower prices. The new innovations will merely increase competition in what is already an exceedingly competitive industry.

Korvettes[112]

When Agache-Willot, a $3.5 billion French textile and retail conglomerate, bought Korvettes from Arlen Realty and Development Corporation for $31 million in April, 1979, the chain consisted of 50 stores with sales totaling about $600 million, but it operated at a loss. Korvettes was trying to upgrade its image from being an outlet emphasizing hard goods to a moderately priced, fashionable soft goods chain. Agache-Willot brought in its own management team to recast the

[112] Example drawn from "The Crisis at Korvettes is Far From Finished," *Business Week* (September 1, 1980). For some fascinating details of Korvettes' decline, see Robert F. Hartley, *Marketing Mistakes* (Columbus, Ohio: Grid, Inc., 1976), pp. 33–44.

chain. The strategy was to turn Korvettes back into a discounter, pare overhead, and narrow inventory costs and the breadth of selection. But the reduction in service, merchandise, and advertising annoyed customers, and the new management's uncompromising style alienated suppliers.

In the spring of 1980, with losses continuing at a rapid rate and with the flow of goods from suppliers slowing significantly, a new chief executive officer, Joseph A. Ris, was brought in by the parent company. Almost immediately after assuming office, Ris met with 15 percent of the chain's 4000 lenders, promising them prompt payment in full and negotiating with the major lenders to restructure the chain's debt. But Agache-Willot balked at the terms negotiated by Ris, which had stipulated that Korvettes would repay about 45 percent of the total debt owed to several major lenders in installments and would give them 25 percent of any future profits through 1987. Also included in the terms was a plan to reduce the number of stores in the chain to 18, all of which were to be centered in the New York metropolitan area. A principal of the parent company described the conditions as "humiliating." While a new agreement was worked out,[113] many suppliers refused to ship merchandise to the chain until the terms were fully agreed upon and understood.

In the face of all this conflict in Korvette's channels, the question became whether, in the long run, *any* agreement would really matter. Korvettes was in need of a major repositioning. The probabilities of success, even with such an effort, were limited at best. (Indeed, some industry experts believe that the parent corporation was always most interested in Korvette's real estate, believing it would be worth $200 million at some future date.) Korvettes' life cycle had expired.

Another question which emerges indirectly from Korvette's fiasco is just how successful foreign investors are likely to be when they begin to become involved in U.S. retailing. The amount of activity by European investors over the past decade has been particularly impressive, as shown in Table 2-6. However, the jury is still out when it comes to making an assessment of their ability to help their acquired firms achieve satisfactory returns.

Levitz[114]

The Levitz family built the largest independent furniture retailing chain in the U.S. by pioneering the sale of large amounts of discount-priced furnishings that customers could carry home immediately. This strategy produced high volume but relatively low margins. When the company sustained a loss during the 1974–75 recession, the family brought in a professional manager, Robert M. Elliott, as presi-

[113] For specifics, see Jeffrey H. Birnbaum, "Weak Chain: Korvettes to Get Aid From French Parent, But Problems Persist," *Wall Street Journal,* August 27, 1980, p. 1. See also Jeffrey H. Birnbaum, "Korvettes Gives Up Plan to Reopen Stores and Will Try to Sell Remaining 23 Sites," *Wall Street Journal,* February 24, 1981, p. 14, which tells of Korvettes' last gasps.

[114] Example drawn from "Levitz: When a Manager Veers from the Owners' Original Plan," *Business Week* (September 1, 1980), pp. 40–41.

TABLE 2–6   European acquisitions of U.S. retailing firms as of 1980

- **A** Grocery Stores
- **B** Department Stores
- **C** Discount Stores
- **D** Clothing Stores
- **E** Variety Stores
- **F** Toy Stores

#		U.S. retailer / Headquarters	Annual sales¹ (millions)	Profitable?	European acquirer / Country	Annual sales¹ (millions)	Main business	Initial investment made	Total investment (millions)	Percent owned
1	A	A&P, Montvale, N.J.	$6,684	No	Tengelmann Group, Germany	$3,576	A	1979	$115	48%
2	A	Grand Union, Elmwood Park, N.J.	$3,138	Yes				1973	$130	100%
3	A	Colonial Stores, Elmwood Park, N.J.	Now a division of Grand Union		Cavenham, Great Britain	$5,062	A	1978	$139	100%
4	A	J. Weingarten, Houston	$567	Yes				1980	$27	100%
5	B	Gimbel Brothers, New York City	$1,190	Yes	BAT Industries, Great Britain	$15,845	Tobacco	1973	$200	100%
6	A	Kohl, Milwaukee	$400	Yes				1972	$90	100%
7	C	Fedmart, San Diego	$1,061	No	Mann GmbH, Germany	$2,076	A	1975	$90	88%
8	A	BI-LO, Mauldin, S.C.	$547	Yes	Ahold NV, Netherlands	$2,761	A	1977	$60	100%
9	A	Scrivner, Oklahoma City	$547	Yes	Franz Haniel, Germany	$2,076	Fuel & shipping	1977	$27	100%
10	A	Alterman Foods, Atlanta	$495	Yes	Delhaize "Le Lion", Belgium	$1,537	A	1980	$36	100%
11	A	Food Town Stores, Salisbury, N.C.	$416	Yes				1974	$27	52%
12	A	Furr's, Lubbock, Tex.	$450*	No	RHG-Leibbrand, Germany	$2,768	A	1979	$24	100%
13	C	Korvettes, New York City	$400*	No	Agache-Willot, France	$3,175	Textiles	1979	$67	100%
14	B	Dillard Dept. Stores, Little Rock	$391	Yes	Vroom & Dreesmann, Netherlands	$3,386	A B	1978	$35	52%
15	A	Red Food Stores, Chattanooga, Tenn.	$265*	Yes	Promodes, France	$2,240	A	1980	$36	100%
16	D	Ohrbachs, New York City	N.A.	Yes				1962	N.A.	100%
17	D	Maurices, Duluth, Minn.	N.A.	Yes	Brenninkmeyer family, Netherlands	$5,190*	D	1978	N.A.	100%
18	D	Hub Distributing, Ontario, Calif.	N.A.	Yes				1980	N.A.	100%
19	E	Winn's Stores, San Antonio	$70	Yes	Heinrich Bauer Verlag, Germany	$779	Magazine publishing	1979	$50	100%
20	E	Macks Stores, Sanford, N.C.	$62	Yes	Koninklijke Bijenkorf Beheer, Netherlands	$1,302	A	1980	$15	100%
21	D	Ups 'n Downs, Secaucus, N.J.	$58	No	Tootal, Great Britain	$858	Textiles	1979	$19	100%
22	A	Lil' Champ Food Stores, Jacksonville	$31	Yes	Docks de France, France	$2,683	A	1978	$3	35%
23	D	Dekon, New York City	$28	No	Mothercare, Great Britain	$352	D	1976	$1	100%
24	F	F.A.O. Schwarz, New York City	$15	Yes	Franz Carl Weber, Switzerland	$125	F	1974	$3	95%

N.A. Not available. *FORTUNE estimate. ¹Latest fiscal year. Foreign currencies have been converted to dollars using the average exchange rate in the official market during the fiscal year.

Source: Robert Ball, "Europe's U.S. Shopping Spree," *Fortune* (December 1, 1980), p. 85.

dent and chief executive officer. Elliott has gradually moved to emphasize conservative growth and higher margins. Furious at this change, the Levitz family, which contols 25 percent of the company's stock, fought to dislodge Elliott.

The Levitzes began their business by experimenting in furniture retailing for over 25 years in Pottstown, Pa. In 1963, the family built a massive warehouse-showroom combination building near a rail siding in that city with a "carton-and-crates" atmosphere of low overhead and low prices. In an industry in which slow delivery is normal, Levitz stocked all its merchandise for immediate pickup. Customers were expected to provide their own delivery services. Growth was phenomenal, from two stores with sales of $21 million in 1964 to 55 stores with sales of $380 million in 1974. But the company suffered from a lack of central controls over inventory, advertising, purchasing, and other functions. The recession that began in 1974 caught the company with $80 million in inventory, much of it low-priced, showy furniture.

When Elliott assumed office, he installed the necessary controls over the operation. But he also began to raise prices and move to higher quality merchandise. In 1976, he complemented Levitz' budget merchandise with "Classic House Galleries," displays of more expensive furniture inside the showrooms. As a result, overall gross margins rose from 40.3 percent of sales to 44.1 percent. In addition, instead of building the typical Levitz unit of 170,000 square feet, he began constructing 64,000-square-foot units aimed at smaller metropolitan markets. He also began a chain of "satellite" stores that are merely showrooms for warehouse stores about 25 miles away. While Elliott did not abandon discounting, he supplemented the technique with furnishings and stores that could, in his estimation, better serve a new rising segment of furniture buyers—the baby-boom generation, which has matured into an affluent group of homeowners concerned with more of a desire and ability to "buy" the "good life." In contrast, the Levitz family believed that by reverting to the original discounting tactics, Levitz could launch itself on a rapid growth path, appealing more broadly to price-conscious buyers.

Clearly, suppliers to the chain are in a quandary, because the outcome of the battle between the Levitz family and Elliott is by no means certain. The uncertainty may breed questions about the long-term viability of the enterprise. Surely, furniture manufacturers are well aware of Korvettes-type scenarios. They realize that market positioning is critical and that Levitz is in the process of changing its image. They fear that the same fate which befell Korvettes and even Sears when they started to upgrade might also befall Levitz.

SUMMARY AND CONCLUSION   Retailing involves the direct sale of goods and services to ultimate household consumers. The overwhelming majority of retail sales is consummated in stores or retail establishments as opposed to other conduits, such as the mail, house-to-house selling, or automatic vending machines.

The primary strategies available to retailers revolve around a variety of operating orientations. The first is concerned with margins and inventory turnover rates. During the twentieth century, a heavy emphasis has been placed on low margin/high turnover/minimum service operations. Such operations have traded off between the services which they perform for consumers and the prices they charge. Consumers have been increasingly willing to participate more heavily in the marketing flows.

The second orientation is concerned with assortments, whereby retailing institutions design and evolve product-mix strategies to suit changing shopping patterns. The third dimension is location. Decreased search-shopping patterns are making the location decision, particularly site selection, even more important. While the emphasis is on convenience, there is a difficult tradeoff between one-stop shopping convenience and spatial convenience for many lines of retail trade. The fourth dimension is customer service. Large-scale retailers are becoming increasingly sophisticated at segmenting their markets into those subsets with high, moderate, and low service requirements and have developed different means (through acquisition or internal growth) to serve each segment.

Retailers face an exceedingly complex and difficult set of environments. The consumer environment is marked by population shifts, the emergence of the ''new'' American family, changes in the age, income, and education levels of the population, and alterations in consumer values. Particularly notable and impactful for retailers have been the ''flight'' to the suburbs, the migration to the sunbelt, the importance of smaller towns as markets, continued mobility, the increase in single-person households and in working wives, and the growing ''poverty of time.'' In addition, such factors as the ''graying'' of America, the existence of a ''permanent'' inflation psychology, and the emergence of the ''me'' generation demand that significant emphasis be placed on life-style segmentation and positioning.

The competitive environment is exceedingly threatening. Increasing intertype competition and the growth of vertical marketing systems and ''free-form'' corporations combined with the acceleration of institutional life cycles mean that no retailer's market is secure from competitive incursions. Also, problems in securing capital, high labor productivity, facilities and real estate, and merchandise are likely to be a part of the retailers' landscape for some time to come. Adoption of new technologies will help considerably, but the risk is high because of the enormous investment required in purchasing and using such systems. Clearly, the need to employ sophisticated and effective management practices in retailing is critical for survival, not to mention growth.

While it is certain that new retailing institutions will continue to emerge and that existing institutions will continue to evolve during the remainder of the twentieth century, there is considerable room for innovative management within the present institutional mix. For example, as Bucklin observes:

> There are substantial frontiers yet to be conquered in tying together the wholesale and retail sectors of the business, improving logistics and inventory control.[115]

[115] Bucklin, *Competition and Evolution . . ., op. cit.,* p. 168.

In the next two chapters, attention is focused on the wholesaling institutions comprising channels and on the management of logistical or physical distribution activities. Following a discussion of those areas, attention is then focused on marketing channel strategy, design, and the effective interorganization management of channel systems, which is viewed as the means by which the "frontiers" will be "conquered."

DISCUSSION QUESTIONS

1.   Paul Valery, a famous author, at one time remarked:

"Once destiny was an honest game of cards which followed certain conventions, with a limited number of cards and values. Now the player realizes in amazement that the hand of his future contains cards never seen before and that the rules of the game are modified by each play."

Relate Valery's statement to the problems facing high-level retail executives today.

2.   One author has described the revolution in retailing as a process of "creative destruction," because of the many new institutions that have appeared in this industry over the years. If, as McCammon suggests, institutional life cycles have shortened to approximately 10 years, what types of institutional forms do you predict will arise in the 1990's to "creatively destroy" the institutions that are emerging as powers in retail trade today (e.g., warehouse technologies and organizations, and extensions of the supermarket concept)?

State fully the reasons behind your answer, including also what impinging environmental factors you believe will help to bring about these changes.

3.   After answering question 2, assume now that you are a high-level retail executive for a major chain of supermarkets. Given your assumptions about the future, what strategies would you initiate to adapt your organization to the impending environment?

If you were a manufacturer of household consumer durables, what action would you take relative to future retail distribution outlets for your products, considering again your assumptions about the environment?

4.   In your opinion, what kind of competition exists in retailing—perfect, monopolistically competitive (atomistic), oligopolistic, or monopolistic? Explain in full, using a variety of different lines of retail trade to illustrate your response.

5.   With the growing trend to scrambled merchandising, and the proliferation of "me, too" retail establishments, existing differences between competing outlets are often perceived as superficial by the consumer with the result that a firm's advertising and promotion may often be attributed to a competitor. Consequently, many analysts believe that store positioning will become the most important retail marketing strategy of the 1980's.

Describe what you believe to be the various positioning strategies of:

(a) B. F. Goodrich.
(b) Burger King.
(c) Meijer's Thrifty Acres (hypermarket).
(d) Cadillac.

Enumerate both the advantages and disadvantages that seem to be associated with each of these strategies.

6. Assume that you are planning on establishing a major department store operation with several nearby branch locations somewhere in the United States. Outline the general steps you would undertake in conducting both an *inter-* and *intraregional* location analysis for your store. Included in your outline should be a list of all the factors (e.g., population, buyer power, etc.) that you would take into consideration for each type of analysis.

What types of locational assistance might you seek from manufacturers and wholesalers whose products you planned to carry?

7. Why is an understanding of the retail buying process important from an *interorganizational* perspective? If, through market research, a manufacturer determined that a retail buyer was using a linear choice model in making his merchandise selection, what general promotional tactics might he employ to help insure his product's selection? How would this differ if the retail buyer was instead using:
(a) A conjunctive model?
(b) A lexicographic model?
(c) A disjunctive model?

On an *a priori* basis, what situational factors might prompt the retail buyer to use one choice model instead of another? (*Hint:* Consider for example, such situational factors as *perceived risk attached to the buyer's decision* and *amount of time available to make the decision.*) An answer to this question requires reading of Appendix 2A.

8. What is meant by merchandising variety and assortment? What are the dimensions of assortment? What purposes does the merchandising budget serve? (See Appendix 2C.)

9. As the retailing environment becomes more and more turbulent, which of the following policy decision areas—location, merchandise selection, or inventory control—do you believe becomes more important, as well as more difficult for the retailer? Offer at least *three* compelling reasons in support of your position.

Appendix 2A

Evaluative procedures (choice strategies) used by retail buyers

The evaluative procedures employed by retail buyers can be classified as particular types of decision rules or *choice strategies*.[116] The actual choice strategy that the retail buyer uses is a direct result of the type of decision problem he faces when making his merchandise selection.[117] Because the buyer must generally select merchandise from among a number of competing brand alternatives, all of which can be described in terms of their various attributes, the situation confronting the buyer can be accurately described as a *multiple-attribute decision problem*.[118] In general, the evaluation of individual brands and their respective sources of supply involves the rating of alternative sources along some or all of the following ten product attributes or performance parameters:[119]

- Demonstrated consumer demand (or projected demand, if a new product)
- Projected gross margin
- Expected volume

[116] Development of the choice strategy concept is found in Peter Wright, "Consumer Choice Strategies: Simplifying vs. Optimizing," *Journal of Marketing Research,* Vol. 7 (February 1975), pp. 60–67.

[117] The authors wish to acknowledge the significant contribution of Lynn W. Phillips to the development of the following discussion.

[118] For an overview of this type of decision problem see Kenneth R. MacCrimmon, "An Overview of Multiple Objective Decision Making," in J. L. Cochrane and M. Zeleny (eds.), *Multiple Criteria Decision Making* (Columbia, S.C.: University of South Carolina Press, 1973), pp. 18–44.

[119] This list is not necessarily in order of importance. Furthermore, the number of attributes considered by the buyer obviously varies from situation to situation. Doyle and Weinberg, for example, in a study of supermarket buyers' decisions, found that buyers examined only eight dimensions, while Montgomery, in a recent study in the same context, reports that 18 different factors were taken into consideration. See Peter Doyle and Charles B. Weinberg, "Effective New Product Decisions for Supermarkets," *Operations Research Quarterly,* Vol. 24 (March 1973), pp. 45–54; and David B. Montgomery, "New Product Distribution—An Analysis of Supermarket Buyer Decision," *Journal of Marketing Research,* Vol. 12 (November, 1975), pp. 255–264.

- Merchandise suitability
- Prices and terms
- Service level offered
- Manufacturer reputation
- Quality of the brand
- Promotional assistance
- Vendor's distribution policy (national, regional, or local; exclusive, selective or intensive)

The choice strategy, then, is the method by which the retail buyer evaluates each multiattribute brand alternative and discriminates it from the others available in order to arrive at a merchandise selection.

There are numerous choice strategies that a buyer might adopt.[120] To illustrate its application, consider the situation of a retail buyer choosing among potential suppliers of wristwatches. The buyer employing a *linear additive* choice strategy would, first, assign subjective weights to each attribute dimension listed above according to the evaluative importance he places on each. For example, in the case of wristwatches, manufacturer's reputation and demonstrated consumer demand might, by some retailers, be deemed more important than a factor such as promotional assistance. Second, the buyer would judge each available alternative according to the extent to which it seemingly possessed each of the attribute dimensions. One brand, for example, might be perceived as being of higher quality than the other brands under consideration. After assessing each alternative relative to each attribute dimension, the retail buyer would then combine each of these unidimensional judgments according to a simple linear rule. This rule would dictate the selection of the supply source offering the highest "global utility index" via a process similar to the one depicted in Table 2A-1. In the wristwatch example, the buyer would choose Brand 4 because of its superior overall evaluation.

On the other hand, the retail buyer might use a *conjunctive* choice strategy in making his selection, and if he did, the results could be different from those arrived at through application of the linear strategy.[121] Using a conjunctive model, the

---

[120] All choice strategies may be carried out overtly, such as via pencil and paper calculation, or cognitively. In fact, most investigations of choice strategy paradigms involve an examination of how well they approximate actual cognitive processes. Although the retail buyer could use either approach, his evaluations of potential suppliers often are done quickly and judgmentally because of the workload he faces. See, for example, Doyle and Weinbert, *op. cit.,* p. 51. One possible strategy is a *linear additive* method of evaluation. For a review of the additive choice model, see William L. Wilkie and Edgar A. Pessemier, "Issues in Marketing's Use of Multi-Attribute Attitude Models," *Journal of Marketing Research,* Vol. 10 (November 1973), pp. 428–441. Empirical evidence indicating that retail buyers may cognitively use a linear additive method of evaluation has been marshalled by Roger M. Heller, Michael J. Kearney, and Bruce J. Mehaffey in "Modeling Supermarket Product Selection," *Journal of Marketing Research,* Vol. 10 (February 1973), pp. 34–37.

[121] Both Wright and Russ offer extended discussions of the nonlinear models presented here. See Peter Wright, "The Simplifying Consumer: Perspectives on Information Processing Strategies," a paper presented at the American Marketing Association Doctoral Consortium, Michigan State University, August 1973; and Frederick Russ, "Consumer Evaluation of Alternative Product Models," *Combined Proceedings of the 1971 Spring and Fall Conferences* (Chicago: American Marketing Association, 1972), pp. 664–668.

TABLE 2A–1   Hypothetical application of a linear additive choice strategy for choosing among alternative brands of wristwatches

Attribute Dimensions Taken into Consideration	Evaluative Importance of the Attribute Dimensions to the Retail Buyer (A)	Judgments about Individual Brands of Wristwatches Across All Attribute Dimensions			
		Brand 1 (B_1)	Brand 2 (B_2)	Brand 3 (B_3)	Brand 4 (B_4)
Demonstrated consumer demand (or projected demand, if a new product)	0.9	0.5	0.9	0.4	0.8
Projected gross margin	0.8	0.6	0.6	0.4	0.6
Expected volume	0.7	0.6	0.7	0.3	0.7
Merchandise suitability	0.6	0.5	0.4	0.4	0.4
Prices and terms	0.5	0.5	0.4	0.6	0.5
Service level offered	0.5	0.5	0.3	0.4	0.5
Manufacturer reputation	0.6	0.6	0.6	0.3	0.8
Quality of the brand	0.7	0.6	0.5	0.3	0.8
Promotional assistance	0.3	0.5	0.4	0.5	0.5
Vendor's distribution policy	0.4	0.5	0.3	0.4	0.7
Global utility index for each alternative		3.22	3.32	2.33	3.90

$$U = \sum_{i=1}^{n} AB_{ij}$$

where

U = overall judged utility of a brand alternative
A_i = *numerical weight assigned to the ith dimension*
B_{ij} = a numerical value for the jth brand alternative on the ith dimension

buyer would establish minimum cutoff values for each attribute dimension and then compare competing brands against these values. If any of the brands were rated below the cutoff value on any of the attributes, it would be rejected as a choice possibility. For example, in Table 2A–1, if the retail buyer established a minimum cutoff value of *0.5* for each of the ten dimensions, Brand 1 would be selected as the best choice, because it is the only brand that meets or surpasses the established cutoff on each attribute.

Another approach that the retail buyer might use is a *lexicographic* choice strategy. Here, the buyer first orders the different attribute dimensions according to importance. Then the buyer compares all the alternative sources of supply on the single most important dimension. If one brand offers a noticeably better outcome on that dimension, it is selected. If, however, a number of alternative brands qualify so that the buyer still cannot discriminate among the various available choices, he then drops down to the second most important attribute dimension and repeats the procedure. This one-dimension-at-a-time process is followed until a choice is identified. In the wristwatch example depicted in Table 2A–1, Brand 2 would now be selected, since it is perceived as surpassing all of the other alternatives on the most important dimension—"demonstrated consumer demand."

There are other choice strategies available to the retail buyer. These, as well as those already mentioned above, are summarized in Exhibit 2A–1. Not presented are the "hybrid" or modified versions that some of these strategies may take on.[122] For example, since it is possible for several alternatives to exceed all established cutoff values when a conjunctive strategy is used, a further discrimination procedure may be necessary to identify a final choice for the retail buyer. One such mode of discrimination is to combine the conjunctive strategy with a satisficing "first choice rule," whereby the brand chosen is the first one that meets all standards. Another mode of discrimination would be a multistage use of strategies, whereby the retail buyer might employ a conjunctive scheme to narrow the number of brand alternatives and then apply a lexicographic or linear strategy as an aid in making the final choice.

As mentioned earlier, the type of choice strategy the retail buyer uses in judging brand alternatives has significant implications for the planning of marketing efforts on the part of suppliers seeking to serve the buyer. For example, if the buyer is using a lexicographic strategy in his evaluation of a certain product class, a supplier would do best by focusing his promotional efforts on affecting the buyer's beliefs pertaining to what the buyer perceives as the product's most important attribute dimension, because the supplier's brand will be chosen if it surpasses all other alternatives on this dimension. However, such an approach may not prove effective if the buyer is, instead, employing a conjunctive decision rule. Convincing the buyer that a supplier's brand is outstanding on one attribute dimension will not be sufficient if the brand falls below standards set for the other dimensions considered. When a linear additive choice strategy is used, marketing efforts could be directed

---

[122] See Hillel Einhorn, "The Use of Nonlinear, Noncompensatory Models in Decision Making," *Psychological Bulletin,* Vol. 73 (1970), pp. 221–230.

**Possible Choice Strategies a Retail Buyer May Employ
When Selecting Sources of Supply**

General Class of Choice Strategy Model	Specific Strategies	Strategy Description
Linear Models	Linear additive	Evaluative weights are assigned to each attribute dimension according to its perceived importance. Each supplier/brand alternative then receives a rating on each attribute dimension. These are combined linearly to form an overall judgment for each supplier/brand alternative that can be used as a comparison basis in making the final selection.
	Linear averaging	Same as linear additive, except that the evaluative weights must sum to one to connote a dependency among the attribute dimensions.[a]
Lexicographic Models	Regular lexicography	All supplier/brand alternatives are compared on the single most important dimension. If one surpasses all others on that dimension, it is selected. If not, the process continues along the other dimensions until the supplier(s)/brand(s) is (are) selected.
	Lexicographic semiorder	Same as regular lexicography, except that, even though a supplier/brand alternative surpasses other alternatives on the single most important dimension, if the difference is not a significant one, the comparison continues along the other dimensions until the supplier(s)/brand(s) is (are) selected.
Multiple Cut-off Models	Conjunctive	All suppliers/brands are compared against some minimum cutoff on each attribute dimension. Those supplier/brand alternatives possessing *below*-cutoff features on any dimension are rejected.
	Disjunctive	Same as conjunctive, except that any supplier/brand alternative possessing an *above*-cutoff feature on any single dimension is accepted.
	Elimination by aspects	Minimum cutoffs are established for each attribute dimension. Supplier/brand alternatives are eliminated which fail to surpass the cutoff on the most discriminating dimension, then the second most discriminating, etc., until all dimensions are exhausted or the supplier(s)/brand(s) is (are) selected. The most discriminating dimension is that one which will eliminate the most alternatives from further consideration.

Sequential elimination	Minimum cutoffs are established for each attribute dimension. Supplier/brand alternatives are eliminated which fail to surpass the cutoff on the most important dimension, then the second most important, etc., until all dimensions are exhausted or the supplier(s)/brand(s) is (are) selected.[b]

[a] For example, the weights, or A_i's in the utility index of Table 2A-1, would have to sum to 1 in order to indicate the *relative* importance of the attribute dimensions, if it were to be an averaging model. An illustration of this choice strategy is presented in Chapter 5 in the discussion of how to choose among alternative channel strategies.

[b] An illustrative application of this choice model is also presented in Chapter 5.

Source: Lynn W. Phillips, "Evaluation Process Models: An Overview," an unpublished doctoral seminar paper, Northwestern University, June 1975.

by a supplier at increasing his brand's rating on any attribute dimension, because, in light of the additive nature of the choice process, the increase would affect, in a positive way, the overall evaluation of the brand.

APPENDIX 2B

A glossary of pricing and buying terms commonly used by retailers

ORIGINAL RETAIL. The first price at which the merchandise is offered for sale.

SALES RETAIL. The final selling price.

MERCHANDISE COST. The billed cost of merchandise less any applicable trade or quantity discounts plus in-bound transportation costs, if paid by the buyer. Cash discounts are not deducted to arrive at merchandise cost. Usually, they are either deducted from "aggregate cost of goods sold" at the end of an accounting period or added to net operating profits. If cash discounts are added to net operating profit, the amount added is treated as financial income with no effect on gross margins.

MARKUP. The difference between merchandise cost and the retail price.

INITIAL MARKUP OR MARKON. The difference between merchandise cost and the original retail value.

MAINTAINED MARKUP OR MARGIN. The difference between the *gross* cost of goods sold and net sales.

GROSS MARGIN OF PROFIT. Gross margin of profit is the dollar difference between the *total* cost of goods sold and net sales.

GROSS MARGIN RETURN ON INVENTORY (GMROI). Gross margin divided by average inventory (at cost). GMROI is used most appropriately in measuring the performance of products within a single merchandise category. The measure permits the buyer to look at products with different gross margin percentages and different rates of inventory turnover and make a relatively quick evaluation as to which are the best performers. The componenets of GMROI are

Gross Margin Percentage	Sales to Inventory Ratio	GMROI

$$\frac{\text{Gross margin}}{\text{Net sales}} \quad \times \quad \frac{\text{Net sales}}{\text{Average inventory (at cost)}} \quad = \quad \frac{\text{Gross margin}}{\text{Average inventory (at cost)}}$$

TOTAL COST.   Total cost of goods sold = Gross cost of goods sold + Workroom costs–Cash discounts

MARKDOWN.   Markdown is a reduction in the original or the previous retail price on merchandise. *Markdown percentage* refers to the ratio of the dollar markdown during a period to the net sales for the same period.

OFF-RETAIL.   Designates specific reductions off the original retail price. Retailers can express markup in terms of retail price or cost. Large retailers and progressive small retailers express markups in terms of retail for several reasons. First, other operating ratios are expressed in terms of percentage net sales. Second, net sales figures are available more frequently than cost figures. Finally, most trade statistics are expressed in terms of sales.

   Markup on retail can be converted to cost base by using the following formula:

$$\text{Markup \% on cost} = \frac{\text{Markup \% on retail}}{100\% - \text{Markup \% on retail}}$$

On the other hand,

$$\text{Markup \% on retail} = \frac{\text{Markup \% on cost}}{100\% + \text{Markup \% on cost}}$$

F.O.B.   The seller places the merchandise "free on board" the carrier at the point of shipment or other predesignated place. The buyer assumes title to the merchandise and pays all freight charges from this point.

DELIVERED SALE.   The seller pays all freight charges to the buyer's destination and retains title to the goods until they are received by the buyer.

FREIGHT ALLOWANCES.   F.O.B. terms can be used with freight allowances to transfer the title to the buyer at the point of shipping, while the seller absorbs transportation cost. The seller ships F.O.B. and the buyer deducts freight costs from his invoice payment.

TRADE DISCOUNT.   Vendors usually quote a list price and offer a trade discount to provide the purchaser a reasonable margin to cover his operating expenses and provide for net profit margin. Trade discounts are sometimes labeled as functional discounts. They are usually quoted in a series of percentages, such as list price less 33%–15%–5%, for different channel intermediaries. Therefore, if a list price of $100 is assumed, the discount applies as follows for different channel members:

List price	$100.00	
Less 33%	33.00	retailer
	$ 67.00	
Less 15%	10.05	wholesaler
	56.95	
Less 5%	2.85	manufacturer's representative
	$ 52.65	

QUANTITY DISCOUNTS. Vendors offer two types of quantity discounts, non-cumulative and cumulative discounts. While noncumulative discounts are offered on volume of each order, cumulative discounts are offered on total volume for a specified period. Quantity discounts are offered to encourage volume buying and, legally, they should not exceed production and distribution cost savings to the seller owing to volume buying.

SEASONAL DISCOUNTS. Seasonal discounts are offered to buyers of seasonal products who place their orders in advance of the season's buying period. This enables the manufacturer to use his equipment more efficiently by spreading production throughout the year.

CASH DISCOUNTS. Vendors selling on credit offer a cash discount for payment within a specified period of time. The cash discount is usually expressed in the following format: 2/10, net 30. This means that the seller extends credit for 30 days. If payment is made within 10 days, a 2 percent discount is offered to the buyer. The 2 percent interest rate for 10 days is equivalent to 36 percent effective interest rate per year. Therefore, the passing up of cash discounts can be very costly. Some middlemen who operate on slim margins simply cannot realize a profit on a merchandise shipment unless they take advantage of the cash discount. Channel intermediaries usually maintain a line of credit at low interest rates to use to pay their bills within the cash discount period.

CASH DATING. Cash datings include C.O.D. (cash on delivery), C.W.O. (cash with order), R.O.G. (receipt of goods), S.D.-B.L. (sight-draft-bill of lading). S.D.-B.L. means that a sight-draft is attached to the bill of lading and must be honored before the buyer takes possession of the shipment.

FUTURE DATING. Future datings include:
(1) Ordinary dating such as "2/10, net 30."
(2) End of month dating such as "2/10, net 30, E.O.M.," where the cash discount and the net credit periods begin on the first day of the following month rather than the invoice date.
(3) Proximo dating such as "2 percent, 10th proximo, net 60" specifies a date in the following month on which payment must be made in order to take the cash discount.

(4) Extra dating such as "2/10—30 days extra" means that the buyer has 70 days from the invoice date to pay his bill and benefit from the discounts.

(5) Advance or season dating such as "2/10, net 30 as of May 1" means that the discount and net periods are calculated from May 1. Sometimes extra dating is accompanied with anticipation allowance. For example, if the buyer is quoted "2/10, 60 days extra," and he pays in 10 days or 60 days ahead, an additional discount is made available to the buyer.

APPENDIX 2C

Merchandise planning and control

Merchandise planning and control start first with decisions about merchandise variety and assortment. Variety decisions involve determination of the generically different kinds of goods to be carried or services to be offered. For example, a department store carries a wide variety of merchandise ranging from men's clothing and women's fashions to sports equipment and appliances. On the other hand, assortment decisions involve determination of the range of choice (e.g., brands, styles or models, colors, sizes, prices) offered to the customer within a variety classification. The more carefully and wisely decisions on variety and assortment are made, the more likely the retailer is to achieve a satisfactory rate of stockturn.

The rate of "stockturn" (stock turnover) is the number of times during a given period in which the average amount of stock on hand is sold and is most commonly determined by dividing the average inventory at cost into the cost of the merchandise sold.[123] To achieve a high rate of stockturn, retailers frequently attempt to limit their investment in inventory which, in turn, reduces storage space as well as such expenses as interest, taxes, and insurance on merchandise. "Fresher" merchandise will be on hand, thereby generating more sales. Thus, a rapid stockturn can lead to greater returns on invested capital.[124]

While retailing firms with the highest rates of turnover tend to realize the greatest profit-to-sales ratios,[125] significant problems may be encountered by adopting high turnover goals. For example, higher sales volume can be generated

---

[123] It is also computed by dividing average inventory at retail into the net sales figure or by dividing average inventory in physical units into sales in physical units.

[124] Delbert J. Duncan, Charles F. Phillips, and Stanley C. Hollander, *Modern Retailing Management,* 8th ed. (Homewood, Ill.: Richard D. Irwin, 1972), p. 324.

[125] *Ibid.,* pp. 326–327.

102

through lower margins which, in turn, reduce profitability; lower inventory levels may result in lost sales due to out-of-stock conditions; purchasing in small quantities may result in additional ordering (clerical) costs and the loss of quantity discounts; and greater expense may be involved in receiving, checking, and marking merchandise. Merchandise budget planning provides the means by which the appropriate balance can be achieved between retail stock and sales volume.

MERCHANDISE BUDGETING.   The merchandise budget plan is a forecast of specified merchandise-related activities for a definite period of time. Although the usual period covered is one season of six months, in practice this period is often broken down into monthly or even shorter periods. Merchandise budgeting requires the retail decision maker to make forecasts and plans relative to five basic variables: sales, stock levels, reductions, purchases, and gross margin and operating profit. Each of these variables will be addressed briefly below.[126]

Planned Sales and Stock Levels   The *first step* in budget determination is the preparation of the *sales forecast* for the season and for each month in the season for which the budget is being prepared. The *second step* involves the determination of the *beginning of the month* (B.O.M.) *inventory* (stock on hand), which necessitates specification of a desired rate of stockturn for each month of the season. If, for example, the desired stock-sales ratio for the month of June is 4 and forecasted (planned) sales during June are $10,000, then the planned B.O.M. stock would be $40,000.[127] It is also important, for budgeting purposes, to calculate the stock available at the end of the month (E.O.M. stock). This figure is identical to the B.O.M. stock for the following month. Thus, May's E.O.M. stock is, if the above example is used, $40,000 (or June's B.O.M. stock).

Planned Reductions   The *third step* in budget preparation is *reduction planning*, which involves accounting for markdowns, shortages, and employee discounts. Reduction planning is critical because any amount of reductions has exactly the same effect on the value of stock as an equal amount of sales. Markdowns vary from month to month, depending upon special and sales events. In addition, shortages are becoming an increasing problem to retailers, amounting to $16 billion in the aggregate during 1970. Shortages result from shoplifting, employee pilferage, miscounting, and pricing and checkout mistakes. Generally, merchandise managers can rely on past data in forecasting both shortages and employee discounts.

Planned Purchases   When figures for sales, opening (B.O.M.) and closing (E.O.M.) stocks, and reductions have been forecast, the *fourth step, the planning of purchases* in dollars, becomes merely a mechanical mathematical operation.

---

[126] It should be noted that all of the variables have been treated more fully elsewhere, should the reader desire more detail. See Phillips and Hollander, *op. cit.*

[127] There are numerous variations used to determine B.O.M. stock. See Duncan, Phillips, and Hollander, *op. cit.*, p. 342.

Thus, planned purchases are equal to planned stock at the end of the month (E.O.M.) + planned sales + planned reductions — stock at the beginning of the month (B.O.M.). Suppose, for example, that the planned E.O.M. stock for June was $67,500[128] and that reductions for June were forecast to be $2500. Then,

Planned E.O.M. stock (June 30)	$67,500
Planned sales (June 1-June 30)	10,000
Planned reductions	2,500
Total	$80,000
Less	
Planned B.O.M. stock (June 1)	40,000
Planned purchases	$40,000

The planned purchases figure is, however, based on *retail prices*. To determine the financial resources needed to acquire the merchandise, it is necessary to determine planned purchases at *cost*. The difference between planned purchases at retail and at cost represents the initial markup goal for the merchandise in question. This goal is established by determining the amount of operating expenses that are necessary in order to achieve the forecasted sales volume, as well as the profits desired from the specific operation, and combining this information with the data on reductions. Thus,

$$\text{Initial markup goal} = \frac{\text{Expenses} + \text{Profit} + \text{Reductions}}{\text{Net sales} + \text{Reductions}}$$

A term frequently used in retailing is "open-to-buy." It refers to the amount, in terms of retail prices or at cost, which a buyer is open to receive into stock during a certain period on the basis of the plans formulated.[129] Thus, planned purchases and "open-to-buy" may be synonymous in instances where forecasts coincide with actual results. However, adjustments in inventories, fluctuations in sales volume, unplanned markdowns, and goods ordered but not received all serve to complicate the determination of the amount that a buyer may spend.[130]

Planned Gross Margin and Operating Profit   The *gross margin* is the initial markup adjusted for price changes, stock shortages, and other reductions. The difference between gross margin and expenses required to generate sales will yield either a contribution to profit or a *net operating profit* (before taxes) depending, of course, on the sophistication of a retailer's accounting system and the narrowness of his merchandise budgeting.

[128] Derived from a desired stock-sales ratio for July of 4.5 and projected sales for July of $15,000. Remember, June's E.O.M. is the same as July's B.O.M.

[129] Duncan, Phillips, and Hollander, *op. cit.*, p. 345.

[130] *Ibid.*

THREE

Wholesaling: Structure and Strategy

WHOLESALING DEFINED

One of the most confusing aspects of marketing channels is related to wholesaling. There are so many different types of wholesaling establishments that it is difficult to get a "fix" on just what wholesaling is. The nomenclature of the distributive trades adds to this confusion. Wholesalers are called jobbers, distributors, and middlemen, among other names. (Some of the names are unprintable, because of the antagonism towards wholesalers which has been built up over the years due to their alleged role in increasing the overall cost of distribution.) As if the name-calling problem were not enough, it has been confounded by the fact that manufacturers' agents, rack jobbers, food brokers, commission merchants, and a host of other functionaries are also members of the wholesaling "industry." Therefore, any attempt to define just what a wholesaler is is bound to apply in some situations but miss the mark in others.

Nevertheless, to avoid semantic debates and to at least attempt a beginning, we can adopt the U.S. Bureau of the Census's definition for starters:

> Wholesaling is concerned with the activities of those persons or establishments which sell to retailers and other merchants, and/or to industrial, institutional, and commercial users, but who do not sell in significant amounts to ultimate consumers.

Of course, accepting this definition as the gospel truth means that every sale made by every organization to anyone but an ultimate consumer is a "wholesale sale." This would include every manufacturing firm (with the exception of the small amount of sales made through factory outlets to household consumers) as well as sales made by such diverse organizations as hotels, insurance companies, and accounting firms when they deal with "industrial, institutional, and commercial" users in booking rooms, arranging pension plans, or preparing annual reports.

In actuality, then, almost all organizations (except those dealing with ultimate consumers) are engaged in wholesale transactions. Taking such a broad perspective in this chapter would force consideration here of every form of marketing at every level in a channel other than retailing. Our intention is not to provide a global view of marketing practices, but to take a brief look at some of the structural and strategic dimensions of wholesale trade—defined quite narrowly to encompass only the operations of specialized independently owned and operated wholesaling institutions and establishments engaged primarily in domestic marketing. About 50 percent of the total output marketed "at wholesale" passes through such institutions and establishments. In addition, the focus in this chapter is largely on so-called "merchant" wholesalers—independently owned firms which purchase goods from suppliers for their own account, operate one or more warehouses in which they receive and take title to goods, store them, and later reship them.[1] By assuming such a narrow focus, it will be possible to become more fully exposed to and examine more thoroughly those channel members normally referred to as "wholesalers," so that when attention is turned to specific approaches to channel management in later chapters, account may be taken of the unique contributions, characteristics, and orientations of these institutions in forming the most beneficial systemwide strategies for the channel.

| RATIONALE FOR THE EMERGENCE OF MODERN WHOLESALERS | The wholesaler's functions are shaped by the vast economic task of coordinating production and consumption or, in Alderson's words, of matching heterogeneous demands for assortments at various levels within distribution.[2] Thus, wholesalers aid in |

bridging the time and space gap between periods and places in which goods are produced and those in which they are consumed or used.

The sorting process of wholesalers is the key to their economic viability. It frequently happens that the quantities in which goods are produced or the characteristics with which they are endowed by nature do not match either the quantities in which they are demanded or the characteristics desired by those who use or consume them. Channel intermediaries (e.g., wholesalers and retailers) essentially solve the problem of the discrepancy between the various types of assortments of goods and services that are required by industrial and household consumers *and* the assortments that are available directly from individual producers. In other words, manufacturers usually produce a large quantity of a limited number of

---

[1] Richard S. Lopata, "Faster Pace in Wholesaling," *Harvard Business Review,* Vol. 47 (July–August 1969), p. 131.

[2] Wroe Alderson, "Factors Governing the Development of Marketing Channels," in Willaim G. Moller, Jr., and David L. Wilemon (eds.), *Marketing Channels: A Systems Viewpoint* (Homewood, Ill.: Richard D. Irwin, 1971), p. 20.

products, whereas consumers purchase only a few items of a large number of diverse products. Middlemen reduce this *discrepancy of assortments,* thereby enabling consumers to avoid dealing directly with individual manufacturers in order to satisfy their needs.

The rationale for a wholesaler's existence boils down to the functions he performs for the suppliers and customers he serves. That is, his economic justification is based on just what it is that he can do for his clientele, whether they be retailers, institutions (e.g., hospitals, schools, restaurants), manufacturers, or any other type of business enterprise. For example, with respect to his customers, a wholesaler can often provide the following services:

- *Physical possession.* A wholesaler can store goods in anticipation of customer needs and can provide quick delivery when the goods are desired because he is usually located closer to customers than more centralized manufacturing facilities.
- *Ownership.* Many wholesalers take title to the goods they store; therefore, they absorb inventory carrying costs for their customers. Customers can purchase from wholesalers in small lots; if they purchase directly, they generally must assume a larger inventory burden.
- *Financing.* A wholesaler finances the exchange process by investing in inventory and by extending credit to customers.
- *Risk-taking.* A wholesaler assumes risk when he takes possession and ownership of products that can deteriorate or become obsolete. He can also assist his customers in absorbing uncertainty by providing information about technical features, appropriate usage, availability, product quality, competitive conditions, and so on.
- *Negotiating.* Wholesalers generally bring together an *assortment* of merchandise, usually of related items, by negotiating with a number of different sources.
- *Ordering.* A wholesaler can anticipate his customers' needs and thereby simplify their buying tasks. Rather than having to negotiate and purchase from a large number of sources, a customer can order from one source the assortment of products required. In addition, a wholesaler may inspect, test, or judge the products he receives for quality, thereby assuming an even greater role in the ordering process for his customers.

Thus, in the case of industrial goods needed in the assembly of a given product (e.g., electronic tubes for radios), it may be less costly for the purchasing organization to place the burden of handling, owning, storing, delivering, and ordering the goods on a wholesaler versus having to order in very large lots directly from the manufacturer, especially if the goods will have to be held a considerable period of time before they are fully used up in the production process. Similar economies are available to purchasers of certain consumer goods, such as toys. For instance, almost 80 percent of all retail toy sales are made during November and December. Although thousands of toys are marketed every Christmas season, probably less than a hundred are best sellers. Because of the fickleness of consumers, retailers cannot accurately predict the demand for toys too far in advance. Therefore, they place numerous reorders of popular toys during the peak selling season. Wholesalers maintain large speculative inventories close to retail markets, thus permitting speedy delivery of toys on short notice.

Pressure on Wholesalers

Wholesalers have been under increasing pressure, however, to prove and improve their economic viability because of several forces threatening their standing in distribution. The three most significant of these forces are, according to Bucklin, (1) the decline of the role and importance of wholesalers in importing and exporting; (2) the fact that manufacturers have expanded the scale of their factories, broadened their product lines, and integrated forward into distribution; and (3) the growth of chain stores.[3] These pressures started building during the late nineteenth century and have not abated since that time. In addition, the wholesaler's unique position in the middle of channels subjects him to the impact of the constant changes and innovations in the whole marketplace.

> Technological advances, product line proliferation, changing retail structures, and social adjustments are only a few of the real problems that complicate the wholesaler's life. Each improved product passing through the wholesale level generates a new demand for investments in warehouse space, market analysis, and sales training, and for myriad adjustments in the wholesaler's information systems. Each major retailing shift designed to satisfy customer needs obliges him to adjust his selling patterns, to review his customer service levels, to study product assortments, and to revise his strategies.[4]

The structure of wholesaling must, therefore, be adaptable and capable of parrying or absorbing these changes.

THE STRUCTURE OF WHOLESALING

Wholesaling may be characterized as an industry in which the degree of specialization has constantly increased as a response to the waves of change mentioned above. In fact, as depicted in Fig. 3–1, as well as in the appendix to this chapter, the amount of institutional variety in wholesaling is tremendous, and, to some extent, overwhelming. Such a variety offers buyers and sellers many channel choices, as dictated by such considerations as size, market segmentation, financial strength, services offered, and chosen method of operation. It also makes possible a high degree of marketing flow or functional shiftability, whereby all wholesaling functions or a small part thereof may be shifted from one type of agency to another.

[3] Louis P. Bucklin, *Competition and Evolution in the Distributive Trades* (Englewood Cliffs, N.J.: Prentice-Hall, 1972), p. 203.
[4] Lopata, *op. cit.*, p. 131.

FIGURE 3–1

The Wholesaling Structure—Types of Wholesale Middlemen

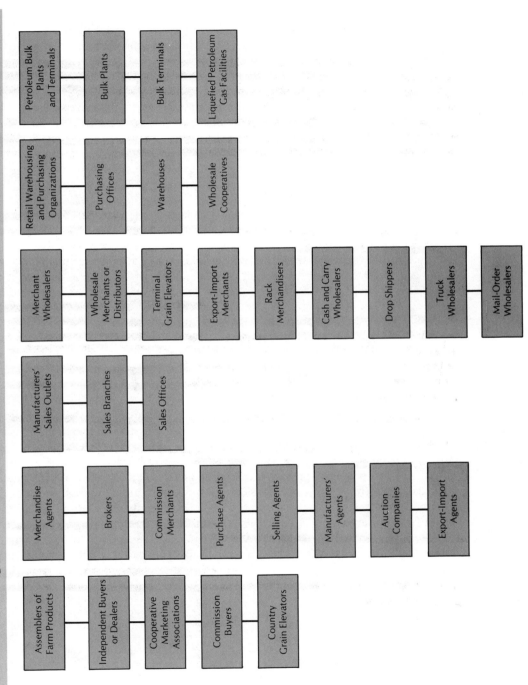

Source: Reprinted from Richard M. Hill, *Wholesaling Management* (Homewood, Ill.: Richard D. Irwin, 1963), p. 25.

From a channel analysis perspective, it is important to understand what specific roles the various types of wholesaling institutions and agencies assume so that when a channel is designed or adjusted, the appropriate kind of organization can be included. An essential piece of information, in this regard, is whether a wholesaler participates in all or only a few of the marketing flows (physical possession, ownership, promotion, negotiation, financing, risking, ordering, and payment). That is, assuming a manufacturer's or a retailer's perspective for the moment, what is it that one could expect to receive from a wholesaler in the way of services performed? Clearly, the more services performed, the higher will have to be the wholesaler's compensation from the channel as a whole. The appendix to this chapter provides a rather detailed, but not exhaustive, listing of the flows participated in by a variety of wholesaling enterprises. Table 3–1 provides a "bare bones" summary of the appendix.

An examination of Table 3–1 indicates that full-function merchant wholesalers participate in all the flows while brokers and manufacturers' agents participate in only a few of them. This fact is reinforced by the knowledge that, appropriate to the functions they perform in the channel, the former incur operating expenses of approximately 15 percent of sales while the latter's operating expenses range, on average, from 3.2 percent of sales for merchandise brokers to 6.6 percent of sales for manufacturers' agents.[5] Therefore, if a manufacturer were to "employ" full-function merchant wholesalers, the discount granted to these wholesalers would have to be considerably more than the commission he would have to pay to manufacturer's agents or brokers for selling his products to end users. But when a manufacturer does not use a full function wholesaler, he does not "save" 15 percent, because he must assume all of the services which the wholesaler would have provided.

In an effort to provide some semblance of order and analysis to what must appear to the onlooker as a chaotic structure, academic scholars, merchants, and the U.S. Bureau of the Census have divided all of the various wholesaling institutions and establishments into the five major types[6] shown in Tables 3–2 and 3–3. Several salient facts can be gleaned about wholesaling in general and about specific types in particular directly from the tables or from computations based on the data contained in them. First, the volume of wholesale trade in *constant dollars* was almost twice as large in 1977 as in 1963.[7] Second, merchant wholesalers continue to hold the largest share of wholesale trade and their share appears to be growing. In addition, an examination of the percentage distribution of merchant wholesaler sales by type of customer (see Table 3–4) indicates that an increasing proportion of their sales is going to industrial, commercial, and government users, as well as to other wholesalers.

[5] U.S. Bureau of the Census, *1977 Census of Wholesale Trade*, Geographic Area Series, Report No. WC77-A-52 (June 1980), p. 52–8.

[6] Definitions of the various types of wholesalers can be found in the appendix to this chapter.

[7] Nationally, aggregate sales by wholesalers are larger than sales by retailers because of the large product flow to industrial markets that does not pass through the retail trade *and* because some products are sold two or more times by wholesale institutions.

TABLE 3-1   Summary of wholesalers' participation in the marketing flows

	Physical Possession	Ownership	Promotion	Negotiation	Financing	Risking	Ordering	Payment
A. Merchant Wholesalers								
1. Full-function or service wholesalers	High	High	High	High	High	High	High	High
2. Limited-function wholesalers								
a) Drop-shipper (desk jobber)	None	High	Low	High	High	High	High	High
b) Cash-carry wholesalers	High	High	Low	High	None	Low	High	High
c) Wagon (truck) jobbing	Low	Low	Low	High	Low	Low	High	High
d) Rack jobbers (service merchandisers)	High	High	Low	High	High	High	High	High
e) Converters	Low	High	Low	High	High	High	High	High
f) Wholesaler-sponsored (voluntary) chains	High	High	High	High	High	High	High	High
B. Retailer-sponsored Cooperatives	High	High	High	High	High	High	High	High
C. Function Middlemen (Agents and Brokers)								
1. Brokers	None	None	High	Low	None	None	High	Low
2. Manufacturers' agents	None	None	High	None	None	None	High	Low
3. Selling agents	None	None	High	High	None	None	High	Low
4. Commission Merchants	High	None	High	High	High	High	High	High

Source: Derived from Appendix 3A.

TABLE 3–2   Annual sales of major types of wholesalers, 1948 through 1977 (in billions of dollars)

	1948	1963	1967	1972	1977
Merchant-wholesalers	$ 76.6	$157.4	$206.1	$353.9	$ 676.1
Manufacturer sales branches and offices	50.7	116.4	157.1	255.7	451.8
Sales branches (with stock)	28.5	54.8	67.2	124.5	221.5
Sales offices (without stock)	22.2	61.6	89.9	131.2	230.3
Petroleum bulk stations	10.5	21.5	24.8	33.3	25.6
Agents and brokers	32.9	53.3	61.3	85.6	130.5
Assemblers	9.9	9.8	10.2	a	a
Total	$180.6	$358.4	$459.5	$728.5	$1284.0

a Included under "Merchant-wholesalers."

Source: U.S. Bureau of the Census, *Wholesale Trade, Summary Statistics,* various years.

Third, there has been a substantial rise in the number of wholesale establishments; between 1963 and 1977, the number of such places of business increased over 12 percent. Over the same period, the number of retail establishments remained relatively constant while retail sales grew at a rate comparable to that for wholesaling. Thus, logically extrapolated, this means that the differential in size between the typical wholesale and retail establishment has been continually declining. If size can be taken as an indicator of vertical market power, such a change may have vast implications for channel leadership. However, despite any of the trends apparent in the data, wholesaling, like retailing, is predominately an industry of small business—86 percent of all wholesale establishments have no more than nineteen employees; the average establishment had only 11 employees in 1977.

Because of their obvious importance in the wholesaling structure, some additional developments within merchant wholesaling and among manufacturers' sales branches and offices are mentioned below.

Merchant Wholesalers

The "merchant wholesalers" category listed in Tables 3–2 and 3–3 includes such service wholesalers as wholesale merchants and distributors, importers, exporters, rack merchandisers, terminal grain elevators, and assemblers of farm products, as well as a group of limited-function wholesalers like cash-and-carry establishments, drop shippers who do not handle the goods in which they deal, and so-called wagon or truck distributors, who combine selling and delivery in one operation. Merchant wholesalers take title to the goods in which they deal (whether they handle them or not) and operate independently from suppliers on the one hand and from retailers and other customers on the other.

The sales of merchant wholesalers have increased significantly over the time

TABLE 3-3 Trends in the share of wholesaling establishments and sales ᵃ

	Establishments (number)				Sales (billions of dollars)			
	1963	1967	1972	1977	1963	1967	1972	1977
Total	308,177	311,464	369,791	394,029	$358.4	$459.5	$728.5	$1284.0
	(percentage of total)				(percentage of total)			
Merchant-wholesalers	67.8%	68.4%	73.4%	78.0%	43.9%	44.8%	48.6%	52.7%
Manufacturer sales branches and offices	9.4	9.9	11.9	10.3	32.5	34.2	35.2	35.2
Sales branches (with stocks)	5.3	5.4	8.4	6.8	15.3	14.6	17.2	17.3
Sales offices (without stocks)	4.1	4.5	3.5	3.5	17.2	19.6	18.0	17.9
Petroleum bulk stations	10.0	9.7	6.3	2.8	6.0	5.4	4.6	2.0
Agents and brokers	8.2	8.5	8.4	8.9	14.9	13.3	10.4	10.2
Assemblers	4.6	3.6	b	b	2.6	2.2	b	b

ᵃ Some of the percentages do not add up to 100 percent due to rounding or absent data.
ᵇ Included in "Merchant-wholesalers."

Source: U.S. Bureau of the Census, *Wholesale Trade*, various years.

TABLE 3-4   Merchant wholesaler sales by type of customer

Type of Customer	1948	1963	1974
Retailers	46.9%	40.8%	37.2%
Industrial, commercial, and government users	31.8	37.6	40.7
Other wholesalers	13.7	14.5	15.0
Consumers and farmers	1.6	1.2	1.3
Foreign buyers	6.0	5.9	5.8
	100.0%	100.0%	100.0%

Source: Bert C. McCammon, Jr. and James W. Kenderdine, "Mainstream Developments in Wholesaling," a paper presented at the 1975 Conference of the Southwestern Marketing Association, p. 3.

TABLE 3-5   Sales of selected durable and nondurable goods by U.S. merchant wholesale groups

Durable Goods	1977 Sales (in billions)
Motor vehicles and automotive parts and supplies	$147.1
Furniture and home furnishings	22.0
Lumber and other construction materials	46.2
Sporting, recreational, photographic, and hobby goods, toys, and supplies	16.5
Metals and minerals, except petroleum	80.3
Electrical goods	70.0
Hardware and plumbing and heating equipment and supplies	30.6
Machinery, equipment, and supplies	165.1
Nondurable Goods	
Paper and paper products	32.5
Drugs, drug proprieties, and druggists' sundries	19.4
Apparel, piece goods, and notions	39.9
Groceries and related products	182.9
Chemicals and allied products	51.7
Petroleum and petroleum products	116.8
Beer, wines, and distilled alcoholic beverages	27.0
Tobacco and tobacco products	11.3

Source: U.S. Bureau of the Census, 1977 Census of Wholesale Trade, Advance Report, March 1980.

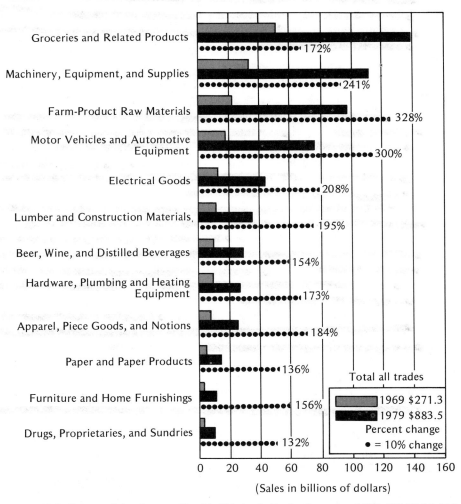

FIGURE 3-2

Sales of Merchant Wholesalers by Kind of Business: 1969 and 1979

Groceries and Related Products — 172%

Machinery, Equipment, and Supplies — 241%

Farm-Product Raw Materials — 328%

Motor Vehicles and Automotive Equipment — 300%

Electrical Goods — 208%

Lumber and Construction Materials — 195%

Beer, Wine, and Distilled Beverages — 154%

Hardware, Plumbing and Heating Equipment — 173%

Apparel, Piece Goods, and Notions — 184%

Paper and Paper Products — 136%

Furniture and Home Furnishings — 156%

Drugs, Proprietaries, and Sundries — 132%

Total all trades
1969 $271.3
1979 $883.5
Percent change
● = 10% change

0   20   40   60   80   100   120   140   160

(Sales in billions of dollars)

Source: U.S. Bureau of the Census, *Monthly Wholesale Trade, December 1979,* BW-79-12 (February 1980), p. 3.

period covered in Tables 3-2 and 3-3. In addition, the proportion of merchant wholesaler establishments increased rather dramatically over the time period relative to the increase in the number of establishments of other wholesaler types. However, while overall growth—in sales and establishments—has been strongly positive, the success of merchant wholesalers has varied widely from the standpoint of individual product class groupings. (Sales of selected nondurable and durable goods by merchant wholesale groups are shown in Table 3–5 and Fig. 3–2).[8]

In addition, some merchant wholesalers have found considerable success by restricting their activities to a limited range of products within a product grouping. In groceries, drugs, hardware, and jewelry, specialty wholesalers have been able to aid retail chains in expanding their product lines in directions unfamiliar to chain buyers and merchandisers (e.g., nonfood items in grocery stores).

Manufacturers' Sales Branches and Offices

Branches are captive wholesaling operations owned and operated by a manufacturer. Branch operations are common, for example, in electrical supplies (e.g., Westinghouse Electric Supply Company) and in plumbing (e.g., Crane Supply Company and Arnstan-American Standard). Captive branch operations are also employed heavily by truck manufacturers, full-line farm equipment manufacturers, and large producers of major appliances.[9]

Manufacturers' sales branches are of two types: those that carry inventories and those that do not. The greatest growth has been among the former type. This development reflects the fact that manufacturers have increasingly been establishing local distribution centers which house sales branches and coordinate the operations of both centrally.[10] For industrial goods marketing, the quantities involved and the need for technical expertise seem to create a need for manufacturers' sales branch operations, irrespective of type.[11]

It is, however, important to note that a fourth of the business done by the branches and sales offices is in sales to other wholesale establishments rather than to customers of merchant wholesalers.[12] In fact, almost 56 percent of the merchant wholesaler's industrial goods volume is obtained from another wholesale institution, according to Bucklin's estimates,[13] and it is very likely that a vast majority of shipments come to these wholesalers from manufacturers' branches. Double wholesaling is even more important for consumer goods, although the channels for

---

[8] Besides product class groupings, wholesalers can also be broken down into customer categories. Thus, there is one broad class of wholesalers who sell to retailers such diverse commodities as food, drugs, tobacco, hardware, dry goods, and appliances. Another class sells such items as food, paper products, medical goods and supplies, and so on, to restaurants and institutions. A third class sells building materials to builders and contractors. A fourth class sells manufacturing supplies such as tools, chemicals, abrasives, and so on, to manufacturers. In the complex automotive parts aftermarket, there are even warehouse distributors who sell only to other jobbers. However, growth generalities are difficult to make here because of the diversity of products included within each class.

[9] Lopata, *op. cit.,* p. 131.

[10] As Bucklin points out, the data on manufacturers' sales branches without stocks do not fully disclose the extent to which the manufacturers may be employing other inventory depots not located directly at the sales office. One regional warehouse, for example, may serve several sales offices. Alternatively, the manufacturer may be employing public warehouse facilities—particularly in small territories—rather than constructing his own. Bucklin, *op. cit.,* p. 214.

[11] *Ibid.,* p. 217.

[12] Theodore N. Beckman, "Changes in Wholesaling Structure and Performance," in Moller and Wilemon, *op. cit.,* p. 126.

[13] Bucklin, *op. cit.,* p. 218.

TABLE 3-6 Sales by agent wholesalers-1967 and 1977 (in millions of dollars)

	1967		1977	
Type of Operation	Volume of Trade	Percentage of Total	Volume of Trade	Percentage of Total
Auction companies	4,792	7.8	10,826	8.3
Brokers	14,030	22.9	30,585	23.4
Commission merchants	14,068	22.9	27,966	21.4
Import agents }			3,920	3.0
Export agents }	6,309	10.3	8,822	6.8
Manufacturers' agents[a]	22,150	36.1	48,369	37.1
Total	61,347	100.0	130,488	100.0

[a]Includes selling agents.

Source: U.S. Census of Business, *Wholesale Trade, Summary Statistics,* 1967 and 1977.

industrial and consumer goods are becoming more similar over the years in this respect.[14]

Agents and Brokers

Finally with regard to the overall structure of wholesaling, the relative decline of agents and brokers shown in Table 3-3 masks the increase in the relative importance of certain categories within this segment, as seen in Table 3-6. Numerous brokers and agents operate very much like salesmen in the field, except that they carry a narrow line of products from a few suppliers related in terms of the needs of their customers.[15] Manufacturers in a few industries have tended to move away from reliance on any type of agent wholesaling organization, because they view such wholesalers as not being service-oriented, controllable, innovative, efficient, or reliable.[16]

ECONOMIC CONCENTRATION IN WHOLESALING

Of some 307,264 establishments owned by 254,651 merchant wholesalers in 1977, only about 9000 were generating over $10 million in annual sales.[17]

In 1977, wholesaler establishments with annual sales over $10 million accounted for 49 percent of total wholesaler sales, up from 14 percent in 1948.[18] In general, however, economic concentration in wholesaling is

[14] *Ibid.,* p. 219.

[15] See the appendix at the end of this chapter for a description of the activities of various agent middlemen.

[16] James R. Moore and Kendall A. Adams, *"Functional Wholesaler Sales: Trends and Analysis,"* in Edward M. Mazze (ed.), *1975 Combined Proceedings* (Chicago: American Marketing Association, 1976), pp. 403-404.

[17] U.S. Bureau of the Census, *1977 Census of Wholesale Trade,* Establishment and Firm Size, Report No. WC77-5-1, pp. 1-17 and 1-97.

[18] *Ibid.*

very low, especially on the national level. For example, the 20 largest merchant wholesalers accounted for only 10.3 percent of 1977 sales by merchant wholesalers. On a product line or a local geographic basis, wholesaling is more concentrated. Thus, 13 firms (including Graybar Electric Company) control 30.4 percent of the business done by electrical supply wholesalers; six firms (including American Hospital Supply Corporation) share 19.6 percent of the business done by wholesalers of hospital supplies; 19 firms (including Joseph P. Ryerson & Sons, Inc.) account for 18 percent of the business done by metal service centers.[19] Bucklin's analysis has shown that in one large geographic area (California), the typical number of wholesalers directly operating within all but the very largest metropolitan area is relatively small.[20]

One factor accounting for the extent of concentration is the existence of multiunit or chain operations within wholesaling. While wholesaling is still very largely an industry comprised of single-unit firms, multiestablishment wholesale firms accounted for 65 percent of all sales and over 30 percent of all establishments in 1977.[21] In a study of 14 product subsectors, Bucklin has shown that the share of chain operations ranges from a low of 28.1 percent in dry goods to a high of 81.4 percent in petroleum bulk stations and terminals.[22]

COMPETITION IN WHOLESALING

Competition, especially in larger market areas, is intense, from the perspective of both price and service. Several factors account for this. First, as in retailing, product line assortments are generally very broad, making price identity among competitors very difficult to maintain within wholesale trade. Second, wholesalers face economically significant retailing, industrial, and business buying organizations, and such organizations are capable of playing wholesalers off against one another as well as threatening to purchase directly from manufacturers if prices are not set to their satisfaction. Although the balance of power can swing in the wholesaler's favor from time to time (as when large wholesaling organizations deal with small retailing firms), any deviance in pricing behavior from that afforded to other channels comprised of organizations purchasing directly from suppliers will rapidly place the wholesaler's channel in a weakened competitive position. In other words, by using his power relative to small retailers and industrial buyers for self-aggrandizement purposes, the wholesaler may be hurting himself in the long run by crippling his customers.

Third, because wholesalers generally deal in large lot size orders, the opportunity for intermarket penetration is high. In wholesaling, market size is generally

---

[19] Bucklin, *op. cit.*, p. 244.

[20] *Ibid.*, p. 245.

[21] U.S. Bureau of the Census, *1977 Census of Wholesale Trade,* Establishment and Firm Size, Report No. WC 77-5-1, p. 1-79.

[22] Bucklin, *op. cit.*, p. 258. For documentation relative to leading industrial distribution chains, see "The Chain of Events in Industrial Distribution," *Marketing News* (January 30, 1976), p. 7.

TABLE 3-7   Profits of selected U.S. merchant-wholesalers and manufacturers, 1979

	Net Profit on Tangible Net Worth[a]	
Durable Goods	Merchant Wholesalers	Manufacturers
Automotive parts and supplies	17.7	21.0[b]
Electrical apparatus and equipment	19.1	21.3[c]
Furniture	20.4	19.6[d]
Hardware	16.9	21.0[e]
Plumbing and hydronic heating supplies	16.7	27.8
Lumber plywood and mill work	21.1	22.1[f]
Metals service centers and offices	20.6	18.6[g]
Nondurable Goods		
Groceries, general line	12.8	11.6[h]
Beer and ale	20.0	8.3[i]
Confectionery	20.6	18.7
Chemicals and allied products	22.2	10.9[j]
Clothing, accessories, and furnishings	20.7[k]	16.7[l]

[a]Median percentages, after taxes.
[b]Motor vehicle parts and accessories.
[c]Electric transformers.
[d]Wood household furniture.
[e]Screw machine products.
[f]Millwork.
[g]Fabricated structural metals.
[h]Canned fruits and vegetables.
[i]Malt liquors.
[j]Agricultural chemicals.
[k]Average of "clothing and accessories, women's and children's" and "clothing and furnishings, men's and boys'."
[l]Average of clothing, footwear, and outerwear categories.
Source: Dun and Bradstreet, Inc., *Key Business Ratios in 125 Industries, 1979.*

determined by transport costs, the bulk of the product, and the value of the product relative to freight charges.[23] The market size is not limited by the extent to which customers will travel to buy goods, as it is in retailing. Thus, enterprising wholesalers can find markets stretched by their willingness to meet or beat prices existing in locations quite distant from their normal trading areas. The efficiency of their operations will, to a large extent, determine just how far their market outreach can extend.

Fourth, entry is relatively easy.

Although the cost of constructing a new warehouse might range upwards of $10 million for the plant alone, entry into some separate product-line category could be effected at

[23] Bucklin, *op. cit.,* p. 266.

119

substantially lower fees. The specialist might compete on some basis other than price (such as faster delivery and unusually deep stocks), but his presence nevertheless brings competitive pressure upon the general-line wholesaler, leaving little room to extract higher than warranted margins.[24]

Finally, the most important factor breeding a high degree of competition in wholesale trade was hinted at in Chapter 2—the continual evolution of new distributive patterns (so-called intertype competition, such as that engendered by retail chain stores, cooperatives, and vertical integration) which narrow the security of the established sellers and bring powerful pressures to bear on wholesale markets. In fact, like large retailers, certain wholesalers are striving to achieve a differential advantage in *multiple* competitive environments.

Consider, for example, the competitive milieu of Stratton & Terstegge, a large hardware wholesaler in Louisville. At the present time, the company sells to independent retailers, sponsors a voluntary group program, and operates its own stores. In these multiple capacities, it competes against conventional wholesalers (Belknap), cash and carry wholesalers (Atlas), specialty wholesalers (Garcia), corporate chains (Wickes), voluntary groups (Western Auto), cooperative groups (Cotter), free form corporations (Interco), and others. Given the complexity of its competitive environment, it is not surprising to observe that Stratton & Terstegge generates a relatively modest rate of return on net worth.[25]

In spite of these five factors, returns for wholesalers in a number of industries have matched those of manufacturers while, in others, competition has taken its toll. (See Table 3–7.)

SELECTING AND USING WHOLESALERS

It is an old axiom of marketing that it is possible to eliminate the wholesaler (or any middleman for that matter), but it is impossible to eliminate his functions. The major question facing a manufacturer is whether, by vertical integration (that is, by establishing his own sales branches and warehouse facilities), he can perform the functions more effectively and efficiently than can a wholesaler. This question is a cause for considerable controversy in distribution. From U.S. Bureau of Census data, it is known that the operating expenses of manufacturers' sales branches (with stocks) average 9 percent of sales, which compares very favorably with the 15 percent indicated for merchant wholesalers.[26] But this comparison must be looked at very critically, because of the differences in pricing procedures which

---

[24] *Ibid.,* pp. 269-270

[25] Bert C. McCammon, Jr., "Future Shock and the Practice of Management," a paper presented at the Fifth Annual Attitude Research Conference of the American Marketing Association, Madrid, Spain, 1973, p. 9. For a comprehensive discussion of the performance of large wholesaling concerns, see Bert C. McCammon, Jr., and James M. Kenderine, "High Performance Wholesaling," *Hardlines Wholesaling,* Vol. 9 (September 1975), pp. 17-57.

[26] U.S. Bureau of the Census, *1977 Census of Wholesale Trade,* Geographic Area Series, Report No. WC77-A-52, p. 52-8.

are employed when selling to a sales branch which is owned outright vs. selling to an independently owned wholesaling firm. Furthermore, sometimes certain marketing costs are not allocated to the sales branch but are instead absorbed by the home office of the manufacturer. In addition, the investment required to establish sales branches and warehouses may be prohibitive, especially for small firms.

The likelihood is that the cost of marketing through wholesalers is not going to be *vastly* different from the funds that a firm would have to expend on its own in order to obtain the same services. If this is so, then what accounts for the large amount of direct selling that goes on? Why is vertical integration of wholesaling functions so popular, especially among large manufacturing and retailing firms? The answer lies not only in *efficiency* considerations (e.g., with very large volume and high turnover factors, very small differences in operating expenses can make a very significant difference in absolute profits) but mainly in *effectiveness* considerations. The fact that a given type of wholesaling firm participates in a number of marketing flows gives some idea about the *potential* for a division of labor in the channel. But the crucial question from a management perspective is how and to what extent (i.e., how *heavily*) does the firm participate? To answer this question, we must first examine what it is that wholesalers can, ideally, provide. Then, we will juxtapose this description against a hard-nosed assessment of the orientation of many wholesalers.

How Can Wholesalers Serve Suppliers? *(MANUFACTURERS)*

Ideally, wholesalers have a great deal of potential as channel partners for suppliers. From an operational perspective, suppliers of both industrial and consumer goods may rely on wholesalers for several key reasons.[27]

1. Wholesalers have continuity in and intimacy with local markets. Being close to customers, they are in positions to take initial steps in the sale of any product, namely, identifying prospective users and determining the extent of their needs.

2. Wholesalers make possible local availability of stocks and thereby relieve suppliers of small-order business, which the latter can seldom conduct on a profitable basis. Also, they tend to have an acute understanding of the costs of holding and handling inventory in which they have made major commitments.

3. Within their territories, wholesalers can provide suppliers with a sales force that is in close touch with the needs of customers and prospects. Also, by virtue of the fact that a wholesaler represents a number of suppliers, he can often cover a given territory at a lower cost than could the manufacturer's own salesmen.

[27] Many of these same points have been made in more detail by Richard M. Hill, *Wholesaling Management* (Homewood, Ill.: Richard D. Irwin, 1963), pp. 10–14. See also Frederick E. Webster, Jr., *Industrial Marketing Strategy* (New York: John Wiley & Sons, 1979), pp. 161–168.

4. Wholesalers perform financial services for suppliers by providing volume cash markets through which they can recover capital that would otherwise be invested in inventories.

From the point of view of the manufacturer, the several salient factors shown in Exhibit 3-1 must be evaluated in determining the type of wholesaling establishment to use; these factors must always be conditioned by the nature of the ultimate market for the goods in question.

How Can Wholesalers Serve Retailers?

Manufacturers are generally self-centered and myopic. Their interest is to encourage retailers to promote and sell their own lines of products. On the other hand, wholesalers have a strong vested interest in building up their retail customers as merchants, since it is quite likely that, particularly in the case of smaller retail establishments, an individual wholesaler would be able to supply a large part of the retailer's requirements for merchandise. It is in the wholesaler's self-interest to spend considerable effort and resources training, stimulating, and aiding retailers to become better managers. Therefore, wholesalers become directly involved in retail merchandise management. In this respect, the benefits to the retailer derived from relying on wholesalers may be described as follows:[28]

1. Wholesalers can give their retail customers a great deal of direct selling aid in the form of price concessions on featured items, point-of-sale material, and cooperative advertising.
2. Wholesalers often can provide expert assistance in planning store layout, building design, and material specifications.
3. Wholesalers generally offer retailers guidance and counsel in public relations, housekeeping and accounting methods, administrative procedures, and the like.

In the toy industry, for instance, many retailers prefer to make some or all of their total annual toy purchases from wholesalers rather than from manufacturers, because, as one retail executive has indicated:

1. In many instances reorders are filled more quickly.
2. Wholesalers guarantee the sale (any items which are not sold can be returned for full credit).
3. Defective products are replaced promptly.
4. The wholesaler extends long-term credit.

---

[28] See Hill, *op. cit.*, pp. 16–21, for more explanation and details.

EXHIBIT 3-1

Criteria of Choice in the Decision of What Type of Wholesaling Establishment to Use—Point of View of the Manufacturer

1. Evaluation of sales efforts of wholesaler
   a. Extent and activity of sales force of wholesaler
   b. Does sales force *sell*, or does it just take orders?
   c. Extent to which manufacturer must supplement wholesaler's sales efforts with own promotion, salesmen, and/or detail men
   d. Number of lines handled by wholesaler
      (1) Does wholesaler handle too many lines to give sufficient attention to manufacturer's line?
         (a) Use of heavy advertising, good margins, realistic pricing to stimulate attention on part of wholesaler
         (b) Preference, sometimes, for more attention to individual line by use of specialty or limited-line wholesalers
      (2) Does wholesaler handle competing lines?
         (a) Use of sales or manufacturers' agents sometimes indicated
         (b) May necessitate creation of exclusive distributorships
2. Evaluation of relationship of wholesaler to channel of distribution for the product
   a. Type of wholesaler that can give widest distribution and assurance of sufficient retail outlets for line
   b. When particular types of retail outlets are desired, what type of wholesaler can best handle them?
   c. Quality and continuity of relationships maintained between wholesaling and retailing firms
   d. Degree to which wholesaler cooperates in promotion, pricing, financing, and other marketing activities
   e. Willingness of wholesaler to maintain continuous relationships with manufacturer

Source: Department of Marketing, University of Pennsylvania, Wharton School of Finance and Commerce.

5. The percentage of mark-up by working through a wholesaler is more than offset by decreased inventory costs and improved service.[29]

Obviously, the foremost advantage for many retailers in relying on wholesalers is the fact that the latter buy in large quantities, break bulk to suit the convenience of their customers, and then pass along the savings effected both in

[29] Richard N. Cardozo and James E. Haefner, "Note on the Toy Industry" (Boston, Mass.: Intercollegiate Case Clearinghouse, No. ICH 14M60, 1970), p. 9.

123

cost and transportation, compared, of course, to the costs of obtaining merchandise directly in small lots from distant points. Thus, by using wholesalers, independent retailers can avoid diluting the energies of their often overtaxed executive staffs. Furthermore, these retailers obtain access through wholesalers to a large group of products of small manufacturers that might not otherwise be available to them. Even in the case of large establishments in certain product lines, reliance on wholesalers allows conversion of dead-weight store space, formerly devoted to merchandise storage, into profit-making selling or customer service space.[30] For example, although supermarket and discount chains can buy at the same price as a rack jobber or service merchandiser, the latter's hold on the market comes from knowing precisely what to buy and minimizing the handling and inventory costs of a variety of nonfood products, such as health and beauty aids, phonograph records, hardware, and sporting goods.

Some of the significant criteria used in evaluating, from the perspective of the retailer, whether and what type of wholesaler to "employ" are listed in Exhibit 3-2. As in the case of the manufacturer or supplier, these criteria are conditioned by the nature of the products that the retailer carries and the market he serves.

How Can Wholesalers Serve the Business User?

Merchant wholesaler sales are divided about equally between retailers and business or industrial users. Although many of the advantages to the business user from relying on wholesalers are exactly the same as those mentioned above relative to retailers, there are some additional factors which are briefly discussed here.

The short "lead" time on deliveries made available through wholesalers are especially important to industrial users. Flexibility in production scheduling can generally be achieved if production planners know that speedy local deliveries can be forthcoming. This factor is why industrial distributors, perhaps more than most types of wholesale firms, are plagued by the problem of small orders. One steel warehouse reported that 31.7 percent of the orders it received averaged $7.50 per order, created 32 percent of its administration cost, and contributed only 6 percent to its total sales.[31]

In addition, many types of wholesalers provide unique forms of technical assistance that are relatively costly to duplicate elsewhere, except in situations where a buyer can purchase in very large quantities. For example, machine tool and accessories wholesalers often have specialists on their staffs who are available to help customers with technical problems pertaining to the use of tools and parts. Indeed, it is not unusual to find such technically trained persons as metallurgists, chemists, draftsmen, and mechanical and civil engineers employed by wholesalers to assist

---

[30] Paul L. Courtney, "The Wholesaler as a Link in the Distribution Channel," in Moller and Wilemon, *op. cit.,* p. 178.

[31] Richard M. Hill, Ralph S. Alexander, and James S. Cross, *Industrial Marketing,* 4th ed. (Homewood, Ill.: Richard D. Irwin, 1975), p. 231.

EXHIBIT 3–2

Criteria of Choice in the Decision of What Type of Wholesaling Establishment to Use—Point of View of the Retailer

1. Lines
   a. Does wholesaler supply all or most of the lines needed by the retailer?
   b. Does wholesaler supply all or most of the brands required by the retailer for each of his lines?
   c. Does the wholesaler stock an assortment of varieties, styles, sizes, and colors sufficient to meet retailer's needs?

2. Services
   a. Can wholesaler assure a continuous and regular supply of merchandise without excessive out-of-stocks or backorders?
   b. Extent of aid given to retailer by wholesaler (e.g., promotion, pricing, inventory maintenance, etc.)?
   c. Extension of credit by wholesaler?
   d. Delivery by wholesaler?
   e. Do types of wholesalers used result in too frequent and time-consuming calls by salesmen?
   f. Help given by salesmen?
   g. Does wholesaler's cost structure permit selling price to retailer such as to allow retailer sufficient margins?

Source: Department of Marketing, University of Pennsylvania, Wharton School of Finance and Commerce.

customers with the problems involved in proper selection and use of products.[32] Even managerial assistance is being increasingly provided to business users by wholesalers. Thus,

> An electronics distributor in Ann Arbor analyzed the stockkeeping methods of one of his industrial customers and recommended revised delivery schedules, prearranged items, packs suitable for assembly line use, and standardized item identification. The customer was able to reduce the possession costs on his stock by 15% of its value.[33]

Business users and retailers alike must be concerned with the overall or *ultimate cost* of the goods that they purchase, handle, and store—not merely with the price at which such goods are obtained. When adequate accounting is made, it can often be found that the *ultimate cost* of dealing with wholesalers is less than the ultimate cost of dealing directly with manufacturers, even though the quantity discounts made available by the latter are not generally available when using wholesalers as suppliers. This *ultimate cost concept* can be applied to justifying the

[32] Hill, *op. cit.,* pp. 22–23.
[33] Lopata, *op. cit.,* p. 140.

125

use of wholesalers in situations where they might not otherwise appear to be economical.[34]

Recognition of the ultimate cost concept by both wholesalers and their customers has led to a phenomenon called "systems selling." As defined by Hannaford,

> Systems selling is a broad, inconclusive term that may be used to describe any form of cooperative contracting relationship between an industrial distributor and his customer for the ordering and distribution of low-value, repetitively used items for maintenance, repair, or operating (MRO) purposes, or for the use in manufacturing original equipment.

Wholesalers offer such purchasing systems in order to alleviate the high cost and paper work facing firms seeking to acquire a wide variety of items, ranging from power tools and welding supplies to lamps, electronic equipment, and hardware. The major means employed by wholesalers' system selling arrangements to solve these problems include (1) shifting the bulk of the customer's on-premises MRO inventory back to the stocking wholesaler, (2) providing for automatic and semi-automatic ordering of these items on an as-needed basis, and (3) one-day delivery of the ordered items.[35] Customer benefits from the arrangement may include:

1. A reduction of the time spent in purchasing low-value items.
2. A reduction in purchasing paperwork.
3. Simplified requisitioning.
4. More free in-plant storage space.
5. Greater harmony and closer ties between customer and wholesaler.

As Hannaford points out,

> A system selling arrangement changes the roles of supplier and customer as traditional channel autonomy is supplanted by the cooperative meshing of resources. Instead of the fragmented purchase of individual items, the system provides complete solutions to the product and service needs/problems of industrial customers.[36]

Indeed, the notion of system selling ranges far beyond applications to items used to support or maintain manufacturing processes. For example, a drug wholesaler located in Columbus, Ohio has provided a system selling arrangement for a major discount chain relative to the chain's needs for health, beauty, and pharmaceutical items. The chain retains very little warehouse or backroom stocks of the items; rather, the wholesaling firm provides all of the services required to

---

[34] The term "ultimate cost concept" was introduced to the authors by Richard S. Lopata and Richard E. Peterson, Principals, SAM Associates, Inc., Chicago, Illinois.

[35] William J. Hannaford, "Systems Selling: Problems and Benefits for Buyers and Sellers," *Industrial Marketing Management,* Vol. 5 (June 1976), p. 139.

[36] *Ibid.,* p. 141.

maintain an adequate assortment of the items on the shelves of each of the chain's stores within its assigned territory. Similar kinds of arrangements exist between medical supply companies, such as American Hospital Supply Company, and a number of hospitals. Hospital inventories are generally not well managed, thereby increasing the need to shift such functions back onto wholesalers.[37]

There are dozens of varieties of systems selling programs in operation. Exhibit 3–3 depicts two types of programs currently used by wholesalers—systems contracting and blanket ordering. While both involve contractual agreements which usually specify the vendor (i.e., the wholesaler) as the sole source for the designated items over the life of the contract, systems contracting goes further by providing a total system of solutions for customer purchasing problems.

The discussion of systems selling above has been included here not because we believe that systems purchasing is always an appropriate arrangement for customers of wholesalers,[38] but because it illustrates, in a specific way, the potential scope of a wholesaler's functions. In particular, it illustrates the ultimate cost concept. Wholesalers will rarely offer the lowest prices, but employing them as channel partners may provide *total cost* savings in the area of supplies procurement through reductions in costs associated with paper work, vendor analysis, requisitioning, inefficient central stores operations, and the like.

A Hard-nosed Assessment

While most of the above descriptions concerning what it is that a wholesaler can do for suppliers, retailers, and business users provide an optimistic picture, the channel analyst should approach the selection of wholesalers as channel partners with a great deal of caution. Despite the fact that wholesalers can spread the costs of participating in the marketing flows over an entire commodity line (e.g., groceries, electrical supplies, plumbing and heating equipment) and do, thereby, have the potential for reducing the overall cost of distribution, they are not, for the most part, aggressive marketers because of their size, their managerial capacity and ability, and their traditional orientations. In fact, wholesaling firms are, in general, much more preoccupied with logistics functions than they are with penetrating markets. The result of this preoccupation has meant that they have been severely out of position as major changes have taken place within certain industries and have had to scramble to maintain viability within them.

While there are significant and numerous exceptions to this generalization, merchant wholesalers, the dominant group among wholesalers both in numbers and in dollar volume, are, for the most part, very small family-owned companies ($1 to $3 million in sales with less than 20 employees) who rely on their contracts with

[37] P. Ronald Stephenson, "Strategic Analysis of Wholesaler Distribution: A Study of the Medical Supply Industry," *Industrial Marketing Management,* Vol. 5 (March 1976), p. 39.

[38] In a survey of 500 wholesalers, Hannaford found that 70 percent claimed to be involved in systems selling but that their systems accounted for 19 percent of their total sales or less. Hannaford, "Systems Selling: Problems and Benefits for Buyers and Sellers," *op. cit.,* p. 140.

EXHIBIT 3–3

Characteristics of Systems Contracting and Blanket Ordering

Characteristics of Systems Contracting	Characteristics of Blanket Ordering

1. Contract terms are relatively loose, founded on distributor-buyer trust and mutual cooperation:
  a. One contract can cover the distributor's entire product line of different MRO items.
  b. Buyer does not specify quantities to be carried by seller and is not committed to buy any specific quantity.
  c. No specific termination date is necessarily required; contract is often subject only to periodic review rather than renegotiation.
  d. Prices are not tied to duration of contract. Escalator clauses allow for price changes after notification and waiting period.
	1. Contracts are usually firm and relatively inflexible. Less cooperation and trust is required:
	  a. Precise and specific single products (or closely related families of items) are specifically named in separate contracts.
	  b. Buyers specify quantities to be carried by seller and agree to buy that quantity over the life of the contract.
	  c. Most contracts have six-month to one-year specified termination date. Contracts up for renegotiation are easily lost to competitors who bid lower prices.
	  d. Prices are fixed for life of contract—a necessity because of fixed expiration date.

2. Vendor assumes financial and warehousing responsibility for contract inventories, guaranteeing specific standards of performance:
  a. Sufficient stocking of contract items on distributor's premises, based on forecast of usage provided by buyer.
  b. 95% item availability at all times.
  c. Guaranteed 48-hour delivery or better; emergency deliveries immediately.
	2. Responsibility for providing materials inventory remains with buyer. No standards of performance are guaranteed or imposed:
	  a. Vendor does not assume customer's stores function.
	  b. 95% in-stock item availability not guaranteed at all times.
	  c. Delivery times not a critical factor: customer has storeroom.

3. Users of MRO items requisition stocks directly from Systems vendor. Purchasing department is not involved, except for general overseeing.	3. Blanket Order releases do not go directly to vendor, but must first be approved by Purchasing Department.
4. One billing transaction (invoice) sent monthly or semi-monthly, covers all requisitions for that time period.	4. Each requisition/delivery requires a separate invoicing procedure. No summary tally sheets for a period's orders.

5. All items under contract are listed in supplier's "catalog" (or tab report, printed list, card file) showing item descriptions, stock numbers, order quantities.	5. No catalog of several items is needed; each contract is for a single, specific item or narrowly defined class of items.

6. Separate cost-reducing services can be provided by the supplier as part of the total package, including:
  a. Information compiled on item usage.
  b. Consultation or technical seminars to educate users.
  c. Constant maintenance and servicing by supplier's salesmen.
	6. No separate services are offered as part of the contract. Major means of cost reduction is through negotiation of lowest possible prices.

7. Entire program and negotiations are often vendor-initiated and center upon the buyer's top financial, accounting, or purchasing management.	7. Program and negotiations are frequently customer-initiated and consist of an invitation to bid on a year's contract. Negotiations center around purchasing agents.
8. Program is sold on the basis of improving customer's total cost of procurement. Price is secondary consideration and is frequently *not* the lowest bid.	8. Purchasing agents insist upon price as the focal point. Total cost of procurement is not the basis of the contract, even if vendor would like it to be so.
9. The cooperative relationship is characterized by a spirit of faith, trust, and harmony. Parties liken it to a marriage or true partnership.	9. The relationship is characterized by a short-term feeling of caution and distrust. Suspicion replaces faith and trust.

Source: William J. Hannaford, "Systems Selling: Problems and Benefits for Buyers and Sellers," *Industrial Marketing Management*, Vol. 5 (June 1976), p. 142.

other small companies, either suppliers or clients, for survival. These companies frequently lack management expertise and an infrastructure capable of putting into practice sophisticated marketing methods. They exist by virtue of the fact that the suppliers and/or customers with whom they are linked simply cannot afford to integrate the wholesaling functions and therefore must rely on such intermediaries to reach markets or obtain supply. Often the link between wholesalers and their clientele is more personal (e.g., family ties) than economic.

Over the past thirty years, the position of wholesalers has been significantly threatened with regard to the marketing of consumer goods. Relatively few wholesalers have been successful in meeting the challenges head on. Although there have been changes in the marketing of industrial goods, too, it appears that wholesalers have, from a managerial perspective, shown greater adaptability and innovativeness in their approaches to industrial goods suppliers and markets than they have in consumer goods. In order to obtain a realistic perspective of wholesaling, it is important to delve briefly into developments in both sectors of the economy as they have affected wholesalers.

CONSUMER GOODS. Retailers have been particularly active in revolutionizing physical distribution practices. They have taken advantage of large volume purchasing, warehousing, and delivery operations through the formation of mass merchandising chain organizations, as discussed in Chapter 2. To a large extent, as the chains grew and prospered, numerous wholesalers selling consumer goods continued to be order-takers rather than developing expertise in marketing strategy and tactics. They relied on manufacturers to stimulate demand for brand-name products among ultimate consumers via advertising and waited for the generated demand to pull the brands through the channel. Indeed, many wholesalers were easily replaceable by retailers, because they no longer offered an economical or effective alternative to achieving sales or logistical services. What mass retailers could not obtain from the manufacturers directly, they could supply to themselves on their own. Wholesalers were quickly relegated to serving small businesses. Because there are still tens of thousands of small manufacturers and retailers in existence, many wholesalers of consumer goods have continued to serve an economic purpose, but to a shrinking portion of the market.

On the other hand, those few wholesalers who saw the handwriting on the wall and acted purposively to secure the marketing and physical distribution advantages of large-scale retail chain operations while permitting local ownership of individual retail units have succeeded rather handsomely. They formed voluntary (wholesaler-sponsored) chains (e.g., Super Valu Stores, Fleming, and Malone & Hyde in groceries), franchised systems (e.g., Midas International and Western Auto in the automotive aftermarket), and administered systems (e.g., Genuine Parts's automotive jobber NAPA network) in order to gain efficiencies in purchasing, advertising, warehousing, accounting, inventory control, and virtually every other business function. They also permitted themselves to become part of retailer-sponsored cooperatives (e.g., Cotter's True Value and Ace Hardware). For example, almost 40 percent of total full-line hardware wholesaler sales are accounted for by so-called dealer-owned wholesalers.[39] The return on investment of many of these various kinds of systems which are organized around wholesalers is frequently above 20 percent.[40] Given that the average return for wholesaling corporations for which public data are available is around 14 percent, as shown in Chapter 11, the performance of these wholesalers is significantly above the norm. In fact, their effect on marketing channels is so important that separate discussion of their activities is saved for Chapter 7, where we examine a number of vertical marketing systems, including those centered around wholesalers, in which purposive interorganization management is being practiced.

Beyond those consumer goods wholesalers who have formed vertical

[39] M. J. Holtzman, "Wholesalers Face Down Challengers," *Hardware Age* (October 1979), p. 64.
[40] See Bert C. McCammon, Jr., and James M. Kenderine, "High Performance Wholesaling," *Hardlines Wholesaling,* Vol. 9 (September 1975), pp. 17–51.

marketing systems, there are others who have been successful without changing their corporate organization. Some have restricted their activities to a limited range of products and have sought out market niches that do not require high sales volume to be competitive. In groceries, drugs, hardware, and jewelry, specialty wholesalers have been able to develop a substantial volume of business. For example, in the grocery trade, such firms supply such products as frozen food, dairy products, fancy or gourmet foods, bread and baked goods, and beverages. As Bucklin points out:

> They exist only to the extent that the inventory, handling, and transport requirements are so specialized that they cannot be duplicated by the chain (or general-line wholesaler) or that their product line is such that these competing organizations cannot attain sufficient volume to offset the costs of handling desirable assortments.[41]

Service merchandisers or rack jobbers have been particularly effective. The more successful specialty wholesalers, like rack jobbers, have been able to serve both large suppliers and large buyers, thus severing the wholesalers' traditional dependence on small-scale retailing.[42]

On the other hand, there have also been a number of general- or full-line consumer goods wholesalers who have achieved viability. Their route to success has been to improve their management and marketing practices in line with strict adherence to stated marketing channel objectives. One of these wholesalers is United Stationers of Maywood, Illinois. Over 70 percent of United's business comes from retail stationers who resell to ultimate consumers and who also employ salesmen who call on commercial accounts. United competes head-on with such manufacturer-integrated wholesaling operations as those run by Boise-Cascade, Champion International, and Zellerbach Paper Company. It has been able to generate over $150 million in sales by adopting an approach which contains the following components:

1. A stated commitment to lower the cost of distribution for its suppliers and its customers.

2. A series of syndicated catalogs made available to its customers which the customers use, under their own names, to sell to their clients.

3. A complete set of pricing services, utilizing microfiche and other media, which permits the continuous updating of prices, especially important during inflationary periods.

4. An on-line order entry system, an on-line inventory system, and an on-line inventory forecasting system.

5. Four regional distribution centers (Forest Park, Ill., Pennsauken, N.J., Livonia, Mich., and Dallas, Tex.) each stocking over 20,000 office products. (The Forest Park facility is over 200,000 sq ft.)

[41] Bucklin, *op. cit.,* pp. 233–234.

[42] *Ibid.,* p. 235. For an excellent example in the magazine and paperback book industry, see Paul Doebler, "Charles Levy-Spawned Company Computerizes the Problems Out of Distribution and Sales," *Publishers Weekly,* Vol. 205 (February 4, 1974).

6. Customer-service representatives assigned to every distribution center who place regularly scheduled WATS telephone calls to retailers within their geographic area at a frequency determined by the retailers individually.

7. A network of ten satellite distribution centers. (Each day, every distribution center ships orders taken over the phone during that day by the customer-service representatives. These shipments travel directly to retailers or their customers, or to the satellite distribution centers. If shipped to the satellites, the orders are available to dealers on a will-call, local delivery, or drop shipment basis.)

8. Quarterly reviews of retailers' purchases via company account executives and specific retailer-oriented printout of purchase records;

9. An automated rebuying procedure.

10. A computerized automatic reorder system for retailers.

Another successful, independent full-line consumer goods wholesaler is Belknap, a hardware firm located in Louisville, Kentucky. Belknap has 20,000 accounts, including hardware stores, home centers, lumber yards, variety stores, furniture stores, and sporting goods stores. It maintains an inventory of 57,000 separate stockkeeping units. Besides having a very strong, high-quality private label program ("Blue Grass" label), Belknap has been able to maintain a service level of 93 percent, despite its enormous inventory. (In other words, 93 percent of the 57,000 items listed in Belknap's catalog can be supplied to retailers on notice.) The company can maintain this service level, plus a highly streamlined order system, because of its reliance on computers, which is similar to United Stationers in intensity. In fact, each of the company's more than 300 sales representatives punches his daily orders into an MSI unit installed in his own home. Belknap's sales are over $100 million per year.

Neither United Stationers nor Belknap are typical of wholesaling firms which sell items for resale. Both are significantly more advanced in their management practices than the norm. And yet neither United nor Belknap could be described as a marketing "giant." That is, while they have certainly developed systems for their retail customers, their major emphasis is on physical distribution—good inventory control and speedy delivery systems. Indeed, marketing for wholesaling is equivalent to selling—the focus is on converting inventory into cash, on generating sales volume, on short-run solutions, on the problems of individual customers, and on the importance of field work (e.g., selling or distribution). There are very few wholesalers who are preoccupied with profit planning, with analyzing long-run trends, threats, and opportunities, with studying customer types and market segment differences, and with developing strong systems for market analysis, planning, and control.[43]

---

[43] For an excellent discussion distinguishing selling from marketing, see Philip Kotler, "From Sales Obsession to Marketing Effectiveness," *Harvard Business Review* (November-December 1977), pp. 67–75. Even Belknap is far from perfect, in this respect. See David P. Garino, "Belknap's New President Shakes Things Up at Strong but Lethargic Hardware Concern," *Wall Street Journal,* August 20, 1980, p. 21.

INDUSTRIAL GOODS. Manufacturers of many types of industrial goods tend to be more engineering-oriented than marketing-oriented. They prefer to allocate resources to research and production rather than to distribution, which they know has historically delivered a much lower return on investment. Given this orientation, it is not surprising that they frequently turn "troublesome" marketing problems over to distribution specialists. This is why, as contrasted with consumer goods, industrial distribution has been a particularly viable sector of wholesaling over the years.

The situation involving industrial distribution is particularly intriguing because, in some respects, it is a microcosm of the dynamics that go on in distribution generally. Industrial distributors are frequently viewed as a special class of merchant wholesaler. According to Frederick Webster, who has performed an extensive study of industrial distributors, this middleman:

> . . . sells primarily to manufacturers. He stocks the products he sells, has at least one outside salesperson as well as an inside telephone and/or counter salesperson, and performs a broad variety of marketing channel functions . . . . The products stocked include: *maintenance, repair, and operating* supplies (MRO items); *original equipment* (OEM) supplies, such as fasteners, power transmission components, fluid power equipment, and small rubber parts, which become part of the manufacturer's finished product; *equipment* used in the operation of a business, such as hand tools, power tools, and conveyors; and *machinery* used to make raw materials and semi-finished goods into finished products.[44]

There are approximately 6500 such distributors, compared to 7600 a decade ago.[45]

On average, industrial distributors are as small as the wholesalers serving retailers, but the median size is increasing as the number of distributors declines and as the market expands. The increase in size means that more firms are able to adopt electronic data processing for inventory control, order processing, and other administrative controls. (However, it is estimated that only 40 percent of such firms use computers,[46] which means that well over half are still operating manual, relatively archaic systems.)

The distributor's importance in the marketing channel for industrial goods is growing for a variety of reasons, including the desire of manufacturers to shift more physical distribution responsibilities to distributors due to inflationary cost pressures; the tendency of a number of products to become commodities (e.g., bearings), a factor which permits distributors more control over the relationship with the customer; and the increased value which distributors are adding to products by performing special services, such as assembly and submanufacturing, for their customers.[47] For example, estimates by Joseph T. Ryerson & Son, Inc., a ma-

---

[44] Frederick E. Webster, Jr., "The Role of the Industrial Distributor in Marketing Strategy," *Journal of Marketing,* Vol. 40 (July 1976), p. 11.

[45] "Parts for all Seasons," *Forbes* (February 15, 1976), p. 44.

[46] Tom O'Boyle, "Industrial Distributors Eye '80's Boom, but Shakeout Could Peril Smaller Firms," *Crain's Chicago Business* (October 29, 1979), p. 19.

[47] Webster, *Industrial Marketing Strategy, op. cit.,* p. 169.

jor metal distributor, indicate that the marketing of processed steels (i.e., steel which is cut or fabricated by the distributor) could go as high as 90 percent of its sales in the near future. The metals "service center" is no longer a "warehouse" where a buyer may go for small lots; it now adds value to the generic products it carries by performing such operations as welding, bending, shearing, and stamping.

Industrial distributors have become more capable at fulfilling their major responsibility in the channel from the supplier's perspective. That is, their job has been primarily to contact present and potential customers and to make the product available—with the necessary supporting services such as delivery, credit, and technical advice—as quickly as economically feasible.[48] In this respect, they may have discouraged the kind of integration of wholesaling functions so prevalent in consumer goods channels. In fact, it is much easier for the industrial goods manufacturer to go "direct" than it is for the consumer goods manufacturer, a point which is expanded upon in Chapter 6. It would, for example, be virtually impossible for General Foods Corporation to sell its products directly to millions of consumers, but it is feasible for Monsanto to sell its products directly to hundreds of industrial end-users. Thus, in consumer goods the major problem for wholesalers is the backward vertical integration of retailers into wholesaling. In industrial goods, the problem is one of manufacturers integrating forward. While such integration is occurring, the problem for wholesalers appears to be more acute relative to consumer goods.

One of the ways in which industrial distributors have maintained and even increased their importance in the marketing channel is by doing something which some of their counterparts selling consumer goods have also done—they have specialized their operations. In 1979, specialists represented more than 70 percent of all industrial distributors, up from 23 percent in 1964.[49] While specialists carry fewer product lines than the general line distributor, the inventory is usually deeper. As Webster points out:

> The trend toward specialization has generally been associated with increased technical competence and product knowledge. The specialist can offer greater depth, including multiple brands, in a given product area. Some general line distributors have agreed to set up specialist departments as a condition for obtaining a leading product line. In other cases, manufacturers report that they are being forced to go to the specialist distributors, because of their wide acceptance in certain product areas.[50]

For example, more than 90 percent of Semiconductor Specialists' $20 million sales come from semiconductors and microprocessors alone. A. M. Castle, a metals distributor, sells more nickel, alloys, and specialty metals than its competitors. And Premier Industrial has 14 completely separate divisions, each with its own sales force, serving distinct markets, from J. L. Holcomb Manufacturing, which sells cleaning agents, brushes, insecticides, and the like, to Certanium Alloys & Research

---

[48] Webster, "The Role of the Industrial Distributor in Marketing Strategy, *op. cit.,* p. 13.

[49] O'Boyle, *op., cit.,* p. 18.

[50] Webster, *Industrial Marketing Strategy, op. cit.,* p. 170.

Co., which sells welding electrodes, brazing alloys, solders, and other welding aids. In addition to specializing their product lines, a number of distributors have hired technical experts, and this development has led to instances where distributor salesmen are more knowledgeable about a given technological area than the manufacturer's own salesmen.

Another way in which industrial distributors have enhanced their role in the marketing channel is via the formation of distributor chains. Individual entrepreneurs have either acquired or established multiple outlets. The result has been that they have been able to secure significant economies of scale by establishing one highly sophisticated central inventory, purchasing, and distribution system.[51] The merger trend is particularly strong among bearing and power transmission distributors. Mergers are often preferred to internal development because personal service in wholesaling is such a strong marketing factor—established distributors have an existing clientele which often can be retained after the merger is completed. Some of the advantages that distributor chains have over small, privately owned, single-warehouse firms are:[52]

1. Inventory power. Chain inventories are not only deeper and cheaper but are also broader and more diversified.
2. Central warehouses. Such warehouses permit adding highly sophisticated computerized systems, purchasing in quantity, and stocking in depth, and result in lower warehousing costs per outlet.
3. Quantity discounts
4. Multiple brand coverage
5. Private labeling. This movement is particularly strong for such product lines as bearings, electrical motors and equipment, and MRO supplies. (For example, private labels account for almost 100 percent of Associated Spring's sales; 75 percent of W. W. Grainger's sales; and 90 percent of Lawson Products' sales.)

Thirteen major publicly traded industrial distribution chains are listed in Exhibit 3–4. These chains plus privately owned chains account for approximately 10 percent of the sales of industrial distributors. Even more impressive than the sales generated is the return on investment earned by some of these companies. For example, Bearings, Inc.'s and W. W. Grainger's return on investment is around 17 percent, while Kar Products' and Lawson Products' return is close to 30 percent.[53]

Clearly, these chains pose a threat for small, single-warehouse distributors. Indeed, "independents" (as single-warehouse distributors are called) have entered into the *shock* and *defensive retreat* phases of the crisis-change model discussed in Chapter 5. In some cases, they have mounted lobbying campaigns against quantity

[51] "The Chain of Events in Industrial Distribution," *Marketing News* (January 30, 1976), p. 7. (This article was reprinted from *Management Practice,* 1976, a quarterly publication.)
[52] *Ibid.*
[53] See Tom O'Boyle, *op. cit.,* p. 19; "Parts for all Seasons," *op. cit.,* p. 44; and McCammon and Kenderdine, *op. cit.,* pp. 28 and 36.

EXHIBIT 3-4

13 Publicly-Traded Industrial Distribution Chains Lead the Field

Company	1974 Net Sales In Distribution	Estimated Number Of Outlets	Area Served	Major Products
Associated Spring Corporation Bristol, Conn. *Distribution Group*	$73.7 million *36% of total company sales*	14 warehouses	U.S. & Canada	Automotive aftermarket, welding supplies, industrial maintenance supplies, industrial aerosols, special purpose hardware and fasteners
Bearings, Inc. Cleveland, Ohio *Bearings, Inc. Dixie Bearings, Bruening Bearings, Inc.*	$156.2 million	131 distribution centers	Essentially national 25 states excluding California	Bearings, industrial power transmission components, specialized seals, lubricants, bearing retaining devices & tools
Curtis Knoll Corp. Cleveland, Ohio	$104.3 million *91% of total company sales*	15 warehouses plus auto jobber outlets	U.S. and foreign	Automotive aftermarket products, and industrial maintenance products such as alloy plate and bar stock; tools; chemicals, cleaning insecticides, and paper
Ducommun, Inc. Los Angeles, Calif.	$210.3 million *97.2% of total company sales*	12 processing centers	U.S. for electronic; Western and Southwestern states for metal	Metals, tools and industrial supplies; and electronic parts and components to industrial users
W. W. Grainger, Inc. Chicago, Illinois	$283.9 million *90% of total company sales*	134 branches	U.S.	Electric motors and accessories, fans, blowers, pumps, air compressors, hand & bench tools, arc welders, material handling & storage equipment
Kaman Corp. Bloomfield, Conn. *Reliable Bearings & Supply Western Bearings, Inc., BIT Co.*	$45.5 million *30.1% of total company sales*	51 outlets	11 Western States, Hawaii & British Columbia	Bearings, seals, hydraulic components, lubricants, rubber products, power transmission, and material handling equipment

Company	Sales	Facilities	Area	Products
Kar Products, Inc. Des Plaines, Ill.	$26.0 million	5 regional warehouses	U.S.	Expendable fasteners, hardware, parts, equipment and supplies, for over-the-road and off-the-road equipment, passenger cars, machinery and plant facilities
Lamson Products, Inc. Niles, Illinois	$33.4 million	5 distribution centers	U.S.	Expendable maintenance, repair, and replacement fasteners; parts, chemicals, electrical supplies, and shop supplies
Motion Industries, Inc. Birmingham, Ala.	$71.9 million	50 sales & warehouse facilities	9 states in South and South West	Bearings, mechanical and fluid power transmission equipment, including hydraulic pneumatic products, material handling components, and related parts and supplies
Noland Company Newport News, Va.	$226.3 million	52 outlets	11 Southeastern States	Plumbing and heating, electrical, industrial, and refrigeration supplies
H. K. Porter Company, Inc. Pittsburgh, Pa. *Banks-Miller Supply Co.* *Tidewater Supply Co.*	$54.0 million *16% of total company sales*	17 warehouses	Southern region	35,000 items of industrial equipment and supplies
Premier Industrial Corporation Cleveland, Ohio *Newark Electronics* *Cadillac Electric Supply*	$137.1 million *90.7% of total company sales*	10 distribution centers	U.S.	Industrial maintenance products such as fasteners, welding supplies, industrial cleaning supplies, specialty oils and greases; electronic and electrical parts, components, and equipment
Union Camp Corporation New York, N.Y. *Moore Handley Corp.*	$123.0 million *13.5% of total company sales*	48 home improvement and building supply centers	South-eastern states	Retail distributor of building materials, appliances and accessories for the home; wholesale distributor of hardware; direct supplier of industrial and electrical supplies and machine tools

Source: "The Chain of Events in Industrial Distribution," *Marketing News,* (January 30, 1976), p. 7. (Originally published in *Management Practice* by CCMP Management Consultants, Inc.)

Note:
Other major publicly-traded companies with industrial chain distribution activities include: Apache Corp. (Beals, McCarthy & Rogers), Gulf & Western (Hendrie & Bolthoff) and IU International (Distribution Services Division, Pittsburgh Gage, Saunders & Co. and Taylor Engineering)

pricing. In others, they have formed "moral consortiums" in which the members provide one another with services and supplies and remain committed to maintaining members' independence through mutual cooperation and regional solidarity. But some independents have *acknowledged* the efficiencies of the chains and have even begun to *adapt* and *change* their modes of operation. For example, an organization of independents called The Midwest 60 has plans for central warehouses in order to help its members compete against power transmission chains. To counter the chains' enormous inventory power, some independents are setting up swapping arrangements on some products. These inventory exchange agreements are aimed at reducing warehousing costs and enhancing the assortments of each member.[54]

From a potential customer's perspective, the chains incorporate many of the attributes which are important to industrial customers in choosing a source of supply. They are able to keep delivery promises, offer a better discount structure, maintain an efficient phone order system, provide stock breadth and depth, offer technical services, enact appropriate sales procedures (e.g., regular sales calls), maintain a strong assortment of brand names, offer quick delivery time, and provide quality assurance. Indeed, because of their capabilities, they have created serious policy questions for manufacturers seeking to employ *both* independent and chain distributors in their channels. Some of these questions are[55]

1. Can we afford to offer exclusives to independents? to chains? If we offer them to independents, is there any way to protect existing exclusives and still sell to chains?

2. How do we sell to chains? Do we need separate sales forces, one for chains and one for independents?

3. Is our volume to chains large enough to permit us to withdraw our branch warehousing support to independents?

4. Should we help independents to pool?

5. How large a reduction in price are we willing to grant chains for assuming the entire warehousing burden?

6. Do we want to sell for private label sales?

7. What kind of discounting structure should we employ?

Despite the significant changes in industrial distribution which have been cataloged above, manufacturers frequently remain frustrated by the low level of management competence among distributors and their lack of management depth, as well as by distributors' inadequate financial management and the frequent lack of provision for management succession.[56] In fact, industrial goods distributors, like their counterparts in consumer goods wholesaling, are viewed as basically noninnovative and unsophisticated, especially from a marketing perspective. Their

[54] "The Chain of Events in Industrial Distribution," *op. cit.*, p. 7.

[55] *Ibid.*

[56] Webster, *Industrial Marketing Strategy, op. cit.*, p. 171.

salesmen are seen more as order-takers than as creative individuals who are interested in finding new accounts and aggressively promoting new products. They are perceived by manufacturers to have little interest in market research and an inadequate source of information about the markets in which they operate.[57] Therefore, though there have been important improvements, industrial distributors, on average, appear to have a long way to go before they can be counted on to perform in accordance with the modern marketing concept.

Wholesalers have, however, been particularly strong in medical supply channels and in other channels whose characteristics are similar to those found in the distribution of medical supplies. Several factors account for the importance of medical supply wholesalers:[58]

1. The large number of potential customers. (There are over 7000 hospitals and approximately 330,000 physicians in the U.S.)

2. The small average manufacturer size. (Average manufacturer sales volume is approximately $2 million. Even the largest firms can obtain only limited market coverage with a direct sales/distribution strategy.)

3. The small average transaction size. (Even in the largest hospitals, average transaction size for one manufacturer's product line is likely to be relatively small. Therefore, selling costs per transaction would be extremely high if products were sold on a direct basis.)

4. The high inventory/service requirements. (Substantial inventories must be carried locally, frequently adequate to support mandatory zero out-of-stock policies. Also, logistics services must be available to support emergency delivery requests.)

Certain wholesalers have been especially successful in this industry—generating over 17 percent return on *assets* (pretax)—by concentrating their efforts on specific market segments.[59] Those who try to serve a number of different segments, such as hospitals, physicians, extended care facilities, and laboratories, generally have lower returns. According to Stephenson:

> (Wholesalers) that concentrate on a particular market segment tend to tailor their operating strategies to the characteristics of that segment. Firms that have near-equal revenues in two or more markets hurt their profit performance by attempting to extend a strategy developed in serving one market to other segments where different strategies are appropriate. For example, firms with strategies historically designed to serve the physician segment will expand into the hospital segment using the same technique. The average physician-oriented strategy has an operating expense ratio of 27 percent of net sales. Average gross margin available in the hospital segment is 19 percent of net sales. Obviously, a differentiated and lower cost strategy is mandatory. One cannot profitably service the two segments with one relatively high cost strategy.[60]

[57] *Ibid.*, pp. 171–172; and Webster, "The Role of the Industrial Distributor in Marketing Strategy," *op. cit.*, p. 14.

[58] Stephenson, *op. cit.*, pp. 38–40.

[59] *Ibid.*, p. 41.

[60] *Ibid.*, p. 42.

Thus, as in all businesses, wholesalers must practice strategic planning in order to achieve target rates of return.

ADV OF WHOLE-SALERS

One of the major reasons accounting for the continued prominence of wholesalers of industrial goods is the "push"-type marketing strategies adopted by industrial goods manufacturers. That is, rather than relying upon "consumer-directed" promotion, such as advertising, coupons, and the like, to stimulate demand at the end user level and thereby "pull" the product through the marketing channel, industrial goods manufacturers place considerable weight on personal selling. Because wholesalers maintain large sales forces and can spread the costs of their sales forces over a number of manufacturers' product lines, it frequently is more economical for manufacturers to look to wholesalers to provide the "push." In addition, it is very expensive to maintain a series of distribution centers around the country which specialize in making a single manufacturer's product available to widely dispersed end-users in a variety of industries. Therefore, the selling and the physical distribution functions performed by wholesalers provide them with a differential advantage in the marketing of many types of industrial goods. Unfortunately, wholesalers have not, on average, fully capitalized on this advantage, primarily because of some of their managerial weaknesses alluded to above.

THE STRATEGIC MANAGEMENT OF WHOLESALING INSTITUTIONS

The two major *financial* factors determining the success of wholesalers, defined in terms of achieving target rates of return on investment or on assets, are the net profit margin and the asset turnover attained.[61]

Margin Management

Net profit margin is a function of gross margin achieved and operating expenses incurred. Net profit is extremely sensitive to the level of gross margin. In wholesaling, a small change in gross margin (either positive or negative) will carry directly through to net profit, producing a disproportionately large change. As a result, gross margin is widely used as a critical decision variable at the wholesale level of distribution. Likewise, net profits are extremely sensitive to expense changes.

The margins that wholesalers receive are highly dependent upon the prices they are able to negotiate with suppliers, the prices that they charge their customers, the mix of products they carry (i.e., their assortments), the market segments they choose to serve, and their desired growth rates. In the long run, strategic decisions surrounding these critical variables commit individual firms to specific gross margin

[61] For an excellent discussion of these factors as related to wholesale distribution in the medical supply industry, see *ibid.,* pp. 40–41.

and operating cost characteristics. For example, in the medical supply industry, Stephenson has observed that:

> A high growth strategy . . . involves commitment (on the part of wholesalers) to the hospital market with relatively low gross margins and the need for highly streamlined operating characteristics producing low average operating costs. On the other hand, emphasis on the physician segment means relatively high available gross margins, but commitment to a high operating cost strategy—high sales/service requirements, increased logistical demands, and relatively small average transaction size.[62]

Margins vary widely by line of trade served, depending, of course, on the needs and requirements of customers served. Thus, gross margins of electrical supply distributors vary from over 25 percent for MRO items sold to industrial accounts to less than 10 percent for household appliances sold to retailers.

Asset Management

In addition, wholesalers can generate high rates of asset turnover through intense asset management. Typically, a very high proportion (over 70 percent, as shown in Table 3–8) of total assets are invested in the current category, primarily in accounts receivable and inventory. Unlike the manufacturer who has heavy investments in fixed plant and equipment, the wholesaler is in a position to exercise

TABLE 3–8   Composition of assets for wholesaling corporations

Assets	Percent
Current assets	
Cash or its equivalent	7.5%
Accounts receivable	30.5
Inventory	33.8
All other	3.5
Total	75.3%
Fixed assets	
Property, plant, and equipment	17.8%
All other	6.9
Total	24.7%
Total assets	100.0%

Source: Federal Trade Commission, *Quarterly Financial Report for Manufacturing, Mining and Trade Corporations, Second Quarter 1980* (Washington, D.C.: U.S. Government Printing Office, September 16, 1980), p. 83.

---

[62] *Ibid.,* p. 41.

strong short-term credit and inventory controls in an effort to achieve desirable asset turnover levels. Futhermore, the overall liquidity of wholesaling operations means that it is very difficult for a wholesaler to go bankrupt. Three factors seem to account for the average wholesaler's buoyancy, irrespective of his marketing failings. First, the typical wholesaler has a multiplicity of suppliers and customers; therefore, he is not dependent on any one source of supply or sales. Second, many wholesalers are able to turn over their inventories about six times a year, on average, which means that they are a minimum of 120 days away from a cash position. Third, they are generally only 90 days away from cash relative to accounts receivable. The question then is not usually how to achieve appropriate asset management for survival purposes, but rather how to generate a high rate of return.

ACCOUNTS RECEIVABLE.   With regard to accounts receivable, it is often the case that 90 percent or more of a wholesaler's sales are made on a credit basis. Proper use of credit in building sales as well as effective employment of the capital invested, therefore, requires careful attention to the management of the credit function. Achieving an adequate cash flow is critical to a wholesaler's operation and demands careful attention to the evaluation and selection of credit risks, collection of accounts, and overall control of credit. For example, the average collection period varies considerably between different kinds of wholesale business, depending in part on the customary terms of sale. (The average collection period for certain grocery wholesalers is only 14 days, as compared with between 45 and 50 days in dry goods, footwear, and floor coverings.)

INVENTORY.   In wholesaling as well as in retailing, achieving a reasonably high inventory turnover rate is one of the prime prerequisites to obtaining an adequate rate of return on invested capital. Higher profits on investment are gained both through the effect that a high turnover rate has on operating expenses (as turnover increases, the costs of possession—interest on capital invested in inventory, insurance, property taxes, and warehousing space—decline) *and* on the amount of capital invested in inventory. However, various surveys and trade conferences suggest that the merchant wholesaler's major problem is inventory control and management.[63] Such a heavy investment in inventory is made necessary by the large number of items that wholesalers must carry in order to serve the needs of their clients. Compounding the problem is the fact that suppliers are generating enormous quantities of new products. For example, the automotive distributor carries over 70,000 identifiable items, as compared with 40,000 ten years ago. Furthermore, many of the items that wholesalers must carry are slow-moving articles that are required infrequently but, when needed, are vital to the operations of the wholesaler's customer.

Some of the wholesaler's reactions to his inventory problems have been (1) to demand that suppliers reduce the size and variety of the lines they offer; (2) to select

[63] Lopata, *op. cit.,* p. 138.

TABLE 3–9   Benefits derived by selected wholesalers by developing management information systems

Performance Measurement	Results Achieved with	
	Conventional Data Processing System	Management Information System
Inventory service level	84.6%	89.6%
Gross margin/net sales	17.3%	20.6%
Average inventory (number of weeks supply)	14.8	13.0
Gross margin/average inventory	73.6%	103.9%
Contribution margin/average inventory	49.6%	79.9%

Source: Management Horizons Data Systems, as reported in Bert C. McCammon, Jr., and James W. Kenderine, "Mainstream Developments in Wholesaling," a paper presented at the 1975 Conference of the Southwestern Marketing Association, p. 7.

only popular items from among a supplier's line (called, by the trade, "cherry picking"); or (3) to select items and set stock levels according to item demand and item movement.[64] In the last case, wholesalers are dropping many slow-moving and/or low-revenue-producing supply items from their assortments while placing stronger sales efforts behind higher-priced product lines with larger dollar volumes. Concomitantly, these wholesalers are retraining salesmen as equipment demonstrators and discouraging them from merely taking small orders.

Clearly, improved management practices are a prerequisite to improved per-

TABLE 3–10   Benefits derived by selected wholesalers by adopting improved management practices

Management Practice	Number Order Lines per Manhour
Minimum order policy	9.3
No minimum order policy	8.8
Out-of-stocks deleted before orders are picked	13.1
Out-of-stocks deleted after orders are picked	8.2
Item location shown on order or pick ticket	9.3
Item location not shown on order or pick ticket	8.6
Picking sequence specified on order or pick ticket	9.4
Picking sequence not specified on order or pick ticket	8.7

Source: Hardware Institute for Research and Development, as reported in Bert C. McCammon, Jr., and James W. Kenderine, "Mainstream Developments in Wholesaling," a paper presented at the 1975 Conference of the Southern Marketing Association, p. 7.

[64] Ibid.

formance in the inventory control area. Such practices must not only encompass the setting of minimum order policies but must include the broader aspect of developing effective management information systems based on the use of up-to-date electronic data processing. Some of the potential benefits available to wholesalers from adapting more sophisticated methods are shown in Tables 3–9 and 3–10. Indeed, the discussion on inventory control in Chapter 4 is exceedingly pertinent to wholesaling; without appropriate management of the marketing flows of ownership and physical possession, the wholesaler will not only derive lower rates of return, but he will also lose a significant amount of his value to the channel as a whole.

CHANNEL MANAGEMENT ISSUES IN USING WHOLESALERS

With the exception of the large, professionally managed wholesaling firms, such as Genuine Parts Company in the automotive industry, Bergen Brunswig Corporation in the drug industry, Foremost-McKesson Company in the drug, grocery, liquor, and health and beauty aid industries, Graybar Electric Company in electrical supply, Fleming Companies, Inc. in groceries, American Hospital Supply Corporation in medical supplies, and Earl M. Jorgensen Co. in metals,[65] most wholesaling firms can, as indicated previously, be categorized as small, entrepreneurially oriented, relatively unsophisticated, and generally risk-averse businesses. Therefore, when a manufacturer turns to a wholesaler for assistance in making his products available for sale and for stimulating demand among industrial, institutional, or commercial end-users or among retailers, he cannot give up his own responsibility for effective marketing, nor can he expect the wholesaler to respond to all his suggestions. Rather, as Webster has observed, the manufacturer must assume new responsibilities for making the wholesaler more effective through programs of product development, careful pricing, promotional support, technical assistance, order servicing, and training for wholesaler salesmen and management.[66] Specifically, manufacturers employing wholesalers must do the following:

1. Make certain that the functions to be performed are clearly understood and that margins fairly reflect the value of these functions to the manufacturer and the cost to the wholesaler of performing them well.

2. Train, supervise, and compensate company salesmen so that they are knowledgeable about working with wholesalers and are motivated to do so.

3. Take an active role in building up the competence of the wholesaler's organization, with particular emphasis on product knowledge, salesmanship, account management, inventory level decisions, product line profitability analysis, and market area analysis.

[65] For a comprehensive listing, see McCammon and Kenderdine, *op. cit.,* pp. 17–51.
[66] Webster, *Industrial Marketing Strategy, op. cit.,* p. 178.

4. Expect to take an active role in marketing, because many activities (such as direct mail promotions, the development of effective catalogs, and local advertising) may be beyond the wholesaler's capabilities.[67]

All of these activities will result in making the wholesaler into a more effective channel partner. In the long run, the manufacturer can expect to deal with a larger and stronger wholesaling organization which he has helped to create. The development of mutual dependencies will produce a more cohesive channel system.

SUMMARY   The significance of the wholesaler's role in a channel of distribution is defined by the efficiency of his sorting function whereby he helps match the heterogeneous output of suppliers on the one hand with the diverse needs of retailers, industrial, and business users on the other. There have been increased pressures on wholesalers to prove their economic viability in this respect.

Many suppliers use wholesalers to reach their customers because they prefer to turn troublesome, supposedly lower-return distribution activities over to specialists. The benefits available to suppliers (manufacturers, growers, etc.) from wholesalers are continuity in and intimacy with local markets, local availability of stocks, coverage of small-order business, lower costs because wholesalers can spread overhead over many suppliers' products, and relief from the burden of holding inventory.

Often wholesalers' perceived self-interests are more directly involved with the well-being of retailers than those of manufacturers; therefore, it is logical to assume that wholesalers would develop approaches to assure the survival of retailers. Many wholesalers do, in fact, offer retailers direct selling aid, expert assistance in all aspects of retail operations, local and speedy delivery, relief from inventory burdens, quick adjustments, credit extension, and, in some cases, guaranteed sales. Business users can receive many of the same benefits, which may be especially important when it comes to production scheduling and technical assistance.

While it has been noted in this chapter that the average wholesaler appears to have some significant weaknesses as a marketing entity, it is important to reemphasize, in any discussion of wholesaling, that a wholesaling firm can be eliminated from a channel of distribution, but that some other institution must be capable of performing the tasks formerly done by the firm. Elimination of a wholesaler is valid from a societal point of view only if the tasks performed by the wholesaler can be either partially eliminated or performed more efficiently by some other institution.

[67] Derived from *ibid.*, pp. 178–179. Although the focus of Webster's discussion is on industrial goods wholesaling, it is the authors' belief that the suggestions Webster makes apply with equal, and sometimes with more, force to consumer goods wholesaling. Therefore, they are presented here as being generic to wholesaling, irrespective of type of goods involved.

DISCUSSION QUESTIONS

1. Distinguish between a "wholesale sale" and a "retail sale" (e.g., sales at wholesale versus sales at retail).

2. Consider the following statement:

> "A wholesaling operation can be eliminated as an entity, but someone must perform the wholesaling tasks and absorb the costs formerly done by the agency, if it is assumed that the wholesaling tasks are necessary."

Take a position on this statement, pro or con, and offer support for your reasoning.

3. Why do manufacturers appear to have a "keener desire to participate more actively in the wholesaling process" as evidenced by the rapid growth of manufacturer sales branches and sales offices?

4. Debate the pros and cons of forward vertical integration, particularly of wholesaling functions.

5. Prescribe what a wholesaler needs to do over the next ten years in order to remain a viable entity. Should he stand pat or make changes? What changes? (Pick specific industries, such as steel, groceries, hardware, drugs, electronics.)

6. Discuss why the predictions of the classical economist's model fail to adequately describe the nature of competition in the wholesale trade.

7. Would you say that inventory control is a more *or* less important policy decision for wholesalers than it is for retailers? How might inventory management and control problems and approaches differ between wholesalers and retailers?

8. Wholesaling is often thought of as being a less than glamorous intermediary venture when compared to other channel intermediary operations, such as retailing. In your opinion, which of these two would be the most difficult to manage—a wholesaling or a retailing operation? Which would seem to have the best chance, on the average, of achieving a high ROI (return on investment) today?

Which line of trade would you say has had to face more challenges to its survival in the last 50 years?

Appendix 3A

Participation in the marketing flows by different types of wholesalers

Wholesaling agencies, their functions, and the marketing flows. *Note:* All of the agencies described below are "pure" types; in real life we often find agencies which are composites of several of these types.

A. *Merchant wholesalers.* Merchants whose principal business is buying goods in "job lots" and reselling them for a profit to customers who (1) resell the goods again to someone else, or (2) consume the goods in the course of operating a profit-making enterprise. The compensation of a merchant wholesaler is a *profit* that is made *on the sale of the goods.*

   1. *Full-function or service wholesalers.* The "traditional" wholesalers who perform all or most of the marketing functions normally associated with wholesaling. Participate directly in all or most of the flows of marketing. Particularly useful in broad retail lines such as groceries and drugs.

   a. *Physical possession flow.*
   (1) Take possession of the goods.
   (2) Maintain storage facilities.
   (3) Maintain stocks of goods sufficient in both variety and quantity to supply customers on regular basis.
   (4) Deliver goods to customer.

   b. *Ownership flow.* Take legal title (ownership) from supplier, pass it on to customer when sale is made.

   c. *Promotion.* May participate in manufacturer's advertising allowances; may print catalogs for trade; may advertise to trade; maintain sales force.

Source: Department of Marketing, University of Pennsylvania, Wharton School of Finance and Commerce.

    d. *Negotiation.* Make contact and negotiate over prices, quality, quantity, terms of sale, etc., with *both* supplier and customer.

    e. *Financing.* Extend credit to customers (thereby financing the customer's inventory.) Help to finance manufacturer to extent that wholesaler relieves manufacturer of burden of carrying large stocks of finished goods.

    f. *Risking.* By taking ownership assume all risks of failure to sell goods and of changes in the prices of the goods. Risk assumption may be offset by manufacturer's willingness to accept returns and/or guarantee price.

    g. *Ordering.* In effect, flow of ordering moves from retailer to manufacturer. In reality, anticipate needs of retailers and order from manufacturer in advance of actual sale to retailer (see "risking").

    h. *Payment.* Accept payment for goods from customers; pass payment minus expenses and profit to supplier. May pay supplier *before* making collection from customer (another form of risk).

2. *Limited-function wholesalers.* Wholesalers who do not perform all of the marketing functions, either by eliminating them entirely or passing them on to someone else. Some limited-function wholesalers *participate* in all of the marketing flows, but their *degree* of participation in any one flow may be considerably less than that of the service wholesaler.

    a. *Drop-shipper (desk jobber).* A wholesale merchant who passes on the order of his customer with instructions to the manufacturer to ship directly to a location specified by the customer. Maintains no warehouse or inventory, *does not come in physical possession* of the goods. Much contact with his customers by telephone, hence may have no sales force and may be much less active in promotional flow. Particulary useful in bulky goods and where merchandise typically moves in carlot quantities. (Sometimes called a "carlot wholesaler.")

    b. *Cash-carry wholesalers.*

        (1) *Financing.* Do not finance customers because of no-credit policy.

        (2) *Physical possession flow.* Same position in this flow as the service wholesaler with exception that customer assumes burden of delivery.

        (3) *Promotion.* Operation, by its nature, is a cost-cutting one. Dealing often in small orders with small retailers, therefore less likely to have an outside sales force.

    c. *Wagon jobbing (truck jobbing).*

        (1) *Wagon jobbers (self-employed merchants).*

            (a) Little capital, often extend no credit to customers.

            (b) May own goods, but often gets them on consignment from supplier.

            (c) Often maintain no warehouse, buy on hand-to-mouth basis.

        (2) *Driver-salesmen (not really wholesalers).* Takes goods on consignment or salary rather than profit.

        (3) Used with perishables and semi-perishables; sometimes with auto parts, cigars and cigarettes, candy, sundries.

    d. *Rack jobbers.* Important in variety and specialty lines, especially in super-markets. Maintain racks stocked with merchandise at the retailer's location.

        (1) *Ownership and risk.* Heavy assumption of risk, since the *jobber keeps* title and the *retailer is billed only for goods sold from the rack.*

        (2) *Finance.* Rack jobbers assume the sole financial burden for the goods, finance customer's inventory by maintaining ownership. Retailer's only investment is in the space allotted to the rack.

        (3) *Promotion.* Deal widely in highly advertised, branded, well-known goods. Have to do little promotion on the goods, which are "self-selling" through display. (*Note:* Use of the well-known brands partially offsets the risks of ownership).

  3. *Other types of wholesale operations, often of a special-purpose nature.*

    a. *Converters.*

        (1) *Ownership.* Purchase cloth from textile mills; process, dye, or print it on contract basis for garment manufacturers.

        (2) *Physical possession.* Cloth frequently finished in outside plants; converter may never touch it.

        (3) *Finance.* Converter may take entire output of textile mill; may extend heavy credit to garment manufacturers.

        (4) *Risking.* Ownership risk assumed by converter heavy because of fluid changes in popularity of patterns and colors; risk also strong when financing small garment manufacturers (high bankruptcy rate).

        (5) *Ordering.* Highly anticipatory of needs of garment makers.

    b. *Franchise wholesalers.* Retailers affiliate with existing wholesaler, who gives them right (franchise) to use certain name or store-front design. Most *voluntary chains* operate under franchises from wholesalers.

        (1) *Promotion.* Wholesaler may furnish advertising material for affiliates, may aid retailers in display and point-of-sale promotion.

        (2) Often operate on a *cost-plus* basis.

        (3) Often use *preprinted order forms;* outside sales force may give service more of an advisory nature to retailers.

        (4) May furnish accounting service for retailers.

        (5) Participation in marketing flows very similar to service wholesaler, except that *more services* are often provided to affiliates.

B. *Retailer-sponsored cooperatives*

  1. Independent *retailers* form an association, which buys or builds wholesale warehouse facilities which they own cooperatively. The *wholesale* operation is thus not a profit-making institution, but exists only as an arm of the associated retailers. *As a unit,* however, it participates in many of the marketing flows.

    a. *Ownership.* As a legal entity, the cooperative takes title to the merchandise. Legal responsibilities will depend on the form of organization.

b. *Physical possession.* Cooperative performs all acts of possession, and physical handling of goods.

c. *Promotion.* Cooperative advertising is executed by the staff of the organization for the membership. Sales force for *selling* purposes often eliminated; outside staff members may render aid to member stores in display, point-of-sale promotion, etc.

d. *Negotiation.* The cooperative negotiates (on behalf of its membership) with suppliers. Cooperative organization usually set up so that members are supplied on *cost-plus* basis. (Landed or invoice cost plus estimated allowable expenses).

e. *Financing.* May carry members' accounts on credit basis, but does not really finance members, since it is the *member's* capital which finances the cooperative.

f. *Risking.* The cooperative, as a unit, may lose money on inventories, but the risk (and profits or losses) are shared by the membership.

g. *Ordering.* The cooperative is, in effect, passing on the orders of the membership to suppliers. Often use *preprinted order forms.*

h. *Flow of payment.* Normal-membership, through organization to suppliers.

C. *Other agencies involved in wholesaling. Functional middlemen,* specializing in performance of one or more specific marketing tasks, especially those concerned with *negotiation.* As a rule, participate in only a *few* of the flows. *Not merchants:* their compensation is in the form of a commission or fee for a service rendered, NOT a profit on the sale of goods.

1. *Brokers.* Agents who specialize in buying or selling goods for a principal. Usually have neither title to, nor possession of, the merchandise.

a. *Ownership and physical possession.* Through making a sale, they *facilitate* changes in ownership and possession. They do not participate directly in these flows.

b. *Promotion.* May advertise in trade journals, have salesmen to call on trade. Broker, himself, may be a salesman.

c. *Negotiation.* Negotiate with customers on price, quantity, quality, terms of sale, etc., within limitations of authority granted by principal. Results of negotiation *binding* on principal so long as broker does not exceed authority given him.

d. *Financing.* Brokers seldom give or receive credit. Financial arrangements between principal and customer.

e. *Risking.* Brokers never own goods, take no risk on them, do not figure in the flow of risk *on the goods.* (Naturally, they take their own risks in choosing whom to represent, etc.)

f. *Ordering.* Customer orders from principal, through broker.

g. *Payment.* Payment for goods usually goes from their customers to the suppliers. They *may* (but not always) collect from customer and deduct their commission.

    h. With free-lance brokers, each sale is a separate and distinct transaction; may frequently change principals whom they represent.

  2. *Manufacturers' agents.* Functional middlemen who sell part of the output of manufacturers on an extended contract basis.

    a. Difference from brokers.

      (1) Represent limited number of principals, whom they represent regularly.

      (2) Usually represent several, noncompeting lines from different manufacturers.

      (3) Territory definite and limited.

      (4) Prices, terms of sale, etc., set by principal.

    b. Involvement in marketing flows similar to broker, except:

      (1) May be more active in promotional aspects of selling (e.g., having outside salesmen) than broker.

      (2) Will often sell in smaller lots than broker.

  3. *Selling (or sales) agents.*

    a. Difference from brokers and manufacturers' agents.

      (1) Normally handle entire output of the principal (thus, in effect, becomes sales force of manufacturer).

      (2) Usually given more complete authority over prices, terms of sale, territory, etc.

      (3) May use manufacturers' agents or brokers in places where they maintain no office.

      (4) May have quite an extensive sales force and promotional program.

  4. *Commission merchants.* (Sometimes called "factors.") Agents who receive goods on consignment for sale on a commission basis.

    a. Maintain a warehouse, involved in physical handling of goods, thus participate in the flow of *physical possession.*

    b. *Ownership.* Receive goods on consignment basis, have no title.

    c. *Promotion.* May maintain full sales force, print catalogs, have sales offices in various cities, advertise in trade magazines.

    d. *Negotiation.* Have full power to negotiate price, terms of sale, etc., with customer.

    e. *Financing.* May extend credit to customers, often assuming the risk of making collections as *del credere* agent.

      (1) *Factoring.* Commission merchants finance their principals, often by *discounting accounts receivable* from buyers.

    f. *Risking.* May assume risk of collecting accounts in factoring; may be responsible for payment to principal prior to collection of discounted account receivable.

    g. *Ordering.* May order entire output of manufacturer on consignment in anticipation of orders from customers.

    h. *Payment.* May collect from customers, forward payment to principal after deduction of expenses and commission.

FOUR

Physical Distribution: Structure And Strategy

In all marketing channels the product must be moved in the right quantity at a specific time to a specific place in order to be delivered most efficiently to the industrial user or final consumer.

The term "physical distribution" is the one most commonly applied to describe, generically, the task of sustaining a physical flow of materials and prod-

FIGURE 4-1
The Scope of Business Logistics

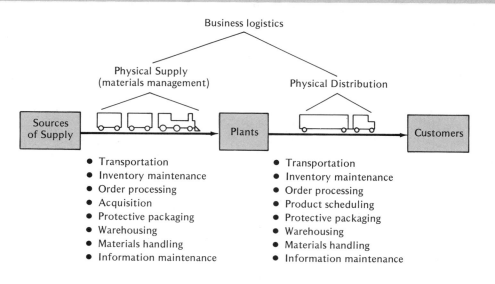

Source: Ronald H. Ballou, *Basic Business Logistics* (Englewood Cliffs, N.J.: Prentice-Hall, 1978), p. 21.

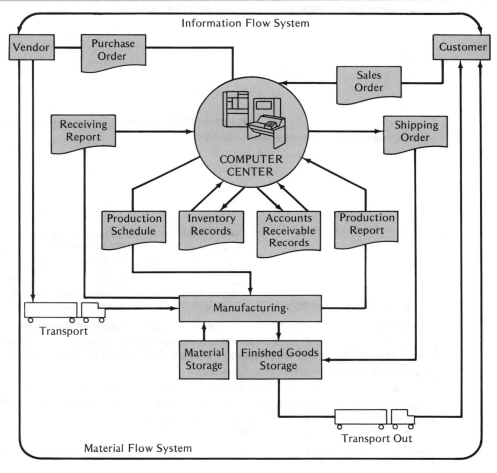

Source: E. Ralph Sims, Jr., "Applying Automation Techniques in Industrial Logistics," *Automation* (November 1967), p. 102.

ucts from their points of extraction or production to their points of final consumption. More accurately, the term "logistics system" should be used since, as shown in Fig. 4-1, a logistics system incorporates both physical supply and physical distribution activities in marketing channels. Although we will use both "physical distribution" and "logistics" alternately, it should be clear here that our use of "physical distribution" is generic, referring to the task of sustaining the physical flows.[1]

[1] For alternative definitions and exploration of the concept see John F. Magee, *Industrial Logistics* (New York: McGraw-Hill Book Co., 1968), p. 2; Ronald H. Ballou, *Business Logistics Management*

Although the term "physical distribution" may imply dealing exclusively with physical movement of goods, the reader should be warned that this perspective is too narrow. Indeed, physical distribution management involves the orchestration of flows of materials or *goods* and flows of information as illustrated in Fig. 4–2.

THE SIGNIFICANCE OF PHYSICAL DISTRIBUTION

The importance of this aspect of marketing channels is highlighted by the fact that the physical distribution of goods from producers to final consumers costs more than $400 billion a year, or 20 percent of GNP.[2] Naturally, the components and significance of distribution cost vary in different sectors of the economy, as demonstrated in Table 4–1. The fact remains, however, that distribution cost averages 13.6 percent of the sales dollars of all manufacturing companies and 25.6 percent of the sales dollars of all merchandising, retailing, and wholesaling companies.[3]

IMPLICATION FOR PHYSICAL DISTRIBUTION MANAGEMENT

If productivity is defined as the provision of goods to ultimate consumers at the lowest possible cost, physical distribution management represents a great potential for improvements in productivity.[4]

Improvements can be achieved in reducing *visible distribution costs* such as direct warehousing, transportation, and materials handling cost as well as indirect costs associated with interest on capital invested in inventory, inventory spoilage and obsolescence, and property taxes on inventories and warehouses. Therefore, one of the challenges of physical distribution management is to keep these visible costs down.

In addition to these visible distribution costs, there are *hidden costs* consisting of lost profit opportunities due to failure to ship the product on time and stockouts resulting in customers switching to competing brands, sources of supply, or stores, cancelled orders, and customer dissatisfaction.[5] Therefore, another challenge of physical distribution management is inherent in improving customer service to

(Englewood Cliffs, N.J.: Prentice-Hall, 1978), pp. 7–8; James L. Heskett, Nicholas A. Glaskowsky, Jr., and Robert M. Ivie, *Business Logistics,* 2nd ed. (New York: The Ronald Press Co., 1973), pp. 8–10; Donald J. Bowersox, *Logistical Management* (New York: MacMillan Publishing Co., 1978), pp. 3–23.

[2] *Measuring Productivity in Physical Distribution* (Chicago: National Council of Physical Distribution Management, 1978).

[3] B. J. LaLonde and P. H. Zinszer, *Customer Service: Meaning and Measurement* (Chicago: National Council of Physical Distribution Management, 1976).

[4] David P. Herron, "Managing Physical Distribution for Profit," *Harvard Business Review* (May–June 1979), p. 123.

[5] Stephen B. Oresman and Charles D. Scudder, "A Remedy for Maldistribution," *Business Horizons* (June 1974), p. 63.

TABLE 4–1   Distribution costs as a percentage of sales dollars

	Outbound trans- portation	Inventory carrying	Ware- housing	Admini- stration	Receiving and shipping	Packaging	Order processing	Total
All manufacturing companies	6.2%	1.3%	3.6%	0.5%	0.8%	0.7%	0.5%	13.6%
Chemicals and plastics	6.3	1.6	3.3	0.3	0.6	1.4	0.6	14.1
Food manufacturing	8.1	0.3	3.5	0.4	0.9	—	0.2	13.4
Pharmaceutical	1.4	—	1.2	0.7	0.5	0.1	0.5	4.4
Electronics	3.2	2.5	3.2	1.2	0.9	1.1	1.2	13.3
Paper	5.8	0.1	4.6	0.2	0.3	—	0.2	11.2
Machinery and tools	4.5	1.0	2.0	0.5	0.5	1.0	0.5	10.0
All other	6.8	1.0	2.9	1.2	1.4	0.4	0.4	14.1
All merchandising companies	7.4	10.3	4.2	1.2	0.6	1.2	0.7	25.6
Consumer goods	8.1	8.5	4.0	1.3	0.9	0.9	0.5	24.2
Industrial goods	5.9	13.7	2.9	0.7	0.2	2.0	1.0	26.4

Source: B. J. LaLonde and P. H. Zinszer, Customer Service: Its Meaning and Measurement (Chicago: National Council of Physical Distribution Management, 1976) as reported in David P. Heiron, "Managing Physical Distribution for Profit," Harvard Business Review (May–June 1979), p. 123.

reduce the hidden costs. The dilemma of physical distribution management can be summarized as follows:

> Customer service and these costs (visible and hidden) are logically interdependent. Improving the service provided by the distribution system should increase costs, and meaningful cost reduction should lower service performance. From this relationship, it appears that the principal problem in effectively managing distribution is to determine the appropriate service level for the business, and then run the distribution as efficiently as possible to achieve that level of service.[6]

GOAL OF PHYS. DIST.

The *physical distribution* or *logistics concept* provides guidelines to achieving this critical balance.

THE PHYSICAL DISTRIBUTION CONCEPT

In a renowned study completed over twenty years ago, it was found that, for a number of companies, 10 to 20 percent of the products carried in inventory accounted for nearly 80 percent of the companies' sales and that half of the products accounted for less than 4 percent of sales.[7] In fact, the bottom half of the product lines were found to impose a vastly disproportionate amount of expense and investment on the various companies' distribution systems because of the costs associated with carrying these more slowly selling items in inventory. Such costs can be highly significant amounting to 25 percent of the average value of inventory on hand.

The researchers argued, based on their findings, that the firms would be better off if they were to *reduce* the amount of inventory of these products being held in *each* of their *regional* warehouses and consolidate much of the remaining inventory in central warehouses. The companies' salesmen protested, saying that *customer service* would decline because of the longer rail or truck transit times associated with the more distant warehouses. To meet this objection, a system was established whereby salesmen could, upon receiving an order for one of the more slowly selling products, telephone the central warehouse, which would then use air freight services to provide overnight delivery to their customers. Thus, by consolidation of products and increased use of air freight, customer service was maintained while total distribution costs (especially inventory holding costs) were drastically reduced.[8]

Emerging from this study was the basic rationale behind the PD concept, which can be described as a *cost-service* orientation, backed by an integrated physical distribution network, that is aimed at *minimizing* the total costs of distribution at a *given level of customer service.* Four main components of the PD

---

[6] *Ibid.*

[7] Howard T. Lewis, James W. Culliton, and Jack D. Steele, *The Role of Air Freight in Physical Distribution* (Boston: Division of Research, Harvard University Graduate School of Business Administration, 1956). See also John F. Magee, "The Logistics of Distribution," *Harvard Business Review,* Vol. 38 (July–August 1960), pp. 89–101.

[8] Lewis, et al., *op. cit.,* p. 155.

concept are (1) a total cost perspective, (2) the understanding of relevant tradeoffs among costs, (3) the notion of zero suboptimization, and (4) the total system perspective, each of which is discussed briefly below.

The Total Cost Perspective

The key to the total-cost approach is to consider all distribution cost elements, visible and hidden,[9] simultaneously when one is attempting to meet specified customer service standards. When alternative approaches are tested, costs of some functions increase, some will decrease, and others will stay the same. The objective is to find the alternative with the lowest *total* cost, given a desired service level.

Cost Tradeoffs

Even though certain costs may increase while others are purposively reduced, the end result, under the PD concept, is that total distribution cost will, it is to be hoped, decline. For example, the Gillette Company, the world's largest producer of safety razors, was faced with an ever expanding assortment of products because it had expanded into a broad range of toiletry products. To give good customer service the company started using air freight, an expensive form of distribution. Upon studying their distribution system, they discovered that their problem was in the slowness with which orders were processed. By simplifying paperwork they were able to reduce the time required to process orders. Gillette was able to return to lower-cost surface transportation and still be able to meet delivery schedules. The cost tradeoff was between order processing costs which *increased* and transportation costs which *decreased;* and the net result was that total distribution costs *decreased.*

The Montgomery Ward Company found that significant inventory reductions could be achieved by consolidating all their slower-moving products into one central warehouse. This facility is located only seven miles from Chicago's O'Hare Airport. When a slow-moving product or part is needed, the Chicago warehouse is notified and the requirement is often sent via air freight to the requesting party. While this procedure greatly increases the transportation charges involved in sending a product or part to a customer, the inventory holding cost reduction more than offsets the increased per-unit transportation charges.[10]

Zero Suboptimization

When one distribution function is optimized, the result will likely be an impairment of the performance of other distribution functions. For example, if a traf-

[9] *Ibid.,* pp. 64–65. See also Oresman and Scudder, *op. cit.,* p. 63.
[10] James C. Johnson and Donald F. Wood, *Contemporary Physical Distribution* (Tulsa, Ok.: PPC Books, 1977), p. 8.

fic manager attempts to optimize the performance of his own department by accumulating merchandise in order to use high-bulk/low-cost modes of transport, he will adversely affect the ability of the inventory manager to keep inventory carrying costs down to a reasonable level.[11] When physical distribution functions are integrated and coordinated, the focus of system management should be to minimize suboptimization, or ideally, reach zero suboptimization. Therefore, in the above examples, the traffic manager may be encouraged to use less than carload shipments and high-speed transportation if necessary to reduce inventory carrying cost and meet customer service requirements.

Total Systems Concept

This concept is an extension of the total cost concept. It extends the total cost concept to cover trading-off the cost of performing different functions throughout the entire marketing channel. For example, price-ticketing of goods is normally performed at the retail level. The process is time-consuming and labor intensive. Some large retailers have resorted to direct negotiations with suppliers to goods to shift the price-ticketing operation to the assembly line at the supplier's production facilities. Retailers provide up-to-date price lists to their suppliers, and the goods are received at the retailer's premises preticketed. Naturally, manufacturers have increased their prices to retailers to compensate for the prolonged production process resulting from the assumption of the price-ticketing function. Usually retailers are ready for these increases, because they are more than offset by the reduction of their own cost. The final result is a reduction in the total distribution cost in the channel system.[12]

In order to implement the PD concept, management must design and implement a physical distribution or logistics system that coordinates and integrates the components of the system, as shown in Fig. 4-3.[13] The core system component is customer service standards, shown in the inner circle. Basic PD system components are shown in the middle circle and supportive system components are shown in the outer circle.

This chapter concentrates on the core and basic system components, i.e.,

1. The determination of customer service standards.

2. The establishment of appropriate number and location for warehousing facilities.

[11] For other examples see Oresman and Scudder, *op. cit.,* p. 64.

[12] For other examples see Ronald H. Ballou, *Basic Business Logistics* (Englewood Cliffs, N.J.: Prentice-Hall, 1978), pp. 34–35.

[13] Discussions of integration and coordination problems and approaches are found in Raymond LeKashman and John F. Stolle, "The Total Cost Approach to Distribution," *Business Horizons,* Vol. 8 (Winter 1965), pp. 34–46; George G. Smith, "Knowing Your P.D. Costs," *Distribution Age* (January 1966), pp. 21–27; John F. Stolle, "How to Manage Physical Distribution," *Harvard Business Review,* Vol. 45 (July–August 1967), pp. 93–100; Charles A. Taff, *op. cit.,* pp. 6 and 14; and Grant Davis and Stephen W. Brown, *Logistics Management* (Lexington, Mass.: D. C. Heath and Co., 1974), pp. 25–44.

FIGURE 4-3

The Dynamics of the Physical Distribution System

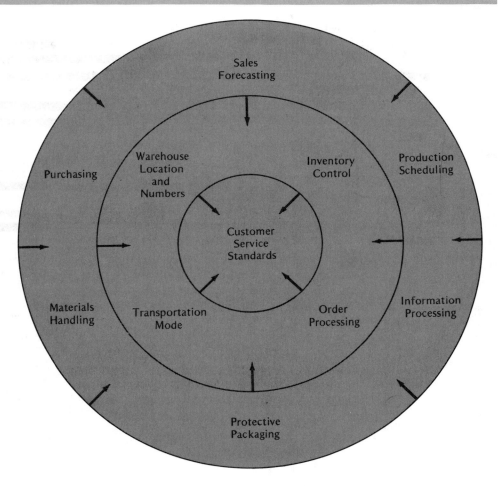

3. The setting of inventory management and inventory control procedures.
4. The design of order processing systems.
5. The selection of transportation modes.

Concentration on these decision areas and components is important, since they are more generalizable to various types of channel members than, say, is a discussion of material handling or protective packaging. More important, however, the four areas selected for emphasis represent the most strategic, as well as the most cost-significant, elements in physical distribution for most channel members.

Once system design is accomplished, attention is needed to PD system management, or the effective melding of all decision areas into a meaningful whole. This is undertaken in the final part of this chapter.

CUSTOMER SERVICE STANDARDS   Although it is repeated throughout this text, it must be continually emphasized that the process of policy and strategy formulation in marketing starts with a determination of customer needs and desires. This "adage" applies with equal force to the setting of physical distribution policies. In fact, certain studies indicate that a number of purchasing managers consider physical distribution service and performance second only to product quality as a factor in their selection decisions.[14]

The key PD service level measures used by manufacturing and merchandising, i.e., retailing and wholesaling, firms are shown in Table 4–2.[15] The critical question confronting the distribution manager is which of these customer service elements are of major importance to his clientele. Answering this question is not an easy task, for empirical evidence suggests that the importance given to each of these various elements varies according to different product/market and purchasing contexts.[16] For example, for some retail buyers, faster average order cycle time (i.e., shorter elapsed time from order placement to order delivery) is not as important as a less variable order cycle. These buyers would accept longer delivery times if the variability of order cycle times were reduced or if price concessions were offered. This situation does not hold, however, for retailers of drug sundries; the latter place a greater emphasis on actual delivery speed.

In addition to variations because of different product/market and purchasing contexts, a recent study confirmed

. . . substantial variation in customer service perceptions between the Transportation and Public Warehousing industries and the firms using these industries. If this lack of agreement is translated into marketing programs by carriers or public warehousemen it would suggest that in some cases the customer service interface between these firms is neither efficient nor effective. The packer-distributor seem to be in general agreement on the importance of product availability and order cycle time. However, on other key elements of customer service there appears to be significant variation in perceptions. This might indicate that manufacturers are not "tuning in"

[14] See Bernard Klass, "What Factors Affect Industrial Buying Decisions," *Industrial Marketing* (May 1961), pp. 33–35; and Harvey H. Shycon and Christopher R. Sprague, "Put a Price Tag on Your Customer Servicing Levels," *Harvard Business Review,* Vol. 53 (July–August 1975), pp. 71–78.

[15] For additional lists, see Heskett, et al., *op. cit.,* pp. 250–251; P. Ronald Stephenson and Ronald P. Willett, "Selling with Physical Distribution Service," *Business Horizons,* Vol. 11 (December 1968), pp. 75–85; and William M. Hutchinson and John F. Stolle, "How to Manage Customer Service," *Harvard Business Review,* Vol. 46 (November-December 1968), pp. 85–96.

[16] For examples of such variability, see James L. Heskett, "Predictive Value of Classroom Simulation," in William S. Decker (ed.), *Emerging Concepts in Marketing* (Chicago: American Marketing Association, 1963), pp. 101–115; Ronald P. Willett and P. Ronald Stephenson, "Determinants of Buyer Response to Physical Distribution Services," *Journal of Marketing Research,* Vol. 6 (August 1969), pp. 279–283; and Hutchinson and Stolle, *op. cit.,* pp. 33–37.

**TABLE 4–2   Selected service level measurements
used by manufacturing and merchandising firms**

Major Category	Sub-Category
Product Availability	Line Item Availability Product Group Availability Invoice Fill Cases/Units
Order Cycle Time	Order Entry Order Processing Total Cycle Time
Consistency	In Order Cycle Time In Shipment Dispatch In Transit Time In Arrival Time In Warehouse Handling
Response Time	Order Status Order Tracing Backorder Status Order Confirmation Product Substitution Order Shortages Product Information Requests
Error Rates	Shipment Delays Order Errors Picking & Packing Errors Shipping & Labeling Errors Paperwork Errors
Product/Shipment Related Malfunction	Damaged Merchandise Merchandise Refusals Claims Returned Goods Customer Complaints
Special Handling	Transshipment Expedited Orders Expedited Transportation Special Packaging Customer Backhauls

Source: B. J. LaLonde and P. H. Zinszer, *Customer Service: Its Meaning and Measurement* (Chicago: National Council of Physical Distribution Management, 1976), p. 184.

their wholesalers or middlemen and integrating customer requirements into total customer service planning. It might also indicate that the packer/processor is using too narrow a view of customer service and/or the distributor is not effectively articulating his customer service requierments to his suppliers.[17]

[17] LaLonde and Zinszer, *Customer Service, op. cit.,* p. 155. For a complete account of variations in perceptions among channel members, see pp. 112–155.

In order to arrive at an appropriate customer service standard, it is useful to approach the problem systematically. A schematic overview for analyzing this type of problem is shown in Fig. 4–4. It summarizes a physical distribution service (PDS) decision model which involves six steps:

1. Define important PDS elements.
2. Determine customers' viewpoints.
3. Design a competitive PDS package.
4. Develop a promotional program to "sell" PDS.
5. Market test the PDS package and promotional program.
6. Establish performance controls.[18]

Of all these tasks, the first three are the most important for the setting of customer service standards.[19] Carrying out this part of the analysis requires the generation of pertinent information through PDS market research. Perreault and Russ suggest a four-phase approach for obtaining the needed information and using it to develop competitive standards.[20]

PHASE ONE: IDENTIFY CURRENT PDS LEVELS AND THEIR COSTS. This phase involves an examination of in-house cost data and the informal questioning of salesmen and clients.

PHASE TWO: IDENTIFY PDS LEVELS FOR FURTHER STUDY. According to Perreault and Russ:

> Three criteria are used to identify PDS areas/elements where change has the greatest potential impact for the firm: the *stated importance* of each element to customers (obtained through informal questioning or a formal survey), the *competitive potential* of changes in each element (determined by questioning the firm's distribution specialists about the difficulty that competitors will face in detecting and copying the changes), and the *relative costs* of making changes in the level of service for a particular element of the PDS package.[21]

---

[18] William D. Perreault, Jr., and Frederick A. Russ, "Physical Distribution Service: A Neglected Aspect of Marketing Management," *MSU Business Topics,* Vol. 22 (Summer 1974), pp. 37–45. See also Hutchinson and Stolle, *op. cit.*; John F. Gustafson and Raymond Ricard, "How to Determine Levels of Required Customer Service," *Transportation and Distribution Management,* Vol. 14 (May–June 1964), pp. 34–37.

[19] The necessary tools and techniques for implementing the last three steps can be found in James L. Heskett, "Controlling Customer Logistics Service," *International Journal of Physical Distribution,* Vol. 1 (June 1971), pp. 140–145.

[20] Perreault and Russ, *op. cit.,* pp. 42–44.

[21] *Ibid.,* p. 42.

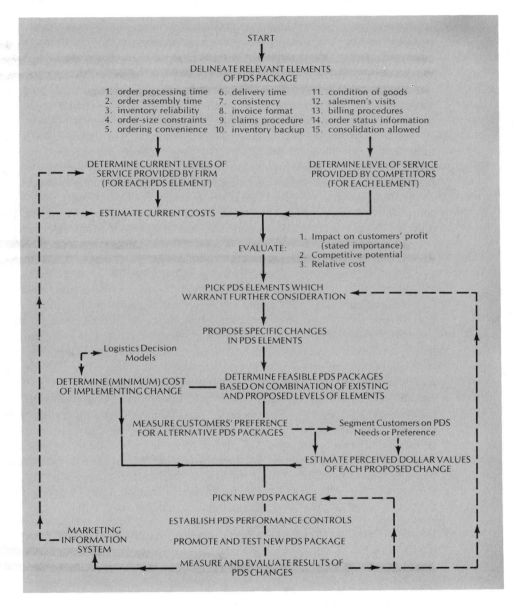

Source: William D. Perreault, Jr. and Frederick A. Russ, "Physical Distribution Service: A Neglected Aspect of Marketing Management," *MSU Business Topics*, (Summer 1974), p. 40. Reprinted by permission of the publisher, Division of Research, Graduate School of Business Administration, Michigan State University.

For example, this part of the analysis might suggest to the manufacturer or middleman that he focus his efforts on changing customer service standards through improvements in order cycle time for rush orders, a reduction in order cycle time variability for regular orders, and a simplification of order placement methods.

PHASE THREE: IDENTIFY FEASIBLE SERVICE PACKAGES. Once the important elements of PDS are established, the next step is to specify possible changes in these elements and identify the costs associated with alternative changes. Certain changes may affect costs that are "visible" in nature; the least cost solution associated with such changes can then be estimated by existing logistics decision models.[22] For example, PDS research may suggest that the firm's present in-stock service level of 95 percent (indicating that, when a customer wants a product, it is immediately available 95 percent of the time) should be increased to 96 percent. However, it is a well-known distribution axiom that the inventory required to render varying levels of service will increase (as will its cost) at an accelerating rate as the desired service level is raised. For example, raising the service level to 96 percent from 95 percent requires 6 percent more safety stock, and raising the service level to 99 percent from 98 percent demands 14 percent more safety stock.[23]

In addition, certain changes in the PDS package may also encompass costs of the "hidden" variety referred to earlier, and thus may be more difficult to estimate. For example, even when a service level is raised to 96 percent, the fact still remains that the product or service will be unavailable 4 percent of the time. Whether or not this is significant depends upon such factors as the degree of brand loyalty on the part of the firm's ultimate customers, the degree of purchaser (e.g., middleman) sensitivity to PD service failures, the relative effectiveness of competitors' service levels, and so on. In fact, an examination of such "hidden" factors might suggest that an increase in service level is unwarranted. It may be the case that the firm's *ultimate* consumers would not consider switching brands even when they are confronted by temporary out-of-stock conditions. Indeed, one study showed that as many as 50 percent of U.S. household consumers, depending on the product and market, could not be sold a substitute brand when "their" brand was missing from the shelf and that as many as 25 percent refused even a different size or color of their own brand.[24] However, for certain frequently purchased convenience goods items that command less brand loyalty, as well as for many industrial goods, the stockout factor is likely to be a costly one and therefore must be taken into account when the range of feasible PDS packages is narrowed.

PHASE FOUR: COLLECT AND ANALYZE PDS CUSTOMER PREFERENCE DATA. The impact that the various changes in the PDS service package can have on profits is a function not only of the costs of the changes to the firm but

[22] For excellent reviews of a variety of logistics decision models geared toward analyzing the cost effects of these types of changes in the "PDS package," see Ronald H. Ballou, *op. cit.*; and Stanley F. Stasch, *Systems Analysis for Marketing Planning and Control* (Glenview, Ill.: Scott, Foresman and Co., 1972).
[23] Shycon and Sprague, *op. cit.*, p. 75.
[24] "The Out-of-Stock Study," *Progressive Grocer* (November 1968), pp. 5–17.

also of the perceived dollar value of the changes to potential or actual purchasers. Implicitly, it is a question of tradeoffs, in that the firm's customers must evaluate how much a change in PDS is worth in terms of the increased price of increased patronage. Determination of the implicit tradeoffs made by the firm's customers requires that they provide a simple preference evaluation of the alternative PDS packages. This can be done by presenting purchasing managers with selected pairs of alternative PDS packages and asking them for an estimate of what proportion of their patronage they would allocate to each member of the pair if they represented the only two alternatives.[25] The preference data obtained in this manner may then be analyzed in such a way as to provide scale estimates of the value of different PDS packages to the firm's customers or estimates of the effect that each particular level of PDS has on the overall preference process.[26] In turn, these estimates may be interpreted as "tradeoff" values, as perceived by the firm's customers, for changes in the PDS package. As Perreault and Russ note:

> The dollar trade-off values estimated in this fashion provide the marketing manager with an index of which changes the customer considers to be important, and more specifically whether the additional revenue (due to the possibility of increased prices or increased demand) exceeds the additional costs incurred by the higher service level. The result of this type of analysis is the pinpointing of the PDS package(s), among all those considered, whose cost increases can best be justified by the potential incremental revenues from its target market.[27]

Once the "best" PDS package is identified, distribution management can plan to reinforce or adjust existing customer service standards so that physical distribution service may become a competitive selling weapon for the company. It may very well be the case that the most competitive PDS package is one which offers a lower level of service accompanied by a lower price. Once this "optimal" package is decided upon, management can then undertake a selection of the appropriate warehousing, inventory, and transportation policies that will assure the proper implementation of the desired customer service standards.

Warehousing represents perhaps the first vital link in the logistics system for carrying out the customer service standards established by the firm. Because efficient production requires that manufacturing operations be conducted as continuously as possible at relatively few locations, warehouses maintained by mid-

[25] It seems that purchasing agents are indeed willing to provide such judgmental data. See Perreault and Russ, *op. cit.,* p. 43.

[26] Two scaling procedures have been applied to this problem area: conjoint scaling and a multifactor variation of Thurstone's model for comparative judgment. See Perreault and Russ, *op. cit.* For a discussion of conjoint measurement in a marketing context, see Paul E. Green and Vithala R. Rao, "Conjoint Measurement for Quantifying Judgmental Data," *Journal of Marketing Research,* Vol. 8 (August 1971), pp. 355–365. For a discussion of multifactor generalizations of Thurstone's law of comparative judgment, see R. Darrell Bock and Lyle V. Jones, *The Measurement and Prediction of Judgment and Choice* (San Francisco: Holden-Day, 1968), pp. 187–211.

[27] Perreault and Russ, *op. cit.,* pp. 43–44.

dlemen or by the manufacturers themselves are needed to accommodate finished-goods inventories. In turn, these warehouses can be strategically located in or near centers of demand in order to facilitate customer service. Furthermore, because it is not possible to perfectly synchronize production with market demand, the inventories held at warehouses act as buffers to variations between production and sales.

MANAGERIAL VARIABLES IN WAREHOUSING DECISIONS

There are two basic types of warehouse facilities available to channel members. These are *privately* owned by the firm and *public* facilities, in which space is leased by the firm. In general, *private* warehousing is desirable when a firm needs flexibility in the design of warehouse facilities, wishes to maintain control over the operation of its warehouses, has special storage and handling requirements, and has a relatively constant, high volume of goods moving through these facilities into large metropolitan areas.[28] In contrast, *public* warehousing is desirable for those firms that wish to free themselves from the investment costs and problems of private operation and thereby obtain professional warehouse management. Public warehousing also permits great flexibility in the location of a firm's inventory, which is desirable if the firm is selling in areas of uncertain, limited, or seasonal market demand. Flexibility in warehouse location is also preferable in regions where rate relationships between different transport modes are subject to significant change. Finally, public warehouses assist firms in obtaining lower freight rates by consolidating the small shipments of various clients into carload lots as well as by receiving pooled car shipments from companies at car- or truck-load rates and then distributing the contents of these shipments to different clients located in its service area.[29] Table 4–3 summarizes and compares many of the basic tradeoffs that are involved in choosing between public and private warehousing arrangements.

Public Warehousing

Whereas private warehouses are often built to suit specialized user needs, public warehouses come in a number of types and offer a wide range of services. Some specialization takes place in public warehousing but only within broad product categories. In general, public warehouses are classified into five basic types.

- *Commodity warehouses.* These are warehouses that limit their services to certain commodity groupings. The warehouses may specialize in storing and handling such commodities as lumber, cotton, tobacco, and grain.

[28] Heskett, et al., *op. cit.,* pp. 607–608.
[29] Charles A. Taff, *Management of Traffic and Physical Distribution,* 4th ed. (Homewood, Ill.: Richard D. Irwin, 1967), p. 7.

TABLE 4–3   Decision variables in choosing among types of warehouses

Decisions Variables	Private Owned	Private Leased	Public
	Types of Warehousing Arrangements		
1. Fixed investment	Very high	Moderate, depends on the lease's terms	No fixed investment is involved
2. Unit cost	High, if volume is low	High, if volume is low	Low, since facilities are on "for hire as needed" and fixed costs are widely distributed among users
3. Control	High	High	Low managerial control
4. Adequacy to product line	Highly adequate	Moderately adequate	May not be convenient
5. Flexibility	Low	Low	High; termination of usage can be easily arranged

- *Bulk-storage warehouses.* Some warehouses offer storage and handling of products in bulk, such as liquid chemicals, oil, highway salts, and syrups. Mixing products and breaking bulk may also be part of the service.
- *Cold-storage warehouses.* These are controlled, low-temperature warehouses. Perishables, such as fruits, vegetables, and frozen foods, as well as some chemicals and drugs, require this type of storage for preservation.
- *Household-goods warehouses.* Storage and handling of household articles and furniture are the specialty of these warehouses. Although furniture manufacturers may use these warehouses, the major users are the household-goods moving companies.
- *General-merchandise warehouses.* These warehouses handle a broad range of merchandise, which usually does not require the special facilities or the special handling noted in the four previous types of warehouses.[30]

In practice hybrid types exist. For example, a general merchandise warehouse handling food products may have to operate a refrigerated section to satisfy the needs of food grocers. By the same token, bulk storage warehouses may handle general merchandise.

The public warehousing industry has been experiencing a steady rate of growth. As of 1975, the industry operated some 15,000 facilities (as compared with approximately 9500 in 1967) and was building new units at the rate of 13 percent an-

---

[30] Creed H. Jenkins, *Modern Warehouse Management* (New York: McGraw-Hill Book Company, 1968), p. 29 as quoted in Ballou, *op. cit.*, p. 207.

nually.[31] Limited data suggest that this trend is especially dominant among household goods and general warehousing operations. One reason for the increased use of public warehousing is the ability of such organizations to provide services to companies with varied distribution needs. For example, Balanced Foods, Inc., a small health food supplier, shifted much of its participation in the physical possession flow to General Warehouse Corporation when it was undertaking a large expansion during the late 1960s. By doing so, it was able to realize multiple benefits, including a greater amount of warehouse space allocated to its products, the use of expensive high-efficiency equipment that the firm itself could not have afforded, a reduction in distribution costs by 15 percent, and a reduction in order cycle time to 24 hours. In turn, these multiple benefits permitted the company to concentrate heavily on its other marketing operations, with the result that its sales volume grew from $3 million to $11 million in five years.[32]

Large companies are also making increased use of public warehouses for a variety of reasons. Mead Johnson & Company has always relied predominantly on public warehousing because of its space flexibility; Tonka Corporation finds public warehousing useful because its space needs fluctuate widely due to the seasonality of the toy business; Alcoa has turned to public warehouses in some areas to speed up its deliveries to customers; Kresge uses public warehouses for a month or two before each of its new store openings to ensure that initial inventories are on hand when needed; Owens-Corning Fiberglas Corporation and Johns-Mansville Corporation have begun to use public warehouses to supplement their own network of private warehouses.[33]

Developments in engineering, data processing, and management control, as well as improved coordination with other warehousemen, have transformed both the image and the task of public warehousing beyond its traditional scope.[34] For example, certain public warehousemen have begun to band together into national associations in an effort to improve and expand the services they offer. One corporate illustration is Distribution America, a network of 12 independent warehouses from coast to coast, which utilizes a computer system to provide an array of shipping and inventory information for its customers.[35] Along similar lines, certain public warehousing operations are beginning to offer a *total* distribution service package on a national scale. One example is USCO Services, the distribution subsidiary of Uniroyal, which developed as a separate entity when Uniroyal reorganized its warehousing operations. Starting as an in-house service with 28 existing warehouses and Uniroyal's sophisticated computer arrangement, USCO entered public warehousing. The company soon began to offer a wide range of ser-

[31] See Walter F. Friedman, "Physical Distribution: The Concept of Shared Services," *Harvard Business Review,* Vol. 53 (March–April 1975), p. 26.

[32] *Ibid.*

[33] *Ibid.*

[34] For a discussion of these trends, see "Meeting Those Distribution Needs," *Handling and Shipping* (July 1975), pp. 37–41.

[35] *Ibid.,* p. 38; Friedman, *op. cit.,* p. 29.

vices in order to utilize its organization more fully and to bring down distribution costs for Uniroyal as well as for its other clients.[36] Other warehousing operations employing similar strategies include Gulf-Atlantic Warehouse Company, Trammell Crow Distribution Corporation, Consolidated Services, and National Distribution Services (NDS), an independent subsidiary of Eastern Air Lines, Inc. Characteristic of all these large public warehousing operations is a broad range of services offered, including inventory management; all physical handling and storage of goods; all transportation (including consolidation of shipments and local delivery to client's customers); all paper work such as purchase orders, invoices, and freight bills; and computer and management systems capabilities that can develop efficient distribution programs for clients.[37]

Private Warehousing

A major development in *private* warehousing is the emergence of *distribution centers*. Distribution centers are distinguished from *conventional* private warehousing operations by the fact that such centers are major centralized warehousing operations that:

- Serve regional markets.
- Process and regroup products into customized orders.
- Maintain a full line of products for customer distribution.
- Consolidate large shipments from different production points.
- Frequently employ a computer and various materials-handling equipment and may be highly automated rather than labor intensive.
- Are large and single-storied, rather than multi-storied.[38]

Clearly, most of these criteria can be met by the more modern public warehousing facilities mentioned above. However, technologically sophisticated public operations are still few in number, and the preponderance of "distribution centers" in operation today are owned or leased for private corporate use.[39] Moreover, there is one other distinguishing characteristic of distribution centers that clearly separates them from the vast majority of public warehousing operations: distribution centers

---

[36] *Ibid.*

[37] Friedman, *op. cit.,* pp. 29 and 36.

[38] See Kenneth Marshall and John Miller, "Where Are the Distribution Centers Going?" *Handling and Shipping*; (November 1965), p. 38; and Marjorie Person and Diane Mitchell, "Distribution Centers: The Fort Wayne Experience," *Business Horizons,* Vol. 19 (August 1975), pp. 89–95.

[39] In fact, one study carried out in Fort Wayne, Indiana, which is one of the U.S. havens for the location of distribution centers, found that 96.2 percent of all distribution centers in the area (26) were owned or leased, with 65.4 percent being company owned and 30.8 percent being leased. See Person and Mitchell, *op. cit.,* p. 92. See also H.G. Becker and Liz Jelenic, "Where the Distribution Centers Are," *H&SM* (November 1980), pp. 52–56.

are primarily established for the movement of goods, rather than their storage.[40] As one marketing executive observed regarding his company's distribution center,

> Our terminal is in constant motion. At no time is merchandise warehoused here . . . we're strictly a distribution terminal.[41]

Thus, the rationale underlying the development of distribution centers is to maintain the company's product in a constant and efficient flow from the moment it leaves production until the day it arrives at its destination.

Many of the world's foremost corporations now operate distribution centers as an integral part of their physical distribution systems. For example, IBM's "World Trade Distribution Center" (WTDC) is one of the largest and most sophisticated of its kind in the world. From its location in New York, the WTDC uses a complex communications network to control the annual movement of more than 23 million pounds of equipment, parts, and supplies.[42] Similarly, Levi Strauss, Inc., operates a huge distribution center in Little Rock, Arkansas, responsible for the rapid movement of its 48,000 product line items from its ten U.S. manufacturing plants to distributors in 70 foreign lands and more than 17,000 stores domestically.[43] Further, from a single distribution center covering 28 acres and more than 1¼ million square feet, the Anchor Hocking Corporation ships 1¼ million pounds of housewares products daily, one of the highest tonnage-shipped-per-day figures in the United States.[44]

Many other firms employing private warehousing operations have also begun to rethink the economics of storage, and to search for ways to boost productivity and save time and money in their distribution pipelines. Probably the single most important development has been the widespread application of computer technology to private warehousing operations. Linked with equipment and lines for rapid transmission of data, the computer has, in fact, become the key element in virtually all distribution center operations. Computers are being used to provide extremely rapid service to customers by determining the availability of items required, issuing the proper order-filling, furnishing shipping and billing documentation, maintaining inventory control records, and in some instances providing an automated order-picking function.

Despite the heavy investment often required for a computer and its accompanying support facilities, cost savings have been generated by numerous firms through an updating of their private storage distribution systems and equipment. One example is Marcor (formerly Montgomery Ward), which achieved significant cost savings in its distribution center operations by utilizing computerization and

---

[40] Marshall and Miller, *op. cit.;* Person and Mitchell, *op. cit.*

[41] "Meeting Those Distribution Center Needs," *Handling and Shipping* (July 1975), p. 37.

[42] Janet Bosworth Dower, "How IBM Distributes—Worldwide," *Distribution Worldwide* (October 1973), pp. 51–54, 58–60.

[43] Jim Dixon, "Streamlining Storage and Distribution," *Distribution Worldwide* (May 1975), p. 32.

[44] *Ibid.,* pp. 28–29.

automated handling.[45] Marcor's savings stemmed from a 60 percent reduction in the number of distribution centers operated, reduced labor costs for order processing, reduction in the number of special orders, modern handling equipment, and the central storage of slow-moving items coupled with air freight for rapid delivery.[46] It seems certain that this trend toward reevaluation and redesign of private warehousing facilities will continue, especially in the light of the increase in income-tax depreciation allowances for capital outlays, which should further encourage firms to search for more productive equipment. In turn, the result for private warehousing is a movement toward increasing sophistication and change.

Storage in Transit

Storage in transit, the time that goods remain in transportation equipment during delivery, reduces the need for and cost of warehousing. The following example is illustrative.

> The United Processors Company harvests and processes a variety of fruits and vegetables in southern and western farming regions of the country. For certain of these products such as strawberries and watermelon, there tends to be strong demand in the East and Midwest just ahead of the local growing season. Because United must harvest earlier than the northern climates, supply builds before demand peaks. Inventories normally build in the growing areas before truck shipments are made to the demand areas. By switching to rail service and the longer delivery times associated with it, the company could, in many cases, ship immediately after harvesting and have the products arrive in the marketplace just as strong demand develops. The railroad serves the warehousing function. The result is a substantial reduction in warehousing costs and transportation costs, too![47]

Therefore, transportation equipment should be viewed as *moving warehouses*.

Determining the Number and Location of Warehousing Facilities

Whether a channel member chooses to employ public or private warehousing operations in his physical distribution system, questions still remain as to how many warehouses should be established and where they should be located. The determination of the number of warehouses to be used is directly dependent upon the customer service levels established by the firm. A channel member faced with high customer service requirements will often establish a series of warehouses. Care must be taken, however, that the number of warehouses employed to ensure customer

---

[45] See "Customer Service Sparks Total Distribution Overhaul," *Handling and Shipping* (May 1968), pp. 55–58.

[46] *Ibid.*

[47] Ballou, *op. cit.,* pp. 216–217.

service is not so great as to raise costs inordinately for other PD functions (e.g., inventory management, traffic, etc.). For example, the number of locations a firm establishes has a cost relationship to several other logistical variables. Thus, the *total costs* associated with the number of warehouses employed must be taken into account. Although the least-cost solution to this problem is unique for each firm because of differences in customer service standards, inventory carrying costs, and so on, the total cost related to the logistical network can be generalized in a manner similar to that shown in Fig. 4-5. The low point on the total *transportation* cost curve in Fig. 4-5 is at a configuration of eight locations. However, total cost related to average *inventory* commitment clearly increases with each additional location. Thus, once the cost tradeoffs have been accounted for, the lowest *total* cost for the overall logistical structure is shown in Fig. 4-5 to be a network consisting of six locations.

The location of warehouse facilities will also have a significant impact on the competitive thrust of an organization and, concomitantly, of an entire marketing channel. Just as the number of warehouses established directly affects the ability of the organization and channel to serve its customers and, at the same time, keep

FIGURE 4-5
Total Cost Logistical Network

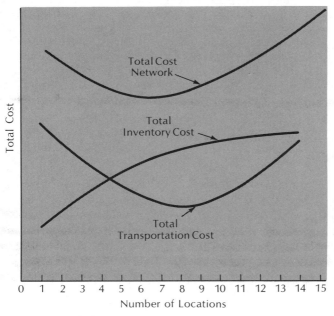

Source: Reprinted from *Logistical Management*, 2nd ed., by Donald J. Bowersox, p. 253. ©1978 by the Macmillan Publishing Co., Inc.

logistical costs in line, so too does the selection of appropriate warehouse locations. A number of warehousing facility location models and solution techniques have been developed over the past two decades which have been important in aiding management to make better decisions.[48] Critical to each are estimates of sales lost because of customer distance from warehouses, the cost of operating warehouses, and transportation cost (both inbound and outbound).

INVENTORY MANAGEMENT AND CONTROL

If it were not for the presence of and need for inventories, there would be no purpose served in discussing warehousing decisions. In fact, although the decisions involving ownership, type, and location of warehouses are obviously important, solutions to problems associated with inventory management and control are crucial to the viability of all commercial channel members, irrespective of the warehousing decisions arrived at. This observation is particularly salient in periods of slow economic growth. In fact, given the economic conditions of the middle and late 1970s, some top-level executives are beginning to disparage personnel in middle management positions who regularly show large annual sales increases in their divisions but smaller gains in profits, while continually needing more cash from their parent companies. According to

[48] Ronald H. Ballou, *Business Logistics Management* (Englewood Cliffs, N.J.: Prentice-Hall, 1973), p. 233; William R. King, *Quantitative Analysis for Marketing Management* (New York: McGraw-Hill Book Company, 1967), pp. 539-40.

Donald J. Bowersox, "An Analytical Approach to Warehouse Location," *Handling and Shipping* (February, 1962), pp. 17-20.

Frank H. Mossman and Newton Morton, *Logistics of Distribution Systems* (Boston: Allyn and Bacon, 1965), pp. 245-56.

Alfred A. Kuehn and Michael J. Hamburger, "A Heuristic Program for Locating Warehouses," *Management Science,* Vol. 9 (July 1963), pp. 643-666. For an extension of this model, see E. F. Feldman, A. Lehrer, and T. L. Ray, "Warehouse Location Under Continuous Economies of Scale," *Management Science,* Vol. 12 (May 1966), pp. 670-684.

Leon Cooper, "An Extension of the Generalized Weber Problem," *Journal of Regional Science,* Vol. 8, No. 2 (1968), pp. 181-197.

Edward H. Bowman and John B. Stewart, "A Model for Scale of Operations," *Journal of Marketing,* Vol. 20 (January 1956), pp. 242-247.

William J. Baumol and Philip Wolfe, "A Warehouse Location Problem," *Operations Research* (March-April 1958), pp. 252-263.

James L. Heskett, Nicholas A. Glaskowsky, Jr., and Robert M. Ivie, *Business Logistics,* 2nd ed. (New York: The Ronald Press Co., 1973), p. 429.

Arthur W. Napolitan, "Determining Optimum Distribution Points for Economical Warehousing and Transportation," *Managing the Materials Functions,* American Management Association, Report 35, 1959, pp. 76-82.

Ronald Ballou, "Dynamic Warehouse Location Analysis," *Journal of Marketing Research,* Vol. 5 (August 1968), pp. 271-276.

Harvey N. Shycon and Richard B. Maffei, "Simulation—Tool for Better Distribution," *Harvard Business Review,* Vol. 39 (November-December 1960), pp. 65-75.

Martin L. Gerson and Richard B. Maffei, "Technical Characteristics of Distribution Simulators," *Management Science,* Vol. 10 (October 1963), pp. 62-69.

these executives, such middle-level managers frequently accept marginally profitable business to build sales volume. To support higher sales volumes and the still larger sales they see ahead, growth-oriented managers often build heavy inventories and plow money freely into plant and equipment. They do not strive for quick payment on receivables, because they do not want to risk irritating customers and losing sales. Thus, the increased emphasis by top corporate executives on achieving adequate returns on investment and on assets as opposed to sales growth during periods of shortages, reduced demand, and high interest rates means that inventory management and control will assume even greater importance in the future than it has in the past.

The magnitude and significance of inventories vary for different members of the marketing channel, as shown in Table 4–4.

In general, inventory control theory deals with the determination of optimal procedures for procuring stocks of commodities to meet future demand. The decision concerning when and how much to order is a matter of balancing a number of conflicting cost functions. The objective is to minimize total inventory costs subject to demand and service constraints. The primary cost functions that must be balanced are those associated with holding inventory, ordering inventory, and risking stockouts. Figure 4–6 shows the tradeoffs among the relevant cost functions and their respective components. Because the fundamental purpose of any inventory control system is to tell a firm (1) how much to reorder, (2) when to reorder, and (3) how to control stockouts at the lowest cost, the discussion below focuses directly on these three key problem areas.

TABLE 4–4   Inventory value as a percent of sales and assets for six types of business firms

Company	% Sales [a]	% Current Assets [b]	% Total Assets [c]	Turnover Ratio [d]
Retailer	14%	45%	20%	4.3
Food Distributor	6	72	45	10.1
Electrical Components Mfg.	18	49	29	4.3
Construction Equipment Mfg.	30	56	39	3.1
Home Furnishing Mfg.	15	33	26	4.6
Metal Fabricator	11	44	16	6.3

[a] Sales valued at the cost of goods sold.
[b] Current assets are those items that can easily be converted to cash and include cash on hand, marketable securities, accounts receivable, and inventories.
[c] Includes current assets plus plant and equipment, investments, and intangible items (trademarks and franchises).
[d] Ratio of net sales to average inventory.

Source: David O. Nellemann, "Profit Improvement Through Inventory Management," *Proceedings of the Thirteenth Annual Conference of the National Council of Physical Distribution Management* (October 13-15, 1975), p. 442.

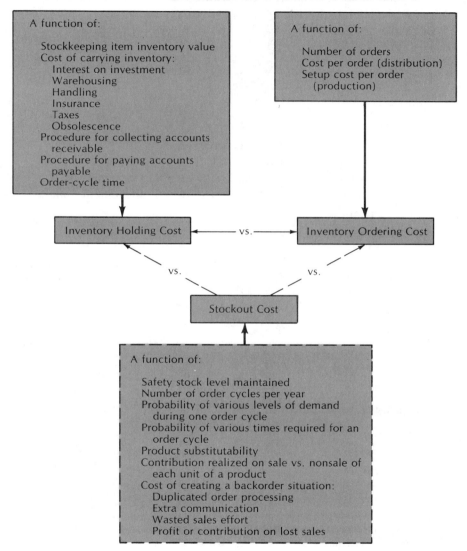

A function of:

    Stockkeeping item inventory value
    Cost of carrying inventory:
        Interest on investment
        Warehousing
        Handling
        Insurance
        Taxes
        Obsolescence
    Procedure for collecting accounts
      receivable
    Procedure for paying accounts
      payable
    Order-cycle time

A function of:

    Number of orders
    Cost per order (distribution)
    Setup cost per order
      (production)

Inventory Holding Cost ←— vs. —→ Inventory Ordering Cost

vs.   vs.

Stockout Cost

A function of:

    Safety stock level maintained
    Number of order cycles per year
    Probability of various levels of demand
      during one order cycle
    Probability of various times required for an
      order cycle
    Product substitutability
    Contribution realized on sale vs. nonsale of
      each unit of a product
    Cost of creating a backorder situation:
        Duplicated order processing
        Extra communication
        Wasted sales effort
        Profit or contribution on lost sales

Source: James L. Heskett, Nicholas A. Glaskowsky, Jr., and Robert M. Ivie, *Business Logistics*, 2nd ed. (New York: The Ronald Press, 1973), p. 313.

175

How Much To Reorder

The quantity to order can be arrived at using an "economic lot size" or "economic order quantity" (EOQ) formula. One of the oldest and most widely accepted economic lot size formulas is stated as follows:

$$Q^* = \sqrt{\frac{2DS}{IC}}$$

where

Q^* = the order quantity in units[49]
D = annual demand in units
S = the order processing cost (cost per order in dollars)
I = annual inventory carrying cost as a percentage of C
C = value of a unit held in inventory (unit price in dollars)

As an illustration, consider an inventory control problem having the following specifications for a particular item:[50]

D = 50 units per week, or $50 \times 52 = 2600$ units per year
I = 10 percent (e.g., this might be derived as shown in footnote[51])
S = \$10
C = \$5

[49] The optimum Q is found by the first derivative of $TC(Q)$, i.e., the total cost equation for an annual period, setting the derivative equal to zero, and solving for Q. Thus,

$$TC(Q) = \frac{D}{Q} S + IC\frac{Q}{2}$$

Taking the derivative and setting it equal to zero, we obtain

$$\frac{dTC(Q)}{dQ} = \frac{-DS}{Q^2} + \frac{IC}{2} = 0$$

Solving for Q gives

$$Q^* = \sqrt{\frac{2DS}{IC}}$$

[50] This example is drawn from Ballou, *op. cit.,* p. 292.

[51]
Interest on investment	4.0%
Obsolescence	3.0
Storage, transportation and handling	0.8
Insurance, taxes	0.2
Depreciation	2.0
	10.0%

The optimum order quantity according to the EOQ formula would be

$$Q^* = \sqrt{\frac{2(2600)(10)}{(0.10)(5)}}$$

$$= 322 \text{ units}$$

Although this classical EOQ formula is straightforward and used widely by many manufacturers and merchant wholesalers, it is likely to be of little help to retailers in carrying out their ordering policies. In fact, after devoting a considerable amount of time and resources to studying the possible application of the classical EOQ formula to a variety of inventory problems, IBM Corporation recommended that the formula should not be used by retailers. The reason for this recommendation was that some of the assumptions underlying the formula were not tenable in retailing situations. The questionable assumptions are listed below along with the reasons that they are not applicable to retailing.[52]

1. *Demand is known, constant, and continuous.* Demand in retail is usually not known. It is rarely constant and is seasonal for most types of merchandise. In fact, order quantities are used to build up or reduce inventory in anticipation of varying seasonal demand. Also, demand is not continuous, because of the existence of such merchandise as end-of-season (that is, merchandise carried only during one season, such as winter or summer jackets).

2. *The only costs significant to reordering decisions are inventory carrying and ordering costs.* Frequently, in managing the inventory of a whole department or classification, other factors, not considered by the classical EOQ equation, become very important. The problem of being out of stock is probably the most important single consideration. Furthermore, the costs for individual stock-keeping units (SKU's)[53] are not as significant for the total department as overall inventory and ordering strategies. The EOQ equation certainly does not include all the costs relevant to retail management objectives.

3. *The marginal cost of an additional order or an additional SKU is fixed, and the marginal cost of carrying an additional unit in inventory is fixed.* Marginal costs are synonymous with variable or incremental costs. In other words, marginal costs are the out-of-pocket costs of an additional order or an additional unit in inventory. These costs are different from fixed, indirect, or overhead costs incurred regardless of ordering strategy.

The most serious problem in applying the classical EOQ equation is the problem of determining costs. In practice the actual ordering costs are not

---

[52] *Retail IMPACT—Inventory Management Program and Control Techniques Application Description,* 6th ed. (White Plains, N.Y.: IBM Technical Publications Department, March 1970), pp. 71–72.

[53] An SKU is a *stockkeeping unit.* It is the lowest level of identification of merchandise. SKU's are usually defined by department, store, vendor, style, color, size, and location.

fixed as required by the classical EOQ equation. Inventory carrying cost can vary, for example, with management's changing estimates of the cost of capital. Both inventory carrying cost and ordering cost, when applied to retail situations, include elements of fixed and variable costs that would be very difficult to separate.

The determination of cost elements has been a problem since the classical EOQ equation was first developed, and many attempts have been made to solve the problem. Quite often the costs used are not representative of the real costs involved. Many of the cost elements in actual use are based on estimates involving management decisions, and are "correct" so long as there is full agreement on the decisions made. In many cases the cost estimates are reduced to subjective assessments because of the excessive, time-consuming studies involved.

4. *The whole order quantity arrives at one time.* Frequently, in retail shipments, such an assumption does not hold true. For many reasons, partial shipments do occur, and serious consideration should be given to them. Retail shipments, like many other activities in a department store, are complicated by the highs and lows of volume from month to month, week to week, and day to day. The order quantities should be sufficiently flexible to permit satisfactory adjustment to partial shipments when they occur.

5. *Transaction sizes are small relative to order quantity.* For two reasons, transaction sizes for some staple merchandise are actually large relative to their order quantity. The first reason is the batching of transactions (usually representing sales for one or two weeks) because of data-handling problems and the convenience that batch processing offers. The second reason involves the retail demand process as reflected in customer buying patterns for slow and medium sellers. Customers frequently buy multiple units for many types of merchandise such as shirts, underwear, women's hosiery, etc.

6. *There are no overriding restrictions in order-quantity size.* The classical EOQ formulation does not include any restrictions on the size of the order quantity. For a fixed review time system, the order quantity should be as large as the expected sales during a review time. The order quantity should be at least one pack size in order to be acceptable to the vendor. In many cases, the order quantity cannot be greater than a specified maximum, such as three months' supply or a year's supply. The EOQ equation does not include any of these constraints, and, therefore, it is frequently impractical to apply the results derived from the formula directly.

Consequently, a different order quantity technique has been developed which offers a better solution for retail inventory problems.[54] This approach, called the modified EOQ, attempts to remove the largest stumbling block—the problem of

[54] *Ibid.*, p. 73.

determining costs. The classical approach explained above attempts to identify and quantify all the "true" costs related to inventory carrying and reordering. The modified approach, however, treats the costs in the EOQ formula as control "knobs." These control knobs are made available to management and are to be used primarily for selecting management policies, such as the amount of investment in total inventory and overall ordering workload. In other words, the classical "costs," transposed now to modern control "knobs," should be viewed merely as one of the policy variables in the inventory management system. Turning the control "knobs" to the "left" or "right" makes it possible to vary the balance between inventory investment, on the one hand, and the number of orders, on the other, thus allowing management to examine many alternate strategies.[55] This approach also implies that costs should not be considered fixed and definite. Management can manipulate the modified EOQ equation in order to get the results that will match goals. Furthermore, management can now view inventories as a total investment, not as an investment in an individual inventory unit.

The derivation of the modified EOQ begins by spelling out the component parts of the classical EOQ formula, as follows:

$$\text{Economic order quantity in units} = \sqrt{\frac{2 \times (\text{cost per order in dollars}) \times \text{Annual sales in units}}{\text{Inventory carrying rate per year in percent} \times \text{Unit price in dollars}}}$$

This equation can be further broken down into:

$$\sqrt{\frac{2 \times (\text{Cost per unit in dollars})}{\text{Inventory carrying rate per year in percent}}} \times \sqrt{\frac{\text{Annual sales in units}}{\text{Unit price in dollars}}}$$

Now, let the expression under the first square root equal K, and rewrite the EOQ formula somewhat differently to obtain the modified EOQ equation:

$$\text{Modified economic order quantity in units} = K \sqrt{\frac{\text{Annual sales in units}}{\text{Unit price in dollars}}}$$

The K factor is the management control "knob" referred to above. Varying the K factor changes the order quantity and, consequently, the number of orders in a year.[56]

---

[55] *Ibid.*

[56] *Ibid.* Two of the many excellent sources that describe EOQ formulae for almost any application are Fred Hanssman, *Operations Research and Inventory Control* (New York: John Wiley & Sons, 1962); and John F. Magee, *Production Planning and Inventory Control* (New York: McGraw-Hill Book Co., 1958).

When to Reorder[57]

In order to determine when to reorder, it is first necessary to know the projected demand or *sales forecast* (derived from a standard forecasting technique) as well as the *delivery lead time* and the *length of the review period*. *Delivery lead time* is usually expressed as the number of days to receive stock in available inventory after the inventory replenishment signal has been given. The main components of lead time are order processing time, order picking and handling time, transit time, and unloading and stocking time. On the other hand, the *length of the review period* is usually expressed as the number of days between forecasts, or the number of days between possible reorder decisions. A good approximation of the length of the review period can sometimes be obtained from the basic EOQ model. If the economic order quantity is Q^*, then the number of orders that should be placed in a year's time is given by dividing projected demand for the year by Q^*. Dividing the number of orders that should be placed in a year into the number of weeks or days in a year will tell how frequently the stock level should be reviewed. Thus, using the data from the previous EOQ example, and letting N^* stand for the optimum order interval, we estimate that the stock level should be reviewed every 6.45 weeks:

$$N^* = \frac{D}{Q^*} = \frac{2600}{322} = 8.07 \text{ orders per year}$$

$$\frac{52 \text{ weeks}}{8.07 \text{ orders per year}} = 6.45 \text{ weeks}$$

In retailing, the review period is often very short (e.g., a week), not because of economic order quantity considerations but rather because sales of many items sold at retail are highly seasonal and fluctuate continuously over time, thus necessitating frequent review. In wholesaling and manufacturing, the length of the review period is typically longer and frequently coincides more closely with estimates derived from EOQ considerations, although the period's length varies widely, depending on the characteristics of the product category under concern.

To compute a reorder point, the projected demand of a product during the review period is added to the projected demand for the product during the delivery lead time. The result is then compared to the quantity of the product available in inventory. The reorder point is reached when the overall projected demand (sales forecast) is greater than the amount available in inventory. For example, assume that a retailer has a review period of seven days, a lead time of ten days, and an available inventory of 110 units.[58] Assume, also, that the sales forecast for the next

---

[57] The following discussion draws heavily from two sources: Edward W. Smykay and Allan D. Dale, "Inventory Control: What Price Service? Part 1," *Handling and Shipping* (July 1966), pp. 48–51; and *Retail IMPACT—Inventory Management Program and Control Techniques Application Description,* 6th ed. (White Plains, N.Y.: IBM Technical Publications Department, March 1970).

[58] This example is drawn from Smykay and Dale, *op. cit.,* pp. 49–50.

180

17 days is 102 units. The projected average daily sales for the 17-day period is, therefore, 6 units (102/17). Because the next review period is seven days away, it can be estimated that 42 units will be sold in that time, leaving 68 units (110 – 42) in available inventory. If the retailer waits until the next review period to reorder, the order will arrive when available inventory is down to 8 units {68 (units in stock at the end of the next review period) *less* [6 (average daily sales forecast) *times* 10 (lead time)]}.

Suppose, however, that the forecast showed that expected sales during the next 17 days were 119 units. If the retailer waited until the next review point to place an inventory replenishment order, he would be out of stock the day before the new stock arrives. Selling seven units a day (119/17), he would need 49 units to cover the period until the next review point. This would leave him with only 61 units (110–49) to cover the ten-day lead time during which he will need 70 units in stock.

Thus, the decision rules for deciding whether to reorder an item held in inventory are the following:

1. If net on hand (available inventory) is greater than the sales forecast, take no action.

2. If net on hand (available inventory) is less than the sales forecast, place reorder.[59]

Forecasting

In determining how much to reorder and when to reorder, the sales forecast is the most critical variable affecting the final outcome. In fact, the short-term sales forecast is the heart of any system designed to solve these problems. For any channel member, the type of forecasting method to be used depends upon the type of demand pattern his customers exhibit.

In general, customer demand patterns can be categorized as (a) regular and highly predictable, (b) irregular but mathematically consistent, and (c) irregular and unpredictable.[60] Regular and highly predictable demand does not require a sophisticated sales forecast system. Type (b) demand (irregular but mathematically consistent) requires statistical forecasting, whereas type (c) demand requires the greatest degree of sophistication in designing an inventory control system.

For most types of customer demand patterns, a short-term computer forecast is the most efficient and most consistent way of obtaining future sales projections. It assumes that the historical sales patterns of a product can be used to predict its future sales, and therefore relies upon such historical data-based forecasting methods as moving averages, weighted moving averages, regression, and exponential smoothing.

[59] *Ibid.*
[60] *Ibid.*, p. 48.

Exponential smoothing, the most popular of these techniques, is explained in Appendix 4A. Although the application of such historical data-based techniques is less reliable for type (c) demand patterns, this problem can be alleviated somewhat by reducing the forecasting interval considerably—say, to one week—which enhances the reliability of the date, and, hence, improves prediction.

Lack of a sales forecast, inaccurate sales forecasting, and/or lack of sales forecast information sharing between retailers, wholesalers, and manufacturers can create inventory problems throughout the marketing channel. First, a sudden increase in sales volume at the retail level creates a ripple effect back through the channel because of time lags of order-processing and flows of goods. For example, as shown in Fig. 4–7, the effect of a sudden 10 percent increase in retail sales causes a 16 percent increase in manufacturer warehouse orders from distributors almost three months after the retail increase takes place. When distributors' orders are placed with manufacturers, they reduce factory inventories by 13 percent. Unfilled orders to replace depleted inventories begin to build up and production does not peak until almost four months after the retail sales increase.

Second, unpredicted sales increases result in stockouts. Frequent stockouts

FIGURE 4–7

Effect of a Sudden 10% Increase in Retail Sales on Inventories and Factory Output

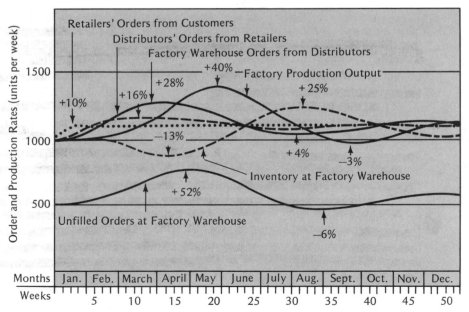

Source: Jay W. Forrester, "Industrial Dynamics: A Major Breakthrough for Decision Makers," *Harvard Business Review* (July–August 1958), p. 43. Copyright © 1958 by the President and Fellows of Harvard College; all rights reserved.

may result in substantial lost sales and the generation of customer ill will, as demonstrated by the following quote:

> Surveys made by *Progressive Grocer* magazine showed large variations among supermarket product lines in the percentage of customers who will buy elsewhere if a product is out of stock and in the gross margin loss if a sale is loss. The product of these two factors gives the expected percentage of gross margin loss per unit out of stock. It ranges over a factor of 10—from 1.9% for canned peaches and peanut butter to 17% for deodorants. Many companies structure their reorder policies to keep all products on the shelf for the same percentage of time; yet obviously such policies make little sense if the profit consequences of stockouts vary so widely from one product line to another.
>
> It is important to keep in mind that loss of a sale entails loss of the entire gross margin on the product, not merely the nominal operating profit, since there is rarely an appreciable saving in overhead when a sales loss occurs. In many cases, better distribution management can increase the expected fill rate and sales level by several percentage points with little or no increase in distribution costs.[61]

Controlling Stockouts

Up to this point in the discussion of inventory control techniques, attention has been focused on the maintenance of "base stocks." If sales forecasting were perfectly accurate, carrying only base stock in inventory would always provide "perfect" inventories; the problem of stockouts would never occur. If, however, it is known in advance that each forecast will have some error in it (as it almost surely will), then action must be taken to ensure that this error does not seriously weaken customer service.

Ideally, a firm would never have a stockout, but maintaining a 100 percent service level is usually prohibitively costly. In order to minimize stockouts at a reasonable cost to the firm, it is necessary to predict the likely forecasting error. The term used for this prediction is the *standard error of the estimate* (S.E.). The standard error is employed to determine how much extra "safety" stock is needed to cushion against customer demand larger than the sales forecast. Figure 4–8 depicts the effect of forecast errors and the insurance, or cushioning, that safety stocks provide.

If it is assumed that sales forecast errors are random and normally distributed, it is possible to set average stockouts at any level desired.[62] If forecast errors are, in fact, random and normally distributed, then adding one S.E. to the average inventory will reduce stockouts from 50 to 16 percent, giving an in-stock frequency of 84 percent. However, additional safety stocks yield diminishing returns in improved customer service levels. For example, adding two S.E. of safety stock to average inventory reduces average stockouts to 2.3 percent, while the third S.E. reduces

---

[61] David P. Herron, "Managing Physical Distribution for Profit," *op. cit.*, pp. 123–124.
[62] The following discussion draws heavily on Edward W. Smykay and Allan D. Dale, "Inventory Control: What Price Service? Part 2," *Handling and Shipping* (August 1966), pp. 60–63.

FIGURE 4–8

Inventory Level with Sales Forecast Errors

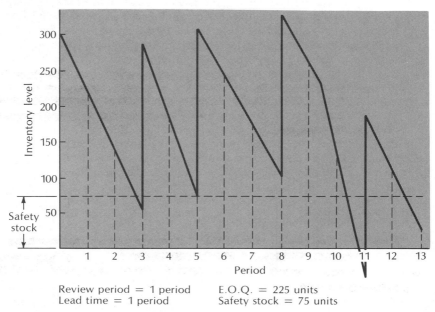

Review period = 1 period   E.O.Q. = 225 units
Lead time = 1 period   Safety stock = 75 units

Source: Edward W. Smykay and Allan D. Dale, "Inventory Control: What Price Service? Part 1," *Handling and Shipping* (July 1966), p. 51.

stockouts to 0.3 percent. Furthermore, adding one S.E. increases inventory in-stock frequency by 34 percent, while the second S.E. brings 11 percent improvement. By adding a third S.E., a less than 2 percent improvement is achieved. Table 4–5 illustrates many of these trade-offs by showing how a hypothetical problem concerning the control of stockouts is solved.

It is important to note that, for inventory control purposes, safety stocks should not be counted with base stocks. When reorder points are computed, for example, the required safety stocks should be subtracted from available inventory before it is compared to the forecast, because safety stocks are only insurance against forecast errors. If they are counted as available inventory, the result is a low forecast that will, in turn, lead to a stockout.

To compute average inventory for decision-making purposes, simply divide base stock by two, and then add safety stocks. This is done because safety stocks are assumed to be the same at the beginning and end of a cycle.

As indicated earlier, every channel member must determine, through PDS research, the customer service level best suited to it by balancing the cost of holding additional safety stock versus the costs of stockouts. The example and graph in Fig. 4–9 show one method of finding the service level that will minimize costs, if different customers' reactions to a stockout have already been determined.

TABLE 4–5   Hypothetical problem dealing with the control of stockouts

Order Cycle	Forecast (stock)	Actual	(Actual-Fcst)^2
1	311	280	961
2	273	260	169
3	191	195	16
4	225	180	2,025
5	300	260	1,600
6	411	385	676
7	306	400	8,836
8	220	280	3,600
	2237	2240	17,883

$$\text{S.E.} = \sqrt{\frac{17,883}{8}} = 47.3$$

$$\text{Average inventory} \frac{2237}{8} = 279.6\ ^a$$

^{a} If this firm were willing to endure stockouts for about 50 percent of its order cycles, it could hold an average inventory of 279.6 units. To increase customer service levels to 84 percent, average inventory would have to be increased to 326.9 units (279.6 + 47.3). To increase customer service levels to 97.7 or 99.7 percent would take an increase in average inventory to 374.2 units and 421.5 units. In this example, a 17 percent increase in average inventory brought a 34 percent increase in customer service levels. The second and third 17 percent increments brought only 14 and 2 percent increases in customer service levels.

Source: Edward W. Smykay and Allan D. Dale, "Inventory Control: What Price Service? Part 2," *Handling and Shipping* (August 1966), p. 60.

In summary, the sequence of events that should be employed by a channel member in instituting an inventory control system include the following twelve steps, which are also shown in flow chart form in Fig. 4–10.

1. Establish customer service level.
2. Establish lead and review times.
3. Gather demand history.
4. Test alternatives to determine best forecasting model.
5. Gather pertinent inventory cost information.
6. Compute EOQ.
7. Forecast demand over review period plus lead time.
8. Forecast safety stock requirement.
9. Deduct required safety stock from on-hand inventory.
10. If net on-hand inventory is greater than forecast, take no action and go to next item.
11. If net on-hand inventory is less than forecast, place reorder.
12. If net on-hand inventory is negative, expedite reorder.[63]

[63] Adapted from Smykay and Dale, "Inventory Control: . . . Part 2," *op. cit.,* p. 62.

FIGURE 4-9

Determination of Minimum-cost Service Levels

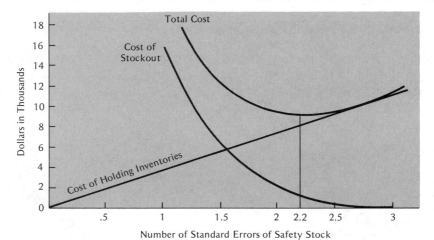

Number of Standard Errors of Safety Stock

In the above illustration the lowest point on total cost curve will show the number of standard errors of safety stock that will minimize costs. Here, 2.2 S.E., or $8800 of safety stock yield the lowest total cost. This quantity will give a customer service level of 98.6% and cost $9200 a year. Carrying any other quantity of safety stock would increase total costs.

Example:
Assume: average number of orders per year is 1000.
    Average order size = $2000
    Profit margin = 15%
    Expected return on investment = 10%/yr.
    Average sales per customer = $4000/yr.
    Order cycle = 1 month
    Inventory holding cost = 20% of inventory value

Customer reaction to stock out:
1. Back order
    Results in a one-month delay in receipt of $2000. Cost of stockout is given by lost earnings on $2000 for 1/12 of one year. Cost of stockout = $2000 x 0.10 x 1/12 = $16.67

2. Cancel order
    Results in loss of profit on $2000 in sales.
    Cost = $2000 x 0.15 = $300

3. Switch to new vendor
    Results in loss of all future profits. Cost is computed by discounting all future profits by 10%.
    $Cost = \dfrac{\$4000 \times 0.15}{0.10} = \$6000$

Assume that 90% of customers will back order, 9% will cancel, and 1% will switch suppliers.

The average cost of a stockout is
    16.67 x 0.90 = $15.00
    300.00 x 0.09 = 27.00
    6000.00 x 0.01 = 60.00
    Average cost $102.00

Assume that one standard error of safety stock is $20,000 of inventory. At a holding cost of 20%, each S.E. costs $4000 per year.

Therefore, this company can have 39.2 stockouts per year ($4000 ÷ $102) given one S.E. of safety stock.

Source: Edward W. Smykay and Allan D. Dale, "Inventory Control: What Price Service? Part 2," Handling and Shipping (August 1966), p. 62.

FIGURE 4-10
A Model of an Inventory Control System

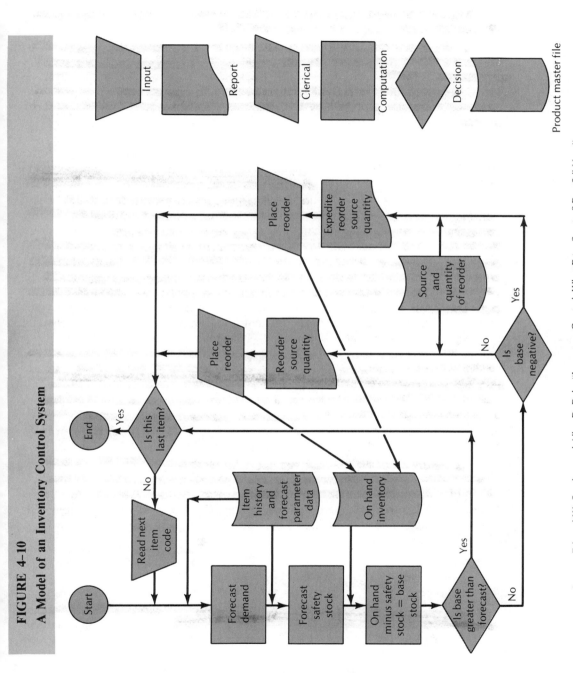

Source: Edward W. Smykay and Allan D. Dale, "Inventory Control: What Price Service? Part 2," *Handling and Shipping* (August 1966), p. 63

Although not discussed in detail here, it should be noted that order processing is as critical to achievement of customer service.

Order processing is as critical to achievement of customer service standards as carrying adequate inventory at appropriate locations and selection of the right transportation mode. Delays in order processing can severely hamper customer service. Many manufacturers, wholesalers, and other suppliers resort to the use of toll-free numbers and electronic data processing to speed the receipt and processing of orders.[64]

TRANSPORTATION DECISIONS

Inadequate transportation service and uncertain transit times can cause a company to hold several days' more inventory than PD plans call for. These problems, in turn, add to the cost of carrying inventory and reduce the number of times that capital in inventory can be turned over during the year, not to mention the undesirable effects they have in terms of poor customer service and missed product promotions. Consequently, the selection of appropriate transportation modes and the maintenance of a concerted effort by PD management to ensure efficient and reliable transportation are both prerequisites to accomplishing distribution objectives. Therefore, in this section, attention is given to describing various transportation modes and the functions that they can perform for various channel members in facilitating the movement of products.

In the United States, the bulk of freight movement is handled by five basic modes of transportation—rail, truck, waterways, air, and pipeline—and is facilitated by various transportation agencies—freight forwarders, parcel post, air express, and shippers' associations. Economical arrangements are often created through the interaction of these carriers and agencies with the result being a coordinated system of transportation, as shown in Fig. 4–11. The various legal forms of transport are discussed in more detail in Appendix 4B.

In making transportation mode selection decisions, distribution managers in the marketing channel consider the speed, availability, dependability, capability, and frequency of the five basic transportation modes available to them. The relative operating characteristics of rail, highway, water, pipeline, and air are examined in Table 4–6. These modes are ranked from one (top ranking) to five (lowest ranking) for each operating characteristic.

Transportation Modes

Market shares of the five basic transport modes have shifted dramatically over time. The railroad continues to be the dominant mode, even though its share in total ton-mileage has dropped from 54 percent in 1947 to 35.9 percent in 1979.[65]

---

[64] For a detailed example see Ballou, *op. cit.,* pp. 350–352.
[65] Transportation Association of America, *Transportation Facts and Trends,* 15th ed., July 1979.

FIGURE 4–11

Transportation System for a Business Logistics System

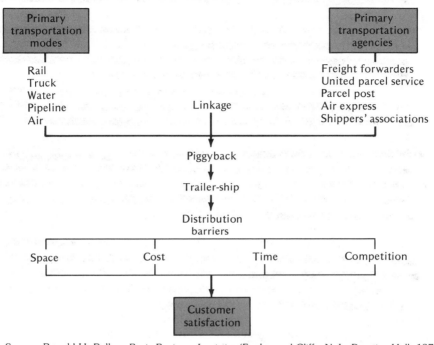

Primary transportation modes

Rail
Truck
Water
Pipeline
Air

Primary transportation agencies

Freight forwarders
United parcel service
Parcel post
Air express
Shippers' associations

Linkage

Piggyback

Trailer-ship

Distribution barriers

Space   Cost   Time   Competition

Customer satisfaction

Source: Ronald H. Ballou, *Basic Business Logistics* (Englewood Cliffs, N.J.: Prentice-Hall, 1978), p. 116. Adapted from William Lazer, "The Distribution Mix—A Systems Approach," in Eugene J. Kelley and William Lazer (eds.), *Managerial Marketing: Perspectives and Viewpoints,* 3rd ed. (Homewood, Ill.: Richard D. Irwin, 1967), p. 529.

TABLE 4–6   Relative operating characteristics—five basic transportation modes

Operating Characteristic	Transportation Mode				
	Rail	Highway	Water	Pipeline	Air
Speed	3	2	4	5	1
Availability	2	1	4	5	3
Dependability	3	2	4	1	5
Capability	2	3	1	5	4
Frequency	4	2	5	1	3

Source: Donald J. Bowersox, *Logistical Management,* 2nd ed. (New York: Macmillan Publishing Co., 1978), p. 120.

Despite the implications of this decline, the railroad is still considered the major long-haul mover of bulk commodities, such as coal and grain. Furthermore, it offers important services to shippers, such as expedited handling to guarantee arrival within a certain number of hours, stop-off privileges, pickup and delivery, and diversion and reconsignment, which enhance its attractiveness as a mover of a large number of products. Although the railroads have experienced significant problems in generating an adequate return on investment, projections made in 1977 by the Department of Transportation estimate that by 1990 the railroad industry will increase its market share in total ton-mileage to 42 percent.[66]

On the other hand, *motor carriers* have some inherent advantages over the railroad, including door-to-door service as well as frequency and availability of service. Trucking is a relatively short-range transportation service which, because of highway safety restrictions on the dimensions of shipments and their weight, is less capable than rail of handling all types of freight. For less-than-truckload (LTL) shipments, however, trucking generally offers more rapid and dependable service than the railroad. In fact, motor carriers handle approximately 90 percent of the country's "small" (less than 10,000 pounds) shipments, which, in turn, account for the major portion of their total business. Partly as a result of their willingness to handle small shipment traffic, motor carriers' share in total ton-mileage has increased from 5.2 percent in 1947 to 24.5 percent in 1979.[67] Nevertheless, due to the current and anticipated high cost of diesel fuel, a drop to 16.5 percent market share by 1995 has been forecasted by the research firm of Frost and Sullivan.[68]

Air transportation is being considered by increasing numbers of shippers for regular service, despite its high rate charges. Over the past two decades, the air transport industry has developed and defined a basic operating system that has been able to increase its total cargo movement 2775 percent. Despite this increase, the airlines moved only 0.20 percent of the total freight in 1979, which is still a very small percentage when compared to other modes of transportation.[69] Since fuel costs now constitute over 30 percent of operating expenses, it is expected that air freight will not make substantial cuts into the trucking industry's market share, as was once predicted. The inherent advantage of air transportation is its unmatched origin-destination speed. However, this speed is not directly comparable with other modes of transportation, because it does not include pickup and delivery times or ground handling time. Thus, a well-managed and coordinated truck-rail operation often can match the schedules of the air transport system.

Historically, *water* transportation was the earliest domestic means for moving cargo in large volumes. It has played a vital role in the economic history of the United States. Although water transportation is comparatively slow, less dependable than other modes, and limited to bulk cargo service along waterways systems,

---

[66] *National Transportation Trends and Choices to the Year 2000,* U.S. Department of Transportation (January 1977), p. 69.

[67] Transportation Association of America, *op. cit.*

[68] *Traffic World* (July 25, 1977), p. 17.

[69] Transportation Association of America, *op. cit.*

it has competitively lower cost. Market share has declined, however, from 31.3 percent of total freight moved in 1947 to 15.7 percent in 1979.[70] This decline can be ascribed to a number of problems that have faced the water carriers in the form of restrictions on automation on the waterfront, escalating fuel prices, wage increases, and selective rate cutting by competing modes of transportation.

Finally, pipeline carriers have significantly increased their share of total ton-miles from 9.5 percent in 1947 to 23.6 percent in 1979.[71] Further, the Department of Transportation estimates that this upward trend will continue through 1990.[72] The increase in the number and capacity of the pipelines is due mainly to the increasing need for economic volume movement systems for fluids and solids in hydraulic suspension. Pipeline transportation provides a very limited range of services and capability because of the physical limitations on the products that can be moved by the pipelines. However, transportation by pipeline is the most dependable service of all transportation modes and has lower rates of loss and damage to the product.

PHYSICAL DISTRIBUTION SYSTEM DESIGN AND MANAGEMENT

The PD System design is a complex task involving the integration of all system components. One of the most popular tools for PD systems design and management is *simulation*. Via simulation, a manager can construct mathematical models of each of the major PD activity areas and their interrelations. Then, by manipulating these models, he can draw conclusions as to appropriate policies and strategies.[73] Simulation permits distribution management to change one or two variables and know that the resulting changes in the system's operation as a whole are due to that manipulation alone. Great savings can be achieved from the use of simulation, because alterations can be made and tested without disturbing the actual system. Moreover, with the speed of computers, changes whose impact might require years to determine can be assessed very quickly.[74]

One of the best-known simulations of a physical distribution system was developed for the H. J. Heinz Company[75] and was later applied to the distribution problems of the Nestlé Company. The simulation provided answers to basic warehouse location questions (e.g., number, location, allocation of demand to

[70] Transportation Association of America, *op. cit.*

[71] Transportation Association of America, *op. cit.*

[72] U.S. Department of Transportation, *op. cit.*

[73] Friedman, *op. cit.*, p. 25. See also James C. Johnson, "An Analysis of the 'Small Shipments' Problem with Particular Attention to its Ramifications on a Firm's Logistical System," *ICC Practitioners Journal,* Vol. 44 (July–August 1972), pp. 646–664.

[74] John Dearden, *Computers in Business Management* (Homewood, Ill.: Richard D. Irwin, 1966), p. 234. For a discussion of the ways of constructing simulation models, see James R. Emshoff and Roger L. Sisson, *Design and Use of Computer Simulation* (New York: Macmillan Publishing Co., 1970).

[75] Harvey N. Shycon and Richard B. Maffei, "Simulation—Tool for Better Distribution," *Harvard Business Review,* Vol. 39 (November–December 1960), pp. 65–75; and Edward W. Smykay, "Anatomy of a Ready-Made PD Simulation Program," *Handling and Shipping* (February 1968), pp. 62–64, (April 1968), pp. 76–77; and (July 1968), pp. 55–57.

warehouses, etc.) by manipulating cost data associated with a variety of physical distribution system variables. The case study of physical distribution system design and management in Exhibit 4–1 best illustrates the steps and complexities involved.

The Problem of "Maldistribution"

Despite the availability of sophisticated techniques such as simulation, many channel members are not effective in managing the physical possession flow. In fact, research shows that companies with comparatively high distribution costs frequently provide *poorer* service than some of their competitors who have lower distribution costs, even though they are supplying essentially the same products to identical markets.[76] This problem—termed "maldistribution"—occurs repeatedly in companies of varying sizes across a wide variety of industries and is estimated to cost, in the aggregate, as much as $10 billion annually.[77]

Exhibit 4–2 lists four signs of maldistribution. If any of these signs appears, a channel member should undertake a careful study of his PD system.

One of the major reasons for the significance of this problem seems to be a lack of top management support and effort in integrating the different areas required for effective PD systems management.[78] Another major reason is the seemingly overabundance of "technique"—or "equipment"—oriented approaches to solving distribution problems as opposed to a truly integrated "systems management" approach. Although specific problems—such as inaccurate sales forecasts, losses from inventory stockouts, inadequate inventory information, and the like—can be "remedied" through the use of sophisticated models, the changes required to implement the remedies often create new unexpected problems that are not accounted for by the models and which generally outweigh any improvements achieved. Thus, in practice, the more popular distribution techniques should be viewed only as aids in solving the complex problems frequently encountered.

Furthermore, management is well advised to adopt periodic audits of PD functions, activities and strategy. The audit may incorporate questions such as the following:[79]

1. What levels of service (a) do our customers expect? (b) do our competitors provide?

2. How do competitors achieve the service levels that we think they achieve?

3. Through how many outlets should we distribute our products? of what type? where?

[76] Oresman and Scudder, *op. cit.*, p. 63.

[77] *Ibid.*

[78] See Robert P. Neuschel, "Corporate Level PD: Creative or Reactive," *Distribution Worldwide* (December 1971), pp. 21–25.

[79] Direct quote from James L. Heskett, "Logistics Essential to Strategy," *Harvard Business Review* (November–December 1977), pp. 90–94.

A large manufacturer of consumer goods was faced with escalating inventories and declining customer service. Over a three-year period, sales had leveled after a decade of explosive growth, yet inventories had continued to climb an additional 30 percent. Customer service had deteriorated over this same period from the traditional 99 percent to less than 96 percent; customer complaints were at an all-time high; and salesmen's morale was seriously affected by the service problem.

Company management had previously made several piecemeal attempts to solve this problem. A linear programming computer model had been developed which had indicated that two more warehouses were needed, an on-line inventory control system had been designed and installed, and various organization changes had been made to focus attention on service and inventories. None of these efforts perceptibly slowed the increase in inventories or decline in customer service. As a result, top management decided that a more innovative approach was required.

The first step taken was to frame the basic question, "How much inventory should we have to provide a competitive level of service, and how can we assure that we achieve that level of service?" With this definition of the scope of the undertaking, a project team was formed consisting of four members: the manager responsible for customer service and warehousing, a line manufacturing manager responsible for production scheduling, a manufacturing systems specialist, and the manager of production and inventory control. This task force was assigned full time to the project, assisted by outside consultants, and made responsible to a steering committee of top management.

The newly organized task force spent its first three months collecting and analyzing operating data and interviewing other company managers to accurately define the problem. Over the three-month data collection and analysis phase, a large number of projects were carried out. In most cases, they were performed by team members themselves, and the tendency to write a computer program to do the work was actively resisted. Most of the work was done with calculators and slide rules.

The following projects are representative of those carried out in the data collection and analysis phase of the project:

A statistical analysis of warehouse shipments by line item measured warehouse variability of demand. The results of this analysis were in turn used to calculate the theoretical inventories required to give 99 percent service. This calculation showed that warehouse inventories were 50 percent higher than required in total, but significantly too low on a handful of products.

A detailed analysis of customer service was based on a sample of invoices and backorders. Although a service problem clearly recognized, the company had no way of measuring the extent of the problem quantitatively. The results of this analysis showed that over a three-year period, service had declined from 99 percent to less than 96 percent. In dollar terms, backorders had risen from an average of $10,000 to more than $500,000.

Manufacturing inventory replenishment was based on the policy of maintaining safety stocks of at least two months' sales. A comparison of actual stock levels with forecasts showed a variance of from one-half to six months instead of the expected two months. This discrepancy prompted further examination which revealed that there were at least two different forecasts for each item—one prepared by the sales and marketing department and another prepared by manufacturing. An analysis of manufacturing schedules showed that in the company's peak summer months only 20 percent of orders were made on time and that the principal component of lead times was waiting time rather than working time.

At the conclusion of the data collection and analysis phase, a number of major problems were identified:

Inconsistent and inaccurate sales forecasts. In addition to the sales and manufacturing forecasts, a third distribution forecast was also uncovered.

Inappropriate inventory levels. The two-month safety stocks policy led to insufficient protection on some items and excesses on others.

Demand on the field warehouses was much more regular and predictable than demand on the plant after the warehouses had translated customer demand into reorders.

The replenishment policy concentrated on freight costs and ignored inventory and storage costs, and, as result, overall costs were increased $100,000 annually.

Capacity was severely overloaded during peak months. The scheduling system did not load by manufacturing departments, and lead times were excessive because the scheduling system allowed for large queues of work before each operation.

Of particular significance in this step was the team's concentration on analysis rather than on techniques. The effort was concentrated on causes rather than on determining if various proposed approaches were desirable. Further, since the managers got into the details themselves, they were forced to discard preconceived notions and thus became aware of preconceptions on the part of others, including top management. Finally, as they all worked together in the same room on various points of the same problem, they developed a strong feeling for the interrelationships among their various functions.

Once the key problem areas had been sharply defined, the specialists on and supporting the team could go to work designing solutions. To correct the problem of multiple inaccurate forecasts, the marketing team member and an operations research specialist developed a sales forecasting system. This system used computerized linear regression techniques to develop a statistical sales forecast, which was then modified by the responsible product manager. The modified forecast was divided by the computer into forecasts for each warehouse to be used in the distribution system and then reassembled by plant to be used in the manufacturing inventory control system.

The manufacturing and inventory control members of the team developed a statistical safety stock system based on the forecast to cover each item in each warehouse. A similar safety stock was calculated for the central warehouses and used in overall inventory control to take advantage of the fact that the variability of demand at the plants would be less than the sum of variability at the warehouses. The problem of lumpy demands from the warehouses was approached by reducing lot sizes of shipments to conform more closely to actual sales demand and by scheduling regular shipments so that freight costs would not increase.

To test the validity of these system design changes, a computer simulation model was constructed to prove that the various elements were truly integrated and that the predicted inventory and service levels were achievable. It was only at this fairly advanced step that emphasis changed to techniques and systems design. Operations research and inventory control techniques were used but only as methods for treating clearly identified problems, not as overall solutions.

The work of the task force did not stop with the development of the solution to the distribution inventory and service problem. Previous analysis had shown that the manufacturing systems could not support even the smoothed demand from the warehouses at certain periods of the year. A new manufacturing and planning system was designed to shorten lead times and to plan capacity on an overall basis so that inventory could be built during slack periods in anticipation of peak demand.

It is obviously essential that manufacturing and distribution work from the same information, but in this step the concept of integrated operations was carried further to raise the question of whether the manufacturing operations could provide the product after they had the proper information. If this last step had not been considered and a new capacity planning and scheduling system designed, much of the previous work would have been for naught.

The changes recommended by the task force were implemented over a period of about one year. The work during the implementation included programming and testing of new computer systems, training of users, and parallel testing of new systems along with old. The impact of the changes was dramatic. Inventories were reduced by 15 percent or almost $8 million. Back orders were reduced from a peak of $500,000 to a more normal level of $10,000 to $20,000. Customer complaints dropped substantially, and operating costs were reduced by more than $300,000 per year, excluding the savings from reduced inventories and improved service.

Source: Stephen B. Oresman and Charles D. Scudder, "A Remedy for Maldistribution," *Business Horizons*, Vol. 19 (June 1974), pp. 66 and 69.

EXHIBIT 4-2

Signs of Maldistribution

① *INVENTORIES THAT TURN SLOWLY.* Distribution inventories should turn between six and twelve times per year in most companies except in unusual product situations; distribution inventories that turn less than six times per year are a frequent sign of control problems.

② *POOR CUSTOMER SERVICE.* Inventory investment equal to about two months of sales should provide about 99 percent service. Investment of about half this amount should provide about 90 percent service. Failure to achieve these levels of results can mean that the inventory is in the wrong products, the wrong location, or both.

③ *INTERWAREHOUSE SHIPMENTS.* Because stock transfers require double handling, distribution managers rarely transship except in emergencies. A significant amount of interwarehouse transfers is a sign of a system in continual trouble.

④ *PREMIUM FREIGHT CHARGES.* A distribution system that relies on premium freight is in trouble for the same reasons. Cost savings are usually significant when the problem is corrected.

Source: Stephen B. Oresman and Charles D. Scudder, "A Remedy for Maldistribution," *Business Horizons*, Vol. 19 (June 1974), p. 72.

4. Are our plants located and focused properly to support corporate strategy?

5. Where is our company on the logistics life cycle for all or a portion of its business?

6. Have we taken advantage of the full potential for postponement and speculation, standardization, consolidation, and differentiation in our logistics programs?

7. To what extent have we assured ourselves that our strategy meets desired levels of costs and services where it counts most, to the end-user?

8. To what extent have we employed "channel vision" in determining who should do what, when, where, and how in our channels of distribution? Have we taken steps to ensure that all parties carry out their functions as planned?

9. What implications do technological trends have for our company?

10. What implications do regulatory trends have for us?

11. Does our logistics strategy support our corporate strategy? To what extent should our strategy be logistics-oriented?

SUMMARY AND CONCLUSIONS

Physical distribution management is a critical factor in the effective and efficient marketing of all products. However, the costs of activities associated with the flow of physical possession are surprisingly high—so high, in fact, that efforts must be expended to reduce them if distributive firms are to reach their profit goals, particularly during economic periods when sales are growing at very slow rates. Underlying effective and efficient physical distribution management is the physical distribution (PD) concept. This concept takes a cost-service orientation that is aimed at minimizing the costs of distribution at a given level of customer service. The tenets in the concept can be achieved only through a coordinated system-wide physical distribution network.

Developing a PD system should begin with a determination of customer service standards. Arriving at an appropriate customer service standard may involve applying a physical distribution service (PDS) decision model which concentrates on the formulation of PDS packages that are congruent with customers' perceived needs for PD services. Once an optimal PDS package is decided upon, management can then undertake a selection of the warehousing, inventory, and transportation policies that will assure the proper implementation of the desired customer service standards.

The two basic categories of warehouses available to channel members are private facilities, which are either owned or leased by the firm, and public facilities, in which space is rented by the firm. The choice between the two often involves tradeoffs between managerial control on the one hand and capital investment on the other. Use of public warehouses appears to be growing rapidly, because the public warehousing industry is becoming more sophisticated in the scope and performance of a wide variety of distributive services. For firms having private warehouses, the development of distribution centers has emerged as a major service factor in physical distribution management. Clearly, the widespread application of data processing technology has significantly increased the ability of warehousing operations of all types to meet the needs of the firms they serve. Determining the number and location of warehouses is a problem the manager faces, irrespective of the private versus public decision. A total cost approach is required, because the solution demands tradeoffs among all physical distribution costs and especially those costs associated with warehouse operation, transportation, inventory, and lost sales resulting from slow service.

Inventory management and control will always play a vital role in the operation of firms directly involved in distribution; however, its significance is even more salient in periods of shortages, slow economic growth, and high interest rates. Inventory control encompasses decisions over how much and when to order as well as how much inventory to keep in stock. The objective of inventory control is to minimize total inventory cost subject to demand and service constraints. In order to determine when to reorder, it is first necessary to know projected demand, delivery lead times, and the length of review periods. The reorder point is reached when the overall projected demand (including demand during the lead time) is greater than the amount available in inventory. The decision on how much to order is primarily a function of demand, the order processing cost, and inventory carrying cost.

Critical to decisions on when and how much to order is an accurate sales forecast. The forecasting model used depends on whether customer demand can be categorized as regular and highly predictable, irregular but mathematically consistent, or irregular and unpredictable. Exponential smoothing models are frequently used by manufacturers and wholesalers, because the demand facing them is generally not highly volatile. Retailers, though, often face fluctuating or, at the least, highly seasonal demand patterns. Therefore, adaptive forecasting is needed to cope with the latter's inventory problems. Furthermore, given the fact that sales forecasts are subject to error, controls must be established so that these errors do not lead to a reduction in customer service standards. In order to minimize stockouts at a reasonable cost to the firm, it is necessary to utilize a standard error of the estimate so that appropriate levels of safety stock can be established.

Problems in transporting merchandise can create difficulties in maintaining proper inventory levels and can impair customer service. Therefore, selection of suitable transportation modes is an integral part of developing a sound PD system. To a large extent, rail, highway, water, air, and pipeline networks each have elements of comparative advantage for different shippers and receivers. However, it appears that highway and air transport are becoming more important, even though rail is still the major means of freight movement in the United States. Increasingly, though, combinations of the various modes are being used. Aided by various transportation agencies, such as freight forwarders, the existing transportation system in the United States presents channel members with a myriad of reasonably efficient transport choices.

A key component in the development of coordinated PD systems is information relative to each of the PD activity areas. To ensure the continuous supply of relevant data, managers should design a logistical information system. Once an appropriate information system is functioning, mathematical techniques, such as simulation, can be applied to aid in solving system-wide logistical problems. Even with sophisticated techniques, however, "maldistribution" is still common in many industries. PD audits must, therefore, be developed in which evaluations of PD systems will be made as soon as indications of "maldistribution" are detected.

DISCUSSION QUESTIONS

1. What is systems analysis and why is it so useful an approach for managing physical distribution activities?

2. The physical distribution manager has been called "a manager of tradeoffs." Explain what this means.

3. Suppose that a firm currently offers the following elements of PDS at the indicated levels and has decided to evaluate how customers view the proposed changes in these levels.

    a. How many feasible PDS packages are there to be considered?

    b. How can the most appropriate combination be systematically determined?

    c. In this example, other PDS elements are explicitly or implicitly held constant. Add two additional service areas to the example above and suggest hypothetical "current" and "proposed" service levels. Then, develop two PDS packages incorporating the new and "old" areas and discuss which package is

Service Area	Service Level	
	Current	Proposed
Average order cycle time (OCT)— rush orders	72 hours	48 hours
OCT variability—regular orders	+3 days	+1 day
Order placement methods	phone call to salesmen	call to plant via incoming WATTS line
Price ($/unit)	$49	$50

likely to be more appealing to you if you were a buyer for a grocery store chain responsible for canned goods purchases. What assumptions did you make in arriving at your answer?

4. Compare and contrast private ownership of storage space with rented storage space with reference to:

a. The services that can be obtained with each.

b. The cost of storage.

c. The degree of administrative control.

d. The flexibility for meeting future uncertainties.

5. Assume that you are employed by a retailing firm. What are the tradeoffs involved in obtaining delivery in three to four days of a given item from a wholesaler versus delivery in three to four weeks from the manufacturer?

6. The following estimates are made about a certain inventory item:

Demand: 100 units per week
Inventory carrying cost: 20 percent
Order costs: $20 per order
Item value: $20
Lead time: 1.5 weeks

Determine the order quantity and reorder point. What would you need to know in order to calculate appropriate levels of safety stocks for the above example?

7. Suppose you are given the following data:

Period	Demand	Forecast (stock)	Overstock/ Understock
1	520	520	0
2	500		
3	470		
4	620		

a. Compute forecasts for periods 2, 3, and 4 using (1) a simple unweighted average: (2) exponential smoothing where weight (α) = 0.8.

b. Compute the average over-/understock.

c. Explain which forecasting method is superior and why.

8. Contrast the following in terms of speed, reliability, availability, and cost of service.

    a. Truck and rail
    b. Rail and inland water
    c. Piggyback and truck
    d. Piggyback and rail
    e. Company-owned trucking with common carrier trucking
    f. Air and truck

9. Since transportation is so largely a regulated industry, there is little to be gained by a shipper having experts on his staff in the fields of traffic and transportation. To what extent do you agree with this statement?

10. In what ways may the computer be applied to the process of physical distribution? How may the computer be used to help solve the problems of "maldistribution"?

APPENDIX 4A

Sales forecasting

Exponential smoothing is one of the most popular statistical forecasting techniques. It is an algebraic method of varying the weight (or importance) that is placed on past demand data. In other words, the older the data, the less weight is put on them, or, alternatively stated, the weights placed on data decline exponentially as the age of the data increases. In order to use exponential smoothing in forecasting, the weights and the mathematical model to be used must first be determined.

Tables 4A–1 through 4A–3 show a simple average (unweighted) forecast compared to two exponentially smoothed models, all using the same data. Table 4A–1 shows that a simple average (unweighted) forecast always results in substantial overstock/understock, with an average in this example of 56.25.

In Table 4A–2, however, a weight of 90 percent is placed on the most recent period's demand. This weighting factor is generally represented by the Greek letter α (alpha) and can vary between 0 and 1 (or between 0 and 100 percent). Here all older data are weighted by 10 percent. To forecast for the next period, multiply the latest period's demand by 0.9 ($= \alpha$). Then multiply the forecast of this period's demand by 0.1 ($= 1 - \alpha$), and add the two results together. For example, to compute demand for Period 4:

$$\alpha \times \text{Period 3 demand} = 0.9 \times 195 = 175.5$$
$$(1 - \alpha) \times \text{Period 3 forecast} = 0.1 \times 262 = 26.2$$
$$175.5 + 262 = 201.7$$

Thus, 201.7 units is the forecast for Period 4.

TABLE 4A-1   **Forecasting with a simple unweighted average**

Period	Demand	Forecast (stock)	Overstock (+) Understock (−)
1	280	280	0
2	260	280	+ 20
3	195	280	+ 85
4	180	280	+ 100
5	260	280	+ 20
6	385	280	− 105
7	400	280	− 120
8	280	280	0
Total	2240	2240	450
Average	280	280	56.25

Decision rule: stock to average demand
Result: average inventory = 280
        average overstock/understock = 56.25

Source: Edward W. Smykay and Allan D. Dale, "Inventory Control: What Price Service? Part 1," *Handling and Shipping* (July 1966), p. 50.

TABLE 4A-2   **Exponential smoothing, I**

Period	Demand	Forecast (stock)	Overstock (+) Understock (−)
1	280	280	0
2	260	280	+ 20
3	195	262	+ 67
4	180	202	+ 22
5	260	182	− 78
6	385	252	− 133
7	400	371	− 29
8	280	397	+ 117
Total	2240	2226	466
Average	280	278.25	58.25

Decision rule: stock to forecast
Result: average inventory = 278.25
        average overstock/understock = 58.25

Model: Forecast = α (new demand) + $(1 - \alpha)$ (old forecast)
        Weight (α) = 0.9

Source: Edward W. Smykay and Allan D. Dale, "Inventory Control: What Price Service? Part 1," *Handling and Shipping* (July 1966), p. 50.

TABLE 4A–3   Exponential smoothing, II

Period	Demand	Forecast (stock)	Overstock (+) Understock (−)
1	280	280	0
2	260	280	+20
3	195	244	+49
4	180	156	−24
5	260	199	−61
6	385	309	−76
7	400	446	+46
8	280	363	+83
Total	2240	2277	359
Average	280	284.6	44.9

Decision rule: stock to forecast
Result: average inventory = 284.6
average overstock/understock = 44.9

Model: 2α (new demand) − $(2\alpha - 1)$ (old forecast)
Weight (α) = 0.9

Source: Edward W. Smykay and Allan D. Dale, "Inventory Control: What Price Service? Part 1," *Handling and Shipping* (July 1966), p. 50.

As shown in Table 4A–2, this method is not much better than the simple average forecast. Average inventories decline slightly from 280 to 278 units, but the overstock/understock figure (58.25) is worse than that achieved via the simple average forecast (56.25).

Table 4A–3 demonstrates the use of a different exponential smoothing equation. This particular model places a weight of 180 percent (2 × 90%) on the latest period's demand, and a weight of minus 80 percent (180% − 100%) on all older data. This forecasting method is the same as in the last example, except that the weighted forecast is subtracted rather than added. Again, using Period 4 as an example, we have

$$2\alpha \times \text{Period 3 demand} = 1.8 \times 195 = 351.0$$
$$(2\alpha - 1) \times \text{Period 3 forecast} = 0.8 \times 244 = 195.2$$
$$351.0 - 195.2 = 155.8$$

Thus, 155.8 units is the forecast for Period 4 demand.

The results obtained in Table 4A–3 are considerably better than those in Tables 4A–1 and 4A–2. Although average inventory increased slightly to 284.6 units, average overstock/understock fell to 44.9 units.

Obviously, the selection of the proper weighting factor, or alpha, is extremely important. In Table 4A–3 any weighting factor other than 0.9 will reduce the accuracy of the forecast. The only way to determine the best model and weighting factor for minimizing forecast errors is to test all feasible alternatives. This is best done by using a computer. As discussed in Chapter 12, IBM has developed a computer program library system that classifies demand patterns in terms of various forecasting models, and then recommends whichever model yields the minimum forecast error.[1]

Although exponential smoothing models such as those discussed above are frequently used by manufacturers and wholesalers, they cannot adequately handle the marked seasonal patterns that exist in the demand for retail merchandise. IBM's Retail IMPACT system, however, employs a forecasting technique called "adaptive forecasting" which incorporates mathematical functions describing retail patterns of demand.[2] In IBM's IMPACT system, six types of forecasting models, each representing a different underlying demand process, are available for use in adaptive forecasting: a *constant model,* a *trend model,* a *seasonal model,* an *end-of-season model,* and a *trend-seasonal model.* The basic nature of each model is described briefly below.[3]

CONSTANT MODEL.   A constant model is used to forecast a demand pattern characterized by an essentially stable level of volume with random fluctuations or noise. The model represents demand as centering around an average value, with variations (noise) which may be attributed to random causes and which exhibit no discernible pattern over time. The fact that sales are below (or above) average for one month does not permit any specific inference about sales in coming months. The mathematical representation can be a single term that represents the average. Figure 4A–1 shows the monthly sales for a "constant demand" item along with a constant demand model.

TREND MODEL.   The trend model represents a demand pattern that consistently increases or decreases over time, with the increase or decrease of sufficient magnitude to be recognizable through the noise. The mathematical representation is composed of two terms, one of which is an average representing the historical sales of the item, while the other represents the direction (up or down) and magnitude of the trend. These elements, in combination with others such as forecast error and an allowance for the possible development of seasonality, are used to project the model into the future for forecasting purposes. The sales of a typical "down-trending" inventory item (SKU) and a corresponding trend model are shown in Fig. 4A–2.

---

[1] *Wholesale IMPACT—Advanced Principles and Implementation Reference Manual,* 2nd ed. (White Plains, N.Y.: IBM Technical Publications Department, May, 1969).

[2] *Retail IMPACT . . . op. cit.,* pp. 43–57.

[3] It is beyond the scope of this book to examine the internal mathematics of each of these models. For a brief, but not comprehensive, description of the mathematics involved in these forecasting processes, see *Retail IMPACT, op. cit.,* pp. 55–57.

Demand Pattern and Appropriate Forecasting Model for a Hypothetical "Constant Demand" Inventory Item (SKU)

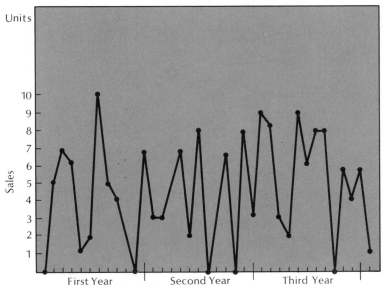

Sales of a "Constant Demand" Inventory Item (SKU)

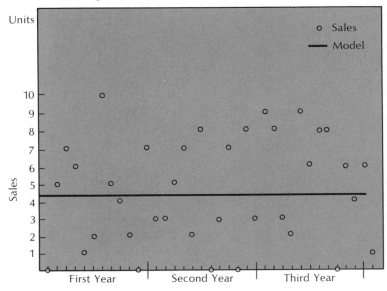

Forecasting Model of a "Constant Demand" Inventory Item (SKU)

Source: Reprinted by permission from *Retail IMPACT—Inventory Management Program and Control Techniques Application,* 6th ed. (White Plains, N.Y.: IBM Technical Publications Department, March 1970), pp. 37 and 44. © 1970 by International Business Machines Corporation.

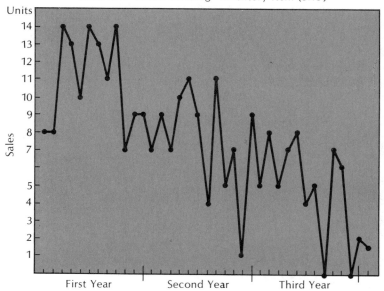

Sales of a "Down-trending" Inventory Item (SKU)

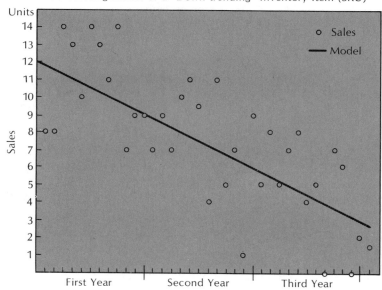

Forecasting Model of a "Down-trending" Inventory Item (SKU)

Source: Reprinted by permission from *Retail IMPACT—Inventory Management Program and Control Techniques Application*, 6th ed. (White Plains, N.Y.: IBM Technical Publications Department, March 1970), pp. 37 and 45. © 1970 by International Business Machines Corporation.

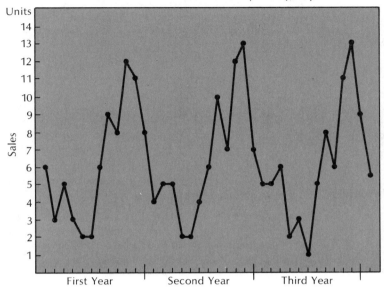

Sales of a "Seasonal" Inventory Item (SKU)

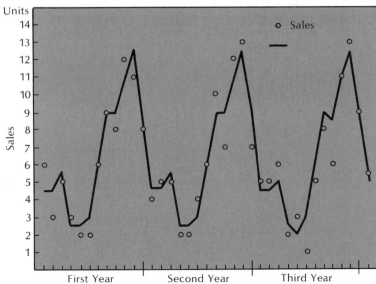

Forecasting Model of a "Seasonal" Inventory Item (SKU)

Source: Reprinted by permission from *Retail IMPACT—Inventory Management and Control Techniques Application,* 6th ed. (White Plains, N.Y.: IBM Technical Publications Department, March 1970), pp. 38 and 46. © 1970 by International Business Machines Corporations.

Demand Pattern and Appropriate Forecasting Model for Hypothetical "End-of-Season" Inventory Items (SKUs)

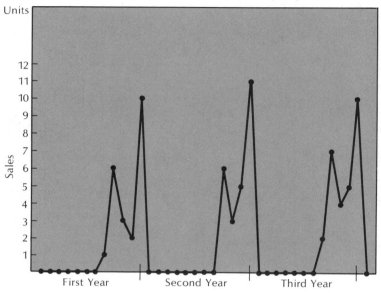

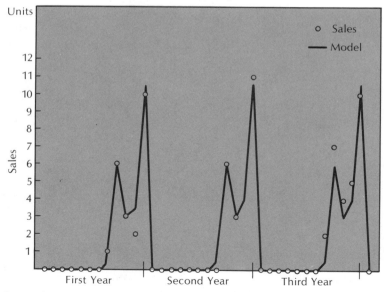

Source: Reprinted by permission from *Retail IMPACT—Inventory Management and Control Techniques Application,* 6th ed. (White Plains, N.Y.: IBM Technical Publications Department, March 1970), pp. 38 and 46. © 1970 by International Business Machines Corporation.

Demand Pattern and Appropriate Forecasting Model for Hypothetical "Trend-Seasonal" Inventory Items

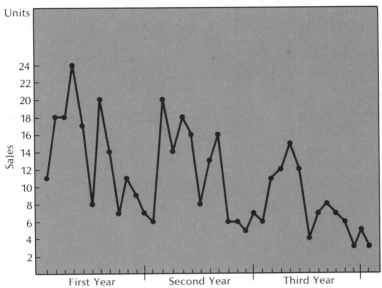

Sales of a "Trend-Seasonal" Item (SKU)

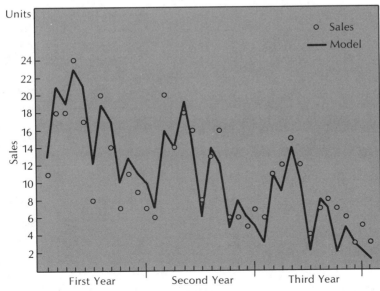

Forecasting Model of a "Trend-Seasonal"
Item (SKU)

SEASONAL MODEL. The seasonal model represents a demand pattern that is characterized by high and low periods that recur as a function of time. These seasonal or cyclic patterns occur at about the same time during each year as a result of external conditions (school opening) or internal factors (January "white sales"). Because of the fact that such seasonal processes are a predominant factor in retailing, special mathematical functions must be used to seek out and describe the underlying demand patterns. The mathematical functions (sines and cosines) incorporated in this adaptive forecasting model are actual patterns themselves, as opposed to simple points, percentages, or comparisons of this year to last year. These functions are combined and superimposed in many ways to form the best approximation of the true demand process. Figure 4A–3 shows a typical sales pattern and corresponding forecast model associated with a seasonal inventory item.

END-OF-SEASON AND TREND-SEASONAL MODELS. The end-of-season model is used to forecast demand for merchandise that is taken off the shelves for a major part of each year so that there are no sales during that time. The trend-seasonal model is used for the same purpose as the seasonal model, but is formulated somewhat differently. Both the end-of-season and trend-seasonal models are determined by combinations of the seasonal technique described above. Examples of end-of-season and trend-seasonal models are shown in Fig. 4A–4 and Fig. 4A–5.

LOW-VOLUME, LUMPY-DEMAND MODELS. These models are used for merchandise that sells at a very low rate and displays very erratic patterns of behavior. In fact, the behavior of individual low-volume and medium-volume inventory items is usually such that no well-defined seasonal pattern can be established. However, if taken at a group level (e.g., a particular style within a store or end sizes within a style, etc.), a seasonal demand pattern may be detected. Thus, by grouping low- and medium-volume inventory items, and thereby making the seasonal demand pattern more pronounced, the adaptive forecasting technique is able to make effective use of its seasonal models.

In general, the IBM Retail IMPACT adaptive forecasting program searches for and develops the appropriate models to best describe the underlying demand process at the retail level. Further, each model may carry additional elements that automatically adapt to changes in the pattern as these changes become significant and discernible to the system.

Appendix 4B

Legal forms of transport

Legal Forms of Transport

Four legal forms of transport currently exist as alternatives for shippers: common carriers, contract carriers, exempt carriage, and private transportation. Freight brokers are sometimes considered as an additional legal form. However, brokers merely "match" freight with carriers without assuming ownership or the risks of operating transport equipment.

COMMON CARRIERS. Common carriers are the most regulated for-hire transport agencies. They are required to charge similar rates for similar services, and to publish and make available to the public all rates charged for their services. A common carrier is any transportation firm that makes its services available to all shippers and accepts responsibility for carrying goods any time, any place, on a fee basis. Therefore, a basic characteristic of common carriers is that their services are offered to all potential shippers without discrimination.

CONTRACT CARRIERS. In contrast with common carriers, contract carriers are those firms who make themselves available for business on a selective basis. They service a limited number of shippers and carry a restricted number of commodities as specified by their operating permits.

Although contract carriers are required to publish the actual rates that they charge shippers, they may charge different rates to different customers for the same service. Operation permits issued to contract carriers are less restrictive than those issued to common carriers. They do specify routes to be utilized and commodities to be transported, however.

EXEMPT CARRIAGE.   The third legal form of transportation embraces a wide variety of transportation activities that are exempt from direct regulation, thus the name "exempt" carriers. Exemptions are usually given on three bases: (1) Geographic area, such as those defined by the Interstate Commerce Commission (ICC) around the periphery of certain cities mainly because of the administrative difficulties of keeping track of the operations of the numerous small, local cartage operators and small delivery trucks. (2) Exempt commodities, under which carriages of "unprocessed" products of agriculture and fishing are largely exempt from economic regulations. Exempt commodities, therefore, are moved at prices lower than those of regulated forms, especially common carriers. (3) Exempt associations, such as agricultural cooperatives and the shippers' associations described later.

PRIVATE TRANSPORTATION.   Carried on as an activity incidental to the primary purpose of a business, private transportation refers to the "common ownership of goods transported and the lease or ownership of the equipment in which they are moved." Private transportation activities fall outside the economic regulation of the ICC. Where volume of shipment is high, private transportation may prove to be an attractive alternative for users who hope to gain better operating performance, availability, and lower cost. Even when the volume is low, some companies are forced to own or contract for transportation to meet their special transportation requirements not commonly available through the purchase of common carrier services.

Transportation Agencies

Transportation agencies offer transportation services to shippers by handling small shipments and consolidating them into vehicle load quantities. They do not own any line haul equipment.

FREIGHT FORWARDERS.   Freight forwarders are considered to be common carriers of freight and, as such, have similar rights and obligations. However, they utilize the services of other common carriers for the long-distance shipments. Their major function is the consolidation of small shipments into large ones, thereby offsetting the differential between LTL and TL (truckload) rates and LCL and CL (carload) rates, respectively.

PARCEL POST AND COMPETITIVE SERVICES.   Parcel post services are offered by the United States Post Office. Directly competitive services are available through such firms as REA Express, Federal Express, United Parcel Service, and Emery. They are designed for small shipments and can be used by nearly everyone. The parcel post uses all air and surface line-haul carriers except pipeline. The rates for air parcel post are usually higher than the surface rates.

SHIPPERS' ASSOCIATIONS.   Shippers' associations are cooperative organizations operating on a nonprofit basis to take advantage of consolidation economies. They perform the same functions as freight forwarders.

Coordinated (Intermodal) Systems

The idea of coordinating the services of two or more transportation modes can be traced to the early 1920's. However, renewed interest in coordinated systems has grown in recent years. Coordinated systems are those operations which offer point-to-point through-movement by means of two or more modes of transportation on a regularly scheduled basis. There are at least seven possible combinations among the rail, water, air, and truck transportation modes. In addition, there are pipeline connections with other modes that are in common use among oil transportation companies.

Examples of coordinated service combinations are listed below.

1. *Piggyback services* are a combination of truck and rail services. This combination is also known as trailer-on-flat-car (TOFC) service. It refers to transporting truck trailers on railroad flat cars over longer distances than trucks normally haul. The cost is usually less than a truck trailer might incur over the road for the same traveled distance. The result of such a coordinated system is the extension of the trucking industry's range of operation.

The TOFC service is offered under different plans to provide operating flexibility to shippers. Plan I calls for common carrier truckers to place their trailers on railroad-owned flat cars. Plan II is similar to Plan I except that the trailers are also owned by the railroads. Shippers deal only with railroads that provide a door-to-door service. Plan III calls for shippers to place their own trailers on rail-owned flat cars and be charged a flat rate. Under Plan IV shippers provide both the trailer or container *and* the rail cars on which they are placed. The railroad charges a distance fee for the use of its pulling power. Finally, Plan V is based on a joint rate quoted by two or more carriers for truck-rail-truck service.

The plan allows for the extension of the territory of each carrier into that served by the other.

2. *Fishyback* is a coordinated truck and water service that includes the combination of truck movement with water movement on inland waterways as well as on coastal and intercoastal routes.

3. *Rail-water* is also called "train-ship" coordinated service.

4. *Truck-air* consists of the cooperation of air carriers with a number of trucking firms. The service is widely available throughout the United States.

5. The pipeline combinations include *truck-pipe, water-pipe,* and *rail-pipe.* Almost all of these services exist in the United States, although they may not be available for all shippers because of the special operating characteristics of pipelines.

PART THREE

CHANNEL MANAGEMENT: PLANNING, COORDINATING, ORGANIZING, AND CONTROLLING

Management is a process involving planning, organizing, and controlling. When we discuss management in marketing channels, however, the concern is less with planning, organizing, and controlling the behavior of individuals and more with planning, organizing, and controlling the behavior of organizations. Indeed, channel management demands an *interorganizational* focus. And it is no easy matter to convince another organization, *as a whole,* to do something it would not normally have done.

As an aid in the implementation of objectives, plans, and programs that will generate competitively viable distribution systems, it is useful, from a managerial/analytical perspective, to think of marketing channels as *superorganizations.*[1] The term "superorganization" implies that channels have characteristics of all complex organizations, even though channels are comprised of collectivities (business firms, day care centers, welfare agencies, and the like) rather than individuals. According to organization theory, *any* complex organization can be operationally defined in terms of the following characteristics:[2]

- A cooperative relationship among its members
- Collective goal(s)

[1] Initial development of this concept may be found in Louis W. Stern and J. L. Heskett, "Conflict Management in Interorganization Relations: A Conceptual Framework," in Louis W. Stern (ed.), *Distribution Channels: Behavioral Dimensions* (Boston: Houghton Mifflin Company, 1969), pp. 288–305. See also Louis W. Stern, "The Interorganization Management of Distribution Channels: Prerequisites and Prescriptions," in George Fisk (ed.), *New Essays in Marketing Theory* (Boston: Allyn and Bacon, 1971), pp. 301–314, and Torger Reve and Louis W. Stern, "Interorganizational Relations in Marketing Channels," *Academy of Management Review,* Vol. 4 (1979), pp. 405–516.

[2] Karl E. Weick, "Laboratory Experimentation with Organizations," in James G. March (ed.), *Handbook of Organizations* (Chicago: Rand McNally, 1965), pp. 194–260.

- Differentiation of function among its members
- A highly formalized unit with explicit rules and policies
- Structural complexity
- Interdependency among its members relative to task performance
- Communication among its members
- Criteria for evaluating the communication
- A stable and explicit hierarchical structure
- Integration through strictly defined subordination

Likewise, within *any* given distribution channel network, almost all of these characteristics can be found. There exists a *cooperative relationship*; otherwise, the network could not exist. There is, however, no assumption made here as to the extent or effectiveness of the cooperation; obviously, cooperation varies widely, and some channel situations are more chaotic and atomistic in this respect than others. For example, many fast-food franchise systems have engendered a high degree of cooperation between franchisor and franchisee (e.g., Kentucky Fried Chicken, McDonald's, 7-Eleven Convenience Stores) while others have witnessed franchisee revolts within the system (e.g., Chicken Delight, Sambo's).

It is also possible to argue that *collective goals* operate within distribution channel networks, even though the goals themselves may not be explicitly noted or constantly accepted. Certainly, the desire to serve the ultimate consumer in a satisfactory manner seems to pervade distribution systems, although there are frequent occasions when one might question whether such a goal is being pursued adequately. In addition, channels represent a grandiose *division of labor* among the institutions and agencies comprising them.

There would be no channels of distribution without transactional routines among members, and for a transaction to be routinized, it must happen according to *explicit rules*.[3] Channel members must understand the rules. Performance rests on the belief that one channel member will behave as another expects him to. Although channels are not often as "formalized" as typical complex organizations, they approach such formalization by the adoption of rules. In fact, within any channel system, positions and duties are generally fairly well ordered and defined. Relationships are also institutionalized. Channels are not simply ad hoc assemblages, but are among the more enduring forms of socioeconomic organization in our society. Explicit rules and policies regarding delivery, billing, order size, standardization, customer care, and the like are the vehicles that permit routinization and the formation of what Alderson termed "organized behavior systems."[4]

It is not necessary to document the self-evident notion that channels are *structurally complex* or that *communication* (and criteria for evaluating it) exists among

[3] Wroe Alderson, "Factors Governing the Development of Marketing Channels," in Bruce Mallen (ed.), *The Marketing Channel* (New York: John Wiley & Sons, 1967), p. 39.
[4] Wroe Alderson, *Dynamic Marketing Behavior* (Homewood, Ill.: Richard D. Irwin, 1965), pp. 37 and 43–45.

their memberships. It is, however, possible to note that many channels are different from complex organizations in that formal chains of command are often lacking within them. Thus, if "a stable and explicit hierarchical structure" and "integration through strictly defined subordination" are required in the formation or identification of a superorganization, surrogates for such a structure or subordination must be located in order to implement interorganization management. Although it is reasonably clear that chains of command exist within vertically integrated systems (e.g., within General Electric's distributor network for air conditioning equipment or among the clinics comprising the Kaiser health maintenance organization in California) and within some franchised systems, such authority networks are not immediately self-evident in the majority of extant distribution channels (e.g., within the furniture, food, and steel industries). Therefore, if the dictates of organization theory are followed, it would seem essential to build into interorganization systems an *informal* system of authority, at the very least. In order to organize the resources of distribution channels, it may be necessary to uncover or develop loci of power, or power centers, within the system.

All told, adopting the perspective of a marketing channel as a "super-organization" and, most especially, as an interorganizational system is important as the reader approaches the next seven chapters. Combined with Chapter 1, the content of the chapters comprises the core of this text. Part III spells out, in considerable detail, what channel management (i.e., the management of interorganizational networks involved in the marketing of goods and services) is all about.

In Chapter 1, attention was focused on why it is that marketing channel structures emerge. At that time, such concepts as sorting, accumulation, routinization, and service outputs were introduced. Using the principles (e.g., postponement-speculation) discussed in Chapter 1, it should be possible to predict when and why intermediaries appear at certain points in the channel.

In Chapter 5, we focus on the strategy and design parts of channel planning. Clearly, planning is the linchpin in the process. Without it, management cannot proceed with any strong assurance of success. In channels, planning means the setting of objectives and the development of strategies, just as it means in any other context. However, the key determinants for channels are the service output levels desired by industrial, institutional, or household users. That is, assessing whether the service outputs can be adequately provided by independently owned institutions and agencies or whether vertical integration is required is a central feature of channel planning. In answering this question, which emanates from other questions concerned with market coverage and support within the channel, management must develop mechanisms for choosing among alternative channel configurations. Overlaid on this entire process are the constraints which management faces because, for example, middlemen think and act differently than do manufacturers or because the firm's products are perishable.

Once having established what is involved with strategy and design, the next important topic on which we focus is how to coordinate the interorganizational system called a marketing channel. Because coordination is so essential (it is the "organizing" of the planning, organizing, and controlling trilogy), Chapter 6 is devoted entirely to an examination of how to achieve it. Here, we turn to the behavioral sciences for some lessons—particularly from psychology, sociology, and political science. The importance of the use of power and the significance of conflict management in the channel is explained, and something which we have called the "coordinative process" is detailed. Chapter 6 provides an essential theoretical backdrop against which to position the various forms of organizing channels examined in Chapter 7.

There are all sorts of ways that one can put together organizations into channel systems. For the sake of clarity of explanation, we have adopted the classification scheme developed by Davidson[5] and McCammon[6] some years ago. Thus, we have divided channels into conventional, administered, contractual, and corporate systems. This scheme permits us to discuss every possible configuration ranging from very loose coalitions of firms to vertically integrated operations. Almost all channels, if they are organized in a purposive fashion, require that social and economic power be used in order to marshal resources and coordinate efforts. The more tightly organized the channel must become, especially in response to competitive or other environmental pressures, the greater the importance of power as a coordinative mechanism.[7]

In many countries around the globe, there are no or minimal governmental restraints on the use of power in commercial transactions. Such is not the case in the United States. Chapter 8 is devoted only to a discussion of federal restraints; however, there are those who believe that state law will begin to dominate federal law in the antitrust area in the 1980s and beyond. It behooves the channel manager to have at least a rough idea of when he/she might be running afoul of the law and to have more than a nodding acquaintance with a very good law firm specializing in commercial and antitrust law.

We realize that the legal chapter is bound to dampen the potential channel manager's enthusiasm. It is a discouraging chapter, indeed. In contrast, Chapter 9, which discusses channel management by various channel participants, shows what has been and might be done to manage the channel and isolates institutions and agencies that seem to be assuming leadership roles. It provides an amalgamation of planning notions combined with organization examples and outlooks. Chapter 10 continues along the same line of thought, but focuses on communication within the channel. Again, emphasis is placed on examples of channel management and how communication opportunities and problems enhance or impair channel organization.

[5] William R. Davidson, "Changes in Distributive Institutions," *Journal of Marketing,* Vol. 34 (January 1970), pp. 7–10.

[6] Bert C. McCammon, Jr., "Perspectives for Distribution Programming," in Louis P. Bucklin (ed.), *Vertical Marketing Systems* (Glenview, Ill.: Scott, Foresman and Co., 1970), pp. 32–51.

[7] Those interested in examining an extremely insightful theory of the relationships among interorganizational coordination, environmental demands, and the use of power, should read Jeffrey Pfeffer and Gerald R. Salancik, *The External Control of Organizations: A Resource Dependence Perspective* (New York: Harper & Row, 1978).

The final chapter in Part III—Chapter 11—examines the "controlling" or auditing aspect of the management process. But, in order to impose management controls, it is first essential to know about performance. That is, in the absence of performance standards, auditing mechanisms are simply academic toys. There are two aspects of performance that should be kept in mind by individuals interested in channels. One is the social welfare or macro aspect. Are marketing channels in fact providing the greatest good for the greatest number, or are they simply encouraging elitism at the expense of the poor and disadvantaged? Are channels producing service outputs that are desired by the society? Are the distributive trades efficient or basically wasteful of resources? The other is the commercial or micro aspect. Are the channels employed by the firm profitable? Do the various channel members earn adequate returns on their investments, or is there a weakness in their earnings which gives evidence of a weakness in their ability to compete?

Once these questions are addressed, it is then useful to explore auditing mechanisms, such as the strategic profit model, the channel audit, and distribution cost accounting. If these mechanisms are successfully applied, they will permit judgments to be made with regard to the efficacy of the firm's entire channel management process.

FIVE

Channel Planning: Strategy and Design

In the late 1970s, Iveco, a European truck manufacturer with an 18 percent share of Western Europe's commercial vehicle market, decided to "crack" the United States market with a line of medium duty diesel trucks.[1] With a proven and dependable product and in the face of increasing demand for gasoline alternatives in the medium truck market, Iveco was confident of its success. However, difficulties in organizing a strong dealer network greatly impeded Iveco's impact. Because reducing downtime is one of the primary concerns of truck owners, a truck manufacturer must establish a strong system capable of servicing its products and maintaining adequate parts inventories. Without such a system, the manufacturer cannot achieve market acceptance—no matter how good its products may be.

Around the same time period, Welch Foods, a producer of grape products, entered the soft drink market with a newly developed grape-flavored soda.[2] Welch attempted to reach food retailers through its existing network of food brokers. This decision was motivated by management's expectation of profitability without the necessity of selecting a new marketing channel. The predominant and firmly established marketing channels of the competition (e.g., Coca-Cola, Pepsi, and Seven-Up) were comprised of franchised soft drink bottlers who primarily distribute soft drinks and who service retail shelves weekly. Welch's food brokers called on retailers only about once a month and provided service for a line of products, of which the new grape-flavored soda was only one. Welch's initial failure to penetrate the soft drink market should have been easily predictable. (Eventually, Welch's management realized the extent and source of their strategic mistake and

[1] "A New Challenger in Trucks," *Business Week* (July 3, 1978), p. 88.

[2] Phil Fitzell, "Distribution: How Welch Cracked the Soft Drink Market," *Product Marketing,* Vol. 6 (June 1977), p. 19.

were later able to enter the market successfully, using their own network of franchised bottlers.)

The Iveco and Welch vignettes could be repeated scores of times by simply changing the names of the companies. In fact, in a recent study, Lambert discovered, after interviewing managers from a total of 18 consumer and industrial goods manufacturers, that there existed a distinct absence of formal planning and evaluation procedures for marketing channels.[3] He found that the majority of channels he studied were not purposively designed but simply evolved over time. Because marketing channels have such an enormous impact on market acceptance and overall economic performance, a formal planning process for designing and selecting channels is imperative. The steps in such a planning process are depicted in Fig. 5-1 and are discussed throughout this chapter.

The Starting Point: Knowledge of Consumer Behavior

The starting point in planning the marketing channel is the industrial, commercial, institutional, or ultimate household consumer. Channel design and selection of channel partners cannot be meaningful unless they take place in the context

FIGURE 5-1
Steps in the Channel Planning Process

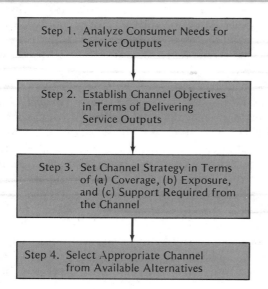

Step 1. Analyze Consumer Needs for Service Outputs

Step 2. Establish Channel Objectives in Terms of Delivering Service Outputs

Step 3. Set Channel Strategy in Terms of (a) Coverage, (b) Exposure, and (c) Support Required from the Channel

Step 4. Select Appropriate Channel from Available Alternatives

[3] Douglas M. Lambert, *The Distribution Channel Decision* (New York: National Association of Accountants; and Hamilton, Ontario: The Society of Management Accountants of Canada, 1978), pp. 56–59.

of the target markets that the designer wishes to serve and the specific needs of the consumers within those markets. This basic "axiom" holds true whether one is considering the decisions of producers relative to middlemen or vice versa. Knowledge about what consumers need, where consumers buy, why they buy from certain outlets, when they buy, and how they buy is critical. The task of planning a marketing channel involves the seller in determining the most profitable and effective ways to reach the markets that he wants to serve, and such a determination is possible only from an understanding of consumer behavior.

An essential feature of studying consumer behavior relative to channel decisions is determining the service output levels desired by consumers. It should be recalled from Chapter 1 that a commercial marketing channel is capable of producing a number of service outputs, among which are lot size, spatial convenience or market decentralization, delivery or waiting time, and product variety or assortment breadth and depth. Once it is ascertained whether the consumers in the target market desire high service output levels, whether they are willing to forego service for lower prices, or whether there are numerous consumers in each set, it is possible to lay out a number of alternative channel designs which would satisfy demand.

Xerox Corporation's decision to open its own retail office equipment stores provides an excellent illustration of what we have been talking about.[4] One of the target markets isolated by Xerox is comprised of small-business customers. Xerox had been unable to serve this market successfully through its existing (direct sales force plus company-owned distribution centers) marketing channels. Because small-business customers are geographically dispersed and do not require large amounts or large pieces of equipment, their needs differ from those of Xerox's directly served, more sizable customers. The development of retail stores was an effort to provide the service outputs desired by small businesses, namely small lot size, market decentralization, quick delivery, and, by Xerox's building of assortments comprised of other manufacturers' office equipment as well as its own, product variety. Consideration of other service outputs, such as technical advice, availability of repair facilities, provision of warranties and/or guarantees, product demonstration, and flexible financing, was equally important in making this decision. Whether Xerox could have accomplished the same ends by marketing through existing retail office equipment outlets rather than via vertical integration, however, is a debatable point. In fact, the corporation decided to test a variety of routes to the small business market after it had made the initial decision to own some of its own outlets.[5]

The determination of the service output levels demanded by consumers plays a

---

[4] "Xerox Corporation Plans Chain of Retail Stores in a Bid for Small Business Customers," *Wall Street Journal,* April 9, 1980, p. 3; and "Xerox Formally Opens Dallas Retail Store, First of Planned Chain," *Wall Street Journal,* April 10, 1980, p. 29.

[5] See "Xerox, in a Change of Tactics, Turning to Outside Dealers," *Wall Street Journal,* September 5, 1980, p. 30. The question of how to serve the small business market is perplexing to computer as well as to copier manufacturers. See Jeffrey A. Tannenbaum, "IBM Will Open Retail Store Chain in U.S. in Effort to Spur Office-Equipment Sales," *Wall Street Journal,* November 18, 1980, p. 5. An excellent discussion of the channel problems involved can be found in "Tapping the 'Mom and Pop' Market," *Business Week* (October 27, 1980), pp. 165–172.

central role in giving direction to management decision making. In fact, it is from the determination of the desired services that objectives for the channel as a whole should be formed. For example, market coverage, efficiency, and effectiveness objectives all emanate from what it is that must be provided to consumers in order to remain viable in a highly competitive environment. And, given the increased difficulty in achieving high corporate growth in a rather lackluster economy, it is also essential that management learn how to adapt to, combat, and challenge competitors by designing new channel systems that are more attractive to consumers or by preempting those channels that are already available.

Developing Channel Strategy

Channel strategy must be derived from channel objectives. The objectives for the channel are derived from an analysis of the service output levels desired by consumers and management's overall long-run goals for the corporation (e.g., in terms of return on investment, market share, absolute level of profits achieved, sales growth, etc.). The reason why the inclusion of global goals is important here is that the design and selection of a channel, once accomplished, are, relative to many other marketing decisions, long-term in nature. In other words, changing channels is a very infrequent (and often highly risky) occurrence. Clearly, a firm may make modifications once in a while, but altering the channel radically is a decision that often requires the approval of the board of directors of a corporation. Channel decisions are costly, complex, long-term, and not easily reversible commitments. In fact, changes in a channel may affect the entire character of an enterprise and the way it is perceived.

The specific (as opposed to global) objectives for the channel must, however, be couched in terms of the service outputs that are needed to meet the demands of the target markets that management has isolated for attack. As mentioned above, if several different segments are isolated, then different sets of service outputs may be demanded by the various segments. The firm will then be involved in something Robert Weigand has called "multimarketing" or the use of multiple channels.[6] In fact, the use of a single channel is becoming rare in today's marketplace. This is true for industrial as well as consumer goods. For example, Illinois Tool Works (ITW), a manufacturer of engineered fasteners and components, electronic products and components, packaging products, and precision tools and gearing, sells directly to large original equipment manufacturers (OEMs) but reaches small customers through industrial distributors. In order to discourage competition between its direct and indirect channels, it prices its products in such a way that distributors cannot provide a differential advantage to large buyers relative to their purchasing directly from ITW. The lower prices which ITW offers to its large customers are a result of the fact that the latter are willing to order individual prod-

---

[6] Robert E. Weigand, "Fit Products and Channels to Your Markets," *Harvard Business Review,* Vol. 55 (January-February 1977), pp. 95–105.

ucts in large lot sizes, hold inventory, receive no spatial convenience, and are willing to wait for delivery. Hence, in terms of the postponement-speculation principle articulated in Chapter 1, they are willing to speculate on ITW's products in return for a favorable price. On the other hand, ITW can postpone the production of large OEM orders until they can be efficiently scheduled. The lower price offered to these customers is offset by the lessened service output levels. The type of service outputs required by small customers cannot be effectively met by ITW's direct channel. Thus, distributors are utilized to provide them with quick delivery time, small lot sizes, spatial convenience, and product variety.

Once channel objectives have been stated in service output terms, it is possible to turn to two critical strategic issues. The first of these has to do with the market coverage required and the degree of support one might expect to receive from the channel based on the adoption of different coverage strategies. For example, the more intensively a manufacturer distributes his products, the less in the way of support he can expect to receive from each channel member employed in his distribution system. The second has to do with ownership. That is, does the firm need to own its entire marketing channel or parts of it in order to ensure that the required service output levels will be achieved? Is the cost of ownership prohibitive, given the extent of market coverage and support needed? The ownership question logically follows the coverage and support question.

COVERAGE AND SUPPORT. One of the key elements of channel strategy, which is evident in the Illinois Tool Works and Xerox examples, is the degree of market coverage, exposure, and channel support necessary to achieve corporate objectives. In other words, it is crucial to know how many sales outlets should be established in a given geographic area and what should be required from each of the outlets relative to their participation in the marketing flows so that the needs of existing, potential, and past customers may be adequately served. Three basic strategic choices appear to be available: (1) *Intensive distribution,* whereby a product or brand is placed in as many outlets as possible, (2) *selective distribution,* whereby a product or brand is placed in a more limited number of outlets in a defined geographic area, and (3) *exclusive distribution,* whereby a product or brand is placed in the hands of only one outlet in a specific area. These choices are applicable to both vertically integrated and nonvertically integrated systems, although clearly the capital required to establish a wholly owned channel characterized by intensive distribution might be staggering. Generally, however, discussion of these strategies is most directly applicable to channels comprised of independently owned institutions and agencies.

Intensive distribution appears to be a rational strategy for goods that people wish to purchase frequently and with minimum effort; examples are tobacco products, soap, newspapers, chewing gum, gasoline, candy bars, and aspirin. Selective distribution can be used for goods that buyers seek out and can range from almost intensive to almost exclusive; examples are certain brands of television sets (e.g., Zenith, RCA), mattresses (e.g., Simmons), cosmetics (e.g., Revlon, Estee Lauder), industrial supplies (e.g., Norton abrasives), and clothing (e.g., Arrow shirts). Exclusive distribution is used to bring about a greater partnership between seller and reseller and is commonly found in the marketing channels for new automobiles, some major appliances, commercial air-conditioning equipment, some brands of apparel, high-priced furniture, and construction and farm machinery. In addition, channel structure tends to interact with the degree of market exposure. For example, the use of numerous wholesale intermediaries (i.e., "long" channel structures) often permits greater market decentralization and thus intensive distribution, while the opposite tends to hold for shorter, more direct channels.

PITFALLS OF INTENSIVE DISTRIBUTION

It could be argued that the more intensive a product's distribution, the greater the sales that product will achieve in the short run. In fact, one could call this statement a "law" of marketing. Thus, if Magnavox, a producer of high-quality stereophonic phonograph consoles, decided to disband its present system of selective distribution in favor of a more intensive arrangement, one could predict, with certainty, that its sales would increase in the short run. But, as Magnavox expanded the number of its outlets to include drugstores (picture Walgreen's selling major stereo consoles, if you will), supermarkets, discount stores, and other outlets, it is highly likely that adverse consequences would take place over the long term. First, because some of the new outlets would undoubtedly begin to use the Magnavox brand as a leader item to attract traffic, retail prices on Magnavox equipment would begin to drop, and valued dealers such as Lazarus in Columbus, Ohio, might have second thoughts about selling a product on which profit margins were becoming slimmer and slimmer.[7] Second, service would deteriorate. Drugstores, supermarkets, and discount stores might not be willing to install service facilities, and repair work under warranty arrangements with consumers would have to be assumed by those stores with such facilities or by the manufacturer. Often, warranty business is not the most lucrative element of a service department's repair work, and leading stores offering such service would become increasingly disaffected at having to handle problems on equipment sold by other concerns. When General Electric decided to adopt a more intensive distribution strategy for its small electrical appliances some years ago, it found that it could not obtain adequate service from its expanded retail network. The company had to institute a nationwide, company-owned chain of service centers in order to solve this significant marketing problem.

Third, it is likely that, because of its intensive distribution strategy Magnavox would find itself assuming a greater participation in a number of the marketing flows. Thus, promotion by the company would probably have to be increased, because dealers who once were willing to promote the product (through advertising

[7] It is interesting to note that when W. T. Grant, a major retail chain, was attempting to avoid bankruptcy in 1975, it decided to drop the lines of major appliances that it was carrying because margins had been competed away on them. While this move did not save Grant's, it did at least permit the chain to concentrate on more profitable lines. Other retailers are having similar problems in selling major appliances at a profit, given the extent of discounting on these items.

TABLE 5–1   Selection of suitable distribution policies based on the relationship between type of product and type of store

Classification	Consumer Behavior	Most Likely Form of Distribution
Convenience store/ convenience good	The consumer prefers to buy the most readily available brand of product at the most accessible store	Intensive
Convenience store/ shopping good	The consumer selects his purchase from among the assortment carried by the most accessible store	Intensive
Convenience store/ specialty good	The consumer purchases his favorite brand from the most accessible store carrying the item in stock.	Selective/exclusive
Shopping store/ convenience good	The consumer is indifferent to the brand of product he buys but shops different stores to secure better retail service and/or retail price.	Intensive
Shopping store/ shopping good	The consumer makes comparisons among both retail-controlled factors and factors associated with the product (brand).	Selective/exclusive
Shopping store/ specialty good	The consumer has a strong preference as to product brand but shops a number of stores to secure the best retail service and/or price for this brand.	Selective/exclusive
Specialty store/ convenience good	The consumer prefers to trade at a specific store but is indifferent to the brand of product purchased.	Selective/exclusive
Specialty store/ shopping good	The consumer prefers to trade at a certain store but is uncertain as to which product he wishes to buy and examines the store's assortment for the best purchase.	Selective/exclusive
Specialty store/ specialty good	The consumer has both a preference for a particular store and for a specific brand.	Selective/exclusive

Source: Louis P. Bucklin, "Retail Strategy and the Classification of Consumer Goods," *Journal of Marketing,* Vol. 23 (January 1963), pp. 50-55. The specific table was developed by and appears in Burton Marcus, et al., *Modern Marketing* (New York: Random House, 1975), p. 550.

and especially through in-store personal selling and display) might find their margins reduced to the point where such efforts on their part were no longer warranted relative to other brands of stereo equipment that they might have in stock. In addition, more of the burden of holding inventory would undoubtedly have to be assumed by Magnavox as smaller outlets were added. In fact, it is possible to conceive of Magnavox's having to sell stereo equipment on a consignment basis in order to secure distribution in outlets where cash flow is a considerable problem.

A circumstance not unlike the hypothetical Magnavox example befell Sony during the late 1970s. Sony built its overall marketing strategy on a high quality, premium pricing plan. When the fair trade laws were repealed, Sony found itself unable to control directly the price of its color television sets or to prevent their resale to what it considered undesirable outlets. Price cutting at the retail level began to undermine the Sony quality image. The problem became so severe that Sony finally had to cancel all of its dealers and selectively accept them back into the channel under a new franchise agreement which provided Sony with the necessary control to prevent dealer resale to other outlets.[8]

Clearly, the type of distribution strategy employed interacts with the product itself (e.g., notice that the Magnavox and Sony examples involve shopping or specialty goods, not convenience items) and with other elements of the marketing mix. Gaining sales volume in the short run is not an appropriate goal for numerous companies, and uncontrolled distribution is likely to bring with it some serious long-term problems.

To aid in the selection of a distribution strategy, it is best to consider the relationship between store and product types. As indicated in Chapter 2, Bucklin has combined the traditional threefold classification of consumer goods (convenience, shopping, and specialty goods) with a threefold classification of outlets according to patronage motives (convenience, shopping, and specialty stores) in order to facilitate decision-making in this area.[9] As can be seen in Table 5–1, knowledge of consumer behavior is again the key in unlocking the problem of distribution strategy.

TRADEOFFS IN SELECTING A STRATEGY

The selection of a distribution strategy involves a consideration of relevant tradeoffs. As indicated above, when a channel member decides to adopt an intensive strategy, he generally relinquishes a significant amount of control over the marketing of his products within the channel. The only way he can reestablish such control in these cases is to assume greater participation in each of the marketing flows. For example, O. M. Scott & Sons Company, a prominent manufacturer of lawn products, decided to adopt a less selective distribution strategy, because it wanted to obtain more exposure for its product line among a large percentage of medium- to upper-income home-owning families who were, according to marketing research study conducted in the 1960s, not users of

[8] See Paul Ingrassia, "In a Color-TV Market Roiled by Price Wars, Sony Takes a Pounding," *Wall Street Journal,* March 16, 1978, p. 1; and "Sony's U.S. Operation Goes in for Repairs," *Business Week* (March 13, 1978), pp. 31–32. Severe problems with distribution strategies that were too intensive have also been experienced by Michelin (see "Michelin: Spinning Its Wheels in the Competitive U.S. Market," *Business Week* (December 1, 1980), p. 121) and Pioneer Electronics (see "U.S. Pioneer Electronics Corporation," Harvard Business School, ICH 9-579-079, Rev. 7/80).

[9] Louis P. Bucklin, "Retail Strategy and the Classification of Consumer Goods," *Journal of Marketing,* Vol. 23 (January 1963), pp. 50–55.

lawn fertilizers.[10] In order to obtain the proper merchandising support and control throughout its expanded reseller base, Scott found it necessary to develop special detailed programs for each retail account. Monthly sales plans were formulated by Scott account executives in terms of the retailers' requirements, and promotional plans were defined for each store. Many of these programs involved more than fifty pages of plans developed for an individual account. As a result of this programmed merchandising, retail store executives rarely had to make a decision that was not covered in detail in the individual account prospectus. Scott's programs were first instituted in department stores and subsequently were developed for supermarkets and other types of mass merchandisers. Therefore, not only did Scott assume the investment burden involved in formulating marketing plans for each channel member, but it was also able, through its store-by-store programmed merchandising efforts, to retain many of the policies it had adopted when its distribution was more selective (e.g., price maintenance, advertising incentives, and the like). Scott relied heavily on its expert power base relative to the marketing of lawn products, as well as the promise of significant rewards in terms of profits, to convince resellers to participate in programs that they would not otherwise have adopted.[11]

On the other hand, as channel members move towards exclusive distribution, role expectations become more sharply delineated. Specific agreements are possible with respect to degrees of participation in the marketing flows. But each of these agreements demands careful bargaining over rights and obligations. For an exclusive distribution strategy, the bargaining points (and relevant tradeoffs) generally concern the following:

1. *Products covered.* The specific items in the line that are to be handled by the exclusive wholesaler or retailer must be clearly delineated. For example, there may be certain products, especially those of a highly technical nature, that a supplier will wish to sell through his own sales force direct to ultimate customers. Other products will be made available for sale through exclusive distributors. To avoid future conflict over the division of product line responsibilities, a clear understanding must be forged among the channel members as to the relevant domains of each with regard to the items in the line. In the cases where an item has been assigned to a distributor, any sales of that item by the supplier in the distributor's territory should be credited to the distributor. Otherwise, a domain violation is obvious.

2. *Classes or types of customers.* Agreement over who is responsible for various types of customers must be arrived at to prevent future dysfunctional conflict. Thus, as in the case of products covered, the supplier may wish to retain the right to sell directly to specific classes of customers, such as the military or to very large commercial accounts (e.g., General Motors). Any sales to customers allocated to distributors or dealers must be credited to the latter if domains are not to be violated. The expectations with regard to who is to serve whom must be clearly understood and/or resolved through bargaining at the outset of the exclusive arrangement.

[10] Ronald D. Michman, *Marketing Channels* (Columbus, Ohio: Grid, Inc. 1974), pp. 152–153.
[11] Programmed merchandising is discussed again in Chapter 7, when attention is given to administered vertical marketing systems.

3. *Territory covered.* Clearly, this is another crucial element in establishing relevant domains. In many cases, agreement on territories can prevent future jurisdictional disputes among the distributors handling the supplier's products. However, tight restrictions here are circumscribed by federal law, as indicated in the chapter dealing with legal limitations.

4. *Inventories.* The questions to be resolved here are who is going to bear the burden of holding inventories and how much and where is the inventory to be held? In situations of fluctuating price levels, these questions become particularly acute. Suppliers may have to enter into price guarantees or may have to consign merchandise when economic conditions are turbulent.

5. *Installation and repair services.* This bargaining issue is obviously relevant for durable goods both in the industrial and consumer goods sectors. Here, questions relative to the handling of warranties are crucial, and the rights and obligations of suppliers and distributors must be clearly specified. Distributors may be asked to commit resources to the training of servicemen, while suppliers may have to assure distributors that service "troubleshooters" will be available on an on-call basis in situations that are beyond the distributors' service capabilities. Considerable conflict among middlemen and manufacturers has been evidenced in the automobile, home appliance, and capital equipment industries due to misunderstandings over inadequate specification of roles relative to installation and repair.

6. *Prices.* Under exclusive distribution policies, the supplier is likely to agree to some form of price or margin guarantee in times of declining market prices. The distributor may agree to maintain "reasonable margins" in its prices to end-users, but legal constraints prohibit any collusion on this matter between the supplier and the distributor.

7. *Sales quotas.* The establishment of unrealistic sales quotas has brought about considerable friction in channel relations. In agreeing to an exclusive distribution arrangement, the parties involved should arrive at a consensus relative to the way in which the quotas are to be calculated. They should also agree on the rewards to be received or punishments to be levied for performance that is above or below the quotas arrived at.

8. *Advertising and sales promotional obligations.* Responsibilities for the development of catalogs, sales aids, display work, local advertising and promotion, etc., must be specified in the agreement. The basis for calculating cooperative advertising allowances should be spelled out in detail so that each party realizes its obligation to the other.

9. *Exclusive dealing.* In some situations, suppliers prefer that their distributors handle no products that will compete directly with their own. If this is the case, then these suppliers will often be called upon to give added promotional support to their distributors in order to assure that the latter will be able to achieve a satisfactory sales volume in the product category affected. As with territorial restrictions, exclusive dealing is also circumscribed by federal law.

10. *Duration, provision for renewal, and termination.* If exclusive distribution arrangements are desired, then it is important that the specifics of each of the previous nine points be agreed upon in writing. The contract established should, however, permit for enough flexibility to meet extraneous events and contingencies, should they arise. In addition, it is important for the parties to agree on the length of time that the agreement is to be in effect and on renewal provisions. Especially important, given the legal implications involved, are specifics regarding when and how the arrangement can be terminated by either of the parties.

The list above is not exhaustive; it merely serves to indicate the detail required in formulating distribution strategy as one moves toward the exclusive end of the spectrum. The reader is encouraged to read the "Distributor Sales Agreement" and the statement of "Distribution Policy and Practices" of Rex Chainbelt, Inc., which have been reproduced in the appendix to this chapter, to obtain a more complete perspective of the specifics involved in establishing such a strategy. It is very important to note, however, that the establishment of such strategies is not a one-way street. In other words, implicit in such agreements is a tone of mutual support—each of the parties gains something by the agreement from the other under each and every point. Thus, benefits and costs are, or should be, divided equitably.

OWNERSHIP.   As is discussed in the next chapter, one of the key elements of channel strategy is determining whether and to what extent a firm can divide labor with others in its attempt to assure delivery of the appropriate service output levels. A basic strategic choice involves the use of independent middlemen or suppliers versus vertical integration of manufacturing, wholesaling, or retailing functions. With a vertically integrated system, control of the channel is accomplished through internal planning and monitoring. Vertical integration or outright ownership is an effective means of securing increased coordination, integration of effort, and heightened channel commitment. However, as pointed out in Chapter 7, where corporate vertical marketing systems are discussed, vertical integration is often an extremely costly undertaking and involves a number of tradeoffs, not the least of which is bureaucratic inflexibility. Therefore, it may not be justified in a wide variety of circumstances.

On the other hand, associating with independent businessmen as channel partners is more difficult, from a managerial point of view, than owning one's own system, because of the existence of divergent goals and expectations which bring about control and coordination problems. However, a nonvertically integrated management allows the producer or the middleman to concentrate on activities within their specific areas of expertise. Thus, channel functions which can be performed more effectively and efficiently by specialized institutions are assigned to various channel members. In certain circumstances and for certain kinds of products, this division of labor may result in lower overall distribution costs than a vertically integrated system.[12]

---

[12] The discussion of whether or not to vertically integrate is a very complex issue which has been oversimplified here. While it is discussed in more detail in Chapter 7, the reader should consult the numerous articles and books in the economics literature for more insights. Particularly useful in providing a conceptual framework is Oliver E. Williamson, *Markets and Hierarchies: Analysis and Antitrust Implications* (New York: The Free Press, 1975).

In a number of cases, marketing channels have the characteristics of vertically integrated systems without actual ownership. Chapter 7 is devoted to a discussion of a variety of such channels. One of the channel systems discussed there is franchising, which is employed by such companies as McDonald's and Southland Corporation (7-Eleven Convenience Food Stores). Through franchising, McDonald's and Southland maintain tight control over the provision of service outputs within their channels without the enormous capital and other resource requirements of outright ownership.

Choosing Among Alternative Channels

Once channel objectives have been set and the coverage, support, and ownership issues associated with channel strategy have been isolated, the marketing manager should be ready to turn his attention to determining which path his organization should follow in making its product or service available to end-users. In fact, because organizations are rarely restricted to one means of reaching their markets or obtaining their supplies, the relevant question to be answered often is: How can managers efficiently arrive at a rational choice regarding which *channels* to employ? Philip Kotler has laid out a number of different approaches for choosing channels.[13] His suggestions, including an example he developed to illustrate them, are summarized here.

Assume that an old line manufacturer of chemicals facing declining profits is considering marketing a product that can be used to kill germs in swimming pools. Assume further that the product is a significant departure from the company's present line—that the company has never done any previous consumer marketing and that its present channels of distribution are far from ideal for tapping the swimming pool market.

The first step in determining the type of middlemen to use in reaching this market would be to itemize alternative ways in which swimming pool owners could purchase this product. For example, the swimming pool owner may obtain the product from at least the five sources listed below:

1. Conventional retail outlets, such as hardware stores and drug stores.
2. Specialized swimming pool supply and equipment retailers.
3. Swimming pool service companies.
4. Mass retailer outlets such as supermarkets, department stores, and discount houses.
5. Direct mail supply companies.

Management will want to assess the relative volumes of swimming pool germicides that move through each of these types of outlets, their relative rates of growth, and their relative profitability as channels. It will also want to find out from swimming

---

[13] Philip Kotler, *Marketing Decision Making: A Model Building Approach* (New York: Holt, Rinehart and Winston, 1971), pp. 290–298.

pool owners the value they place on price, convenience, packaging, germicide effectiveness, etc., in order further to assess the relative standing of the various outlets in facilitating the delivery of these features. For this example, it is assumed that management has the option of using one or more of these sets of outlets.

The next step in the analysis of alternatives is to specify the primary channel paths the company might follow in reaching these various outlets or in tapping the various markets. Five radically different paths the company might take to market the new product are:

1. Market through the present distributors of its industrial chemicals (*present distributors alternative*).
2. Marketing through new distributors already selling to the swimming pool trade (*new distributors alternative*).
3. Buying a small company already in this market to utilize its distributors (*acquisition alternative*).
4. Selling the chemical in bulk to companies already in this market (*private brand alternative*).
5. Packaging and selling the chemical through mail campaigns directed at swimming pool owners (*direct mail alternative*).

Each of these alternatives has, obviously, drawbacks as well as strengths. In order to assess these in an analytical manner, however, it is useful to go beyond qualitative debate as to their merits and demerits. Thus, the third step in the channel alternative assessment process is to attempt to quantify the relevant factors in the consideration of each.

A number of different decision techniques can be fruitfully applied to this problem. For example, all of the multiattribute choice models specified in the appendix to Chapter 2 are directly applicable to the problem of channel design. Here, we first focus on the three methods suggested by Kotler—the linear averaging method, the sequential elimination method, and the simulation method.[14] Then, we will describe a fourth method suggested by Corstjens and Doyle.[15]

Linear Averaging Method[16]

This method calls upon management to list the major factors or attributes that the company should consider, to assign weights to reflect their relative importance, to rate each distribution alternative on each factor, and to determine the overall global utility index for each alternative. In this way, the five distribution alternatives can at least be ranked and the lowest ranked ones can be dropped.

[14] *Ibid.*

[15] Marcel Corstjens and Peter Doyle, "Channel Optimization in Complex Marketing Systems," *Management Science,* Vol. 25 (October 1979), pp. 1014–1025.

[16] Kotler calls this method the "weighted factor score method." It is also known as the expectancy value method. We have, however, chosen, for reasons of consistency, to use the terminology introduced to the reader in Appendix 2B.

An example of this method is shown in Table 5–2 relative to the "present distributors alternative." Clearly, different factors might be selected and different weights applied to each factor. It has been assumed here that the relevant factors involve an alternative's likely effectiveness in reaching the target market, its profitability, the experience that the company will gain in consumer marketing, the level of investment required to implement the alternative, and its ability to aid the company in cutting short its losses on other operations. It should be noted that the factor weights sum to 1.00; thus, they reflect the *relative* importance of each factor to management.

Although this method represents an improvement over simply listing the pros and cons of each alternative and is particularly useful in the early stage of evaluation when little data are available, it is subject to a number of statistical limitations, the major one of which is that the method misleadingly uses an interval scale for data that are properly only ordinal.[17] The sequential elimination method avoids this criticism.

TABLE 5–2 Linear averaging method applied to distribution of swimming pool germicide: present distributors alternative

Factor	(A) Factor Weight	(B) Factor Score .0	.1	.2	.3	.4	.5	.6	.7	.8	.9	1.0	Rating (A × B)
1. Effectiveness in reaching swimming pool owners	.15				✓								.045
2. Amount of profit if this alternative works well	.25						✓						.125
3. Experience company will gain in consumer marketing	.10			✓									.020
4. Amount of investment involved (high score for low investment)	.30									✓			.240
5. Ability of company to cut short its losses	.20								✓				.140
	Σ 1.00					Global Utility Index							.570

Source: Philip Kotler, *Marketing Decision Making: A Model Building Approach* (New York: Holt, Rinehart and Winston, 1971), p. 293.

[17] See, for this and additional limitations, Wroe Alderson and Paul E. Green, *Planning and Problem Solving in Marketing* (Homewood, Ill.: Richard D. Irwin, 1964), p. 206.

Sequential Elimination[18]

This method calls for management (1) to rank, not rate, the five factors or attributes in order of importance, (2) to set a minimum level from 0.00 to 1.00 for each factor that a distribution alternative must satisfy in order to be considered, and (3) to examine all distribution alternatives against the first important factor, then the second, etc., eliminating those strategies at each stage that fail to satisfy that factor.

An example is presented in Table 5-3 using the swimming pool germicide example. Note that the factors have been reordered according to the factor weights shown in Table 5-2. For each factor, a minimum pass level is established by management. In this example, all but one distribution alternative scored at or above the pass level. Thus, alternative 3 is eliminated from further consideration, because it requires too much investment. Alternative 5 is eliminated when the second most important factor is considered, because it fails to promise enough profits. The procedure is continued by bringing in successively less important factors until, as Table 5-3 indicates, only alternative 2 remains. The relative standings of the five alternatives are shown in the bottom row.

Although this method probably comes close to reflecting how many managers tend to think about choosing among alternatives, it gives no credit to how well a particular distribution alternative exceeds a minimum level required by some factor. A particular strategy may be almost perfect on the most important criterion and slightly below the minimum level on a minor criterion and as a result be eliminated. In these situations, it may be necessary for management to adopt another choice strategy, such as one of those suggested in the appendix to Chapter 2, which would more equitably discriminate between the options under consideration.

Both the weighted factor score and the hierarchical preference ordering methods fail to produce an actual estimate of profit and risk for each alternative. To accomplish this, it would be desirable to create a simulation model for examining the estimated monetary consequences of each alternative under different assumptions and sets of data.

Simulation Method

Plausible data were developed by Kotler and Vialle relative to the problem specified above.[19] These data are shown in Table 5-4. For example, the acquisition alternative was considered to require the highest investment, while the private brand alternate required the lowest level of investment. Furthermore, each distribution alternative involves a somewhat different pricing policy and contribution margin as well as different levels of advertising expenditures and effectiveness. Thus, under

---

[18] Kotler calls this method the "hierarchical preference ordering method." As with the linear averaging method, we have chosen, for consistency, to use the terminology introduced to the reader in Appendix 2B.

[19] Kotler, *Marketing Decision Making . . . , op. cit.,* p. 296.

TABLE 5-3   Sequential elimination method applied to five distribution alternatives

Factors in Order of Importance	Minimum Pass Level	Alternative 1	Alternative 2	Alternative 3	Alternative 4	Alternative 5
1. Amount of investment involved	.3	.8 = P	.6 = P	.2 = F	.9 = P	.9 = P
2. Amount of profit if this alternative works well	.5	.5 = P	.8 = P	.6 = —	.5 = P	.4 = F
3. Ability of company to cut short its losses	.5	.7 = P	.6 = P	.1 = —	.8 = P	.8 = —
4. Effectiveness in reaching swimming pool owners	.3	.3 = P	.7 = P	.8 = —	.6 = P	.3 = —
5. Experience company will gain in consumer marketing	.4	.2 = F	.5 = P	.6 = —	.2 = F	.4 = —
Ranking		3rd	1st	5th	2nd	4th

Note: P = Pass
F = Fail

Source: Philip Kotler, *Marketing Decision Making: A Model Building Approach* (New York: Holt, Rinehart and Winston, 1971), p. 295.

TABLE 5–4   Example of data input for simulation of alternative distribution strategies

| | Distribution Strategies | | | |
| | (1) | (2) | (3) | (4) |
Variables	Present Distributors Alternative	New Distributors Alternative	Acquisition Alternative	Private Brand Alternative
Investment	$300,000	$500,000	$2,500,000	$100,000
Price per bag	$2.70	$2.50	$2.70	$2.20
Contribution margin per bag	$1.20	$1.00	$1.20	$0.70
Mean monthly advertising budget	$5,000	$50,000	$10,000	$5,000
Advertising effectiveness coefficient	1/2	1/1.8	1/1.9	1/2
Initial number of distributors	80	20	60	60
Growth rate per month in number of distributors	0.02	0.04	0.01	0.02
Maximum number of distributors permitted	150	150	150	150
Distribution effectiveness coefficient	1/2.5	1/2.0	1/2.2	1/2.2

Source: Philip Kotler, *Marketing Decision Making: A Model Building Approach* (New York: Holt, Rinehart and Winston, 1971), p. 296.

the new distributors alternative, the initial number of distributors would be low but the growth rate would be high, because it is assumed that potential distributors would react favorably to the large advertising budget and the higher margin given to them under this alternative.

Other inputs used by Kotler and Vialle, but not shown in Table 5–4, were (1)

TABLE 5–5   Results of simulation of alternative distribution strategies

| | (1) Present distributors alternative | | (2) New distributors alternative | | (3) Acquisition alternative | | (4) Private brand alternative | |
Criterion	Value	Rank	Value	Rank	Value	Rank	Value	Rank
Pay-back period (months)	14	3	8	1	25	4	9	2
Share of potential	44%	4	100%	1	62%	2	43%	3
Accumulated discounted profit (millions)	3.25	3	6.10	1	5.60	2	1.99	4

Source: Philip Kotler, *Marketing Decision Making: A Model Building Approach* (New York: Holt, Rinehart and Winston, 1971), p. 297.

the rate of growth in demand expected under the different distribution alternatives, (2) a provision for substantial competitive reaction if the company's market share starts to exceed a certain figure, and (3) a provision for the effect of test marketing before making a decision. The particular distribution alternatives were simulated for a 48-month period; the results, in terms of three different measures of performance, are shown in Table 5–5. "Pay-back period" refers to how many months will pass before the accumulated revenue covers the accumulated cost to the company. The "share of potential" refers to the percentage of the company's potential share of the market that is realized by the particular distribution alternative. "Accumulated discounted profit" refers to the present value of 48-month earnings stream discounted at 10 percent. Clearly, the new distributors alternative is superior relative to the performance criteria.

Geometric Programming Method

A fourth method for choosing among alternative channels has recently been suggested by Corstjens and Doyle.[20] In order to assist a confectionery manufacturer in determining which channels to concentrate on, how many outlets to develop within any given channel, and what margins to seek in each channel, Corstjens and Doyle developed a channel optimization model employing general (or signomial) geometric programming. The manufacturer owned some of his own retail outlets but also sold through other channels. In all, there were five different channel alternatives—large wholly owned stores, small wholly owned stores, franchising, export, and private label.

Under the geometric programming approach, problem formulation starts with the manager seeking to select a distribution policy which maximizes profits, subject to constraints on the relevant decision variables. The objective function, i.e., the focal organization's total profit, is composed of a set of demand and cost functions as follows:

Total Demand Structure

$$Q = \sum_{i=1}^{K} \alpha_i \, (p_i)^{\beta_i} \prod_{\substack{j=1 \\ j \neq 1}}^{K} (p_j)^{\delta_{ij}} \, (N_i)^{\epsilon_i} \tag{1}$$

where Q represents the sales of the focal organization; K is the channels available to the organization; β_i represents the direct elasticity with respect to price (p_i) for an average outlet in channel i; δ_{ij} refers to the cross price elasticity between channels i and j, and ϵ_i represents the economies $(\epsilon_i > 1)$ or diseconomies $(\epsilon_i < 1)$ from increasing the number of outlets (N_i) within channel i.

[20] Marcel Corstjens and Peter Doyle, *op. cit.*, pp. 1014–1025.

Total Cost Structure

$$\text{TC} = \sum_{i=1}^{K} \omega_i (q_i)^{\nu_i} (N_i)^{\tau_i}. \tag{2}$$

where q_i is the sales per outlet in channel i and ν_i represents economies of scale in the cost function. If $\nu_i < 1$, the average cost curve is decreasing. Parameter τ_i is the possible economy resulting from increasing the number of outlets in channel i, e.g., unit savings in buying, transportation, and production costs.

The constraints on the relevant decision variables include a capacity constraint, a control constraint, a system inflexibility constraint, and a nonnegativity constraint, as shown below.

Capacity Constraint

$$\sum_{i=1}^{K} q_i (N_i) \leq Q^* \tag{3}$$

where Q^* is the corporate production capacity constraint.

Control Constraint

$$q_i N_i \leq z Q^*. \tag{4}$$

where z is percentage of production capacity.

System Inflexibility Constraint

$$N_i^L \leq N_i \leq N_i^U \quad \text{and} \quad p_i^L \leq p_i \leq p_i^U. \tag{5}$$

where superscripts L and U refer to the lower and upper bounds of the decision variables.

Nonnegativity Constraint

$$q_i \geq 0; \quad p_i \geq 0 \quad \text{and} \quad N_i \geq 0 \text{ for all } i. \tag{6}$$

The reason for the capacity constraint is because, in the short run, there will likely be some upper bound on potential output. The control constraint ensures that sales through any single channel are limited to some discretionary percentage (set by management) of production capacity. For example, a supplier may wish to avoid being dependent on any single channel for more than a given fraction of sales. The system inflexibility constraint limits the number of outlets opened in a channel and the price charged to that channel to within feasible ranges. In other words, it limits the amount of adaption and discretion a manager has over any channel system. Some channels will be closed to him, as pointed out below, while others will have output restrictions. The nonnegativity constraint simply ensures reasonable solution values. The constraints can be modified to model other issues of importance, such as channel power and conflict.[21] For example, the control constraint can be formulated in such a way to permit investigation of optimal levels of dependency among channel members.

Because of the nonconvex and nonlinear structure of their optimization model, Corstjens and Doyle could not employ traditional optimization techniques or linear programming. General or signomial geometrical programming places no constraints on the structure of the objective function or on the type of constraints; therefore, it was used to achieve a solution.[22] However, a weakness of this approach—which is present in the other approaches as well—is that estimation of the parameters relies heavily on the subjective judgment of managers. Unfortunately, satisfactory objective data are rarely available for the solution of channel problems.[23]

QUALITATIVE CRITERIA. Although it should be clear that the methods described above are useful means for determining the most profitable channel alternative, other considerations of a more qualitative nature must enter into the

[21] For an excellent start at developing an optimization model incorporating relevant behavioral factors, see Leigh McAlister, "An Optimization Model of Distribution Channels Incorporating Behavioral Constructs," University of Washington (Seattle) Graduate School of Business Administration, February 1980.

[22] See Corstjens and Doyle, *op. cit.*, pp. 1019–1020 and 1023–1024 for an explanation of the rationale for using signomial geometric programming and for a discussion of the solution procedure. It should be noted, however, that there may be some serious problems with the demand function in Cortsjens and Doyle's model. Zoltners and Becker have pointed out the following:

> When the distribution strategy decision is incorporated into the model, solutions for which $N_i = 0$ become admissible. As would be expected, the i-th channel's sales contribution to the manufacturer will drop completely out of the demand equation when $N_i = 0$. However, the price cross-elasticities δ_{ij} are not a function of N_i and N_j. Hence, if $N_i = 0$ the sales volumes in other channels are still affected by the price charged in channel i. This is due to the fact that $p_i^{\delta_{ij}}$ does not drop out of the equation, since $p_i > 0$ and $\delta_{ij} \neq 0$. Consequently, total demand is a function of the prices charged in channels that are not being used. This undermines the demand equation. The cost and capacity equations are also questionable since they, likewise, employ price cross-elasticities.

See Andris A. Zoltners and Robert J. Becker, "A Decision Framework and Model for Distribution Channel Design," Northwestern University Department of Marketing Working Paper, September 1980, p. 24.

[23] Corstjens and Doyle list four reasons for the unavailability of satisfactory data: (1) Few companies have seen the value of systematically recording over time information on all the relevant variables. (2) Use of conventional budgeting methods and rules of thumb mean that there is commonly a lack of variability across and within channels in the key marketing instruments to statistically estimate their effects. (3) Generating the data by experimental methods is usually viewed by managements as too costly, time-consuming, and problematical. (4) The marketing environment since the mid-1970s may have been subject to such significant shifts that past observations are seen as of questionable relevance to the future business environment. *Ibid.*, p. 1020.

analysis as well.[24] Simplistically put, the choice among channel alternatives in the discussion above comes down to judgments on the basis of mainly economic criteria. Thus, if it were possible to assume that two alternative channels (for example, employing one's own sales force versus using manufacturers' representatives or developing a wholly owned system of warehouses versus renting space in public warehouses) produce the same sales, a straightforward breakeven analysis could be developed to aid in making the decision between the two.[25] Figure 5-2 portrays the average costs associated with these alternatives. The average cost of using manufacturers' representatives (or public warehouses) is constant over the range of sales, while the per unit cost of employing one's own sales force (or owning one's own warehouses) declines as the level of sales increases (if it is assumed that the salesmen are paid on a straight salary basis or that the warehouses are bought outright and not leased back).

In this highly simplified example, the breakeven point between the various alternatives is at X. Thus, at sales levels less than Q_c the decision maker should

FIGURE 5–2

Breakeven Cost Chart: Manufacturers' Representatives versus Own Sales Force and Public Warehouses versus Own Warehouses

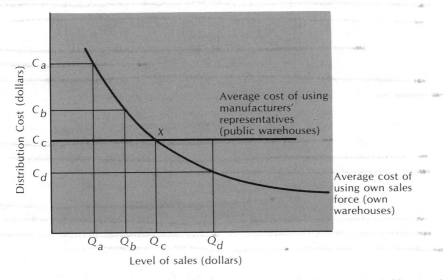

[24] A theoretical treatment of this subject matter is found in Frederick E. Balderston, "Design of Marketing Channels," in Reavis Cox, Wroe Alderson, and Stanley Shapiro (eds.), *Theory in Marketing* (Homewood, Ill.: Richard D. Irwin, 1964), pp. 176–189. See also Ronald Artle and Sture Berlund, "A Note on Manufacturers' Choice of Distribution Channels," *Management Science* (July 1959), pp. 460–471; and Helmy H. Baligh, "A Theoretical Framework for Channel Choice," in P. D. Bennett (ed.), *Economic Growth, Competition, and World Markets* (Chicago: American Marketing Association, 1965), pp. 631–654.

[25] A similar approach can be found in Kotler, *Marketing Management . . . , op. cit.*, pp. 575–578.

employ manufacturers' representatives (or use public warehouses) and at sales levels greater than Q_c, he should hire his own sales force (or purchase his own warehouses).

There is, however, a constraint present in the marketplace that is not readily apparent when one is considering economic variables alone—it is likely that channel alternatives will be limited for new entrants to a market. Thus, when sales are at level Q_a, the manufacturer (or middleman, in the case of alternatives available to intermediaries) may be forced to integrate the personal selling or the warehousing function even though the breakeven analysis indicates otherwise, because the volume that he can generate is not sufficiently attractive to independent intermediaries. The missionary effort that the latter would have to expend on the new entrant's product or service might not, in their eyes, be justified by the returns they would receive. Therefore, the shifting of marketing flows within the channel may be restricted until the market becomes larger—when the sales level reaches Q_b. The division of labor in channels may be limited by the extent of the market.[26]

Management's desire to exert sufficient control over channel members' activities so as to assure adequate performance throughout the channel system frequently modifies decisions based on economic criteria alone. Management may be willing to trade off short-term economic benefits in order to gain a long-term ability to manipulate the channel. In conventional channels of distribution, the members are independent businessmen. Therefore, each is primarily interested in maximizing his own profits, which can sometimes lead to suboptimization within the system, as pointed out in Chapter 1. Suboptimization refers to the fact that each channel member may make a set of decisions on the various elements of marketing strategy (e.g., price, advertising, and physical distribution) which maximizes his profits but which conflicts with the ability of the entire system to perform most efficiently or effectively. As Stasch has observed, the remedy to this problem is to seek an adjustment of the strategy decisions of each member so that total channel performance (measured in terms of profits, market share, or some other commonly shared goal) will be higher.[27] The greater the difference between present channel performance and projected channel performance under the systems approach, the greater will be the incentive of channel members to pursue joint planning.

ADAPTABILITY. Another critical noneconomic factor in choosing among alternative channels is the ability of various potential or existing channel members to adapt to changing conditions. Problems of adaptability are most evident during times of economic downturn or when a channel is being threatened by import or in-

[26] For a discussion of this point, see George J. Stigler, "The Division of Labor is Limited by the Extent of the Market," *Journal of Political Economy,* Vol. 59 (June 1951), pp. 185–193. For an application to distribution problems, see Reed Moyer, "The Structure of Markets in Developing Economies," *MSU Business Topics,* Vol. 12 (Autumn 1964), pp. 43–60. The breakeven analysis presented above is directly consistent with the concepts of postponement-speculation and functional spinoff which were introduced in Chapter 1 to show how channel structure emerges and evolves.

[27] Stanley F. Stasch, *A Method of Dynamically Analyzing the Stability of the Economic Structure of Channels of Distribution,* an unpublished doctoral dissertation, School of Business, Northwestern University, 1964, p. 63ff.

tertype competition of an innovative nature. Indeed, adaptability for most marketing institutions is a slow and tortuous process. Most marketing institutions are relatively rigid and conservative and, therefore, tend to go into "shock" and/or "defensive retreat," as described in Exhibit 5-1, when faced by a threat rather than acknowledging it and creatively adapting to it. Given the volatility of the economic environment over the past decade, it is likely that (1) ability and (2) willingness to make adaptations may be among the foremost criteria in choosing among channel alternatives and in selecting specific channel partners.

Selecting Specific Channel "Partners"

The choice of a specific channel partner(s) is, of course, the ultimate determinant of success or failure of the channel relationship. All of the planning suggested up to this point means absolutely nothing if the right parties cannot be found to execute it.

To aid a supplier in the selection process, Mauser has developed a checklist of 21 questions,[28] each of which must be assessed carefully by the supplier prior to making a final decision (see Exhibit 5-2). The reader is encouraged to construct choice models using this checklist, as well as to develop a comparable checklist taking the perspective of middlemen selecting suppliers with whom they might deal.

Constraints on Channel Strategy and Design

Aside from the strong stipulation that channel planning starts from an understanding of consumer behavior and, in particular, consumer demand for service outputs levels, there are several critical factors which place constraints on and, in a number of cases, are instrumental in determining channel organization. These factors are discussed in some detail in basic marketing and marketing management texts and, therefore, will be reviewed only briefly here.[29]

ENTRY BARRIERS. It is important to realize at the outset that the choice of outlets, in the case of manufacturers, and of suppliers, in the case of middlemen, is frequently highly restricted. For example, in the automotive passenger tire industry, a new manufacturer would find it extremely difficult to find retail outlets for his replacement tires, because most of the suitable outlets have already been secured by the existing manufacturers (e.g., Goodyear, Firestone, Goodrich, General, and Uniroyal). In order to generate sales volume and thus achieve scale economies in production, a new tire manufacturer would probably have to vie for private label business. The manufacturer would likely be forced into an unequal bargaining posi-

---

[28] Ferdinand F. Mauser, *Modern Marketing Management* (New York: McGraw-Hill, 1961), p. 338.

[29] See, for example, Philip Kotler, *Marketing Management: Analysis, Planning, and Control,* 4th ed. (Englewood Cliffs, N.J.: Prentice-Hall, 1980), pp. 431–443; Burton Marcus, et al., *Modern Marketing* (New York: Random House, 1975), pp. 546–555; and David J. Schwartz, *Marketing Today: A Basic Approach* (New York: Harcourt Brace Jovanovich, 1973), pp. 279–284.

EXHIBIT 5-1

The Crisis-Change Model

The crisis-change model isolates four distinct phases through which organizational systems pass as they adapt to crisis situations. According to this theory, adaptation begins with an initial period of "shock," is followed by a period of "defensive retreat," then by "acknowledgment," and finally, by a process of "adaption and change."

THE SHOCK PHASE. An organization is considered to be in crisis when any factor critical to the viability of the total system of which it is a part is threatened. The "shock" phase occurs when members of a channel become aware of a threat to the survival or to the objectives of the system, such as when a new type of competing retailing institution emerges. At this point, individual survival is the paramount objective of each member of the total system, which, in turn, leads to a fragmentation of intergroup (intrachannel) relations. The primary focus is, therefore, placed upon the threat, and day-to-day operations become irrelevant. It is during this stage that the established system loses ground to its new competitor as the individual members contemplate *noncompetitive means* of destroying the source of crisis. An illustrative example is the emergence of the chain grocery store and the threat it posed to the independent grocer. When chains first developed, independents spent their efforts predicting the former's eventual demise; their energies were absorbed in developing rationalizations for the "short-term" predicament.

THE DEFENSIVE RETREAT PHASE. This stage is marked by the established system mobilizing its forces by imposing controls designed to reduce the threat. These controls do not provide a resolution of the crisis, but merely a means of postponing a confrontation, possibly on another plane. Thus, during the period of the emergence of the chain store, the "defensive retreat" phase was marked by lobbying for legislation to curtail chain store activities. The small grocer realized that he could not compete in the marketplace with the chain and, therefore, felt that he had to eliminate or weaken the chains by subjecting them to crippling controls. Collectively, the small grocers carried out this objective by seeking legislation that would restrict the activities of the newer, more progressive, and more efficient organization and, thereby, curtail its effectiveness. The result in the grocery trade was the passage of chain store taxes and the Robinson-Patman Act. Although the threatened system survives during this phase, such defensive actions eventually become self-defeating, because they are not consistent with the goals and objectives of long-term organizational growth.

THE ACKNOWLEDGMENT PHASE. During the acknowledgment phase, the individuals in the threatened system engage in a process of self-examination and interpersonal confrontation. It is here that the individual members of the system search for new and better ways of communication, ways which ultimately lead to a genuine understanding and a sharing of information. Leadership and decision-making now become open to a wider range of influences, which are given fair consideration. Problems are explored and are not assumed to be manageable by some simple formula. As a result, solutions become more attuned to the nature of the problems. During the "acknowledgment" phase, the established system comes to doubt the validity of its own traditions and begins to experiment with some new alternatives, but in a rather cautious manner. As some structural changes are tried out, the system becomes less and less dependent upon its past history and more in touch with current developments. It begins to discover ways of using structure to facilitate the functions it must perform, rather than attempting to fit functions into preestablished structures. In the previous example, the independent grocer finally came to the realization that he would have to innovate in order to survive. The result of the crisis was the birth of the Independent Grocers Alliance (IGA) and other wholesaler- and retailer-sponsored cooperatives. Overall, then, characteristic of the acknowledgment phase is an increasing excitement about the discovery of something new and better as well as a certainty that it is undesirable, if not impossible, to return to the former patterns of operation.

THE ADAPTION AND CHANGE (GROWTH) PHASE. The processes that characterize the period of "adaption and change" reflect effective coping, and they sharply contrast with those that characterize the "defensive retreat." The "adaption and change" phase represents a renewal of the growth process. In this sense it is not really a phase but a rebirth of an ongoing state of development. By the time the system has reached this phase, it has, to a large degree, disposed of dysfunctional behavior in that the subsystems are working interdependently, and each institution complements the total system. It is here that cooperatives like IGA begin to mature and prosper, not only with respect to isolated functions, such as quantity purchases, but throughout the entire realm of the business. The final result is that the new system triggers the "shock" phase for the system that posed the original threat.

Source: Stephen L. Fink, Joel Beak, Kenneth Taddeo, "Organizational Crisis and Change," *Journal of Applied Behavioral Science,* Vol. 7 (January-February 1971), pp. 15-37.

tion relative to his prospective customers, because in such situations, middlemen can usually play suppliers off against one another and thereby are able to establish highly favorable terms of trade on private label arrangements.[30] On the other hand, wholesalers are obviously foreclosed from many channels in which direct distribution is practiced (e.g., automobiles, computers), and specific retailers may find themselves similarly foreclosed because of the policies of suppliers to deal with only

[30] Federal Trade Commission, *Economic Report on the Manufacture and Distribution of Automotive Tires* (Washington, D.C.: U.S. Government Printing Office, 1966).

EXHIBIT 5-2

**A Checklist of 21 Questions for Rating Prospective
Applicants for a Distributorship (Dealership)**

   1. What is the caliber of the person who is the head of the distributor's (dealer's) organization? Does the firm have the respect and confidence of the community?

   2. Do they have conflicting lines or products?

   3. Do they have a well-trained, smoothly running organization?

   4. Are they adequately financed?

   5. Are they making money?

   6. Do they have plant, equipment, and facilities for handling the line?

   7. Do they have an adequate and well-informed sales team?

   8. Do they have other products that fit in and harmonize with our line?

   9. Do they have a sales training program? Do they allow suppliers to participate in their training program?

   10. What is the average educational background of their personnel?

   11. Are they marketing-minded? Do they have the interest and ability to promote our product?

   12. Are they willing to appoint one executive to concentrate on our lines and be responsible for it? Who would he be and what are his qualifications?

   13. Do they cover their territory thoroughly?

   14. Do they penetrate through to customers, executives, engineers, and operating people, or do they cover only the purchasing agents?

   15. Will they accept a quota and make a reasonable effort to meet it?

   16. Will they accept and use our promotional materials in accordance with our marketing program?

   17. Do they have the courage to maintain reasonable margins when times are tough?

   18. Do they have a good setup for giving continuing service to customers in order to maintain customer goodwill for our product?

   19. Will they welcome our executives for conferences and sales meetings?

   20. Will they give us the names and home addresses of their inside and outside salesmen, so we can quickly send information to them?

   21. If our line is small, are they willing to feature it and push it?

Source: Ferdinand F. Mauser, *Modern Marketing Management* (New York: McGraw-Hill, 1961), p. 338.

certain types of outlets (e.g., Schwinn bicycles and Stiffel lamps are not sold through discount houses). While the problem associated with channel choice is particularly vexing for new, unestablished organizations, it is also worrisome for units wishing to diversify or to broaden their distribution. Certainly, the extent of financial and other sources of power held by a channel member seeking to enter or enlarge a distribution network will have a strong effect on the amount of freedom of choice available to him.

MIDDLEMAN ORIENTATION.   The pros and cons of particular distribution policies from a middleman's point of view may differ radically from those of manufacturers. Wittreich has presented examples of the brewing, appliance, and building products industries to show that small retailers speak a different language from and are not as growth-oriented as the large manufacturers whose products they sell.[31] In fact, it is likely that the perceptions and outlook of wholesalers are more congruent with retailers and vice versa than are the manufacturers' with either.

Marketing programs can fail because managers at the manufacturer's level do not tailor their programs to the capabilities and orientations of their middlemen. For example, a promotion campaign may be too complicated for middlemen to understand or implement properly. The number of calls per customer required by a manufacturer from his wholesalers may exceed the wholesalers' capacity, or the minimum orders specified by the manufacturer may be beyond the inventory handling and storage facilities of a middleman.

In general, the "independence" of independent middlemen can work at cross-purposes to the desires of manufacturers. First of all, the middleman is in business to satisfy his customers.[32] In consumer goods marketing, there are relatively few exceptions to the statement that consumers buy products from retailers, not from manufacturers. Thus, retailers possess "veto power" over virtually all marketing programs.[33] (An analogous situation holds when manufacturers of industrial goods employ industrial distributors or manufacturers' representatives.) Although the manufacturer could theoretically market his products directly to consumers, consumer buying behavior and distribution economics often preclude this possibility. As Star observes:

> While retailers *can* influence brand sales significantly in most product categories, such influence is clearly a more decisive factor in some product categories than in others. Conceptually, we would expect such influence to be most important in product categories (1) where the buying process is very unimportant to the consumer (e.g., frequently purchased, low-priced staple commodities), and (2) where the buying process is

[31] Warren J. Wittreich, "Misunderstanding the Retailer," *Harvard Business Review,* Vol. 40 (May-June 1962), pp. 147–159. This communication problem among others is examined in detail in Chapter 12.
[32] For an interesting discussion of the weaknesses inherent in assuming too much about middlemen's orientations, see Philip McVey, "Are Channels of Distribution What Textbooks Say?" *Journal of Marketing,* Vol. 24 (January 1960), pp. 61–65.
[33] Steven H. Star, "Obtaining Retailer Support for Marketing Programs," Project Description P-82 (Cambridge, Mass.: Marketing Science Institute, August 1973), p. 1.

extremely important to the consumer (e.g., infrequently purchased, high-priced products perceived to be differentiated along complex dimensions). In the first case, the consumer's need for information is so low that manufacturers are generally unable to create strong brand preference. As a result, retailers are free to carry any brand(s) they wish without fear of lost sales or lessened consumer goodwill. In the second case, the consumer's need for information is so great that manufacturers can directly satisfy the need only partially. Under these circumstances, the retailer must provide additional information in order to "close" a sale. In the process of providing this information, the retailer has considerable opportunity to influence the consumer's ultimate brand choice.[34]

Thus, the manufacturer is continuously engaged in seeking support from middlemen, especially for the kinds of products mentioned by Star (and their analogues in the industrial market). Such support is not, by any means, automatically available.

Second, independent middlemen are in business for themselves, not for manufacturers.[35] For example, retailers resort to selling private brands to increase their independence from manufacturers of branded merchandise and to guarantee a continuous source of supply of products they desire to provide for their customers. Third, middlemen generally have existing lines of products. The manufacturer seeking to "employ" a specific middleman must develop a product that closely fits the line that the middleman handles. Finally, in the case of retailers, the middleman allocates display space, which is, indeed, a scarce resource, given the number of items desiring placement.[36] Although some manufacturers have gained considerable control over the display space allocation process in the grocery trade (e.g., Kraft relative to certain dairy products, Campbell relative to soup, and Nabisco relative to crackers and cookies), and in the sale of cosmetics through department stores, the majority of manufacturers must vie for this space by granting significant concessions or by investing heavily in consumer promotions of various kinds.

In addition, a manufacturer seeking to market through middlemen must recognize and sell to three publics. The first are the middlemen's customers. The second are the managements of the various intermediary organizations. The third are the salesmen employed by the latter. Successful wooing of management does not automatically mean that market penetration will be forthcoming. A middleman's salesmen have to be convinced of the merits of the product, and thus manufacturers must engage themselves in selling to the salesmen via sales training programs, sales contests, special promotions, and other incentives.

On the other hand, a manufacturer may have considerable power in his at-

---

[34] *Ibid.,* pp. 4–5.

[35] McVey, *op. cit.*

[36] For some interesting and useful empirical work on this subject, particularly relating to shelf space in supermarkets, see Ronald C. Curhan, "The Relationship Between Shelf Space and Unit Sales in Supermarkets," *Journal of Marketing Research,* Vol. 9 (November 1972), pp. 406–412; and Robert D. Buzzell, Walter J. Salmon, and Richard F. Vancil, *Product Profitability Measurement and Merchandising Decisions* (Boston: Harvard University Graduate School of Business Administration, Division of Research, 1965).

tempt to recruit and influence channel intermediaries. Instead of trying to *push* his brand through a channel and pursuing a hard-sell policy with regard to middlemen, he has the option of trying to *pull* his brand through the channel by advertising heavily to gain consumer preference. If the latter strategy works, middlemen may actually solicit the manufacturer to carry his brand, and reseller support is likely to be available to him. However, the alternative costs must be carefully assessed in a manner similar to that specified earlier. The different strategies require varying amounts of capital investment. The key problem is to determine whether greater channel performance can be generated by manufacturers assuming more participation in the marketing flows *or* by shifting more of the work of the channel to middlemen or consumers.[37]

CUSTOMER CHARACTERISTICS.   The number, size, and geographic concentration of customers will have a direct effect on channel design. Thus, if customers are few in number, large in size, and geographically concentrated, direct channels of distribution are likely to be feasible. If the opposite conditions hold, the mechanics of distribution become more cumbersome; the employment of a large number of intermediaries on the part of a seller will probably be required.

PRODUCT CHARACTERISTICS.   Product characteristics will directly influence channel design. Perishable products require direct marketing or at least the use of middlemen who can assure rapid turnover of merchandise. Bulky products require channels that minimize shipping distance and excessive handling. Unstandardized products that call for technical expertise in their sale may require direct selling because of the need for specialized attention. Nonperishable, nonbulky, standardized products can be handled more readily by indirect channels.

OTHER CHARACTERISTICS.   Middleman, competitive, company, and environmental characteristics also influence channel design.[38] Thus, in certain lines of trade (e.g., furniture), manufacturers' representatives are particularly well adapted to serve producers and customers because of their ability to carry full lines of complementary products assembled from a variety of manufacturers. For shopping goods, comparisons as to style, price, and suitability are significant to consumers, and, therefore, the selection of appropriate channels is dictated, to a large degree, by the need to provide such comparisons. Furthermore, companies obviously vary in their financial strength, the breadth of their product mix and assortments, the orientation of their marketing policies, and their experience with certain types of outlets or suppliers. All of these latter factors constrain channel design. Finally, economic conditions and legal restrictions are influential in determining the amount of channel strategy discretion an organization will have. An entire chapter of this

[37] For a discussion of the financial considerations involved in this decision, see Eugene W. Lambert, Jr., "Financial Considerations in Choosing a Marketing Channel," *MSU Business Topics,* Vol. 14 (Winter 1966), pp. 17–26.

[38] For a complete discussion of each of these constraints, see Kotler, *op. cit.,* pp. 567–568.

text has been devoted to legal restrictions.[39] While there is some semblance of stability in the antitrust laws surrounding distribution (in spite of the fact that there have been some important recent Supreme Court decisions and FTC actions), there seems to be very little stability in the environmental picture. Fluctuating interest rates, periods of growth and stagnation, and increased international competition, along with inflation and energy problems, are likely to be hallmarks of the environment of the 1980s and 1990s. In the face of such uncertainty, it would be foolish to attempt to generate any universal "principles." Each channel situation must be measured carefully against the altering environment. The final outcome will vary in each case.

SUMMARY AND CONCLUSIONS   Channel strategy and design are critical elements of marketing strategy. The starting point in the channel planning process is at the consumer level, irrespective of the type of goods and services involved. Channel objectives must emanate from a knowledge of the service output levels desired by the end-user. Once objectives are established for the channel, attention can then focus on questions of channel strategy. Specific objectives are concerned with the degree of market coverage, exposure, and support an organization's products require. Channel strategy involves determining, broadly, how adequate coverage, exposure, and support can be obtained (e.g., via independent middlemen or vertical integration).

Market coverage and exposure issues focus on a determination of both the number of suppliers *and* the number of retailers with whom to deal. As the marketing manager looks down the channel (from manufacturer to wholesaler to retailer), the three basic strategic choices seem to be intensive, selective, or exclusive distribution. It is likely that the more intensive the distribution of a product or brand, the greater its sales will be in the short run. However, there is an important tradeoff between sales and control over the channel, which must be taken into consideration by the manager. Lots of control can result in lower long-term profits.

Development of an appropriate distribution strategy for consumer goods requires consideration of the relationship between type of good and type of store. Again, as in choosing the relevant middlemen, knowledge of consumer purchasing behavior is critical.

If channel strategy dictates a more exclusive type of distribution policy, specific agreements are possible with regard to the allocation of marketing effort among channel members. An appropriate allocation is arrived at through bargaining over products covered, class or types of customers, territory covered, inventories, installation and repair services, prices, sales quotas, advertising and sales promotional obligations, and exclusive dealing. These agreements should be put in writing, reviewed on a yearly basis, be reasonably flexible, and contain information

---

[39] See Chapter 8.

on the duration, renewal, and termination of the agreement. The forging of such an agreement, if it is to be functional over the long term, must reflect mutual support and an equitable division of benefits and costs in carrying forward distribution. It involves the specification of the rights and obligations of each of the parties.

Once channel objectives are established and the basic parameters of channel strategy have been isolated, it is possible to begin the task of choosing among alternative channels. There are four basic steps involved in this process:

1. Itemizing the alternative ways in which ultimate (household or industrial) consumers can purchase the product in question and assessing the relative volume of the product class moving through the purchase outlets, their relative rates of growth, and their relative profitability. Underlying this step is a thorough evaluation of consumer preferences.

2. Specifying the primary channel paths that can be used in reaching these various outlets or in tapping the relevant markets for the product.

3. Quantifying the relevant factors in the consideration of each channel path by employing the linear averaging method, the sequential elimination method, the simulation method, the geometric programming method, or some other systematic choice modeling process.

4. Evaluating qualitative criteria relative to the amount of control and adaptability desired.

Channel choice may, however, be highly restricted. Not every wholesaling and retailing establishment is available to every supplier, and vice versa. Achieving distribution through Sears is not a foregone conclusion for manufacturers, just as obtaining clothing supplies from Hart, Schaffner, and Marx is not a certainty for middlemen.

Despite efforts on the part of managers to organize an efficient and effective channel system, such efforts are sometimes futile, because they do not fully account for the differences in perspective and orientation of independent middlemen. The latter are in business to satisfy their customers and are not in business to satisfy the desires of other channel members. In addition, middlemen generally have existing product lines from which they frequently do not wish to deviate. Finally, middlemen, especially retailers, control display space and the process by which it is allocated. Therefore, gaining reseller support is often not a simple matter, to say the least.

Along with entry barriers and the orientation of middlemen, there are a number of additional constraints which oftentime determine exactly how a channel is (or should be) designed. They include customer, product, competitive, company, and environmental characteristics. All of these constraints clearly will influence the distribution strategy to be employed in any specific situation. They place boundaries around channel management or, as examined in the next chapter, the means available to coordinate the activities of marketing institutions and agencies.

DISCUSSION QUESTIONS

1. Explain how the characteristics of the following consumer and industrial goods affect the channels for them:

Consumer Goods	Industrial Goods
Bread	Typewriter ribbons
Breakfast cereal	Uranium (for nuclear power plants)
Women's hats	Cement
Refrigerators	Data processing equipment

2. Use the linear averaging (weighted factor score) method to evaluate the acquisition alternative in the swimming pool germicide example, using the factors and weights suggested in Table 5–1. Suppose the acquisition alternative receives the following ratings on the five factors: 0.8, 0.6, 0.7, 0.2, and 0.5. What is the total score for this alternative?

3. A prestigious designer of men's fashions (suits, pants, shirts, ties, etc.) has just decided to manufacture his own designs, but has no experience in distribution methods. (a) Conceive of four alternative retail outlets for his line of merchandise. (b) Conceive of four major alternative distribution strategies for his line.

4. A weakness of the hierarchical preference ordering method is that a particular strategy may be almost perfect on the most important criterion and slightly below the minimum level on a minor criterion and as a result be eliminated. Which of the choice strategies outlined in Chapter 2 would eliminate this problem? How would it eliminate the problem?

5. What additional variables should have been included in the simulation of alternative distribution strategies shown in Table 5–4? How would you obtain relevant input data on these variables in order to use them in the simulation?

6. Under the "new distributor's alternative" in Table 5–5, the share of potential is said to be equal to 100 percent. Is this realistic, given that there are likely to be competitive products available on the market?

7. In Table 5–4, tell the meaning of the data associated with the variables "Advertising effectiveness coefficient" and "Distribution effectiveness coefficient."

8. Name and discuss four different variables that might prohibit a manufacturer from gaining distribution through a prestige department store. Name and discuss four different variables that might prohibit a discount department store chain from obtaining a manufacturer's product line. Finally, name and discuss four different variables that might prohibit a manufacturer from gaining distribution through an industrial wholesaler.

9. Debate the pros and cons of intensive versus selective versus exclusive distribution for the following product classes: (a) panty hose; (b) drill presses; (c) tractors; (d) toasters.

10.   Develop a checklist, comparable to that shown in Exhibit 5-2, taking the perspective of middlemen selecting suppliers with whom they might deal.

11.   Develop a checklist, comparable to that shown in Exhibit 5-2, that would apply to the problem of deciding which specific outlet (Store A versus Store B) a manufacturer might select to market his product.

APPENDIX 5A

Rex Chainbelt's Distributor Sales Agreement for the bearing division

REX CHAINBELT INC., a Wisconsin Corporation (herein called REX CHAIN-BELT), having its principal place of business in Milwaukee, Wisconsin, is pleased to submit this Agreement to

_____

of

_____

(herein called DISTRIBUTOR). Under this Agreement, DISTRIBUTOR will act as an authorized stock-carrying distributor for the products listed in this Agreement for the purpose of actively soliciting and serving users of REX CHAINBELT products in DISTRIBUTOR'S territory to secure satisfactory sales of these products from each type of industry.

The purpose of this Agreement is to set forth the basis on which DISTRIBUTOR and REX CHAINBELT INC. agree to do business together, and to insure understanding and cooperation between both parties.

Source: National Industrial Conference Board, *Building a Sound Distributor Organization* (New York: National Industrial Conference Board Experiences in Marketing Management, No. 6, 1964), pp. 20-31.

Appointment and Territory

1. REX CHAINBELT hereby appoints

_____

its distributor in

_____

_____

(a) While DISTRIBUTOR may sell outside of the above area, REX CHAINBELT will furnish sales promotion and field selling assistance only in the area described in this Agreement. Since this area is not exclusive, REX CHAINBELT will not pay commissions or other compensation for sales or shipments made into the DISTRIBUTOR'S area except by specific arrangements in connection with individual orders.

(b) REX CHAINBELT will follow the general policy of not appointing additional stock-carrying distributors other than such as we already have in the described area for those products listed in attached Supplement A provided the volume of business developed by DISTRIBUTOR is satisfactory and reasonable, taking into consideration prevailing business conditions. DISTRIBUTOR will be consulted whenever changes in distribution in his trading area seem necessary.

Products

2. The products covered in this Agreement are listed in attached Supplement A. Any new or different products which REX CHAINBELT may from time to time manufacture or sell are expressly excluded except by REX CHAINBELT'S specific consent.

Sales Coverage

3. The area of DISTRIBUTOR'S primary sales responsibility will be the Industrial Consumer and reselling accounts. REX CHAINBELT will sell directly to Original Equipment Manufacturers and Contract Engineers. While it will be REX CHAINBELT'S policy to direct sales from consumer accounts to the distributor

255

best able to handle the sale, REX CHAINBELT reserves the right to make sales direct to any consumer when this seems necessary in the best interests of customer service.

Prices and Terms

4. REX CHAINBELT shall sell to DISTRIBUTOR the products listed in Supplement A at prices set forth in the schedule of published net distributor prices then prevailing, or according to discounts applicable to the prevailing REX CHAINBELT price lists. Terms and conditions of sale are set forth in the section entitled, "Conditions of Sales" for the Industrial Equipment Section in the prevailing REX CHAINBELT price lists.

Changes in Prices, or Terms, etc., of Sale

5. REX CHAINBELT will endeavor to give DISTRIBUTOR advance notice of changes in price, discounts, and terms and conditions of sale, but reserves the right to make such changes without prior notice if circumstances necessitate it.

Quality

6. The DISTRIBUTOR is authorized to extend to his customers on the resale of REX CHAINBELT products the same warranty then being made by REX CHAINBELT in prevailing price lists (see paragraph on Quality in Standard Conditions of Sale). DISTRIBUTOR is not authorized to make any other warranty.

Stock Requirement

7. To perform the proper distribution function, DISTRIBUTOR will carry an adequate inventory of REX CHAINBELT products as outlined in Paragraph 10 of the Statement of Policy attached.

Return of Stock

8. DISTRIBUTOR may, during the term of this sales Agreement, return any standard REX CHAINBELT products purchased under this Agreement according to the provisions of Paragraph 11 of the Statement of Policy attached.

**Sales Promotion
and Sales Coverage**

9. Distributor shall at all times vigorously promote the sale of REX CHAINBELT products by means of:

(a) an adequate number of qualified salesmen for good market coverage.
(b) an adequate stock and warehouse services.
(c) sales promotion activity including effective use of catalogs and advertising.

REX CHAINBELT will cooperate with DISTRIBUTOR in promoting the sale of REX CHAINBELT products, and will supply DISTRIBUTOR with catalogs, product bulletins, and other sales promotion aids. REX CHAINBELT District Sales Engineers and Representatives will provide the DISTRIBUTOR with field sales assistance in the promotion of REX CHAINBELT products, but will be free to contact directly all customers to demonstrate, promote and otherwise advertise REX CHAINBELT products.

Acceptance of Orders

10. All orders placed by DISTRIBUTOR are subject to acceptance or refusal by REX CHAINBELT, at its originating plants, and delivery is F.O.B. the originating plant.

Adherence to Manufacturer's Policy

11. Distributor agrees to follow the policies of REX CHAINBELT as announced in the Policy Statement attached herein as well as subsequent changes in such policies.

Construction of Agreement

12. This Agreement does not constitute DISTRIBUTOR as the legal representative or agent of REX CHAINBELT for any purpose, nor authorize DISTRIBUTOR to transact business in REX CHAINBELT'S name. The rights and privileges of DISTRIBUTOR under this Agreement are personal, cannot be assigned and will not inure to the benefit of any receiver, trustee in bankruptcy or any other legal representative, unless consented to by REX CHAINBELT INC. This Agreement supercedes all previous agreements and constitutes the entire Agreement between the parties.

Effective Date, Term and Termination

13. This Agreement shall become effective when formally signed and accepted by DISTRIBUTOR and REX CHAINBELT and shall continue until _____. Execution of orders after said date shall not constitute a renewal of this Agreement.

(a) Termination of this sales agreement can be made by either party. Notice of intent to terminate shall be made by letter by either party to the other's headquarters. The mailing date of such letter shall be considered the date of said notice. Termination shall become effective thirty (30) days after date of notice.

(b) In the event of termination by REX CHAINBELT, DISTRIBUTOR may within thirty (30) day termination period, return for credit all standard stock items. Credit will be issued at current prices for all such returned items which are current, unused and salable, less any cost of reconditioning.

(c) In the event of termination by DISTRIBUTOR, REX CHAINBELT will have the option of purchasing within thirty (30) days at current prices any or all of REX CHAINBELT products in DISTRIBUTOR'S inventory at the time of termination. Reshipment transportation charges shall be paid by the party terminating the Agreement, and shall not exceed those for transportation back to REX CHAINBELT'S originating plant.

_____

(Distributor's Corporate or Firm Name)

By_____

Date of Distributor's Signature _____ 19____

REX CHAINBELT INC.

By _____

(Authorized Official)

Date of Acceptance by
REX CHAINBELT INC. _____ 19____

258

REX CHAINBELT'S DISTRIBUTION
POLICY AND PRACTICES FOR THE
BEARING DIVISION

Objectives

1. Our primary objective in the distribution of REX CHAINBELT products is to provide:
    a. Prompt availability to all customers.
    b. Assistance to distributors in carrying out their part of our marketing program.

In order to -

    c. Sell the largest possible share of the market at the lowest possible cost.
    d. Provide a fair return to REX CHAINBELT and its Distributors.
2. Our Sales Agreement covers our fundamental sales relationship. The following paragraphs are intended to explain recommended procedures and to serve as a guide in directing our mutual selling efforts.

REX CHAINBELT Indirect Sales Through Distributors

3. The purpose of our Distributor Policy is to provide the most effective sales coverage to produce the largest share of available business in each trading area and to permit distributors to obtain maximum sales volume. To accomplish this purpose, REX CHAINBELT'S Standard Industrial Products as shown in the current merchandise catalog are sold to all consumer accounts and to all resale or jobber accounts through the following Distribution channels:
    a. Industrial Supply and Power Transmission Distributors
    b. Bearing Specialist Distributors
    c. Special Industry Distributors in market not satisfactorily covered by 3-a

REX CHAINBELT Direct Sales

4. To accomplish the sales objectives previously mentioned, REX CHAINBELT sells directly as follows:
    a. Original Equipment Manufacturers and Contract Engineers
    b. Agencies and offices of the U.S. Government or subcontracts for such agencies and offices.

259

Definition of Territory

5. The basic territory definition is given in Article 1 of our Distributor Agreement.

6. Distributors may sell REX Standard Products to all Consumer and Resale or Jobber accounts in their regularly traveled area. Any questions concerning area assignment should be cleared through the REX District Office.

7. When two or more REX Distributors in the same trading area solicit the same account, the REX District Office will provide product application assistance as required but will maintain impartiality in respect to each distributor's position with such accounts.

Selective Distribution

8. REX CHAINBELT'S objective is to appoint the minimum number of Distributors necessary to obtain satisfactory market penetration in each trading area. Generally only one Bearing Specialist distributor will be appointed in a small size trading area. Where heavy industry concentration or unusual market conditions make additions or changes in distribution seem necessary, the Distributor affected will be consulted before any action is taken.

Handling of Inquiries and Orders

9. a. REX CHAINBELT, where practical, will refer orders and inquiries from consumer accounts to the Distributor best equipped to service the account. However, inquiries and orders received directly will be handled directly where such handling seems necessary in the best interests of customer service.

b. When such inquires are handled directly by REX CHAINBELT INC., whenever possible, copies of the inquiry and reply will be furnished to the Distributor, and the customer will be advised of the services available from the Distributor.

c. In the case of orders received and shipped directly to such consumer accounts, we will advise the consumer account of the service available from the Distributor and recommend that their future orders be placed with the distributor.

d. All orders and inquiries received from resale or jobber accounts will be referred to the local Distributor on an impartial basis.

e. Customer preferences will be major influencing factors in all inquiry or order referrals.

Distributor's Inventory of REX CHAINBELT Products

10. The Distributor will be required to carry an adequate stock of REX products to perform the proper distribution function in his trading area. The stock should amount to *not less* than (_____%) of the Distributor's current annual purchases.

This percentage is based on the relation between a Distributor's out-of-stock and direct sales. The out-of-stock sales should account for a minimum of (____%) of the Distributor's volume resulting in an inventory of no less than (____%) of annual purchases to achieve a desirable inventory turnover of four times. In no case should the Distributor's inventory be less than ($_____) to adequately service the industries in Distributor's Marketing area.

The (____%) or ($_____) minimum Distributor inventory will apply to each branch warehouse location of the Distributor's operation.

Review and Return of Distributor Stock

11.   Periodically, at least every twelve (12) months, the Distributor stock should be reviewed and a list of slow moving, unaltered stock items submitted to the REX District Office or Representative. Credit for return stock will be allowed in accordance with the following provisions:

a. Written approval has been obtained from REX CHAINBELT INC.

b. Full credit at current prices less any original transportation allowance will be allowed on current standard catalog items in good salable condition. Credit on this basis will be issued upon receipt of an order for stock material equal to the dollar value of the credit.

c. Where returned stock as outlined in 11-b is not to be accompanied by an order of equal dollar value, credit will be allowed as under 11-b except that a 10% handling charge will be deducted from the value of the credit.

d. The credit on returned stock in any one year should not exceed 3% of the average of the Distributor's annual purchases for the preceding three years.

e. If it is necessary for REX CHAINBELT to recondition any stock returned under 11-b or 11-c, all reconditioning costs will be deducted from any credit issued.

f. The Distributor will prepay return transportation charges on all returned material.

g. Each request for return of slow moving stock must be accompanied by a complete stock analysis sheet.

h. In event of termination of our Agreement with a distributor, return of stock will be in accordance with Article 13 of REX CHAINBELT Distributor Agreement.

Sales Coverage

12. The Distributor will provide sufficient qualified salesmen properly trained to sell REX BEARING Division products, covered in Supplement A of the REX CHAINBELT Distributor Sales Agreement, to consumer and reselling accounts in his trading area.

REX CHAINBELT will cooperate with the Distributor in training Distributor's organization in the sales and application of BEARING Division products.

The Distributor is expected to cooperate in reporting sales volume to selected accounts in order to help in evaluation of account coverage.

The Distributor is also expected to cooperate in reporting sales activities of Bearing Division products from each individual branch warehouse to assist in the evaluation and increased effectiveness of territory coverage.

Sales Training

13. a. Each Distributor should hold a minimum of two sales meetings annually in cooperation with the REX District Sales Engineer or Representative. It is strongly recommended that the sales meetings be held more frequently in the more active marketing areas. The meetings will be held to instruct the Distributor personnel in the selling and application of Bearing Division products, and the meetings will be so conducted as to be closely related to each Distributor's marketing problem.

b. The Distributor will be asked to hold sales meetings wherever necessary to tie in with REX's sales promotion plans on any product line. Meetings should be arranged at least two weeks in advance and generally will be approximately one and a half hours in length.

Field Sales Assistance

14. The REX District Sales Engineer or Representative will provide field sales assistance to the Distributor through cooperation on local sales meetings and through field sales calls with Distributor salesmen.

All field sales call schedules should be carefully planned in advance. Distributor management should cooperate with the REX District Sales Manager or BEARING Representative in setting up agendas for such calls. The agenda should show, insofar as possible, the problems and subjects which the Distributor salesman intends to cover with the customer.

REX CHAINBELT and the Distributor must recognize the continued need for application selling and the creation of brand preference, and the responsibility of the REX Field Sales organization in this regard. Therefore, our sales organization shall be free to contact all customers in a Distributor's territory to demonstrate, promote and apply REX products. Where practical, calls on the Distributor customers will be made with the Distributor salesman. In the case where such calls are made without Distributor salesmen, the Distributor involved will be informed of the results of such calls and suggestions will be made by our sales organization for follow-up action required by the Distributor to gain the maximum benefits from such REX CHAINBELT direct contacts.

Pricing

15. Individual net price schedules are furnished for each trade classification.

Occasionally, the Distributor may submit inquiries or orders for special products, repair parts, or requirements for major modifications to existing products. In such cases, the prices and discounts will be determined from manufacturing and engineering costs and current market conditions. The Distributor margin on such products may not be the same as the discount on standard products in the same product class.

Price Protection

16. REX CHAINBELT'S standard practice is to hold prices firm for orders that are on our books on the effective date of a price increase, provided shipment is requested, scheduled and made within sixty (60) days from date of price change. However, we reserve the right to make price changes without advance notice; in such cases, Distributors will be notified not later than effective date.

Resale Prices

17. REX CHAINBELT strongly recommends the maintenance of suggested resale prices. Such prices are based on providing Distributors with a gross margin adequate for maintaining a reasonable operating profit based on current average Distributor operating costs.

Advertising and Sales Promotion

18. a. Distributors will be furnished regularly with information about REX promotion plans and lists of available literature and bulletins and necessary requisition blanks. The Distributor should maintain a stock of sales literature applicable to his marketing area. The REX District Sales Engineer or Representative will assist the Distributor wherever possible in selecting the literature to be requisitioned.

b. REX CHAINBELT will assist the Distributor in preparing the material for use in Distributor Catalogs but will not pay any of the cost incurred for the actual publication of this Distributor Catalog. Available inserts for catalog use will be furnished at no charge.

c. REX CHAINBELT will furnish suitable displays for Distributor Open Houses and Exhibits. REX personnel will cooperate in manning the displays wherever possible, but will not share the cost of exhibition space. The displays will be shipped by REX CHAINBELT prepaid to the Distributor and the Distributor will prepay the freight in return shipment of display.

d. REX CHAINBELT will cooperate with the Distributor in furnishing visual aids and other program material for product clinics which the Distributor conducts before special groups such as Plant operating and engineering personnel or technical societies.

The REX World

19. The REX World is a REX CHAINBELT publication providing customers with information on the use of REX products. It includes good reference material and is

also a valuable advertising piece. The use of the REX World is beneficial to the Distributor. REX World issues are available to the distributor in bulk quantities for him to distribute through his own mailing facilities.

Customer Service

20. In addition to supplying product information and carrying adequate stocks of REX BEARING Division products, the Distributor should render any other service which the customer may expect or require.

REX CHAINBELT Warehousing

21. REX District Warehouses are strategically located so that there is a warehouse stock available to practically all REX Distributors. Warehouse stock lists are printed to show the range of stocks available for any one or more of the warehouses which can be drawn on by each Distributor to serve his trading area. It is important that each Distributor Salesman be familiar with the warehouse stocks available, and that his name be placed on the warehouse stock mailing list.

REX CHAINBELT Distributor Advisory Board

22. The REX CHAINBELT Distributor Advisory Board consists of one management representative from twelve REX Distributors selected from varied geographical areas. Membership is composed of individuals from power transmission, bearing specialist, and general line houses. One third of the Board is succeeded each year by new members. The function is advisory in relation to current and contemplated REX Distributor programs and policies.

DISTRIBUTOR Personnel Mailing List

23. REX CHAINBELT will maintain list of all Distributor personnel to insure prompt receipt of product and pricing information, stock lists, and other important releases by proper parties. The Distributor should cooperate with the Rex District Sales Engineer or Representative in periodically furnishing an up-to-date list of personnel.

Financial Responsibility

24. The Distributor will be expected to furnish REX CHAINBELT, upon request, any financial information having a direct bearing on our mutual relationship. In turn, the REX CHAINBELT Credit Department will be happy to confer with the Distributor at any time on matters of finance.

The Distributor should immediately refer any questions of policy or procedure not covered by this Statement or our Agreement to the REX District Office. A clear understanding of mutual objectives is imperative.

SIX

Mechanisms for Achieving Channel Coordination

In order to improve or maintain the competitive viability of any marketing channel, it is essential that the activities and flows within it be coordinated and controlled in an effective and efficient manner. It is only through purposive *interorganizational* coordination that channels can obtain their full potential as systems involved in producing satisfactory outputs for ultimate, business, and industrial consumers.[1] In this chapter, a process for achieving effective coordination is presented. Emphasis is placed on understanding the relevant behavioral dimensions of interorganizational relations, because it is through such an understanding that the manager can learn how to organize, manipulate, and exploit the resources available to him in the commercial channel system of which his firm is a part.[2] The

---

[1] It should be noted that the coordinative approach advocated here and in later chapters is heresy when viewed from a classical economics perspective. This is so because the classical model implicitly denounces collective action and concentration of resources. However, in the United States and around the world, it has been shown, consistently and over time, that those entities that are capable of organizing collective and consistent approaches to their respective markets have been most successful in garnering the rewards of "free" enterprise. On the other hand, those units that have permitted themselves to be buffeted by the whims of the marketplace without making concerted efforts to satisfy those whims through coordinated activities with other channel members or through vertical integration of one form or another have been left at the starting gate. See Johan Arndt, "Toward a Concept of Domesticated Markets," *Journal of Marketing,* Vol. 43 (Fall 1979), pp. 69–75. For an example of where channel coordination has been particularly successful in what otherwise would have been a highly fragmented and vulnerable industry, see "The Billion-Dollar Farm Coops Nobody Knows," *Business Week* (February 7, 1977), pp. 54–64.

[2] The fields of organizational behavior and sociology are giving increased attention to the subject of interorganization relations. For some relevant reading, see Merlin B. Brinkerhoff and Philip R. Kunz (eds.), *Complex Organizations and Their Environments* (Dubuque, Iowa: Wm. C. Brown Co., 1972); John G. Maurer (ed.), *Readings in Organization Theory* (New York: Random House, 1971); Andrew H. Van de Ven, et al., "Frameworks for Interorganizational Analysis," *Organization and Administrative Sciences,* Vol. 5 (Spring 1974), pp. 113–129; Karen S. Cook, "Exchange and Power in Interorganizational Relations," *Sociological Quarterly,* Vol. 18 (Winter 1977), pp. 62–82; Howard E. Aldrich, *Organizations and Environments* (Englewood Cliffs, N. J.: Prentice-Hall, 1979); and Jeffrey Pfeffer and

approach taken is prescriptive rather than descriptive; the focus is on how the economic, social, and political relationships within channels should be managed so as to assure their long-term competitive success.

THE COORDINATIVE PROCESS

The long-run objective of channel management is to achieve, at a reasonable cost, the greatest possible impact at the end-user level so that the individual members of the channel can obtain satisfactory returns (e.g., profits, market share, or other rewards) as compensation for their specific contributions. Channel performance is determined by channel structure and by individual channel member behavior. The specific channel designs available to marketing managers have been discussed in previous chapters, especially in Chapters 1 and 5. We can now turn our attention to the process required for organizing the relationships within channels—that is, for ensuring that, within any given structural arrangement, channel member behavior is conducive to achieving high-yield performance.

Once the marketing management of an organization isolates the market targets that the organization should attack and the products and services which it must supply in order to satisfy needs and wants in those various segments, attention can be turned to the question of how best to make the products and services available for consumption by the various end-users comprising the targeted segments. As indicated in Chapter 5, the *first* step in management answering this question is determining the level of the service outputs demanded by end-users of the commercial channel system.[3] The *second* step involves specifying which marketing tasks must be undertaken in order to generate the requisite service outputs and which of the wide variety of channel members potentially available to be employed in forming a delivery system are equipped to perform the tasks. Sometimes such an assessment concludes with the finding that existing institutions and agencies are inadequately performing the required tasks. It is then the job of management to determine whether, through the use of appropriate influence or channel control strategies, it will be able to adjust the behavior of potential or present channel partners or whether it will be compelled to vertically integrate channel functions and flows so that the desired service outputs are provided to end-users. Even if functions and flows are vertically integrated, there is no guarantee that

---

Gerald R. Salancik, *The External Control of Organizations: A Resource Dependence Perspective* (New York: Harper & Row, 1978).

[3] The commercial channel is the subset of the entire channel that excludes the consumer. Institutions and agencies within the commercial channel can be organized in such a way as to enhance competitive abilities, that is, to satisfy consumer needs and wants in a more complete way than less organized systems might. The focus is on *consumer (end-user)* needs, not on channel member needs. To some extent, the U.S. automobile industry got into its major difficulties in the early 1980s because manufacturers were more concerned with their dealers' desires than their consumers' during the 1970s. See Jack Honomichl, "Consumer Signals: Why U.S. Auto Makers Ignored Them," *Advertising Age* (August 4, 1980), pp. 43 and 44.

plans to provide the outputs will be successful. Therefore, the *third* step in the coordinative process is to determine exactly which influence strategies should be used to accomplish the hoped-for results, irrespective of whether management decides to invest in integrating functions or whether it decides to deal with independently owned companies.

The *fourth* and final step of the coordinative process involves setting up mechanisms to deal with conflict issues which inevitably arise in channels so that the channel will continue to provide the desired service outputs even in the face of disagreements among channel members.

In the following sections of this chapter, each step of the coordinative process depicted in Exhibit 6–1 is detailed and elaborated on.

EXHIBIT 6–1

Steps in the Coordinative Process

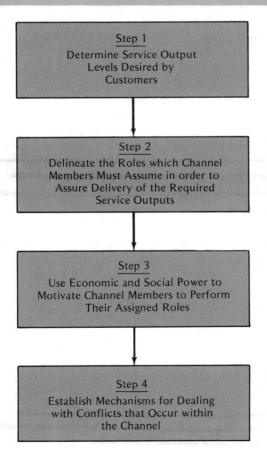

Step 1
Determine Service Output Levels Desired by Customers

Step 2
Delineate the Roles which Channel Members Must Assume in order to Assure Delivery of the Required Service Outputs

Step 3
Use Economic and Social Power to Motivate Channel Members to Perform Their Assigned Roles

Step 4
Establish Mechanisms for Dealing with Conflicts that Occur within the Channel

STEP 1. DETERMINING SERVICE OUTPUT LEVELS As emphasized in Chapter 5, a primary consideration in designing a marketing channel is an estimation of the service output levels required by end-users. The service outputs that are among the most significant in distribution are (1) lot size, (2) delivery or waiting time, (3) market decentralization or spatial convenience, and (4) breadth and depth of product or service assortment. The relevant list of service outputs to consider depends, of course, on the buying situation, e.g., for complex products, technical assistance, demonstration, and flexible financing may be called for, while for more simple products, emphasis may be placed on availability and delivery factors.

EXAMPLE 1: CIGARETTES. In order to estimate the appropriate output levels which should be built into any channel system, it is imperative to perform an in-depth study of consumer demand with respect to the outputs. For example, consumers wish to purchase cigarettes in very small lot sizes (one package per purchase, generally), desire immediate delivery of the product once requested, prefer as many outlets as possible from which to purchase, and want the broadest and deepest possible assortment from which to choose. Therefore, channels which provide these outputs have been designed to meet these needs. Individual packages of cigarettes are available for purchase from widely placed outlets which offer almost every conceivable type (filtered, nonfiltered, etc.) and brand. Delivery time is instantaneous. However, in order to provide these outputs, the channel is generally long and complex. It includes distribution centers of manufacturers which ship to tobacco and grocery wholesalers or chain warehouses which, in turn, ship to individual retail outlets (e.g., stores, vending machines, restaurants, etc.). In addition, because of high turnover, the supplies at the retail level have to be continuously replenished, making the labor costs of maintaining point-of-purchase stocks very high. The end result is that retail cigarette prices are extremely high relative to the cost of manufacturing cigarettes.

EXAMPLE 2: AUTOMOTIVE REPLACEMENT PARTS. A similar situation is found in the marketing of automotive replacement parts. When a consumer takes his car to a service station in order to have a worn-out gasket replaced, the price of the gasket is, even exclusive of labor charges for its installation, several times greater than the cost of manufacturing it. The reason for the high price of automotive parts can be traced to the service output levels demanded by consumers. The consumer wants to have the gasket replaced as quickly as possible, but the service station does not generally maintain an inventory of gaskets. In this circumstance, the mechanic will call a local automotive parts jobber, who will deliver the part in a very short period of time (usually within an hour) to the service station. Furthermore, consumers demand to purchase such parts in small lot sizes (one gasket at a time) but do not want to travel long distances to obtain them. The channel system must, therefore, maintain an enormous, widely decentralized inventory of parts to support the anticipated demands of consumers. It is, thus, no mystery why such parts cost what they do. And it is also clear why consumers, in increasing numbers, have begun to purchase automotive parts from discount stores and perform their own service. The do-it-yourselfers are willing to forego some of the service outputs available from the traditional automotive repair channel in order to achieve a lower cost of car maintenance. (Clearly, if the consumer were to place a higher value on his time, the cost savings might not be as great.)

EXAMPLE 3: GROCERIES. What appears to be happening in distribution is that alternative channel systems have been erected which provide varying levels of service outputs within any given line of trade. This is because markets have become more and more segmented. For example, there are consumers of groceries who still demand "full service" and shop at local butcher shops or specialized produce stores. However, most consumers prefer to forego such service in order to obtain the lower prices available at supermarkets, even though they must travel by car to reach the supermarkets and generally purchase in larger lot sizes during any one transaction period. And there are other consumers who are willing to provide even more of their own labor (by bagging their own groceries, for example). These latter consumers prefer to shop at limited assortment ("box") stores where prices are discounted because service outputs are significantly curtailed (e.g., stores are not as conveniently located as supermarkets, assortments are narrower and not as deep, and other services, such as check cashing, are eliminated).

EXAMPLE 4: STAINLESS STEEL. The analogy can be carried to industrial goods marketing as well. If the purchaser of stainless steel sheet prefers to purchase in large lots, is not concerned about speed of delivery, desires only one or a limited number of grades of sheet, and is willing to transact business over long distances as opposed to dealing with someone located around the corner, he is likely to be much better off, pricewise, in doing business with a direct channel of distribution (buying from the steel mill, for example) than he would be if he purchased from an indirect channel (i.e., a local wholesale steel service center).

As pointed out in Chapter 5, there is a wide variety of factors which influence channel design beyond the determination of service output levels demanded by end-users. However, in the process of managing channel relationships, knowledge of consumer demand for service outputs is critical. Once this is known, the channel manager can proceed with ferreting out the specific institutions and agencies which are capable of providing the desired outputs.

STEP 2. DELINEATING ROLES IN THE CHANNEL

Service outputs are provided by organizing the marketing functions and flows—physical possession, ownership, promotion, negotiation, financing, risking, ordering, and payment—in a wide variety of unique ways. Each channel member participates in at least one flow; otherwise, it would have no reason for its existence. Most channel members participate in several flows, and some participate in all of them. In the cigarette example mentioned above, it is imperative that a large number of channel members participate in the flows of physical possession and ownership in order to provide the lot sizes, spatial convenience, and delivery times demanded by consumers. Therefore, almost every channel member will have to maintain an inventory. On the other hand, not all cigarette channel members have to invest heavily in the flow of promotion. In fact, the normal procedure in the purchase of cigarettes is self-selection. The media advertising aspect of the promotion flow has been assumed almost totally by the manufacturers. This is not the case in the marketing of consumer durables, where retailers are expected to play a much more significant role in promotion via local advertising and personal selling.

Therefore, a major issue in channel management relates to where and to what extent marketing flow participation should be assumed in order to generate the requisite service outputs. If automobile buyers need financing, for example, the manufacturer (e.g., General Motors Acceptance Corporation), the retailer, or some outside intermediary (e.g., Chase Manhattan Bank or Beneficial Finance) can provide it. But the output (in this case, variety in lending services) must be readily available if the consumer is going to feel comfortable in considering a specific purchase requiring financing. In the situation where no channel intermediary is willing to accept the risk of financing, the initial supplier may have to assume the flow. But, in many instances, the supplier would prefer to allocate tasks in the channel. That is, he would prefer to specialize in those flows which he can perform best and rely on others to invest their capital in flows which they can perform at a comparative advantage. To a large extent, this is why it is possible to think of a marketing channel as a mechanism for dividing labor on a macro scale.

The Demand for Specialization

In the marketing of many goods and services, there is a network formed of specialized institutions and agencies. Indeed, channel members choose positions in the channel (e.g., manufacturer, wholesaler, retailer) based on their capacities, interests, goals, expectations, values, and frames of reference. This is particularly true for independent entrepreneurs. For example, one such individual markets an orange breakfast drink nationally. He holds a patent right on the drink formula and contracts its manufacturing to a contract packer. He has engaged five brokers to call on dairies, which he franchises to sell his product via their home delivery routes. In explaining his rationale for selecting this system, he has been quoted as saying:

> I simply do not like to be involved with that mess of manufacturing. It involves lots of detailed work. You've got to worry about the darn machines breaking down and stuff like that. I once owned a soft drink bottling plant, and it was all dirty detail work. We got bogged down all the time in operations and maintenance. It is a mess. You know what I like? I love to fool around with product development, and promotion is my bag.[4]

[4] Robert A. Robicheaux and Adel I. El-Ansary, "A General Model for Understanding Channel Member Behavior," *Journal of Retailing,* Vol. 52 (Winter 1975–76), p. 18.

Given this drive towards specialization, it is clear that, in order to deliver the service outputs required, channel members are highly interdependent with respect to the performance of marketing tasks. Therefore, in a system in which parties must cooperate in order to achieve an end, it is imperative, for the effective functioning of that system, that the role which each party will assume within the system regarding participation in the marketing flows be understood and clearly defined.

The Significance of Role Prescriptions

In specifying role relationships among channel members, prescriptions for role behavior evolve. Basically, role prescriptions are determined by the norms or behavioral standards (values and commonly shared ideals) of channel members for each other. Role prescriptions define certain levels of cooperation and coordination in the performance of marketing tasks. For example, a wholesaler has a set of role prescriptions for his position as well as for the positions of his suppliers and customers. The wholesaler may expect the manufacturers who supply him to stimulate ultimate consumer demand, to provide consistent levels of product quality, to consider the impact that major product additions and deletions would have upon his business, and to furnish up-to-date information about inventory conditions. By the same token, the wholesaler may expect the retailers to whom he sells to forecast their needs adequately, to cooperate with manufacturer-sponsored cooperative advertising programs, and to participate in wholesaler-sponsored training programs. In actuality, role prescriptions indicate what each member desires from all channel members, including himself, relative to their respective degree of participation in the various marketing flows.[5]

The Relationship Between Roles and Compensation

From a channel management perspective, the extent to which any given institution and agency within the channel participates in the various flows should determine the compensation received by that unit for its role in the total channel system. It would seem obvious that channel members should be paid only for what they actually do within the system. However, such is not always the case. In many lines of trade, standard trade discounts have been established based on the position (e.g., wholesaler, retailer, carrier) that an institution occupies within the system. Although these discounts are frequently called "functional" discounts, they are often based not on what flows a specific institution is performing and its coverage of these flows but rather on trade tradition. For example, one manufacturer has been known to grant large discounts to his distributors on the basis of the warehousing (physical possession) functions they perform. In an analysis of distributors' financial positions, it was found that they were earning returns on

---

[5] For a discussion of role theory as applied to marketing channels, see Lynn E. Gill and Louis W. Stern, "Roles and Role Theory in Distribution Channel Systems," in L. W. Stern (ed.), *Distribution Channels: Behavioral Dimensions* (Boston: Houghton Mifflin Co., 1969), pp. 22–47.

their investments of 50 to 100 percent. While middlemen are entitled to earn satisfactory returns, the amounts generated by these distributors were inordinate and indicated that the distributors were "coasting" quite comfortably on the high level of market demand for the product of the channel. Upon further investigation, it was found that undue compensation was being granted for the warehousing operations of the distributors because the manufacturer was, in actuality, consigning much of the component inventory needed for the installation of the product to public warehouses located near the distributors. The manufacturer was also assuming a large portion of the expense associated with the leasing of the space in the warehouses. The conclusion was apparent—the manufacturer had been overcompensating the distributors for their rather minimal participation in the flows of physical possession, ownership, and financing.

Role behavior within the channel is the most critical variable in determining whether appropriate service output levels will be generated, whether high-yield performance will be achieved, and whether individual channel members are being adequately compensated for their contributions to the delivery of the requisite service outputs to end-users. Therefore, a central task for channel management is to *specify* the appropriate roles for each of the various system members so that performance goals will be attained. In order to achieve this end, channel managers must employ economic and social power.

STEP 3. USING POWER TO SPECIFY ROLES

Simply put, *power* is the ability of one channel member to get another channel member to do what the latter would not otherwise have done.[6] More rigorously stated, one channel member's (A's) power over another (B) can be defined as the net increase in the probability of B's enacting a behavior after A has made an intervention, compared to the probability of B's enacting the behavior in the absence of A's intervention.[7] There are several implications of this formal definition that should be noted:

1. **In stating a power relationship,** it is not sufficient to say, "A is powerful"; rather, A must be powerful over someone else (e.g., B). (Think of Sears relative to Tinkertoy versus Sears relative to Goodyear.)

2. **The definition makes no distinction** as to the means of getting B to do what he would not otherwise have done. The range of available means—coercion, rewards, expertise, identification, and legitimacy—are discussed below.

---

[6] Much of the following discussion on power is developed from Frederick J. Beier and Louis W. Stern, "Power in the Channel of Distribution," in Louis W. Stern (ed.), *Distribution Channels: Behavioral Dimensions, op. cit.,* pp. 92–116.

[7] John Schopler, "Social Power," in Leonard Berkowitz (ed.), *Advances in Experimental Social Psychology,* Vol. 2 (New York: Academic Press, 1965), p. 187. See also Robert A. Dahl, *Modern Political Analysis* (Englewood Cliffs, N. J.: Prentice-Hall, 1964), p. 40; and Kjell Grønhaug, "Power in Organizational Buying," *Human Relations,* Vol. 32 (1979), pp. 159–180.

3. The definition does not require each application of power by A to result in overt reactions by B in order to be considered successful. Power attempts may only increase the probability of desired overt action on the part of B. Additional efforts may be required to achieve the actual movement of B.[8]

In addition, power can be viewed in terms of the extent to which one channel member depends upon another. The more highly dependent B is on A, the more power A has over B. For example, a small neighborhood retail druggist may be much more dependent upon his wholesaler than the wholesaler is on the druggist. According to Emerson, the dependence of B on A is (1) directly proportional to B's motivational investment in goals mediated by A, and (2) inversely proportional to the availability of those goals to B outside of the A-B relation.[9] That is, the more A can directly affect B's goal attainment and the fewer the number of alternatives there are open to B to obtain what he needs in order to function properly, the greater the power A has over B.[10] The importance of the dependency concept is nowhere more evident than in the automobile industry. In the past, automobile manufacturers kept most of their parts suppliers in the dark about new-product plans and forced their suppliers to operate on very low margins by requiring them to engage in competitive bidding for contracts each year. But now General Motors, Ford, and Chrysler are all openly courting their suppliers with purchasing contracts that run for two to three years, with negotiated arrangements, and with communication about product plans. The reason for this change is that the manufacturers are going to have to spend over $100 billion to make their cars and trucks safer, cleaner, and more efficient as the result of government-mandated guidelines and foreign competition, and they need the expertise of the suppliers to help them reach their goals. However, the suppliers have become less dependent on the manufacturers over time by diversifying away from heavy reliance on the passenger-car original equipment business. As one industry executive has stated, "You won't have a lot of suppliers scrambling for the auto business any more. I think the car people will be seeking suppliers for a change." And another executive has observed: "We're moving into the realm of partnership, rather than arm's length dealings, as it was in the days of competitive bids in the auto-supply business."[11]

[8] J. L. Heskett, Louis W. Stern, and Frederick J. Beier, "Bases and Uses of Power in Interorganization Relations," in Louis P. Bucklin (ed.), *Vertical Marketing Systems* (Glenview, Ill.: Scott, Foresman & Co., 1970), p. 76. See also Ian Wilkinson and David Kipnis, "Interfirm Use of Power," *Journal of Applied Psychology,* Vol. 63 (1978), pp. 315–320.

[9] Richard M. Emerson, "Power-Dependence Relations," *American Sociological Review,* Vol. 27 (February 1962), pp. 32–33.

[10] See, for further discussion, Adel I. El-Ansary and Louis W. Stern, "Power Measurement in the Distribution Channel," *Journal of Marketing Research,* Vol. 9 (February 1972), pp. 47–52. A number of empirical studies have been performed which have examined the use and effects of power in marketing channels. See Torger Reve and Louis W. Stern, "Interorganizational Relations in Marketing Channels," *Academy of Management Review,* Vol. 4 (July 1979), pp. 405–416, for a listing.

[11] "Detroit's New Face Toward Its Suppliers," *Business Week* (September 24, 1979), p. 140.

Bases of Power

The use of power by individual channel members to affect the decision making or the behavior of others is the mechanism by which congruent and effective roles become specified, roles become realigned, when necessary, and appropriate role performance is enforced. As indicated above, there are a number of bases of power that may be available to one channel member in his attempts to influence another and vice versa. These involve using:[12]

REWARDS.   Reward power is based on the belief by B that A has the ability to mediate rewards for him. The effective use of reward power rests on A's possession of some resource that B values and which B believes he can obtain by conforming to A's request. Specific rewards that may be used by individual channel members may include the granting of wider margins, the allocation of various types of promotional allowances, and the assignment of exclusive territories. For example, if a group of hospitals is willing to link itself to American Hospital Supply's order entry system and purchase a fixed minimum volume of its products per year (say, $2500), AHS will guarantee that future price increases will not rise above a preset ceiling.[13] Thus, reward power is being employed by AHS, which enables hospital groups to fight inflationary pressures and contain costs.

COERCION.   Coercive power stems from the expectation on the part of B that he will be punished by A if he fails to conform to A's influence attempt. Coercion involves any negative sanction or punishment that a firm is perceived to be capable of. Examples would be reductions in margins, the withdrawal of rewards previously granted (e.g., an exclusive territorial right), the slowing down of shipments, and the like. In fact, coercive power can be viewed as the "other side of the coin" relative to reward power. It should be noted, however, that the threat and use of negative sanctions can often be viewed as "pathological" moves and may be less functional over the long run than other power bases that may produce more positive side effects.[14] Therefore, coercion should be employed only when all other avenues to evoke change have been travelled.

Coercive power is often used in situations where there is an extreme imbalance of power within the channel, e.g., where very large and well-financed retailers face small, highly dependent manufacturers and vice versa. Thus, Sears and Revlon have both been known to make coercive demands on their smaller channel partners. Sears' coercive strategies, especially with regard to its forcing suppliers to hold and

[12] John R. P. French and Bertram Raven, "The Bases of Social Power," in Dorwin Cartwright (ed.), *Studies in Social Power* (Ann Arbor, Mich.: University of Michigan Press, 1959), pp. 150–167.

[13] "American Hospital Supply's Pricing Promise," *Sales & Marketing Management* (January 14, 1980), p. 24.

[14] David A. Baldwin, "The Power of Positive Sanctions," *World Politics,* Vol. 24 (October 1971), pp. 19–38; Robert F. Lusch, "Channel Conflict: Its Impact on Retailer Operating Performance," *Journal of Retailing,* Vol. 52 (Summer 1976), pp. 3–12; and Robert F. Lusch, "Sources of Power: Their Impact on Interchannel Conflict," *Journal of Marketing Research,* Vol. 13 (November 1976), pp. 382–390.

finance "over-age" inventory—i.e., goods that Sears has ordered and is obligated to buy, but that it does not step up and take—have been well documented.[15] Revlon has been described as a company that "just can't compromise." Apparently, retailers view Revlon as a company with numerous set policies, such as insisting that retailers add new space for new products prior to supplying the products and demanding that shelf space be allocated to products that are not selling well. While retailers have the final say in what happens, the Revlon approach "comes off like blackmail."[16]

When coercive power is continuously applied, countervailing power will eventually develop in the channel. Thus, Florida citrus growers have formed associations to counteract the coercive activities of processors and grocery chains. Franchisees in the fast-food, petroleum, and automotive industries have formed dealer associations. In virtually every instance where coercive power is used over time, the result has been resistance, conflict, and, if not remedied through more judicious management practices or government reaction, the decline of the channel as a competitive force.

EXPERTNESS.   Expert power is based on B's perception that A has special knowledge. Examples of channel members assuming expert roles are wide-spread. It has become rather common, for example, for small retailers to rely heavily on their wholesale suppliers for expert advice. For example, in the drug, grocery, and hardware trades, merchant wholesalers generally provide retailers with sales promotion counsel and aids, sales training for store employees, information about other retailers' promotions, advice on getting special displays, advice on store layout and arrangement, information on sources of items not stocked by the wholesaler, and managerial counselling. Such services may also be provided by manufacturers in the form of management training for marketing intermediaries.[17]

In American Hospital Supply's order-entry system for hospital groups referred to above in the discussion of reward power, teams of experts arrive to analyze a hospital's inventory needs, brand-name preferences, and materials flow once it joins AHS's plan. Then an order transmitter linked to a central computer at the company's headquarters is installed. Benefits to the hospital include reduced inventory requirements, improved cash flow, less paperwork, and 24-hour delivery on the great majority of orders.[18]

Another example of the use of expert power in marketing channels is provided by Sweda International Inc., the cash register subsidiary of Litton Industries, Inc. Sweda uses 200 independent dealers to sell its high-technology products. Such a

[15] See, for example, Carol J. Loomis, "The Leaning Tower of Sears," *Fortune* (July 2, 1979), pp. 78–85. Using coercive power with general merchandise suppliers is not limited to Sears. See Jeffrey H. Birnbaum, "Major Department Stores are the Focus of an FTC Probe Over Buying Practices," *Wall Street Journal,* November 20, 1980, p. 4.

[16] "Management Realists in the Glamour World of Cosmetics," *Business Week* (November 29, 1976), p. 48.

[17] John Howard, *Marketing Management,* rev. ed. (Homewood, Ill.: Richard D. Irwin, 1963), p. 336.

[18] "American Hospital Supply's Pricing Promise," *op. cit.,* p. 24.

policy is often frowned upon, because customers generally question the sophistication and responsiveness of independent dealers. Sweda has overcome this concern by intensive dealer training. The strategy appears to have paid off. For example, an executive of McCrory Corp., which purchased 2000 Sweda electronic cash registers for 750 departments stores, has been quoted as saying: "We have found in some locations that Sweda's dealers are better than the company's employees."[19]

However, the durability of expert power presents a problem in channel management. If expert advice, once given, provides the receiver with the ability to operate without such assistance in the future, then the expertise has been transferred and the power of the original expert in the relationship is reduced considerably. The receiver's dependence on his tutor is lessened or eliminated. In order for a firm to retain, over the long run, expert power over other firms in a given channel, any training or advice offered would have to be of a specialized nature so that the subject could not apply it to any other relationship except the one with which he is presently involved. For example, a manufacturer might retain his expert power by periodically offering to middlemen unique, well-planned, multifaceted promotional programs each time he introduces a new product. In those cases where expertise can be readily transferred to "outsiders," marketers have sometimes taken rather drastic action to protect it. Burger King Corporation filed a suit against Horn & Hardart Company, one of its largest franchisees; at issue was Horn & Hardart's plan to become the Manhattan franchisee for Arby's, a roast-beef chain owned by Royal Crown Company of Atlanta. Burger King informed Horn & Hardart, which operated 20 Burger Kings in the New York City area, that it was terminating several of its franchises, claiming that Horn & Hardart's plan to open the Arby's units violated its franchise agreement and would be a conflict of interest.[20] Similarly, McDonald's contract with its franchisees specifies that McDonald's may take over a restaurant without advance notice for cause if a franchisee discloses confidential McDonald's documents. The contract also forbids franchisees from investing in another restaurant business. Both Burger King and McDonald's guard, with considerable fervor, the expertise which they have developed and have no desire to share it with others.[21]

Crucial to the retention of expert power is the ability of a channel member to position himself well with respect to the flow of communication and information within a channel system. For example, manufacturers may be highly dependent on the balance of the channel for information concerning consumer demand. Retailers and industrial distributors occupy preferred positions in this regard because of their close contacts with consumers of the manufacturers' products.[22] By gathering, in-

[19] "Sweda: Aggressive Marketing Produces a Spirited Turnaround," *Business Week* (March 31, 1980), p. 101.

[20] "Burger King Sues Firm Controlled by President of Horn & Hardart Co.," *Wall Street Journal,* November 9, 1979, p. 17.

[21] Paul Merrion, "Tougher Pact Riles Big Mac Owners," *Crain's Chicago Business,* Vol. 2 (September 17, 1979), p. 33.

[22] Robert W. Little, "The Marketing Channel: Who Should Lead this Extracorporate Organization," *Journal of Marketing,* Vol. 34 (January 1970), pp. 31–38.

terpreting, and transmitting valuable market information, a channel member can absorb uncertainty for other channel members. Through the process of *uncertainty absorption*[23] the latter become more dependent upon the former relative to obtaining inferences about market developments. For example, General Foods performed a massive study of materials handling in distribution warehouses and then made its results and recommendations available to wholesalers through a group of specialists carefully trained to help implement the recommendations. The company also undertook a major study of retail space profitability and then offered supermarket owners the opportunity to learn a new way of space-profitability accounting.[24]

IDENTIFICATION.   Identification and referent power are, according to French and Raven, linked in a cause and effect sense.

> The referent power of A over B has its basis in the identification of B with A. By identification, we mean a feeling of oneness of B to A, or a desire for such an identity. . . . If A is an attractive group, B will have a feeling of membership or a desire to join. If B is already closely associated with A, he will want to maintain this relationship.[25]

As an illustration, picture the situation where an individual is simultaneously offered a Mercedes Benz dealership and a Subaru dealership. If he discovers, through careful analysis, that both dealerships will yield him the same rate of return on his investment and that the management of both companies will give him comparable support in promotion, training servicemen, finding a location, and the like, it is possible to conjecture that the individual will choose the Mercedes Benz dealership and that, in turn, the Mercedes Benz organization will be able to exercise referent power relative to its new dealership. The existence of referent power within many channels is undeniable, especially in situations where wholesalers or retailers pride themselves on carrying certain brands (e.g., Schwinn bicycles and Estee Lauder's perfumes) and where manufacturers pride themselves on having their brands carried in certain outlets (e.g., Nieman-Marcus and Saks Fifth Avenue). And in certain industrial selling situations, it has been found that industrial purchasing agents' and chemists' responses to sales presentations are strongly influenced by the reputation of the company which the salesman represents. In general, the salesman for the

[23] See James G. March and Herbert A. Simon, *Organizations* (New York: John Wiley, 1958), p. 165. The implementation of uncertainty absorbing techniques could also be viewed more broadly as the use of *information power* rather than the enhancement of *expert power*. Informational influence or persuasion is involved when A provides information not previously available to B or when A points out contingencies of which B had not been aware. B may do what he might not otherwise have done, because, with the new information, he may view the specific action suggested by A to be in his best personal interest, aside from any consideration for A or possible rewards and punishments that A might mete out. Thus, information power is based on the acceptance by B of the logic of A's arguments rather than on A's perceived expertise. See Bertram H. Raven and Arie W. Kruglanski, "Conflict and Power," in Paul Swingle (ed.), *The Structure of Conflict* (New York: Academic Press, 1970), p. 73.

[24] Theodore Levitt, "Marketing Success Through Differentiation—of Anything," *Harvard Business Review* (January-February 1980), p. 89.

[25] French and Raven, *op. cit.*, p. 161.

company with the better reputation always obtains a more favorable response to his presentation.[26]

LEGITIMACY. Legitimate power stems from the values internalized by B which give him a feeling that A "should" or "has a right" to exert influence and that he (B) has an obligation to accept it. The appearance of legitimate power is most obvious in *intra*organizational relations. That is, when a supervisor gives a directive to a subordinate, the latter feels that the former has a right to direct him in a certain manner, and therefore, he will generally conform to the superior's desires. Such legitimized power is synonymous with authority.

Within a nonintegrated marketing channel, there is no formal hierarchy of authority. However, individual firms may perceive that such a hierarchy exists. For example, the largest firm could be considered the leader by other channel members. If this is the case, then legitimate power may be available to that firm. It is highly likely that the scope of legitimate power may be limited; that is, the number of marketing flows over which a given firm may be thought to have a right to exert influence may be quite small (e.g., wholesalers may have legitimate power relative to elements of physical possession, retailers relative to the flow of local promotion and pricing, and the like).

Obviously, the system of laws allows firms to maintain agreements, such as franchises and other contracts, that confer legitimate power. In addition, patent and trademark laws give the owner a certain amount of freedom and justification in supervising the distribution of his products. Another example of this type of legitimate power is the protection afforded a manufacturer and his dealers when the former adopts an exclusive distribution policy.[27]

Combining the Power Bases

The above discussion of power bases has treated each separately. In reality, however, the power bases are used in combination. For example, Digital Equipment Corporation, one of the largest computer manufacturers in the world, has instituted a Commercial Distributor Program, which incorporates a variety of influence strategies, using mainly reward, referent, and expert power bases. Its program includes the following features, among others:

- A Trade Show Program, which supports distributors' participation in trade shows.
- An Open House Program, which provides assistance in attracting prospects and creating new sales leads for distributors.
- A Product Guide, which contains the latest information on Digital products, prices, configurations, and environmental requirements.
- Executive Seminars for distributor personnel.

[26] Theodore Levitt, *Industrial Purchasing Behavior: A Study of Communications Effects* (Boston: Division of Research, Graduate School of Business Administration, Harvard University, 1965), pp. 31–32.

[27] Exclusive distribution and other policies involving legal issues are discussed in Chapter 8.

- A Demonstrator Program, which allows distributors to purchase a Digital computer for demonstration and development purposes at a premium discount.
- A Warehouse Program, which assures shipment of certain standard small business systems and computer peripherals within seven working days.
- A Commercial Operations Guide, which contains recommended guidelines for handling customer surveys, detailed specifications, proposals, contracts, acceptance criteria, warranties, and user documentation.
- An Authorized Digital Computer Distributor Logo, which authorized distributors may use on all sales, stationery, sign, collateral, and advertising materials.
- A Cooperative Advertising Program, under which Digital will reimburse 40 percent of approved advertising expenditures to authorized distributors.

Certain synergistic effects may be operative when power bases are used in combination; e.g., legitimacy may enhance expertise and vice versa, identification may increase with the use of rewards, and coercion may sometimes be necessary to reinforce legitimacy. On the other hand, there may be conflict between certain bases; for example, the use of coercion by a channel member may destroy any referent power that member might have been able to accumulate.

In addition, it should be understood that there are economic, social, and political costs associated with the use of the various power bases which must be taken into account prior to the implementation of programs in which they are incorporated. Influence attempts are also constrained by norms that exist within channel systems. These norms, which are, in fact, "rules" of the competitive "game," aid in defining appropriate industrial behavior and can be even more restrictive than public laws in certain types of situations. For example, during periods of short supply in the steel industry, many buyers are willing to pay above "normal" prices for steel. This alternative is less expensive than shutting down production. Because of short supply, steel distributors in the established marketing channels can command higher prices; however, they frequently refrain from doing so, because they feel that their customers expect certain restraints from them, even though some of their customers go outside the legitimate, established channel structure and purchase higher-priced steel from so-called gray market sources.[28] The established distributors also refrain from using coercive power, such as boycotts, relative to the latter customers, because the norms of market behavior among them do not sanction such actions.

Scope and Significance of the Use of Power

The bases of power can be used to shift the marketing flows among institutions and agencies within the channel, thereby creating a more efficient and effective allocation of resources. The control achieved by some firms over selected deci-

[28] Louis Kriesberg, "Occupational Controls Among Steel Distributors," in Stern (ed.), *Distribution Channels: Behavioral Dimensions, op. cit.,* pp. 48–62.

FIGURE 6-1

Model of a Power Relationship Between Two Firms

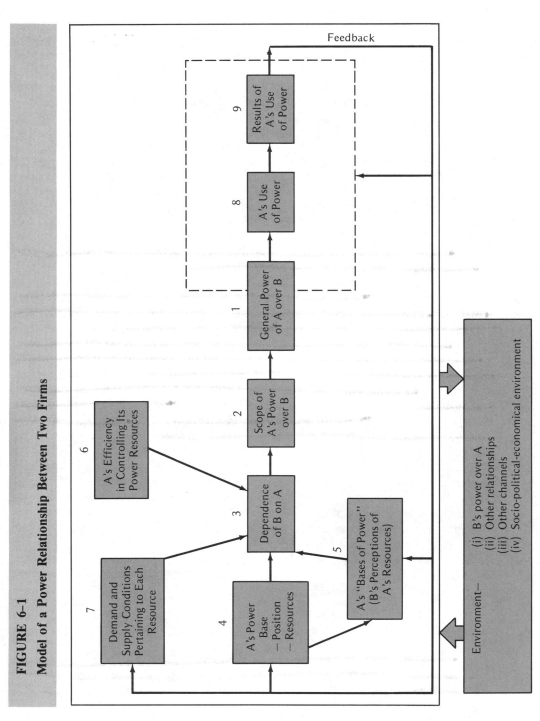

Source: Ian Wilkinson, *Power in Distribution Channels* (Bedfordshire, England: Cranfield Research Papers in Marketing and Logistics, Session 1973-1974), p. 17.

sion variables or marketing efforts of others is a major factor determining the level of performance obtained by the channel as a whole and by each of its individual members. It should, however, be noted that the scope of control does not have to be broad in order for success to be achieved. In fact, within most channels, because of the degree of specialization referred to earlier, the scope of any channel member's power over others may be limited to only a few of the marketing flows. For example, transportation agencies are likely to have little desire to influence promotional activities in the channel, while many manufacturers do not wish to concern themselves greatly with problems associated with financing ultimate consumers' purchases.

The main factors involved in the use of power are summarized in Fig. 6-1 in terms of the relationship between two firms (A and B), where A is the power holder and B is the power subject.[29] Beginning in the middle of the diagram, the general power of A over B (Box 1), which is related to the power A has over B in specific policy areas (Box 2), is shown to stem from the dependence of B on A (Box 3). In turn, this dependence derives from a combination of factors: the resources controlled by A (Box 4); B's perceptions of A, the "bases of power" (Box 5); the efficiency with which A controls his power resources (Box 6); and the demand and supply conditions pertaining to each resource (Box 7). A's use of power (Box 8), which relates in part to the amount of power A has over B (Box 1), leads to certain results (Box 9). The results of A's use of power, i.e., the specification of roles in the channel and, ultimately, the success (sales volume, profitability, market share, etc.) of the relationship, produces certain feedbacks. As a consequence of these feedbacks, the various sources of power may be changed, such as the enhancement or depletion of some resources due to the use of rewards, punishments, expertise, and the like. Finally, the nature of the environment surrounding the relationship is likely to affect a number of elements in the model. For example, the demand and supply conditions pertaining to the resources in A's power base will be affected by the availability of substitutes from other firms. Furthermore, the cultural setting in which the relationship exists, including the past history of interactions in the channel, will affect the way in which power is used and the way the firms perceive one another. The environment comprises many elements—B's power over A, relationships the firms have with other firms, other channels for competing or complementary goods, and the general socio-political-economic environment.

STEP 4. DEALING WITH CHANNEL CONFLICT

As indicated above, channel members tend to specialize in performing certain functions; that is, they have, at least in part, unique roles. Thus, manufacturers specialize in production and national promotions while retailers specialize in merchandising, distribution, and promotions on the local level. This specialization results in the creation of a significant

---

[29] The figure and the discussion of it can be found in Ian Wilkinson, *Power in Distribution Channels* (Bedfordshire, England: Cranfield Research Papers in Marketing and Logistics, Session 1973–1974), pp. 16–18.

amount of operational interdependence among channel members. Each channel member becomes dependent on the other members to realize his organizational objectives. For example, both the manufacturer and the retailer are dependent on each other to reach the final consumer. Members are "pushed" into such interdependencies because of their need for resources—not only money, but specialized skills, access to particular kinds of markets, and the like. Thus, functional interdependence requires a certain minimum level of cooperation in order to accomplish the channel task. Without this minimum cooperation, the channel ceases to exist. Such cooperation allows channel members to find means to coordinate their planning, information, and decision-making and to arrange the payoff structure so that each member can justify joint goals on independent criteria.[30]

There is, however, as Gouldner asserts,[31] a strain toward organizations maximizing their autonomy; therefore, the establishment of mutual interdependencies creates conflicts of interest. In channels comprised of independently owned institutions and agencies, the strain toward autonomy will be juxtaposed to the desire to cooperate; that is, a mixture of motives will be present. It is, therefore, possible to predict with certainty that distribution channels will exhibit evidence of conflict. The relationship between interdependence and conflict has been documented in the social science literature,[32] Fig. 6-2 depicts this relationship. The greater the level of interdependence, the greater will be the opportunity for interference of goal attainment,[33] and hence the greater the potential for conflict among organizations. However, cognitive and affective states generally precede the taking of overt opponent-centered actions on the part of either party to a conflict situation. That is, the parties must usually first become aware or cognizant of the conflict situation as well as personalize the conflict so that hostile feelings develop.[34]

Conflict Over Role Performance

Obviously, role behavior or performance frequently deviates from the prescriptions established by various channel members. While this deviation occurs for many reasons, the most likely causes of the deviation are specific situational factors (e.g., a price war in a retailer's trading area), incompatible organizational

---

[30] Matthew Tuite, Roger Chisholm, and Michael Radnor (eds.), *Interorganizational Decision Making* (Chicago: Aldine Publishing Co., 1972), p. vi.

[31] Alvin Gouldner, "Reciprocity and Autonomy in Functional Theory," in L. Gross (eds.), *Symposium on Sociological Theory* (New York: Harper and Row, 1959), pp. 241–270.

[32] See, for example, Henry Assael, "Constructive Role of Interorganizational Conflict," *Administrative Science Quarterly,* Vol. 14 (1969), pp. 573–582; John M. Dutton and Richard E. Walton, "Interdepartmental Conflict and Cooperation: Two Contrasting Studies," *Human Organization,* Vol. 25 (1966), pp. 207–220; Stuart M. Schmidt and Thomas A. Kochan, "Conflict: Toward Conceptual Clarity," *Administrative Science Quarterly,* Vol. 17 (1972), pp. 359–370; and James D. Thompson, *Organizations in Action* (New York: McGraw-Hill, 1967).

[33] Schmidt and Kochan, *op. cit.,* pp. 361–363.

[34] Louis R. Pondy, "Organizational Conflict: Concepts and Models," *Administrative Science Quarterly,* Vol. 12 (September 1967), pp. 296–320.

FIGURE 6-2
The Conflict Field

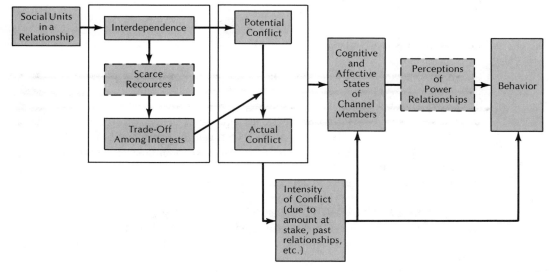

Source: Reprinted from Fuat A. Firat, Alice M. Tybout, and Louis W. Stern, "A Perspective on Conflict and Power in Distribution," in Ronald C. Curhan (ed.), *1974 Combined Proceedings of the AMA Fall and Spring Conferences* (Chicago: American Marketing Association, 1975), p. 436.

objectives, lack of clear and open communication flows between channel members, and differences between the deviating channel member's personal expectations and other members' expectations.[35] Furthermore, it is extremely important to understand that these problems are not confined to relationships in channels comprised of independently owned institutions and agencies. In fact, it is possible that they can be as sharply experienced in vertically integrated systems as they are in nonvertically integrated ones. For example, many of Sears' problems in the 1970s were created because of significant differences in objectives and expectations between its

[35] See Warren J. Wittreich, "Misunderstanding the Retailer," *Harvard Business Review,* Vol. 40 (May–June 1962), pp. 147–152. Contemporary examples of such conflict can be found in the following articles, to mention only a few: John Koten, "Chrysler Corp. Starts Pressuring Its Dealers to Buy More Cars, Citing Danger to Profits," *Wall Street Journal,* October 10, 1980, p. 27; Gail Bronson and Jeffrey H. Birnbaum, "Soaring Interest Rates Pit Manufacturers Against Retailers on Timing of Payments," *Wall Street Journal,* December 8, 1980, p. 3; Leonard M. Apcar, "Burroughs Strikes Back Against Militant Customer," *Wall Street Journal,* November 25, 1980; Jeffrey A. Tannenbaum and Richard E. Rustin, "Commodore International's Shareholders May be Happy, but Many Dealers Aren't," *Wall Street Journal,* December 18, 1980, p. 46; Bill Paul, "Are Oil Giants Twisting Arms to Push Gasoline?" *Wall Street Journal,* September 16, 1980, p. 33; Terry Atlas, "Oil Companies to Reshape Marketing," *Chicago Tribune,* Section 5, February 2, 1981, p. 9; Jeffrey H. Birnbaum, "Suppliers Accuse Big Department Stores of Fudging on Bills Due and Paying Late," *Wall Street Journal,* February 11, 1981, p. 48; and Daniel Machalaba, "Harcourt Brace to Ban Return of Books By Stores for Full Credit Starting Jan. 1," *Wall Street Journal,* November 3, 1980, p. 6.

retail stores, its vertically integrated distribution centers, and its merchandising and buying offices in its Chicago headquarters. Each of the subunits of the organization operated in a semi-autonomous way. Centralized planning was minimal, and conflict was enormous, both within the organization and with its suppliers.

Causes of Channel Conflict

Channel conflict is a situation in which one channel member perceives another channel member(s) to be engaged in behavior that is preventing or impeding him from achieving his goals.[36] It is, in essence, a state of frustration brought about by a restriction of role performance.[37] The amount of conflict is a function of goal incompatibility, domain dissensus, and differences in perceptions of reality among channel members.[38] Furthermore, as channel member interdependence increases, it is likely that even relatively minor incompatibilities in goals, domain definitions, and perceptions can create situations of relatively intense conflict.

GOAL INCOMPATIBILITY. Each channel member has a set of goals and objectives that are very often incompatible with those of other channel members. For example, among the most common conflict issues which arise between manufacturers and industrial distributors are (1) how to handle large accounts, (2) required inventory stocking levels for the distributor, (3) the quality of distributor management, (4) overlapping distributor territories, (5) size of distributor margins, and (6) the philosophical question of whether the distributor's primary obligations and loyalty are to the customer or the supplier.[39] Clearly underlying many of these issues are differences in goals, aims, or values among the channel members involved in the marketing of industrial goods. Furthermore, in consumer goods marketing, there are literally tens of thousands of small retailers served by large manufacturers. Large manufacturers tend to be growth-oriented, whereas small retailers are more interested in maintaining the status quo.[40] The likelihood of conflict is high in such situations because, in their pursuit of policies that are congruent with "dynamic" goals (e.g., increased market share and higher investment returns), the former will

---

[36] Raymond W. Mack and Richard C. Snyder, "The Analysis of Social Conflict—Toward an Overview and Synthesis," *Journal of Conflict Resolution,* Vol. 1 (June 1957), pp. 212–248.

[37] Louis W. Stern and Ronald H. Gorman, "Conflict in Distribution Channels: An Exploration," in Louis W. Stern (ed.), *Distribution Channels: Behavioral Dimensions, op. cit.,* p. 156.

[38] See Louis W. Stern and J. L. Heskett, "Conflict Management in Interorganization Relations: A Conceptual Framework," in Louis W. Stern (ed.), *op. cit.,* pp. 293–294; Larry J. Rosenberg and Louis W. Stern, "Conflict Measurement in the Distribution Channel," *Journal of Marketing Research,* Vol. 8 (November 1971), pp. 437–442; Michael Etgar, "Sources and Types of Intrachannel Conflict," *Journal of Retailing,* Vol. 55 (Spring 1979), pp. 61–78; Ernest R. Cadotte and Louis W. Stern, "A Process Model of Dyadic Interorganizational Relations in Marketing Channels," in Jagdish N. Sheth (ed.), *Research in Marketing,* Vol. 2 (Greenwich, Conn.: Jai Press, 1979); and Reve and Stern, *op. cit.*

[39] Frederick E. Webster, Jr., "The Role of the Industrial Distributor in Marketing Strategy," *Journal of Marketing,* Vol. 40 (July 1976), p. 11.

[40] Wittreich, *op. cit.* See Chapter 9 in this text for a fuller discussion of the communication problems encountered between large manufacturers and small retailers.

likely adopt innovative programs that contradict the more static orientation of the latter.

DOMAIN DISSENSUS.   In addition, conflict arises over domain definitions and role performance via the process depicted in Fig. 6–3. Domain dissensus is often present in so-called dual distribution situations, such as these:[41]

> Independent businessmen who fabricate finished products made from steel, copper, aluminum, and other metals widely report that they must compete with outlets that are owned by their suppliers. These fabricator middlemen must purchase much of their supplies from those with whom they compete, but must also meet the prices established by their suppliers' outlets.
>
> The major refiners of petroleum own and operate their own retail outlets but also sell through independents who either own their own stations or lease the property from their major supplier. The refiners have opened their own directly-operated private brand stations in addition to the regular brand stations. Mobil has about 600 stations

FIGURE 6–3
The Process of Conflict over Roles (Domains)

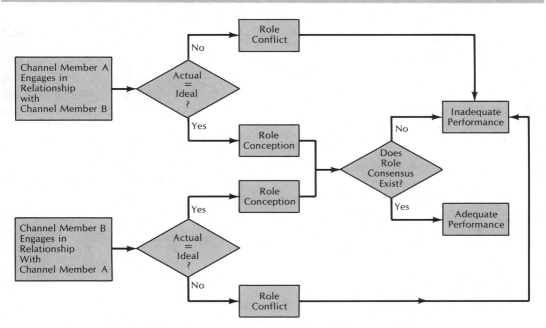

Source: John R. Walton, Assistant Professor of Marketing, University of Minnesota.

[41] The first three examples are presented in Robert E. Weigand, "Fit Products and Channels to Your Markets," *Harvard Business Review* (January–February 1977), pp. 95–105.

selling under such names as Sello and Big-bi. Gulf has 485 private-brand stations that sell under such names as Go-Lo and Ez-Lo.[42]

Automobile manufacturers market the bulk of their output through franchised retailers, but they sell directly to major leasing and rental companies. Hertz buys from the factory and regularly resells part of its slightly used fleet through more than 100 retail outlets throughout the country. Some of the Hertz outlets are located near franchised new car dealers.

In some instances Sears asks its suppliers to procure their raw materials through Sears; for example, Sears might buy corduroy in bulk from textile mills and then resell it to companies that make clothing for it. Sears' traditional justification of this practice is that it helps to ensure quality, supply, and the rock-bottom prices available to a volume buyer. "I've never believed that," one apparel supplier has stated. "I've always thought they were just trying to make a markup on the goods."[43]

Conflict may also occur when a channel member is assigned a role that he does not have the capacity to fulfill, when demands are made upon the channel member that are more than can be expected from the position within the channel that the member holds, and when a channel member feels he must relate to two reference groups and cannot decide which role is dominant.[44] There is also a strong likelihood that a channel member will define his own domain—the population to be served, the territory to be covered, the technology to be employed, and the functions or duties to be performed—in a way which is, at least in part, incongruent with those with whom he deals. For example, in the outdoor power equipment industry (e.g., lawn mowers, garden tractors, rotary tillers, and snow blowers), there is considerable conflict among manufacturers, wholesalers, and retailers over such issues as (1) overlapping territories, (2) where inventory will be held in the channel, (3) who will provide service facilities and handle warranty claims, (4) inadequate levels of spare parts at different levels in the channel, (5) inadequate inventory control, especially at the retail and wholesale levels, and (6) inadequate financing throughout the channel.

DIFFERING PERCEPTIONS OF REALITY. Differing perceptions of reality are also important sources of conflict, because they indicate that there will be differing bases of action in response to the same situation. As a result, behaviors stemming from these perceptions are likely to frustrate and produce conflict. Illustrative of the perceptions that have traditionally led to poor supplier/retailer relations are retailer perceptions that:

- Supplier salespeople oversell without regard to production and delivery capability;

[42] "The Oil Majors Retreat from the Gasoline Pump," *Business Week* (August 7, 1978), p. 51. See also Neil Ulman, "Service Stations Give Oil Firms Tough Fight Over Gas-Only Outlets," *Wall Street Journal,* June 16, 1977, p. 1.

[43] Carol J. Loomis, "The Leaning Tower of Sears," *op. cit.,* p. 81.

[44] Alvin L. Bertrand, *Social Organizations: A General Systems and Role Theory Perspective* (Philadelphia: F. A. Davis, 1972), pp. 173–177.

- Supplier salespeople lack an understanding of the retailer's goals and merchandising philosophy;
- Supplier salespeople do not provide adequate in-store service;
- Suppliers do not offer a planned approach to promoting and merchandising products.

And supplier perceptions that:

- Retail buyers are preoccupied with "chiseling" the best prices out of suppliers;
- Retail buyers lack decision-making autonomy;
- Retail buyers ignore or move too slowly in accepting promotional deals and other allowances;
- Retail buyers handle too many product lines to be effective product managers and ignore merchandise once an order is placed;
- Retailers refuse to cooperate for fear of being "locked-in" to a supplier.[45]

Differing perceptions are also a major cause of a number of conflict issues between manufacturers and industrial distributors.[46] Incongruent perceptions of reality can be attributed to technical problems of communication,[47] as well as to differences in goals and orientations.[48]

In an attempt to develop a comprehensive measure of channel conflict, Etgar formulated the questionnaire items found in Exhibit 6–2.[49] A reading of them provides an extremely useful picture of the depth and breadth of conflict which potentially exists in all marketing channels. For the purposes of effective questionnaire construction, some of the questionnaire items were worded positively so as to prevent leading the respondents to express negative reactions about their channel partners. In his study, Etgar found that disagreements about channel roles, expectations, perceptions, and channel communications were the most important ones in the conflict situations he investigated.[50]

[45] Ronald L. Ernst, "Distribution Channel Detente Benefits Suppliers, Retailers, and Consumers," *Marketing News,* (March 7, 1980), p. 19.

[46] Frederick E. Webster, Jr., *Industrial Marketing Strategy* (New York: John Wiley & Sons, 1979), p. 172.

[47] See, for example, James G. March, "The Power of Power," in David Easton (ed.), *Varieties of Political Theory* (Englewood Cliffs, N. J.: Prentice-Hall, 1966), pp. 39–70; Clagett G. Smith, "A Comparative Analysis of Some Conditions and Consequences of Intra-Organizational Conflict," *Administrative Science Quarterly,* Vol. 11 (1966), pp. 504–529; and Kenneth W. Thomas, Richard E. Walton, and John M. Dutton, "Determinants of Interdepartmental Conflict," in Tuite, Chisholm, and Radnor (eds.), *op. cit.,* pp. 45–69.

[48] See, for example, Assael, *op. cit.*; Dutton and Walton, *op. cit.*; Bert C. McCammon, Jr., and Robert W. Little, "Marketing Channels: Analytical Systems and Approaches," in George Schwartz (ed.), *Science in Marketing* (New York: John Wiley & Sons, 1965), p. 322; Joseph C. Palamountain, *The Politics of Distribution* (Cambridge: Harvard University Press, 1955); C. G. Smith, *op. cit.*; Stern and Gorman, *op. cit.*; and Wittreich, *op. cit.*

[49] Michael Etgar, "Sources and Types of Intrachannel Conflict," *Journal of Retailing,* Vol. 55 (Spring 1979), pp. 61–78.

[50] Data for Etgar's study were collected in 1976 from 138 furniture, stereo equipment, life insurance, shoe, liquor, and automobile dealers who operate in large, northeastern metropolitan areas. *Ibid.,* pp. 68 and 69.

EXHIBIT 6-2

Questionnaire Items Used to Measure Channel Conflict

GOALS DIVERGENCE

1. The leading manufacturer often wants to prod dealers to buy more products than are good for the dealers.

2. The manufacturer often complains that dealers prefer maintaining their professional status over improving their modes of operation.

3. The manufacturers often demand that dealers concentrate fully on their brands, while it is to the dealer's advantage to add major sidelines to his business.

4. A major function of a dealer is to advise and counsel its customers as to which products they should choose while manufacturers consider dealer's major function to be developing contacts with buyers and sellers.

5. Manufacturers are often too concerned with market shares to ensure proper profitability for their products.

6. Manufacturers often do not recognize that there is an optimal size for retailers' operations and that expanding beyond that brings the retailer losses and not profits.

DRIVE FOR AUTONOMY

1. My leading manufacturer influences strongly my choice of other suppliers.

2. In this industry, through couponing, discounting, and advertising, etc., manufacturers practically dictate to dealers the type of promotion the latter will use in their stores.

3. Most of the dealers selling in this channel are forced to adjust their inventories according to the decision of the manufacturers.

4. In this industry retailers have little choice on pricing but to follow manufacturer's suggested retail price.

COMPETITION OVER CHANNEL RESOURCES

1. The manufacturer restricts considerably dealers' use of cooperative advertising monies.

2. The manufacturer often allocates insufficient share of choice items to a dealer.

3. The manufacturer often ties-in less desirable items with orders for choice items.

4. The manufacturer and his dealers often disagree about the size of territories allocated to the dealers.

5. Allocation of shelf space/showroom space is a major issue of negotiations between the manufacturer and his dealers.

6. The manufacturer often attempts to sell directly to large accounts and in this way to circumvent the dealers.

7. The manufacturer does not allow too many dealers to operate in one territory.

ROLE CLARITY

1. In this industry, the duties of the manufacturers and dealers are well defined; only rarely is it not known who should perform a specific function.[a]

2. In this industry there is no agreement as to who should pay for merchandise damaged on the way to the retailer.

3. My leading manufacturer has clear-cut rules about returning unsold merchandise.[a]

4. With some bargaining, dealers get better credit terms from their suppliers.

NONFULFILLMENT OF ROLES BY MANUFACTURERS

1. In this industry, manufacturers often attempt to take over activities which rightfully belong to the dealers.

2. Production innovation by the manufacturer is relatively poor.

3. My leading manufacturer provides enough sales assistance (advertising, salesmen training, etc.) to his dealers.[a]

4. The product line provided by the manufacturer is broad enough to allow his dealers to compete effectively in the market.[a]

5. The manufacturer often prices his products too high and reduces the competitive advantage of the dealers.

6. The delivery scheduling of the products by the manufacturer leaves much to be desired.

NONFULFILLMENT OF ROLES BY DEALERS

1. The manufacturer often complains that dealers do not stock enough of his items.

2. The manufacturer has few complaints about the aggressiveness of the dealers sales people.[a]

3. The manufacturer is highly satisfied with the servicing provided by his dealers to the customers.[a]

4. The manufacturer often complains that the dealers do not promote his products sufficiently.

5. The manufacturer is in general very satisfied with the quality of dealer's sales force.[a]

[a] *Ratings were reversed.*

PERCEPTIONS DIVERGENCE

1. In my opinion, the leading manufacturer treats his dealers very fairly.[a]

2. Dealers are often more knowledgeable about their market than manufacturers expect.

3. A manufacturer and dealer often view each other as rivals where one can only gain at the expense of another.

4. The manufacturers in this industry erroneously think that they are irreplaceable.

5. Manufacturer and dealers often have different opinions about the real nature of competition in this industry.

6. The manufacturer rarely helps the dealer when competition in his area is getting rough.

EXPECTATIONS DIVERGENCE

1. Manufacturers usually expect their products to perform better than they actually do.

2. The manufacturer and dealers often have different opinions about the future of this industry.

3. The manufacturer often relies too much on planned operations and is not ready to adjust rapidly to changing market conditions.

4. The manufacturers rely too much on their own promotional campaigns.

INTRACHANNEL COMMUNICATIONS NOISE

1. My leading manufacturer often does not bother to inform his dealers early enough about out of stock items or discontinuation of models.

2. Manufacturer's salesmen and detail men are well equipped to serve dealers promptly.[a]

3. The manufacturer is often late in informing dealers about the introduction of new products.

4. In this industry, dealers often aggravate manufacturers by cancelling early orders.

5. Dealer's complaints are well taken care of by the manufacturer.[a]

6. Orders forwarded to the manufacturer often get mislaid or misdirected.

Source: Michael Etgar, "Sources and Types of Intrachannel Conflict," *Journal of Retailing*, Vol. 55 (Spring 1979), pp. 76-78.

The Required Inducements-Contributions Balance

A commercial channel system continues to function as long as the subsystems are willing to remain in the system. Each unit is induced to participate in a channel of distribution by the offering of certain rewards for its supposed unique potential contributions. The basic problem, then, is to achieve an inducements-contributions balance for each of the channel members—that is, a channel condition where the rewards offered by the channel system to a channel member are commensurate with the efforts expended by that member. Theoretically, this is accomplished when a channel member is successfully utilizing the distribution system of which he is a part for the achievement of his own organizational objectives, while at the same time the distribution system is effectively employing this individual channel member to attain its objectives. If either of these conditions is not fulfilled, a satisfactory inducement-contributions balance cannot be affected, since dissatisfaction will flow from such a disparate channel system-channel member relationship. Thus, conflict will inevitably result when there is an imbalance between inducements and contributions.

Pathological Conflict

Generally, conflict is thought to be dysfunctional and, therefore, is often defined as behavior designed to destroy, injure, thwart, or control another party in an interdependent relationship.[51] However, such a view is too negatively oriented, because it is clear that the existence of conflict is frequently highly functional—without it, systems might become passive, noninnovative, and eventually nonviable. Thus, even though conflict is opponent-centered behavior,[52] the conflict bred by the dependency relationship is not all "bad." What one must seek to avoid is *pathological conflict,* or, colloquially, moves that are malign for the parties involved and for the entire system itself.[53]

In international relations, wars may be viewed as a pathological conflict—in the process of engaging in behavior designed to thwart another country, the aggressor also kills off its own young men and women. In distribution channel relations, examples of pathological moves are less vivid but nonetheless are easily defined. Thus, when retail druggists were pressing manufacturers to maintain retail prices on their brands through the policing of Fair Trade laws, Lever Brothers found it difficult to control the pricing behavior of "pine board" (cut rate) drug stores relative to Pepsodent, the best-selling brand of toothpaste at the time. In retaliation, the druggists removed the brand from their shelves, thereby forcing consumers to request packages each time they wanted to replenish their household

---

[51] Raymond W. Mack and Richard C. Snyder, "The Analysis of Social Conflict—Toward an Overview and Synthesis," *Journal of Conflict Resolution,* Vol. 1 (June 1957), pp. 212–248.

[52] Although conflict can be viewed as opponent-centered behavior, competition is behavior that is object-centered, and cooperation involves joint-striving. For a discussion of each type of behavior, see Louis W. Stern, "Antitrust Implications of a Sociological Interpretation of Competition, Conflict, and Cooperation in the Marketplace," *The Antitrust Bulletin,* Vol. 16 (Fall 1971), pp. 509–530.

[53] Kenneth E. Boulding, "The Economics of Human Conflict," in Elton B. McNeil (ed.), *The Nature of Human Conflict* (Englewood Cliffs, N. J.: Prentice-Hall, 1965), pp. 174–175. See also William P. Dommermuth, "Profiting From Distribution Conflicts," *Business Horizons* (December 1976), pp. 4–13; and Lewis A. Coser, *The Functions of Social Conflict* (Glencoe, Ill.: The Free Press, 1956). For contrary evidence, see Robert F. Lusch, "Channel Conflict: Its Impact on Retailer Operating Performance," *Journal of Retailing,* Vol. 52 (Summer 1976), pp. 3–12 and 89.

supplies.[54] Surely this was a pathological move in a conflict situation, for in the process of "hurting" Lever Brothers, the druggists hurt themselves by foregoing sales volume and by inconveniencing their customers. The entire system suffered as the result of the boycott.

More recently, when Sears' suppliers complained in 1978 about the great pressure they were under as Sears abruptly changed strategies, began to reduce inventories, and sharply cut back its promotional efforts, they were advised publicly and testily by Sears' new Chairman, Edward R. Telling, that the company had its own business to run and did not owe them a living.[55] Similar situations are found when a supplier slows up deliveries if a reseller is slow with his payments or does not follow some kind of policy dictate of the supplier.

Effective Conflict Management

A central task in channel management is to seek ways to manage conflict. In other words, ways must be found to keep conflict from becoming dysfunctional and to harness the energies in conflict situations to produce innovative resolutions. If conflict within marketing channels is to be managed, it will eventually be necessary for the members involved to come to grips with the underlying causes of the conflict issues that arise among them. The specific strategy employed will depend not only on the cause of the conflict but also on the weight of power of the channel member seeking to manage the conflict.[56] Therefore, the effective use of power is not only required in specifying roles within the channel; it is also essential in dealing with conflicts that inevitably arise among channel members.

Several strategies for use in channel relations are suggested briefly below, each of which can be modified depending upon the situational variables present in and the structural dimensions of a specific channel.[57]

DIPLOMACY. In an analogy from international relations, channel *diplomacy* is the method by which interorganizational relations are conducted, adjusted, and

[54] Joseph C. Palamountain, Jr., *The Politics of Distribution* (Cambridge, Mass.: Harvard University Press, 1955).

[55] Carol J. Loomis, "The Leaning Tower of Sears," *op. cit.,* p. 79.

[56] The "weight" of power is a specification of how much A influences B. When the weight of A's power over B is at the maximum, it may be referred to as control. At this point, A can predict with certainty that B will respond in the desired manner.

[57] For a more detailed discussion and citations related to each of the conflict management strategies listed here as well as additional strategies, see Louis W. Stern, "Potential Conflict Management Mechanisms in Distribution Channels: An Interorganizational Analysis," in Donald N. Thompson (ed.), *Contractual Marketing Systems* (Boston: Heath-Lexington Books, 1971), pp. 111–146. For empirical research results relating to superordinate goals and exchange of persons as conflict management strategies, see Louis W. Stern, Brian Sternthal, and C. Samuel Craig, "Managing Conflict in Distribution Channels: A Laboratory Study," *Journal of Marketing Research,* Vol. 10 (May 1973), pp. 169–179; and J. David Hunger and Louis W. Stern, "An Assessment of the Functionality of Superordinate Goals in Reducing Intergroup Conflict," *Academy of Management Journal,* Vol. 19 (December 1976), pp. 591–605. For additional ideas, see Larry J. Rosenberg, "A New Approach to Distribution Conflict Management," *Business Horizons* (October 1974), pp. 67–74.

managed by "ambassadors," "envoys," or other persons operating at the boundaries of member organizations. Channel members engage in, cultivate, and rely upon diplomatic procedures, especially in nonintegrated systems. The functions of a channel "diplomat" should, in the widest interpretation, be to help shape the policies he is to follow, to conduct negotiations with channel members to whom he is assigned, to observe and report on everything that may be of interest to the firm employing him, and to provide information concerning his firm to the operatives in counterpart channel organizations.

The presence of individual diplomats or of diplomatic committees is common in distribution channels, e.g., the use of business management specialists in the automobile industry and of factory specialists in the U.S. electrical equipment industry.[58] Perhaps the best example of channel diplomacy can be found, however, in the U.S. food industry. Manufacturers appoint "liaison men" who represent and interpret company policy to wholesalers and retailers. According to an official of one major grocery manufacturer, the use of liaison executives in this industry has resulted in a resolution of many conflicts before they have matured.[59]

Because of some well-documented strains on boundary personnel,[60] it would probably be best to place the diplomat position at an executive level within organizations. It is essential that the status of the diplomat be high enough so that the power that the diplomat holds is at least relatively obvious to the parties with whom the diplomat interacts.[61] This caveat would probably exclude salesmen or purchasing agents in most companies as candidates.

JOINT MEMBERSHIP IN TRADE ASSOCIATIONS.   There are numerous instances where membership in the trade associations of channel counterparts has proven to be extremely beneficial in managing conflict situations. The U.S. television receiver industry provides one prominent example:

> . . . the lack of communications in the channel of distribution was one of the major dealer complaints. Another was the lack of product knowledge and the lack of understanding of the dealers' problems on the part of the distributor salesmen. The approach used to correct the lack of communications was to invite the manufacturers to become members of the National Appliance and Radio TV Dealers Association (NARDA). Twelve of the major manufacturers are now members, and representatives of these and other companies now attend NARDA conventions. Manufacturers' rela-

---

[58] Apparently, some of the "diplomats" in the automobile industry have used their positions for personal gain by helping dealers to falsify warranty claims and then blackmailing the dealers in return. Clearly, then, effective monitoring is required when this strategy is used, particularly when the diplomats are given considerable power by their firms. See "General Motors is Countersued by Ex-Dealer," *Wall Street Journal,* July 10, 1975, p. 4.

[59] Albert Adler, Herbert Johnson, Jr., and William Meschio, "The Food Industry," in Henry Assael (ed.), *The Politics of Distributive Trade Associations: A Study in Conflict Resolution* (Hempstead, N. Y.: Hofstra University, 1967), p. 195.

[60] Robert L. Kahn, Donald M. Wolfe, Robert P. Quinn, and J. Diedrick Snoek, *Organizational Stress: Studies in Role Conflict and Ambiguity* (New York: John Wiley & Sons, Inc., 1964), pp. 123–124.

[61] *Ibid.,* p. 393.

tions meetings are a regular convention feature. Executives of manufacturing organizations are regular speakers at NARDA training seminars and at the regular convention.[62]

Another example is the close relationship that has been forged between the Grocery Manufacturers of America (GMA) and the National Association of Food Chains (NAFC). Besides making certain that channel-wide problems are addressed at the annual conventions of both organizations via joint presentations, the two associations formed a committee comprised of manufacturers and retailers which was responsible for developing the Universal Product Code. The code is now found on almost all packaged goods sold through supermarkets and represents one of the major innovations in the food industry in the past thirty years.[63] Other programs are underway which combine the talents of various channel members from both associations in resolving conflict issues in distribution.

Interaction among the various representatives in trade association-sponsored events is, however, infrequent. What is more desirable is the creation of a network of primary relations among channel members. But even on a relatively infrequent basis, the arranging of interorganizational collaboration of a common task jointly accepted as worthwhile and involving personal association of individuals as operating equals should result in more effective coordination and lessened hostility among organizations. Perhaps one of the most meaningful conflict management mechanisms, in this respect, might be an "exchange of persons" program among channel members, similar to those implemented in international relations.

EXCHANGE OF PERSONS. This conflict management strategy involves a bilateral trade of personnel for a specified time period. The technique involved in such programs is essentially the same as role reversal, a procedure where one or both of the participants in a discussion present the viewpoint of the other. Conflict theorists have long suggested that role reversal would create a greater understanding of the other party's position than merely presenting one's own side of the issue.[64]

In distribution channels, exchange of persons could take place on several different levels of an organization or at all levels. Thus, as part of the initial executive training program, the marketing recruit (perhaps fresh from college) could spend a prescribed period of time working in the organization of suppliers, middlemen, and/or customers. Gallo has worked out just such a program with the independently owned wine wholesalers it employs in its marketing channels. In like fashion, sales, purchasing, traffic, and inventory personnel could be exchanged, as well as other line and staff personnel. For certain types of employees, it has been possible to work out a sabbatical system similar to that at universities, so that these individuals could assume temporary positions either closer to or farther away from

[62] Robert G. Biedermann and Richard L. Tabak, "The Television Receiver Industry," in Assael (ed.), *op. cit.,* p. 287.

[63] The functions and potential impact of the Universal Product Code are addressed in some detail in Chapter 9.

[64] For relevant citations, see Louis W. Stern, C. Samuel Craig, and Brian Sternthal, "Conflict Management in Interorganizational Relations," *Journal of Applied Psychology,* Vol. 60 (August 1975).

the ultimate market in which the product of the particular channel is sold. For example, Illinois Central Gulf Railroad conducts employee exchanges with DuPont, U.S. Gypsum, Exxon, and Shell Oil. Similarly, Weyerhaeuser Company has an exchange program with General Electric Company.[65]

While such exchanges require clear guidelines because of the possible disclosure of proprietary information, persons participating in such exchanges take back to their "home" organizations a view of their job in an interorganizational context and a personal and professional involvement in the channel network, as well as added training. In addition to learning something of the complexities of another channel member's organization and mission, participants in such programs have the opportunity of coming together with channel counterparts who share specific tasks, professions, and interests. These shared tasks form the basis of continuing relationship that are extraorganizational in content and interorganizational in commitment. It is highly likely that positive changes in attitudes toward other channel members would occur.

An exchange of persons program in a distributions channel would be of little significance, however, if the only individuals with whom the "exchangee" comes into contact are no potential threat to channel cooperation or are already "converted" to an interorganizational view of channel relations. Furthermore, the "best" type of exchange might involve not merely a transfer of persons but common enterprises, jointly initiated and carried out on a relatively large scale. That is, optimally, the individuals participating in the exchange should participate in major projects concerned with policy-making within the channel.

COOPTATION.   Cooptation is the process of absorbing new elements into the leadership or policy-determining structure of an organization as a means of averting threats to its stability or existence.[66] For example, some members of the Independent Grocers Alliance (IGA) system have used cooptation successfully for a long period of time. A number of wholesalers within the IGA system have formed retailer advisory councils. Although the composition and functions of the councils vary from region to region, depending on the desires of the wholesaler serving the retailers in each region, the councils generally meet four times a year with the wholesaler and are comprised of elected representatives of the retailers in the region. At each meeting, the council members discuss a wide variety of merchandising and logistics subjects and raise questions that concern the retailers they represent. When council members return to their own stores, they inform their "constituency" of what happened at the meeting. If a new program was presented, they tell their retailers about the program and recommend whether it should be accepted or rejected.[67]

[65] "Executive Swapping: Experiments Pay Off at Some Major Firms," *Wall Street Journal,* April 24, 1973, p. 1. For a discussion of some of the possible pitfalls in exchange programs, see "When Bureaucrats and Executives Swap Jobs," *Business Week* (February 18, 1980), pp. 99 and 103.

[66] Philip Selznick, *TVA and the Grass Roots* (Berkeley, Calif.: University of California Press, 1949), p. 13.

[67] "The Retail Senate," *IGA Grocergram,* Vol. 51 (October 1977), p. 31.

The positive attributes of cooptation as a conflict resolution strategy are many. Cooptation may permit the achievement of ready accessibility among channel members in that it requires the establishment of routine and reliable channels through which information, aid, and requests may be brought. Administration of the channel may become more centralized so that the execution of a broad policy is adapted to local market conditions by utilizing the special knowledge of individuals attached to distributive organizations located in diverse markets. Cooptation also permits the sharing of responsibility so that a variety of channel members may become identified with and committed to the programs developed for a particular product or service.

There are, however, some real dangers in implementing this device, especially for the coopting organization. Selznick states:

> The significance of cooptation for organizational analysis is not simply that there is a change in or a broadening of leadership, and that this is an adaptive response, but also *that this change is consequential for the character and role of the organization or governing body.* Cooptation results in some constriction of the field of choice available to the organization or leadership in question. The character of the coopted elements will necessarily shape the modes of action available to the group which has won adaptation at the price of commitment to outside elements.[68]

Thus cooptation makes inroads on the process of deciding goals and means. Not only must the final choice be acceptable to the coopted channel member(s), but to the extent that cooptation is effective, it places an "outsider" in a position to determine the occasion for a goal decision, to participate in analyzing the existing situation, to suggest alternatives, and to take part in the deliberation of consequences.[69] When, in 1979, Chrysler Corporation made the decision to nominate the president of the United Auto Workers for a seat on its board of directors during its financial crisis, a New Jersey-based automobile dealer organization immediately requested that a Chrysler dealer be added to the board as well.[70] If both labor and dealers are represented on the board, the likelihood is that the decision-making powers of Chrysler's management will be severely circumscribed. Furthermore, as Etzioni warns, cooptation may be used to create a semblance of communication from others to those in control without effective communications really existing. Manipulated or fictitious cooptation only conceals the need for real communication and influence.[71] Establishing dealer and distributor advisory councils, for example, is merely patronizing if the firms convening such councils pay only lip service to

[68] Selznick, *op. cit.,* pp. 15–16.

[69] James D. Thompson and William J. McEwen, "Organizational Goals and Environment," in Amitai Etzioni (ed.), *Complex Organizations: A Sociological Reader,* 2nd ed. (New York: Holt, Rinehart and Winston, Inc., 1969), p. 194.

[70] "Chrysler May Face Rush of Candidates For Seats on Board," *Wall Street Journal,* October 29, 1979, p. 14.

[71] Amitai Etzioni, "Administration and the Consumer," *Administration Science Quarterly,* Vol. 3 (September 1958), p. 261.

what the participants say. In many cases, however, especially for such firms as Prudential Insurance and Belden, these councils or advisory boards have represented the use of cooptation in its most effective sense.

MEDIATION.   Mediation is the process whereby a third party attempts to secure settlement of a dispute by persuading the parties either to continue their negotiations or to consider procedural or substantive recommendations that the mediator may make. Mediation essentially involves operating on the field of the conflicting parties in such a way that opportunities or trading moves are perceived that otherwise might not have been perceived. Solutions might be given an acceptability simply by being suggested by the mediator and hence acquire a degree of saliency that is important in making them mutually acceptable. Effective mediation succeeds in clarifying facts and issues, in keeping parties in contact with each other, in exploring possible bases of agreement, in encouraging parties to agree to specific proposals, and in supervising the implementation of agreements.

A worthwhile investment in industries with a record of distribution conflicts might be to place on retainer respected individuals (e.g., retired judges, professors, and consultants) to aid in mediation with the consent of the parties. Many trade associations attempt to play the role of mediator, but their usually slanted interest makes them inappropriate for the task (aside from the possible antitrust implications of their actions).

ARBITRATION.   Arbitration can be compulsory or voluntary.[72] Compulsory arbitration is a process wherein the parties are required by law to submit their dispute to a third party whose decision is final and binding. In a channel context, the government (or the courts) have served to settle disputes, as was the case when the automobile dealers and manufacturers clashed publicly over certain distribution policies. Voluntary arbitration is a process wherein parties voluntarily submit their dispute to a third party whose decision will be considered final and binding. Examples of such arbitration are found by reviewing the Trade Practice Conferences of the Federal Trade Commission. One case is the television receiver industry. The Federal Trade Commission, in concert with television set manufacturers, distributors, and dealers, set up 32 industry rules to protect the consumer and to reduce distributive conflicts. Five distribution conflict areas were arbitrated: (1) tie-in sales, (2) price-fixing, (3) mass shipments used to clog outlets and foreclose competitors, (4) discriminatory billing, and (5) special rebates, bribes, refunds, and discounts.[73]

An important development regarding this conflict management strategy was enacted under a recent Federal Trade Commission order. Airco, Inc., a producer of industrial gases, settled Federal Trade Commission antitrust charges by agreeing to permit its distributors to take disputes over purchases of certain Airco products to

[72] Robert E. Weigand and Hilda C. Wasson, "Arbitration in the Marketing Channel," *Business Horizons* (October 1974), pp. 39–47.
[73] Biedermann and Tabak, *op. cit.*, pp. 280–282.

private arbitration.[74] Under the order, Airco agreed that, among other things, if it refused to sell any gas or welding product to a distributor, the distributor could demand arbitration to determine if Airco's action was in reprisal for the distributor's election to purchase from a supplier other than Airco. The order states that arbitration must be held in accordance with the Commercial Arbitration Rules of the American Arbitration Association, unless otherwise agreed by the parties, and that the decision of the arbitrators would be final and binding on both parties.

It should be noted, though, that the whole question of relying on law and law enforcement to manage conflicts in distribution is suspect, because it is doubtful whether permanently legislated solutions can be equitably applied to future conflicts in different channel contexts. As Assael has found, "internal" (intrachannel) conflict resolution has proven, historically, to be more satisfactory, from both a micro and a macro viewpoint, than "external" or legally imposed resolution.[75]

ADOPTING SUPERORDINATE GOALS.   Superordinate goals are those ends greatly desired by all those caught in dispute or conflict, which cannot be attained by the resources and energies of each of the parties separately, but which require the concerted efforts of all parties involved.[76] Conflict resolution of a relatively permanent nature requires an integration of the needs of both sides to the dispute so that they find a common goal without sacrificing their basic economic and ethical principles. The difficult task is, obviously, to articulate a goal or common interest on which all parties can agree.

A superordinate goal can be an explicit desire by channel members to resist a threat to the channel's survival or growth from some outside pressure (e.g., competitive, legal). In such situations, the channel members may set aside their differences for the sake of defense. The process of meeting a threat external to the system will serve to displace or transfer hostility between and among channel members to the "common enemy." However, a major question remains: When the outside threat is removed, will the internal conflicts return? In other words, is the cohesion ephemeral and is the prior conflict among channel members merely postponed?

The unified reaction on the part of channel members to an outside threat can be viewed as a behavior change, and as behavior changes, attitudes are usually altered to become more consistent with the new behavior. These new attitudes may remain once the threat is removed. In addition, during the process of countering the threat, information will be exchanged, some of which may have a bearing on sources of conflict beyond that posed by the threat. Because of the information ex-

[74] "Airco Agrees to Settle Disputes With Distributors Through Arbitration," *FTC News Summary* (April 13, 1979), p. 3.

[75] Henry Assael, "The Political Role of Trade Associations in Distributive Conflict Resolution," *Journal of Marketing,* Vol. 32 (April 1968), pp. 21–28. See also S. Macaulay, "Non-Contractual Relations in Business," *American Sociological Review,* Vol. 28 (1963), pp. 55–70.

[76] Muzafer Sherif, *Social Interaction* (Chicago, Ill.: Aldine Publishing Company, 1967), p. 457; see also Muzafer Sherif, O. J. Harvey, B. Jack White, William R. Hood, and Carolyn W. Sherif, *Intergroup Conflict and Cooperation: The Robbers Cave Experiment* (Norman, Ok.: The University of Oklahoma, 1961), p. 202.

changed and because of the monetary and psychological costs jointly borne by the parties during the time of combating the threat, future relationships between the parties may be significantly different than they were during previous interactions. Channel members may gain empathy by seeing, perhaps for the first time, other channel members' points of view, even though these viewpoints are presented in a different context than under "normal" circumstances. Finally, the original conflict issues—prior to the threat occurrence—may decay over time as energies are directed at the outside threat.[77]

On the other hand, there is a strong possibility that the prior conflict will reemerge, unaffected by the temporary unity of the parties. Blake, Shepard, and Mouton have observed that:

> The condition under which superordinate goals will produce cooperative effort, *without resolving the intergroup relations* problem, is when the assumed *superordinate goal is really a superordinate threat.* . . . In this circumstance, the groups put aside their own conflict until the greater enemy has been annihilated. But the differences that were set aside earlier return once the threat or superordinate need has been removed. In truth, then, the problem has not been solved. It has only been deferred under conditions of more pressing need for cooperative effort.[78]

Thus, establishing superordinate goals on the basis of threats from the outside, whether conjured up or real, can be a double-edged sword. Extended periods of integrated effort may be achieved only when the institutions and agencies within a given channel come to grips with the underlying causes for their conflict and attempt to resolve them. The strategies previously discussed, if employed wisely, could lead channel members to the eventual adoption of *positive* superordinate goals, such as those emphasizing the necessity of increasing the efficiency of moving a product through the channel, with the result that greater sales volume would be obtained at lower, or at least stable, distribution costs.

THE NEED FOR CHANNEL LEADERSHIP

The most significant output of effective implementation of the four steps of the channel management process is improved performance of the channel system. Indeed, a concomitant result is likely to be increased satisfaction of the individual members of the system with their roles within it. Studies of distribution channels have found owner-manager satisfaction

---

[77] For additional discussion on superordinate goals, see Stern, Sternthal, and Craig, *op. cit.,* and Hunger and Stern, *op. cit.* An excellent illustration of the significance of a superordinate goal as a conflict management mechanism is provided by the aggressiveness of Pepsi Cola, especially during the late 1970s and early 1980s, and the effect of that aggressiveness on the relationship between Coca-Cola and its bottlers. See Anthony Ramirez, "Coke Adopts a Style That Blunts Rivalry of Pepsi and Makes Peace With Bottlers," *Wall Street Journal,* December 22, 1980, p. 7.

[78] Robert R. Blake, H. A. Shepard and Jane S. Mouton, *Managing Intergroup Conflict in Industry* (Houston: Gulf Publishing Co., 1964), p. 89.

to be highly correlated with high levels of organizational performance.[79] Although it is difficult to specify causal relationships between performance and satisfaction (it is not known whether high satisfaction causes high performance or vice versa), it is possible to assert that effective channel management strategies should produce benefits relative to both variables and thus, in the long run, should be a key determinant in ensuring the survival and growth of any given channel system.

In order to achieve effective channel management and thus improved coordination and performance within a channel system, it will be necessary to locate an institution or agency within the system that is willing to assume a leadership role, that is, an organization that will use its power bases to aid in overcoming the spontaneous variability of individual channel member behavior and to allocate the resources within the system so as to enhance the system's viability. Thus, channel leadership can be viewed as the use of power to intentionally affect the behavior of other channel members in order to cause them to act in a manner that contributes to the maintenance or achievement of a desired level of channel performance.[80] In fact, the system may have to gravitate to one where control is required.

Channel control is the ability of a channel member to predict events and achieve desired outcomes in his relations with other channel members.[81] Channel control can result from channel leadership. Furthermore, like channel power, the level of channel control achieved by one firm over others in a channel may be issue specific. For example, while the manufacturer may have control over pricing, retailers may have control over inventory levels in the channel. Whether or not control can be exerted depends, of course, on the power at the command of the channel leader, on the drive for autonomy on the part of the members over whom control is being exerted, and on the latter's tolerance for control. Channel members exhibit different levels of willingness to exert power and to tolerate power when exerted by others. Therefore, effective channel management requires that the deployment of power resources to influence other channel members must be undertaken in magnitudes that are tolerable by them.

Certainly, numerous intra- and extrachannel factors will determine how successful leadership attempts can be. Some of these factors include the demand and supply conditions pertaining to each source of power held by the potential channel leader, his efficiency in controlling his resources, the attractiveness of alternatives, the activities of other competitive channels, and developments in the socio-political-economic environment of which the channel in question is a part.[82]

Clearly, the "proof of the pudding" for channel leadership is whether or not

---

[79] Hal B. Pickle and Brian S. Rungeling, "Empirical Investigation of Entrepreneurial Goals and Customer Satisfaction," *Journal of Business,* Vol. 46 (April 1973), pp. 268–273. See also Ian F. Wilkinson, "Power and Satisfaction in Channels of Distribution," *Journal of Retailing,* Vol. 55 (Summer 1979), pp. 79–94.

[80] Channel leadership is examined more fully in Chapter 9.

[81] Adel I. El-Ansary and Robert A. Robicheaux, "A Theory of Channel Control: Revisited," *Journal of Marketing,* Vol. 38 (January 1974), pp. 2–7.

[82] Ian F. Wilkinson, "Power and Influence Structure in Distribution Channels," *European Journal of Marketing,* Vol. 7 (1973), pp. 119–129.

FIGURE 6-4
A Behavioral Framework for Channel System Performance

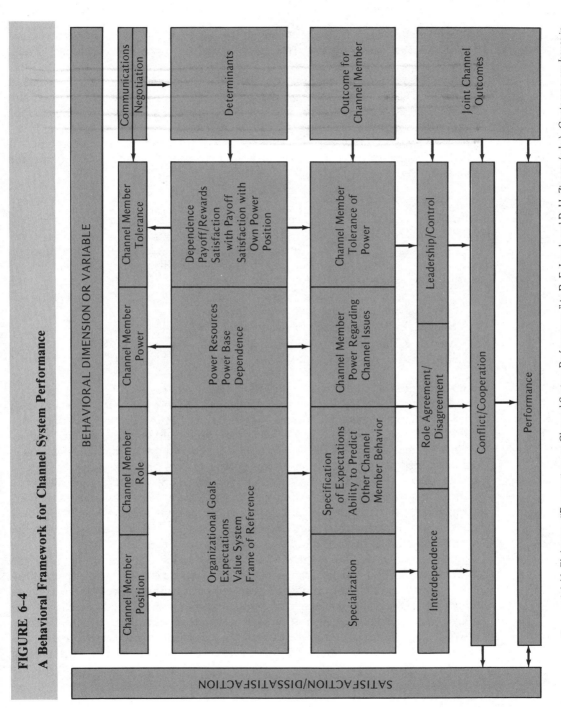

Source: Adel I. El-Ansary, "Perspectives on Channel System Performance," in R. F. Lusch and P. H. Zinszer (eds.), *Contemporary Issues in Marketing Channels* (Norman, Ok.: The University of Oklahoma Printing Services, 1979), p. 50.

the performance of the channel is strong or weak. Strong channel performance depends on the purposive specification of roles throughout the channel. Thus, channel performance is a result of (a) the effectiveness of channel control and (b), possibly, the satisfaction or dissatisfaction of channel members with the channel relationship. Channel control is a function of a channel member's power base and resources, the dependency in the system, the actual use of power, the tolerance for control among channel members, the desire on the part of a channel member to influence others, and leadership effectiveness. All of these factors can be combined to provide a behavioral framework for channel system performance, such as the one depicted in Fig. 6-4.

SUMMARY AND CONCLUSIONS   The central theme of this chapter is that a high degree of interorganizational coordination is required within a marketing channel if that channel is going to have a long-run impact on the markets that it serves.[83] The basic coordinative process involves four key steps:

Step 1. Determining service output levels
Step 2. Delineating roles in the channel
Step 3. Using power to specify roles
Step 4. Dealing with channel conflict

Each component of the process is briefly summarized below.

All marketing effort should begin with assessing the needs and wants of end-users. It is the responsibility of marketing management to encourage the development of goods and services that will satisfy the needs and wants of defined market segments. Once relevant markets have been isolated and appropriate products have been developed and tested, it then becomes critical to ask how the products will be made available to potential end-users for consumption. In order to answer this question, it is essential to know the service output levels demanded of the commercial channel by the consumer. Then a channel can be constructed which will deliver these outputs. Important service outputs are lot size, delivery or waiting time, market decentralization, and product variety, among others.

Once the marketing manager knows the service outputs which must be delivered, he/she can begin to search about in the firm's environment for potential channel partners which are capable of generating the outputs. Because the services can be generated only by organizing the marketing flows and functions, the manager must delineate which roles various channel members should perform relative to their participation in the flows. In the process of specifying role relationships, a series of prescriptions for role behavior evolves. Role prescriptions indicate

[83] For an application of the concepts introduced in this chapter to a specific industrial setting (i.e., property and casualty insurance) by an industry executive, see F. Dean Hildebrandt, Jr., "The American Agency System: It's More Than a Partnership," *Best's Review,* Vol. 81 (December 1980), pp. 12ff.

what each member desires from all channel members relative to their degree of participation in the various marketing flows.

Power generally must be used in a marketing channel to specify appropriate roles, assure role congruence, gain cooperation, and induce satisfactory role performance. Power is the ability of one channel member to get another channel member to do what the latter would not otherwise have done. Power is synonymous with dependence; the more highly dependent one channel member is on another, the more power the latter has relative to the former. Available to channel members are several power bases that they may use to evoke change or to gain continued cooperation; these include rewards, coercion, expertness, identification, and legitimacy. They are most potent when used in combination. There is a cost associated with their use, however, which must be included as an integral part of the analysis in the development of interorganization management programs.

There is a strong likelihood that role performance will deviate, at least occasionally, from prescriptions because of situational factors, differing objectives, communication problems, and differing personal expectations among channel members. More generally, conflict is brought about because of the operational interdependence of channel members. The need to cooperate is juxtaposed to the desire to retain autonomy, and thus channels can be characterized as systems encompassing mixed motives. Channel conflict can be defined as a state in which one channel member perceives another channel member to be engaged in behavior that is impeding or preventing him from achieving his goals. Conflict is caused by goal incompatibility, domain dissensus, and differences in perceptions of reality as well as by the level of interdependence in the system. It results when there is an imbalance between the rewards a member receives from and the contribution he makes to the channel. While conflict is a positive social force which breeds adaptation and innovation, efforts are required to manage it, because it has the potential of preventing a system from achieving effectiveness and efficiency in providing service outputs.

Perhaps one of the most significant functions of channel management is the generation of conflict management strategies, given the fact that conflict is an inherent phenomenon in interorganizational systems. Therefore, employing channel diplomacy, joint membership in trade associations, exchange of persons programs, cooptation, mediation, and arbitration, and establishing superordinate goals should prove highly beneficial. The implementation of these strategies is likely to bring forth more rational and functional collective decision-making within the channel.

In order to activate effective interorganization management, it is likely that channel leadership will be a prerequisite. It is even possible that control will need to be exercised within the system. The only means remaining for achieving control in certain situations will be vertical integration. There are, however, a number of interorganizational programs that can be enacted prior to actually acquiring a variety of channel institutions and agencies. Such programs (such as franchising and programmed merchandising) are discussed in the next chapter.

The approach to the marketplace advocated here is very different from one that might be put forth by a welfare economist who believes that pure or perfect competition among and within the various levels of distribution will produce the greatest good for the greatest number. Although the latter argument may be valid, it would be foolish for the manager to ignore reality. Reality is that organized approaches to the marketplace have historically been permitted to exist, that such approaches have been commercially successful, and that it is unlikely, even in the very long run, that anything approximating pure or perfect competition will exist in industrialized societies. Thus, in order to insure long-term viability, interorganization management is critical for marketing channels.

DISCUSSION QUESTIONS

1. What is the value of a prescriptive model for the interorganization management of distribution channel systems?

2. Distinguish between the terms "position," "role," "role behavior," "role prescription," "role conflict," and "role consensus." Develop a diagram of a wholesaler-retailer relationship that highlights the interrelationships between these terms. What other variables must be included in such a diagram in order to make it a complete pictorial description of the relationship?

3. Generate a list of potential sources of conflict in distribution channel relations. Give examples of each of these potential sources by relating them to any channel situation with which you are familiar.

4. "All conflict in channel relations is undesirable." Critically evaluate this statement.

5. Why is the use of power double-edged? Does conflict provoke the use of power, or does the use of power provoke conflict? Of the various bases of power, which would tend to produce less (more) conflict? Why?

6. Describe what you believe should be the executive background requirements and task obligations for the hypothetical corporate position of Vice-President—Interorganizational Relations. For what types of industries, as well as for what types of channel organization, would such a position seem necessary? How might the position's requirements and obligations change as channel structure changes?

7. Develop a list of likely role conflicts within channels of distribution. Discuss how such conflicts are or might be resolved.

8. How is the process of uncertainty absorption related to the amassing of power? When can the process of uncertainty absorption lead to less rather than more power for the absorber?

9. Describe the manufacturer-dealer system in automobiles in terms of power and role relationships. What are the dominant bases of power that are likely to be employed by either party in this particular channel system?

10. With recent deteriorations in consumer disposable income, more and more buyers are placing emphasis on product warranties and product service in their purchasing decisions. However, warranty programs have long been a source of conflict in marketing channels for consumer durables, especially in the appliance, automobile, and television industries, with the ultimate result often being poor warranty program performance. Typically, conflict arises from dealer dissatisfaction with the warranty programs, stemming from such issues as increased dealer parts-inventory costs, the overloading of dealer-service capabilities, and the attendant substandard service levels these problems cause at the consumer level.

Select any of the above mentioned industries, and develop at least *five* specific and realistic manufacturer-dealer conflict issues involving a warranty service program. Then describe what you believe to be the most effective conflict management strategies that might be employed in dealing with each issue. Justify your selection.

SEVEN

Organizational Patterns in Marketing Channels

A traditional or conventional marketing channel can frequently be described as a piecemeal coalition of independently owned and managed institutions, each of which is prompted by the profit motive with little concern about what goes on before or after it in the distributive sequence. As McCammon notes:

> Goods and services in the American economy have historically been distributed through highly fragmented networks in which *loosely* aligned manufacturers, wholesalers, and retailers have bargained with each other at arm's length, negotiated aggressively over terms of sale, and otherwise behaved autonomously. For the most part, the firms participating in these provisional coalitions have traditionally operated on a relatively small scale and performed a conventionally defined set of marketing functions.[1]

From an interorganization management perspective, such coalitions have no inclusive goals. The locus of decision-making and authority is exclusively at the unit or individual channel member level. There is no formally structured division of labor, and commitment is only to one's own organization. In fact, there is little or no prescribed systemwide orientation of the members.[2] The members are almost totally self-oriented as they pursue their goals.

In contrast with the conventional channel, vertical marketing systems can be described as:

> . . . professionally managed and centrally programmed networks (that are) preengineered to achieve operating economies and maximum market impact. Stated

[1] Bert C. McCammon, Jr., "Perspectives for Distribution Programming," in Louis P. Bucklin (ed.), *Vertical Marketing Systems* (Glenview, Ill.: Scott, Foresman and Company, 1970), p. 43.

[2] The basis for this perspective can be found in Roland L. Warren, "The Interorganizational Field as a Focus for Investigation," in M. B. Brinkerhoff and P. R. Kunz, *Complex Organizations and Their Environments* (Dubuque, Iowa: Wm. C. Brown Company, 1972), p. 316.

alternatively . . . vertical marketing systems are rationalized and capital intensive networks designed to achieve technological, managerial, and promotional economies through the integration, coordination, and synchronization of marketing flows from points of production to points of ultimate use.[3]

Thus, the emergence of vertical marketing systems implies the existence of a power locus in the system that provides for channel leadership, role specification, coordination, conflict management, and control.

In this chapter, the organization and design of such systems are explained in some detail. Comparisons and contrasts between conventional marketing channels and the various types of vertical systems (administered, contractual, and corporate) are enumerated. In order to provide a basis for comparison, it is first necessary briefly to elaborate on the opening paragraphs of this chapter, which discussed the organization of conventional channels.

CONVENTIONAL MARKETING CHANNELS[4]

As mentioned above, conventional marketing channel networks are generally comprised of isolated and autonomous units, each of which performs a traditionally defined set of marketing functions. Coordination among channel members is primarily achieved through bargaining and negotiation. The operating units within such channels are frequently unable to achieve systemic economies. Furthermore, there is usually a low index of member loyalty and relatively easy entry to the channel. The network, then, tends to be relatively unstable. As Etgar points out:

> . . . firms at each level only concern themselves with the distribution of a product to the next adjacent level. (Conventional channels) are coordinated through the operation of prices and the related modes of market mechanisms; the types and variety of products to be handled, levels of promotion, and location of retail outlets are determined by the interaction of manufacturers and distributors as buyers and sellers in intermediary markets.[5]

Within conventional channels, there are a large number of decision makers who tend to be preoccupied with cost, volume, and investment relationships at a *single* stage of the marketing process. Decisions are often tradition-oriented, and decision makers are frequently emotionally committed to established patterns of operation and interaction.

The distribution channel for motion pictures provides an excellent example of the dysfunctional consequences of conventional channel organization.[6] The com-

[3] McCammon, *op. cit.,* p. 43.

[4] With the exception of the motion picture example, this section is based largely on McCammon, *loc. cit.,* p. 44.

[5] Michael Etgar, "Effects of Administrative Control on Efficiency of Vertical Marketing Systems," *Journal of Marketing Research,* Vol. 13 (February 1976), p. 12.

[6] Gene Siskel, "Five Powerful Pieces Set into Place," *Chicago Tribune,* Section 6 (February 23, 1975), pp. 2, 3, and 8. See also Paul Hirsch, "Processing Fads and Fashions: An Organization-Set Analysis of Cultural Industry Systems," *American Journal of Sociology,* Vol. 77 (January 1972), pp. 639–659.

mercial channel for movies is comprised of companies that make movies (producers), distributors, and theatre owners. Prior to 1948, the channel was almost totally integrated—the companies that made the movies also owned the theatres that played them. In 1948, the United States Supreme Court ordered the five major film production-distribution companies to divest themselves of their movie theatres.[7] During the years since 1948, the locus of power in the channel has shifted from the distributor to the theatre owner and back to the distributor. As described by Siskel:

> At first, the new, independent theatre chains were able to bully producers and distributors suddenly bedeviled by television. In recent years, however, the distributors have gained the upper hand. With fewer and fewer pictures being made, the movie world has become a seller's market. The distributors have a limited number of films to rent, and the theatre owners are competing furiously with each other to land the few prize attractions.[8]

Siskel reports, ". . . there has never been any love lost between the major distributors (companies like Universal, Twentieth Century-Fox, and United Artists) and theatre owners. For example, one Chicago representative of a distribution company has been quoted as telling a theatre owner, 'If you make any money on this deal, I'm not doing my job right.' "[9]

While the remark by the representative is obviously facetious, the actions taken by distributors show that there is considerable truth behind it. Apparently, the drive for a good cash flow position is stimulating distributors to ask theatre owners to give them advances or guaranteed money *before* a picture even opens. As a consequence, the public suffers, because only the large downtown movie houses and a few shopping center theatres are able to afford the large, first-run, advance guarantee costs. Smaller theatres are squeezed. Particularly disadvantaged are people who live near the small theatres typically located between downtown and the suburbs.

Furthermore, the major distributors are much less active as producers than they were some years ago. They still produce some pictures on their own (Twentieth Century-Fox Film Corp. and *Star Wars*), but they also frequently participate with independents under various percentage-of-profit arrangements. In many cases, the "majors" rent their lots and equipment to, and distribute pictures produced by, independent companies. Often the stars and directors form their own companies to produce one or more pictures, with distribution through a major company. Clearly, though, this places the "majors" in an even more powerful position. When producers Michael Douglas and Saul Zaentz took the script for *One Flew Over the Cuckoo's Nest* to the major studios for backing, they were turned down by every

---

[7] *United States v. Paramount Pictures, Inc.,* 334 U.S. 131 (1948); also see *Theatre Enterprises, Inc. v. Paramount Film Distributing Corp.,* 346 U.S. 537 (1954).

[8] Siskel, *op. cit.,* p. 2.

[9] *Ibid.*

one of them. Only when United Artists acquired the *finished* film from Douglas and Zaentz was it assured any distribution at all.[10]

Suboptimization within the marketing channel for movies has severely impaired the output of the channel from the consumer's perspective. Certainly, distributors could use their power in more constructive ways to provide for more effective competition vis-a-vis television, but rather than practice interorganization management, distributors are obviously maximizing their own interests and thereby engendering a high degree of conflict within the channel. In his excellent article, Siskel describes additional evidence of myopic behavior on the part of distributors, the existence of which has placed both the consuming public and the theatre owners in somewhat untenable positions.[11] As a reaction, a countervailing force has emerged within the channel in the form of the recently organized Association of Specialized Film Exhibitors. The association is comprised of 34 members who run art theatres all over the United States. While still in its formative stages, the association hopes to improve the availability of films for its membership. However, until it can amass enough power to specify roles and manage conflict, the channel for motion pictures will retain all of the negative attributes of many other conventional marketing channels.

Conventional marketing channels rely heavily on unrestricted open market forces, especially via the price mechanism, to bring about a division of labor among channel members. Such channels are, in terms of numbers, among the most common forms of distribution in capitalistic societies. However, these channels may run into severe problems, particularly when human failings, such as opportunistic

---

[10] Tom Shales, "The Selling of 'Cuckoo's Nest'," *Morning Advocate,* Baton Rouge, La., April 19, 1976, p. 6-C. (Copyrighted story by *The Washington Post,* 1976.)

[11] *Ibid.,* pp. 2, 3, and 8. See also "Warner Bros. Inc., Theatre Rentals Spur U.S. Action," *Wall Street Journal,* April 5, 1976, p. 4; "Movie Industry's Distribution Practices May Spark Antitrust Action, U.S. Warns," *Wall Street Journal,* April 4, 1977; "*Star Wars* Sparks a War with Producers," *Business Week* (August 29, 1977), p. 30; "Theatre Owners Work to Ban Blind Booking," *Business Week* (April 17, 1978); Mitchell C. Lynch, "Movie Theatres Face Obsolescence by '85, Researcher Asserts," *Wall Street Journal,* July 18, 1977, p. 6; "FTC Opens Probe of Major Film Makers, Export Unit for Anti-Competitive Activity," *Wall Street Journal,* May 24, 1979, p. 8; Earl C. Gottschalk, Jr., "Theatre Chains Revolt Against Hollywood's Method of Marketing," *Wall Street Journal,* August 9, 1979, p. 1; "A Film Sale to TV Stings Theatres," *Business Week* (May 5, 1980), p. 46; and Stephen J. Sansweet, "With Ticket Sales Off, Some Movie Exhibitors Project a Bleak Future," *Wall Street Journal,* August 19, 1981, p. 1.

There seems also to be a considerable amount of similar activity taking place in the television industry. See, for example, "Justice Agency and NBC Agree to Settle Suit," *Wall Street Journal,* November 18, 1976, p. 2; "Antitrust Unit Urges Broad FCC Inquiry Into Role and Power of 3 Big TV Networks," *Wall Street Journal,* November 24, 1976; "FCC to Probe Accusations That Networks Exercise Unfair Control of TV Programs," *Wall Street Journal,* January 17, 1977, p. 6; "NBC's Plan to Settle U.S. Antitrust Suit on TV Programming Approved by Court," *Wall Street Journal,* December 2, 1977, p. 4; Boris Becker, "The Future of Television Networks: Boom or Gloom?" *The Collegiate Forum* (Fall 1978), p. 10; Barry R. Litman, "The TV Networks vs. the Program Producers: A Study of Monopoly Power," *The Collegiate Forum* (Spring 1978), p. 3; "Producers Name 3 TV Networks in Antitrust Suit," *Wall Street Journal,* September 12, 1978, p. 5; Burt Schorr, "Over-the-Air Pay TV Builds Subscribers, May Give Cable and Networks Headaches," *Wall Street Journal,* September 25, 1979, p. 40; "For Network TV, A Sudden Case of Future Shock," *Business Week* (October 29, 1979), p. 176; and Television's Fragmented Future," *Business Week* (December 17, 1979), pp. 60 ff.

tendencies and bounded rationality, are combined with technological and environmental complexities and uncertainties.[12] When there is a high degree of uncertainty facing the members of conventional channels due to environmental changes (e.g., new regulations, shortages, slow growth, competition from other channels, technological breakthroughs, etc.) coupled with opportunistic modes of exchange among the members, the economic and sociopolitical costs associated with transacting business across unrestricted markets become very high, and conventional channels begin to fail to remain viable.[13] In an effort to eliminate or penalize the suboptimization that frequently exists in conventional channels and thus to improve channel effectiveness and efficiency, several significant modes of channel organization have emerged. Each limits open market activities so that transaction costs, defined very broadly to include costs associated with the allocation of marketing activities and the establishment of the terms of trade among channel members, are held to reasonable levels. We discuss each of these modes in turn, starting with the least integrated (in a formal, ownership sense) and moving, by steps, to the most highly integrated form. It should be noted at the outset, however, that as one moves closer to formal vertical integration, there are powerful tradeoffs between the control achieved *and* the investment and bureaucracy required to maintain the system.

ADMINISTERED SYSTEMS

Administered vertical marketing systems are one step removed, in an analytical sense, from conventional marketing channels. In an administered system, coordination of marketing activities is achieved through the use of programs developed by one or a limited number of firms. In such systems, administrative strategies combined with the exercise of power are relied on to obtain systemic economies. Successful administered systems are conventional channels in which the principles of effective interorganization management have been correctly applied.

In administered systems, units can exist with disparate goals, but a mechanism exists for informal collaboration on inclusive goals. Decision-making takes place by virtue of the effective interaction of channel members in the absence of a formal inclusive structure. The locus of authority still remains with the individual channel members. The latter are structured autonomously but are willing to agree to an *ad hoc* division of labor without restructuring. As in conventional channels, commit-

---

[12] Oliver E. Williamson, *Markets and Hierarchies: Analysis and Antitrust Implications* (New York: Free Press, 1975). See also Louis W. Stern and Torger Reve, "Distribution Channels as Political Economies: A Framework for Comparative Analysis," *Journal of Marketing,* Vol. 44 (July 1980), and Michael Etgar, "Effects of Administrative Control on Efficiency of Vertical Marketing Systems," *Journal of Marketing Research,* Vol. 13 (February 1976), pp. 12–24.

[13] Williamson has shown how four factors—environmental uncertainty, small numbers bargaining, opportunism, and bounded rationality—can jointly cause markets to fail. Because few transactions can, over time, be typified by large numbers bargaining due to first-mover advantages and because bounded rationality is likely to be descriptive of almost all channel situations, reference here mainly focuses on environmental uncertainty and opportunism. See Williamson, *op. cit.,* pp. 1–40.

ment is self-oriented, but there is at least a minimum amount of systemwide orientation among the members.[14]

As McCammon has observed:

> Manufacturing organizations . . . have historically relied on administrative expertise to coordinate reseller marketing efforts. Suppliers with dominant brands have predictably experienced the least difficulty in securing strong trade support, but many manufacturers with "fringe" items have been able to elicit reseller cooperation through the use of liberal distribution policies that take the form of attractive discounts (or discount substitutes), financial assistance, and various types of concessions that protect resellers from one or more of the risks of doing business.[15]

A number of concessions available to suppliers are listed in Exhibit 7-1.[16]

While administration of the channel can flow backwards from retailer to manufacturer (e.g., Sears, Montgomery Ward, J. C. Penney, and McDonald's[17] administer many of the channels in which they are engaged without committing themselves totally to a program of vertically integrating manufacturing facilities), the application of the concept has, as indicated above, been most frequently undertaken by suppliers. For example, Kraftco has developed facilities management programs to administer the allocation of space in supermarket dairy cases. Kraft's power stems from the fact that the company accounts for 60 percent of dairy case volume, exclusive of milk, eggs, and butter. In addition to facilities management programs, some manufacturers and wholesalers have developed modular merchandising programs, coordinated display programs, and automatic replenishment programs.[18] The latter have been used with a high degree of success by Corning Glass and Genuine Parts, a major auto parts wholesaler. In fact, the long-term viability of many wholesaling firms is dependent upon their administration of such programs for the small retailers, other wholesalers, jobbers, and industrial customers with whom they deal. Wholesalers in the drug, hardware, sporting goods, and phonograph records industries have been particularly successful in this respect. Administered systems are important in financing flows as well. Such companies as General Electric Credit Corporation have played significant roles in helping wholesalers and retailers cope with cash flow problems. Furthermore, many in-

---

[14] See Warren, *op. cit.*, p. 316.

[15] McCammon, *op. cit.*, p. 45.

[16] Even Procter & Gamble has become more involved with developing better deals for retailers. We say "even" because it has been thought in the past that P&G did not need to offer lucrative enticements to the trade; stores were forced to carry P&G brands due to great consumer demand stimulated by media advertising. See Nancy Giges, "P&G Tests Better Retailer Deals," *Advertising Age* (March 17, 1980).

[17] For a description about how McDonald's administers its supply channels, see Peter J. Schuyten, "How Keystone's Handshake Turned Golden," *Fortune* (March 13, 1978), pp. 78–82.

[18] National Biscuit Company has long been an expert in such merchandising. Like Kraftco, which distributes Pillsbury's refrigerated dough products, it also distributes other manufacturers' products. See G. S. Miller, "Nabisco Sees Its Salesforce Providing Promotional Sources for Other Firms," *Wall Street Journal,* April 21, 1980, p.17.

EXHIBIT 7-1

Selected Concessions Available to Suppliers When Seeking To Gain Reseller Support of their Marketing Programs

I. *"Price" Concessions*
   A. Discount Structure:
      trade (functional) discounts
      quantity discounts
      cash discounts
      anticipation allowances
      free goods
      prepaid freight
      new product, display, and advertising allowances (without performance requirements)
      seasonal discounts
      mixed carload privilege
      drop shipping privilege
      trade deals
   B. Discount Substitutes:
      display materials
      premarked merchandise
      inventory control programs
      catalogs and sales promotion literature
      training programs
      shelf-stocking programs
      advertising matrices
      management consulting services
      merchandising programs
      sales "spiffs"
      technical assistance
      payment of sales personnel and demonstrator salaries
      promotional and advertising allowances (with performance requirements)

II. *Financial Assistance*
   A. Conventional Lending Arrangements:
      term loans
      inventory floor plans
      notes payable financing
      accounts payable financing
      installment financing of fixtures and equipment
      lease and note guarantee programs
      accounts receivable financing
   B. Extended Dating:
      E.O.M. dating
      seasonal dating
      R.O.G. dating

III. *Protective Provisions*

    A. Price Protection:
       premarked merchandise
       "franchise" pricing
       agency agreements

    B. Inventory Protection:
       consignment selling
       memorandum selling
       liberal returns allowances
       rebate programs
       reorder guarantees
       guaranteed support of sales events
       maintenance of "spot" stocks and fast delivery

    C. Territorial Protection:
       selective distribution
       exclusive distribution

Source: Bert C. McCammon, Jr., "Perspectives for Distribution Programming," in Louis P. Bucklin (ed.), *Vertical Marketing Systems* (Glenview, Ill.: Scott, Foresman and Company, 1970), pp. 36-37.

dustrial distributors have also committed themselves to program management, as shown in Table 7-1.

One of the most innovative approaches to developing administered systems has been the emergence of programmed merchandising agreements. Under this concept, manufacturers formulate specialized merchandising plans for each type of outlet they serve.

TABLE 7-1 **Percentage of industrial distributors providing various programs and services to their customers, 1973**

Stockless purchasing programs	64%
Systems engineering programs	38%
OSHA, pollution control consulting services	37%
Fabrication	31%
Consignment buying programs	23%
Preventive maintenance programs	21%
Operator training programs	15%
Equipment leasing programs	8%
Scrap reclamation programs	5%

Source: Bert C. McCammon, Jr., and James W. Kenderine, "Mainstream Developments in Wholesaling," a paper presented at the 1975 Conference of the Southwestern Marketing Association, p. 6.

EXHIBIT 7-2

Plans and Activities Covered in Programmed Merchandising Agreements

1. Merchandising Goals
   a. Planned sales
   b. Planned initial markup percentage
   c. Planned reductions, including planned markdowns, shortages, and discounts
   d. Planned gross margin
   e. Planned expense ratio (optional)
   f. Planned profit margin (optional)
2. Inventory Plan
   a. Planned rate of inventory turnover
   b. Planned merchandise assortments, including basic or model stock plans
   c. Formalized "never out" lists
   d. Desired mix of promotional versus regular merchandise
3. Merchandise Presentation Plan
   a. Recommended store fixtures
   b. Space allocation plan
   c. Visual merchandising plan
   d. Needed promotional materials, including point-of-purchase displays, consumer literature, and price signs
4. Personal Selling Plan
   a. Recommended sales presentations
   b. Sales training plan
   c. Special incentive arrangements, including "spiffs," salesmen's contests, and related activities
5. Advertising and Sales Promotion Plan
   a. Advertising and sales promotion budget
   b. Media schedule
   c. Copy themes for major campaigns and promotions
   d. Special sales events
6. Responsibilities and Due Dates
   a. Supplier's responsibilities in connection with the plan
   b. Retailer's responsibilities in connection with the plan

Source: Bert C. McCammon, Jr., "Perspectives for Distribution Programming," in Louis P. Bucklin (ed.), *Vertical Marketing Systems* (Glenview, Ill.: Scott, Foresman and Company, 1970), pp. 48-49.

Programmed merchandising is a "joint venture" in which a specific retail account and a supplier develop a comprehensive merchandising plan to market the supplier's product line. These plans normally cover a six-month period but some are of longer duration.[19]

Such programming generally involves the activities listed in Exhibit 7-2 for each brand and for each store included in the agreement. Manufacturing organizations

[19] McCammon, *op. cit.,* p. 48.

currently engaged in programmed merchandising activities include: General Electric (on major and traffic appliances), Baumritter (on its Ethan Allen furniture line in nonfranchised outlets), Sealy (on its Posturepedic line of mattresses), Villager (on its dress and sportswear lines), Scott (on its lawn care products), and Haines (on its L'eggs pantyhose and L'Erin cosmetics).

In order to develop effective merchandising programs, the supplier-distributor relationship must be characterized by a high degree of cooperation. Planning, communication of intentions, and coordination of effort are imperatives.[20] This places

---

EXHIBIT 7-3

Comparison of Characteristics of Supplier/Distributor Relationships in a Conventional Channel vs. a Programmed System

Characteristics	Conventional Channel	Programmed System
Nature of contacts	Negotiation on an individual order basis	Advanced joint planning for an extended time period
Information considered	Supplier sales presentation data	Distributor's merchandising data
Supplier participants	Supplier's territorial salesperson	Salesperson and major regional or headquarters executive
Distributor participants	Buyer	Various executives, perhaps top management
Distributor's goals	Sales gain and percent markup	Programmed total profitability
Supplier's goal	Big order on each call	Continuing profitable relationship
Nature of performance evaluation	Event centered; primarily related to sales volume and other short-term performance criteria	Specific performance criteria written into the program

Source: Ronald L. Ernst, "Distribution Channel Detente Benefits Suppliers, Retailers, and Consumers," *Marketing News* (March 7, 1980), p. 19.

---

[20] Ronald L. Ernst, "Distribution Channel Detente Benefits Suppliers, Retailers, and Consumers," *Marketing News* (March 7, 1980), p. 19.

an administered or programmed system in sharp contrast to a conventional marketing channel, as pointed out in Exhibit 7-3. As Ronald Ernst has observed,[21] the key benefits to various channel members from engaging in programmed merchandising are:

TO THE SUPPLIER

- The development of maximum sales and profit potential without competing for it on a day-to-day basis.
- Continuity of promotion and sales for more economic scheduling of production and distribution activities.
- Improved sales forecasting ability for manufacturing and distribution planning.
- Achievement of maximum product exposure by middlemen.
- Achievement of a totally coordinated, planned, and controlled marketing approach to reach the end-user.
- Clearly specified middleman inventory requirements, thus allowing inventory management and control efficiencies.

TO THE DISTRIBUTOR   (wholesaler or retailer or both)

- Adequate and timely availability of merchandise.
- Preferential consideration from key resources.
- Assortment planning and merchandise control assistance.
- Clearly specified inventory investment requirements.
- The security of merchandising on a price maintained basis.
- High levels of vendor service with regard to product quality and general account maintenance.
- Economy and efficiency through shifting functions, such as ordering, to the supplier.

An example provided by Ernst in his discussion of programmed merchandising is the Norwalk (Ohio) Furniture Corporation.[22] Norwalk is one of the few upholstery furniture manufacturers that can guarantee 30-day delivery on all special orders due to a unique type of manufacturing facility. In 1977 the company instituted a total-effort dealer program which contained the following key elements:

1. Total-effort dealers agree to display Norwalk furniture in nine out of ten upholstered-furniture room settings.

[21] *Ibid.*

[22] *Ibid.*

2. Total-effort dealers agree to operate on a special order basis and not sell floor samples which would jeopardize future sales.

In turn, Norwalk

1. Guaranteed 30-day delivery.
2. Provided customized ad materials, catalogs, and extra large fabric swatches.
3. Conducted an annual factory authorized sale.
4. Provided floor plan financing.
5. Provided an advertising allowance.
6. Conducted sales meetings for floor sales personnel.
7. Provided in-store merchandising assistance.

Because all dealer sales are made on a custom-order basis with 30-day guaranteed delivery, the only inventory the dealer needs to carry is in floor samples. Also, because all sales under the program are special orders, the dealer typically experiences higher gross margins as a result of reduced risks of carrying poor selling items. Markdowns are minimized, and lower warehousing and handling costs are achieved.

The concept of channel administration through institution systemic programs is also being applied in the logistics field. For example, Ryder System, Inc., has instituted a program that eliminates several intermediate warehousing operations for its truck-leasing customers. Ryder offers its trucks as rolling warehouses. Newly manufactured goods usually go first into the manufacturer's warehouse, next are shipped to a retailer's warehouse, and then are shipped once again either to the store or to the retailer's customer. This process often leads to a minimum of six loadings and unloadings into warehouses before the goods get to their final destination. By using trucks as warehouses, and thereby minimizing loadings and unloadings while speeding up the shipment cycle, Ryder claims it can reduce a customer's trucking needs by 20 percent.[23]

CONTRACTUAL SYSTEMS

Often organizations desire to formalize role obligations within their channel networks by employing legitimate power as a means of achieving control. In these situations, vertical coordination is frequently accomplished through the use of contractual agreements. According to Thompson:

> Independent firms at different levels can integrate their programs on a contractual basis to achieve systemic economies and an increased market impact . . . Contrac-

[23] "Marketing When the Growth Slows," *Business Week* (April 14, 1975), p. 50. Another logistics company that has administered its channels in a unique and profitable way is CAST, a Canadian shipping company. See James O'Shea, "Rival Calls U.S. Shippers Lazy," *Chicago Tribune,* Section 5, April 20, 1980, pp. 1 and 2.

tual integration occurs where the various stages of production and distribution are independently owned, but the relationships between vertically adjacent firms are covered in a contractual arrangement. . . .[24]

While virtually every transaction among businesses and between businesses and individuals is covered by some form of contract, either explicit or implied, the primary function of the contracts in these vertical marketing systems is that they specify, in writing, the marketing roles to be assumed by each party to the contract.[25]

Contractual integration takes a variety of forms, as shown in Exhibit 7-4. However, the three principal forms of contractual integration are wholesaler-sponsored voluntary groups, retailer-sponsored cooperative groups, and franchise systems. The focus here is primarily on these three forms.

From an interorganization management perspective, contractual vertical marketing systems can be viewed as networks in which the members have disparate goals but where there exists some formal organization for inclusive goals. Decision-making is generally made at the top of the inclusive structure but is subject to the ratification of the members. The locus of authority in such networks resides primarily (but not exclusively) with the individual members. The latter are structured autonomously, but will generally agree to a division of labor that may, in turn, affect the basic structure of the channel. In such networks, norms of moderate commitment to the channel system exist, and there is at least a moderate amount of systemwide orientation among the members.[26] Clearly, along each of the above mentioned dimensions, contractual systems are more tightly knit than administered systems. To a significant extent, channel members are willing to trade some degree of autonomy in order to gain scale economies and market impact.[27]

Voluntary and Cooperative Groups

A wholesaler, by banding together a number of independently owned retailers in a voluntary group, can provide goods and support services far more economically than these same retailers could secure acting solely as individuals. Perhaps the most well-known wholesaler-sponsored voluntary is the Independent Grocers Alliance (IGA). In the hardware field, Pro, Liberty, and Sentry are examples of wholesalers who provide retail establishments with services similar to those found in the IGA system. Other examples of voluntary groups are found in the automobile

---

[24] Donald N. Thompson, "Contractual Marketing Systems: An Overview," in D. N. Thompson (ed.), *Contractual Marketing Systems* (Lexington, Mass.: Heath Lexington Books, 1971), p. 5.

[25] For an excellent example, see Appendix 5A for Rex Chainbelt's Distributor Sales Agreement for the Bearing Division.

[26] Warren, *op. cit.,* p. 316.

[27] William R. Davidson, "Changes in Distributive Institutions," in W. G. Moller, Jr., and D. L. Wilemon (eds.), *Marketing Channels: A Systems Viewpoint* (Homewood, Ill.: Richard D. Irwin, 1971), p. 389. For an interesting example in a service industry context, see Laurel Sorenson, "Smaller Banks Join to Form Own Banks," *Wall Street Journal,* February 20, 1981, p. 23.

EXHIBIT 7–4

Principal Types of Contractual Vertical Marketing Systems

Contractual Systems Involving Forward Integration
Wholesaler-sponsored voluntary groups
Wholesaler-sponsored programmed groups
Supplier franchise programs for individual brands and specific departments
Supplier franchise program covering all phases of the licensee's operation
Nonprofit shipping associations
Leased department arrangements
Producer marketing cooperatives
Contractual Systems Involving Backward Integration
Retailer-sponsored cooperative groups
Retailer/wholesaler-sponsored buying groups
Retailer-sponsored promotional groups
Nonprofit shipping associations
Retailer/wholesaler resident buying offices
Industrial, wholesale, and retail procurement contracts
Producer buying cooperatives

accessory market (Western Auto) and in the notions and general merchandise market (Ben Franklin). Some of the largest voluntary groups in the drug and hardware industries are listed in Table 7–2. The principal services provided by seven major hardware "voluntaries" are shown in Table 7–3.

Automatic Service, Genuine Parts, Super Valu, Malone & Hyde, and Canadian Tire are also leading proponents of the voluntary group concept.[28] Automatic Service sponsors a voluntary group program for vending machine operators. Genuine Parts is the largest member of the NAPA (auto parts) network, and Super Valu and Malone & Hyde are leading voluntary group wholesalers in the food field. Canadian Tire is the largest voluntary group wholesaler that supplies affiliated stores with a variety of lines, including automotive parts and accessories, hardware, housewares, small appliances, and sporting goods. A typical Canadian Tire outlet contains approximately 25,000 square feet of space and carries over 20,000 items in inventory.[29] The performance of selected voluntaries is shown, in strategic profit model terms, in Table 7–4.

The retailer-sponsored cooperative is also a voluntary association, but the impetus for the cooperative comes from the retailers rather than from a wholesaler. The retailers organize and democratically operate their own wholesale company,

[28] Bert C. McCammon, Jr., "The Changing Economics of Wholesaling: A Strategic Analysis," a paper presented at the 1974 Annual Conference of the Southern Marketing Association, p. 6.

[29] Bert C. McCammon, Jr., and William L. Hammer, "A Frame of Reference for Improving Productivity in Distribution," *Atlanta Economic Review,* Vol. 24 (September–October 1974), p. 12.

TABLE 7-2   Selected voluntary groups in the drug and hardware fields

	Voluntary Group	Number of Affiliated Stores
Drug Field (1974)	Economost	5,000
	Good Neighbor Pharmacies	1,400
	Associated Druggists	1,132
	United Systems Stores	744
	Family Service Drug Stores	350
	Triple A	300
	Velocity	250
	Community Shield Pharmacies	200
	FIP	200
	Sell-Thru Guild	200
	Total	9,776
Hardware Field (1979)	Sentry	4,700
	Western Auto	4,300
	Pro	3,120
	Trustworthy	1,775
	Coast-to-Coast	1,200
	Gamble-Skogmo	965
	Stratton & Terstegge	850
	Farwell, Ozman, Kirk & Co.	460
	American Wholesale Hardware	330
	Total	17,700

Source: Bert C. McCammon, Jr., and Albert D. Bates, "Reseller Strategies and the Financial Performance of the Firm," in H. B. Thorelli (ed.), *Strategy + Structure = Performance* (Bloomington, Ind.: Indiana University Press, 1977), p. 161; and *Hardware Age* (October 1979), p. 77.

which then performs services for the member retailers. Historically, retailer-sponsored cooperatives have been important in the marketing of foods (e.g., Topco Associates, Associated Grocers, and Certified Grocers). For example, Topco Associates, Inc. is an organization owned on a cooperative basis by a group of supermarket chains and grocery wholesalers located in various markets throughout the country. Topco's central function is to serve its owner-member companies in the purchasing, product development, quality control, packaging, and promotion of a wide variety of private label (controlled brand) food and nonfood products. Its brands include Top Frost, Gaylord, and Food Club, among others. Its owner-members represent over $3 billion in retail sales volume, and include such firms as Big Bear Stores in Columbus, Ohio, Dillon Stores in Hutchinson, Kansas, and Fred Meyer, Inc. in Portland, Oregon.

Retailer-sponsored cooperatives have also become prominent in the hardware

TABLE 7-3   Principal services provided by seven major hardware wholesaler-sponsored voluntary groups

	Sentry	Trustworthy	Pro	Gamble-Skogmo	Coast To Coast	Stratton & Terstegge	American Wholesale Hardware Company
Store Identification	yes	yes	yes	yes	yes	yes	yes
Telephone Ordering	yes	yes	*	yes	yes	yes	yes
Microfiche	yes	yes	yes	yes	no	yes	yes
Catalog Service	yes	yes	yes	yes	yes	yes	yes
Circular Programs	yes	yes	yes	yes	yes	yes	yes
Private Label Merch.	yes	yes	*	yes	yes	yes	no
Merchandising Aid	yes	yes	yes	yes	yes	yes	yes
Basic Stock Lists	*	yes	yes	yes	yes	yes	yes
Direct/Drop Ship Programs	yes	yes	yes	yes	yes	yes	yes
Pool Orders	yes	yes	yes	yes	yes	yes	yes
Consumer Advertising	yes	yes	yes	yes	yes	yes	yes
Co-Op Advertising Programs	yes	yes	yes	yes	yes	yes	yes
Advertising Planning, Aid	yes	yes	yes	yes	yes	yes	yes
Reprinted Order Forms	yes	yes	yes	yes	yes	yes	yes
Data Processing Programs	yes	yes	yes	yes	yes	yes	yes
Inventory Control Systems	yes	yes	yes	yes	yes	yes	yes
Accounting Services	*	yes	no	yes	yes	yes	*
Mgmt. Consultation Services	yes	yes	yes	yes	yes	yes	*
Employee Training	*	*	yes	yes	yes	yes	yes
Dealer Meetings	yes	yes	yes	yes	yes	yes	yes
Volume Rebates/Dividends	yes	yes	yes	no	yes	yes	yes
Store Planning, Layout	yes	yes	yes	yes	yes	yes	yes
Financing	*	yes	*	yes	yes	no	yes
Insurance Programs	no	yes	yes	yes	yes	yes	yes
Field Supervisors/Slsmen	yes	yes	yes	yes	yes	yes	yes
Dealer Shows	yes	yes	yes	yes	yes	yes	yes

* Limited service, or offered by some member wholesalers.

Source: Hardware Age Survey of Hardware Wholesalers, Hardware Age Verified Directory of Hardlines Distributors, *Hardware Age* (October 1979), p. 79.

TABLE 7-4 Strategic profit model profiles for leading wholesalers engaged in voluntary group progams

Company	Net Profits to Net Sales (percent)	Strategic Profit Model Ratios, 1977				Compound Annual Growth Rates 1973-1977	
		Net Sales to Total Assets (times)	Net Profits to Total Assets (percent)	Total Assets to Net Worth (times)	Net Profits to Net Worth (percent)	Net Sales (percent)	Net Profits (percent)
Genuine Parts Company	4.5	2.7	12.0	1.5	18.1	13.2	17.0
Super Valu Stores, Inc.	1.2	6.6	7.7	3.2	24.2	15.7	34.7
S & T Industries	4.2	1.9	8.2	2.5	20.5	17.1	36.5
Malone & Hyde, Inc.[a]	1.3	6.9	9.0	1.0	17.5	17.8	18.7

[a] Malone & Hyde has pursued a vigorous diversification policy in recent years and currently obtains a significant share of its earnings from company-owned stores and related ventures.

Source: Bert C. McCammon, Jr., "Financial Profile of New Wave Wholesalers," prepared for the 1979 Doctoral Consortium of the American Marketing Association held at the University of Wisconsin—Madison, August 1979.

business, where they now account for approximately 35 percent of total wholesale sales. The membership and sales of the largest hardware retailer-sponsored (dealer-owned) cooperatives are shown in Table 7-5. Except for ownership differences, however, wholesaler- and retailer-sponsored contractual systems operate in much the same ways. The members join with the understanding that they will purchase a substantial portion of their merchandise from the group and will standardize retail advertising, identification, and operating procedures as necessary to conform with those of the group to obtain economies and better impact. Members usually contribute to a common advertising fund and operate stores under a common name.

These contractual systems are not new forms of channel organization. Voluntary and cooperative groups emerged in the 1930s as a response to the appearance of chain stores. However, the scope of the cooperative effort has expanded from concentrated buying power to the development of a vast number of programs involving centralized consumer advertising and promotion, store location and layout, training, financing, accounting, and, in some cases, a total package of support services. For example, Malone & Hyde serves 1600 stores in 15 southern states, and is the nation's fifth largest food wholesaler, outranked by two voluntaries, Super Valu Stores, Inc. and Fleming Companies, and by two retailer-sponsored cooperatives, Certified of California and Wakefern Foods. It has achieved its strong position by instituting efficient, innovative procedures which enable it to serve its customers better. Some of these procedures include the following:

- When Malone & Hyde's customers place an order, it is accompanied by a signed blank check, virtually eliminating the wholesaler's collection problems and giving it the use of cash for several extra days. This procedure allows Malone & Hyde to pay cash for whatever it buys.
- Using electronic inventory devices, supermarket operators can place an entire week's order directly with the Malone & Hyde computer in minutes by telephone instead of waiting for a salesman to visit. Groceries in all but one of the firm's nine warehouses are stacked according to family groups, just like the groceries in supermarket aisles. This means that orders can be filled without backtracking by warehouse workers.
- The company has developed a labor-saving system whereby cases in the warehouse are stacked on a cart that can be rolled directly onto a truck, into the supermarket, and down the aisles.
- In addition to distributing food and other items to the retailer, the company provides the retailer with such services as store design, site location, insurance, inventory and accounting controls, and group advertising.
- The company will lease a site location and turn it over to an independent operator. It will also sell the operator equipment and initial inventory on credit and may also inject a sizable amount of operating cash into the store. In return, the new owner-operator completely commits to the store whatever assets he has.[30]

[30] Richard A. Shaffer, "Why Farm-Price Dips Don't Help You Much at the Grocery Store," *Wall Street Journal,* May 8, 1975, pp. 1 and 17.

TABLE 7-5 Retailer-sponsored (dealer-owned) cooperatives in the hardware trade

	1968		1973		1976		1979	
	Members	Sales[a]	Members	Sales[a]	Members	Sales[a]	Members	Sales[a]
Cotter & Co. (True-Value)	3,009	$192	4,400	$400	5,500	$700	6,500	$978
Ace Hardware Corp.[b]	1,300	110	2,500	240	3,489	380	3,800	505
Hardware Wholesalers, Inc.	832	50.5	1,300	138	1,809	240.6	2,349	426
American Hardware Supply	1,200	50	2,000	117	2,800	202	3,500	312
Our Own Hardware Co.	625	32	700	42	800	70	912	100
United Hardware Distributing Co.	465	17.7	600	33	569	50	700	63
Handy Hardware Wholesale, Inc.	69	2	155	5.5	250	11	350	20
Bay Cities Wholesale Hardware Co.	181	5.5	200	6	190	9.5	280	10
General Mercantile & Hardware Co.	85	1.6	110	2.9	163	5.5	230	7.7
Connecticut Hardware Supply Co., Inc.	40	1.5	50	2.5	45	3.6	44	3.8
Master Hardware Distributing, Inc.	80	1.5	60	1.5	72	1.8	87	2.1
Dash Sales, Inc.	100	1	150	2	75[c]	2[c]	75	2
Allied Wholesalers, Inc.	N/A	N/A	N/A	N/A	N/A	N/A	30	0.5
Wisco Hardware Co.[d]	300	5	300	4	—	—	—	—
Totals	8,286	470.3	12,525	994.4	15,762	1,676	18,857	2,439.2

[a] Sales in millions of dollars.

[b] Ace figures for 1969 and 1973 included for purposes of comparison although at those times firm was a franchise operation rather than dealer-owned as it was in 1976 and 1979.

[c] Estimated figures.

[d] Wisco no longer doing business.

Source: Hardware Age (October 1979), p. 83.

Contractual systems have experienced phenomenal growth. For example, IGA now operates more stores than A & P, and Super Valu outlets' annual sales are higher than Kroger's. In fact, nationally, the share of grocery store sales enjoyed by voluntary and cooperative groups combined is equal to that held by corporate chains. One of the reasons for this successful growth is the "clarity of total offer" made possible by the implementation of systemwide programs. Once the customer sees the store sign, there is a clear understanding of the outlet's marketing orientation, including the product, service, and atmosphere.[31]

Generally, wholesaler-sponsored voluntary groups have been more effective competitors than retailer-sponsored cooperatives, primarily because of the difference in channel organization between the two. In the former, a wholesaler can provide strong leadership, because he represents the locus of power within the voluntary system. In a retailer-sponsored cooperative, power is diffused throughout the retail membership, and therefore role specification and concomitant allocation of resources are more difficult to accomplish. In the voluntary groups, the retail members have relinquished some of their autonomy by making themselves highly dependent on specific wholesalers for expertise. (It should be recalled from an earlier chapter that the more one party depends upon another, the more power the latter has relative to the former.) In retailer cooperatives, individual members tend to retain more autonomy and thus tend to depend much less strongly on the supply unit for assistance and direction.

Before we turn to a discussion of perhaps the most popular form of contractual vertical marketing system—franchising—it is important to note that one other type of cooperative has played a major role in distribution in the U.S.—the farm cooperative.[32] While the subject of the emergence and growth of farm cooperatives could fill an entire textbook, suffice it to say here that organizations such as Farmland Industries, Associated Milk Producers, Agway, and Land O'Lakes have become extremely powerful forces in behalf of their memberships in organizing both the farm equipment and supply market as well as the markets into which farmers sell their produce. Indeed, farm cooperatives are channel administrators par excellence. Over the last decade, dairy coops, for example, increased their share of the wholesale dairy market from 65 percent to a commanding 80 percent. And coops market 37 percent of the nation's cotton crop. On the supply side, coops have a 42 percent share of the retail fertilizer market, a 40 percent share of the farm petroleum market, and a 40 percent share of the retail market for agricultural chemicals. While some farm coops have vertically integrated both backwards and forwards within their marketing channels, they are primarily wholesalers of goods and services, and administer the channels that they control with the approval of the farmers who own them.

---

[31] Bert C. McCammon, Jr., Alton F. Doody, and William R. Davidson, *Emerging Patterns of Distribution* (Columbus, Ohio: Management Horizons, Inc., 1969), pp. 5–6.

[32] For an excellent discussion of the power of farm cooperatives, see "The Billion-Dollar Farm Co-ops Nobody Knows," *Business Week* (February 7, 1977), pp. 54 ff. On the other hand, consumer cooperatives have never achieved significant power in U.S. distribution. See "Consumer Co-ops Win Some Aid," *Business Week* (July 31, 1978), p. 105.

FRANCHISE SYSTEMS Franchise systems comprise major components of the distribution structure of the United States. In 1980, sales of goods and services by all franchising companies (manufacturing, wholesaling, and retailing) exceeded $300 billion. Approximately 32 percent of all U.S. retail sales flow through franchise and company-owned units in franchise chains. There are roughly one-half million establishments employing 4½ million people in franchise-related businesses.[33] Because of their growing importance, their makeup, design, and orientation are examined in considerable detail in this section.[34]

Franchising as it is generally known today is a form of marketing and distribution in which a parent company customarily grants an individual or a relatively small company the right, or privilege, to do business in a prescribed manner over a certain period of time in a specified place.[35]

> The parent company is termed the *franchisor*; the receiver of the privilege the *franchisee*; and the right, or privilege itself, the *franchise*. The privilege may be quite varied. It may be the right to sell the parent company's products, to use its name, to adopt its methods, and to copy its symbols, trademarks, or architecture, or the franchise may include all of these rights. The time period and the size of the area of business operations, which are specified, may also vary greatly. The rights that are granted and the duties and obligations of the respective parties, the franchisor and the franchisee, are usually spelled out in a written contract.[36]

The franchisor may occupy any position within the channel. For example, the franchisor may be: (a) the manufacturer, as in the case of Midas Mufflers; (b) a service specialist, as in the case of Kelly Girl; or (c) a retailer franchising other retailers, as in the case of Howard Johnson's during its early years of operation.

There appear to be four basic types of franchise systems:[37]

1. *The manufacturer-retailer franchise* is exemplified by franchised automobile dealers and franchised service stations.

2. *The manufacturer-wholesaler franchise* is exemplified by Coca-Cola, Pepsi Cola, Royal Crown Cola, and Seven-Up, who sell the soft drink syrups they manufacture to franchised wholesalers who, in turn, bottle and distribute soft drinks to retailers.

---

[33] Data on franchising obtained from U.S. Department of Commerce, Industry and Trade Administration, *Franchising in the Economy 1978–80* (Washington, D.C.: U.S. Government Printing Office, January 1980).

[34] For additional detail, see Urban B. Ozanne and Shelby D. Hunt, *The Economic Effects of Franchising* (Washington, D.C.: U.S. Government Printing Office, 1971); Donald N. Thompson, *Franchise Operation and Antitrust* (Lexington, Mass.: Heath Lexington Books, 1971); Donald N. Thompson, *Contractual Marketing Systems, op. cit.;* and Charles L. Vaughn, *Franchising* 2nd Ed. (Lexington, Mass.: Heath Lexington Books, 1979).

[35] Vaughn, *op. cit.,* pp. 1–2.

[36] *Ibid.,* p. 2.

[37] William P. Hall, "Franchising: New Scope for an Old Technique," *Harvard Business Review,* Vol. 42 (January–February 1964), pp. 60–72.

3. *The wholesaler-retailer franchise* is exemplified by Rexall Drug Stores and Sentry Drug Centers.

4. *The service sponsor-retailer franchise* is exemplified by Avis, Hertz, and National in the car rental business; McDonald's, Chicken Delight, Kentucky Fried Chicken, and Taco-Tio in the prepared foods industry; Howard Johnson's and Holiday Inn in the lodging and food industry; Midas and AAMCO in the auto repair business; and Kelly Girl and Manpower in the employment service business.

There is no general agreement as to which channel arrangements should be included as franchise systems. For example, some classification schemes include wholesaler-sponsored voluntary chains as franchise systems. Others include channels in which a retailer or a wholesaler is franchised to sell a product in a specified territory along with other products obtained from other sources. The latter interpretation more accurately describes the franchise method of distribution rather than franchise *systems*. This confusion leads to inaccurate statistics on the number of franchisors and franchisees as well as the sales volume of franchise systems. One of the major sources of confusion is the variety of franchise agreements, which take many forms, as shown in Exhibit 7-5.

A *franchise system* is defined for our purposes here to denote the licensing of an *entire* business format where one firm (the franchisor) licenses a number of outlets (franchisees) to market a product or service and engage in a business developed by the franchisor using the latter's trade names, trademarks, service marks, know-how, and methods of doing business. While heavily circumscribed by law, as pointed out in Chapter 8, the franchisor may sell the products, sell or lease the equipment, and/or sell or lease the premises necessary to the operation.[38] For example, McDonald's insists that all of its units purchase from approved suppliers, provides building and design specifications, provides or helps locate financing for its franchisees, and issues quality standards that each unit must abide by in order to hold its franchise. However, the following warning of James T. Halverson, former Director of the Federal Trade Commission's Bureau of Competition, should be carefully heeded by all those seeking to understand the future of channel arrangements, in general, and franchise relationships, in particular.

(Antitrust) is moving in the direction of ensuring larger numbers of independent decision-makers at all levels of distribution, and this means greater freedom of choice and action by customers and franchisees. . . . manufacturers and franchisors will find it becoming increasingly difficult, absent vital business justifications, to exert an influence on the businessmen who deal in their products and on the markets in which their products are sold. The law is making it easier for customers to choose alternative suppliers and for distributors to establish their own geographic markets, to do business with whom they choose, and to establish their own prices. And the more a supplier or

---

[38] In addition to reviewing Chapter 8, the reader interested in the extent of restrictions on tying agreements should see Shelby D. Hunt and John R. Nevin, "Tying Agreements in Franchising," *Journal of Marketing,* Vol. 39, (July 1975), pp. 20–26.

EXHIBIT 7–5

Types of Franchise Systems

Type	Explanation
Territorial franchise	The franchise granted encompasses several counties or states. The holder of the franchise assumes the responsibility for setting up and training individual franchisees within his territory and obtains an "override" on all sales in his territory.
Operating franchise	The individual independent franchisee who runs his own franchise. He deals either directly with the parent organization or with the territorial franchise holder.
Mobile franchise	A franchise that dispenses its product from a moving vehicle, which is either owned by the franchisee or leased from the franchisor. Examples include Tastee Freeze and Snap-On Tools.
Distributorship	The franchisee takes title to various types of goods and further distributes them to subfranchisees. The distributor has exclusive coverage of a wide geographical area and acts as a supply house for the franchisees who carry the product.
Co-ownership	The franchisor and franchisee share the investment and profits. Examples include Aunt Jemima's Pancake Houses and Denny's Restaurants.
Co-management	The franchisor controls the major part of the investment. The partner-manager shares profits proportionately. Examples include Travelodge and Holiday Inn in the motel business.
Leasing	The franchisor leases the land, buildings, and equipment to franchisees. This is used in conjunction with other provisions.
Licensing	The franchisor licenses the franchisee to use his trademarks and business techniques. The franchisor either supplies the product or provides franchisees with a list of approved suppliers.
Manufacturing	The franchisor grants a franchise to manufacture its product through the use of specified materials and techniques. The franchisee distributes the product, utilizing the franchisor's techniques. This method enables a national manufacturer to distribute regionally when distribution costs from central manufacturing facilities are prohibitive. One example is Sealy.
Service	The franchisor describes patterns by which a franchisee supplies a professional service, as exemplified by employment agencies.

Source: Based on Gerald Pintel and Jay Diamond, *Retailing* (Englewood Cliffs, N.J.: Prentice-Hall, 1971), pp. 23–26.

franchisor attempts to resist these trends by making it difficult for franchisees to exert their independence in legally permissible ways, the harder it becomes to terminate the franchise relationship without inviting a law-suit.[39]

The franchise system is present in almost all business fields, as indicated in Exhibits 7–6 and 7–7.[40] It can be readily seen that the franchise system covers a wide variety of goods and services—accounting service, auto accessories, auto rentals, campgrounds, child care, computer services, dance studios, dry cleaning, employment agencies, fast foods, convenience food markets, sewer cleaning, home care, movie theatres, book stores, construction, industrial and commercial chemical products, and vending machine operations. It has also become a highly significant form of organization in the real estate industry.[41] Despite this diversity, automotive and petroleum franchise systems dominate the franchise industry. As reflected in Table 7–6, they account for about 41 percent of all franchised outlets and 73 percent of sales.

MODES OF OPERATION.[42]   All franchisees are expected to provide a continuing market for a franchisor's product or service. The product or service offering is, in theory, differentiated from those offered by conventional outlets by their *consistent* quantity and quality and strong promotion. Through his market- and image-building promotional strategy, which is instituted at an early stage of a franchise system's development, a franchisor hopes to gain automatic and immediate acceptance on the part of prospective franchisees and the public.

Franchisors provide both *initial* and *continuous* services to their franchisees. *Initial* services include:

- Market survey and site selection
- Facility design and layout
- Lease negotiation advice
- Financing advice
- Operating manuals
- Management training programs
- Franchisee employee training

The extent to which these initial services are provided is shown in Table 7–7. While the amount of involvement with franchisees is clearly high in many cases, it should be noted that the fact that a franchisor provides an initial service does not indicate anything about the depth of his involvement. For example, over 95 percent

[39] James T. Halverson, "What's in Store at the Federal Trade Commission," *Franchising and Antitrust* (Washington, D.C.: International Franchise Association, 1975), p. 25.

[40] Sketches presented in Exhibit 7–7 were developed by Henry Bullock in conjunction with his course work at Northwestern University.

[41] See "Franchising the Local Realty Broker," *Business Week* (September 13, 1976), p. 13; and Gary Washburn, "Forget Big Mac and the Colonel, Real Estate Gets the Franchise Prize," *Chicago Tribune*, Section 12, October 9, 1977, p. 1.

[42] This section is based largely on National Industrial Conference Board, *Franchised Distribution* (New York: National Industrial Conference Board, 1971).

EXHIBIT 7-6

Business Classification of Franchise Organizations and Representative Examples in Each Classification

Accounting and Tax Services
  Business Management Systems
  Edwin K. Williams & Co.
  H & R Block, Inc.

Agricultural
  Harvestall Industries
  Harvestore Products, Inc.

Art Galleries
  Continental Art Galleries, Ltd.
  Heritage Galleries International, Ltd.
  Original Oils, Ltd.

Automotive Accessories and Parts
  Firestone Tire & Rubber Co.
  Goodyear Tire & Rubber Co.
  Western Auto Supply Co.
  White Stores

Automotive Repair and Service
  Brake-O International, Inc.
  AAMCO Transmission, Inc.
  Midas Muffler

Auto Wash, Products and Equipment
  Johnson Waxway Centers
  Robo Wash, Inc.

Auto Rental
  Airways Rent-A-Car System, Inc.
  Budget Rent-A-Car Corp.

Building Construction
  Structural Concepts, Inc.
  Pieper Electric, Inc.

Campgrounds
  Holiday Camps, U.S.A.
  Kampgrounds of America, Inc.

Child Day Care Centers
  Mary Moppet's Day Care Schools, Inc.
  Pied Piper Schools, Inc.

Gas Stations
  Shell Oil
  Mobil Oil

Health Aids and Services
  Unihealth

Industrial and Chemical Products
  Tuff-kote International, Inc.

Industrial Supplies
  Vulcan Tools, Inc.

Motels and Hotels
  Alamo Plaza Hotel Courts
  Holiday Inns, Inc.
  Quality Court Motels, Inc.

Coffee Service
  Coffee Clubs of America, Inc.
  International Coffee Service, Inc.

Computer Services
  Automated Management Systems
  Binex Data Centers

Convenience Food Markets
  E/Z Food Shops

Collection and Credit
  Action Credit Bureau
    International, Inc.
  Credit Service Co.
  Check and Balance, Inc.

Dance Studios
  Fred Astaire Studios

Drug Stores
  Rexall Drug Co.
  Sentry Drug Centers

Dry Cleaning and Laundry Services
  Maytag Co.

Employment Agencies
  Manpower, Inc.
  Snelling & Snelling, Inc.
  Tempositions, Inc.

Food Operations
  Kentucky Fried Chicken
  Korn Kettle, Inc.
  Mr. Donut of America
  Burger King
  McDonald's
  Baskin Robbins 31 Flavors Stores
  Orange Julius of America
  International Pancake House
  Bonanza International, Inc.
  Ramada Inns, Inc.
  Rodeway Inns of America
  Travelodge International, Inc.

Pest Control	Theatres
Redd Man Services	Jerry Lewis Cinemas
Printing & Duplicating	Vending Operations
Kopy Kat, Inc.	Vend Marketing, Inc.
Kwik-Kopy, Inc.	

Source: National Franchise Directory, 1972 (Denver, Colorado: Continental Reports, Inc., 1972).

of all franchised outlets are built from the ground up. That is, similar and ongoing businesses did not previously exist on the current franchisee's location. However, the degree of involvement a franchisor exercises in site location and development varies widely. On the one hand, McDonald's does all locational site analysis and most land acquisition and development; on the other hand, Budget-Rent-A-Car merely assigns a territory and allows the franchisee to build where he pleases, subject to franchisor review and advice. Also, franchisee employee training varies in length based on the complexity of the operation and also the degree to which the franchisor uses this service to enhance the stability of a franchise. For instance, training by Hilton Hotels is a major selling point of its franchise program. In fact, Hilton provides such a host of training services that it never fully escapes the personnel difficulties inherent in company-owned, service-related outlets.[43] As an example of the comprehensiveness of some initial services, information from Southland Corporation, the franchisor of 7-Eleven Convenience Food Stores, is reproduced in the appendix to this chapter.

Continuous services include:

- Field supervision
- Merchandising and promotional materials
- Management and employee retraining
- Quality inspection
- National advertising
- Centralized purchasing
- Market data and guidance
- Auditing and record keeping
- Management reports
- Group insurance plans

Table 7–8 presents data on the extent to which continuing services are provided by franchisors.[44] Almost all franchisors have a continuous program of field services. Field representatives visit the franchise outlet to aid the franchisee in everyday operation, check the quality of product and service, and monitor performance.

[43] Examples provided by Henry Bullock. The authors gratefully acknowledge the data he gathered in interviews with executives of some major franchise companies.

[44] See also Michael Etgar, "Differences in the Use of Manufacturer Power in Conventional and Contractual Channels," *Journal of Retailing*, Vol. 54 (Winter 1978), pp. 49–62.

EXHIBIT 7–7

Thumbnail Sketches of Selected Franchise Systems

Budget Rent-A-Car System

Budget-Rent-A-Car has a fleet of 80,000 trucks and automobiles, ranking it third in the rental vehicle industry. Budget, unlike competitors, is essentially a franchisor. It retains a nucleus of company-owned operations to assist in developing and piloting operating and marketing programs. The company and its licensees provide the same automobile rental service as major competitors, but generally at lower cost. Budget began its operations in off-airport, downtown, and suburban locations and remains the leader in those markets. Major emphasis has now been placed upon expanding into airport locations. At the end of 1978, Budget had in-terminal facilities at 160 U.S. airports serving approximately 70 percent of all U.S. de-planing passengers.

Hilton Hotels Corporation

Hilton Hotels Corporation is operating in three separate areas. First are company-owned and -operated hotels and casinos. Hilton Hotels owns and operates 16 such operations, all of which are 1000 rooms or more. These operations are principally in resort locations and large metropolitan areas and accounted for roughly $360 million in revenue in 1977, $130 million of which was accountable from their two casino operations in Las Vegas. Second, Hilton Hotels enters into management contracts with smaller hotel operations, generally of 500 to 1000 rooms and in which they may or may not have partial equity interest. Hilton Hotels has a management arrangement with a total of 30 hotels, 11 of which are 50 percent owned by Hilton Hotels Corporation. These operations accounted for approximately $10 million in revenues for Hilton Hotels in 1977. Third is Hilton Hotels interest in franchise operations. Hilton has 126 franchised hotels. Franchise fees and royalty payments accounted for slightly above $5 million in revenue in fiscal 1977.

Midas-International

Midas originated the concept of the exhaust specialty shop with the opening of the first Midas Muffler Shop in 1955. Today Midas is a leader in the automotive aftermarket. Midas shops offer mufflers and exhaust systems to fit virtually every make and model of vehicle in the U.S. market. Midas shops are involved in other product areas including shock absorbers, brakes, and other front end services. There are now more than 1100 Midas Muffler shops, most in the U.S., with some in Canada, England, Australia, and Central and South America. Midas International Corporation is a wholly owned subsidiary of IC Industries. Since IC's takeover in 1972, the number of Midas shops has grown 72 percent—an increase of 460 outlets. Although muffler shops are the single most important component of Midas-International Corporation, the subsidiary itself is involved in diversified endeavors in support of these shops.

Sir Speedy, Inc.

Sir Speedy, Inc. has been engaged in franchising instant print centers since its incorporation in 1968. As of December 30, 1977, Sir Speedy became a majority-owned subsidiary of Kampgrounds of America, Inc. As of February 1, 1979, there were 239 franchised Sir Speedy Instant Printing Centers operating in 25 states. Sir Speedy Instant Printing Centers (SSIPC) are retail printing establishments which provide photo-offset printing for a range of needs, including office forms, brochures and booklets, manuals, stationery, and legal briefs. The services provided by Sir Speedy Instant Printing Centers are used by the general public as well as by small to medium commercial establishments. SSIPC faces competition from independent print shops, financial printers, and other franchisors of photo-offset print shops, including Postal Instant Press (440 outlets) and Kwik-Copy (350 outlets). SSIP and the instant print industry are unusual, since they are characterized by three franchisors of roughly equivalent size. Each offers nearly identical services in outlets which yield an unusually high return on investment. The domestic market is still growing rapidly for these services, while the international markets remain virtually untapped.

All franchisees are usually required to report monthly or semi-monthly on key elements of their operations, e.g., weekly sales, local advertising, employee turnover, profits, and other financial and marketing information. The regular reporting is intended to facilitate the various financial, operating, and marketing control procedures.

As might be expected, the reaction of franchisees to field services and operating controls is not always positive. Franchisees are independent businessmen, even though they have signed contractual agreements with franchisors. When conflict over supervision exists within their systems, franchisors have tended to rely on their field representatives to act as channel diplomats. However, these representatives not only are responsible for field service and liaison with franchisees but also must recruit additional franchisees. Complaints are often heard that the franchisor is providing too little attention to franchisees' management problems, especially when the field representatives have too many conflicting responsibilities.[45]

[45] For documentation of conflict issues in franchising, see Shelby D. Hunt and John R. Nevin, "Power in a Channel of Distribution: Sources and Consequences," *Journal of Marketing Research,* Vol. 11 (May 1974), pp. 186–193. See also, for an interesting case example, the conflicts that have arisen in soft drink bottling in such articles as Bill Abrams and John Koten, "New York Coke Agrees to Amend Franchise Accord," *Wall Street Journal,* April 17, 1979, p. 13; and John Koten, "Some Coca-Cola Bottlers Seek to Make Their Own Syrup for Sale to Restaurants," *Wall Street Journal,* February 27, 1979, p. 14.

TABLE 7-6   **Number and sales of franchised outlets by type of franchised system, 1979**

	Number of Units (thousands)	Percentage of Total	Sales (billions)	Percentage of Total
Manufacturer-retailer	202.5	41.1%	217.5	72.8%
Automobile and truck dealers	31.5	6.4	154.6	51.8
Gasoline service stations	171.0	34.7	62.9	21.0
Manufacturer-wholesaler	2.0	0.4	111.3	3.8
Soft drink bottlers	2.0	0.4	11.3	3.8
Wholesaler-retailer	99.7	20.2	18.4	6.2
Automotive products and services	53.4	10.8	8.0	2.7
Retailing (including drugs, hardware, paints, etc.)	46.3	9.4	10.4	3.5
Service-sponsor retailing	188.2	38.2	51.5	17.2
Business aids and services	46.6	9.5	5.2	1.7
Construction and remodeling, home cleaning, etc.	15.4	3.1	1.4	0.5
Convenience grocery stores	16.3	3.3	5.2	1.7
Educational products and services	2.6	0.5	0.3	0.1
Fast food restaurants	65.6	13.3	25.4	8.5
Food retailing (other than fast food and convenience stores)	15.3	3.1	4.0	1.3
Hotels and motels	5.8	1.2	6.1	2.0
Laundry and drycleaning	3.1	0.6	0.3	0.1
Recreation, entertainment, and travel (including campgrounds)	6.2	1.3	0.5	0.2
Rental services	9.2	1.9	2.8	1.0
Miscellaneous (beauty salons, carpet cleaning, etc.)	2.1	0.4	0.3	0.1
Total, all franchising	492.4	100.0%	298.7	100.0%

Source: Adapted from U.S. Department of Commerce, Industry and Trade Administration, *Franchising in the Economy 1977-79* (Washington, D.C.: U.S. Government Printing Office, January 1979), p. 34.

TABLE 7-7   Initial services to franchisees, as reported by franchisors

Type of Service Provided	Total, All Companies	Fast-food & Beverage	Non-food Retailing	Personal Services	Business Products & Services
		Franchisors Reporting			
Operating manuals	100.0%	100.0%	100.0%	100.0%	100.0%
Management training	100.0	100.0	100.0	100.0	100.0
Franchisee employee training	88.3	83.9	83.7	90.9	100.0
Market/surveys and site selection	84.4	98.2	93.0	83.6	42.3
Facility design and layout	80.0	100.0	83.7	81.8	26.9
Lease negotiation	62.7	78.5	72.0	58.1	23.0
Franchisee fee financing	37.7	25.0	37.2	47.2	46.1
All other services	21.1	21.4	25.5	20.0	15.3

Note: Based on information reported by 180 franchise companies. Includes 56 franchisors of fast-foods and beverages, 43 of nonfood consumer products, 55 of personal services, and 26 of business (or industrial) products and services.

Source: National Industrial Conference Board, *Franchised Distribution* (New York: National Industrial Conference Board, 1971), p. 23.

Another source of conflict is the fact that many franchisors own a number of their outlets and some of these outlets compete with those owned by franchisees. In managing a franchise system, however, efforts are made to avoid the problems generally associated with dual distribution. Besides the necessity of owning certain outlets because of bankruptcy problems on the part of some franchisees (franchisors may be the only available source of funds for ownership in these cases), there are a number of other reasons why a franchisor might wish to vertically integrate. First, franchisor-owned and -operated units serve as models for the rest of the system and can be used for research and training purposes. Second, such units may facilitate accelerated network growth, especially during the initial development period. Third, wholly owned units may be profitable. They will also permit the franchisor first-hand insight into day-to-day operating problems. Finally, court decisions and legislation may force franchisors to own more and more of their outlets if they wish to maintain strong control over the operations of the system as a whole. Although there is some feeling that the number of company-owned outlets is increasing,[46] the move to company-owned operations is *highly* significant only in the fast-food restaurant field, where the percentage of company-owned outlets rose from 19.4 in 1972 to 26.1 in 1979 and in the nonfood retailing area, where the

[46] See Donald W. Hackett, *Franchising: The State of the Art,* (Chicago: American Marketing Association Monograph Series No. 9, 1977), p. 41, and Vaughn, *op. cit.,* pp. 9, 61–70.

TABLE 7-8 Continuing services to franchisees, as reported by franchisors

Type of Service Provided	Franchisors Reporting				
	Total, All Companies	Fast-food & Beverage	Nonfood Retailing	Personal Services	Business Products & Services
Field supervision	96.1%	92.8%	100.0%	100.0%	89.6%
Merchandising and promotion materials	94.5	94.6	100.0	96.3	79.3
Franchisee employee retraining	85.1	78.5	83.3	94.5	82.7
Quality inspections	79.6	98.2	80.9	69.0	62.0
Advertising	66.4	62.5	61.9	83.6	48.2
Centralized purchasing	65.3	64.2	73.8	61.8	62.0
Market data and guidance	62.6	48.2	69.0	67.2	72.4
Auditing and recordkeeping	51.0	48.2	57.1	52.7	44.8
Group insurance plans	48.9	50.0	47.6	58.1	31.0
All other continuing services	13.1	8.9	21.4	12.7	10.3

Note: Based on information reported by 182 franchise companies. Includes 56 franchisors of fast-foods and beverages, 42 of nonfood consumer products, 55 of personal services, and 29 of business (or industrial) products and services.

Source: National Industrial Conference Board, *Franchised Distribution* (New York: National Industrial Conference Board, 1971), p. 24.

percentages for 1972 and 1979 were 14.5 and 27.9, respectively.[47] However, the percentage of company-owned stores for *all* franchising was 18.2 in 1979 compared to 17.4 in 1972, certainly not a dramatic increase.[48]

As an example of some of the significant conflict issues that exist between franchisors and franchisees, Exhibit 7-8 details a small bit of the recent history of Burger King, now a subsidiary of Pillsbury Co.

SOURCES OF FRANCHISOR REVENUE.   Sources of franchisor revenue and their relative importance are illustrated in Fig. 7-1. The various sources include:

1. *Initial franchise fees.* Many franchisors charge an initial fee to new franchisees. The fee ranges from $1000 to $100,000, with the mode falling between

---

[47] U.S. Department of Commerce, Industry and Trade Administration, *op. cit.,* pp. 34 and 39. Nonfood retailing franchise systems include general merchandise, wearing apparel, hardware, paints and floor covering, drugs, electronics, and cosmetic items, among others.

[48] *Ibid.* For an example of a fast-food franchise chain that has moved to company-owned outlets, see ''Denny's: A Brisk Turnaround,'' *Business Week* (December 15, 1980), p. 101.

EXHIBIT 7–8

Conflicts in Franchising: A Case Example—Burger King

- 1489 Burger King restaurants out of a total of 2726 are operated by franchisees who own the land and buildings themselves, or rent them from someone other than Pillsbury. In contrast, McDonald's owns or leases nearly all of the land and buildings used by its 5747 restaurants. The advantages of ownership to the franchisor are compelling. The land is an appreciating asset and the building a source of depreciation writeoffs. Equally important, however, is the fact that, as the franchisee's landlord, the franchisor has power. McDonald's franchisees, for example, are not allowed to own any other fastfood restaurants, and they have no territorial rights or protection. On the other hand, until relatively recently, Burger King granted exclusive rights to large territories and allowed franchisees to buy land and build as many stores as they liked. A franchisee was free to sell sections of his territory to others if he wanted; he could even diversify into other fast-food businesses.

- The consequence of Burger King's early policies has been that some of its franchisees have grown so large that they are very difficult for the franchisor to control. Two of its franchisees—Chart House, Inc. and Horn & Hardart Co.—have engaged in all-out battles with Pillsbury over such issues as expansion and diversification into other restaurant businesses. (Chart House owns Cork 'N Cleaver, the Chart House group in California, and over 350 Burger King restaurants. Horn & Hardart operates its famous Automats as well as a number of Arby's restaurants in addition to over 20 Burger King restaurants.)

- Burger King has established a far more demanding contract with its franchisees. Franchisees must now agree not to own any other fast-food business and to live within an hour's drive of their Burger King restaurants, which makes it difficult for a franchisee to own more than a dozen restaurants.

- Burger King franchisees are interested in their restaurants' profits and losses. Pillsbury is more interested in their sales. (Apart from a one-time franchise fee of $40,000, Pillsbury obtains most of its revenue from the franchisee's sales—3½ percent of sales as royalty; 4 percent for the marketing fund; and, if Pillsbury owns the land and building, an additional 8½ percent as rent. McDonald's levies a franchise fee of $12,500, a royalty of 3 percent, a marketing fee of 3 percent and rent of 8½ percent.) There is a potential incompatibility of goals in almost all franchise arrangements, including Burger King's, especially when increasing sales pushes costs so high that the franchisee's profit goes down. For example, many Burger King franchisees originally strongly resisted Pillsbury's desire that they shift to multiple lines, such as McDonald's was using, in existing restaurants. The franchisees believed that the additional cash registers and extra help would cost more than the increased sales would justify.

Source: Lee Smith, "Burger King Puts Down Its Dukes," *Fortune* (June 16, 1980), pp. 90-98. As an epilogue, see "Horn & Hardart Co., Burger King Settle Franchise Dispute," *Wall Street Journal,* November 5, 1980, p. 12.

FIGURE 7-1

Principal Sources of Franchise Company Revenue

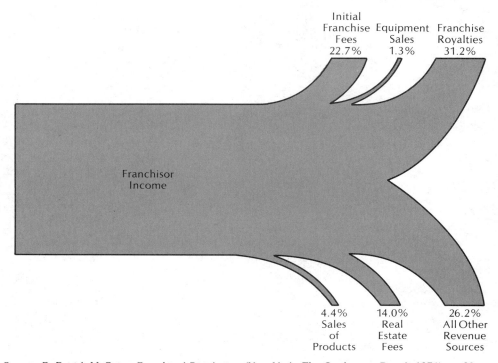

Source: E. Patrick McGuire, *Franchised Distribution* (New York: The Conference Board, 1971), p. 20.

$10,000 and $25,000. The fee is charged to cover the franchisor's expenses for site locations, training, setting operating controls, and other initial services as well as developmental costs in building the system. Initial fees tend to rise as a franchise becomes more successful.

2. *Royalty fees.* Many franchisors charge a royalty fee or commisson based on the gross value of a franchisee's sales volume. Five percent of gross sales is the most common royalty agreement in franchising. Some franchisors require a minimum payment of $150 to $200 per month. In certain cases, the royalty rate decreases as sales volume increases while in others, the royalty fee is a flat rate regardless of the sales volume. Some franchisors collect a royalty on a unit-of-sale basis. For example, motel franchisors charge a fee per room; soft ice cream franchisors charge a fee for each gallon of mix sold to the franchisee; car wash equipment franchisors charge a fee per car washed. Figure 7-2 presents survey results regarding franchise royalty practices.

3. *Sales of products.* Some franchisors function as wholesalers in that they

FIGURE 7-2
Franchise Company Royalty Practices

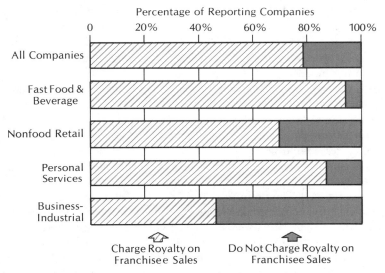

Percentage of Reporting Companies

Note: Survey of 185 franchise companies, including 56 fast-foods and beverages, 45 nonfood retail, 56 personal services, and 28 business/industrial franchisers.

Source: E. Patrick McGuire, *Franchised Distribution*, (New York: The Conference Board, 1971), p. 21.

supply franchisees with raw materials and finished products. Other franchisors manufacture their products; for example, as mentioned earlier, Holiday Inns owns furniture and carpeting manufacturing facilities, and a significant amount of Coca-Cola's revenue is derived from the sale of its soft drink syrups to its franchised bottlers. In some cases, the franchise company sells the equipment needed by the franchisee. These practices are circumscribed by recent court decisions, however, as is pointed out in the chapter on legal limitations.

4. *Rental and lease fees.* The franchise company often leases the building, equipment, and fixtures used in its outlets. Some franchise contracts involve an escalator clause that requires the franchisee to increase his lease payment as sales volume increases.

5. *License fees.* The franchisee sometimes is required to pay for the use and display of the franchisor's trademark. The license fee is used more in conjunction with industrial franchises, where a local manufacturer is licensed to use a particular patent or process.

6. *Management fees.* In a few cases, franchisees are charged fees for consulting services received from the franchisor such as management reports and training.

THE SOCIAL VIEW OF FRANCHISING. A number of arguments have been raised, pro and con, relative to the socioeconomic and legal consequences of franchising.[49] On the pro side, for example, it has been contended that franchising greatly increases the opportunity for individuals to become independent businessmen, even though it is becoming more difficult to qualify for a franchise.[50] Hunt estimates that if franchising did not exist, approximately 52 percent of the owner-managers he surveyed would not be self-employed.[51] It has also been argued, without support one way or the other, that franchised businesses have lower failure rates than other businesses. Furthermore, to various observers, franchising seems to decrease economic concentration by providing a viable alternative to completely integrated corporate vertical marketing systems.

On the con side, some claim that: (1) franchise agreements are one-sided in favor of protecting the franchisor; (2) franchisors employ unethical techniques in selling franchises, including "pyramid" distribution schemes,[52] celebrity promotion of franchises, and misrepresentation of the potential profitability of the franchise; and (3) franchising is an anticompetitive system of distribution. Most of these contentions, especially the last one, involve legal as well as socioeconomic factors.[53]

The bulk of evidence seems to be in support of the contention that franchise agreements favor the franchisor. Franchise contracts involve termination clauses, provisions on operating manual changes at the prerogative of the franchisor, and "covenants not to compete" clauses that prohibit a franchisee from practicing his trade for a specified time period within a specific geographic area after franchise termination. Sixty percent of sample contracts examined by Hunt included such clauses.[54] Observed in these contracts were also clauses requiring the franchisee to buy supplies and equipment from the franchisor, restricting the franchisee's right to sell, and prohibiting the franchisee from joining any union of franchisees. Lack of arbitration clauses was evident in 77 percent of the contracts examined. It is in-

---

[49] See Shelby D. Hunt, "The Socioeconomic Consequences of the Franchised System of Distribution," *Journal of Marketing,* Vol. 36 (July 1972), pp. 32–38. Also see Charles G. Burck, "Franchising's Troubled Dream World," *Fortune* (March 1970), pp. 116 ff.

[50] See Gary Washburn, "Franchising Good but Hard to Enter," *Chicago Tribune,* Section 2, September 21, 1975, p. 13. See, also, Sanford L. Jacobs, "Operating a Franchise Often Pays But Demands on Buyer Are Great," *Wall Street Journal,* November 3, 1980, p. 27.

[51] Hunt, "The Socioeconomic Consequences. . .," *op. cit.,* p. 33.

[52] A pyramid distribution scheme is one in which a parent company sells the right to a territory to an individual, who in turn has the right ("franchise") to sell the right to operate under him or her. The procedure may be repeated in turn at several descending levels and has been used to amass fortunes in the cosmetics field, and especially by Glenn W. Turner with firms he named "Koscot Interplanetary" and "Dare-to-Be-Great," Vaughn, *op. cit.,* p. 23.

[53] For a discussion of socioeconomic factors, see Bruce Mallen, "Channel Power: A Form of Economic Exploitation," *European Journal of Marketing,* Vol. 12, No. 2 (1978), p. 198; and Robert F. Lusch, "Franchisee Satisfaction: Causes and Consequences," *International Journal of Physical Distribution,* Vol. 7 (1977), pp. 128–140,

[54] Hunt, *op. cit.,* p. 37. See also Paul Merrion, "Tougher Pact Riles Big Mac Owners," *Crain's Chicago Business,* Vol. 2 (September 17, 1979), p. 1; and Stanley Penn, "Franchisees Form Militant Trade Groups to Meet Fears About Power of Licensers," *Wall Street Journal,* August 8, 1979, p. 8.

teresting to note, however, that 40 percent of the sample of franchisees responding to Hunt's survey did not consult a lawyer prior to signing a contract.[55]

Partly as a result of some of the above-mentioned practices on the part of franchisors, the Federal Trade Commission approved in 1979 a trade regulation rule titled "Disclosure Requirement and Prohibitions Concerning Franchising and Business Opportunity Ventures," which requires sellers of franchises to disclose a wide variety of information to franchise buyers. The rule bars misrepresentations of actual or potential sales, income, or profits. It requires the disclosure of information about the franchise seller, such as its business experience, the business experience of its key management personnel, its bankruptcy and litigation history, and its certified balance sheet for the most recent year. In addition, the seller is mandated to disclose:

- Costs, both initial and recurring, that will be required to be paid by the franchisee.
- Restrictions placed on the franchisee's conduct of business.
- Termination, cancellation, and renewal provisions of the franchise agreement.
- Statistical information about the number of franchises and their rates of termination.
- Training programs for the franchisee.[56]

The trade regulation rule, which went into effect on October 21, 1979, does not preempt state laws governing franchises. In fact, there is a multiplicity of regulatory rules and statutes both at state and local levels which govern the actions of franchisors and their franchisees.[57]

The use of unethical techniques in selling is, obviously, not restricted to franchising. The FTC is, however, cracking down on pyramid schemes, and several states have declared such schemes to be an unfair trade practice. Relative to inflated estimates of profitability, Hunt's study showed that 73 percent of the franchisees had incomes below the minimum projected by the pro-forma income statement; 92

[55] Hunt, *op. cit.,* p. 37.

[56] "FTC Gives Details on Requirements and Coverage of Franchise Rule," *FTC News Summary* (August 3, 1979), p. 2. See also "FTC Will Require Sellers of Franchises to Disclose Variety of Data to Buyers," *Wall Street Journal,* December 21, 1978, p. 2; "Oil and Auto Concerns Receive FTC Franchise-Rule Exemptions," *FTC News Summary* (August 1, 1980), pp. 2 and 3; and "FTC Seeks Comment on Request from Wholesale Grocers for Franchise-Rule Exemption," *FTC News Summary* (February 20, 1981), p. 3.

[57] For example, only a very few states have a so-called "fractional franchise" exemption from state disclosure laws, even though such an exemption is available relative to the federal rule. The federal exemption has two requirements: first, it requires that the parties reasonably anticipate that the sales which will arise from the relationship which they are about to begin will not exceed 20 percent of the total dollar sales volume of the reseller in the coming year. The second requirement is that the reseller must have been in the same type of business represented by the franchise relationship for at least two years. For further discussion of federal and state disclosure laws, see Shelby D. Hunt and John R. Nevin, "Full Disclosure Laws in Franchising: An Empirical Evaluation," *Journal of Marketing,* Vol. 40 (April 1976), pp. 53–62; and U.S. Department of Commerce, Industry and Trade Administration, *op. cit.,* pp. 20–31.

percent had incomes below the average projected figures; and 99 percent had incomes below the maximum projected incomes.[58]

Franchising generally involves tying agreements, territorial restrictions, and uniform pricing policies. These legal issues and related case rulings are discussed in detail in the next chapter on legal limitations to interorganization management. Hunt's study reported that 50 percent of the fast-food franchisors responding to his survey specified prices for the franchisee's products, 28 percent required the franchisee to buy paper goods from the franchisor, and 85 percent assigned an exclusive territory.[59] All of these practices may be viewed by antitrust enforcement agencies as restricting competition.

THE RATIONALE FOR FRANCHISING. Before we address the organizing strategy involved with vertical integration or corporate vertical marketing systems, it is important to pause for a moment and consider why it is that franchise systems evolve, if they are so loaded down with controversy. Tightly controlled franchise systems represent the extreme form of limiting the market, short of outright ownership. That is, through the stipulations in the contract which they sign, the parties purposively subvert and circumscribe the marketplace existing between them. Schedules are set, programs are constructed, and commitments are made so that, in the end, the end-user can receive the product of the synergistic (it is to be hoped) efforts of the franchisor and franchisee. Thus, in theory at least, the franchise system is used to provide substantial franchisee training, sales, service, promotional, and capital assistance so that overall system performance will be enhanced.

In addition, franchise systems facilitate the flow of critical market information between franchisors and franchisees so that consumer preferences, complaints, and purchasing intentions can more quickly be reflected in marketing and production planning. Routinizing information flows is also important when it is necessary to monitor compensation claims, such as those for warranty work. The long-run mutual interest fostered by routinization of information flows reduces incentives for exaggerated compensation claims, while the uniform accounting and reporting procedures and greater access to information permit effective monitoring of the entire franchise system.

Finally, the franchise system provides needed investment incentives by making substantial sales, service, and management assistance readily available to potential franchisees; by harmonizing interdependent investment decision making through realignments of business risks; and by mitigating opportunities for the exploitation of invested capital by free-rider franchisees.[60] For example, in the automobile industry, there are significant costs incurred by dealers in providing point-of-sale ser-

---

[58] Hunt, *op. cit.,* p. 38.

[59] *Ibid.,* p. 36.

[60] Discussion of externalities, economies of scale in information processing, and investment incentives as applied to franchise systems in the automobile, tire, and petroleum industries can be found in Thomas G. Marx, "Distribution Efficiency in Franchising," *Business Topics,* Vol. 28 (Winter 1980), pp. 5-13. The free-rider problem is also addressed in Chapter 8 of this text.

vices (showrooms, demonstration vehicles, sales assistance, etc.). Limited service dealers could obtain cost advantages over full service rivals by obtaining a free ride on their investments in these service facilities. A dealer with only a price list and an order form could underprice full service competitors, and consumers could realize substantial savings by shopping at full service dealerships and purchasing at limited service dealerships.[61]

Given the clear desire of a wide variety of manufacturers, wholesalers, and service-oriented organizations to control their marketing channels by establishing franchises or some other form of contractual marketing system, the next logical question would seem to be: Why don't they go all the way and vertically integrate the relevant marketing flows? The answer to this question is pursued below as we examine corporate systems.

CORPORATE SYSTEMS   Corporate vertical marketing systems exist when channel members on different levels of distribution for a particular product are owned and operated by one organization. Corporate forward integration occurs frequently when a manufacturing firm decides to establish its own sales branches, distribution centers, and/or wholesale outlets, as when Evans Products Company (a manufacturer of plywood) purchased wholesale lumber distributors in order to more aggressively promote its products through retail lumber establishments.

In Chapter 3, it was pointed out that manufacturers may have both efficiency and effectiveness incentives to establish their own wholesaling operations. For example, as shown in Chapter 3, the operating expenses of manufacturers' sales branches (with stocks) average 11 percent of sales versus 15 percent for merchant wholesalers. Even more important is the control that manufacturers achieve over distribution activities. Forward vertical integration may also occur when a manufacturer takes over both the wholesale and retail functions by establishing its own system of retail outlets. Although integration of wholesaling functions alone is more common, evidence of complete forward vertical integration is found in such diverse companies as Singer, Sherwin-Williams (which owns and operates over 2000 retail outlets),[62] Hart, Schaffner, and Marx (which operates over 275 stores),[63] Eagle (which generates 30 percent of its volume from captive locations), International Harvester, Goodyear, and Sohio.[64] In fact, complete forward vertical in-

---

[61] Marx, *op. cit.*, p. 10.

[62] For an interesting discussion of some of Sherwin-Williams' problems and opportunities in maintaining a corporate vertical marketing system, see "A Paintmaker Puts a Fresh Coat on its Marketing," *Business Week* (February 23, 1976), pp. 95–96.

[63] In 1979, 62 percent of Hart, Schaffner & Marx's sales volume of $631 million came from retailing. The corporation owns such chains as Silverwoods, Baskin, Chas. A. Stevens, Wallachs, R. J. Boggs, Zachry, and Hastings, among others.

[64] While the extent of vertical integration in the petroleum industry is great (including crude oil production, refinery operations, and wholesaling), most major oil companies moved away from direct service station operation by the mid-1930s. Chain store taxes, the threat of unionization, and the chance to shift

tegration by manufacturers seems to be on the increase. Among the largest producers to develop corporate systems through to the retail level of distribution in recent years are Edmos (yarns and knits), Pepperidge Farms (baked goods), Eaton (auto parts), Dannon (yogurt), Texas Instruments and Hewlett-Packard (calculators), and GAF (duplicating supplies and services) plus hundreds of manufacturers who are quietly opening retail warehouse outlets.[65] One of the latter is Keller Industries, Inc., of Miami, which makes carpeting, tubular furniture, and aluminum doors, windows, and other products for residential construction. Managers of such newly formed corporate systems see forward integration as a good way to increase sales volume in a slow growth economy while also letting the consuming public know about all of the various products they offer.

Corporate backward integration occurs in distribution when either a retailer or a wholesaler assumes ownership of institutions that normally precede them in the marketing flow of goods and services. To many, corporate systems are regarded as roughly synonymous with integrated chain store systems.[66] While all chain store organizations have integrated wholesaling functions, many of them also own some manufacturing facilities. For example many food chains obtain 15 to 20 percent of their requirements from company-owned processing facilities.[67] Sears and Safeway are important examples of backward vertical integration. Both organizations offer unusually good values in the product categories in which they elect to compete, with value being defined to include all dimensions of the product and service offer. Both companies have created vertical systems to coordinate the procurement and redistribution process.

For example, in 1974, Sears had a financial interest in 31 of its 12,000 suppliers.[68] The companies ranged from small companies with less than 100 employees to large corporations listed on the New York Stock Exchange, including Armstrong Rubber Co., Whirlpool Corp., and De Soto, Inc. The 31 "affiliated manufacturing sources," as Sears refers to them, had combined sales of $4.2 billion and supplied about 28 percent of Sears' purchases.[69] Examples of its affiliated manufacturing sources are shown in Fig. 7–3. In most cases, Sears has a minority interest in terms of common stock ownership, but may account for a large percentage of their sales, as indicated in Table 7–9. According to company executives, Sears' interest in maintaining factory ownership, a practice which dates back to 1906, is to provide its retail and catalog outlets with "a reliable and continuous supply of merchandise,

the burden of low returns from retailing to others were important factors in this decision. Sohio is an exception to the rule, owning approximately 30 percent of its stations. The other majors operate fewer than one percent of their outlets with company employees. For example in 1973 Gulf operated only 32 stations out of 29,540 and Shell only 171 out of 20,464 stations. Fred C. Allvine and James H. Patterson, *Highway Robbery* (Bloomington, Ind.: Indiana University Press, 1974), p. 25.

[65] "Marketing When the Growth Slows," *Business Week, op. cit.,* p. 48. See also "General Host: Vertical Integration to Save a Subsidiary It Couldn't Sell," *Business Week* (January 19, 1981), p. 103.

[66] See, for example, Davidson, *op. cit.,* p. 388.

[67] McCammon, "Perspectives for Distribution Programming," *op. cit.,* p. 45.

[68] William Gruber, "Sears' Success Affects Many," *Chicago Tribune,* Section 2, September 2, 1975, p. 7. See also Carol J. Loomis, "The Leaning Tower of Sears," *Fortune* (July 2, 1979), pp. 78–85.

[69] Gruber, *op. cit.,* p. 7.

FIGURE 7–3

Examples of Sears' Affiliated Manufacturing Sources

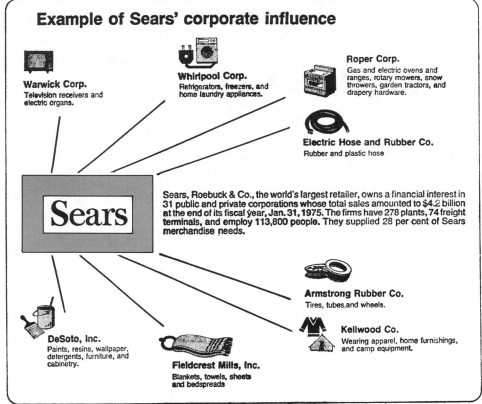

Example of Sears' corporate influence

Warwick Corp.
Television receivers and electric organs.

Whirlpool Corp.
Refrigerators, freezers, and home laundry appliances.

Roper Corp.
Gas and electric ovens and ranges, rotary mowers, snow throwers, garden tractors, and drapery hardware.

Electric Hose and Rubber Co.
Rubber and plastic hose

Sears, Roebuck & Co., the world's largest retailer, owns a financial interest in 31 public and private corporations whose total sales amounted to $4.2 billion at the end of its fiscal year, Jan. 31, 1975. The firms have 278 plants, 74 freight terminals, and employ 113,800 people. They supplied 28 per cent of Sears merchandise needs.

Armstrong Rubber Co.
Tires, tubes, and wheels.

Kellwood Co.
Wearing apparel, home furnishings, and camp equipment.

DeSoto, Inc.
Paints, resins, wallpaper, detergents, furniture, and cabinetry.

Fieldcrest Mills, Inc.
Blankets, towels, sheets and bedspreads

Tribune graphics by Bill Salovic

Source: William Gruber, "Sears' Success Affects Many," *Chicago Tribune*, Section 2, September 7, 1975, p. 7. Reprinted, courtesy of the Chicago Tribune.

built to our specifications, delivered in the right quantities at the right time and at the lowest possible cost."[70] However, Sears will become interested in a manufacturing investment only when it "insures continuity of sound management, quality, service, price and design obtainable in no other way."[71] In fact, there are nine criteria that Sears uses to determine whether to establish an investor relationship with a supplier. They include:

> . . . a competent management, adequate facilities, an accurate cost accounting system that permits both management and Sears buyers to know the actual cost of each

[70] *Ibid.*

[71] *Ibid.*

TABLE 7-9 Sears' ownership of and extent of purchases from selected affiliated manufacturing sources in 1974

Affiliated Manufacturing Source	Sears' Ownership of Stock (percent)	Total Sales of Source (millions)	Sears' Share of Total Sales (percent)
DeSoto, Inc.	32.0%	$271	64%
Roper Corp.	41.4	366	71
Whirlpool Corp.[a]			
Parent company	4.7		
Heil-Quaker subsidiary	20.0	1260	62
Warwick Electronics subsidiary	25.5		
Kellwood Co.	23.0	400	79
Armstrong Rubber Co.	10.0	259	36
Globe-Union Co.[b]	2.6	276	33
Fieldcrest Mills	4.2	NA[c]	NA
Electric Hose and Rubber Co.	5.6	NA	NA

[a] Includes trash compactors, vacuum cleaners, home heating equipment, and home entertainment units, in addition to the products listed in Fig. 10-3.

[b] Globe-Union supplies Sears with automobile batteries and other electronic components.

[c] NA = not available

Source: William Gruber, "Sears' Success Affects Many," *Chicago Tribune*, Section 2, September 7, 1975, p. 7.

product, effective production and budget controls, enlightened personnel policies, a sound sales policy, creative research and development programs, profitable factory operations, and "acceptance by the merchandising departments of their full merchandising responsibility."[72]

According to a famous study by Kaplan, Dirlam, and Lanzillotti, Sears' method of operation at one time produced selling prices ranging from about 15 percent to 30 percent below the retail list prices of less integrated competitors in such product lines as water heaters, refrigerators, men's shoes, house paint, garden hoses, shotguns, and girdles.[73]

Some major wholesalers are engaged in successful backward vertical integration as well. For example, W. W. Grainger, Inc., an electrical distributor with sales of $498 million and a return on net worth of 18 percent in 1973, operates seven manufacturing facilities and has an aggressive private brand program. American Hospital Supply Corporation is both a major distributor and a manufacturer of health care products and services; its sales amounted to $1.5 billion in 1977, and its return on net worth was 13.5 percent. In addition, a number of steel wholesalers

[72] *Ibid.*

[73] A. D. H. Kaplan, Joel B. Dirlam, and Robert F. Lanzillotti, *Pricing Big Business* (Washington, D.C.: The Brookings Institution, 1958), pp. 194–195.

(e.g., Joseph T. Ryerson & Son, Inc., A. M. Castle & Co., and Earle M. Jorgenson Co.) have become metal service centers, offering a wide variety of preprocessing services, including slitting, welding, and forming. These service centers now dominate the wholesale segment of the steel market.

By virtue of ownership, a channel member can achieve operating economies and *absolute* control over the marketing activities of other channel members. From the perspective of organization behavior, corporate systems are those in which units are organized for the achievement of inclusive goals where the locus of both inclusive decision-making and authority is clearly delineated within the structure. Thus, decision-making is *not* subject to unit ratification as it is in contractual systems. Wholly owned channel members are structured for a division of labor within the inclusive organization. Norms of commitment are high. Most important, perhaps, the systemwide orientation of the members is greater than in other vertical marketing systems.[74]

As indicated earlier in this chapter, administered and contractual systems are the result of joint efforts made by channel members to limit, subvert, and/or circumscribe the market which lies between them. By organizing the market, their costs of transacting business are likely to be lower and the effectiveness of their marketing is likely to be higher than it would be if the functioning of a perfectly free market were the resource allocating mechanism between them. However, it should be noted that while the market has been "tampered" with, it still exists for parties in administered and contractual systems. In corporate systems, markets do *not* exist, unless they are simulated. (Some divisions of vertically integrated companies set transfer prices, for example, on the basis of the existing market price levels between nonintegrated buyers and sellers with whom they compete.) In fact, the existence of corporate systems means that, for the corporation involved, the market has "failed." That is, from the perspective of management, the channel cannot aid the corporation in attaining its goals unless it is fully integrated into the corporation.

According to Oliver E. Williamson, markets fail when the costs of completing transactions become unbearable.[75] They are at this level when there exists a high degree of uncertainty surrounding transactions because of environmental factors *and* when channel members do not trust one another because generally deceptive behavior has become commonplace among them. Under these conditions, exchange occurs between channel members only with the protection of iron-clad contracts, lengthy specifications of obligations accounting for all possible contingencies of an uncertain future, and extensive auditing of performance. When this happens, vertical integration will be preferred to the relatively greater costs of market transactions. Williamson believes that a wholly integrated operation is more capable of suppressing opportunistic tendencies, resolving conflicts, and monitoring performance than is one that relies on market transactions. In fact, it could be argued that the only reason for the existence of a corporate vertical marketing system is its

[74] Warren, *op. cit.,* p. 316.

[75] Williamson, *Markets and Hierarchies, op. cit.,* pp. 20–40.

ability to achieve transactional efficiency. Thus, the formation of a corporate system will tend to reduce the suboptimization which often prevails in more fragmented and decentralized systems. Such a system will usually have better opportunities to exploit economies of scale through increased programming of distribution activities. Also, it is likely that corporate systems will allow more free and rapid communication between the various distributive levels.

The development of corporate systems assures a channel member strong and long-term contact with customers and/or suppliers. Through this form of channel organization, the member may secure adequate representation in a market, reduce the cost of goods purchased, secure relatively scarce supplies, reduce production costs, gain greater inventory control and more pertinent market information, and employ excess funds that have been generated in effective ways.[76] Vertical integration may permit a manufacturer, for example, to set and maintain the price at which his goods are sold at wholesale or retail. In addition, the vertically integrated firm may find it easier to control the quality of the product, engage in selective store promotions, or sell to its various retail outlets at different prices for the purpose of achieving greater market penetration in selected geographic areas. During 1979 and 1980, interest rates skyrocketed to over 20 percent. Many firms restricted retail lending because they could not charge enough to make money. In durable goods marketing, this lack of financing was particularly disastrous. In the automobile industry, the manufacturers' vertically integrated finance companies, e.g., Ford Motor Credit Company and General Motors Acceptance Corporation (GMAC), were called upon to fill the gap. General Motors gave its finance company a $500 million interest-free loan to help the unit operate smoothly.[77] The other automobile companies made similar arrangements with their finance companies. Although the latter are supposed to operate as profit centers, they are mandated to make certain that automobile sales do not dry up because of lack of available financing.

The integrated firm may also find it easier to protect its good will and trademarks than otherwise might be the case if it were to depend on a large number of independently owned middlemen who simply use its name. For example, one of the major reasons why Church's Fried Chicken Inc., an 830-store chain based in San Antonio and concentrated mostly in the South and Southwest, has become one of the most profitable companies in the fast-food industry is because of the control it maintains over its primarily company-owned outlets. The company has, for the most part, avoided franchising in order to maintain meal quality by directly owning and managing the operations side of the business.[78]

One of the most interesting developments involving the formation of corporate systems in recent years has been the decision of such firms as Digital Equipment Corporation, NCR, and Xerox to penetrate the small-business market by

---

[76] Frederick D. Sturdivant, et al., *Managerial Analysis in Marketing* (Glenview, Ill.: Scott, Foresman and Company, 1970), pp. 649–653.

[77] Amanda Bennett, "Auto Makers' Finance Units Squeezed Between Fund Costs, Duty to Aid Sales," *Wall Street Journal,* May 12, 1980, p. 16.

[78] "Church's: A Fast-Food Recipe That is Light on Marketing," *Business Week* (February 20, 1978), pp. 110 and 112.

IMPLICATIONS / IBM CASE

opening retail stores.[79] (See the advertisement for Digital's Computer Stores in Exhibit 7–9.) As the cost of computers and copiers declines and the cost of selling and servicing them rises, computer and copier companies are turning away from the traditional way of selling through individual salesmen in order to provide the service outputs required by very small firms, family companies, and professional offices. Xerox was the first copier company to approach the small-business market through stores of its own. In addition to copying machines priced less than $1200, the Xerox stores sell word-processing equipment, facsimile equipment, telephone-answering devices, electronic calculators, and other types of office equipment in the price range of small companies and home offices. Most is made by manufacturers other than Xerox. These moves to vertical integration were taken to counter the moves of competitors who have relied mainly on independent distributors to reach the small-business market. For example, Texas Instruments, Inc. and a number of foreign computer companies, such as Wang, sell their low-cost models for industrial and business use through a network of original equipment manufacturers, or OEMs, that buy computers from makers, add software, and resell them to users. Other companies, like Digital Equipment Corporation, have established both types of channel systems.

The advantages of corporate marketing systems have been explored by a number of economists and marketing scholars.[80] The major emphasis of most of the studies on the subject is placed on the ability of such systems to achieve economies of scale through standardization, automation, and better streamlining of channel operations.[81] It has been argued, though, that in order to achieve scale

ADV.

---

[79] Liz Roman Gallese "Computer Concerns Look to Retail Selling to Tap Lucrative Small-Business Market," *Wall Street Journal,* August 3, 1979; and Jeffrey A. Tannenbaum, "Xerox Corporation Plans Chain of Retail Stores in a Bid for Small-Business Customers," *Wall Street Journal,* April 9, 1980, p. 3.

[80] See, for example, R. H. Coase, "The Nature of the Firm," in G. J. Stigler and K. Boulding (eds.), *Readings in Price Theory* (Homewood, Ill.: Richard D. Irwin, Inc., 1952), p. 331; Arthur R. Burns, *The Decline of Competition* (New York: McGraw-Hill Book Company, 1936); Melvin G. de Chazeau and Alfred Kahn, *Integration and Competition in the Petroleum Industry* (New Haven, Conn.: Yale University Press, 1959); Nugent Wedding, *Vertical Integration in Marketing* (Urbana, Ill.: University of Illinois Bureau of Economic and Business Research, 1952); Oliver E. Williamson, "The Vertical Integration of Production: Market Failure Considerations," *American Economic Review,* Vol. 61 (May 1971), pp. 112–123; Lars Mattson, *Integration and Efficiency in Marketing Systems* (Stockholm, Sweden: Stockholm School of Economics, 1969); Louis P. Bucklin, "The Economic Base of Franchising," in Donald N. Thompson (ed.), *op. cit.,* pp. 33–62; Samuel H. Logan, "A Conceptual Framework for Analyzing Economies of Vertical Integration," *American Journal of Agricultural Economics,* Vol. 51 (November 1969), pp. 836–848; and Michael Etgar, "Determinants of Structural Changes in Vertical Marketing Systems," Working Paper No. 201, School of Management, State University of New York at Buffalo, December 1974.

[81] Michael Etgar, "Effects of Administrative Control on Efficiency of Vertical Marketing Systems," *Journal of Marketing Research,* Vol. 13. (February 1976), pp. 12–14. In an excellent treatment of the strategic benefits and costs of vertical integration, Porter has isolated the following: (a) benefits—secure economies of combined operations, internal control and coordination, information, avoiding the market, and stable relationships; tap into technology; assure supply and/or demand; offset bargaining power and input cost distortions; enhance ability to differentiate; elevate entry and mobility barriers; enter a higher-return business; and defend against foreclosure; (b) costs—overcoming mobility barriers; increased operating leverage; reduced flexibility to change partners; higher overall exit barriers; capital investment requirements; foreclosure of access to supplier or consumer research and/or know-how; maintaining balance; dulled incentives; and differing managerial requirements. See Michael E. Porter, *Competitive Strategy* (New York: The Free Press, 1980), pp. 300–323.

If you employ from 5 to 100 people, Digital has a computer designed to save you money every day you own it.

The DDS-408 computer is for business people who don't like high interest rates and who want to save money right now—by cutting down on their borrowing. The DDS-408 can really help, and here's how.

First, it gets your bills out quicker and keeps better track of who owes you money, so you recover receivables faster. It gets your statements out on the first of the month, when they're supposed to get out. Also, you take discounts because you manage your cash better. And you gain a tighter grip on inventory, increasing turns and cutting down on dead inventory.

Digital's DEC Datasystem 408 (DDS-408) small business computer. From $9445.*

All of which means, with the DDS-408, you borrow less because your cash flow improves.

Best of all, the DDS-408 is from Digital, the world's largest manufacturer of small computers. So you'll have the service and support of more than 13,000 people.

Come in to Digital's Computer Store today and ask for a demonstration. With preprogrammed applications, you'll be surprised how easy it is to use.

Digital's Computer Stores

Whether you manage 5 employees or 100, employ the best means possible to save money. Digital's DDS-408 computer.

*Basic accounting system. Word processing computer with Letter Quality Printer from $12,545. Preprogrammed software and destination charges not included.

digital

Atlanta: 25 Park Place N.E., Trust Company Tower. (404) 523-2105. Mon.-Fri., 9-5.

Stores in: Atlanta/Boston/Chicago/Cincinnati/Cleveland/Columbus/Costa Mesa CA/ Dallas/Denver/Detroit/Garden City NY/Houston/Los Angeles/Manchester NH/ Minneapolis/New York/Philadelphia/Phoenix/Pittsburgh/St. Louis/San Diego/ San Francisco/Schaumburg IL/Seattle/Sherman Oaks CA/Washington DC

economies, there must also be a concomitant reduction in the level of services provided to consumers. For example,

> . . . standardization implies a decline in the product variety offered as retailers reduce breadth of their product line. Similarly, automation and the introduction of self-service reduces personal selling service; while the quest for economies of scale implies that retail outlets have to be larger, and have to draw their buyers from larger trade areas reducing the location convenience of the consumers.[82]

Although corporate integration has, on paper at least, many advantages, a number of reasons can be advanced that specify why a firm might want to avoid taking such a significant step. First and foremost, vertical integration can be exceedingly expensive. From a manufacturer's perspective, distribution is a relatively low-profit activity; if the manufacturer can obtain the desired degree of control without assuming full investment responsibility, he may be able to employ his capital more profitably elsewhere.[83] In this respect, retailers and wholesalers have more incentive to integrate backward in the channel than manufacturers have to integrate forward. However, if a channel member finds that he must make the required investment in order to secure the control, then, as Sturdivant points out,

> . . . the hoped-for advantages . . . (may) prove illusory. The product mix and the marketing style of firms on different levels of the channel are, of necessity, quite different. To alter strategy in one level to meet the needs of another level may result in disaster simply because survival on the annexed level cannot be maintained in this manner.[84]

Indeed, distribution is typically a multiproduct activity, with the product mix of distributors substantially different from that of any one manufacturer and, for that matter, often from other channel members engaged primarily in distribution activities. Vertical integration under these circumstances involves a substantial broadening of the corporation's product responsibility as well as its functional role. Picture, if you will, the changes in orientation that would have to ensue if, in order to secure greater control over the marketing of its products at point of sale, General Foods were to purchase Safeway Corporation. Or if Marshall Field & Company were to purchase Brown Shoe Corporation to ensure adequate supplies. In addition, the local managerial problems and personal service content of wholesaling and retailing often discourage manufacturers from integrating forward, just as mechanical production problems discourage distribution firms from acquiring manufacturing concerns.

Finally, there is a host of organizational behavior problems which are encountered when corporate systems are formed. As Ouchi has observed, organiza-

---

[82] *Ibid.*

[83] Lee E. Preston, "Restrictive Distribution Arrangements: Economic Analysis and Public Policy Standards," *Law and Contemporary Problems,* Vol. 30 (1968), p. 512.

[84] Sturdivant, et. al., *op. cit.,* p. 653.

tions must permit subunits to adapt to local ecological demands in order to cope with environmental uncetainty.[85] However, as they do, the subunits (i.e., the vertically integrated channel members, such as distribution centers, sales branches, retail outlets, and the like) develop differentiated objectives, standards of performance, and underlying values. According to Ouchi,

> This leads to heterogeneity of interests, which undermines trust and thus gives rise to opportunistic behavior. In extreme circumstances, the option of close performance auditing is also lost because the parties cannot agree even on what constitutes acceptable performance. Under this condition, organizations fail. . . .[86]

Furthermore, humanistic social psychologists have long argued that formal organizations, such as corporate systems, will "fail" when (1) workers are placed in a dependent state which denies them the possibility of psychological success, (2) when lack of trust between employees distorts cooperation and communication, (3) when jobs are specialized to the point of dehumanization, and (4) when control is based exclusively on following a set of rules.[87]

Some of these reasons explain why automobile and tire manufacturers, for example, have not integrated more extensively down to the retail level. Marx points out that forward integration in these industries was limited by "the superior market incentives for entrepreneurial performance and the mechanisms for decentralized decision making at the retail level."[88] The large firm has developed refined incentive instruments of a long-run employment nature, but, as Williamson notes, "such incentives are poorly suited to satisfy the entrepreneurial appetites of individuals who are prepared to risk their personal savings and careers in pursuit of big stakes."[89] Also, a large number of complex on-the-spot decisions must be made at the retail level in these industries. Again, as Marx observes:

> The information and communications systems necessary to coordinate the millions of complex transactions, evaluate the multitude of possibilities, and provide the pricing flexibility needed to meet each transaction would have placed a heavy burden on an integrated firm.[90]

Dealings with customers may require a flexibility or discretion in negotiating individual transactions that is relatively high to entrust to a salaried employee—as in bargaining on the price of an automobile or a set of steel-belted radial tires.[91]

[85] William G. Ouchi, "An Organizational Failures Framework," Graduate School of Business, Stanford University, May 26, 1978, p. 16. This paper, in significantly different form and content, was published in the *Administrative Science Quarterly*, Vol. 25 (1980), pp. 129 ff.

[86] *Ibid.*, pp. 16–17.

[87] *Ibid.*, p. 8.

[88] Thomas G. Marx, "Distribution Efficiency in Franchising," *MSU Business Topics,* Vol. 28 (Winter 1980), p. 10.

[89] Williamson, *Markets and Hierarchies, op. cit.,* p. 201.

[90] Marx, *op. cit.,* p. 12.

[91] Richard E. Caves and William F. Murphy II, "Franchising: Firms, Markets, and Intangible Assets," *Southern Economic Journal,* Vol. 42 (April 1976), p. 575.

Other managerial problems that may attend the formation of corporate vertical marketing systems include the likelihood that more employees may be needed to serve the various levels of distribution, and this can mean higher payroll, more insurance, and perhaps involvement with different unions. The firm must also consider the possible diseconomies of inventory control and, in the case of manufacturers, whether the product is marketed more efficiently by more diversified wholesale and retail outlets. Integration may also require increased warehousing and storage capacities and showrooms with adequate floor and shelf space to achieve reasonable product exposure. Furthermore, as corporate systems grow in size, diseconomies set in, especially with regard to the ability of management to absorb and process information. This problem is particularly acute in industries that depend heavily on advanced technology and rapid product improvement. The risks of integrating backward into the manufacturing of integrated circuits, for example, are extremely high for firms making calculators and computers.[92] Finally, as is pointed out in the chapter on legal limitations, there are certain restrictions on corporate integration, particularly when such integration is accomplished via merger or acquisition.

SOURCES OF DIFFERENTIAL ADVANTAGES TO VERTICAL MARKETING SYSTEMS	As contrasted with conventional channels, vertical marketing systems are networks comprised of interconnected units, each of which, in theory, participates in an optimum combination of the marketing flows. Coordination is achieved through the use of detailed plans and comprehensive programs;

channel members are, in fact, programmed to achieve systemwide economies. Entry is rigorously controlled by the system's requirements and by market conditions. In the case of contractual and corporate systems, membership loyalty is assured through the use of specific agreements or ownership. As a result, the network tends to be relatively stable. The limited number of strategists in such systems are preoccupied with cost, volume, and investment relationships at *all stages* of the marketing process. There is likely to be a heavy reliance on relatively "scientific" decisions, and the decision makers are generally committed, in a philosophical and analytical sense, to sophisticated marketing concepts and the formation of viable systems rather than emotionally committed to established business methods and traditional approaches.[93]

Unlike many conventional channels, the tasks of vertical marketing systems are routinized. As Bucklin has observed:

> Of the many dimensions that form the relationship between agencies on different levels of a distribution channel, perhaps the most important is the extent of the role of day-to-day market pressure. Day-to-day market forces comprise the panoply of shifting

[92] See "Varadyne Switches to a Single Product," *Business Week* (March 25, 1972), p. 52; and "Why They're Integrating into Integrated Circuits," *Business Week* (September 28, 1974), pp. 55–58.

[93] This paragraph is based on McCammon, "Perspectives for Distribution Programming," *op. cit.,* p. 44.

prices, deals, allowances, promotions, and minor competitive crises that constitute the most visible strains of a market agency's work. Their presence in the interfirm relationship is manifested by detailed negotiations for each contract for the sale of goods to provide continuous adjustment to these prices. They disappear when goods are transferred as part of long-range plans where the issue is not optimal profit on each sale, but the means of better exploiting the market for mutual advantage of both parties.

If the importance of day-to-day forces is defined as a continuum ranging from one pole, where each transaction is negotiated separately in the light of market conditions, to the other, where the movement of goods is an automatic element part of a long-range marketing plan, then franchising as a mode of distribution may be said to occupy the middle ground. At the planned end of the continuum is to be found the integrated system (corporate vertical system); at the day-to-day pole is the independent (conventional) system.[94]

Vertical marketing systems seem to capitalize on programmed organization, economies of scale, and economies of standardization that exist within activities at the various levels of distribution. On the other hand, although the absence of long-term planning in independent channels results in higher distribution cost, it must be recognized that the independent retailer is free to tap supplies from a number of manufacturers and wholesalers in order to better adapt to his market. Thus, as pointed out above, although distribution cost is lower for corporate chains, for example, chain store managers are heavily circumscribed when it comes to adaptation to their markets. The franchise operator seems to occupy the middle ground on both the cost and adaptation fronts. While cost advantages work in the favor of vertical marketing systems, independent operators seem to have a differential advantage when it comes to ability to adapt to heterogeneous market opportunity.[95] The standardized level of performance achieved within vertical marketing systems is, though, rarely attained in conventional channels. Both industrial and household consumers prefer uniformity in the quality of goods and services they purchase, which gives systems capable of delivering such uniformity a strong differential advantage.

From a managerial perspective, vertical marketing systems are developed in order to achieve a degree of control over the cost and quality of the functions performed by various channel members. The strength of such systems lies in their capitalization on role specification through shifting and allocating the marketing flows. In theory, the performance of a vertical marketing system can approximate the performance of Bucklin's "normative channel"[96] in that institutions can be grouped and organized in such a way so that no other type of grouping could create greater profits or more consumer satisfaction per dollar of product cost.

[94] Louis P. Bucklin, "The Economic Base of Franchising," in Donald N. Thompson (ed.), *Contractual Marketing Systems* (Lexington, Mass.: Heath Lexington Books, 1971), p. 33. (Parentheses supplied.)

[95] *Ibid.*, pp. 33–62.

[96] Louis P. Bucklin, *A Theory of Distribution Channel Structure* (Berkeley, Calif.: Institute of Business and Economic Research, University of California, 1966), p. 5; Louis P. Bucklin, "A Normative Approach to the Economics of Channel Structure," in Louis P. Bucklin (ed.), *Vertical Marketing Systems, op. cit.*, pp. 164–173; and discussions of Bucklin's theory earlier in this book.

In conventional channels, power is often diffused among channel members.[97] In corporate systems, power is concentrated at one channel level through ownership. At least a moderate degree of expert and reward power must exist at the administrator's level in administered systems, whereas legitimate power obviously resides with the initiator of the legal agreements in contractual systems.[98] All in all, unlike conventional marketing channels, vertical marketing systems contain a locus of power, and as was pointed out in earlier chapters, such a locus is a prerequisite for channel leadership.[99] Because power is centralized, role specification and conflict management are more likely to accomplished, and thus greater channel performance can be expected.

Implicit within the concept of a vertical marketing system is the fact that management recognizes the entire channel to be the relevant unit of competition. In conventional channels, independent members tend to believe that competitive viability is the result solely of actions taken on their specific levels of distribution.

THE MARKET IMPACT OF VERTICAL MARKETING SYSTEMS

As McCammon observes:

> The autonomy of operating units in conventional marketing channels frequently results in duplicative programming, scheduling inefficiencies, and high selling costs. Similarly, the persistence of small units results in the sacrifice of scale economies . . . And, perhaps most importantly, the functional rigidity characteristic of most conventional marketing channels ignores the economies that can be achieved by realigning activities within the network . . . Consequently, it is not surprising to observe that planned vertical marketing systems are rapidly displacing conventional marketing channels as the dominant mode of distribution in the American economy.[100]

As evidence of the market impact of vertical marketing systems, it is known that retailers affiliated with contractual systems (wholesaler-sponsored voluntary groups, retailer-sponsored cooperatives, and franchise networks) account for over 40 percent of retail sales and that corporate chains represent another 32 percent of the market.[101] Although no figures are available for administered systems, other forms of corporate systems, or for the industrial market, it is obvious that a large percentage of trade is enjoyed by vertical marketing systems of all types.

Given the competitive advances made by vertical marketing systems, it is blatantly obvious that members of conventional channels will be forced to evoke

---

[97] For an example, see Adel I. El-Ansary and Louis W. Stern, "Power Measurement in the Distribution Channel," *Journal of Marketing Research,* Vol. 9 (February 1972), pp. 47–52.

[98] Other bases of power are also in evidence in contractual systems as shown in Hunt and Nevin, *op. cit.*

[99] See also Louis W. Stern, "The Interorganizational Management of Distribution Channels: Prerequisites and Prescriptions," in George Fisk (ed.), *New Essays in Marketing Theory* (Boston, Mass.: Allyn and Bacon, Inc., 1971), pp. 301–314.

[100] McCammon, "Perspectives for Distribution Programming," *op. cit.,* p. 43.

[101] McCammon and Hammer, *op. cit.,* p. 13.

fresh strategies if they are going to survive. A few suggested strategies are advanced below. The first three can be implemented in the short term, but the fourth requires long-run adjustments.[102] In fact, an implementation of the latter would begin to position the channel within the set of vertical marketing systems.

> **1. Develop programs to strengthen** customers' competitive capabilities. This alternative would involve manufacturers and wholesalers in such activities as sponsoring centralized accounting and management reporting services, formulating cooperative promotional programs, and co-signing shopping center leases.
>
> **2. Enter new markets.** For example, building supply distributors have initiated cash-and-carry outlets. Steel warehouses have added glass and plastic product lines to their traditional product lines. Industrial distributors have initiated stockless buying plans and blanket order contracts so that they may compete effectively for customers who buy on a direct basis.
>
> **3. Effect economies of operation by developing management information systems.** For example, some middlemen in conventional channels have installed the IBM IMPACT program to improve their control over inventory.
>
> **4. Determine, through research, the locus of power in the channel and urge the channel member** designated to undertake a reorganization of the marketing flows. The potential channel leader may be located on any level of the channel, as is discussed in Chapter 9.

SUMMARY AND CONCLUSIONS

Conventional marketing channels comprised of independently owned institutions and agencies frequently suffer from several weaknesses, the foremost among them being the absence of a systemwide orientation and inclusive goals. If a locus of power is also absent, the specification of roles and the management of conflict in conventional channels are likely to be difficult, at best. Even when a locus of power is present (as in the marketing channel for motion pictures), there is no guarantee that the performance of the channel will be any better than when power is diffused.

Vertical marketing systems have emerged as significant forms of channel organization and represent, for the most part, sophisticated attempts on the part of management to overcome the inherent weaknesses of conventional channels. Administered vertical marketing systems are those in which coordination of marketing activities is achieved through the use of programs developed by one or a limited number of firms. Administrative strategies combined with the exercise of power are relied on to obtain systemic economies. Such strategies have been most frequently adopted by suppliers and by carriers. They have involved the use of facilities management, modular merchandising, coordinated display, and automatic replenishment programs as well as programmed merchandising agreements.

Contractual vertical marketing systems are those in which independent firms

---

[102] The first three suggestions were adapted from McCammon, Doody, and Davidson, *op. cit.*, pp. 9–10.

EXHIBIT 7-10

Organizational Dimension of Conventional and Vertical Marketing Systems

Dimension	Conventional	Administered	Contractual	Corporate
Relation of units to an inclusive goal	No inclusive goals	Units with disparate goals, but informal collaboration for inclusive goals	Units with disparate goals but some organization for inclusive goals	Units organized for achievement of inclusive goals
Locus of inclusive decision making	Within units	In interaction of units without a formal inclusive structure	At top of inclusive structure, subject to unit ratification	At top of inclusive structure
Locus of authority	Exclusively at unit level	Exclusively at unit level	Primarily at unit level	At top of hierarchy of inclusive structure
Structural provision for division of labor	No formally structured division of labor within an inclusive context	Units structured autonomously, may agree to *ad hoc* division of labor, without restructuring	Units structured autonomously, may agree to a division of labor, which may affect their structure	Units structured for division of labor within inclusive organization
Commitment to a leadership subsystem	Commitment only to unit leaders	Commitment only to unit leaders	Norms of moderate commitment	Norms of high commitment
Prescribed collectivity-orientation of units	Little or none	Low to moderate	Moderate to high	High

Source: Adapted from Roland L. Warren, "The Interorganizational Field as a Focus for Investigation," *Administrative Science Quarterly,* Vol. 12 (1967), pp. 396–419.

at different channel levels integrate their programs on a contractual basis to achieve systemic economies and increased market impact. They include, among other forms of organization, wholesaler-sponsored voluntary groups, retailer-sponsored cooperative groups, and franchise systems. By virtue of the use of legitimate power in their formulation, contractual systems tend to be more tightly knit than administered systems.

Corporate vertical marketing systems are those in which channel members on different levels of distribution are owned and operated by one organization. In fact, such systems are synonymous with both forward and backward vertical integration. Forward integration is on the increase, even within franchise systems. Backward integration has long been typified by corporate chain store systems. The key tradeoffs in instituting any corporate vertical marketing system are the investment required plus the flexibility lost, on the one hand, versus the control secured over marketing activities of channel members plus the operating economies gained, on the other.

The organizational dimensions of conventional and vertical marketing systems are summarized in Exhibit 7-10. From a managerial perspective, vertical marketing systems appear to offer a series of differential advantages over conventional channels. The former employ a systemic approach and are committed to scientific decision-making while engendering channel member loyalty and network stability. Tasks are routinized, and economies of standardization are likely within them. Because a locus of power is available and utilized in a positive manner, it is possible to gain at least some control over the cost and quality of the functions performed by various channel members. Furthermore, inherent within systems management is the notion that the channel itself is the relevant unit of competition.

DISCUSSION QUESTIONS

1. According to Bucklin, the issue of channel performance focuses on the major conflict that exists between two major dimensions of channel performance. On the one hand, consumers and users are primarily concerned with lowering costs of the goods and services sold and therefore on reducing the costs of distribution. On the other hand, consumers want to benefit from and receive some marketing services in conjunction with the good or service they purchase. However, provision of these services increases the cost of distribution.

Evaluate conventional, administered, contractual, and corporate systems relative to the performance dimensions mentioned by Bucklin. Which, if any, would tend to be superior on an overall basis?

2. It has been argued that the price mechanism is the formal means through which vertical coordination is achieved in conventional or fragmented channels. What does this mean and what are its consequences for channel performance, both from a macro- and micro-perspective?

3. Suggest three ways in which the marketing channel for motion pictures might be improved.

4. What are the advantages of administered systems versus contractual systems? What are the disadvantages of administered systems that might be overcome by forming contractual systems?

5. Classify the selected concessions available to suppliers when seeking to gain reseller support of their marketing programs (Exhibit 7-1) by the various bases of power (coercive, reward, expert, referent, and legitimate).

6. Which of the various concessions listed in Exhibit 7-1 are likely to be useful in marketing through supermarkets? Through department stores? Through catalog showrooms? Through warehouse showrooms? Through industrial (full-function) distributors?

7. Which type of cooperative—wholesaler-sponsored, retailer-sponsored, or consumer-sponsored—would you expect to be most successful? Why have consumer cooperatives never enjoyed widespread popularity in the United States?

8. After studying Table 7-4, can you pinpoint any factors which seem to differentiate the operating styles of the five leading wholesalers, simply on the basis of the financial data presented in the table?

9. Write a plan for starting your own franchising operation. What would be the essential ingredients of the plan? What specific points would you include in the contractual arrangement you establish with your franchisees?

10. From 1973 to 1975, Sears experienced lower-than-normal returns. What factors accounted for these low returns? What changes would you suggest to Sears to improve its returns from its merchandising operations? (Do you feel, for example, that the company has too many affiliated manufacturing sources?)

11. Assume that you are the manufacturer of a broad line of moderately priced furniture. When would you seriously consider forming a corporate vertical marketing system for your line? What factors would you take into account in making your decision?

12. Montgomery Ward describes its supplier investments as "very minimal" and says it will consider such relationships "only as a last resort in order to meet the company's requirements for satisfying its customer needs." According to a Ward's executive, the firm's only major supplier investment is in the Standard T Chemical Co., which manufactures paint. (William Grauber, "Sears' Success Affects Many," *Chicago Tribune,* Section 2, September 7, 1975, p. 7)

Compare and contrast Ward's philosophy with that of Sears. Which would you endorse as an overall corporate policy, if you were running a comparable retailing organization (e.g., Penney's)?

13. Name two additional survival (or growth) strategies that you might suggest to members of conventional channels, beyond those mentioned at the end of Chapter 7.

Appendix 7A

Initial information to inquiries for a 7-Eleven Store franchise

7-Eleven . . . A Way of Life

7-Eleven is, to busy people of all ages, the friendly little store that's "just around the corner." It's the convenient place to stop for a loaf of bread, quart of milk, package of cigarettes, groceries, beverages, picnic supplies, candy, "hot to go" foods, or everyone's favorite ice drink . . . Slurpee. 7-Eleven Stores are small, compact, easily accessible, and usually open for business 24 hours a day, 7 days a week. Their convenient locations, fast service, and friendly image have combined to make 7-Eleven shopping a familiar part of the American lifestyle.

7-Eleven is a division of The Southland Corporation, pioneer of the convenience store and a recognized leader in the food and dairy industries. More than 5,000 7-Eleven Stores are located virtually throughout the nation and, in some areas, stores are available for franchise to qualified applicants.

7-Eleven offers a business system in a ready-to-operate store on a carefully selected site. It includes training, counseling, bookkeeping, financing, and merchandising assistance. This brochure, which briefly introduces the 7-Eleven System, is your invitation to meet with a company representative to discuss in detail how you and your family can become a part of 7-Eleven.

Real Estate

7-Eleven's real estate representatives research an area and select the sites which, based upon population, traffic flow, convenience to homes, and competition, are most likely to produce sales. 7-Eleven buys or leases these sites, and leases the completed 7-Eleven Stores to franchisees.

Equipment

All equipment in the stores, including heating and air conditioning, vaults, shelving, cash registers, and refrigerated cases, are included in the lease to the franchisee, who is responsible for maintenance of the equipment.

Merchandise

7-Eleven arranges for the initial inventory of merchandise in the store. Thereafter, the franchisee orders and stocks his own merchandise. 7-Eleven recommends vendors who, we believe, offer the best service and the highest quality merchandise at the lowest costs. Franchisees are, however, free to purchase from any vendors they choose. The franchisee receives credit for all discounts on merchandise purchased.

In addition, 7-Eleven prepares for the franchisee lists of recommended merchandise and suggested retail selling prices. These lists are based upon the company's many years of experience in convenience store merchandising and appear to afford the greatest potential for profit. Some recommended vendors may be affiliated with 7-Eleven, and some suggested merchandise may be produced by divisions of The Southland Corporation. However, franchisees are free to purchase the merchandise they choose and establish the retail prices they prefer.

Advertising

Advertising plays a significant role in assisting franchisees in building the sales and profits of their 7-Eleven Stores. For many years, 7-Eleven advertising has received widespread recognition.

"OH, THANK HEAVEN FOR 7-ELEVEN"
"IT'S ABOUT TIME"
"IF IT'S NOT AROUND THE HOUSE,
IT'S JUST AROUND THE CORNER"

Franchisees are, of course, free to further advertise at their own expense.

Training

Prior to opening the stores, applicants for 7-Eleven Franchise are required to attend a 7-Eleven training school to learn the mechanics of the day-to-day 7-Eleven Store operations. Following the one-week classroom training program, the franchisee is trained on-the-job for one week in a training store under 7-Eleven's supervision. Successful completion of the training programs is a prerequisite for final acceptance by 7-Eleven of an applicant. Additional in-store training is also provided the franchisee from time to time as deemed necessary by local management. An initial training fee and (in addition) a store set-up fee are required.

Employees

Although most franchised 7-Eleven Stores are family operated, it is usually necessary for the franchisee to employ additional part-time and full-time help.

It is the franchisee's responsibility to hire and train his employees. The franchisee is responsible for all payroll expenses, including employee taxes. Based on the franchisee's authorization and his employees' time cards, 7-Eleven prepares his payroll checks.

Personal Insurance

7-Eleven franchisees, their families and employees are eligible to participate in the 7-Eleven Franchise Trust which provides financial relief in the event of sickness, disability, or death. An H. R. 10 Retirement Plan is also available in most areas at the option of the franchisee.

Bookkeeping

7-Eleven keeps bookkeeping records on the franchisee's operation of the 7-Eleven Store. Franchisees make their own daily cash deposits of sales receipts. From these, 7-Eleven pays all expenses appoved by the franchisee in connection with operations of the stores. The franchisee purchases his merchandise and, upon his approval of the invoices, 7-Eleven will make payment on their behalf.

Investment

The investment requirements for a 7-Eleven Store Franchise include the cost of the inventory and the cash register fund. The exact amounts vary depending upon the location of the store and the inventory requirements. Average investments range from $17,000 to $25,000, a portion of which 7-Eleven wil! finance for qualified applicants.

Franchisees Can Most Affect Profits By:

- General management aptitude
- Ability to hire and train competent employees
- Control of employee and customer pilferage
- Creative salesmanship

- Sincere customer relations
- Ability to create a friendly store atmosphere
- Keep a clean and orderly store profile

Profits

A local 7-Eleven representative will discuss the financial history of the store being considered and other stores in the nearby area.

The GROSS PROFIT of the store is shared by the franchisee and 7-Eleven.

The percentage of GROSS PROFIT paid by the franchisee to 7-Eleven is a continuing charge for the rental of the store building and equipment, utilities, advertising, bookkeeping and merchandising and general management assistance.

From the remainder of the GROSS PROFIT split the franchisee pays all other operating expenses such as:

- Payroll
- Payroll taxes
- Supplies
- Laundry
- Telephone
- Interest
- Business taxes and licenses
- In-store maintenance
- Landscaping maintenance
- Bad checks
- Cash variation
- Inventory variation

The NET PROFIT after payment of the operating expenses is the franchisee's net income.

Source: The Southland Corporation, *The 7-Eleven Franchise*, promotional brochure. (Reprinted with the permission of the Southland Corporation.)

EIGHT

Legal Constraints on the Interorganization Management of Marketing Channels

In order to institute effective interorganization management, the use of power is, as pointed out in the preceding chapters, a necessary predicate. There are, however, significant legal constraints on the manner in which power may be employed in the marketing channel. Prior to developing and implementing interorganizational strategies and programs, it is imperative that marketing managers at all levels of distribution comprehend the intention and the scope of these constraints so that any strategy or program that is promulgated will not meet with a negative reaction from the various antitrust enforcement agencies.

The focus in this chapter is on federal legislation, even though it is recognized that there are a myriad of international, state, and local laws that directly affect distribution practices. In addition, attention is given here only to legislation directly affecting relations among commercial channel members. Excluded from the discussion is mention of consumer-oriented legislation, even though such legislation obviously tempers certain kinds of activities among and between commercial channel members.[1]

---

[1] The Federal Trade Commission has attacked thousands of devious schemes in distribution that directly affect the consumer. The largest categories have been fictitious pricing, wherein goods are falsely advertised as bargains; "bait and switch" advertising, by which customers, lured into a store by a spectacular bargain not intended to be sold, are "switched" to other more expensive purchases; exaggerated claims for the efficacy of drugs and cosmetics; the selling of used products as new; failure to disclose the limitations of guarantees; and misrepresentations of the quality of products. In addition, the FTC polices the labeling of furs and textiles so that a buyer can be sure the product is made of the material claimed on the label, the Flammable Fabrics Act to protect consumers from dangerously flammable clothing, the Fair Packaging and Labeling Act to inform the consumer as to the net contents of a package, the Truth in Lending Act, which enables consumers to shop for credit by comparing the finance charges and the annual percentage rates of creditors, the Fair Credit Reporting Act, which seeks to protect consumers from

TABLE 8–1   Principal laws affecting the interorganization management of marketing channels

Act	Key Provisions
Sherman Antitrust Act, 1890	1. Prohibits contracts or combinations in restraint of interstate and foreign commerce. 2. Makes monopoly or attempt at monopoly a crime in interstate or foreign commerce.
Clayton Antitrust Act, 1914	Where competition is substantially lessened it prohibits: 1. Price discrimination in sales or leasing 2. Exclusive dealing 3. Tying contracts 4. Interlocking directorates among competitors 5. Intercorporate stockholding
Celler-Kefauver Act, 1950	Prohibits purchase of assets of another firm if competition is lessened.
FTC Act, 1914	1. Prohibits unfair trade practices injurious to competition or a competitor. 2. Sets up FTC to determine unfairness.
Robinson-Patman Act, 1936	1. Discriminatory prices are prohibited if they reduce competition at any point in the channel. 2. Discriminatory prices can be given in good faith to meet competition. 3. Brokerage allowances are allowed only if earned by an independent broker. 4. Sellers must give all services and promotional allowances to all buyers equally if the buyers are in competition. Alternatives must be offered. 5. Buyers are prohibited from knowingly inducing price discrimination. 6. Price discrimination can be legal if it results from real cost differences in serving different customers. 7. Prohibits agreement with competitors to charge unreasonably low prices to destroy competition.
State Sales Below Cost	Prohibits selling below cost or without minimum markup.
FTC Trade Practice Rules	1. Enforced by FTC. Define unfair competition for individual industries. These practices are prohibited by FTC. 2. Define rules of sound practice. These rules are not enforced by the FTC, but are recommended.

the reporting of erroneous personal information by credit bureaus, and the Consumer Product Safety Act, which attempts to minimize the number of physical injuries to consumers caused by dangerous or defective products. Major federal consumer legislation is reviewed in Burton Marcus, et al., *Modern Marketing* (New York: Random House, 1975), pp. 680–683. Also see Laurence P. Feldman, *Consumer Protection: Problems and Prospects* (St. Paul, Minn.: West Publishing Co., 1976); and Joe L. Welch, *Marketing Law* (Tulsa, Ok.: PPC Books, 1980).

Although all legislation may be said to affect the legitimate power of channel members, the legal constraints examined below basically confine the use of coercive and reward power in channel management. In situations where vertical integration is employed to achieve the goals of a given distribution system, there are additional laws that inhibit the means by which such integration is accomplished and practiced. Therefore, the following discussion centers on legal limitations to the use of coercive and reward power *and* to vertical integration. The principal laws constraining interorganization management in marketing are listed in Table 8–1.

LEGAL LIMITATIONS ON THE USE OF COERCIVE POWER

If a firm desires intensive distribution for its product, it will try to put it into as many channels as possible. This leads to relatively few legal problems in the area of customer selection, since *intrabrand* competition, or competition among resellers of the same brand, is usually unrestricted under these conditions. If, however, a firm wishes to limit the distribution of its product to certain outlets or to limit the freedom of its outlets in their methods of doing business, legal problems are more likely to arise. In such situations, a firm's refusal to sell or its adherence to distribution control policies may ultimately restrict intrabrand competition and lead to conflict with the antitrust laws. Each of the distribution policies and practices discussed below involves the use of coercive power in its implementation and enforcement, and each is circumscribed by law.

Exclusive Dealing

Exclusive dealing is the requirement by a seller or lessor that its customers sell or lease only its products, or at least no products in direct competition with the seller's products. If the buyer does not comply, the seller may invoke negative sanctions by refusing to deal with the buyer. Thus, such arrangements clearly reduce the freedom of choice of the buyer. In establishing exclusive dealing provisions, suppliers ensure that their products will be merchandised with maximum energy and enthusiasm. As Scherer points out: "The dealer confined to a single manufacturer's line can scarcely be indifferent as to whose brand consumers purchase."[2] The buyer, however, will generally receive some benefits from the arrangements, such as promotional support. He also avoids the added inventory costs that go with carrying multiple brands.[3]

Exclusive dealing contracts are legal under some circumstances and illegal in others. Section 3 of the Clayton Antitrust Act provides that this kind of restriction

---

[2] F. M. Scherer, *Industrial Market Structure and Economic Performance,* 2nd ed. (Chicago: Rand McNally College Publishing Co., 1980), p. 586.

[3] W. F. Brown, "The Effect of Federal Legislation upon Marketing Channels," in R. M. Clewett (ed.), *Marketing Channels for Manufactured Products* (Homewood, Ill.: Richard D. Irwin, 1954), pp. 485–486.

on wholesalers or retailers is unlawful if the effect of the contract may be substantially to lessen competition or to tend to create a monopoly in any line of commerce. These contracts have also been attacked under Section 5 of the Federal Trade Commission Act.

Exclusive dealerships do tend to lessen competition and create monopoly, since other sellers are excluded from the particular outlet. Whether this is considered substantial by the courts depends on two major factors:

1. Whether the volume of the product in question is a substantial part of the total volume for the product type.

2. Whether the exclusive dealership excludes competitive products from a substantial share of the market.

When either of these conditions obtains, the agreement is subject to attack as a restraint of competition. Both of these conditions depend on the relative size of the firms in their respective markets.

In the Brown Shoe case,[4] the Supreme Court decided that Brown Shoe Company, one of the world's largest shoe manufacturers, could be prohibited by the FTC from using exclusive dealerships as an unfair trade practice under the FTC Act. According to the Court, the contracts were in conflict with the spirit of the Sherman and Clayton Acts; therefore, the FTC was not required to prove actual or potential injury to competition as required by either of these acts. This finding means that exclusive dealerships or franchises will be more vulnerable in the future to prosecution under Section 5 of the FTC Act than under provisions of the other antitrust laws.[5]

In the Standard Oil of California case, exclusive dealership arrangements between the company and its independent stations were declared illegal by the Supreme Court under Section 3 of the Clayton Act on grounds that competitors had been foreclosed from a substantial share of the line of commerce affected.[6] At the time, these exclusive dealerships accounted for only 7 percent of the total sales of petroleum products in the area.[7] The use of exclusive dealing contracts by Standard and other companies had, however, foreclosed over 50 percent of the market to independent oil refiners and wholesalers. The court declared "that exclusive dealing contracts as such are not illegal and that they might be a useful competitive device when employed by smaller firms, particularly when entering the market, but that their use by large, established firms might constitute an unwarranted restriction with consequent 'substantial lessening of competition.' "[8] Therefore, it becomes

---

[4] *Brown Shoe Co., Inc. v. Federal Trade Commission,* 384 U.S. 316 (1966).

[5] R. O. Werner, "Marketing and the United States Supreme Court, 1965–1968," *Journal of Marketing,* Vol. 33 (January 1969), pp. 18–19.

[6] *Standard Oil Company of California and Standard Stations Inc. v. U.S.,* 337 U.S. 293 (1949).

[7] Ernest Gellhorn, *Antitrust Law and Economics in a Nutshell* (St. Paul, Minn.: West Publishing Co., 1976), p. 292. See also T. N. Beckman, W. R. Davidson, and J. F. Engel, *Marketing,* 8th ed. (New York: The Ronald Press Co., 1967), p. 406.

[8] *Standard Oil Company of California, loc. cit.*

apparent that the use of exclusive dealerships by several firms in a market may be relevant to the legality of their use by one firm.[9]

Exclusive dealing can be imposed by the use of coercive power even in the absence of an explicit agreement. For example, tires, batteries, and accessories have been sold in gasoline stations of major oil companies in two different ways:

1. *Purchase-Resale Agreements.* Under this plan, the products are purchased from the manufacturer by the oil company and resold to the gasoline wholesalers and retailers.
2. *Sales Commission Plans.* Under these plans, the products are sold directly to the gasoline wholesalers and retailers by the manufacturer. The oil company receives a commission on all sales, and in return it assists with promotion.

In three cases ending in 1968, the courts held that the sales commission plan is inherently coercive because of the control that the oil company has over its dealers.[10] Market exclusion of other brands will result, and thus the plans are an unfair practice whether illegal intent is shown or not. In the Atlantic Refining case the Supreme Court confirmed this view.[11] The merits of purchase-resale agreements were not ruled upon by the courts.

A seller has the right to choose his own customers, but no coercion or intimidation can be used against the dealer to insure exclusive dealing.[12] Exclusive dealing arrangements are legal when they are entered into for reasons not connected directly with lessening competition. In the Sinclair case, the Supreme Court held that oil companies could forbid the sale of competing brands of gasoline from equipment supplied to the dealers by the companies.[13] The purpose of the plan was to prevent the dealers from switching brands without the knowledge of the consumers.[14] In addition, the dealers were not prohibited by the agreement from having other pumps devoted to competing brands, so competition was not foreclosed.[15]

The Federal Trade Commission is also using Section 5 of the FTC Act to challenge retailers to stop making, carrying out, or enforcing anti-competitive leasing agreements. Similar to exclusive dealing arrangements, such agreements have given a retailer the right to be the only retailer of its kind (e.g., drugstore) in a shopping center, the right to reject or accept the opportunity to operate an additional outlet in a shopping center where it already has one ("rights of first refusal"), the right to prohibit or control the entrance of tenants into shopping centers, and the

---

[9] Brown in Clewett, *op. cit.,* p. 489.

[10] D. F. Dixon, "Market Exclusion and Dealer Coercion in Sponsored TBA Sales," *Journal of Marketing,* Vol. 35 (January 1971), pp. 62–63.

[11] *Atlantic Refining Co. v. Federal Trade Commission,* 381 U.S. 357.

[12] M. C. Howard, *Legal Aspects of Marketing* (New York: McGraw-Hill Book Company, 1964), p. 98.

[13] *Federal Trade Commission v. Sinclair Refining Co., et al.,* 261 U.S. 463 (1923).

[14] Beckman, et al., *op. cit.,* pp. 406–407.

[15] Brown in Clewett, *op. cit.,* p. 476.

right to restrict the business operations of other tenants in shopping centers.[16] For example, FTC consent orders in 1976 and 1979 prohibited Sears Roebuck[17] and Federated Department Stores,[18] respectively, from making or enforcing any agreement with shopping center developers that:

- prohibits entry into centers of particular tenants or classes of tenants (e.g., discount stores) or allows Sears or Federated to approve tenant entry;
- grants Sears or Federated the right to approve floor space of others or their use of it;
- specifies that tenants shall sell their merchandise at any particular price, or within any range of prices, fashions, or quality (when the latter terms connote price);
- limits discount advertising, pricing, or selling;
- limits the types of merchandise or services which tenants may sell;
- prescribes minimum hours of operation;
- grants Sears or Federated the right to approve tenant location; or
- provides for radius restrictions upon tenants.

These prohibitions apply to all shopping centers, including those developed and built by Sears' wholly owned subsidiary, Homart Development Company.

In addition, requirements contracts are a variant of exclusive dealing contracts. They are agreements that a purchaser will buy all or a specified portion of his requirements for a good from a specified seller for a stipulated time period.[19] They may violate either the Sherman Act or Section 3 of the Clayton Act if it can be shown that the seller has some kind of coercive power over the buyer.[20]

Tying Contracts

Tying contracts are often found in exclusive dealing and franchising arrangements. These contracts require a buyer to take other products in order to obtain a product which he desires. These contracts can be held to be illegal under Section 3 of the Clayton Act when it can be shown that the seller has so much coercive

---

[16] "Order Against Drug Chain Bans Shopping Center Lease Restrictions," *FTC News Summary* (October 10, 1975), p. 1. See also "Antitrust Action in the Shopping Malls," *Business Week* (December 8, 1975), p. 51. In survey results released by the FTC on March 13, 1981, it was pointed out that "larger stores in shopping centers have generally abandoned the practice of exercising excessive power over smaller stores and discounters in lease arrangements." In "Shopping Centers Complying with an FTC Decision on Leasing Practices," *FTC News Summary* (March 20, 1981), p. 2.

[17] "Order Against Sears, Roebuck Bans Anticompetitive Shopping Center Conduct," *FTC News Summary* (October 29, 1976), p. 1.

[18] "FTC Shopping Center Order Would Ban Control by Department Stores," *FTC News Summary* (January 19, 1979), p. 1.

[19] L. W. Stern and J. R. Grabner, Jr., *Competition in the Marketplace* (Glenview, Ill.: Scott, Foresman and Co., 1970), pp. 133–134.

[20] Howard, *op. cit.,* p. 99.

power with respect to the tying product that he can restrain competition relative to the tied product *and* that a substantial portion of interstate commerce is affected.[21] Furthermore, a tying arrangement which is not covered by the Clayton Act (e.g., because it does not involve a tangible "commodity") can be illegal under Section 1 of the Sherman Act if the seller has market power in the tying product and if the arrangement forecloses a substantial volume of the market for the tied product.[22] The classic case in this area was *Thomson Manufacturing Co. v. Federal Trade Commission.* Thomson leased rivet setting machines at a low rental, but required its customers to purchase all rivets from the company at a price higher than that in the open market. Rivet makers who did not provide machines were excluded from the market. The court ruled, ". . . the practical effect is to preclude the use of supplies of a competitor and thus substantially lessen competition."[23]

Certain types of tying contracts are legal. If two products are made to be used jointly and one will not function properly without the other, the courts have ruled that the agreement is within the law.[24] In other cases, if a company's goodwill depends on proper operation of equipment, a service contract may be tied to the sale or lease of the machine. The practicality of alternatives to the tying arrangement appears to be crucial. If a firm will suffer injury unless it can protect its product, and there is no feasible alternative, the courts go along with tying agreements.[25] However, even though these exceptions are recognized, the general rule is that tying agreements are inherently anticompetitive in their impact and, thus, are illegal per se.[26]

Serious legal questions regarding tying agreements have been raised in recent years relative to the franchising of restaurants and other eating places, motels, and movie theatres, among others. Under franchise agreements, an individual or group of individuals (the franchisee) is usually permitted to set up an outlet of a national chain in return for a capital investment and a periodic fee to the parent company (the franchisor).[27] In some cases, the parent company also requires the franchise holders to buy various supplies, such as meat, baked goods, and paper cups in the case of restaurants, either from the corporation or an approved supplier. In franchising, the tying product is the franchise itself and the tied products are the supplies that the franchisee must purchase to operate his business. Companies with such requirements have argued that they are necessary in order to maintain the quality of their services and reputation. However, critics of such agreements assert

---

[21] Stern and Grabner, *op. cit.,* p. 132.

[22] *Times-Picayune v. U.S.,* 345 U.S. 594 (1953).

[23] Beckman, et al., *op. cit.,* p. 406.

[24] Stern and Grabner, *op. cit.,* p. 132. See *ILC Peripherals Leasing Corp. v. International Business Machines Corp.*; *Memorex Corp., MRX Sales and Service Corp. v. International Business Machines Corp.*; CCH #61, 992 (D.C. N. Calif., April 1978).

[25] Stern and Grabner, *op. cit.,* p. 132.

[26] See *Fortner Enterprises, Inc. v. United States Steel Corporation,* 394 U.S. 494 (1969); and *Heatransfer Corp. v. Volkswagen, A. C., et al.,* CCH #61, 473 (CA-5, June 1977): BNA ATRR No. 819 (June 23, 1977), A-10, E-1.

[27] Franchising as a form of channel organization is described in some detail in Chapter 7 of this text.

that franchisors often require franchisees to purchase supplies and raw materials at prices far above those of the competitive market.[28] The potential for a conflict of interest on the part of franchisors is high, especially when the volume of revenue generated by sales of supplies is taken into account, as shown in Table 8–2.

Such tying agreements have been sustained by the courts and the antitrust enforcement agencies only when franchisors have been able to prove that the tied product is, in fact, essential to the maintenance of quality control. For example, in a lawsuit against Carvel (a soft ice cream franchise), the court concluded that Carvel's ingredient-supply restrictions were justified by the need for quality control connected with the problem of ingredient secrecy.[29] In addition, in a lawsuit involving Dunkin' Donuts, the court stated that such tying agreements may be justified not only when the franchisor is attempting to maintain product quality but also when it is attempting to enter a new market or industry *or* to preserve its market identity.[30]

In a decision involving the Chock Full O' Nuts Corporation, it was held that the franchisor "successfully proved its affirmative defense (to tying charges) of

TABLE 8–2   Sales of supplies by franchisors to franchisees, 1974

Franchisees by Industry	Amount Spent with Franchisors (millions of dollars)
Shoe stores, apparel shops, florists, photo stores	$2200
Auto accessory stores, repair services, car washes, tire stores	1500
Convenience stores	330
Fast-food restaurants (hamburgers, chicken, pizza, ice cream, donuts)	325
Includes:	
Food ingredients $206	
Supplies (paper) 81	
Equipment (nonfood) 38	
Do-it-yourself stores, cleaning services, repair shops	109
Travel facilities (hotels, motels, etc.)	50
Copying services, income tax preparation, employment services	33

Source: U.S. Department of Commerce, *Franchising in the Economy, 1972-1974* (Washington, D.C.: U.S. Government Printing Office, 1974).

[28] *The Impact of Franchising on Small Business,* Hearings before the Subcommittee on Urban and Rural Economic Development (Washington, D.C.: U.S. Government Printing Office, 1970), p. 5.

[29] *Susser v. Carvel,* 332 # F. 2d 505 (1964).

[30] *Ungar v. Dunkin' Donuts of America, Inc.,* 68 F. R. D. 65 (1975). See also W. L. Trombetta and A. L. Page, "The Channel Control Issue Under Scrutiny," *Journal of Retailing,* Vol. 54 (Summer 1978), p. 44.

maintaining quality control with regard to its coffee and baked goods.''[31] On the other hand, Chock Full O' Nuts was unsuccessful in defending its tying practices with respect to a number of other products (e.g., french fries, soft drink syrups, napkins, and glasses). The latter adverse finding paralleled that in an antitrust case involving Chicken Delight.[32] The parent company's contract requiring Chicken Delight franchisees to purchase paper items, cookers, fryers, and mix preparations from the franchisor was declared to be a tying contract in violation of Section 1 of the Sherman Act. Chicken Delight failed in its attempt to convince the court that its system should be considered a single product. The paper products were viewed as illegally tied to the franchise because they were easily reproducible. The issue of the cookers, fryers, and spice items was less clearcut, and the court left it to a jury to decide whether they were justifiably tied on the basis of quality control of the finished product. The jury eventually determined that quality control could have been effected by means other than a tie-in and thus rejected the franchisor's claims.

A survey conducted by Hunt and Nevin indicated that about 70 percent of over 600 fast-food franchisee respondents were required to purchase at least some of their operating supplies from their franchisors and that the supplies so obtained represented 50 percent of the franchisees' total purchases.[33] Furthermore, almost half of those respondents who purchase supplies from their franchisors believed that they were paying higher prices for the supplies than they would have had to pay in the open market.[34] There is, no doubt, a very great need for conflict management within a number of fast-food franchising systems with regard to this issue.

Tying agreements were also involved in the previously mentioned Brown Shoe Company Case.[35] Under Brown's franchise plan, held to be unfair and illegal by the FTC, independent dealers were given what was admittedly a valuable package of services—architectural plans, merchandising records, the help of a Brown field representative, and an option to participate in inexpensive group insurance—in return for a simple promise of the dealer-franchisee to concentrate on the Brown Shoe line and not to handle competing lines. Justice Hugo Black, in writing the Supreme Court's decision, stated that the records showed "beyond doubt" that Brown's program required shoe retailers, "unless faithless to their contractual obligations with Brown, substantially to limit their trade with Brown's competitors.''[36] The conclusion in this case was that franchising poses a restraint to trade if the parent company places unreasonable limitations on the right of the franchisee to make his own business decisions.

---

[31] *In re Chock Full O'Nuts Corp. Inc.,* 3 Trade Reg. Rep. 20, 441 (October 1973).

[32] *H. Siegal, et al. v. Chicken Delight, et al.,* 448 F. 2d 43 (1971).

[33] S. D. Hunt and J. R. Nevin, "Tying Agreements in Franchising," *Journal of Marketing,* Vol. 39 (July 1975), pp. 24–25.

[34] *Ibid.*

[35] *Brown Shoe Co., Inc. v. Federal Trade Commission,* 384 U.S. 316 (1966). For critical discussion of the Court's ruling in this case, see John L. Peterman, "The Brown Shoe Case," *Journal of Law and Economics,* Vol. 18 (April 1975), pp. 81–146.

[36] S. D. Hunt, *op. cit.,* p. 35.

Full-line Forcing

Full-line forcing is a requirement that a middleman carry a full line of a manufacturer's product if he is to carry any single items in the line. Contracts of this kind are not illegal unless the dealer is prevented from handling competitors' products. In the case of a farm machinery manufacturer, a court held that the practice was within the law, but inferred that full-line forcing which caused the exclusion of competitors from this part of the market might be illegal if a substantial share of business were affected.[37] This might be termed *de facto* exclusive dealing. In 1976, E. & J. Gallo Winery, the largest seller of wine in the U.S., consented to a Federal Trade Commission order prohibiting the company from, among other things, requiring its wholesalers to distribute any Gallo wines in order to obtain other kinds.[38] And, in 1977, Union Carbide Corporation agreed to a consent order prohibiting the company from requiring its dealers to purchase from it their total requirements of six industrial gases (acetylene, argon, helium, hydrogen, nitrogen, and oxygen) and from making the purchase of the six gases a prerequisite for dealers buying other gases or welding products.[39]

CUSTOMER RESTRICTIONS

A supplier may wish to impose restrictions on to whom a wholesaler or retailer may resell his goods and services. These arrangements may be very desirable for manufacturers or distributors in the marketing of some goods, since they can reserve certain large customers to themselves for direct sales and can also control the reselling of their goods through the channel.

Contracts of this type become illegal when it can be shown that their effects tend to reduce competition. At the present time, however, there are no clear guidelines which determine just how far a supplier may go in dictating to wholesalers or retailers the classes and kinds of customers to whom they may resell his product or brand. The reason for this confusion is due, primarily, to the fact that the Supreme Court in its decision in the Sylvania case[40] did not distinguish between customer (resale) restrictions and territorial restrictions. The former are basically exercises of coercive power (e.g., prohibitions on selling to discount houses) while the latter are basically exercises of reward power (e.g., the granting of a monopoly with respect to the sale of a brand within a defined territory). Discussion of the Sylvania decision is reserved for later when we examine restrictions on reward power, because, in the Sylvania case, the issue directly related to location agreements and not to customer restrictions. Suffice it to say here that resale restric-

---

[37] Beckman, et al., *op. cit.,* p. 409.

[38] "Gallo Winery Consents to FTC Rule Covering Wholesaler Dealings," *Wall Street Journal,* May 20, 1976, p. 15; and "Consent Agreement Cites E & J Gallo Winery," *FTC News Summary* (May 21, 1976), p. 1.

[39] "Union Carbide Settles Complaint by FTC on Industrial-Gas Sales; Airco to Fight," *Wall Street Journal,* May 20, 1977, p. 8.

[40] *Continental T.V., Inc. v. GTE Sylvania, Inc.,* 433 U.S. 36 (1977).

tions are viewed as a restraint of trade and, therefore, are directly challengeable under the Sherman Act. But, given the *Sylvania* decision, their legality is to be judged under a rule-of-reason approach. That is, they will be considered *legal* if they have not substantially lessened competition.

Some of the legal limits to resale restrictions were defined in the General Motors[41] case, which preceded the Sylvania case but which was not overturned by it. General Motors used location restrictions to prevent dealers in the Los Angeles area from selling new cars through discount houses. The Chevrolet franchise agreement provided that dealers could not change the location of their businesses or open at new locations without permission by the company. When several dealers started to sell spare parts through discount houses, the company found them in violation of the location clause and forced them to suspend the practice.[42] A key element in the case was that other Chevrolet dealers in the area helped G.M. to police the ban and, indeed, complaints from them had been a primary motive of General Motors' enforcement actions. The court ruled that the cooperation between G.M. and the other dealers was a conspiracy to eliminate a class of competitors and was, therefore, illegal. This decision indicates that enforcement of resale restrictions must be absolutely unilateral if they are to be legal.

Reciprocity

Reciprocity is the practice of making purchasing decisions at least partly on the basis of whether the vendor is also a customer. In some cases the relationship may be more complex, involving three or more customer-vendors in a circular arrangement. Reciprocity comes down to doing business with your friends.[43] Business reciprocity has come under antitrust scrutiny, especially if there is an inequality of bargaining power in the relationship. This may arise from differences in the relative sizes of the firms.[44] The antitrust laws regulate reciprocity, because sellers influence their customers to buy not only on the basis of marketing competition but also because the buyer wishes to sell his own products to the seller.

There is a body of cases that determines the division between illegal and legal reciprocity. In general, reciprocity is illegal under two circumstances.[45]

1. Coercive reciprocity involving the use of pressure may be illegal as an unfair trade practice.

2. A merger that may cause a reciprocity program to be formed will violate Section 7 of the Clayton Act if the reciprocity may reduce competition.[46]

[41] *U.S. v. General Motors Corp., et al.,* 384 U.S. 127 (1966).

[42] Stern and Grabner, *op. cit.,* p. 135.

[43] R. Moyer, "Reciprocity: Retrospect and Prospect," *Journal of Marketing,* Vol. 34 (October 1970), p. 47.

[44] Howard, *op. cit.,* p. 93.

[45] Moyer, *op. cit.,* p. 48.

[46] See *FTC v. Consolidated Foods Corp.,* 380 U.S. 592.

This latter circumstance can come about when a firm that operates a reciprocity program merges with another firm and one of the two has a customer that sells to the other. In some cases a corporate policy against reciprocity will shield a merger from Section 7.[47] We will return later in this chapter to the issue of reciprocity stemming from mergers when vertical integration is discussed.

Noncoercive reciprocity is legal so long as the policy is not aggressive, is outside of a merger context, and is not supported with elaborate records of purchases and sales from and to other firms. The Federal Trade Commission has held that where reciprocity is prevalent and systematized and where a substantial amount of commerce is involved, there is a violation of Section 5 of the Federal Trade Commission Act.[48] A 1971 case in which a major tire manufacturer and its three subsidiaries were barred from any reciprocity purchases from their suppliers confirmed this view.[49] In many respects, reciprocity is analogous to tying agreements. However, it is very difficult to draw a line between so-called "coercive" reciprocity and the situation where two firms do business "voluntarily" with each other because it is to their mutual advantage.

Price Maintenance

Resale price maintenance was one of the few channel policy areas where the use of coercive power was sanctioned, in a positive manner, by federal laws. State resale price maintenance (fair trade) laws were set up to enable manufacturers to fix resale prices for their goods if they chose to do so. Although on the surface such laws seemed to support a manufacturer's desire to influence prices at the retail level, their initial development was due to the coercive power of coalitions of small, independent retailers who wished to be protected from the direct price competition of mass merchandisers and discounters.[50]

Fair trade laws now represent an historical curiosity, because, early in 1976, a bill went into effect that repealed the Miller-Tydings Act and the McGuire Act, laws that Congress had passed in 1937 and 1952 exempting retail price-fixing by manufacturers from the federal antitrust laws in states which permitted such vertical pricing arrangements. If manufacturers are to have any influence on the prices of resellers, they now have to use power bases other than coercion and will, clearly, have to be extremely cautious in doing so. Maintaining prices, in the absence of fair trade laws, may prove very difficult indeed, given the growing significance of mass merchandisers in retailing. Emphasis will have to be placed on "moral suasion" relating to the consequences of widespread price-cutting on both the wholesale and

---

[47] Moyer, *loc. cit.*

[48] "Federal Trade Commission Statement on Reciprocity," *Journal of Marketing,* Vol. 35 (April 1971), pp. 76–77.

[49] "United States v. General Tire and Rubber Co., Aerojet-General Corp., A. M. Byers Co., and RKO General Inc.," *Journal of Marketing,* Vol. 35 (April 1971), p. 71.

[50] J. C. Palamountain, Jr., *The Politics of Distribution* (Cambridge, Mass.: Harvard University Press, 1955), pp. 235–253.

retail level, segmenting markets into those typified by inelastic and elastic demands, or keeping gross margins so low that room for price-cutting does not exist.[51] However, it should be emphasized that each and every attempt to specify or maintain resale prices will likely be scrutinized very closely by the antitrust enforcement agencies. For example, the FTC has obtained consent order agreements from garment, high fidelity component, carpet, detergent, cookware, and ski equipment manufacturers relative to their vertical pricing activities.[52] In a number of cases, the consent orders prohibit the manufacturers from:

- fixing or controlling resale prices;
- suggesting or recommending resale prices to customers for a set number of years;
- preticketing products with resale prices;
- policing customers' resale prices;
- communicating with any customer or prospective customer concerning a deviation from any resale price;
- terminating or taking any other action against customers because of their resale prices; or
- withholding advertising or other allowances from customers because of their resale prices.

Furthermore, it makes no difference whether maximum[53] or minimum prices are set. Price-fixing in any form is illegal.

On the other hand, still in effect in a number of states are unfair practices acts which regulate the right of sellers to sell below costs or below specified markups on some or all products. These laws are designed to prevent deep and predatory price cuts or "loss leader" selling.[54] Marketing managers whose firms operate in states having such laws must be familiar with the provisions of the laws of each state,

---

[51] See Louis W. Stern, "Approaches to Achieving Retail Price Stability," *Business Horizons,* Vol. 7 (Fall 1964), pp. 82–84.

[52] "Jonathan Logan Apparel Subject of Consent Order Affecting Sales Practices," *FTC News Summary* (May 18, 1979), p. 1; "FTC Complaint Against Levi Strauss Alleges Price Fixing and Other Anticompetitive Acts," *FTC News Summary* (May 14, 1976), p. 1; "Public Comment on Two Orders Banning Price Fixing of Hi-Fi Components Accepted and Invited," *FTC News Summary* (May 7, 1976), p. 3; "Consent Order Banning Resale Price Fixing of Rugs and Carpet Issued," *FTC News Summary* (August 27, 1976), p. 2; "Two Clothing Companies Agree Not to Set Retail Prices, Says FTC," *FTC News Summary* (August 31, 1979), p. 3; "FTC Order Forbids Resale Price-Fixing by Amway," *FTC News Summary* (May 25, 1979), p. 2; "FTC Accepts and Invites Comment on Consent Order Banning Resale Price Fixing by Copco, Inc.," *FTC News Summary* (May 6, 1977), p. 2; "FTC Accepts and Invites Comment on Consent Order Banning Resale Price Fixing by Olin Ski Co., Inc.," *FTC News Summary* (May 10, 1977), p. 2; "The Pricing Police Take a Sterner Line," *Business Week* (June 14, 1976), p. 27.
The Justice Department has also become more active in the vertical price fixing area. See Robert E. Taylor, "Livack Gets Attention of Business with Novel Antitrust Prosecution," *Wall Street Journal,* October 31, 1980, p. 27; and "Cuisinarts Is Fined on Felony Charges in Antitrust Case," *Wall Street Journal,* December 22, 1980, p. 9.

[53] For a court ruling on the setting of maximum prices, see *Albrecht v. Herald Co.,* 390 U.S. 145 (1968).

[54] Beckman, et al., *op. cit.,* pp. 529–531.

since they vary. Sales made for charitable purposes, to relief agencies, for clearance, closeout, liquidation of business, or sales of goods whose marketability is declining are usually exempted from these laws.[55]

Price Discrimination by Buyers

When a seller discriminates in his pricing between two customers, such an action can be viewed as an attempt to exercise reward power relative to the customer receiving the lower price. However, when one of the customers uses his power to force a discriminatory price from the seller, then such an action may be viewed as coercion on the part of the customer. The latter situation is addressed here; the former is left to the next part of the chapter, which deals with limitations on the use of reward power.

Section 2(f) of the Robinson-Patman Act makes it unlawful for a person in commerce knowingly to induce or receive a discrimination in price. To violate this section, a buyer must be reasonably aware of the illegality of the price he has received. This section prevents large, powerful buyers from compelling sellers to give them discriminatory lower prices.[56] It is often enforced by means of Section 5 of the Federal Trade Commission Act on grounds that this use of coercive power is an unfair method of competition. Likewise, it is illegal for buyers to coerce favors from suppliers in the form of special promotional allowances and services.[57]

In addition, large buyers (like A&P) have been known to set up "dummy" brokerage firms as part of their businesses in order to obtain a brokerage allowance from sellers which, in effect, permits them to receive lower prices than their competitors. This form of coercive power is deemed illegal under Section 2(c) of the Robinson-Patman Act, which makes it unlawful to pay brokerage fees or discounts or to accept them except for services rendered in connection with sales or purchases. It also prohibits brokerage fees or discounts paid to any broker who is not independent of both buyer and seller.[58]

Refusals to Deal

A seller can select his own dealers according to his own criteria and judgment. He may also announce in advance the circumstances under which he would refuse

[55] Howard, *op. cit.*, p. 45.

[56] *Ibid.*, pp. 73–75.

[57] See "Order Against Retail Chain Bans Inducement of Preferential Treatment," *FTC News Summary* (February 6, 1976), p. 9; "Fred Meyer Inc. Pays $200,000 Fine to Settle an FTC Complaint," *Wall Street Journal,* January 30, 1976, p. 2; "FTC Law Judge Bars Gibson Retailers from Boycotting Suppliers Who Rebuff Gibson Trade Shows," *FTC News Summary* (March 30, 1979), p. 3; "FTC Says Foremost-McKesson Disobeyed '73 Antitrust Order, Asks for Penalties," *Wall Street Journal,* January 12, 1979, p. 8; "Zayre Consents to Ban on Coercing Suppliers to Be In Trade Shows," *Wall Street Journal,* September 11, 1978, p. 12; and "FTC Finds A&P Violated Robinson-Patman Act," *FTC News Summary* (May 28, 1976), p. 2.

[58] Stern and Grabner, *op. cit.*, p. 119.

to sell to dealers. These two commercial "freedoms" were granted in *U.S. v. Colgate & Co.* in 1919 and referred to as the "Colgate Doctrine."[59] The doctrine was formally recognized by Congress in Section 2(a) of the Robinson-Patman Act, which reads that ". . . nothing herein contained shall prevent persons engaged in selling goods, wares, or merchandise in commerce from selecting their own customers in *bona fide* transactions and not in restraint of trade." Although the selection of dealers poses little problem from a legal perspective, the cutting off or termination of a dealership does. The use of such coercive power is possible only when the refusal to sell involves no joint action or conspiracy in the channel (as discussed in the General Motors case earlier under "Customer Restrictions") or when the end sought by the refusal is not itself illegal.[60]

Clearly, refusal to deal is a major "punishment" underlying a channel member's coercive power. It is, however, heavily circumscribed, as the following quotation indicates:

> . . . (Sellers') right to terminate dealerships is somewhat qualified. In general, sellers can drop dealers "for cause." But they cannot drop dealers, for example, if the latter refuse to cooperate in a dubious legal arrangement, such as exclusive-dealing or tying arrangements. The acuteness of this problem in the automobile industry led to the passage of the Automobile Dealers Franchise Act in 1956, which established the rights of automobile dealers to secure a judicial determination whenever they feel a manufacturer has not acted toward them in good faith.[61]

Despite the numerous limitations discussed above on the use of coercive power in channel relations, it should be emphasized that it is still feasible for both sellers and buyers to employ negative sanctions in interorganizational management. The use of such sanctions has not been outlawed, except in highly extreme forms. For example, exclusive dealing and tying agreements are illegal only if it can be shown that through their implementation, competition is substantially lessened, and proving *substantial* lessening is a difficult task, indeed. As pointed out in Chapter 6, it is, however, generally more functional, from a long-run interorganization management perspective, to mediate rewards rather than punishments in attempting to influence a channel member to do something he would not otherwise have done. Whereas fear, anxiety, and resistance are typical responses to negative sanctions, the typical responses to positive sanctions are hope, reassurance, and attraction.[62] Furthermore, if a channel member uses negative sanctions in the present, it is likely that the member being influenced will be less willing to cooperate in the future, whereas the opposite is true when positive sanctions are employed.[63]

---

[59] *U.S. v. Colgate & Co.,* 250 U.S. 300 (1919).

[60] Stern and Grabner, *op. cit.,* p. 131.

[61] Philip Kotler, *Marketing Management: Analysis, Planning, and Control,* 2nd ed. (Englewood Cliffs, N.J.: Prentice-Hall, 1972), p. 834.

[62] David A. Baldwin, "The Power of Positive Sanctions," *World Politics,* Vol. 24 (October 1971), p. 32.

[63] *Ibid.,* p. 33.

LEGAL LIMITATIONS
ON THE USE
OF REWARD POWER

In this section, we consider those situations in which the use of reward power is limited by law. As was the case with coercive power, the laws do not prevent a channel member from employing rewards as a central component of his interorganizational strategy; rather, they place restrictions around how certain enticements or incentives might be used.

Territorial Allocations

In order to influence a wholesaler or retailer to make necessary investments in plant, equipment, or inventory relative to a product or brand on which the investment might not otherwise be forthcoming *or* to provide important support activities (such as repair services or promotion in local areas) *or* to achieve the widest and deepest possible coverage of a market, a manufacturer may offer the wholesaler or retailer a territory in which to sell his product or brand which is, at least to some extent, removed, isolated, or "protected" from other wholesalers or retailers also selling the manufacturer's items. In effect, the manufacturer is attempting to provide the reseller with a monopoly relative to the sales of his brand within a defined geographic area. These arrangements are intended to make the manufacturer's line so attractive to individual resellers that they will concentrate their efforts on his brands and not concern themselves unduly with competition from other dealers selling the same brands. From an interorganization management perspective, the attempt to dampen *intra*brand competition in order to strengthen *inter*brand competition makes a lot of sense. A manufacturer would often rather have the middlemen handling his brand compete with those of other brands than to slug it out among themselves.

Territorial allocations or restrictions range from absolute confinement of reseller sales intended to completely foreclose intrabrand competition to "lesser" territorial allocations designed to inhibit such competition. These lesser allocations include areas of primary responsibility, profit pass-over arrangements, and location clauses.[64]

Absolute confinement involves a promise by a reseller that he will not sell outside his assigned territory. Often combined with such a promise is a pledge by the supplier not to sell anyone else in that territory. Such a pledge is known as the granting of an *exclusive* distributorship or franchise. When absolute confinement is combined with an exclusive distributorship, the territory can be considered "airtight."[65] On the other hand, an area of primary responsibility requires the reseller to use his best efforts to maintain effective distribution of the supplier's goods in the territory specifically assigned to him. Failure to meet performance targets may

[64] For a complete discussion of these restrictions and the legal issues surrounding their use, see ABA Antitrust Section, *Vertical Restrictions Limiting Intrabrand Competition* (Chicago: American Bar Association, 1977).

[65] See Robert Pitofsky, "The *Sylvania* Case: Antitrust Analysis of Non-Price Vertical Restrictions," *Columbia Law Review,* Vol. 78 (January 1978), pp. 3–4.

result in termination, but the reseller is free to sell outside his area, and other wholesalers or retailers may sell in his territory.

Profit pass-over arrangements require that a reseller who sells to a customer located outside his assigned territory compensate the reseller in whose territory the customer is located. Such compensation is ostensibly to reimburse the second reseller for his efforts to stimulate demand in his territory and for the cost of providing services upon which the first reseller might have capitalized. Finally, a location clause specifies the physical site of a reseller's place of business. Such clauses are used to "space" resellers in a given territory so that each has a "natural" market to serve comprised of those customers who are closest to the reseller's location. However, the reseller may sell to any customer walking through his door. Furthermore, the customers located closest to him may decide to purchase at more distant locations than his.

As indicated earlier in this chapter, the antitrust enforcement agencies' attitude is that effective competition involves *both* intrabrand and interbrand competition. Consequently, any attempts to confine wholesalers' or retailers' selling activities to one area may be viewed by these agencies as either restraints of trade or as unfair methods of competition and therefore may be challenged under the Sherman Act or under Section 5 of the FTC Act.

For example, in 1958, the Justice Department brought suit against the White Motor Company, charging, among other things, that its franchises, which limited the area in which its dealers could sell or solicit customers, constituted an agreement to restrain trade. The decision by the lower courts concurred with the Justice Department's argument and held that such exclusive territorial arrangements were illegal *per se,* regardless of their competitive effects.[66] The Supreme Court demurred and suggested a retrial.[67] Before a retrial could be held in the lower courts, White accepted a consent decree to drop the exclusive territorial provisions in its franchise agreements.[68]

Another court case involving this issue concerned Sealy, Inc., a company which licensed other firms to manufacture and sell its products (mattresses) under the Sealy trademark at uniform prices and in specified areas.[69] However, the Sealy licensees were in reality the owners of Sealy, Inc. The courts held that the exclusive territorial restraints were simply a collusive means of horizontal price-fixing and policing, in *per se* violation of Section 1 of the Sherman Act.

In the Schwinn Case,[70] the same line of reasoning that was applied against Schwinn's resale restrictions regarding to whom its wholesalers and retailers could sell its bicycles was used relative to its territorial restrictions. Both customer and territorial restrictions were found to be *per se* violations of the Sherman Act unless Schwinn was willing to retain title, risk, and dominion over its product—that is, to

---

[66] *White Motor Co. v. U.S.,* 194 F. Supp. 562 (1961).

[67] *White Motor Co. v. U.S.,* 372 U.S. 253 (1963).

[68] Stern and Grabner, *op. cit.,* p. 135.

[69] *U.S. v. Sealy, Inc.,* 388 U.S. 350 (1967).

[70] *U.S. v. Arnold Schwinn and Co., et al.,* 388 U.S. 365 (1967).

sell them on a consignment basis or vertically integrate.[71] It should be noted, however, that when the actual remedy was imposed by the District Court, Schwinn was not prohibited from designating areas of prime responsibility for its distributors nor from designating the location of the place of business in its franchise agreements. Schwinn also retained the right to select its distributors and franchised dealers and to terminate dealerships for cause so long as such arrangements did not involve exclusive dealing clauses.[72]

The decision in the Schwinn case proved to be immensely unpopular among businessmen, legal scholars, and even among judges. Therefore, when the Supreme Court handed down a decision in the Sylvania[73] case on June 23, 1977, which overturned the Schwinn decision, there was cause for celebration. The Schwinn decision had established a rule of *per se* illegality for customer (resale) and territorial restrictions; the Sylvania decision held that such restraints should be judged by the "rule of reason" on a case-by-case basis. Because of the significance of the Sylvania case to the establishing of distribution policies, it is important to devote some time to understanding what transpired in it.

Prior to 1962, Sylvania, a manufacturer of television sets, sold its sets through both independent and company-owned distributors to a large number of independent retailers. RCA dominated the market at the time with 60 to 70 percent of national sales, with Zenith and Magnavox as major rivals. Sylvania had only one to two percent of the market. In 1962, Sylvania decided to abandon efforts at "saturation distribution" and chose instead to phase out its wholesalers and sell directly to a smaller group of franchised retailers. Sylvania retained sole discretion to determine how many retailers would operate in any geographic area and, in fact, at least two retailers were franchised in every metropolitan center of more than 100,000 people. Dealers were free to sell anywhere and to any class of customers, but agreed to operate only from locations approved by Sylvania.

Continental TV was one of Sylvania's most successful retailers in northern California. After a series of disagreements arising from Sylvania's authorizing a new outlet near one of Continental's best locations, Continental opened a new outlet in Sacramento, although its earlier request for approval for that location had been denied. Sylvania then terminated Continental's franchise. Continental brought a lawsuit against Sylvania, citing the precedent established in the Schwinn decision regarding the per se illegality of territorial restrictions. The Court sided with Sylvania, which argued that the use of its territorial allocation policy permitted its marketing channels to compete more successfully against those established by its large competitors.

While the situation in the Sylvania case did not involve customer restrictions, the Supreme Court found that the intent and competitive impact of the retail customer restriction in the Schwinn franchise agreement wherein Schwinn pro-

[71] See Betty Bock, *Antitrust Issues in Restricting Sales Territories and Outlets* (New York: The Conference Board, 1967), for a complete discussion of the case.
[72] "U.S. v. Arnold Schwinn and Co., et al.," *Journal of Marketing*, Vol. 33 (January 1969), p. 107.
[73] *Continental T.V., Inc. v. GTE Sylvania Inc.,* 433 U.S. 36 (1977).

hibited its franchised retailers from selling its products to nonfranchised retailers (e.g., discount stores) were indistinguishable from the territorial restriction (i.e., the location clause) in the Sylvania franchise agreement. Furthermore, in its decision, the Court favored the promotion of *inter*brand competition even if *intra*brand competition were restricted. It indicated that customer and territorial restrictions encourage interbrand competition by allowing the manufacturer to achieve certain efficiencies in the distribution of his products. And, in a footnote, the Court recognized that marketing efficiency is not the only legitimate reason for a manufacturer's desire to exert control over the manner in which its products are sold and serviced, because society increasingly demands that the manufacturer directly assume responsibility for the safety and quality of his products.

Thus, the upshot of the Sylvania decision is that customer and territorial restraints will not be found to be per se illegal if they do not have a "pernicious effect on competition without redeeming value." Increased interbrand competition appears to be of sufficient "redeeming value." Of course, such restraints may still be attacked as unreasonable restraints in violation of Section 1 of the Sherman Act or Section 5 of the Federal Trade Commission Act, but the burden will be on the plaintiff to prove that they are unreasonable. It appears, however, that the status of such restraints imposed by successful marketers with substantial market power will remain clouded pending further court decisions.[74] Also, court decisions challenging such restraints will likely be more complex and costly due to the requisite economic evidence that will be required to prove certain restraints unreasonable. The effect of this should be to reduce the amount of private litigation involving such restraints.[75]

Incentives for Resellers' Employees

The Federal Trade Commission originally took the position that one firm could not reward (via the use of "push" money[76] or similar incentives) the employees of their commercial customers for reselling its product. The Commission considered these incentives a violation of Section 5 of the FTC Act, alleging that competing products suffered a disadvantage under such schemes. In 1921, the courts declared that the practice was legal if the employer consented to it, because, it was curiously reasoned, if a seller sold his goods outright to a reseller, the relevant

---

[74] The FTC has brought suit against the exclusive territorial restrictions used by Coca-Cola and Pepsi Cola. The case is still in the courts. See *Coca-Cola Co.,* 91 F.T.C. 517, appeal docketed, 78-1364 (D.C. Cir. 1978). For a suggested approach in such cases, see E. F. Zelek, Jr., L. W. Stern, and T. W. Dunfee, "A Rule of Reason Model After *Sylvania,*" *California Law Review*, Vol. 68 (1980), pp. 801–836.

[75] Many of these conclusions have been drawn from James G. Hiering and Richard L. Reinish, "Vertical Restraints on Distribution: Continental TV, Inc. v. GTE Sylvania, Inc.," office memorandum of Keck, Cushman, Mahin & Cate, Chicago, Ill., July 1, 1977. See also Robert E. Weigand, "Policing the Marketing Channel—It May Get Easier," in R. F. Lusch and P. H. Zinszer (eds.), *Contemporary Issues in Marketing Channels* (Norman, Ok.: University of Oklahoma, 1979), pp. 105–111.

[76] "Push money" is extra monetary payment from a manufacturer to a customer's salesman for "pushing" the manufacturer's brand.

competitive market was now the reseller's. Thus, the original seller was no longer in the competition under consideration once title passed to the reseller.[77]

The Federal Trade Commission has issued trade practice rules that forbid push money if the employer does not consent, if the payment involves a lottery, where competitive products are affected severely, where competition is lessened, or where the inducements are not available to salesmen of all competing resellers.

Push money payments transferred to the employers are subject to restrictions under the price discrimination articles of the Robinson-Patman Act, discussed below.

Commercial Bribery

Commercial bribery is the practice of paying the employees of customers to purchase from the payer. After it was discovered in 1975 that several major U.S. corporations had been involved in making illegal or questionable payoffs to foreign nationals in order to obtain business abroad, there has been an intensified drive, especially by the Securities and Exchange Commission (SEC) and the Internal Revenue Service (IRS), to uncover kickbacks and other questionable or illegal payments both domestically and internationally.[78] The SEC's interest is in the possibility that publicly owned companies engaged in illegal activities may be violating the securities laws if they do not disclose that fact to the investing public. The IRS's interest is founded on the fact that bribery is not a legitimate business expense and that bribery payments may be buried in income tax statements under such seemingly innocuous items as "cooperative advertising allowances." During the 1975–1978 period, federal agencies located over $1 billion of dubious payments by more than 500 companies.[79] It is to be hoped that the problem is becoming less acute as the result of the SEC and IRS efforts and because of the Foreign Corrupt Practices Act of 1978, which has stiffened prohibitions against secret bank accounts and has instituted criminal penalties for bribing foreign-government officials.

The Federal Trade Commission is also getting involved in bribery issues by applying Section 5 of the FTC Act (which prohibits unfair methods of competition) to situations involving questionable payments both domestically and abroad.[80] Its first

---

[77] Howard, *op. cit.,* pp. 135–136.

[78] Burt Schorr, "Questionable-Payments Drive Stimulates Competition, Tougher Internal Controls," *Wall Street Journal,* June 23, 1978, p. 30; and Carol H. Falk, "SEC May Uncover More Domestic Bribes using Foreign-Payoff Detection Methods," *Wall Street Journal,* March 10, 1976, p. 4.

[79] Schorr, *ibid.,* p. 30. For examples of domestic bribery in marketing channels, see "SEC Accuses Jacquin, 2 Aides of Making Payoffs to Retailers to Sell Its Liquors," *Wall Street Journal,* October 18, 1977, p. 11; "Schlitz Brewing, as Expected, Is Indicted for Illegal Practices in Marketing Beer," *Wall Street Journal,* March 16, 1978, p. 12; "National Distiller Says That Liquor Unit Paid Kickbacks of $4 Million to Retailers," *Wall Street Journal,* January 31, 1977, p. 5; Frederick C. Klein, "Beer Firms Are Target As Agencies Extend Bribery Probes to U.S.," *Wall Street Journal,* June 10, 1976, p. 1; "Two Gum-Rack Firms Plead Guilty in Case Linked to Kickbacks," *Wall Street Journal,* April 14, 1978, p. 10; and "Restaurant Firm Discloses Payoffs By Its Suppliers," *Wall Street Journal,* March 23, 1977, p. 16.

[80] Burt Schorr, "FTC Staff Action Against Aircraft Firms May Set Precedent for Fighting Payoffs," *Wall Street Journal,* October 18, 1977, p. 2.

attempt to apply Section 5 in such situations was in 1976.[81] Prior to that time, the FTC was successful in barring payola to disc jockeys as an unfair trade practice unless the listening public is informed of the payment.[82] It is likely that the FTC will become more active in policing bribes, because its staff lawyers believe that the federal securities and tax laws leave loopholes for continued payoffs that can be closed only by the antitrust laws.[83]

Price Discrimination by Sellers

Section 2(a) of the Robinson-Patman Act states,

> It shall be unlawful for any person engaged in commerce, . . . either directly or indirectly, to discriminate in price between different purchasers of commodities of like grade and quality, where either or any of the purchases involved in such discrimination are in commerce, where such commodities are sold for use, consumption, or resale within . . . (any area) . . . under the jurisdiction of the United States, and where the effect of such discrimination may be to substantially lessen competition or tend to create a monopoly in any line of commerce, or to injure, destroy or prevent competition with any person who either grants or knowingly receives the benefit of such discrimination, or with customers of either of them.

It goes on to allow price differentials due to differences in the cost of serving different customers, up to the amounts justified by the cost savings. However, cost-justified quantity discounts can be limited by the Federal Trade Commission. Other provisions of the Robinson-Patman Act are that sellers can select their own customers unless in restraint of trade, and that price changes due to market value, marketability of goods, distress sales, or discontinuance of business are allowed.

1. LIKE GRADE AND QUALITY. Where products are of different materials or workmanship level, they are not ordinarily considered to be of "like grade and quality," but where differences are small and do not affect the basic use of the goods, then selling at price differentials has been attacked.[84]

In cases where competition between two buyers from a single seller is under consideration, products of the same composition have been declared of like grade and quality even if the brand preference shown to one of them in the market is significant. In the Borden Case,[85] the Supreme Court held that evaporated milk sold under the Borden label and evaporated milk manufactured by Borden and sold

[81] "FTC Accuses Service Corp. International of Paying Bribes to Get Funeral Business," *Wall Street Journal,* February 5, 1976, p. 2.
[82] Howard, *op. cit.,* pp. 137–138.
[83] Schorr, *op. cit.* (1977), p. 2; John S. Estey and David W. Marston, "Pitfalls (and Loopholes) in the Foreign Bribery Law," *Fortune* (October 9, 1978), pp. 182–188.
[84] Stern and Grabner, *op. cit.,* pp. 112–113.
[85] *U.S. v. Borden Co.,* 383 U.S. 637 (1966).

under "private" labels were of like grade and quality, illustrating the point that "perceived" product differentiation fails to constitute an "actual" difference in grade and quality under the law's interpretation.

In cases where two sellers are in competition for the same buyer, the Federal Trade Commission has held that brand identification by the public is a difference in grade and quality, so that cutting the price on a product labeled as "premium" to the same level as others charge for a standard (nonpremium) product is actually undercutting the competitor's price. Price discrimination to do this, then, is not protected by the "meeting competition" defense.[86]

2. TO SUBSTANTIALLY LESSEN COMPETITION.

There is an important difference between injury to competitors and injury to competition. A loss of sales by one firm and their gain by another is the essence of competition, and the object of each competitor is to outsell his rivals. Evidence of predatory intent to destroy a competitor may indicate an injury to competition. Other factors to consider are the number of firms in the market and the market share of the discriminating seller.[87]

In the Anheuser-Busch case, the Court of Appeals ruled that injury to competition and not injury to competitors was a critical factor in determining the legality or illegality of price discrimination.[88] The injury to competition need not be actual to be unlawful, but a remote possibility of injury is not sufficient for illegality.[89]

Because of the requirement of injury to competition, a time and space dimension must be applied in price discrimination cases. In one case, for example, a sulphur producer had a ten-year contract with a fertilizer manufacturer to supply a fixed quantity of sulphur every year at a specified price, or at the price charged to the fertilizer firm's competitors, whichever was lower. In times of high prices, the stipulated price was lower than that charged to other customers. Therefore, the sulphur firm attempted to have the contract declared illegal as unlawful price discrimination. The court ruled that the lower price was legal so long as the other firms were offered the same prices and terms at the time the contract was made.[90]

Price discrimination among customers who are not in competition is not illegal. The Federal Trade Commission has issued an advisory opinion that an apparel manufacturer may grant extended credit terms to new stores in ghetto areas, even though other classes of customers would be excluded from the plan. The FTC justified its decision on grounds that there should be little competition between favored and nonfavored stores in this case.[91]

---

[86] Stern and Grabner, *op. cit.,* pp. 113–114.

[87] Howard, *op. cit.,* pp. 54–55.

[88] *Anheuser-Busch, Inc. v. Federal Trade Commission,* 265 F. 2d 677 (7th Cir. 1959), 363 U.S. 536 (1960), 289 F. 2d 835 (7th Cir. 1961).

[89] Howard, *op. cit.,* p. 55.

[90] "Texas Gulf Sulphur Co. v. J. R. Simplot Co.," *Journal of Marketing,* Vol. 34 (April 1970), p. 82.

[91] "Federal Trade Commission Advisory Opinion No. 253," *Journal of Marketing,* Vol. 33 (January 1969), p. 105.

Injury to any of three levels of competition may bring price discrimination under the prohibition of the Robinson-Patman Act.

a. *Primary Level.* Competition between two sellers may be injured when one of them gives discriminatory prices to some customers. This was the situation in the Utah Pie Case.[92] The Utah Pie Company was a local concern that sold its frozen pies in the Salt Lake City market at low prices due to its low costs. It had 66 percent of the market. Several national concerns competed with Utah Pie in that market. They cut their prices in Salt Lake City below those that they charged in other markets. In some cases these prices were below full cost.[93] The Supreme Court ruled that the evidence in the case was sufficient for a jury to decide whether the defendants had engaged in predatory tactics and whether competition had been lessened, even though Utah's market share had declined only to 45 percent and its sales had expanded.[94] In this case the dominant local firm was protected from discriminatory price cutting by national firms.[95]

b. *Secondary Level.* Competition between two customers of a seller may be affected if the seller differentiates between them in price. In effect the seller is aiding one customer and harming the other in their mutual competition, and this is sufficient to cause substantial lessening of competition.[96]

c. *Tertiary Level.* If a manufacturer discriminates in prices between two wholesalers such that the customers of one wholesaler are favored over those of the other, the competition is being injured by the price discrimination.[97]

3. IN COMMERCE.   Price discrimination is illegal only if the discriminatory sales are in commerce. In one case, a court held that National Food Stores could advertise and sell certain items at one store at lower prices than they charge at others. The court ruled that the sales were not in commerce since they were to anyone who came in and were completed on the premises.[98] Furthermore, discrimination in pricing can be lawful when the products involved are not identical, when a product is sold for different uses, when separate markets are involved, when sales of the product(s) take place at different times, and when sales are made to government agencies[99] as well as in the situations where the cost justification or the good faith defense can be applied, as described below.

[92] *Utah Pie Co. v. Continental Baking Co., et al.,* 386 U.S. 685 (1967).
[93] R. O. Werner, "Marketing and the United States Supreme Court 1965-1968," *Journal of Marketing,* Vol. 33 (January 1969), p. 17.
[94] *Utah Pie Co. v. Continental Baking Co., et al.,* 386 U.S. 685 (1967).
[95] Werner, *loc. cit.*
[96] Howard, *op. cit.,* pp. 53-54.
[97] *Ibid.*
[98] "Plotken's West Inc. v. National Food Stores, Inc.," *Journal of Marketing,* Vol. 35 (January 1971), pp. 79-80.
[99] Donald V. Harper, *Price Policy and Procedure* (New York: Harcourt, Brace & World, 1966), pp. 105-106.

4. COST JUSTIFICATION DEFENSE. Price differences between customers are permitted if they can be justified by differences in the costs of sale or delivery to the different customers. The burden of proof of cost differences is on the seller. However, the courts have been reluctant to accept the cost figures as valid.[100] As one author puts it, "The record shows that few firms have been able, in litigation, to justify price differences on the basis of cost."[101] The difficulties lie in ascertaining exactly what costs are to be included in the calculation and how overhead and joint costs are to be allocated.[102]

5. QUANTITY DISCOUNTS. Are permitted under Section 2(a) to the extent that they are justified by cost savings. The Supreme Court has ruled that quantity discounts must reflect cost savings in deliveries made to one place at one time.[103] This places limitations on the use of cumulative quantity discounts. Furthermore, quantity limits may be placed on discounts on some commodities by the Federal Trade Commission, if it can be determined that only a few very large buyers can qualify for the largest discount category in a seller's pricing schedule.[104]

6. GOOD FAITH DEFENSE. Section 2(b) of the Robinson-Patman Act allows a firm to charge lower prices to some of its customers than others, if it is done "in good faith to meet an equally low price of a competitor." This defense is valid even if there is substantial injury to competition, but the burden of proving good faith falls on the defendant.[105]

> **a.** The price being met must be lawful and not a price produced by collusion. A seller does not have to prove the price that he is meeting is lawful, but he must make some effort to find out if it is.[106]
>
> **b.** The price being met must really exist,[107] and the price must be met and not undercut.[108] As mentioned previously, price reductions on a "premium" product to the level of "standard" products can be a form of illegal price discrimination. If the public is willing to pay a higher price for the "premium" product, the equal prices may be considered beating and not meeting competition.[109]

[100] Stern and Grabner, *op. cit.*, p. 114.

[101] Howard, *op. cit.*, p. 62.

[102] *Ibid.*

[103] Stern and Grabner, *op. cit.*, p. 121.

[104] *Federal Trade Commission v. Morton Salt Company*, 334 U.S. 37 (1948). Although the FTC may establish maximum discounts or quantity limits, its only attempt to use this power was unsuccessful because of a basic discrepancy between the FTC's order and the evidence on which it was based. See *Federal Trade Commission v. B. F. Goodrich et al.*, 242 F. 2d 31 (1957).

[105] Howard, *op. cit.*, p. 56.

[106] *Ibid.*, pp. 60–61.

[107] *Standard Oil Co. v. FTC*, 340 U.S. 231 (1951).

[108] Howard, *op. cit.*, pp. 56–59.

[109] Stern and Grabner, *op. cit.*, p. 116.

c. The competition being met must be at the primary level. Granting a discriminatory price to some customers to enable them to meet their own competition is not protected.[110]

The question of whether the good faith defense is applicable to gaining new customers as well as to retaining old customers is basically unsettled. The Federal Trade Commission has argued that a company is only allowed to grant price discriminations "in good faith" to retain old customers.[111] However, the 7th Circuit Court overruled this view in holding that the law does not distinguish old and new customers.[112]

Because of the difficulty encountered by companies in trying to apply the above-mentioned defenses and the likelihood that, in certain instances, the Act merely protects competitors from competition, there is considerable question about its ultimate value and equity. In fact, there have been efforts made to gain a repeal of the Act.[113]

Promotional Allowances and Services

Section 2(d) of the Robinson-Patman Act prohibits the payment of any special allowances to customers for their services in connection with the processing, handling, selling, or offering for sale of any products sold by them, unless the allowances are available to all other competing customers on proportionately equal terms. Section 2(e) makes the same prohibition of discrimination among purchasers in the giving of services or facilities to aid them in reselling the goods.

These sections forbid the creation of price discrimination among customers indirectly by the granting of special promotional allowances to some but not all customers. It is not illegal to give promotional allowances or services, but the seller must grant them to all competing customers on "proportionately equal terms." Both of these prohibitions are absolute and are not dependent on injury to competition, and cost justification of the discrimination is not a defense.[114]

There are several points to be considered before allowances and services are judged illegal.[115]

a. The customers among whom the discrimination has taken place must be in competition with each other; thus, the markets in which the customer-resellers sell are a consideration. These markets may be local, regional, or national,

---

[110] *Federal Trade Commission v. Sun Oil Co.,* 371 U.S. 505 (1963).

[111] Stern and Grabner, *op. cit.,* p. 115.

[112] Howard, *op. cit.,* p. 57.

[113] Stanley Cohen, "Bigger 'n' Better Doesn't Always Mean Cheaper," *Advertising Age* (July 28, 1975), p. 54; and "Justice Department Urges an Overhaul of Key Trust Law," *Wall Street Journal,* January 18, 1977, p. 8.

[114] Howard, *op. cit.,* pp. 69–73.

[115] *Ibid.*

depending upon the particular customer involved. A time dimension is also involved.

b. The type of customer is a consideration. For the purposes of the law, a wholesaler whose customers compete with retailers buying direct from the manufacturer is entitled to promotional allowances if the retailers are granted them.

The Fred Meyer case illustrates the difficulties involved in avoiding discrimination when dual distribution is used. The Supreme Court ruled that if Fred Meyer was granted promotional fees and allowances as a direct buying retailer, then its retail competitors who purchased through wholesalers were entitled to them also; and it was the duty of the supplier to see that the competing retailers actually received them.[116] The Federal Trade Commission has issued a new set of guidelines for advertising and other allowances and services that implement the key elements of the decision. The seller may enter into agreements with distributors or other third parties to guarantee the performance of the seller's obligations to the customers of wholesalers, but the legal responsibility is on the seller.[117]

c. The law requires allowances to be granted to all on proportionately equal terms. The Federal Trade Commission guidelines indicate that the allowances should be based on the quantity of goods purchased or on the dollar volume of sales in a given time. In some cases, promotional services such as demonstrators in stores are not practical for all customers. When this happens, a substitute for this service must be made available to those unable to use the demonstrators, and the availability of the alternative must be made known.[118]

When promotional allowances or merchandising services are provided, the FTC has stipulated that they should be furnished in accordance with a written plan. Besides making certain that the services or payments are available on some proportional basis to all competing customers, the seller should take steps to make sure that all customers are informed of the plan, that all services are actually performed, and that he is not overpaying for the services.

Functional Discounts

Each level in the marketing channel performs certain specific tasks and takes certain risks as labor is divided among the various institutions and agencies responsible for making goods and services available to end-users. Historically, when there was little vertical integration and when independent wholesalers sold to numerous, relatively small retail outlets, each level in the channel was rewarded differently

---

[116] *Federal Trade Commission v. Fred Meyer et al.*, 390 U.S. 341 (1968). Also see "Fred Meyer, Inc. Pays $200,000 in Settlement of Civil Penalty Suit," *FTC News Summary* (January 30, 1976), p. 1.

[117] Federal Trade Commission, *Guides For Advertising Allowances and Other Merchandising Payments and Services*. Promulgated May 29, 1969, amended August 4, 1972.

[118] Howard, *op. cit.,* pp. 69–73.

(e.g., the wholesaler got a larger price discount from the manufacturer than the retailer). In addition, each level in the channel dealt with a specific class of customer; i.e., the wholesaler sold only to retailers, and retailers only to consumers. Therefore, the discounts given to wholesalers and retailers, called functional discounts because they were payments for unique functions performed,[119] could differ without being an antitrust violation. However, in more recent years, the distinctions in distribution systems have blurred as wholesalers have formed voluntary chains and as retailers have integrated wholesaling functions; therefore, the antitrust questions are much more difficult.

Although functional or trade discounts are not specifically referred to in the Robinson-Patman Act, they are lawful under the Act as long as they are offered on the same terms to all competing buyers of the same class and as long as the discounts granted do not exceed cost savings of the seller. This suggests that different discounts can in fact be granted to wholesalers than are granted to retailers without being considered a violation of the Act. However, as Harper points out:

> The problem arises when sellers attempt to distinguish between various kinds of retailers, such as chain-store companies, department stores, mail-order houses, and independent retailers, in their trade-discount structures or when they attempt to distinguish between different kinds of wholesalers, such as drop shippers and full-service wholesalers. Since retailers may be in competition with one another regardless of these distinctions and since wholesalers of different types may compete with one another, it can be construed that competition is injured if different competing retailers or different competing wholesalers are charged different prices by means of trade discounts.[120]

For example, Mueller Company sold products for water and gas distribution systems to wholesalers, some of whom inventoried certain items and some of whom did not. Mueller gave the first set of wholesalers an additional 10 percent discount on the inventoried items. The Federal Trade Commission found this action to be a violation of the Robinson-Patman Act because, it reasoned, Mueller had given these wholesalers a business advantage (i.e., having the high-volume items on hand for immediate delivery to customers) by subsidizing them.[121] But the FTC also found that the opportunity to be an inventory-carrying wholesaler was not open to all wholesalers but only open to those selected by Mueller. If the opportunity were available to all, then the functional discount might not have been viewed as blatantly discriminatory. In any case, the legal status of functional discounts is cloudy, given the fact that the functions of marketing channel members are scrambled and that classes of trade (i.e., manufacturers, wholesalers, and retailers) will continue to overlap considerably as intertype competition intensifies.

---

[119] Wholesalers and retailers can receive *both* functional discounts *and* quantity discounts. Functional discounts are a reward for functions performed, while quantity discounts are a reward for amount purchased.

[120] Donald V. Harper, *Price Policy and Procedure* (New York: Harcourt, Brace & World, 1966), p. 289.

[121] *In the Matter of Mueller Co.,* 60 F.T.C. 120 (1962).

The murkiness of the functional discount issue was further increased by a complaint dated May 9, 1980 filed by the Federal Trade Commission charging the Boise Cascade Corporation with knowingly receiving illegal discounts from its office-products suppliers.[122] Boise Cascade purchases office supplies from manufacturers and resells them to both retail dealers and large commercial users. In selling to commercial users, Boise competes against retail stationers and other office products dealers who buy from the same manufacturers. The FTC charged that, on goods purchased for resale to commercial users, Boise's Office Products Division receives discounts that are not available to other retail dealers, giving Boise a competitive advantage.

It appears that there are two legal standards which might be applied by the FTC to this case.[123] One of them arises from a 1955 FTC lawsuit involving the Doubleday Co. In that case, the FTC indicated that discriminatory prices may be legal if justified by special services or functions performed for manufacturers by the company receiving the discount. This might include such things as carrying a complete line of products or keeping a warehouse fully stocked. The other standard stemming from the above-mentioned Mueller decision says that an otherwise illegal price discrimination can be justified only if the discount matches actual cost savings the manufacturer derives from special services the buyer performs. In the Mueller case, the FTC expressly overturned its Doubleday ruling.

Delivered Pricing

Delivered prices are the quotation of prices so that all customers within a given area pay the same price for a product regardless of differences in shipping costs from the seller to the buyer. These systems have been popular over the years and have been used to promote price stability in some industries. On some occasions, they have been attacked successfully by the Federal Trade Commission in the courts.[124]

Delivered pricing systems are legal under some circumstances.[125]

> *When a seller acts independently and not in collusion with competitors, provided that individual actions of a variety of competitors do not result in a systematic matching of delivered prices,* a delivered pricing plan or policy of freight absorption is legal under any of the following qualifying conditions:
>
> **1.** If the seller is willing to sell on an f.o.b. basis when a purchaser so requests.
> **2.** If the seller maintains a uniform delivered price at all points of delivery . . . as when he charges nationwide uniform delivered prices.
> **3.** If the seller absorbs freight costs, or some portion of them, in order to meet competition, as when his factory price plus actual freight to destination is higher than the

[122] "Boise Cascade Charged with Receiving Illegal Discounts," *FTC News Summary* (May 9, 1980), p. 2.
[123] *Ibid.*
[124] Stern and Grabner, *op. cit.,* p. 117.
[125] Beckman, et al., *op. cit.,* pp. 518–519.

amount a customer would have to pay when procuring the goods from a competitor.
4. If the buyers and/or their customers are noncompetitive.

LEGAL LIMITATIONS
REGARDING VERTICAL
INTEGRATION

The marketing manager is faced with another set of legal constraints when considering vertical integration. Vertical integration in the channel may come about through forward integration by a producer, backward integration by a retailer, or integration in either direction by a wholesaler or other intermediate level of distribution. Integration may be brought about by the creation of a new business function by existing firms (internal expansion) or by acquisition of the stock or the assets of other firms (mergers).

The two methods of creating integration are fundamentally different in their relationship to the law. Internal expansion is regulated by Section 2 of the Sherman Act, which prohibits monopoly or attempts to monopolize any part of the interstate or foreign commerce of the United States. External expansion is regulated by Section 7 of the Clayton Act and its amendment, the Celler-Kefauver Act, which prohibits the purchase of stock or assets of other firms, if the effects may be to substantially lessen competition or tend to create a monopoly in any line of commerce in any part of the country. Internal expansion is given favored treatment under the law.[126] The theory seems to be that internal expansion expands investment and production, and thus increases competition, whereas growth by merger removes an entity from the market.[127]

Integration, whether by merger or internal expansion, may result in the lowering of costs and make possible more effective interorganizational management of the channel. It may also be a means of avoiding many of the legal problems previously discussed, because an integrated firm is free to control prices and allocate products to its integrated outlets without conflict with the laws governing restrictive distribution policies.

Vertical Integration by Merger

The major legal consideration in a vertical merger is the effect the merger will have on competition among firms at the various distributive levels involved in the merger. That is to say, if the merger will tend to foreclose a source of supply to independent firms at the buyer's level or to foreclose a market to other firms at the

---

[126] Under the wording of Section 7 of the Clayton Act, it is not necessary to prove that the restraint involved has actually restrained competition. It is enough that it ''may'' tend to substantially lessen competition.

[127] E. T. Grether, *Marketing and Public Policy* (Englewood Cliffs, N.J.: Prentice-Hall, 1966), p. 104. In order to show their goodwill relative to preserving competition, some companies relinquish their voting privileges on the stock they acquire in merger activities. For a discussion of merger theory, see T. W. Dunfee and L. W. Stern, ''Potential Competition Theory as an Antimerger Tool Under Section 7 of the Clayton Act: A Decision Model,'' *Northwestern Law Review,* Vol. 69 (January–February 1975), pp. 821–871.

seller's level, the merger can be questioned. This kind of situation comes about when either level contains only a few firms, so that the merger of one in each level can make it difficult for third parties to obtain suppliers or outlets that are not competitors as well.[128] The merger of the Brown Shoe Company and the G. R. Kinney Company, the largest independent chain of shoe stores, was declared illegal by the Supreme Court because it was believed that the merger would foreclose other manufacturers from selling through Kinney.[129]

In determining whether a merger will reduce competition, the two critical variables involved are the definition of the line of commerce and the market involved. If either is defined narrowly enough, almost any merger can be questioned. For example, the critical nature of the definition of the relevant market is apparent in vertical merger cases in the cement industry. The Federal Trade Commission has long been interested in the trend of such mergers and has required firms to give notice to the Commission before the consummation of any merger involving a ready-mixed concrete producer. The Commission will attempt to block the merger if it feels that the merger has anticompetitive features.[130] This happened when the OKG Corporation acquired 88 percent of Jahnke Service, Inc. Jahnke produces building materials, including ready-mixed cement, while OKG is a producer of cement and other products. At the time of the merger, Jahnke's purchases of cement were about 27 percent of the total in the New Orleans metropolitan area and about 4 percent of the total in the Southern Louisiana, Mississippi, and Pensacola areas combined. The Federal Trade Commission decided, first, that the relevant market was the smaller one, and second, that even if it had accepted the larger market as the relevant one, the extent of market foreclosure would violate the Clayton Act. It then ordered OKG to divest itself of Jahnke.[131]

Over time, it appears that the courts have adopted a rule of reason analysis in the vertical merger area, balancing efficiency claims against anticompetitive claims. What it amounts to is that a defendant must argue many elements, attempting to show that anticompetitive effects are not unreasonable. Among the relevant elements are market shares, the total quantitative amount of business involved, the efficiencies involved, the trend to concentration in the industry, whether or not the defendant would have entered the market without a merger, the possibility of price or supply squeezes, the barriers to entry into the industry, and the existing level of concentration in the industry. Thus, Ford Motor Company's merger of Autolite was found to be unlawful because (1) the merger foreclosed 10 percent of the spark plug market to other sellers (i.e., Ford's purchases represented 10 percent of the market for spark plugs); (2) Ford was going to start its own manufacture of spark plugs, but bought Autolite instead; (3) the automotive after-market normally replaced the same type of spark plug put in the original equipment; therefore, the acquisition of Autolite by Ford would mean that the spark plug market would

---

[128] Stern and Grabner, *op. cit.,* p. 95.
[129] *Brown Shoe Co. v. U.S.,* 370 U.S. 294, Vertical Aspects, 370 U.S. 323 (1962).
[130] Stern and Grabner, *op. cit.,* pp. 95–96.
[131] "In re OKG Corporation, et al.," *Journal of Marketing,* Vol. 35 (April 1971), pp. 69–70.

become exactly like the concentrated car market; and (4) the barriers to entry for new spark plug firms would be extremely high after the acquisition.[132]

As indicated earlier, vertical mergers creating the opportunity for forcing reciprocal buying agreements upon suppliers or buyers are also subject to attack under the Clayton Act.[133] For example, Consolidated Foods, a large processor and distributor of food products, purchased Gentry, Inc., a processor of dehydrated onion and garlic, putting Consolidated in a position to require its suppliers to obtain onion and garlic from Gentry as a condition of doing business with Consolidated. The FTC objected to such uses of reciprocity, and filed suit to force Consolidated to divest itself of Gentry. The court found that the particular practice in this situation was moving in the direction of coercion and "foreclosure" as well as possible "price squeezing," and stated, ". . . the establishment of the power to exert pressure on customers because those customers are also suppliers, when such power was acquired by merger, is in violation of Section 7 of the Clayton Act."[134]

Vertical Integration by Internal Expansion

This form of integration is limited only by the laws preventing monopoly or attempts to monopolize. A firm is ordinarily free to set up its own distribution and retailing system unless this would overconcentrate the market for its product.[135] Section 7 of the Clayton Act specifically permits a firm to set up subsidiary corporations to carry on business or extensions thereof if competition is not substantially reduced.

Problems Created by Dual Distribution

The term "dual distribution" describes a wide variety of marketing arrangements by which a manufacturer or a wholesaler reaches its final markets by employing two or more different types of channels for the same basic product. However, a dual arrangement that often creates controversy is the one that involves marketing through competing vertically integrated *and* independent outlets on either the wholesale or the retail level.[136] This kind of practice is customary in some lines of trade, such as the automotive passenger tire, paint, and petroleum in-

---

[132] *Ford Motor Co. v. U.S.,* 405 U.S. 562 (USSC, 1972).

[133] Stern and Grabner, *op. cit.,* p. 96.

[134] *Federal Trade Commission v. Consolidated Foods Corp.,* 380 U.S. 592 (1965).

[135] "Industrial Buildings Materials v. Interchemical Corp.," *Journal of Marketing,* Vol. 35 (July 1971), p. 76.

[136] Grether, *op. cit.,* p. 84. The issue of dual distribution was a "hot topic," under the Carter Administration. For the first time, the U.S. Department of Justice was prepared to bring criminal charges against dual distribution arrangements. Using the Sherman Act, the Justice Department was looking for price fixing, geographic allocations, customer restrictions, and other potential violations which dual distribution might have been enforcing. See "Justice Takes Aim at Dual Distribution," *Business Week* (July 7, 1980), pp. 24–25.

dustries. Dual distribution also takes place when a producer sells similar products under different brand names for distribution through different channels.[137] This latter kind of dual distribution comes about because of market segmentation, or because of sales to distributors under "private" labels. In all dual distribution situations, conflict among channel members is likely to be relatively high.

Dual distribution may have undesirable effects on independent distributors, and in turn on competitors, as the independent channels are replaced by integrated channels, and the competitor's markets are dried up. A second possible negative effect is the creation of a price squeeze on the independent distributors by the primary supplier. He can charge a high price to the resellers and a relatively low price as a competitor to the reseller. If alternative sources of supply are not reasonably available, the real profits of the distributor can be taken by the integrated firm. This can be called a quasi-monopoly. A committee of the United States House of Representatives has investigated dual distribution, and has recommended that firms in dual distribution should maintain sufficient price differentials to prevent substantial injury to competition.[138]

Dual distribution in itself is not illegal under the antitrust laws, but the courts have begun to draw lines between illegal and legal practices in this area. For example, in one case the court of appeals reversed a district court and held that, where a manufacturer has dominant or monopoly power over a given product, it must preserve the independent distributor of its products. According to the court of appeals, the public benefits by being able to buy from a distributor who may handle competing products. A dominant manufacturer may replace a distributor, but he may not enter into competition with him and destroy him.[139]

A highly significant Supreme Court action in the dual distribution area occurred in 1978, when the Court upheld a Maryland law that prohibits oil producers or refiners from directly operating gasoline outlets.[140] The law, which permits oil companies to own retail stations so long as they do not use their own employees or agents to run them, also forbids discrimination among dealers in the supply and price of gasoline. The Maryland law, which is analogous to legislation proposed in numerous other states, was designed to halt the trend of oil companies opening their own cut-rate, gasoline-only stations in competition with dealer-operated stations. The specific impetus for the law was dealer complaints that oil companies gave their own stations preferential treatment when gasoline was in short supply at the time of the 1973 Arab oil boycott. Because the supply situation has not improved markedly, the pressure for similar legislation is likely to continue.

In another dual distribution situation, a group of 20 independent film pro-

[137] L. E. Preston and A. E. Schramm, Jr., "Dual Distribution and Its Impact on Marketing Organization," *California Management Review,* Vol. 8 (Winter 1965), p. 61.

[138] *Ibid.,* pp. 66–67.

[139] "Industrial Building Materials Inc. v. Interchemical Corp.," *Journal of Marketing,* Vol. 35 (July 1971), p. 76.

[140] Carol H. Falk, "Justices Uphold Bar to Oil Firms' Retail Outlets," *Wall Street Journal,* June 15, 1978, p. 3; and "The Oil Majors Retreat from the Gasoline Pump," *Business Week* (August 7, 1978), pp. 50–51.

ducers filed a $180 million antitrust suit against the three major television networks, charging them with restraint of trade and monopolization of news and public affairs programming.[141] In their suit, the producers seek a court decree that would bar the networks from owning or producing their own news and public affairs programming or "magazine" programs. They want a ruling that would stipulate that these programs be produced by independents and licensed to the networks for airing. The critical issue for the court to decide will be whether, because of the networks' alleged refusal to purchase outside programs due to their vertical integration policies, they have foreclosed competition from the market and thereby monopolized an important segment of the programming industry.

SUMMARY AND CONCLUSIONS

In order to institute effective interorganizational management programs that will not conflict with antitrust enforcement agency programs, the marketing manager must become intimately familiar with the various legal constraints on the manner in which power may be employed in the marketing channel.[142] It is also imperative that he have a clear understanding of the restrictions imposed on vertical integration, should he decide that interorganization management is best accomplished through ownership rather than persuasion. The focus in this chapter has been on federal legislation that directly affects relations among commercial channel members.

Legal limitations on the use of coercive power are addressed primarily to the following distribution policy areas.

1. *Exclusive dealing.* The requirement by a seller or lessor that its customers sell or lease only its products or at least no products in direct competition with the seller's products. Such a policy is illegal if the requirement substantially lessens competition and is circumscribed by the Clayton and FTC Acts.

2. *Tying contracts.* The requirement by a seller or lessor that its customers take other products in order to obtain a product that they desire. As with exclusive dealing, such a requirement is illegal when it substantially lessens competition. The policy is directly limited by Section 3 of the Clayton Act.

3. *Full-line forcing.* The requirement by a seller that its customers carry a full line of its products if they are to carry any of them. Such a policy is a variant of tying agreements and is, therefore, subject to similar scrutiny.

4. *Resale restrictions.* The requirement by a seller that its customers can resell its products only to specified clientele. Such a policy is illegal when competition is substantially lessened.

5. *Reciprocity.* The requirement by a buyer that those from whom he purchases must also by buyers of his products. Such a policy is prohibited by Sec-

---

[141] "Producers Name 3 TV Networks in Antitrust Suit," *Wall Street Journal,* September 12, 1978, p. 5.

[142] For in-depth treatment of the relationship between power and the law, see Macaulay Stewart, *Law and the Balance of Power* (New York: Russell Sage Foundation, 1966).

tion 5 of the FTC Act when a substantial amount of commerce is involved and where reciprocity is prevalent and systematized.

6. *Price maintenance.* The requirement by a seller that a buyer can resell his products only above a specific price or at a stipulated price. Price maintenance (fair trade) laws have been nullified by the repeal of the Miller-Tydings and the McGuire Acts. Similar in intent to now obsolete state fair trade laws are unfair practices acts, which regulate the right of resellers to sell below costs or below specified margins.

7. *Price discrimination by buyers.* The requirement by a buyer that a seller offer him a price lower than that offered or available to his competitors. Such a policy is covered under the Robinson-Patman Act if it substantially lessens competition and under the FTC Act as an unfair method of competition.

8. *Refusals to deal.* The right of the seller to choose his own customers or to stop serving a given customer. This threat obviously underlies the enforcement of the above-mentioned policies. Although its use is permitted under Section 2a of the Robinson-Patman Act, it is strictly forbidden if it fosters restraint of trade or is employed so as to substantially lessen competition.

Reward power is employed in establishing the specific distribution policies listed below, each of which is limited by federal law.

1. *Exclusive territories.* The granting by a seller of a geographical monopoly to a buyer relative to the resale of his product or brand. Such a policy is circumscribed by the Sherman Act and Section 5 of the FTC Act.

2. *Incentives for resellers' employees.* The offering of special incentives (e.g., push money) by a seller to buyers' employees. While generally permitted, the providing of such incentives is limited by Federal Trade Commission Trade Practice Rules and by the Robinson-Patman Act if they can be shown to injure competition substantially.

3. *Commercial bribery.* The offering of bribes by a seller to a buyer in order to induce the buyer to purchase his products. Although such bribery is viewed as an unfair trade practice under the FTC Act, it is difficult to enforce because of the liberal use of gratuities and entertainment to promote sales. Bribery has historically been policed by the SEC and the IRS.

4. *Price discrimination.* The offering of different prices by a seller to two competing resellers on merchandise of like grade and quality. Such a policy is illegal when it substantially lessens competition, but is legal when it can be justified on the basis of cost differentials or as being adopted in "good faith" to meet competition. It is directly circumscribed by the Robinson-Patman Act.

5. *Promotional allowances and services.* The granting by a seller of payments to resellers for services rendered in connection with processing, handling, selling, or the offering for sale of any of his products sold by them. In order to be legal, such payments must be offered on proportionately equal terms to all resellers and must be used for the purpose for which they were intended (e.g., advertising allowances must be used for advertising). Again, the Robinson-

Patman Act directly limits the way in which such allowances may be employed.

6. *Functional discounts.* The granting by a seller of price reductions to resellers on the basis of their positions in the channel and the nature and scope of their marketing functions. Although no law directly deals with such discounts, they are circumscribed indirectly by the Robinson-Patman Act and the FTC Act in circumstances where they are allocated unfairly in such a way as to substantially lessen competition.

7. *Delivered pricing.* The quotation of prices by a seller so that all customers within a given area pay the same price for his product regardless of differences in shipping costs from the seller to the customers. Delivered pricing policies are viewed as restraining trade and lessening competition if their effect is similar to that of price collusion among sellers. Such pricing policies have been attacked under the Federal Trade Commission Act and under the Sherman Act.

Vertical integration via internal expansion seems to be positively sanctioned by the antitrust enforcement agencies so long as it does not lead to monopolization in restraint of trade, a Sherman Act offense. On the other hand, vertical integration by merger is much more heavily scrutinized and may be viewed rather negatively by the agencies and the courts. In the case of such mergers, Section 7 (the Celler-Kefauver Amendment) of the Clayton Act comes into play and can be used if the agencies believe that there may be a tendency for the merger, once consummated, to substantially lessen competition. Thus, the agencies can challenge such mergers in their incipiency.

The policy of vertically integrating often leads to dual distribution conflicts when sellers become competitors of some of their independently owned resellers. Although there are no additional laws beyond those mentioned earlier circumscribing the practice of dual distribution, this phenomenon has undergone considerable scrutiny in Congress, and it is not at all unlikely that legislation may be forthcoming to limit its practice, especially if it can be shown that small independent middlemen are being severely hurt by it.

With regard to most of the legal limitations referred to above, it should be noted that the antitrust enforcement agencies have been highly successful in terms of the number of court cases they have won when they have brought suit against alleged offenders. Furthermore, in order for a firm to defend itself adequately once charged with a violation, it would doubtless have to spend a large sum of money preparing its case, given the complexity of the defenses available. The costs involved may, in fact, exceed the benefits of winning. Therefore, marketing managers might spare themselves considerable difficulties by devoting energies to avoid being in conflict with the antitrust laws or with the edicts of the antitrust enforcement agencies.[143]

[143] Marketing managers would also be well advised, however, to watch current developments very carefully, because the Reagan Administration has given signals that it intends to be highly permissive with respect to vertical restrictions in distribution. See, for example, Robert E. Taylor and Stan Crock, "Reagan Team Believes Antitrust Legislation Hurts Big Business," *Wall Street Journal,* July 8, 1981, p. 1.

It should also be noted that this chapter has focused only on federal law. The states have become much more active in the antitrust arena over the past decade, and thus, the marketing manager would make a serious mistake if he were to ignore the vast outpouring of legislation regulating distribution practices in each of the states in which the products of his company are sold. Unfortunately, no comprehensive compendium of state laws regulating distribution is available. The marketing manager must, therefore, rely on a state-by-state analysis in order to uncover relevant guidelines.

DISCUSSION QUESTIONS

1. What laws affecting distribution are more likely to be protecting competitors rather than competition? Is the distinction important? Why?

2. Why might manufacturers wish to engage in resale price maintenance practices? What tactics could they employ to maintain prices, other than invoking the fair trade laws?

3. Which is preferable—intrabrand or interbrand competition? Can there be one without the other? Where do you stand on the issue of intrabrand competition—is it necessary in order for there to be viable general competition from a macroperspective? Discuss these questions in the context of resale restrictions and the granting of exclusive territories.

4. Explain the relationship between vertical "arrangements" and horizontal competition.

5. How does the Celler-Kefauver Amendment (Section 7) to the Clayton Act relate to vertical mergers? What are the key issues involved in these situations?

6. Do you believe that the Robinson-Patman Act should be stricken from the laws of this country? Debate the pros and cons of this question and come out with a position on it.

7. The president of an automobile accessory manufacturing business wants to purchase a chain of automotive retail stores. What legal issues might this raise?

8. Discuss the similarities and differences between a tying contract and the business practice of reciprocity. Do the practices, on balance, appear to be significantly different?

9. Name five uses of coercive power that would be legal in interorganization management. Name five uses of reward power that would be legal.

10. Can you think of any instances where the use of expert or referent power in interorganization management might be illegal?

11. Which conflict management strategies that were suggested in Chapter 6 might be questionable from a legal perspective? Why?

12. Opposition to dual distribution is another example of entrenched institutions trying to protect themselves against competition by resort to law. Is this true in whole or in part?

NINE

Channel Management by Channel Participants

At this point in this text, it should be clear to the reader that some form of interorganization management is necessary and desirable if a channel is to maintain or achieve satisfactory performance as a competitive entity. Thus, the discussion here focuses not on the need for management but rather on delineating the variables that impact on channel control and the institutions that are capable of assuming managerial roles within commercial channel systems. In this chapter, a framework for a channel leadership and control is presented and consideration is given to the leadership potential of manufacturers, wholesalers, retailers, and physical distribution agencies. Clearly, the question of leadership hinges, to a large degree, on the locus of power within various systems, and, therefore, considerable attention is devoted to this subject. The reader should be forewarned, however, that attempts to generalize are often misleading, since each system will, in reality, vary widely in its composition and orientation. Only through an in-depth empirical analysis is one likely to discover the best answer to the question, "Who should lead the channel?"

A FRAMEWORK FOR CHANNEL LEADERSHIP AND CONTROL

The extent to which the channel of distribution is managed by a leader(s) who can stipulate marketing policies to other channel members and therefore control their marketing decisions hinges upon a number of interrelated factors and conditions, as shown in Fig. 9–1. A discussion of these factors, their interrelationships, and related research findings follows.

FIGURE 9-1

A Framework for Channel Leadership and Control

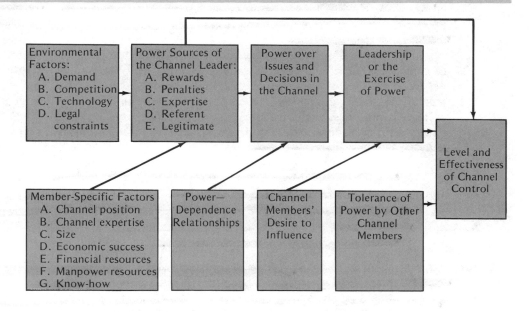

Explanation

- Power sources accrue to channel members as a result of environmental factors and/or the specific characteristics of the channel member.
- Power is issue-oriented. Power over issues and decisions is a function of sources of power accumulated by a channel member and his power-dependence relationships vis-a-vis other channel members.
- Leadership, or the exercise of power, can materialize only when a channel member has power over issue(s) and desires to exercise his power.
- The level and effectiveness of channel control achieved is a function of the quality of leadership, nature, and magnitude of power resources deployed, and the tolerance of power by other channel members.

Source: Based, in part, on Michael Etgar, "Channel Environment and Channel Leadership" *Journal of Marketing Research* (February 1977), p. 70

Channel Environment and Channel Leadership

The ability of a channel member to exercise control stems from his access to power resources. According to Etgar, the accrual of such power-generating resources to a channel leader may be the result of the specific characteristics, experience, or history of the firm and its management. Alternatively, power sources (or their absence) may reflect particular characteristics of the environmental forces impinging upon the channel (demand, technology, competition, legal constraints, etc.) and the channel member's ability to capitalize on these forces. Therefore, the power of a channel leader may reflect both the characteristics of his environment and his own characteristics.[1]

The relationships between the various environmental variables and the degree of control exercised by a channel leader over other members in a distribution channel were the foci of a cross-sectional study conducted by Etgar.[2] Four environmental variables were chosen for empirical analysis: the stage in a product's life cycle, demand uncertainty, extent of use of personal services in marketing, and intensity of interchannel competition. The results of the study indicated that the control of a channel leader is greater:

1. Under conditions of declining rather than growing demand.
2. If demand is more unstable than stable.
3. In situations where the importance of personal selling and of postsales servicing is high.
4. When interchannel competition is strong.

Jointly, these results imply that channel leaders tend to emerge in distributive channels when the environment is threatening. However, it should be noted that the environmental variables *as a group* explained only a relatively *small* amount of the variance in the control variables. Other factors, especially those reflecting the specific characteristics of the channel leader and his channel position, apparently are more important in explaining the variance.

The Use of Coercive and Noncoercive Sources of Power

A channel member has to command sources of power, e.g., reward, coercion, expertise, referent or legitimate, before he can effectively attempt to control other channel members. There are indications in the literature that, as pointed out in Chapter 6, under different circumstances the deployment of certain sources of power can be more effective than others. For example, on the basis of the research study, Etgar suggests that in conventional channels involving highly independent dealers who also hold countervailing powers, control over these dealers can best be

---

[1] Michael Etgar, "Channel Environment and Channel Leadership," *Journal of Marketing Research* (February 1977), p. 70.

[2] *Ibid.*, pp. 74–75. It should be noted that most of the channels studies reported in this chapter suffer from some serious methodological deficiencies. For a thorough critique, see Lynn W. Phillips, *The Study of Collective Behavior in Marketing: Methodological Issues in the Use of Key Informants,* unpublished Ph.D. dissertation, Northwestern University, June 1980.

accomplished through an exchange process, where agents agree to give up a certain degree of independence in return for services offered by the suppliers. Power tradeoffs were shown to be more effective in achieving control than reliance on the use of coercion and threats.[3]

Similarly, Lusch found on the basis of research investigating the effects of the use of coercive and noncoercive power that noncoercive power is directly related to the frequency of intrachannel conflict. The study suggested that coercive sources may increase the frequency of intrachannel conflict and decrease dealer satisfaction,[4] although no causal relationship or direction was established.

The Use of Economic and Noneconomic Sources of Power

In another study, Etgar evaluated the relative effectiveness of the deployment of economic- and noneconomic-based power sources in achieving channel control over different channel decisions, as shown in Table 9–1. The results of the study indicate that:

> . . . out of the array of power-generating vehicles, economic rewards and penalties have an important advantage over noneconomic ones like legitimacy, expertise, and identification. The former were found to be positively linked to channel leaders' power and therefore useful for control generation; the latter were found to be inversely related to power.[5]

Etgar further concluded that the effectiveness of a power source will be affected by: (1) the extent to which it can be applied on an individual basis and targeted to specific channel members (selectivity), and (2) the extent to which it can be related to specific performance by channel members (directedness). Expert, referent, and legitimacy power sources may be less flexible and can often be viewed as being unrelated to specific performance by channel members. For example, legal constraints may not allow a channel leader to discriminate among similar channel members and may require them to offer identical or equal rewards to all. Meanwhile, economic power sources can be applied on an individual basis and can be related to specific performance.[6] There are, however, serious side effects attending the use of reward and coercive power, such as the conflict generated. These factors were discussed in Chapter 6 and in Chapter 8.

---

[3] Michael Etgar, "Channel Domination and Countervailing Power in Distributive Channels," *Journal of Marketing Research* (August 1976), p. 260.

[4] Robert F. Lusch, "Sources of Power: Their Impact on Intrachannel Conflict," *Journal of Marketing Research* (November 1976), p. 388.

[5] Michael Etgar, "Selection of An Effective Channel Control Mix," *Journal of Marketing* (July 1978), p. 57.

[6] *Ibid.*, pp. 54–55.

**TABLE 9-1 Measures of power
and sources of power**

Measures of Power	Measures of Power Sources	
Insure Control Over	Economic	Noneconomic
1. Retail pricing 2. Choice of retail location 3. Minimum order size 4. Mix of units ordered 5. Retail advertising 6. Provision of credit to customers 7. Ability to buy from other suppliers 8. Salesmen training 9. Salesmen hiring 10. Physical layout of the store 11. Participation in professional & trade associations 12. Selling policies — territorial & customer restrictions	1. Financial assistance at start 2. Financial assistance on a current basis 3. Help in retail advertising 4. Assistance in store management 5. Provision of market information 6. Provision of sales leads 7. Promptness of delivery 8. Frequency of delivery	1. Selection of products 2. Assistance in training 3. Rate of development of new products 4. Backup by advertising 5. Level of expertise 6. Team association

Source: Michael Etgar, "Selection of An Effective Channel Control Mix," *Journal of Marketing* (July 1978), p. 56.

Basic Control Issues in the Channel

Channel control on the part of the producer focuses on a number of important issues including:

- Can suppliers use tied product arrangements?
- What kind and degree of pricing discretion exist in stipulating price throughout the channel?
- How can a supplier maintain control over his product through the channel?
- Can middlemen sell the products of two competing suppliers?
- Can suppliers impose exclusive dealing arrangements on distributors?
- Are exclusive territories and allocations valid for restricting where a product can be sold?[7]

Regardless of the tolerance levels of wholesalers and retailers to control attempts by producers over these issues, producers are constrained by legal restrictions, as discussed in greater detail in Chapter 8. It is appropriate at this juncture to indicate that since legal restrictions are based on recent court decisions, it behooves a channel leader to keep abreast of these as they may change over time.

THE CHANNEL CONTROL PROCESS. Channel members use different power bases to achieve control. The selection of specific bases depends on prior experience, organizational structure and resources, managerial preference, and goals of the channel member attempting to exercise leadership. For example, research evidence pinpoints the fact that there are

> . . . significant differences between the types of power used by manufacturers who control conventional channels and those used by manufacturers who control contractual channels. Manufacturers in conventional channels were found to rely primarily on product-related means of power (i.e., width of product selection, promptness of delivery, development and introduction of new products, frequency of delivery, and supplier's product expertise) which conform to the traditional role of manufacturers in channels while the manufacturers in contractual channels were found to rely on retail assistance (i.e., assistance in training sales people, assistance in store management and layout, and provision of sales leads) which stems from a nontraditional view of the role of the manufacturer in the distributive channel.[8]

The effectiveness of channel leadership in achieving channel coordination and control hinges to a large extent on:

[7] William L. Trombetta and Albert L. Page, "The Channel Control Issue Under Scrutiny," *Journal of Retailing* (Summer 1978), p. 43. Also see Dwight L. Gentry and Milton M. Pressley, "Distribution Channel Control: The Interests of Producer and Consumer," *University of Michigan Business Review* (September 1977), p. 27.

[8] Michael Etgar, "Differences in the Use of Manufacturer Power in Conventional and Contractual Channels," *Journal of Retailing* (Winter 1978), p. 59.

1. Whether the channel members perceive a channel of distribution system or are merely concerned with their immediate suppliers and customers. If channel members do not perceive themselves as members of a total system, it is more likely for suboptimization to be the rule and the more difficult channel coordination gets.

2. How the members perceive the control process within the channel. Differences in perceptions are indicative of a strong potential among channel members to have differing bases of action in responding to similar situations.

3. Which marketing strategy variables are perceived as controlled by each channel member. Control is not exercised over a range of issues as some type of total control. Rather, channel member power is over specific issues or marketing decision(s) variables. Unless channel members share common perceptions as to who is controlling what, random attempts to control may result in chaos and further misunderstanding instead of the desired coordination and control.[9]

An exploratory research study by Speh and Bonfield, designed to explore the above issues, reported that

1. Retail personnel do not firmly grasp the concept of a total channel system.

2. There are differences in the way owner/managers and sales personnel perceive the pattern of overall channel control. Both tend to look toward the member directly adjacent to themselves in the channel as the most important influencer.

3. There are differences in the way owner/managers and sales personnel perceive control over specific marketing variables. Additionally, within each group of respondents, different channel members were seen to have different amounts of influence over the marketing variables.

4. There is no overall retail firm viewpoint on control perception. Owner/managers and sales personnel differ in how they view influence patterns in the channel.[10]

The above findings underscore the difficulties involved in channel management and the necessity of the development of a channelwide communication and information system to broaden the base of common understanding and promote commonality of perception among channel members. Without such effort, attempts to control the channel can be mere shots in the dark. The development of channel communication and information system is the subject of Chapter 10.

The above discussion focused on variables that influence channel members' leadership and control potential. A better understanding of these variables can be achieved through an examination of key channel members.

---

[9] Thomas W. Speh and E. H. Bonfield, "The Control Process in Marketing Channels: An Exploratory Investigation," *Journal of Retailing,* pp. 14–16.

[10] *Ibid.,* p. 25.

CHANNEL MANAGEMENT BY MANUFACTURERS

Too often it is automatically assumed that the manufacturer or producer will be the channel leader and that middlemen will be the channel followers. As Mallen points out, manufacturers have not always been the channel leaders:

> The growth of mass retailers is increasingly challenging the manufacturer for channel leadership, as the manufacturer challenged the wholesaler in the early part of this century.[11]

Underlying Mallen's statement, however, is the assumption (or belief) that either manufacturers or mass retailers will manage the interorganizational relations within channels. Although this assumption has a great deal of appeal, as will be shown below, it is not necessarily valid in all cases and need not be valid in the future.

Large manufacturers can always be considered potential leaders of channels because, by definition, they have amassed a significant amount of reward and coercive power, given their size and dominance in the markets in which they compete. Their power emanates from their considerable financial resources, which enable them to maintain superior product research and development, cultivate consumer franchises through promotion, maintain continuous flows of market information, offer high margins and support to middlemen, and retain control over their products until they reach the point in the channel where ultimate consumers or industrial buyers can purchase them.

However, small manufacturers may, as Little observes, also serve as potential sources of control and direction of an interorganizational channel network.[12] Limited economic resources hamper their opportunity, but a good product offers control possibilities.[13] Such possibilities are manifestations of their legitimate, referent, and, to some extent, expert power. The manufacturer with an outstanding product may have, from the perspective of those purchasing it, a "right" to dictate how it should be sold and consumed, an image with which others seek to identify, and probably a greater assumed knowledge about the market for his product than anyone else. Furthermore, those in the position of controlling a new product that is desired by many consumers—irrespective of whether they are large or small—can elect to offer or withhold their product from various middlemen and therefore exercise reward or coercive power.

In general, the traditional viewpoint of manufacturer dominance in the marketing channel flows from an emphasis on production economies that can be achieved only by increases in sales. As sales grow, a manufacturer realizes the benefits of large-scale operations and is able to spread his overhead costs over a

[11] Bruce Mallen, "Conflict and Cooperation in Marketing Channels," in Bruce Mallen (ed.), *The Marketing Channel: A Conceptual Viewpoint* (New York: John Wiley & Sons, 1967), p. 127.

[12] Robert W. Little, "The Marketing Channel: Who Should Lead This Extracorporate Organization," *Journal of Marketing,* Vol. 34 (January 1970), p. 34.

[13] Neil H. Borden, *Acceptance of New Products by Supermarkets* (Boston, Mass.: Division of Research, Graduate School of Business Administration, Harvard University, 1968), p. 13.

large number of units. In fact, Mallen argues that the manufacturer must control the channel in order to assure himself of adequate sales volume and thereby justify the investment risk he alone must take relative to development and production.[14] In addition, it has also been asserted that as long as a manufacturer has the legal right to select the middlemen with whom he will deal, then he should be able to specify roles and allocate resources within the system that he selects for the marketing of his product.[15] Thus, the manufacturer-directed channel concept is based primarily on the belief that because the manufacturer creates and produces the product and designs the network through which it passes on its way to consumers, he is entitled, on the basis of legitimacy if nothing else, to impose his marketing policies on other channel members and to direct the activities of the channel.

Although it is the case that a number of channels are manufacturer-dominated for just these reasons (especially when the manufacturers in question have considerable economic power), the question of channel leadership is not as easy to answer as the above discussion would imply. There are many other factors that must be considered before manufacturers are deemed the logical channel managers. First, the manufacturer is not always eager to concern himself with the matters of channel management. His sole concern may simply be with the firms above and below him in the channel. After all, the manufacturer's dealings are usually with his immediate suppliers and customers and not with any of the other resellers of his products. The manufacturer may not care at all about the problems of other channel members as long as his own needs are satisfied. Similar assertions could be applied to middlemen as well. A manufacturer, it must be noted, is not unique in this respect. Furthermore, the manufacturer may prefer to concentrate his efforts on product research and development because of limited marketing management capacity or capability. As was shown in an earlier chapter, this latter factor accounts for the heavy reliance on wholesalers in a number of industrial goods industries.

Second, as pointed out later in this chapter, the manufacturer may simply not be powerful enough, in relation to other channel members, to impose his marketing policies on them. This is particularly true if the manufacturer is interested in employing large wholesaling and retailing institutions. In general, middlemen have as much, if not more, freedom of choice as the manufacturer. They do not have to handle the manufacturer's product if they do not desire to do so, especially if substitutes are readily available. Given limited display and warehouse space as well as the need for immediate cash flow on the part of many resellers, manufacturers must often curry the favor of middlemen in order to assure that adequate inventories of their products are maintained, not to say promoted. In addition, middlemen frequently can develop a great deal of local strength in their particular markets so that customers become more loyal to them than to the various brands they carry.

In summary, manufacturer dominance of the marketing channel is not an ab-

---

[14] Mallen, *op. cit.*, p. 129.
[15] Eli P. Cox, *Federal Quantity Discount Limitations and Its Possible Effects on Distribution Channel Dynamics,* (unpublished doctoral dissertation, University of Texas, 1956), p. 12.

solute certainty for several reasons. Among these are the manufacturer's own reluctance to lead and the relative strength of middlemen in the channel. On the other hand, *if* the manufacturer possesses a relatively unique product with a strong consumer demand (or can provide unique services that enhance the use of his products) and *if* middlemen are relatively weak (e.g., if they have limited options and limited resources), then it is likely that the manufacturer could assume the channel management role quite easily.

Methods of Manufacturer Dominance

Of the many methods that the manufacturer can use to dominate the channel, perhaps the most common is, as indicated above, the development of strong consumer attraction or loyalty to his products. This factor is particularly important in the case of products sold through convenience retail outlets, where little or no sales assistance in the form of salesperson interaction is provided with the sale and where the locational density of outlets is high. Porter has explained how manufacturers amass power in these situations:

> For products sold through convenience outlets, low unit price and frequent purchase of the product reduce the desire of the consumer to expend effort on search. The consumer demands a nearby retail outlet, is unwilling to shop around, and needs no sales help, thus the consumer considers the purchase relatively unimportant. Since the purchase is not perceived to be important, the consumer is willing to rely on less objective criteria (attributes) accordingly. . .
>
> In view of these characteristics, the manufacturer's prime strategy for differentiating his product is to develop a strong brand image through advertising. If the manufacturer can develop a brand image, the retailer has very little power because (1) the retailer is little able to influence the buying decision of the consumer in the store; (2) a strong manufacturer's brand image creates consumer demand for the product, which assures profits to the retailer from stocking the product and at the same time denies him the credible bargaining counter of refusing to deal in the manufacturer's goods.[16]

A manufacturer may also use coercive methods or policies, such as refusing to deal with particular middlemen or limiting sales to them unless they conform to his desires. He can also employ resale restrictions, exclusive dealing, and tying contracts. When legal, these latter methods work only when middlemen strongly desire to carry a manufacturer's product line, and therefore they must generally be coupled with significant brand identification, the availability of few comparable product sources, and the opportunity for sizeable rewards. In addition, other methods of manufacturer dominance are forward vertical integration and/or the use of contractual agreements.

If a manufacturer can amass sufficient expert, referent, and/or legitimate power, it is possible that he will be able to assume a position of channel leadership.

[16] Michael E. Porter, "Consumer Behavior, Retailer Power and Market Performance in Consumer Goods Industries," *The Review of Economics and Statistics,* Vol. 56 (November 1974), p. 423.

In such cases, he must have made a long-term commitment to gathering and disseminating crucial market information (i.e., to absorb uncertainty for other channel members) as well as to ensure continual innovation in products and managerial practice so that other channel members seek to identify with him and come to believe that he has a right to direct their activities. It should be obvious, though, that such efforts, with the exception of new-product development, are not necessarily unique to manufacturers. If channel members at other levels choose to undertake them, the mantle of leadership (or the rights of dominance) may fall to them. Thus, it should not be surprising that, in at least some industries, channel management is practiced by wholesalers and retailers and not by manufacturers, because the former have done a more effective job of accumulating a significant amount of power within their channel networks than have the manufacturers supplying them.

CHANNEL MANAGEMENT BY WHOLESALERS

The wholesaler's management role in the modern marketing channel is greatly reduced from what it once was. During the early stages of economic development in the United States (prior to the mid-1800s), the merchant wholesaler was in a natural position to assume leadership, because he was generally flanked by small manufacturers and small retailers who had little interest in delineating the various actors in their respective channel networks, let alone engaging in interorganization management. However, by the late 1800s, the country was caught up in a period of rapid industrial growth, and large manufacturers and retailers were beginning to develop. Increased pressure was placed on wholesalers. Manufacturers often felt that, given their increased production capacities, they could more effectively market their own goods without using wholesalers. And retailers, as their size increased, were more capable of buying direct from manufacturers, obtaining discounts and allowances that normally went to wholesalers.

From a historical and comparative perspective, the wholesaler has been able to remain in a dominant channel position only in those industries where the buyers and producers are small in size, large in number, relatively scattered geographically, and where manufacturers are financially weak and lack marketing expertise.[17] Except in a limited number of fields, these conditions no longer exist in the United States. The fact that wholesalers are still a significant factor in distribution, as was shown in detail in an earlier chapter, attests to their success in readjusting to their changing environment, at least to some degree.

Despite this rather gloomy description of the wholesaler's opportunity for channel leadership, it is shown below that there are certain circumstances in which wholesalers do, in fact, engage in strong and effective interorganization manage-

---

[17] Edwin H. Lewis, "Channel Management by Wholesalers," in Robert L. King (ed.), *Marketing and the New Science of Planning* (Chicago, Ill.: American Marketing Association, 1968), p. 138.

ment. However, it is equally important to observe that not every institution can or should assume a leadership position within a channel and that efficient followership is as essential to a channel's long-term viability as the existence of a centralizing force.

Methods of Wholesaler Dominance

One form of channel organization that has been particularly successful for wholesalers in strengthening their positions has been the voluntary chain, especially in the marketing of grocery products. As noted in the preceding chapter, wholesalers are clearly the leaders of these contractual vertical marketing systems. Retailers obtain the benefits of centralized buying, private brands, the identity of the group, large-scale promotion, and other management aids, while the wholesalers allocate the resources of their respective voluntary systems in such a way as to enhance their overall performance relative to competitive systems. However, there is evidence that wholesaler-sponsored voluntary chains have not been uniformly successful. According to Lewis:

> Voluntary chains in hardware have been rather loosely knit, compared with those in groceries, and the sponsoring wholesalers frequently continue to service nonaffiliated stores. Furthermore, some of these organizations also operate centrally-owned chains. In these cases, the voluntary-group stores tend to be located in communities where it would not be profitable to establish chain stores.
> The hardware trade has experienced a greater amount of inter-type competition than the grocery field. Mail order houses with their retail chains, and more recently, discount houses have been major competitors of independent hardware merchants and wholesalers. Also, the wide range of lines carried in the hardware trade places wholesalers and retailers alike in a position of competing with several types of stores.[18]

Besides voluntary groups, wholesalers have also been active in franchising. The wholesaler-franchisor clearly dominates his channel by exercising strict control over and surveillance of operations at the retail level. Also, because he is rarely tied to brand names, a wholesaler-franchisor's purchasing power combined with the maintenance of alternative sources of supply enable him to influence the marketing activities of his suppliers and thus to specify roles throughout the entire franchise system.

Another method used by wholesalers to achieve dominance has been the development of their own private brands.[19] The promotion of private brands by wholesalers appears to be successful mainly in fields where the products are relatively undifferentiated, frequently purchased, and where demand for the product has already been established. However, the fact that the products are relatively

[18] *Ibid.,* p. 139.
[19] *Ibid.,* p. 140.

undifferentiated forces the wholesaler to use price as the primary appeal in order to sell his brand. In addition, unless the wholesaler can develop a private brand in each of his key lines, the control he may enjoy will be slight. The development of private brands also requires considerable capital and substantial promotion as well as products of relatively high quality. Therefore, the use of private brands to secure dominance is obviously far from an easy task. Perhaps the most successful wholesalers, in this respect, have been those who have established multiunit operations, such as McKesson in the drug field. Multiunit organizations, like their chain counterparts in the retail field, can secure buying leverage both with respect to manufacturer's brands and private labels. When the convenience and quick delivery attributes of multiple locations are combined with a strong private label program, it is likely that wholesalers can play a leadership role in their various channels. It is important to note, however, that the majority of wholesalers actually do not attempt to gain significant control in their channels but instead seek merely to maintain the foothold that they already have. Significant means of maintaining their present positions include selective distribution, reduction of competing product lines, reduction of some service, the development of new and improved services, and improved operating procedures.[20] The development of computerized interorganizational data systems (IDS) is seen by some as a means that wholesalers could use to recapture positions of dominance in specific channels. For example:

> . . . in a channel characterized by a loose coalition of independent retailers and wholesalers, where no middleman is particularly dominant, one of the wholesalers may take the lead in developing IDS, thereby "tying" a number of the retailers to him. As a consequence, it is likely that the market will sustain a "shakeout" with a few large wholesalers emerging and displacing the smaller ones. Those wholesalers who do not establish a clientele large enough to support an IDS will probably fail. In a channel situation similar to that posed above, the member(s) best able to establish strong dependency bonds and limit alternatives for those with whom they deal will dominate, and IDS is seen as a means to this end.
>
> Positionally, wholesalers are probably best able to assume leadership in the development of IDS in such channels. It would not be feasible, from an economic perspective, to maintain a great number of parallel (communication) flows, since each data link represents a cost. In any channel with more than two retailers and more than two manufacturers, the number of links can be minimized by employing a wholesaler. With a large number of possible links, the saving can be substantial. The emergence of wholesalers as power loci is an example of technological determinism. Ipso facto their position in distribution channels bestows power on them in this regard.
>
> Interorganizational data systems portend great promise for wholesalers in another area—computer services. A wholesaler is in an ideal position to help smaller retailers with inventory management, accounts receivable, payroll, and other applications beyond the capabilities of the latter's own equipment . . . . Moreover, with the wholesaler-retailer links established, the wholesaler can readily build on the wholesaler-manufacturer links. With a large exclusive domain of retailers, a wholesaler will be able to exert power over manufacturers. By controlling inventories, maintaining receivables,

---

[20] *Ibid.*

and helping to prepare the payroll, the wholesaler will further entrench himself in the retailer's operation.[21]

In summary, it would seem that wholesalers are not qualified to lead channels in many of today's highly developed markets. The methods they use have enabled them to dominate channels in only a few industries (e.g., hardware, drugs, motion pictures, liquor, auto accessories and parts, and industrial supplies). It seems that the strength of wholesalers lies in their role as builders of assortments, integrators of product lines, and reliable sources of merchandise for their customers. In order simply to hold their present positions, they must maintain their differential advantage in performing this role. Otherwise, they will become increasingly vulnerable and will eventually be bypassed.

CHANNEL MANAGEMENT BY RETAILERS

A significant number of retailers have grown in size to a point where they rival or even dwarf many large manufacturers. It is likely, therefore, that these retailers may want to exert some control over the channels in which they are members.

The large retailer is, in reality, a multilevel merchandiser (MLM).[22] That is, such retailers have integrated the wholesaling functions within their channels and a number of them have, as was pointed out in the preceding chapter, integrated backwards to the manufacturing level.[23] Similar to large manufacturers, MLM's have considerable coercive, reward, and expert power that can be employed in an effort to control channels. As Little observes:

> They can control resources, "buy" time by utilizing staff specialists, and employ their resources in a manner to help the channel reduce conflict arising from any of the basic sources of organizational conflict. For example, (they) can employ research personnel to learn more about customers and markets and therefore reduce uncertainty and improve communications throughout the channel. They have the economic power to communicate and enforce a greater recognition of the system's common goals which are congruent with some goals in each member firm. They have the ability to enforce, through economic sanction, a reward and penalty system within the interorganizational structure. They are thus able to design and administer joint-decision efforts and responsibilities in a manner that can lead to less conflict than would likely be the case without their intervention.[24]

Large retailers have unique overlapping attributes that may give them an edge in the struggle (if there is one) for channel control. First, by virtue of their close

[21] Louis W. Stern and C. Samuel Craig, "Interorganizational Data Systems: The Computer and Distribution," *Journal of Retailing,* Vol. 47 (Summer 1971), pp. 83–85.

[22] See Little, *op. cit.,* p. 33.

[23] Wholesalers can also be characterized as multilevel merchandisers when they sponsor voluntary groups.

[24] Little, *op. cit.,* p. 34.

proximity to local markets, they have an opportunity to accumulate expert power by continuously assessing the needs of consumers within their communities. While other members of the channel could perform the same information-generating and uncertainty-absorbing tasks, they would undoubtedly have to expend more effort in data collection than large retailers, simply because of the latter's locational advantage. Second, retail-directed MLM's have ready access to large markets that manufacturers are desirous of reaching. In effect, they are gatekeepers. The larger the markets that they serve, the more important they become to manufacturers, and thus the stronger their potential leadership becomes. Third, so long as MLM's can maintain alternative sources of supply, manufacturers will tend to be more dependent on them, especially in cases where a generic demand for a given product class has been established. Dickinson has observed that it is reasonable to assume that, under most conditions, the supplier has more to gain by selling to the retailer than the retailer has to gain by buying from the supplier.

> . . . the manufacturers usually have (or think they will have) excess capacity . . ., and when they operate at full capacity it is only for a small part of the year. This is even truer of wholesalers. For manufacturers and wholesalers, then, no sale nearly always means no profit. Retailers, on the other hand, are sitting on a scarce resource whether they make a particular purchase or not. That resource is shelf space, the battle for which is so fierce that some suppliers even pay to have space reserved for them. Moreover, if a particular supplier does not sell to a particular retailer, the loss to the retailer is only relative, since there is always another supplier with other goods for a particular unit of space. In fact, it may be no loss at all, since in retailing most products can be replaced without great loss of profit by the retailer.[25]

Interestingly, channel management is not always practiced by large retailers, even though they often have the necessary power to do so. Instead, they frequently seem more concerned with obtaining specific types of concessions than they do in exerting a strong influence over aspects of new product development, promotional and inventory policies of the entire channel, and the like.[26] As a result of their self-selected task of serving wide markets, the managers of MLM's concentrate the majority of their efforts on selecting and maintaining stocks and providing and merchandising the services that accompany them.[27] Therefore, two very important functions that might be considered within the domain of channel leaders—product development and demand stimulation—are, to a large extent, left unattended by large retailers. Even though the latter are, by dint of their closeness to and contact with ultimate consumers, in the best position of any channel members to discover exactly what the preferences of consumers are, they are much too engrossed with the details of their own operations to consider performing these functions on a

---

[25] Roger A. Dickinson, *Retail Management: A Channels Approach* (Belmont, Calif.: Wadsworth Publishing Company, 1974), p. 37.

[26] Roger A. Dickinson, "Channel Management by Large Retailers," in Robert L. King, *op. cit.,* p. 128.

[27] Little, *op. cit.,* p. 35.

channelwide basis. Thus, by default, they frequently leave channel leadership to manufacturers.

Methods of Retailer Dominance

The large retailers or MLM's have at their disposal a variety of means by which they could secure dominance in their channels. As with manufacturers, the most prominent means is the building of a consumer franchise through advertising, sales promotion, and branding.[28] The strong patronage motives relative to shopping at stores like Hudson's, Filene's, Bullock's, Sears, Gold Circle, I. Magnin, and Safeway have been established as the result of the assembling of an assortment of merchandise appropriate to each store's target market, the adequate promotion of that assortment, and the provision of ancillary services. In other words, the successful retail operations have achieved positions of power within their markets through effective programming of the retailing mix elements, just as manufacturers have achieved success by combining the various elements of the marketing mix in unique ways.

In addition, many MLM's have generated private-label programs that reinforce or further the establishment of strong patronage motives. Although it is possible that some MLM's have probably overemphasized their private-label programs,[29] there can be little doubt that such programs can be a means for securing channel control.[30] However, as in wholesaling, retailers' brands are economically feasible only after widespread market acceptance of the product has been established.[31] On the other hand, if generic product acceptance exists, then the MLM not only can decide to enter the market with its own brand, but it can decide which of the leading brands it will stock and thus be able to play off one supplier against another in order to achieve various concessions.[32]

---

[28] Mallen, *op. cit.*, p. 131.

[29] A&P distributes no fewer than 1500 varieties of private label grocery, dairy, bakery, and fish products that account for 15 percent of the chain's total sales. Its overemphasis on private labels has been one of the factors responsible for its decline over the past 25 years. See "Can Jonathan Scott Save A&P?" *Business Week* (May 19, 1975), p. 133. It is also likely that both Sears and Wards will be carrying more manufacturers' brands in the future in order to increase the potency of their assortments and to provide on-the-spot price comparisons for consumers between their privately branded products and manufacturers' brands.

[30] See Louis W. Stern, "The New World of Private Brands," *California Management Review*, Vol. 8 (Spring 1966), pp. 43–50; Victor J. Cook and Thomas F. Schutte, *Brand Policy Determination* (Boston: Allyn and Bacon, 1967); Ray A Goldberg, *Agribusiness Coordination* (Boston: Division of Research, Graduate School of Business Administration, Harvard University, 1968), pp. 181–184; and Victor J. Cook, "Private Brand Mismanagement by Misconception," *Business Horizons*, Vol. 11 (December 1968), pp. 63–74. Weiss has argued that private brands will increase in importance over the next decade due to the growth of "giant" retailing and the advertising support that such retailers give to their private-label programs. See E. B. Weiss, "Advice to Suppliers: Private Labels Will Loom Large; Don't Hold Back," *Advertising Age* (August 4, 1975), p. 10.

[31] Little, *op. cit.*, p. 35.

[32] *Ibid.*, p. 36.

In the absence of the development of a strong consumer franchise for their brands on the part of manufacturers, power is clearly weighted in favor of large-scale retailers in many of the channels where they are strong participants. As pointed out above, however, these retailers are not always willing to assume leadership roles, and therefore the task of marshalling the resources of the various channel systems falls to other parties. Given the prerequisites to the application of interorganization management that were specified earlier in this book, channelwide organization may be very difficult under these circumstances, because the units with the most power are often simply not willing to take an active part in specifying roles and managing conflict. It is likely, though, because of the power that they hold, that they retain veto power over attempts to reallocate resources throughout the channel.

Small Retailers as Channel Leaders

Even though small retailers, on an individual basis, generally lack sufficient power to assume leadership roles within their channels, dominance may accrue to them, as well as to larger retailers, because of the nature of the buying process itself. For example, the retailer becomes very powerful when a manufacturer selling through convenience outlets is unable to develop a brand image through advertising. In such situations, the manufacturer's ability to achieve product differentiation in the eyes of the consumer is severely limited. The manufacturer becomes highly dependent on retailers, because many outlets must stock the product in order for the former to achieve an efficient density of market coverage.[33] Furthermore, in situations where retail outlets provide significant sales assistance and the outlets are selectively rather than densely located, it is also possible to hypothesize that retailers, irrespective of size, will be dominant. As Porter points out:

> For products sold through nonconvenience outlets, the consumer considers the purchase relatively important and is willing to expend effort in shopping and comparing products.
> For products sold through nonconvenience outlets, the retailer is influential in the consumer's purchase decision. Although advertising can lead the consumer to consider a particular brand, it will not prevent him from considering other brands and shopping several outlets. The retailer can negate the effect of advertising by changing the consumer's mind in the store.[34]

Thus, in the case of shopping goods, the retailer exerts considerable influence on the purchase decision of the consumer in several ways. First, the retailer controls or is a proxy for some of the attributes that the consumer may desire. The reputation, image, physical amenities, and attendant services (e.g., credit, billing, delivery, warranty, repair) of a retail store can sway consumer purchase decisions. Second, the retailer can influence the sale of products sold through nonconvenience outlets

---

[33] Porter, *op. cit.*, p. 423.
[34] *Ibid.*, p. 424.

through the provision of information via a selling presentation, advice solicited by the consumer, the perceived expertise of the salesperson with respect to the product, or any combination of all of these.[35] In fact, as the retailer's influence on product differentiation increases, the bargaining power of the retail stage vis-a-vis the manufacturer or the wholesale supplier increases.

Collectively, small retailers have been known to exert considerable pressure on channel activities. They have been instrumental in gaining particularistic legislation on the local, state, and national levels that has had the effect of restraining competition or of providing impediments to change.[36] They have colluded to prevent marketing activities that they have perceived to be threatening to their survival. Through their legislative and collusive actions, they have sometimes been able to influence marketing strategy throughout the channel. Thus, there exist state and local restrictions on entry, licensing requirements, antipeddler and anti-itinerant vendor ordinances, chain store taxes, evening and Sunday closing laws, advertising restrictions (particularly price-posting regulations), as well as a whole host of other small retailer-inspired and -promoted laws that are designed to soften or curb competitive impacts.[37] Clearly, this form of negative leadership is not laudatory. It is fortunate that the effect of these impediments has been short-lived, in many situations, and that they have been unable to effectively restrain many innovations in distribution.

On the other hand, small retailers have attempted to exert positive channel leadership through the development of retailer-sponsored cooperatives. The retailer cooperative is an obvious effort to overcome the size and thus the buying disadvantages faced by individual small retailers. However, as indicated in the preceding chapter, retailer-sponsored cooperatives face some very serious problems. Within them, power is diffused, and therefore, there is considerable doubt whether they can provide the tightly knit control needed to compete successfully with corporate and voluntary chains. As Hollander points out,

> Membership turnover can be high. Coordination is difficult. Investment in manufacturing or processing facilities may be hazardous and inadvisable, since acceptance of the output may not be assured. Financing problems may inhibit growth, since the members may have little interest in financing newcomers, and particularly in helping potential competitors. Risk allocation difficulties tend to deter experimentation. Personality conflicts can exacerbate many of the cooperative's problems. None of these difficulties is entirely absent from the corporate chain sector, but quite obviously, their impact is substantially reduced when ownership, risk, and control are centralized.[38]

Evidence of the need for greater control is found in the fact that a significant number of the member supermarkets in the successful Wakefern-Shop Rite retail

[35] *Ibid.,* pp. 420–421.

[36] Stanley C. Hollander, *Restraints upon Retail Competition* (East Lansing, Mich.: Bureau of Business and Economic Research, Michigan State University); and Stanley C. Hollander, "Channel Management by Small Retailers," in Robert L. King (ed.), *op. cit.,* pp. 132–134.

[37] Hollander, "Channel Management by Small Retailers," *op. cit.,* p. 133.

[38] *Ibid.,* p. 135.

food cooperative located in New Jersey are owned by internal corporate chains, for example.

| CHANNEL MANAGEMENT BY PHYSICAL DISTRIBUTION AGENCIES | Although not normally considered as potential managers of channel relations, common carriers could possibly assume such roles if they were to utilize more effectively the power bases at their disposal. In fact, logistical institutions of all types occupy unique positions in this respect, because |

they have the advantage of being *neutral* relative to many of the channel policies and activities of major concern to manufacturers, wholesalers, and retailers.[39] While the latter channel members may have difficulty in looking beyond their immediate suppliers and customers, logistical institutions can take a broader perspective of channel problems.

Consideration of common carriers as channel leaders serves to focus attention on a salient characteristic of all channel relations. That is, leadership is possible with regard to each of the marketing flows taken separately or to all of the flows. Thus, it is clear that common carriers can assume an interorganizational management stance relative to the flow of physical possession, but their influence relative to the remaining flows is likely to be minimal. In other words, the scope of a common carrier's power is limited to those activities with which it is directly concerned.

Figure 9–2 illustrates the position occupied by common carriers within a generalized channel arrangement and some of the power bases that are available to them.[40] Some specific examples of the reward and expert power bases that could be, and sometimes are, used by common carriers have been enumerated by Beier.[41] These include:

- Reductions in rates charged to shippers. (However, because of competitive reaction, such reductions are likely to have limited impact over the long run.
- Reductions in the overall cost of transportation by eliminating loss and damage claims, special schedules, and/or minimum weight requirements.
- Providing special arrangements such as rent-a-train services whereby carriers rent specialized equipment designed to serve particular clients. The provision of specialized equipment increases the dependence of shippers on carriers.

[39] J. L. Heskett, "Costing and Coordinating External and Internal Logistics Activities," in Donald J. Bowersox, Bernard J. LaLonde, and Edward W. Smykay (eds.), *Readings in Physical Distribution Management* (New York: The Macmillan Company, 1969), pp. 81–83.

[40] For an extended example, see J. L. Heskett, "Interorganizational Problem Solving in a Channel of Distribution," in Matthew Tuite, Roger Chisholm, and Michael Radnor (eds.) *Interorganizational Decision Making* (Chicago: Aldine Publishing Co., 1972), pp. 152–161. See also J. L. Heskett and Ronald H. Ballou, "Logistical Planning in Inter-Organization Systems," in M. P. Hottenstein and R. W. Millman (eds.), *Research Toward the Development of Management Thought,* Papers and Proceedings of the 26th Annual Meeting of the Academy of Management, San Francisco, December 27–29, 1966, pp. 124–136.

[41] Frederick J. Beier, "The Role of the Common Carrier in the Channel of Distribution," *Transportation Journal,* Vol. 9 (Winter 1969), pp. 12–21.

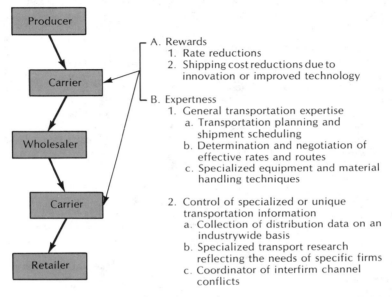

A. Rewards
 1. Rate reductions
 2. Shipping cost reductions due to innovation or improved technology

B. Expertness
 1. General transportation expertise
  a. Transportation planning and shipment scheduling
  b. Determination and negotiation of effective rates and routes
  c. Specialized equipment and material handling techniques
 2. Control of specialized or unique transportation information
  a. Collection of distribution data on an industrywide basis
  b. Specialized transport research reflecting the needs of specific firms
  c. Coordinator of interfirm channel conflicts

Source: Frederick J. Beier, "The Role of the Common Carrier in the Channel of Distribution," *Transportation Journal,* Vol. 9 (Winter 1969), p. 19.

- Providing consulting services to shippers whereby staff specialists assigned to a particular industry advise shippers in that industry about rates, routing, and LTL and LCL loading-in-transit privileges. Traditionally, carriers have acted as advisors relative to plant locations in their operating areas.
- Making available part of a carrier's large computing facilities in order to institute a channelwide communication system relative to information about shipments. (Carriers are in a position to draw sample data with regard to product movements from a broader population than is generally available to individual shippers. Thus, they could operate as uncertainty absorbers within the channel).
- Providing information with regard to the transportation and material-handling requirements of other channel members. (Carriers can thereby suggest compatible handling systems that would lead to more efficient coordination of the physical and information interface between channel members).

Similarly, it is suggested that the distribution center may play an important role in channel management if it deploys its expertise and informational resource bases.

> The distribution center manager. . . is familiar with marketing-related objectives and patterns of distribution not only of his customers, but also of his customers'

customers and of the carriers and other institutions in the distribution chain. He knows their needs, wants, aspirations, and operations. As he fulfills these services, the user becomes more dependent upon him and he becomes more powerful.[42]

At this juncture it should be noted that channel control is a dynamic process. The following anecdote is illustrative of power dynamics in the grocery industry:

> Manufacturers once held the upper hand because of the tremendous advertising and promotion budgets they deployed to "pull" consumers into stores. Supermarkets deferred to suppliers' merchandising suggestions and relied on their data to determine what products to stock. "There was a job that needed to be done and manufacturers stepped into the breach," says Willard Bishop, a grocery consultant.
>
> But retailers aren't willing to continue as silent conduits between manufacturers and consumers. "Just spending an enormous amount of money on TV doesn't cut the ice anymore," says David Nichol, president of Loblaw's Canadian supermarkets. Adds Len Daykin, director of merchandising for the Foote, Cone & Belding advertising agency, "In a battle between giants like Procter & Gamble and Safeway, five years ago, P&G would have prevailed. Now Safeway can call the tune."
>
> Even small retailers are more assertive. Genuardi's, a Pennsylvania chain of 14 stores, recently warned its suppliers that their products would be dropped if they didn't bear clear universal product code symbols.
>
> Retailers are also resisting the glut of products competing for scarce shelf space. Sloan's supermarkets in New York says it has a choice of 22 laundry soaps, each in six sizes ranging from seven ounces to 211 ounces. Of that field of 132, Sloan's carries 51. When recently offered four sizes of Pert, a new Procter & Gamble shampoo, the chain took two.[43]

Therefore, there are no guarantees that those who control the marketing channel today will continue in command tomorrow. There is no substitute for an analysis of the dynamics of power and its structure in an industry to reach plausible conclusions as to who controls the marketing channel.

WHO SHOULD LEAD THE CHANNEL?

Although the question as to which institution or agency should lead the channel has been debated in the literature for many years and by a variety of scholars,[44] there exists no single satisfactory answer. The fact is that the answer

---

[42] James A. Constantin, Jack J. Kasulis, and Robert F. Lusch, "The Distribution Center: A Potential Locus of Power," in Robert J. House and James F. Robeson (eds.), *Interfaces: Logistics, Marketing and Production,* proceedings of the Sixth Annual Transportation and Logistics Educators Conference (Columbus, Ohio: Transportation and Logistics Research Fund, The Ohio State University and NCDPM, 1976), p. 42.

[43] "Food Chains Pressure Suppliers, Altering Industry Power Balance," *Wall Street Journal,* August 21, 1980, p. 25.

[44] For a variety of different arguments and perspectives, see the following: David Craig and Werner Gabler, "The Competitive Struggle for Market Control," *The Annals of the American Academy of Political and Social Science* (May 1940), pp. 84 ff. [reprinted in Howard J. Westing (ed.), *Readings in Marketing* (Englewood Cliffs, N.J.: Prentice-Hall, Inc. 1953), pp. 84–107]; John K. Galbraith, *American Capitalism,* rev. ed. (Boston: Houghton Mifflin Co., 1956), pp. 110–114, 117–123; Bruce Mallen, *op. cit.,* pp. 127–134; Robert W. Little, *op. cit.,* pp. 31–38; Richard B. Heflebower, "Mass

demands empirical evidence from *specific* settings. It is necessary to look closely at the issues involved in each industrial setting and to define the scope of power of each commercial channel member with respect to each of the marketing flows. It may even be necessary to break the flows down into component parts in order to perform an adequate analysis. For example, the flow of physical possession incorporates both transportation and storage of merchandise. One channel member may be able to exert more influence with regard to the first component, while another may have more power with respect to the second. Clearly, the analysis—based on empirical findings—must account for the tolerance levels in the channel for control by each of the members as well as the payoffs that accrue to each as a result of control.[45] Anecdotal evidence can be accumulated that leads an individual to suspect that one particular institution is the most logical leader in a particular situation, but such evidence rarely permits the generation of counter-intuitive findings. In such an important area as this—where concern is over the allocation of resources throughout an entire distributive system—opinions and hearsay are not satisfactory in making the appropriate selection. Furthermore, allowance must be made for the influence of elements in a commercial channel's task environment (e.g., consumers and government) in determining or constraining the leadership question. With the emergence of consumerism as a vital force in marketing relations and with the increased interest in distribution matters on the part of government, it would be foolhardy to think that the decision on leadership (or even the use of interorganization management techniques generally) will be free from scrutiny or limitations. It should, however, be clear from the discussion in this chapter that each commercial channel member has at least the potential for leadership with regard to one or more of the marketing flows, because each has amassed or is capable of amassing power of one form or another relative to other channel members. The ultimate answer as to who should lead must, however, be left to an empirical analysis of power and the relevant payoffs from its use on a case-by-case basis.

A Methodology for Determining the Locus of Channel Power

Some tentative steps have been taken towards developing a methodology that permits a determination of the locus of power within specific marketing channels. The approach reported below was first employed by the authors of this text[46] and

---

Distribution: A Phase of Bilateral Oligopoly or of Competition?'' *American Economic Review,* Vol. 47 (May 1957), pp. 274–285; Valentine F. Ridgway, ''Administration of Manufacturer-Dealer Systems,'' *Administrative Science Quarterly,* Vol. 1 (March 1957), pp. 464–483; and Louis P. Bucklin, ''A Theory of Channel Control,'' *Journal of Marketing,* Vol. 37 (January 1973), pp. 39–47. These authors present various anecdotal evidence and/or analytical models for arriving at particular choices.

[45] Adel I. El-Ansary and Robert A. Robicheaux, ''A Theory of Channel Control: Revisited,'' *Journal of Marketing,* Vol. 38 (January 1974), pp. 4–7.

[46] Adel I. El-Ansary and Louis W. Stern, ''Power Measurement in the Distribution Channel,'' *Journal of Marketing Research,* Vol. 9 (February 1972), pp. 47–52.

has been subsequently applied, in modified forms, by Hunt and Nevin,[47] by Etgar, by Wilkinson, and by Lusch.[48]

For purposes of research on isolating potential or actual leaders of channels, the power of a channel member can be operationally defined as the member's ability to control the decision variables in the marketing strategy of another member in a given channel at a different level of distribution. For this control to qualify as a power, it should be different from the influenced member's original level of control over his own marketing strategy.

As indicated in Chapter 6, power can be viewed as a function of dependence. The power of a wholesaler over a retailer, for example, is related to the dependence of the retailer on the wholesaler. In addition, the magnitude of a power source can be employed as an index of influence. For example, a manufacturer who advertises directly to consumers maintains an influence base or power source relative to retailers who distribute his brand. A measure of the magnitude of advertising and the resulting consumer preference might be used as an index of the manufacturer's power over his retailers. Thus, the power of any given channel member is a function of the sources of power available to him at any given time. As explained previously, the sources or bases of power can be classified as reward, coercive, expert, referent, and legitimate. Based on this reasoning, a fundamental model underlying research into power relationships within a given marketing channel may be depicted by the equations listed in Table 9–2.

Measures of power, dependence, and sources of power can be developed from gauging the self-perceptions of various channel members and attributions about them by other channel members.[49] A questionnaire can be constructed that probes self-perceptions and attributions of each channel member with respect to (1) control over marketing strategy variables, (2) the relative importance of each of the various marketing strategy variables, (3) the extent of dependency, and (4) sources of power.[50] For example, the marketing strategy variables can relate to such elements as inventory policy, order size, pricing, sales promotion, cooperative advertising, distribution policies (e.g., selective versus intensive), delivery, credit, quality of installation work, salesmen's training, sales meetings, service schools, and participation in the activities of professional associations. A raw power score can be ob-

[47] Shelby D. Hunt and John R. Nevin, "Power in a Channel of Distribution: Sources and Consequences," *Journal of Marketing Research,* Vol. 11 (May 1974), pp. 186–193.

[48] Michael Etgar, *An Empirical Analysis of the Motivations for the Development of Centrally Coordinated Vertical Marketing Systems: The Case of the Property and Casualty Insurance Company,* an unpublished Ph.D. dissertation, University of California at Berkeley, 1974. See also Ian Wilkinson, "Power in Distribution Channels," Cranfield [England] Research Papers in Marketing and Logistics, Session 1973–1974; and Lusch, *op. cit.*

[49] Support for such an approach can be found in El-Ansary and Stern, *op. cit.,* p. 48. For an extension of the self-perception, attribution approach, see Fuat A. Firat, Alice M. Tybout, and Louis W. Stern, "A Perspective on Conflict and Power in Distribution," in Ronald C. Curhan (ed.), *1974 Combined Proceedings* (Chicago, Ill.: American Marketing Association, 1975), pp. 436–438.

[50] A five-point Likert-type scale can be used as a measuring tool. The five points of the scale could be "nonexistent or of no importance," "of insignificant importance," "of some importance," "of significant importance," and "of very significant importance." See El-Ansary and Stern, *op. cit.,* p. 49.

TABLE 9–2   A model of power relationships in marketing channels[a]

Power of channel member i over member j	Power of channel member i over all other members, n
(1) $P_{ij} = C_{ij}$	$P_i = \sum_{j=1}^{n} C_{ij}$
(2) $P_{ij} = f(D_{ij})$	$P_i = f\left(\sum_{j=1}^{n} D_{ij}\right)$
$\quad P_{ij} = \alpha D_{ij}$	$P_i = \sum_{j=1}^{n} \alpha D_{ij}$
(3) $P_{ij} = f(S_{ij})$	$P_i = f\left(\sum_{j=1}^{n} S_{ij}\right)$
$\quad P_{ij} = \beta S_{ij}$	$P_i = \sum_{j=1}^{n} \beta S_{ij}$
(4) $P_{ij} = f(D_{ij}, S_{ij})$	$P_i = f\left(\sum_{j=1}^{n} D_{ij}, \sum_{j=1}^{n} S_{ij}\right)$
$\quad P_{ij} = \alpha D_{ij} + \beta S_{ij}$	$P_i = \sum_{j=1}^{n} \alpha D_{ij} + \sum_{j=1}^{n} \beta S_{ij}$

where:

P_{ij} = power of channel member i over member j.

C_{ij} = control of i over the decision variables in the marketing strategy of j.

P_i = power of i over all other members with whom i is vertically linked.

D_{ij} = dependence of i on j.

α = direction coefficient of dependence[b]: if $D_{ij} > 0, \alpha = -1$; if $D_{ij} < 0, \alpha = +1$.

S_{ij} = sources of power held by i relative to j.

β = direction coefficient of power sources: if $S_{ij} > 0, \beta = +1$; if $S_{ij} < 0, \beta = -1$.

[a]Although the model is stated in static terms, some implicit notion of history (past relations) should be read into it.

[b]D_{ij} is undefined at zero; if $D_{ij} = 0$, no channel relationship exists.

Source: Adel I. El-Ansary and Louis W. Stern, "Power Measurement in the Distribution Channel," *Journal of Marketing Research,* Vol. 9 (February 1972), p. 48.

tained by summing the power scores of the strategy variables for each channel member. Next, each channel member can be asked to specify the relative importance of each marketing strategy variable in his total marketing strategy. A weighted power score can be generated by multiplying the basic information on control over marketing strategy variables (the raw power score) by the weight of relative importance given to each variable and then summing the weighted power scores for each channel member.

Dependency can be viewed as a function of (1) the percentage of a channel member's business which he contracts with another member and the size of the contribution which that business makes to his profits; (2) the commitment of a channel member to another member in terms of the relative importance of the latter's marketing policies to him; and (3) the difficulty in effort and cost faced by a channel member in attempting to replace another member as a source of supply or as a customer. A dependence score can be obtained by summing the scores of the various dependency issues for each member.

Finally, sources of power could include such factors as customer preference, completeness of line, financial and business advice, sharing advertising expenditures, product sales meetings, service schools, salesmen's training, image and reputation in the community, prompt delivery and service, access to market information, selective distribution, promotion programs, large lot buying, ability to buy directly, ability to control customer's brand choice, middleman brand support, and competitive pricing. A sources-of-power score can then be obtained by summing the scores of the various sources for each channel member.

In sum, for every channel member four basic scores can be obtained: (1) a (raw) power score, (2) a weighted power score, (3) a dependence score, and (4) a sources-of-power score. If a power structure exists within a channel, there should be a significant, *positive* correlation between self-perceptions of power (i.e., control over marketing strategy variables) and attributions of power. Likewise, the means of perceptions and attributions should be highly similar. There should also be a significant, *negative* correlation between a channel member's self-perceived power over another member and the latter's perception of the former's dependence on him as well as between attributed power and self-perceived dependence. Finally, if a well-defined power structure exists, there should be a significant positive relationship between a channel member's self-perceived power over another channel member and the sources of power attributed to the former by the latter. In addition, a similar relationship should be found between the power that one member attributes to another and the sources of power that the latter perceives himself as possessing.

SUMMARY AND CONCLUSIONS

This chapter has focused on factors influencing the leadership and control processes in marketing channels and the potential of manufacturers, wholesalers, retailers, and physical distribution agencies to assume the role of channel managers or leaders. In coming to grips with this issue, a crucial consideration is the amount and kinds of power available to each institution.

The potential channel management role of manufacturers appears to hinge on the strength of their products, brands, and services as viewed by ultimate consumers, both on the household and industrial levels. In other words, their power relative to other channel members is derived primarily from the final marketplace. The traditional manufacturer-directed channel concept is based on the belief that because the manufacturer creates and produces the product and designs the network through which it passes on its way to consumers, he is entitled to impose his marketing policies on other channel members and to direct the activities of the channel.

From a historical perspective, wholesalers have been able to remain in dominant positions only in those industries where the buyers and producers are small in size, large in number, relatively scattered geographically, and where manufacturers are financially weak and lack marketing expertise. Wholesalers have, however, been particularly successful in strengthening their positions by organizing voluntary groups and franchising systems as well as by developing private label programs and interorganizational data systems.

The potential of large (multilevel) retailers as channel leaders appears to stem from their close physical proximity to consumers, their roles as gatekeepers relative to market access, and their maintenance of alternative sources of supply. Their continuous control over display space within their outlets, the development of strong patronage motives, and their use of private-label programs have enhanced their power considerably.

Small retailers have, collectively, been able to assume leadership in the channel—but primarily from a negative perspective. Through collusion, they have been able to secure particularistic legislation, which has restrained competition and impeded change. The most positive step they have taken has been the formation of cooperatives.

Common carriers and distribution centers could possibly assume a greater role in channel leadership if they were to utilize more effectively the reward and expert and informational power at their disposal. Their influence would, however, generally be limited to activities involved in the flow of physical possession, even if they were to become more aggressive within the channels in which they participate.

The question as to who should lead the channel cannot be answered without an in-depth empirical analysis of channels on a case-by-case basis. Because each and every institution has at least some power relative to the various marketing flows, leadership may take the form of control over or management of only one or a few of the flows, depending of course on the scope of power enjoyed by the various institutions comprising a given system. Furthermore, leadership will clearly be constrained by consumerism issues and by the increased interest of antitrust enforcement and regulatory agencies (particularly the Consumer Protection Agency and the Federal Trade Commission) in distribution practices.

Power relationships within the channel can be measured by gauging the perceptions and attributions of individual channel members through the use of survey research techniques. Such measurements might focus on the relationship between perceptions and attributions of power (i.e., control over marketing strategy variables), the relationship between power and dependence, and the relationship between power and sources of power.

If channel management is going to be instituted, it will be necessary for appropriate information and communication systems to be established. Such systems are particularly crucial if a variety of institutions take a role in channel leadership. The dovetailing of decision-making must form an essential part of the overall channel management job; otherwise, suboptimization of the marketing flows can be expected. The marketing flows, taken as a whole, comprise a system; they must be combined in such a way as to permit strong impact of the channel on its environment. This combination can only be achieved through the sharing of relevant data among channel members. Therefore, the next chapter is concerned with the development of effective communication within channels.

DISCUSSION QUESTIONS

1. How do you account for the persistence and survival of some distribution channels without a channel leader, captain, or manager? Does a channel have to have a leader in order to survive over the long term?

2. What are the consequences of increased "scrambled merchandising" for power and leadership in the channel? How will such product line diversification on the retail level affect the positions of manufacturers, wholesalers, and retailers relative to their potential for channel leadership?

3. If, within the channels in which it participates, a major department store chain is the most powerful member, what might the chain do to gain increased coordination and cooperation throughout each of the channels serving it?

4. It has been stated by one writer, "The more a retailer can concentrate his purchasing, the more dominating he can become; the more he spreads his purchasing, the more dominated he becomes." Do you agree?

5. Do private brands come into being as a result of a conflict situation between manufacturers and middlemen? Describe the issues and factors surrounding a decision to market private brands on the part of both manufacturers and middlemen.

6. In those cases where the absolute number of retail buyers for a manufacturing industry's product are small and the size of these retailers is large, it has been argued that retailer power flows conventionally from buyer concentration. Explain what this statement means, from the perspective of power, dependence, and sources of power.

7. An important structural characteristic of retailing is the presence or absence of multiple forms of retailers selling a given industry's product (e.g., drugstores and supermarkets). Explain the consequences of this structural characteristic for channel management.

8. It has been stated that "as the retail outlet (establishment) becomes more specialized and carries fewer product categories, its power to influence the sale will generally increase." Give examples that support this statement. Then give examples that would support the reverse of this statement.

9. In general, which type of institution—manufacturer, wholesaler, or retailer—should lead the channel of distribution for the following products:

Toys
Automobiles
Stainless steel
Health and beauty aids

What assumptions did you have to make in order to arrive at an answer for each product category? What were the relevant variables you considered in each case?

10.   In view of the emphasis on consumerism issues, do you think that the consumer will eventually be the channel leader in many consumer goods industries? If yes, which industries? How will the leadership be made manifest?

TEN

Channel Communications and Information Systems

Regardless of whether particular institutions or agencies assume leadership roles with respect to specific marketing flows within distribution channels, communication in one form or another provides the means by which the work of channels is coordinated. Poor or ineffective communications can prove to be a major roadblock to coordinative efforts. As such, vigilance should be exercised to ensure that problems of this nature do not develop. Nevertheless, omission and distortion of messages are, in reality, frequent occurrences within channels. In fact, inadequate communication or miscommunication is often not only a major stimulator but also an outcome of deep-rooted and dysfunctional channel conflict.

In this chapter, attention is focused directly on problems arising from the lack of effective communication within channels. The difficulty in securing adequate communication in channels generally centers around a wide variety of structural and activity issues. Therefore, we shall deal with problems arising because of the length of channels as well as with difficulties associated with transportation modes and storage facilities, determining inventory levels, promotional programs, product assortments, and pricing practices. Moreover, throughout our discussion, we suggest possible solutions to these problems, which should permit a significant start toward the development of sound interorganizational information systems.

RUDIMENTS OF CHANNEL INFORMATION SYSTEMS

At the outset, it should be understood that the successful development and operation of a channel communication system is frequently limited by the legality, availability, cost, and confidentiality of the information flow. Furthermore, any attempt to achieve a distortion-free communication system is doomed to failure because manufacturing, wholesaling, retailing, and logistical firms are obviously comprised

428

of individual human beings who will always perceive situations in different ways. Nevertheless, construction of even a moderately successful system seems mandatory, because, as Gross points out,

> Cross-purpose activities, redundant operations, blunted impact of uncoordinated promotional activities, (reseller) resentment when not invited to participate in available promotional allowances and aids, unbalanced inventories, and other difficulties that are the outcome of poor communication procedures are burdensome and expensive.[1]

FIGURE 10-1

Direct and Indirect Communications Media Available to Merchandise Sources and Resellers

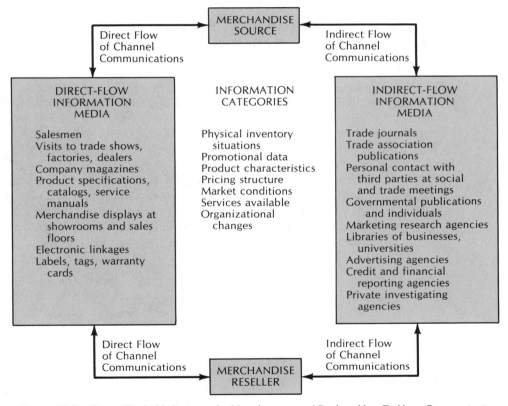

Source: Walter Gross, "Profitable Listening for Manufacturers and Dealers: How To Use a Communication System," in *Marketing Channels: A Systems Viewpoint*, eds. William G. Moller, Jr. and David L. Wilemon (Homewood, Ill.: Richard D. Irwin, Inc., 1971), p. 346.

[1] Walter Gross, "Profitable Listening for Manufacturers and Dealers: How to Use a Communication System," in William G. Moller, Jr., and David L. Wilemon (eds.), *Marketing Channels: A Systems Viewpoint* (Homewood, Ill.: Richard D. Irwin, 1971), p. 351.

To facilitate the development of information relative to all marketing flows, the variety of direct and indirect media listed in Fig. 10–1 is available to merchandise sources (factories and/or wholesalers) and resellers (wholesalers and/or retailers). However, as Gross has observed,

> The adequacy of the vertical channel communication systems that have evolved within various firms and industries varies considerably. Two reasons appear fundamentally to account for a weak system: (1) the profitability potential of providing certain data to associated firms in the channel may not have been analyzed, or (2) if the profitability is recognized, a *standard* procedure for such data communication has not been established.[2]

The development of an effective information system will probably result in a higher degree of loyalty and commitment on the part of the channel members to a particular channel arrangement. Furthermore, the firm that is instrumental in originating and maintaining the system may acquire more power within the channel as the other members become more dependent on the data transmitted. Hence, there is more than one incentive for firms to play an active role in formulation and maintenance of a channel communications system.

Before efforts to develop an interorganizational information system take place, it is necessary that individual channel members develop smooth-functioning intraorganizational systems. For most firms this means the connection of several internal systems such as a merchandise information system, a system for financial management, credit management, and other management functions. Emphasis is placed on the merchandise or inventory information system because it is the component over which most channel interaction takes place.

A comprehensive treatment of channel information system development is more meaningful when undertaken in the context of the communication problems with which the information system is designed to deal. These problems are related to the length of the channels, transportation and storage flows, inventory management, promotional programs, product assortments, and pricing practices.

THE LENGTH OF CHANNELS

Clearly, the longer a channel—the more middlemen involved in the distribution of a given product, brand, or service—the more likelihood there is of omission and distortion of message contents taking place, all other things being equal. The number of links in a communication network is inversely related to accurate reception.[3] Perceptual and secrecy problems are compounded as more and more channel members become involved in the uncertainty absorption process. Consider, for example, the case of a pharmacist for a large public hospital who complained to the president of a drug wholesaling firm that manufacturers did not

[2] Gross, *op. cit.,* p. 352.

[3] See, for example, Alex Bavelas, "Communication Patterns in Task-oriented Groups," *Journal of the Acoustical Society of America,* Vol. 22 (1950), pp. 725–730; and Harold Guetzkow and Herbert Simon, "The Impact of Certain Communication Nets upon Organization and Performance in Task-oriented Groups," *Management Science,* Vol. 1 (April–July 1955), pp. 233–250.

keep him well informed about their new products. He wanted to know why he was not detailed promptly on new ethicals (prescription drugs) as they were developed and why the manufacturers did not provide him with printed materials. As explained by Cox, Schutte, and Few:

> The wholesaler agreed that the manufacturers were "falling down on their job," but when he interviewed detail men for several manufacturers, he found that they, too, were frustrated. They had more than adequate information to give out—written and oral. To them, the pharmacist himself was the villain. They were fed up with waiting as much as four hours to conduct a detail call. "That pharmacist thinks he is God," one salesman said. "He couldn't care less about how long he makes the salesman wait." The wholesaler took the initiative, told the pharmacist what the real problem was, and made appointments for him to see the detail men at given hours.
>
> But note that it is the manufacturer's communication line that has broken down, not the wholesaler's. The manufacturer has depended upon detail men to tell the potential pharmacist buyer about his products, which could then be sold and delivered by wholesalers to the buyer. The wholesaler's responsibility in communication was only to tell prospective buyers that they had the manufacturer's products available. Obviously, the manufacturer's feedback was inadequate in that it took a wholesaler to straighten out the manufacturer's communication problem.[4]

Thus, as Cox, Schutte, and Few imply, the longer the channel, the more highly developed the feedback system available to each channel member and especially to the channel leader must be. Furthermore, in such situations, there is obviously a need for a mechanism permitting the bypassing of messages. That is, a working information system should be established that permits the directly affected and conflicting parties to avoid one or more links in the normal communication network so that such a bottleneck situation can be eliminated, especially during the period of crisis within the system.[5]

Reliance on indirect communication links frequently multiplies chances for distortion.[6] This problem is exemplified by the case of a leading manufacturer of electronic products who had received *indirect* complaints about his order-filling service. From these complaints, certain key executives concluded that most of the

---

[4] Reavis Cox, Thomas F. Schutte, and Kendrick S. Few, "Towards the Measurement of Trade Channel Perception," in Fred C. Allvine (ed.), *Combined Proceedings 1971 Spring and Fall Conferences* (Chicago: American Marketing Association, 1972), pp. 190–191.

[5] Discussion of the various communication noise-reduction mechanisms throughout this chapter and in Chapter 6 is largely based on John R. Grabner, Jr., and L. J. Rosenberg, "Communication in Distribution Channel Systems," in Louis W. Stern (ed.), *Distribution Channels: Behavioral Dimensions* (Boston, Mass.: Houghton Mifflin Co., 1969), pp. 238–249.

[6] Technological advances are significant in reducing the need for indirect communication. The development of electronic funds transfer systems (EFTS) in the banking industry is an example of the substitution of direct for indirect communication links. Banks and savings and loan associations are placing electronic terminals in supermarkets, making it possible for customers to pay for their groceries via a transfer of funds from their accounts to that of the store. In these situations, the supermarket becomes the financial and operational medium between the customer and the bank. The supermarket does not, however, become a financial institution, according to some, because the terminal is only a means of communication; the actual transfer of funds takes place inside the bank's computer, which is, of course, located inside the bank and not at the supermarket. The consequences of such a development could be profound, especially for the banking industry. See "Bank Cards Take Over the Country," *Business Week* (August 4, 1975), pp. 44–54. See also Robert M. Lilienfeld and Diane Wolgemuth, *Consumer Reactions Toward an Electronic Funds Transfer System in Supermarkets* (Chicago: Super Market Institute, Inc., 1975).

customers were dissatisfied because of the length of time elapsing between the sending of an order and the receipt of goods. The executives laid detailed plans to remedy this "perceived" problem, and included among them was a plan to establish an elaborate system of regional warehouses. Shortly before instituting these plans, the president of the company suggested gathering some additional information directly from customers. The results of a preliminary field survey that was conducted at his request indicated that the original information was completely erroneous—that most of the company's customers were highly satisfied with the service they were receiving. While the customers indicated that shorter turnaround time would be welcomed, they were impressed with the consistency of the manufacturer's service. That is, they said they could count on the receipt of goods from the company a specified number of days after orders had been placed and that such consistency was extremely important to them.[7] Thus, in this situation, the company in question was saved from making a considerable investment in both time and money. Future problems of this sort, however, could be eliminated or mitigated only by assuring adequate feedback from the field, by instituting bypassing mechanisms, and by ensuring repetition of messages that bear such heavy consequances for the firm's operations.

Two approaches which may be helpful to the manufacturer and other channel members in ensuring the conveyance of accurate and pertinent information within the channel are (1) research studies conducted by outside parties, and (2) distributor advisory councils. In the case of the former, it is suggested that studies executed by an agent who is not a channel member offer a greater insurance of objectivity in information gathering. Hence, the chances of obtaining complete and accurate data are increased. In the case of the latter, the formation of advisory councils consisting of representatives from the top management of all channel members gives members the opportunity to voice their sentiments on matters of mutual importance, enables them to outline any problems or needs they might have as individual channel entities, and allows them to participate in the planning process surrounding matters which directly affect their own welfare. In this manner, a feedback system within the channel is institutionalized, a method for bringing to light problems and needs which are not always transmitted through the regular channel information flow is provided, and overall channel communication is improved.[8]

TRANSPORTATION AND STORAGE PROBLEMS

Communication with regard to transportation and storage is clearly a critical feature of interorganizational relations in marketing. Inadequate communications between shippers and their selected transportation modes or storage facilities can lead to excessive inventories, poor customer service, erratic production scheduling, poor material handling, and costly transportation expenditures.

---

[7] This example was drawn from Cox, Shutte, and Few, *op. cit.*, p. 191.

[8] Bert Rosenbloom, "Motivating Independent Distribution Channel Members," *Industrial Marketing Management* (1978), pp. 276–277.

Transportation information systems should concentrate on appropriate queuing and sequencing of messages. To a large extent, specialized languages via advanced technology such as Electronic Data Interchange (EDI) are the major means by which communication noise can be reduced and coordinative mechanisms can be established between shippers and their respective transport modes. Intercompany information transactions with EDI are electronic transmissions in which information in certain prescribed formats is either requested from or given to another company. These transactions are related to operational requirements and are initiated by some process in the participant's internal Electronic Data Processing (EDP) system. By means of such a system, the computer of a manufacturer, having received an order for goods from the computer of a wholesaler, would prepare the necessary documents—order form, pickup form, shipping label, etc.—and establish contact with the computer of an outside shipper, making arrangements for transportation of the goods. Once the order is shipped, the manufacturer's computer relays the information to the wholesaler's computer. Both systems then, through communications with the shipper's computer, keep track of the shipment until it reaches its destination. Thus, the entire transaction is performed with little need for human interference, with a significant reduction or elimination of duplicative activities within the channel, and with extremely fast and accurate interorganizational communication.

Some transportation companies already have applied EDI to certain aspects of the distribution process. For example, Missouri Pacific Railroad has developed a railcar management program known as CoMPubill, which is an automated system for preparing bills of lading. Under this system:

> . . . the shipper who has a railcar ready for pickup enters a so-called shipper instruction message into his own computer, which has a data link with the rail carrier's computer. This message is received by the rail computer, and it automatically prepares a bill of lading and any other necessary documents.[9]

Although EDI offers the opportunity for significant improvements in channel productivity, widespread adoption by shippers, carriers, and receivers is yet to be realized due to the incompatibility of internal data systems and formats currently being utilized. In order to remedy this problem, the Transportation Data Coordination Committee (TDCC) has been given responsibility for developing a standardized format by which different organizations can communicate data. It would seem that the successful completion of this task will eliminate a major barrier to industrial adoption of EDI.

In the meantime, the continued use of specialized languages in EDP has aided various companies in solving shipping problems. For example, General Mills has developed a "Shipment Status system" (called S–3 by the company), which was established to eliminate certain problems it was having in moving its products via its

---

[9] "Computer Interface: The Giant Step and EDP to EDI," *Distribution Worldwide* (February 1978), p. 57.

major transport mode, the railroad.[10] Specifically, in order to assure on-time delivery from the railroad, General Mills, in consultation with railroad management, established standard times along every route relative to the number of days or hours required for a shipment from a company plant or distribution center to reach various checkpoints. Under S–3, General Mills' computer communicates with railroad computer terminals on a daily basis to determine if particular freight cars have arrived at designated checkpoints. Electronic scanners positioned at railroad stations are used to examine reflective identification tape on the cars and report the status and location of the cars to the railroad computer terminal, which, in turn, reports to General Mills' computer. If a car fails to arrive at a designated checkpoint within a one-day grace period, General Mills reports this fact on computer "exception" sheets to railroad management personnel who then track down the car and correct the situation. As a result of the S–3 system, General Mills has achieved the highest rate of on-time delivery service (76 percent) in the company's history.

Similar types of coordinative communication systems have also been established with motor carriers. For example, General Electric's Insulating Materials Product Section has developed a "Ship-By-Number" system.[11] Under this system, each GE shipment container is marked with a large, highly visible bill-of-lading number (as opposed to plain tab-on stenciled addresses with no bill of lading). The presence of this "specialized language" enables truckers to better match freight with the proper bill-of-lading form, thus minimizing the confusion on shipping docks and in carrier terminals. The result for General Electric has been improved customer service, both from the point of view of misdirected shipments as well as speed of receipt of merchandise.

Transportation companies themselves are instituting communication-enhancing systems, which frequently involve shared services. Such efforts are exemplified by the National Association of Freight Payment Banks whose service simplifies the clerical and accounting tasks associated with freight payment.[12] In addition, TransporData Corps., Inc., has initiated a nonprofit shipper-oriented freight-bill payment service in the Northwest region of the United States that not only aids in solving payment problems but also performs data collection operations as well.[13]

The idea of shared services has been extended beyond transportation-oriented problems to other areas in physical distribution. As Friedman observes:

> . . . shared data-processing services for all distribution functions have come into common use. These services offer expensive computer hardware and sophisticated software systems to individual warehouses and other users who would not be able to afford the same kind of information on a private basis. A service of this type usually includes

[10] Information concerning S–3 was received from James C. Johnson, Associate Professor of Transportation and Traffic at the University of Tulsa, via personal correspondence.

[11] See Jim Dixon, "Streamlining Distribution and Storage," *Distribution Worldwide* (May 1975), pp. 30–31.

[12] Walter F. Friedman, "Physical Distribution: The Concept of Shared Services," *Harvard Business Review*, Vol. 53 (March–April 1975), p. 26.

[13] *Ibid.*

invoicing, billing, credit checking, accounting, inventory control, storage and retrieval, and other scheduling.[14]

For example, a communication system called STORE (an acronym for Storage, Transmission, Order-Entry, Receiving, and Enquiry) has been developed by USCO, a large public warehousing company, which permits customers to have a direct computer link-up to USCO's warehouses.[15] Through this linkup, customers can obtain prompt and complete reports relative to billing, inventory control, and customer service. Customers tie into the communications network via teletypewriter, phone, or mail. The system is particularly adaptable to shippers who have limited but nationwide physical distribution requirements, fluctuating physical distribution needs, or commitments to rapid service.[16] STORE is programmed to generate weekly inventory summaries, shipments-by-suppliers reports, and monthly unit movement reports and can, if used effectively, result in reduced order preparation and shipment times, lowered accounts receivable, and improved cash flow.

The potential for shared services in physical distribution is enormous. Clearly, they can increase the effectiveness of communication markedly through the reduction of communication overload. The feedback systems that are fostered by such services can lead to better control, and, thus, lower cost distribution or, at least, improved customer service at the same cost. It is, however, the efficiency of such services that provides the greatest benefits. Through them, duplication of effort is circumscribed, thereby permitting each firm in the interorganizational network to concentrate more heavily on those marketing activities for which it has a comparative advantage.[17]

INVENTORY
PROBLEMS

As was clearly witnessed during the recessions of 1974 and 1980, problems with inventory can pose tremendous difficulties for all members of a marketing channel. In fact, the poor profit performance of both Sears and Penney's during the earlier recession can be directly traced to problems of inventory management and control, which led to the steep markdowns that were taken by both firms to reduce excessive stocks of merchandise.[18] Inventory management is a channelwide problem and demands channelwide communication. As Gross has observed:

> . . . the manufacturers, wholesalers, and retailers can control physical stock problems better when each knows about changes in the quantity and the location of the

---

[14] *Ibid.*

[15] "Meeting Those Distribution Center Needs," *Handling and Shipping Management* (July 1975), pp. 37–38.

[16] *Ibid.*

[17] For an interesting example of the shared services concept in the fast-food industry, where merchant wholesalers have provided so-called "third party physical distribution," see "Fast Food," *Distribution Worldwide* (May 1975), pp. 29–33.

[18] The consequences of Sears' and Penney's 1974 inventory problems are documented in Alvin Nagelberg, "Retailers Eye Very Merry Christmas," *Chicago Tribune,* Section 2, May 25, 1975, p. 11; and in "Why Sears' Profits Tumbled," *Business Week* (April 21, 1975), pp. 32–33.

others' inventory. To be complete, . . . physical inventory should cover more than the number of units located at premises owned by manufacturers or resellers. It is equally important to know how much merchandise is stored in public warehouses, how much is in transit, and what is on display in wholesale showrooms and on retail sales floors.[19]

Not only will such information aid the manufacturer's production scheduling, but it will also have a direct impact on a retailer's or wholesaler's buying plans, because the latter will be able to anticipate the length of order lead times. For example, one furniture manufacturer's study revealed that his shipments were uncoordinated with dealers' needs—some merchandise was shipped out too late to prevent out-of-stock situations, and other items were delivered before the dealers expected them, causing unanticipated handling problems. The situation came to a head when one retailer dropped the manufacturer's line after concluding that the inventory and warehousing problems associated with it generated costs that more than offset the advantages of the line.[20]

As the example above indicates, inventory problems are intimately tied to ordering, shipping, and delivery difficulties. The first step in eradicating the problems causing inventory mismanagement is the development of an *intra*organizational information system. Without doubt, the greatest aid to the management of inventories has been the introduction and adaptation of programs associated with the use of high-speed electronic data processing equipment. By utilizing such programs, manufacturers can systematize their production, shipping, and delivery operations, and middlemen can maintain up-to-date inventory records. Implementation of Electronic Data Interchange (EDI) to allow channel hookups via computer between manufacturer, wholesaler, and retailer similar to those used for communication about transportation and storage problems will provide optimum automatic ordering systems. Current predictions are that in the near future the entire process for reordering products will be triggered by computers. Computerized inventory information systems can lead to greater inventory turnover, reduction in freight costs, better buying decisions, rapid assessment of physical inventory, availability of disaggregated sales data, and reduction in clerical costs.

One of the most sophisticated inventory control systems exists at Motorola's Fossil Creek assembly plant in Fort Worth, Texas. The plant is unique in that the building specifications were drawn around a proposed materials control system. As shown in Exhibit 10–1, by combining the use of computers and conveyers, the system provides for completely automated parts movement from receipt to production, and efficiently integrates production and physical distribution.

Materials are tracked from dock to stock to shipping with scheduled and random human checks along the way to verify the computer's inventory tallies.[21]

---

[19] Gross, *op. cit.,* p. 344.

[20] This example was drawn from Gross, *op. cit.,* p. 341.

[21] Patrick Gallagher, "An Unbeatable System," *Handling and Shipping Management* (October 1979), p. 55.

EXHIBIT 10-1

Layout of Motorola's Fossil Creek Plant

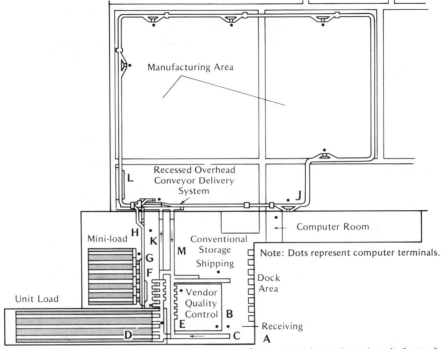

Manufacturing Area

Recessed Overhead
Conveyor Delivery
System

L

J

Mini-load

Computer Room

H

K

M

Conventional
Storage

Note: Dots represent computer terminals.

G

Shipping

F

Dock
Area

Unit Load

Vendor
Quality
Control

B

D

E

Receiving

C

A

All vendor supplied parts and components from other Motorola plants arrive at receiving dock A.

Necessary information on incoming material is Input to minicomputer terminal B and a code ticket is printed and applied to the item.

The material is placed on a slave pallet and immediately sent via conveyor C to Unit Load storage D. The computer assigns a storage location for the pallet, sends it to the proper aisle, and commands the Unit Load machine to pick the pallet off the conveyor spur and store it.

When the Vendor Quality Control (VQC) department is ready to inspect the material, the computer is notified and it directs the load out of storage onto a VQC input spur E. After inspection the pallet load is returned to storage, removed from VQC quarantine status and made available for manufacturing use.

Unit Load pallets are called out to replenish the Mini-Load storage system which originates the parts kits for manufacturing. Pallets are broken down for input to Mini-Load storage at the picking spurs F.

Parts are put into tubs and set in front of the Mini-Load aisles G. The Mini-Load storage machines bring forward bins with empty storage space for the parts. The computer notifies operators where to place the parts in the bins and then has the S/R machines return the bins to storage.

A reverse sequence is performed when parts kits are to be made up for manufacturing. Under computer direction, the Mini-Load operators set an escort memory code on the kit tubs and place them on an output delivery conveyor H.

The tubs move through the overhead conveyor delivery system and are automatically diverted down elevators J at the proper "drop zones." Drop zone operators notify the computer of kit receipt.

Some bulk items on slave pallets may be commanded by the computer to be delivered to manufacturing directly out of Unit Load storage via conveyor K. Finished products are packaged at station L and returned on slave pallets to conventional storage for shipping on conveyor M. The slave pallets are then returned to the Unit Load system.

Source: Patrick Gallagher, "An Unbeatable System," *Handling and Shipping Management* (October 1979), p. 55.

The system also provides absolute real-time inventory tracking, and a materials requirements planning system which enables management to know not only what is in storage but also what is the work-in-process. On that basis and on the basis of forecasted demand, the system generates materials requirements. Implementation of the system has been so successful that Motorola is now shipping ahead of its delivery schedule and delinquent customer orders have been eliminated.[22]

IBM's IMPACT

As indicated in Chapter 4 in the discussion of inventory policy, International Business Machines Corporation has been at the forefront in the development of inventory management and control techniques tailored to each level in the marketing channel. Through its IMPACT[23] the company has been able to formulate advanced methodologies to solve basic inventory problems.

In IMPACT, two types of models are of major concern: a forecast model and an order model.[24] As discussed in the appendix to Chapter 4, the forecast model identifies the essential and underlying demand for an item, classifying demand patterns in terms of three models: horizontal, trend, and seasonal. The program recommends, whichever model yields the minimum forecast error. However, the IMPACT forecast model suffers from the same problems as many other forecasting models in that it cannot anticipate the effect of short-term influences on demand, such as the promotion of an item through additional, short-run sales effort, advertising, or special prices. Furthermore, it does not solve the difficult problems associated with forecasting the demand for new items, fads, style goods, etc.

To overcome some of these limitations, IBM has developed the Retail IMPACT fashion system.[25] Retail IMPACT detects fast- or slow-moving styles rapidly and recommends to the retail buyer that they be reordered, returned, marked down, or, in the case of chain operations, transferred to another store. In inventory management and control, the sales forecast is crucial in providing the basis for future order quantities. With fashion goods, where styles change rapidly, the forecast depends greatly on subjective human judgment. Thus, even with compensating features programmed into the model, it is still possible for a retailer's in-

---

[22] *Ibid.,* p. 54.

[23] IMPACT stands for Inventory Management Program and Control Techniques.

[24] These models are described in detail in *Wholesale IMPACT—Advanced Principles and Implementation Reference Manual,* 2nd ed. (White Plains, N.Y.: IBM Corporation Technical Publications Department, May 1969).

[25] For a complete description of the Retail IMPACT fashion system, as well as an IMPACT system for stable merchandise, see *Retail IMPACT—Inventory Management Program and Control Techniques Application Description,* 6th ed. (White Plains, N.Y.: IBM Technical Publications Department, March 1970).

ventory to become quickly out of line, requiring manual readjustment, revised forecasting, and reprogramming. Also, unexpected longer or shorter seasons, fads on which individual initiative must be taken, and fluctuations in the large number of other variables a retail manager must "manage" relegate fashion models to the category of decision aids. They are certainly not a panacea to achieving optimum turnover with minimum stockouts.

The *order* models used in IMPACT are concerned mainly with identifying the relevant costs incurred by ordering decisions so that management can determine when to buy (using the forecasts developed by IBM's forecasting system referred to above) and how much to buy. The IMPACT Computer Program Library provides the means of analyzing, for each vendor, various alternative order models that take all pertinent factors into account [e.g., economic lot size (EOQ) adjusted for the availability of quantity discounts and desired safety stock], and of selecting the best of the alternatives based on the criterion of lowest total cost.[26]

Automatic Reordering

Many retailing organizations use computerized inventory control and management systems to establish automatic reorder procedures. Although originally developed by manufacturers, such procedures are increasingly being employed by retailers to control their basic stocks. Some shoe chains, for example, have set up carefully determined basic stocks for each store and control each store's inventory on a central basis. A card placed in each shoe box is removed when a sale is made, and the cards representing a day's sales are returned to the main office. Each store's stock is then automatically replenished on the basis of the store's sales and the individual item's reorder point. Similar procedures are used by variety stores. Department stores also use automatic replenishment procedures for such merchandise as men's shirts, sheets and pillow cases, women's hosiery, etc. Both the shipping of merchandise from the warehouse and the reordering of merchandise are controlled automatically. By maintaining a vendor name and address card file, the store can use the system to generate purchase orders automatically.

As reported by manufacturers, wholesalers, and retailers, computerized automatic reorder systems have resulted in the following benefits:[27]

   1. Retailers' sales have increased as a result of having the right quantities of the right stock on their shelves, fewer stockouts, faster turnover, and rapid service from the manufacturer or wholesaler.
   2. Simplified reordering saves time and work for retail store personnel.

---

[26] See *Wholesale IMPACT . . . , op. cit.,* pp. 64–75.
[27] *Guide to Inventory and Material Accounting* (White Plains, N.Y.: IBM Technical Publications Department, September 1969), p. 31.

3. Errors in orders and shipments are greatly reduced.

4. Changes in colors, styles, and models can be handled quickly, with minimum confusion to the retailer.

5. Production planning and control, billing, shipping, and accounts receivable are simplified and stabilized for the manufacturer.

6. Periodic order analyses are easily obtained.

7. Because of systematic and frequent reordering, fewer customers are lost to competitors, and sales and deliveries tend to be constant rather than having infrequent peaks.

It should be noted, however, that, on the retail level, automatic reorder systems are especially applicable to grocery retailing, where there is generally a continual demand for relatively staple items with a steady turnover. Automatic reordering applied to all but the most staple items in a department store would be limited, because of the many variables that the manager must balance. In addition, for general merchandise operations, the on-hand quantities with which the computer works may be inaccurate because of clerical error at the point of purchase, marking room errors, shoplifting, spoilage or deterioration, and errors in entering merchandise as it is received. Also, although speed may be increased if orders are processed automatically, the goal of speedier arrival of the merchandise is still constrained by the speed of the transportation mode used for delivery of the merchandise from the manufacturer to the retailer.

Point-of-sale (Front-end) Systems

Of all the remarkable advances in the field of electronic data processing related to *intra*organizational inventory management and control, none has the potential impact of those information systems that permit data retrieval at the point-of-sale at the retail store level. These computerized cash register systems provide data processing, merchandise-processing, and point-of-sale functions at both chain headquarters and at individual stores in the chain. At the store level, a variety of terminals is used for sales and checkout and for the accounting functions associated with the processing of merchandise and the management of the store.[28]

While performing these functions, the terminals record comprehensive data on their activity. A store controller (minicomputer) coordinates the activity of the terminals, collects data from the terminals, and performs additional specific store-level functions. It also communicates with a computer at area headquarters (the host), pro-

[28] Here, attention is focused on electronic systems with laser scanners. There have been a number of technical breakthroughs in recent years involving cash registers prior to the use of scanners. These include "stand alone" electronic cash registers and electronic registers with some information processing capabilities. For a discussion of these, see Gordon F. Bloom and Ronald C. Curhan, "Technological Change in the Food Industry," Marketing Science Institute Working Papper P-63 (Cambridge, Mass.: Marketing Science Institute, December 1974), pp. 29–34.

viding it with data collected from the terminals, receiving store-level system support and other communication from it, and communicating interactively with it when required.[29]

In supermarkets, a significant benefit available from such point-of-sale or "front-end" systems, beyond those directly related to the production of up-to-the-minute inventory and store management data, is that of checker productivity. As indicated in earlier chapters, the trend in food retailing over the past several decades has been toward increased operating expense, which has been caused primarily by the rise of labor cost relative to productivity. Technology has recently provided an adequate device to address the productivity requirement of the supermarket checkstand—the *laser checkout scanner*. The scanner contains a light source to illuminate and automatically identify each premarked item as it passes across the checkstand. In April, 1973, the supermarket industry established a novel identifier for all supermarket items made in the United States and Canada: the *Universal Product Code* (UPC) symbol that enabled economic use of scanners for checkout.

The Universal Product Code

The UPC symbol is, typically, a unique, 12-digit item identification number, marked both in decimal characters and in bar-coded form that can be read by an optical scanner (see Fig. 10–2). When front-end systems are installed, all the codes in a supermarket's inventory can be maintained at the store controller in a file of price description records that contain both the prices and alphabetic descriptions of the items. The code item is invariant, even though its price may vary among stores. Prices are marked on the shelf but not necessarily on the merchandise, since the system reads the code of an item at the checkstand, retrieves its price and description, and displays that information to the shopper, while also printing it on his

FIGURE 10-2

A Sample of the Universal Product Code, Found on the Side of a Food Package, which Will Be Read by the Scanner of a Computerized Register at the Checkout Counter

[29] P. V. McEnroe, H. T. Huth, E. A. Moore, and W. W. Morris III, "Overview of the Supermarket System and the Retail Store System," *IBM Systems Journal,* Vol. 14 (1975), pp. 3–4. Much of the discussion regarding the supermarket and general merchandise systems in this chapter is based on information supplied in this article.

receipt tape. At headquarters, the front-end system provides item-movement data so that management can implement optimal inventory policies and shelf allocation procedures, which, in turn, should lead to a reduction of both backroom inventory and stockouts, increased turnover because of more efficient shelf allocation, and a reduction in ordering cost as a consequence of the adoption of automatic reordering procedures.

Widespread adoption of UPC-oriented systems at the retail level has not taken place at anywhere near the rate which was projected when the Kroger Company first experimented with the scanner in 1972. This has been largely due to the fact that a rather substantial capital outlay is necessary to implement the system. Equipment manufacturers are quoting a cost of $120,000 to $150,000 per supermarket—including scanners, computers, and cash register. The capital requirement alone for a regional chain or division of a national chain with 150 stores has been estimated at $21 million, or $140,000 per store.[30] Evidence suggests, however, that the sale of electronic registers with scanners is fast accelerating. Prior to 1985, nearly 300,000 electronic registers will have been installed by food retailers, and a rapidly increasing percentage of these registers will be attached to scanners.[31]

This significant upturn in sales is largely due to the increasing use of the UPC. More than four-fifths of supermarket items are now marked with the code by their packager.[32] Stores making use of scanner systems have found that in addition to increasing checker productivity and eliminating price-marking, the information provided by the computer to which most scanners are linked has allowed them to fine-tune labor schedules, cut the number of items out of stock at any one time, track the sales of new items, and plot the effectiveness of advertising or price promotions.[33] Some of the potential benefits of the system are listed in Exhibit 10–2.

While effective use of the UPC was initially thought to have its greatest potential benefit at the retail level, recent developments have shown that it is also a valuable tool for marketing research. With a greater number of supermarkets now investing in scanning devices, prominent market research firms—A. C. Nielsen, Time, Inc.'s Selling Area Marketing, and TeleResearch Item Movement, among others—are beginning to offer expanded scanner-based services. A. C. Nielsen's ScanTrack service, which combines sales data with regular staff visits to supermarkets to monitor display and other in-store promotions, links electronic checkout scanning systems on a nationwide basis. Such a network gives clients data from a comprehensive cross section of stores with scanning devices in operation.[34] For brand managers and promotion executives this kind of information is most advantageous. Reliable and fast sales information enables them to make any needed corrections as quickly as possible.

---

[30] The $140,000 figure includes installation costs for new cableways, etc., in existing stores and costs for in-store symbol marking equipment. Bloom and Curhan, *op. cit.,* p. 37.

[31] "Electronic Registers Satisfy Need for Good Data: Becker," *Marketing News* (March 23, 1979), p. 5.

[32] "Supermarket Scanners Take Hold," *Business Week* (April 23, 1979), p. 46B.

[33] *Ibid.* See also "Checkout Scanners Soon Will Revolutionize Market Research, Packaged Goods Marketing," *Marketing News* (December 12, 1980), p. 5.

[34] "Market Research by Scanner," *Business Week* (May 5, 1980), p. 116.

EXHIBIT 10-2

Potential Benefits to Food Retailers from Adoption of UPC-Oriented Systems

Front-end Benefits	Merchandising Benefits
Improved throughput	Point-of-sale item movement data
Checker productivity	Advertising analysis
Reduced misrings	Vendor analysis
Tender reconciliation	New item performance analysis
Cash reporting	Location analysis (for items within
Store funds control	stores and between stores)
Check authorization	Price management

Store Operations Benefits	Inventory Management Benefits
Eliminates price marking and remarking	Shelf-space allocation
Permits routine ordering	Reduced out-of-stock
Reduce shrinkage	Reduced backroom inventory

Warehouse and Transportation Workload Balancing

Source: IBM Corporation, November 1975.

A service which goes beyond the simple provision of aggregate sales movement data by supplying detailed consumer research information is BehaviorScan, which was developed by Information Resources, Inc. Rather than wait for supermarkets to install scanners in geographically desirable research areas, Behavior-Scan, at a cost of $2.5 million, provided the equipment free in two cities which are ideal test markets: Marion, Indiana and Pittsfield, Massachusetts.[35]

> BehaviorScan works like this: 3,000 households in two experimental markets (50,000 to 100,000 population centers in Northeast and Midwest), are given special identification cards which are used to track their purchases in local supermarkets, which have Automated Front End (AFE) scanner systems. (The ID card is scanned along with groceries.)
>
> The households in the project receive all their television programming via cable relay from nearby metropolitan areas. Commercials are controlled by means of a cable "split." For example, half the households may see a Wheaties breakfast cereal commercial during the 6 p.m. newscast while the other half watches a Cheerios ad.[36]

By means of this system, all the grocery purchases of a representative sample of households can be measured along with how these consumers react to certain promotional tools such as coupons, free samples, price adjustments, television commercials, newspaper ads, and point-of-purchase displays. Needless to say, the implications of this development for manufacturers and food processors are enormous.

[35] *Ibid.*, p. 113.
[36] "New 'BehaviorScan' System Ties Grocery Sales to TV Ads," *Marketing News,* (December 12, 1980), p. 7.

General Merchandise Codes

Similar advances have been made relative to the management of general merchandise items sold throught department, variety, and discount stores. The development of a Standard Merchandise Classification (SMC) by the Controllers Congress of the National Retail Merchants Association permits benefits similar to those available to supermarkets via UPC. However, even with SMC, each general merchandise retailer usually tickets merchandise in a manner that best suits his own environment. The retail sales ticket contains a great deal more information (e.g., stock-keeping unit number, buying division, selling division, class, size, and price) than that required in a supermarket identification system. There is also much variability both in size and content of such tickets. The front-end information systems developed for general merchandise retailers contain the capability of making and reading a variety of tickets, because they often include point-of-sale terminals with magnetic wands and magnetic ticket units.[37] It is possible, though, that, in general merchandise retailing, the utilization of product codes and more routinized operations will not lead to a more streamlined operation and greater clerk productivity due to the relatively complicated nature of general merchandise transactions compared with the normal "cash and carry" transactions in supermarkets. Because there are many more information bits that must be entered for a transaction, including the sales-person number, specific credit plan, additional services attending the sale (e.g., delivery, warehouse pickup, layaway, etc.), return adjustments, allowances for defective merchandise, and the like, implementing the laser scanner reduces the time associated with information input only by a small amount.

Consequences of the Point-of-Sale Breakthroughs

These truly innovative *intra*organizational systems have the potential of alleviating much of the "noise" present in *inter*organizational communication dealing with stock levels and shipments. They should permit more effective queuing and sequencing of messages among channel members as well as nearly instantaneous feedback relative to item movement. Most significantly, these innovations indicate the potential for more functional communication via the development of specialized languages (e.g., UPC and SMC) and the altering of technology. Machines are substituted for people, and a portion of the communications task is delegated to units specializing in a crucial aspect of the communication process.

There are also numerous economic, social, and political consequences of such innovations. First, if retailers' willingness to purchase and perfect front-end systems

---

[37] A magnetic hand-held scanner, or wand, is normally a more accurate and faster data entry device than the cash register keyboard when many characteristics of data are to be entered.

is assumed,[38] market data critical to the functioning of channels of distribution will be instantaneously retrievable by retailers. Unless manufacturers, wholesalers, carriers, and warehousing firms can somehow tie into the retail systems, they will become highly dependent on retailers for updated information. The uncertainty absorbing attributes of the retail store information systems are profound, and thus, the opportunity for retailers to assume channel leadership roles will undoubtedly be greatly magnified.

Second, it is likely that manufacturers, wholesalers, and logistical institutions will recognize the potential economic benefits as well as the above-mentioned political consequences of these *intra*organizational devices and will, therefore, begin to accelerate efforts to develop *inter*organizational data systems. Evidence of computerized interorganizational data connections was present even before front-end systems became a reality. Electronic linkages such as data phones have emerged as significant communication media for the transmission of ordering, billing, and inventory data among channel members. Order cycles can be reduced markedly when orders are transmitted instantly under real-time information system conditions. Inventory costs can be lowered for all members because less inventory is needed throughout the channel. As Gross has observed:

> Manufacturers, wholesalers, and retailers are moving toward lower and lower stock ratios as almost immediate transmittal of financial and inventory data becomes feasible. A hardware wholesaler in Texas has established a Data-phone connection with certain customers; Kellogg's warehouses are linked directly with warehouses of Safeway Stores and of the Wakefern Food chain; the Pillsbury Company has electronic hookups with Spartan Stores.[39]

Once interorganizational data systems are instituted within a distribution channel, the most immediate and obvious change will be an increase in the speed with which communication takes place.[40] When a retail stockout occurs, or an order point is reached, it will not be days or hours before the appropriate supplier knows about it, but seconds. This linkage brings each level of the channel temporarily closer together. It is not only the retailer who will be able to perceive shifts in ultimate consumer markets as they happen, but all key members of the channel. In addition to the greater speed with which data will be sent through the channel, greater accuracy of data transmittal can be effected.

Channel management would be enhanced if all *intra*organizational data

---

[38] Clearly, adoption will be relatively slow, given the investment required. Furthermore, the systems, especially those designed for supermarkets, are likely to be most feasible when installed in large stores, irrespective of the total number of stores in a chain. See Bloom and Curhan, *op. cit.,* pp. 35–38, for estimates of the rate of diffusion of these systems.

[39] Gross, *op. cit.,* pp. 350–351.

[40] The discussion here is based on Louis W. Stern and C. Samuel Craig. "Interorganizational Data Systems: The Computer and Distribution," *Journal of Retailing,* Vol. 47 (Summer 1971), pp. 81–82. See also Felix Kaufman, "Data Systems That Cross Company Boundaries," *Harvard Business Review,* Vol. 44 (January–February 1966), pp. 141–155.

systems were compatible and able to communicate freely with one another. However, social orientations (e.g., the desire for privacy, the maintenance of trade secrets) and technical requirements (e.g., computer hardware and software) vary from firm to firm. If patterns of data processing development continue such as they have in the past (i.e., most systems are tailored to the individual firm's specifications), computers and programs will continue to be unique. Also, computer manufacturers have a vested interest in maintaining unique systems. This problem was evident in the early development of supermarket checkout systems. According to Bloom and Curhan:

> . . . during the mid-1960's, various companies, including RCA, Zellweger, IMS Marketron, and others, had begun to develop automated checkout systems incorporating scanning technologies, using their own proprietary symbols. For the most part, these various symbols were incompatible in that they could not be read by devices of other equipment manufacturers.[41]

Unless trade associations and computer manufacturers exert considerable pressure for a high degree of standardization, members in the same channel will not be able to interact freely and speedily. Firms will not be able to switch to competitive systems without substantial changes.

From an interorganizational management perspective, it is, however, encouraging to note that the development of the new codes and classification schemes (UPC and SMC) was the result of interorganization cooperation in the marketing channels for both food and general merchandise. In fact, the Grocery Manufacturers of America *pioneered* the UPC and the computerized checkout.[42] In 1970, food processors, wholesalers, and retailers established the Grocery Industry Ad Hoc Committee to determine the design and feasibility of a code, and more than $1 million was obtained from various members of the food industry to support the work of the committee.[43] As indicated earlier, the Transportation Data Coordination Committee is currently working to develop a standardized format for electronic data interchange. Thus, it appears that the desire for systemwide inventory management and control—and for increased productivity at the point-of-sale—is nearly universal among commercial channel members in these industries.

Third, there are a number of economic, ethical, and legal issues that will have to be assessed relative to the further development of both *intra-* and *inter*organizational information systems of the nature described above. On one hand, the antitrust enforcement agencies will, quite naturally, be concerned about the potential anticompetitive effects generated by closer and closer ties between channel members, by an increase in the power of large retailers through the installation of such systems, and by the fact that numerous firms may be placed at a severe com-

---

[41] Bloom and Curhan, *op. cit.,* p. 21.

[42] "Electronic Pricing Faces an Uphill Fight," *Business Week* (March 31, 1975), p. 23.

[43] Bloom and Curhan, *op. cit.,* p. 20, Also see Willard R. Bishop, Jr., "New Approaches to Improving Social Productivity in Food Distribution," in Ronald C. Curhan (ed.), *1974 Combined Proceedings* (Chicago: American Marketing Association, 1975), pp. 299–303.

petitive disadvantage if they do not adopt or tie into these systems. On the other hand, the connection of the more than 2500 separate data-processing networks now operating could reduce the cost of such systems to a level that smaller business could afford.[44] Additionally, negative reaction to the supermarket front-end systems and the concomitant elimination of price markings, which was initially voiced by members of the Retail Clerks International Union and by consumers, has resulted in passage of laws mandating the retention of item-pricing in seven states and many municipalities. In response to this problem, most major unionized chains have made an agreement with the union that they would not eliminate item-pricing. Since that time there have been no major labor disputes over the issue. Although the matter appears dormant for now, the question is a potentially explosive one, and any attempts to try new methods of price-marking could bring it to the fore once again.[45]

Controlling Inventory by Limiting Stocks

Aside from the innovations in electronic data processing and the consequences of their use, some retailers have limited their stocks in order to secure higher stockturns. Manufacturers have been critical of retailers for taking such actions, because they believe that, by limiting stocks, retailers are failing to provide adequate amounts of their products to meet customer demand. Manufacturers are also increasingly concerned about retailers' hesitancy to stock new items until demand has been stimulated at the consumers' level. On the other hand, retailers must constantly be aware of the need to "tailor" their lines to promote profitable turnover for their generally limited market areas. Instituting informational assistance appears to be one means by which dysfunctional conflict has been avoided over this issue in certain channels. As reported by Duncan, Phillips, and Hollander:

> . . . some manufacturers, aware of the retailer's need for strict inventory control, have developed stock-control plans providing a reasonable display of their products and also yielding a good turnover figure to the retailer. One skirt manufacturer, for instance, helps the retailer set up a model stock, has his salesmen take a weekly inventory, and offers to replace slow-selling items with fast-selling ones. Such assistance is of particular value to smaller retailers who often lack the stock-control programs of larger firms.[46]

Such interorganizational arrangements are essential if perceptual differences and their accompanying "noise" are going to be reduced relative to inventory problems.

[44] "Computers' Marriage to Communications To Yield Big Benefits—If It Ever Occurs," *Wall Street Journal,* Nov. 2, 1977, p. 46.

[45] "Supermarket Scanners Take Hold," *op. cit.*

[46] Delbert J. Duncan, Charles F. Phillips, and Stanley C. Hollander, *Modern Retailing Management,* 8th ed.(Homewood, Ill.: Richard D. Irwin, 1972), p. 326.

PROMOTIONAL PROBLEMS

Communication failures weaken or nullify promotional efforts of both manufacturers and resellers.

For example, a well-known tire manufacturing company, which prided itself on its dealer point-of-purchase promotional pieces, learned, after conducting a research study on the subject, that its promotional programs were largely wasted; dealers did not want the promotional materials and discarded them almost immediately upon receipt. The tire company found that dealers were primarily concerned with getting customers into their stores and not with selling the consumers once they entered the stores.[47]

The communication problem in this case was clearly one of omission—the manufacturer really did not know what it was the dealers needed and had not taken the trouble to find out until he had spent considerable resources on the wrong kind of materials. The remedy for the problem may be the instituting of appropriate feedback mechanisms. The manufacturer's sales force should be tapped for information on this subject on a regular basis.[48] The problem could have been compounded as a result of communication overload, which occurs when one channel member supplies more material than another can effectively assimilate. The remedy here would be appropriate sequencing of communications.

The problem could also have arisen because the dealers and the manufacturer were operating at crossed purposes and using confused languages. In this respect, corporate management's point of view is generally characterized by a growth psychology, whereas the typical small retail dealer is more concerned with maintenance of the status quo than he is with growth.[49] The executives in a major corporation constantly strive for more income, status, power, security, fame, or self-satisfaction; small retailers may have similar goals, but each goal has a relatively easily defined end point. Furthermore, the language of modern industry often revolves around words like profit, profit margin, profitability, merchandising, marketing, promoting, and the like. Small retailers talk in terms of "making money" and of "giving their customers what they ask for." Some of the problems faced by the tire manufacturer with his dealers are no doubt similar to those described by Wittreich relative to brewers in their interaction with tavern owners:

> . . . a situation of conflicting interests and misunderstanding exists between the brewer and the tavern owner. The latter generally does not feel that brewers are genuinely interested in his problems. He sees industry "take-home" advertising as undermining his business. He sees the individual brewer as primarily interested in pushing his own brand—something in which the tavern operator is not interested because pushing one brand over another does not really add to *his* over-all business.[50]

[47] This example was drawn from Cox, Schutte, and Few, *op. cit.,* p. 191.

[48] For a detailed discussion of the potential feedback roles of salesmen, see Louis W. Stern and J. L. Heskett, "Grass Roots Market Research," *Harvard Business Review,* Vol. 43 (March–April 1965), pp. 83–96.

[49] Warren J. Wittreich, "Misunderstanding the Retailer," in Louis W. Stern (ed.), *Distribution Channels: Behavioral Dimensions, op. cit.,* pp. 254–255.

[50] *Ibid.,* p. 258.

Integral to solving the communication problems in these cases would be a willingness on the part of the "sender" (1) to deal with the "receiver" on the latter's own level, within the framework of the latter's value system, and (2) to discuss promotional strategy in down-to-earth, concrete language that the latter understands.[51] The role of the salesman is critical in these situations.

Clearly, poor communication with regard to promotion results in duplication of effort and dilution of promotional impact. For example, all channel members advertise, but frequently retailers are not fully informed about the assistance that they can obtain from manufacturers in the planning and implementation of campaigns. Also, both the manufacturer and the retailer may be advertising at the same time in the same market with no benefit to either in media purchases or unified campaign themes for maximum impact. Institutional advertising directed at retailers may not be coordinated with wholesalers' personal selling efforts directed at the same retailers. By the same token, manufacturers need information about intermediaries' promotional needs. For example, manufacturers can help in planning anniversary and other special sales by providing specially designed displays and even products. Manufacturers and wholesalers may combine efforts with retailers to push their particular brands during such occasions.

Communication "noise" can lead to serious conflicts regarding other promotional areas as well, such as packaging, sales incentives, and merchandising aids. Consider the following examples:

- A manufacturer's research indicated that consumers wanted a package that would be easier to open. Accordingly the product (bubble gum balls) was packaged in a redesigned box with a simple tear-open feature. Retailers became highly upset with the new package because it led to free sampling by children as well as display floor clean-up problems.[52]

- An appliance manufacturer provided his distributor and dealers with promotional incentives including travel prizes and free merchandise for their outstanding salesmen. Difficulties ensued when the travel prizes aggravated the middlemen's personnel shortages during peak sales periods and when the middlemen learned that their salesmen were selling the free merchandise to customers on company time.[53]

- An advertising agency recommended that one of its clients—a national food manufacturer—use odd-shaped cents-off coupons (e.g., poodle-shaped for dog food). The manufacturer enthusiastically endorsed the recommendation, but found his retailers up-in-arms about the promotional scheme. If enacted, retailers would have found it extremely difficult to stack, sort, and store the coupons.[54]

[51] *Ibid.,* p. 260.

[52] This example was drawn from Gross, *op. cit.,* p. 341.

[53] This example was drawn from Gross, *op. cit.,* p. 342

[54] This example was drawn from Stephen Baker, "Wild Shapes, Sizes Are Today's Look in Coupons," *Advertising Age* (August 4, 1969) and was paraphrased in Reavis Cox and Thomas F. Schutte, "A Look at Channel Management," in Philip R. McDonald (ed.), *1969 Full Conference on Proceedings* (Chicago, Ill.: American Marketing Association, 1970), p. 102.

It is reasonably safe to assume that, in each case cited above, problems could have been alleviated or perhaps would not even have arisen if there had been adequate and continuous (or at least periodic) feedback throughout the system.[55]

Besides judiciously using salesmen for this purpose (which involves developing a sales-force compensation system that would motivate salesmen to perform such a crucial function), a number of other conflict management strategies might also be employed, as outlined earlier in Chapter 6. These strategies include formation of dealer and distributor advisory councils, exchanging personnel, purposive uncertainty absorption techniques, and cooptation.[56] In addition, certain middlemen, such as merchant wholesalers, manufacturers' representatives, and brokers, could perform mediating roles with respect to such problems. However, it would probably be better, over the long term, for retailers, wholesalers, and manufacturers alike to establish channel diplomat positions within their firms in the form of trade relations departments or distribution specialists in order to avoid the conflicts of interest that often plague salesmen and independent middlemen when they seek to perform conflict management functions.[57]

PRODUCT PROBLEMS   Many of the same problems that exist in the transmittal of promotional information are found for product information as well. For example, appliance retailers and manufacturers do not often mean the same thing when they discuss product quality. The former are concerned with the consequences of product quality; they want an item that results in a high level of consumer satisfaction and that minimizes consumer complaints and servicing problems. The latter are concerned with technical features. Thus, refrigerator manufacturers see quality as reflected in such things as maintenance of constant temperature and avoidance of excessive "frosting," while television set manufacturers measure quality in terms of picture clarity, pulling power, and tonal effect.[58] This problem of confused languages can be remedied only by the similar kinds of feedback and interpenetration mechanisms suggested above for promotional problems.

Typical of some of the recurring problems faced by channel members when they fail to communicate effectively about product policy are the following examples:

- A well-known manufacturer of consumer paper products decided to introduce a giant economy size box of one product in its line. Although consumers desired the box—especially after the manufacturer had engaged in heavy pro-

---

[55] It should also be understood, however, that too much feedback can create as much "noise" as too little feedback. See Grabner and Rosenberg, *op. cit.,* pp. 247–248.

[56] See Chapter 6 for a discussion of each of these interpenetration strategies.

[57] See Chapter 6 for additional discussion of this point.

[58] Wittreich, *op. cit.,* pp. 261–262.

motion of it—retailers stocked it reluctantly because it did not fit existing shelf space, and thus they were forced to place it on the floor.[59]

- A manufacturer of outdoor braziers introduced a high-priced and high-quality line into a certain market area. After an introductory sales increase, sales volume started dwindling, even though the product was of superior quality. A special study revealed that newly hired sales personnel in retail outlets were not informed about the distinctive features of the line, let alone that these features needed to be demonstrated to prospective buyers. Although brochures and other training materials were available for retailers, they were not read. The sales personnel simply used the high-priced superior line to promote other, less expensive lines.[60]

- A major producer of electric appliances hired a well-known actress to present new items on a television program. When she announced a new electric frankfurter cooker, it was not only news to the consumer; it was also news to retailers and even to the manager of a wholesale subsidiary owned by this manufacturer.[61]

Obviously, retailers and wholesalers need advance notice of forthcoming model and style changes and new-product introductions. A whole series of steps necessarily precedes successful introduction at the local level, not the least of which is adequate training of sales personnel. For example, it would be useful, from a training perspective, if distinctions could be drawn between "features" and "benefits" of products. A feature is a technical attribute (31–100 wide-ratio derailer on bicycles), whereas a benefit is a feature translated into everyday salable terms (wide-range gears for easier peddling). Although it is standard practice for many manufacturers to keep channel members abreast of developments by sending out a stream of newsletters and other information-giving mail pieces, the problem of communication overload quickly becomes evident, especially if many suppliers are following the same course and if new product introductions are relatively frequent. As with promotion, the salesman must play a key role in carrying salient information. Otherwise, the messages are likely to become damped by the noise surrounding middlemen, which often reaches uncomfortable decibel levels.

Similarly, problems of inadequate product supply within the channel must be handled by means of special communications efforts. For example, not long after the introduction of its new bubblegum product, Hubba Bubba, the William Wrigley, Jr. Company found itself saddled with a heavy backlog of orders due to a demand for the product which exceeded the company's most optimistic forecast.[62] To cope with the situation, the company removed Hubba Bubba from sale to all customers in its Eastern and Mid-Atlantic regions but continued to market the product on a full-scale basis in other parts of the country. Letters of apology were

---

[59] This example was drawn from Cox and Schutte, *op. cit.,* p. 100.

[60] This example was drawn from Gross, *op. cit.,* p. 341.

[61] This example was drawn from Gross, *op. cit.,* p. 348.

[62] Information concerning Hubba Bubba was received from Ronald O. Cox, Vice President of Sales and Marketing at the William Wrigley, Jr., Company, via classroom presentation.

sent to all retailers and jobbers advising them of this action. To compensate for the inconvenience, a premium of 50¢ per box was sent for all unshipped orders placed on or before a specified date. Salesmen were then sent to visit the retailers and jobbers to answer any questions which may have arisen in connection with the problem. Further, during the period of time in which the product supply was cut from the two regions, the company continued to advertise the product. Special TV commercials such as "Don't Blame Your Storekeeper" and "Be Patient" covered the out-of-stock situation and maintained brand awareness. When production levels made reintroduction of the product possible, trade letters were again sent offering a discount of 25 percent off invoice price as an inducement to retailers and jobbers to restock the gum. As a result of its policy of openness in its communication with channel members and its effective employment of promotional tools, the Wrigley Company was again able to market the product successfully in the two regions.

It is incumbent on middlemen to communicate local environmental nuances to their suppliers so that products can be adapted to fit the needs of specific markets. The dealer and distributor advisory notion appears to be ideally suited to such interchanges with respect to both industrial and consumer goods.[63] Wholesalers and retailers are in a position to provide suppliers with information about demographic changes, competitive activities, and changes in consumer preferences and shopping habits in local market areas. For their part, manufacturers who have developed quotas for their own salesmen can readily supply middlemen with estimates of what they should be able to sell.[64] In fact, the process of uncertainty absorption is a mutual one, especially as it relates to product problems.

Another area where communication in marketing channels has tended to be weak has to do with new product warranties. Retailers, wholesalers, and even manufacturers themselves have been confused as to role relationships here, and "noise" within channels regarding the issue of warranties has sometimes been deafening. Problems with warranty arrangements have surfaced in almost all consumer durable goods industries,[65] but perhaps the automobile industry has been the one most frequently plagued with difficulties. In an effort to eliminate warranty-claim discrepancies on the part of its dealers, which came glaringly to the surface during 1975 when certain dealers were found to be charging General Motors for service under warranties which they never performed, GM instituted a new franchise agreement with its dealers that was much more stringent in specifying dealer obligations.[66] Clearly, the problems GM faced with respect to warranties made the com-

[63] For examples of the effective use of dealer and distributor councils, see Chapter 6; H. Thomas Douglas. "I-E and Its Distributors Communicate for Profit," *Industrial Marketing* (February 1970), pp. 51–53; "Belden Co. Airs its Distributors' Views," *Industrial Marketing* (November 1969), pp. 56–58; and R. D. Brown, "Selling Through—Not to—Retailers," in Malcolm P. McNair and Mira Berman (eds.), *Marketing Through Retailers* (New York: American Management Association, 1967), p. 60.

[64] Gross, *op. cit.,* p. 349.

[65] *Product Warranties,* Report of the Sub-Council on Warranties and Guarantees of the National Business Council for Consumer Affairs (Washington, D.C.: U.S. Government Printing Office, 1972).

[66] Terry P. Brown, "GM's Relations with Dealers Are Roiled as Some Dealers Call New Pack Unfair," *Wall Street Journal,* October 30, 1975, p. 34. See also Terry P. Brown, "GM Offers Dealers Special Explanation of Controversial Franchise Agreement," *Wall Street Journal,* February 10, 1976, p. 2.

pany rethink its means of communicating with and gathering intelligence at the retail level. While the problems that have occurred in automobile marketing may be extreme, there are similar problems in other industries, although they do not necessarily revolve around false claims. In the long run (and perhaps even in the short run), consumers are the ones who are injured, because the lack of domain consensus over warranty arrangements places them squarely in the middle. Although the Warranties Improvement Act of 1975 may help to alleviate these problems somewhat by giving consumers more power to deal with inadequate warranty service and unclear warranty claims, it is obvious that commercial channel members must involve themselves more deeply with this issue.[67] Unfortunately, the mechanisms for effective bargaining over it often seem to be lacking, with the result that the courts are called upon too frequently to arbitrate matters which would be better handled by a well-functioning intrachannel conflict management system.

PRICING PROBLEMS   Effective communication between channel members on pricing policy matters is of vital importance to channel operations. Problems relative to this element of the marketing mix are especially acute in periods of inflation and recession, as evidenced during the 1974–1976 stagflation.[68] Prices have a direct effect on the ability of firms within the channel to successfully manage their inventories and maintain adequate assortments; considerable "hedging" is necessary if firms are going to avoid often catastrophic results relative to profits.

Typically, a manufacturer's price list is an inaccurate and misleading communication medium. The net price available to middlemen includes a host of additional factors, some of which are only vaguely transmitted to existing and potential buyers. As Gross points out,[69] allowances may be made to defray advertising and/or to cover shipping, warehousing, internal chain-unit distributing, merchandise defects, and other middleman costs. Special pricing may be available for quantity purchases, for preferred shelf and floor positions, and for trade show market specials. Dating plans, price adjustment guarantees, and other incentives to early ordering are frequently available, but are often not explicitly included in sales presentations or, if presented, are cumbersome and confusing in many cases. In actuality, pricing traditions have given rise to specialized languages (e.g., credit terms, chain discounts), which may lead to more efficient communication but are sometimes subject to considerable interpretation.[70]

[67] C. L. Kendall and Frederick A. Russ, "Warranty and Complaint Policies: An Opportunity for Marketing Management," *Journal of Marketing,* Vol. 39 (April 1975), pp. 36–43. See also Stanley E. Cohen, "FTC Gears Up for Rule-Making Task; Engman Cites Public's Frustrations," *Advertising Age* (July 16, 1973), p. 1.

[68] See, for some excellent examples, "Marketing When the Growth Slows," *Business Week* (April 14, 1975), pp. 44–50; and "Pricing Strategy in an Inflation Economy," *Business Week* (April 6, 1974), pp. 43–48.

[69] Gross, *op. cit.,* p. 349.

[70] Frederick E. Balderston, "Communication Networks in Intermediate Markets," *Management Science,* Vol. 4 (January 1958), pp. 167–168.

Wholesalers and retailers need such information to help them plan their buying effectively. For example, middlemen may decide to place preseason orders, thereby financing manufacturing operations, if they can be convinced that the discount savings available are greater than inventory carrying costs and if manufacturers are willing to guarantee price levels, especially in times of unstable economic conditions. Conversely, manufacturers need information about the price structure at retail and wholesale levels in order to be assured that their pricing is in line with competition, that they are receiving their fair share of price specials at local levels, and that realistic margins are being maintained on their lines so as to avoid price "footballing" situations and thus the possible disaffection of valued distributors and dealers.

Evidence of ineffectiveness in pricing communication and execution is found with regard to the thousands of "trade deals" or temporary price reductions that are offered to retailers by manufacturers. Manufacturers, especially in the food industry, employ a number of different types of short-term inducements in order to encourage increased purchases and/or promotional support by retailers. The most common trade deals in the food industry are "off-invoice" and the "bill-back" allowances; the former are applied directly to reduce billed costs, while the latter are paid retroactively for all purchases within a specified period. The hope of the manufacturers granting these allowances is that retailers will pass along at least part of their savings to consumers and/or that they will erect special displays for and advertise the brands on which prices have been reduced. On the other hand, retailers who participate in trade deals hope to increase total direct profit through higher unit sales of the products being promoted. It is suggested that in many cases neither party receives the most mileage from these deals; often they merely serve to engender or increase the potential for conflict with the channel.

Conflict over trade deals between manufacturers and retailers may manifest itself in several forms. Often the trouble may arise over the form and amount of deals. Retailers may take the view that manufacturer-initiated promotions merely encourage profitless brand switching rather than increase sales or profits. Manufacturers, on the other hand, may accuse retailers of taking advantage of the price reductions without passing the benefits along to the consumer. Promotion of the product may thus never take place at the retail level.[71] Additionally, conflict may arise if a temporary promotion proves to be unsuccessful. In this case, the outcome of the promotion may be unfavorable to either the retailer, the manufacturer, or both. The retailer may find himself saddled with increased inventory carrying costs as a result of his failure to sell the promoted merchandise. He may blame the manufacturer for the predicament, charging him with inadequate promotional support and misleading advice. The manufacturer may thus find himself with a damaged reputation.[72]

---

[71] Michel Chevalier and Ronald C. Curhan, "Temporary Promotions as a Function of Trade Deals: A Descriptive Analysis," Marketing Science Institute Report No. 75-109 (Cambridge, Mass.: Marketing Science Institute, May, 1975), p. 13.

[72] Ibid.

Another example of a potentially conflicting situation presents itself in deals which are favorable to the manufacturer but not to the retailer. This may happen when a manufacturer of branded products possessing strong consumer loyalty uses this power within the channel by offering small purchase inducements to retailers, who, fearful that their competitors will take advantage of the same deal, accept the inducement even though the promotions involved may prove relatively costly for them. It should be noted that while the manufacturer may derive short-term advantages from such a strategy, benefits which are realized at the expense of the retailer may be eroded in the long run through loss of good will. Thus, it is clear that optimal trade deals are those which are structured so that they induce temporary promotions which yield incremental profit for both the retailer and the manufacturer.[73]

In reality, it appears that manufacturer-initiated trade deals do seem to be relatively profitable for the retailer but not necessarily for the manufacturer. It is important to point out, however, that it is difficult to assess the precise impact of temporary promotions on retailer profit due to the fact that:

1. Promoted items may yield less direct product profit per unit sold.
2. Sales of temporarily promoted items may be offset in part by reduced sales of substitutable products during the period of promotion.
3. There may be forward buying during the promotional period.
4. Customers induced to shop in a store because of promoted items may buy other merchandise as well.

Chevalier and Curhan found, after monitoring a total of 1043 trade deals offered to one supermarket chain over a 24-week period, that only 33 percent of those manufacturer-brand items for which deals were recorded received significant advertising mention by the retailers, only 37 percent received an important price cut (only 17 percent excluding in-ad coupons redeemed at the retail store), and only 22 percent were given special displays.[74] In fact, for over 50 percent of the deals that were recorded, the brands involved received *no* price reductions at the retail level.[75] Similar negative results were found with regard to advertising mention and displays. In a considerable understatement of their findings, Chevalier and Curhan concluded that:

> In this particular situation, the retailer promoted only a limited number of items for which he accepted deals. It is unlikely that manufacturers realized the support to which they probably considered themselves entitled.[76]

There are indications that manufacturers are making an effort to correct some of the problems which are inherent in trade deals. For example, Procter & Gamble

[73] Ibid.
[74] Ibid., p. 13.
[75] Ibid., p. 12.
[76] Ibid., p. 28.

only recently began to offer retailers merchandising agreements which would give them money up front for performance-related deals, rather than require them to follow the traditional bill-back procedure. Under this agreement, retailers are required to prove that they have performed the services as promised. If they fail to do so, they must return any money which they have received within 30 days. Should other marketers follow Procter & Gamble's lead and the practice become widespread, retailers could thus have use of millions of promotional dollars as much as six weeks earlier than before.[77]

The pricing area is one that is often shrouded in secrecy. The bargaining that usually ensues with respect to final price makes communications about prices subject to a wide variety of omissions and distortions. To some extent, these problems are alleviated by the kind of information exchange that takes place among channel members at trade shows and trade association meetings as well as through trade journals and trade association publications. There are, however, immense legal obstacles to such exchanges, because they can be viewed by antitrust enforcement agencies as efforts to conspire to fix prices. In fact, there has periodically been a concerted effort by the Justice Department, with full support of the President's office, to "crack down" on price conspiracies.[78] The latter tend to become more prevalent and more overt in a period of recession coupled with inflation when profits are squeezed hardest. The cause for concern by the Justice Department seems warranted, especially if the following examples are typical of practices in other areas and industries.[79]

- More than 100 suits have recently been filed by the Justice Department, state, and private companies charging dozens of paper concerns with fixing prices of corrugated boxes, folding-cartons, stationery, and other paper products.
- Nationwide Mutual Insurance Co. filed suit in Wilmington charging nine auto repair shops in New Castle County, Del., and two trade associations with conspiracy to fix prices on auto body repairs. The suit charged that the company and its policyholders have been forced to pay higher than competitive prices for collision damage repairs.
- For allegedly conspiring with other large retailers to fix prices paid for wholesale beef, A & P, in 1974, was fined $32.7 million for damages.
- A number of suits by building owners and stage governments were set off when a terminated distributor sued his supplier and other members of an alleged conspiracy and settled out of court for $300,000. The franchised distributor was terminated by his supplier because he refused to go along with anticompetitive bidding practices instituted by other distributors in the building materials market.

While the guilt or innocence of a number of the above-mentioned companies charged with price conspiring remains to be determined in the courts, it is clear that

[77] "P & G Tests Better Retailer Deals," *Advertising Age* (March 17, 1980).
[78] "Price-Fixing: Crackdown Under Way," *Business Week* (June 2, 1975), p. 42. See also Bill Neikirk, "Probers Find Price Fixing is Pervasive in America," Chicago Tribune, Section 2, March 7, 1976, p. 9.
[79] These examples were drawn from "Price-Fixing: Crackdown Under Way," *op. cit.,* pp. 42-48.

channel members on all levels of distribution must be very cautious when discussing pricing arrangements of any type, including those dealing with credit and discount terms. In addition, it is likely that any vertical price maintenance arrangements will come under deep scrutiny, as a result of the repeal of Fair Trade.[80]

By now it should be obvious that meaningful communication relative to all marketing flows is essential if the practice of interorganization management is to be successful. The steps required in designing a marketing channel information system are shown in Exhibit 10-3. Availability of timely information is necessary for purposes of channel planning, organization, coordination, and control through careful assessment of channel member and structure performance. While aspects of chan-

EXHIBIT 10-3

Steps in Designing a Marketing Channel Information System

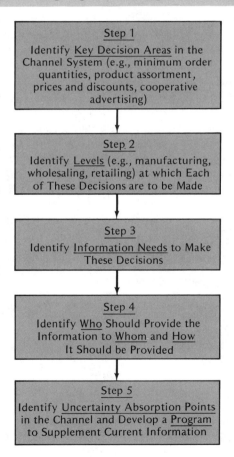

Step 1
Identify Key Decision Areas in the Channel System (e.g., minimum order quantities, product assortment, prices and discounts, cooperative advertising)

Step 2
Identify Levels (e.g., manufacturing, wholesaling, retailing) at which Each of These Decisions are to be Made

Step 3
Identify Information Needs to Make These Decisions

Step 4
Identify Who Should Provide the Information to Whom and How It Should be Provided

Step 5
Identify Uncertainty Absorption Points in the Channel and Develop a Program to Supplement Current Information

[80] See discussion of price maintenance in Chapter 8.

nel planning, organization, and coordination were examined in earlier chapters, assessing channel performance is the subject of the following one.

SUMMARY AND CONCLUSIONS

Inadequate or inappropriate communication, or miscommunication can lead to wasted resources and stimulate interorganizational conflict. The development of a working information system is a prerequisite to securing efficient channel coordination. However, an information system will always be imperfect, because its construction will be impeded by legal, cost, and privacy constraints. Information systems, no matter how carefully developed, are also always subject to distortion, given the perceptual bias inherent in all individuals.

Problems in channel communications generally center around structural and activity issues having to do with the length of the channel, inventory levels, promotion, products, and prices.

The longer the channel, the more highly developed the feedback system available to each channel member must be. Also, there should be mechanisms permitting the bypassing of messages in the channel. There is also likely to be a need for the repetition of messages, given the number of links in the channel that can distort message contents.

Inventory management is a channelwide problem and demands channelwide communication. Inventory difficulties are intimately tied to problems associated with ordering, shipping, and delivery. To solve these problems, the first step must be the development of an effective *intra*organizational information system. Programs associated with the use of high-speed electronic data processing have revolutionized management's capability to deal with problems of inventory management and control. An especially significant innovation has been the introduction of computerized point-of-sale or front-end systems. These various systems have the potential for facilitating the queuing and sequencing of *inter*organizational messages relative to inventory management and control as well as providing instant feedback throughout a marketing channel. They represent communication breakthroughs whereby a significant amount of "noise" can be reduced via the formation of specialized languages and the alteration of technology. However, the economic, social, ethical, and political issues surrounding the widespread adoption of such systems are profound and must be carefully assessed and/or accounted for as the development of such systems progresses.

Beyond computerized systems, and perhaps in conjunction with them, there is a strong need for informational assistance programs, especially on the part of the larger firms in the channel for the smaller ones, who are less able to afford sophisticated inventory programs. Obviously, such assistance will be self-serving if it is successful.

Coordinated systems involving transportation modes and storage facilities demand appropriate queuing and sequencing of messages if communication noise attending timing problems is to be reduced in physical distribution. The development of specialized languages and the aid of computer technology have been significant in securing on-time delivery and adequate inventory, billing, and shipment informa- tion for a number of companies. The application of the concept of shared services also is likely to help reduce redundancy in physical distribution services and com- munication.

Adequate feedback is critical to the solution of promotion problems. Here, the sales force of channel members—or other personnel operating at the boundary of channel organizations—are in key positions to observe difficulties associated with promotion and to enhance the communication process, except, of course, in situations where they themselves are involved in impeding the information flow. When conflicts of interest are suspected, use should be made of other interpenetra- tion strategies, such as channel diplomacy. Clearly, poor communication with regard to promotion results in duplication of effort and dilution of promotional im- pact.

Difficulties associated with channel communication about product features are similar to those faced in reference to promotion, and therefore require similar types of attention and solution. However, understanding the significance of mutual uncertainty absorption may be even more crucial when one is dealing with product design changes and product innovation. In addition, a high degree of domain con- sensus appears to be a prerequisite to conflict management regarding warranty ar- rangements and can only be achieved through effective communication between channel members relative to rights and obligations with regard to the performance of in-warranty service.

Although pricing presents continual problems in channels, communication about prices is particularly cumbersome during stagflationary periods. Price lists are often inaccurate, misleading, and/or frequently out of date. However, sharing information in this area is dangerous, because the probability of being accused of conspiring to fix prices is increasing, even if conversations about pricing problems are informal and seemingly innocuous.

The channel management process is incomplete without the institution of mechanisms to audit and assess the performance of channel members. The develop- ment and deployment of channel performance assessment and auditing mechanisms assumes the availability of free-flowing and error- and distortion-free information moving through the channel information and communication system. While this chapter examined the types of problems associated with the gathering and dissemination of channel information, the following chapter deals with the specification of "hard" data necessary for the evaluation of the performance of channel members and channel structures, and the incorporation of this information in channel performance assessment and channel audit mechanisms.

DISCUSSION QUESTIONS

1. In long channels, it has been suggested that there is a need for mechanisms permitting the bypassing of messages. Suggest three possible mechanisms that might be used for "by passing" purposes. Then discuss how, in such situations, conflict might be avoided relative to a "bypassed" channel member.

2. In what ways can the computer be used to make communication in marketing channels more efficient and effective? What effect will such data systems have on power relationships in channels? On the roles of channel members?

3. Compare and contrast the problems and opportunities of supermarkets and department stores in installing and utilizing front-end systems. What benefits will each receive from such systems? What difficulties will each face in fully utilizing them?

4. Debate the pros and cons of the adoption of UPC-code-oriented systems from a consumer's perspective and from society's perspective. Develop a position on such systems that you could present to the city council of your home town, assuming that the council is considering an ordinance banning such systems.

5. It has been argued by some that the major manufacturers of data processing equipment have embarked on different competitive strategies to further differentiate themselves, create "safe" market niches, lessen the chances for interorganizational hookups, and generally confuse users. IBM has even been accused of making word processing so complex that users think they need IBM to help them. Suggest some conflict management strategies that might be used by channel members to alleviate this situation.

6. What is the concept of "shared services"? In what ways might it be applied to transportation and storage problems, other than those directly mentioned in the text? What is the relationship between shared services and efficient intrachannel communications?

7. In dealing with false warranty claims on the part of its dealers, General Motors' new contract with its dealers requires dealers to keep two years of records available for inspection by GM instead of one, and it permits GM to provide copies to courts or governmental agencies whenever it decides the information is pertinent. According to the *Wall Street Journal* (October 30, 1975, p. 34), some dealers have complained that their business privacy is thus being eroded. As a result of these provisions, one dealer in the New York area has observed that GM has granted itself wider power to investigate its dealers, or to help others investigate them. What problems in communications within the channel is this situation evidence of? What solutions are there to these problems? Does the new contract provision seem equitable?

8. If you were a brand manager for a consumer goods manufacturer, what would you do in order to increase implementation of your trade deals at the retail level?

9. One author has observed that repositioning, scheduling/synchronization, simplification, access, and scale economies are the most important factors explaining the emergence and growth of vertical marketing systems. Explain what you believe is meant by each term, using examples to do so. Then explain what role information systems have had, relative to each factor.

10. Specify four separate distribution channels that might be used by a manufacturer of typewriters which are sold both for consumer and industrial use. Then, specify how each of the following costs might be allocated to the various channels: (1) billing, (2) district sales manager's expenses, (3) national magazine advertising, (4) marketing research, and (5) storage.

11. A wholesaler conducts a distribution cost study to determine the minimum-size order for breaking even. After finding this size, should the wholesaler refuse to accept orders below this size? What issues and alternatives should be considered.

ELEVEN

Assessing the Performance of Channel Institutions and Structures

The variety of institutions that form the primary components of channels and the factors that influence the way in which they link up with one another to comprise channel structures have been examined, described, and explored in previous chapters. The channel management process is not complete without assessment of the performance of the institutions and the channel structures in which they have been housed.

Performance is a multidimensional concept. As shown in Fig. 11-1, the performance of marketing channels and institutions thereof can be assessed by considering a number of dimensions including effectiveness, equity, productivity, and profitability. Performance assessment can be made from both a macro-, or societal perspective and a micro-, or business-oriented perspective. Often the perspectives overlap, and the macro view provides insights into operational features of individual enterprises.

Here, the performance of distribution channel structures and institutions is evaluated in terms of (1) system effectiveness, (2) system equity in serving various markets, (3) system productivity, and (4) system profitability. While attention will be given to historical performance or track record of some key channel members, e.g., wholesalers and retailers, our effort is extended to present a number of alternative managerial and channel audit mechanisms which are or can be used in evaluating channel performance.

CHANNEL SYSTEM EFFECTIVENESS

As indicated in earlier chapters, the marketing flows (physical possession, ownership, promotion, negotiation, financing, risking, ordering, and payment) are organized by institutions and agencies making up commercial channels of distribution in such a way as to provide goods and services in desired quantities (lot

FIGURE 11-1
Performance Measurement in Marketing Channels

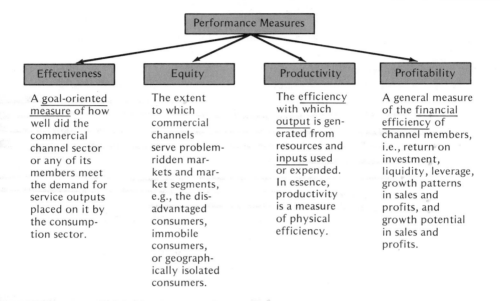

Performance Measures			
Effectiveness	**Equity**	**Productivity**	**Profitability**
A goal-oriented measure of how well did the commercial channel sector or any of its members meet the demand for service outputs placed on it by the consumption sector.	The extent to which commercial channels serve problem-ridden markets and market segments, e.g., the disadvantaged consumers, immobile consumers, or geographically isolated consumers.	The efficiency with which output is generated from resources and inputs used or expended. In essence, productivity is a measure of physical efficiency.	A general measure of the financial efficiency of channel members, i.e., return on investment, liquidity, leverage, growth patterns in sales and profits, and growth potential in sales and profits.

size) when needed (delivery time). These goods and services are made available at a number of different locations (market decentralization) at which they are displayed and generally combined with complementary and substitutable items (assortment breadth) in accordance with marketplace demand. Therefore, the "output" of a given commercial channel of distribution may be conceptualized as lot size, delivery time, market decentralization, and assortment breadth.[1] Household consumers and industrial and business users are key actors in distribution channels because they participate directly in the marketing flows. However, the lower their degree of participation in the flows, the more work must be done by commercial channel members in providing the "output," and thus the higher will be the final price of goods and services. If consumers were willing to increase the amount of search and selection time they devote to purchasing and thus absorb part of the marketing task, prices could probably be reduced.

Unfortunately, there are no quantitative measures available that provide an insight into aggregate performance regarding system output, beyond global estimates of the dollar and physical amount of goods and services passing through the

[1] This model and discussion of system output draws heavily from Louis P. Bucklin, "Marketing Channels and Structures: A Macro View," in Boris W. Becker and Helmut Becker (eds.), *American Marketing Association Combined Conference Proceedings* (Chicago, Ill.: American Marketing Association, 1973), pp. 32–35.

distribution system.[2] Qualitatively, though, it is possible to point to a number of historical changes.

First, as mentioned in the chapter on retailing institutions, there has been a significant increase in the size of the average retail transaction over time.[3] Consumers are, therefore, buying in larger lots, requiring less marketing flow participation and "output" from commercial channel systems in this respect. The increase in transaction size permits retailers to buy in larger lots, which, in turn, reduces the need for wholesaler services. In turn, these developments permit lower distributive costs since commercial channel service outputs are reduced, and thus lower prices to consumers are possible. Similarly, the development of the automobile and improved road networks has, as Bucklin observes, reduced the need for highly decentralized retail systems for *convenience* goods.[4] Offsetting this, however, has been an increase in decentralization for *shopping* items with the emergence of the planned regional shopping center.

Second, there has been no obvious reduction in the willingness of either ultimate household consumers or industrial and business users to accept longer delivery times for the products they desire to buy. Shortages of raw materials may alter this somewhat; in the future, users may have to wait longer in order to be assured of appropriate supplies.[5] The willingness of consumers to postpone and ration purchases of products in short supply (e.g., petroleum), or to accept longer delivery times, will be rewarded, not by lower prices, but merely by being able to secure and consume the scarce commodities.

On the other hand, rising affluence has increased the range of products household consumers would like to buy at a single stop, raising the requirement for broader store assortments and increased speculative inventories within channel systems. Commercial channel "output" has had to rise here; the increase in store size, for example, has been caused by the expanding number of items being stocked.[6] There are, however, serious problems associated with the increase in available assortments relative to desirable levels of consumer choice. If one considers the number of brands to be an element of assortment, then it is possible that there is "overchoice" in the marketplace. In a study of this problem, Settle and Golden surveyed household consumers on their choice perceptions; ideal and perceived assortment size were compared to the actual choices available at the retail level.[7] It was found that actual choices were greater than perceived and ideal

[2] See the chapters on retailing and wholesaling in this text for relevant statistics on the volume of goods and services passing through the distribution system.

[3] David Schwartzman, *The Decline of Service in Retail Trade* (Pullman, Wash.: Washington State University, Bureau of Economic and Business Research, 1971).

[4] Bucklin, *op. cit.,* p. 33.

[5] See Philip Kotler, "Marketing During Periods of Shortage," *Journal of Marketing,* Vol. 38 (July 1974), pp. 20–29.

[6] Bucklin, *op. cit.,* p. 33.

[7] R. B. Settle and L. L. Golden, "Consumer Perceptions: Overchoice in the Marketplace," in Scott Ward and Peter Wright (eds.), *4th Annual Conference Proceedings* (Association for Consumer Research, 1973), pp. 29–37.

choices. This overabundance of brands can lead to inefficiencies in the use of resources and higher prices to consumers. Furthermore, consumers are becoming increasingly confused as to which brands and package sizes of various products represent the "best buys," from a purely economical perspective. This confusion was demonstrated by Friedman in an experiment on consumer choice in which 33 young married women were asked to select the most economical (largest quantity for the price) package for 20 different categories of typically purchased products on sale at a selected supermarket.[8] Among other findings, Friedman reported that the sampled consumers were, on the average, unable to select the most economical package 43 percent of the time. Thus, even though assortment breadth is generally a desirable output of commercial channel operations,[9] there may be threshholds above which more choice becomes dysfunctional or wasteful.

The broader assortments required on the retail level have, to a significant extent, been responsible for the continued growth and survival of wholesalers and have offset, at least partially, the negative effect on the use of wholesalers caused by the increase in retail transaction size. Specialized wholesalers, such as rack merchandisers, who carry broad assortments of limited lines, have, as pointed out in Chapter 3, been especially successful in supplying food stores with nontraditional items (e.g., phonograph records, magazines, and health and beauty aids).[10] In the industrial goods sector, there has also been an increase in demand for wholesaler services, especially because of the growth in sales of items for which wholesaler support has long been relied upon by suppliers and customers, such as machinery, equipment, and supplies. Offsetting this somewhat has been the tendency to move away from "double wholesaling" in the industrial sector as more and more suppliers find themselves capable of absorbing promotional flows for their products. The latter change has had the greatest negative impact on agent middlemen.[11]

If hard evidence is scant for assessing commercial channel "output" (viewed in terms of lot size, waiting or delivery time, market decentralization, and product assortment), it is virtually nonexistent for assessing how well the heterogeneous production capacity of an industry is fitted by the sorting processes to the heterogeneity of consumer tastes and incomes.[12] There have, however, been some data gathered on this subject relative to disadvantaged consumers.

[8] Monroe Peter Friedman, "Consumer Confusion in the Selection of Supermarket Products," *Journal of Applied Psychology,* Vol. 50 (December 1966), pp. 529–534.

[9] For example, Buzzell feels that "most businessmen *and* most academicians would agree that the performance of an industry or company is higher, other things being equal, to the degree that it provides *choice* to customers and to the degree that it manifests *flexibility* in altering its offerings response to changes in demand." Robert D. Buzzell, "Marketing and Economic Performance: Meaning and Measurement," in Fred C. Allvine (ed.), *Public Policy and Marketing Practices* (Chicago, Ill.: American Marketing Association, 1973), pp. 154–155.

[10] The increase in commercial channel output relative to such items comes at a cost to the consumer, however, in the form of higher prices.

[11] Bucklin, *op. cit.,* pp. 33–34.

[12] A channel audit, as specified in Chapter 1, might provide a means for criticizing channel performance along these output dimensions. The end result should produce insights for social as well as business policy.

**EQUITY IN SERVING
VARIOUS MARKETS** Given the profusion of wholesaling and retailing institutions in the United States, it is difficult to imagine pockets of the population that are not adequately served by the distributive trades, at least in terms of the availability of goods and services at fairly reasonable prices. Yet it has been carefully documented by a number of scholars that the poor in the United States, especially those individuals living in ghetto areas of major cities and in rural communities, are disadvantaged by the distributive system as well as by other aspects of our economy and society.[13] While there is some evidence of outright discrimination against minority groups by merchants in their pricing and credit practices,[14] the primary reasons for the absence of broad assortments of reasonably priced merchandise and services seem to be related more to the structure of trade in these areas than to any purposive strategy of racial or socioeconomic bias. For example, it has been shown that food chain prices do not vary significantly between ghetto and suburban locations within a given trading area, although there is still some controversy as to whether quality differs among outlets of a given chain organization.[15] Rather, it is the absence of food chain and major department store operations in the ghetto and rural areas that prohibits the residents of these areas from obtaining the benefits available to their suburban counterparts. The mobility of the poor is limited, so they must rely on the stores within their communities. While these stores have been known to charge high prices and to extend credit at usurious rates, their profitability is very low, which indicates that their costs of doing business are extremely high.[16] A summary of reasons cited by retailers as barriers to successful ghetto distribution is presented in Table 11-1.

A partial explanation of this inequity in distribution is the fact that ghetto retailers in particular are offering "services" of some importance to their constituents, most of whom, according to Goodman, are aware of the high prices being paid. Among these services are high-risk credit, small-lot transactions, convenient purchasing, and a persuasive (often deceptive) rationale to buy goods poor con-

[13] See, for example, David Caplovitz, *The Poor Pay More* (New York: The Free Press, 1963); Louise G. Richards, "Consumer Practices of the Poor," in Lola M. Irelan (ed.), *Low-Income Life Styles* (Washington, D.C.: U.S. Department of Health, Education, and Welfare, Welfare Administration, Publication No. 14), pp. 67–86; Frederick D. Sturdivant and Walter T. Wilhelm, "Poverty, Minorities, and Consumer Exploitation," *Social Science Quarterly,* Vol. 49 (December 1968), pp. 643–650; and Frederick D. Sturdivant (ed.), *The Ghetto Marketplace* (New York: The Free Press, 1969).

[14] See Sturdivant and Wilhelm, *op. cit.*

[15] Donald E. Sexton, Jr., "Do Blacks Pay More?" *Journal of Marketing Research,* Vol. 8 (November 1971), pp. 420–426; Charles S. Goodman, "Do the Poor Pay More?" *Journal of Marketing,* Vol. 32 (January 1968), pp. 18–24; Donald F. Dixon and Daniel J. McLaughlin, Jr., "Low-Income Consumers and the Issue of Exploitation: A Study of Chain Supermarkets," *Social Science Quarterly,* Vol. 51 (September 1970), pp. 320–328; and Louis W. Stern and William J. Sargent, "Comparative Prices and Pedagogy: Towards Relevance in Marketing Education," *Journal of Business Research,* Vol. 2 (October 1974), pp. 435–46.

[16] *Economic Report on Installment Credit and Retail Sales Practices of District of Columbia Retailers* (Washington D.C.: Federal Trade Commission, 1968), p. 18; and Frederick C. Klein, "Black Businessmen Running Ghetto Store Can Be a Survival Test," *Wall Street Journal,* January 31, 1977, pp. 1 and 13.

TABLE 11-1   Reasons cited by retailers as barriers to successful ghetto distribution

1. Higher risk of store damage from vandalism, leading to higher insurance premiums.
2. Low sales per square footage of space.
3. Low inventory turnover.
4. Exploitive image: "If something goes wrong in the neighborhood, someone would always find an excuse to blame us."
6. Higher credit losses due to bad checks.
7. Higher costs of logistics such as material handling and transportation due to, among other things, poor location and smaller lots.
8. Higher personnel costs since "they must be given an incentive to work in a ghetto location."

Source: Iqbal Mathur and Subbash Jain, "Inequality in the Ghetto Distribution Structure and Opportunity Equalization for the Ghetto Dweller," in Ronald C. Curhan, (ed.), *New Marketing for Social and Economic Progress and Marketing's Contribution to the Firm and Society* (Chicago, Ill.: American Marketing Association Combined Proceedings, 1974), p. 281.

sumers would like to have but cannot really afford.[17] Table 11-2 summarizes factors identified as important in explaining neighborhood store patronage by ghetto residents.

From a competitive perspective, the structure of retailing in ghettos is highly atomistic. There are many small stores offering similar merchandise. Barriers to entry, as Sturdivant points out, are also quite low.[18] Therefore, on the basis of economic theory,[19] one would predict that performance from a macroperspective, would be higher in ghetto areas than in the suburbs, where there are generally fewer outlets of larger size. The fact that marketing practices and performance are generally unbearably bad in the ghetto calls into question the assumptions of industrial organization economists about the benefits that derive from atomistic competition.[20] In fact, this questioning is supported by the findings of scholars who have studied less highly developed economies where similar structural conditions appear to hold. For example, in their critique of distributive systems for eggs, milk,

[17] Charles S. Goodman, "Whither the Marketing System in Low-Income Areas," *Wharton Quarterly* (Spring 1970).

[18] Sturdivant, "Distribution in American Society . . . ," *op. cit.,* pp. 102–103.

[19] See the arguments presented by Joe S. Bain, *Industrial Organization,* 2nd ed. (New York: John Wiley & Sons, 1968); and Richard Caves, *American Industry: Structure, Conduct, and Performance,* 2nd ed. (Englewood Cliffs, N.J.: Prentice-Hall, 1967). These positions have been summarized in Stern and Grabner, *op. cit.* Also see John F. Cady, "Competition and Economic Dualism," in Alan R. Andersen, *Marketing: Research Challenges* (Chicago, Ill.: American Marketing Association, 1977), pp. 56–71.

[20] See Stern and Grabner, *op. cit.,* pp. 36–40, for a summary of the assumed benefits. Bucklin and Carman have, implicitly at least, raised similar questions regarding the performance of the present "atomistic" health care delivery system in the United States. See Louis P. Bucklin and James M. Carman, "Vertical Market Structure Theory and the Health Care Delivery System," in Jagdish N. Sheth and Peter L. Wright (eds.), *Marketing Analysis for Societal Problems* (Urbana-Champaign, Ill.: University of Illinois, Bureau of Economic and Business Research, 1974), pp. 7–39, and Chapter 14 of this book.

TABLE 11-2   Some factors identified as important in explaining neighborhood store patronage by ghetto residents

1. Immobility.
2. Habit.
3. Availability of credit.
4. Community spirit.
5. Lack of knowledge that prices would be lower elsewhere.
6. Lack of assurance of acceptance outside the ghetto.
7. Too-frequent shopping due to inability to budget their money and lack of available food storage space.

Source: Igbal Mathur and Subbash Jain, "Inequality in the Ghetto Distribution Structure and Opportunity Equalization for the Ghetto Dweller," in Ronald C. Curhan, (ed.), *New Marketing for Social and Economic Progress and Marketing's Contribution to the Firm and Society* (Chicago, Ill.: American Marketing Association Combined Proceedings, 1974), p. 282.

and produce in sections of South America, Riley, Harrison, Slater, *et al.,* concluded that

> . . . excessive atomistic competition hampers productivity improvements by stifling technological innovations and inhibits the agricultural and marketing development process by fostering market uncertainty, high transaction costs and excessive market wastes and by preventing the effective transmission of incentives to firms in the production-marketing system.[21]

While it is no doubt the case that the reluctance of food chains, department stores, and regional shopping centers, among others, to enter the ghetto and poor rural areas can be traced to high occupancy costs, crime rates, and/or lack of discretionary income to support new, large-scale ventures, the fact remains that these areas are truly disadvantaged relative to other shopping areas and that, as long as they remain so, there will exist a high degree of inequity in the distributive system.[22] In this situation, only the institutionalization of a significant amount of interorganizational coordination between government agencies, chain organizations, wholesalers, manufacturers, and various facilitating agencies (such as insurance companies) will bring about needed change. Many suggestions relative to solutions on the supply side have been forthcoming, such as tax incentives for chain organizations entering the ghetto, investment credits, and the like,[23] but few have been enacted on a sufficiently large scale to have any major impact. On the demand side, it will obviously be necessary to elevate the incomes and increase the mobility

[21] Harold Riley, Kelly Harrison, Charles C. Slater, et al., *Market Coordination in the Development of the Cauca Valley Region—Columbia* (East Lansing, Mich.: Michigan State University, Latin American Studies Center, 1970), p. 189.

[22] It is possible that shopping areas adjacent to many university campuses are subject to many of the same problems as those found in ghetto communities. See, for example, Stern and Sargent, *op. cit.*

[23] See Frederick D. Sturdivant, "Better Deal for Ghetto Shoppers," *Harvard Business Review,* Vol. 46 (March-April 1968), pp. 130–139.

of ghetto and rural residents so that they can have a modicum of bargaining power to use in their dealings with merchants located in their communities.

CHANNEL SYSTEM PRODUCTIVITY*

Productivity is a measure of efficiency in using inputs, e.g., labor and capital, to generate outputs, e.g., sales volume, gross margins, and value added. Ideally, productivity is a measure of physical efficiency; therefore, productivity analysts attempt to remove the impact of price changes on figures used, e.g., sales volume, by deflating them to generate real outputs. Developing an understanding of productivity in the distributive trades requires scrutiny of measures of productivity used and an analysis of correlates of productivity in wholesaling and retailing.

In terms of measures of output, productivity analysts rely heavily upon sales volume data. While gross margin or value added would be closer to ideal measures of output, wide differences exist in average gross margin percentages in the different sectors in wholesaling and retailing. Such differences lead to distortion in results. Additionally, gross margin and value added data are not as available nor as easily obtainable as sales volume data.

In terms of measures of input, productivity analysts rely heavily on labor man-hours because the distributive trades are labor intensive. As a matter of fact, persons engaged in trade represent 22 percent of the labor force in the U.S.[24] Therefore, productivity in the distributive trades is usually measured in terms of sales per man-hour. Most productivity figures are presented as average annual percentage rates of change to portray comparisons between components under study over a period of years. Usually, productivity figures in the distributive trades are compared with those of other sectors in the economy, particularly manufacturing, as shown in Table 11-3.

Despite the impact of developments in retailing—e.g., computerization, increase in transaction size, and reductions in level of services provided per transaction—and in wholesaling—e.g., computerization, warehouse modernization, and employee training—productivity increases in wholesaling and retailing are lagging behind other sectors in the economy, as indicated in Table 11-3. The exception to this statement is the mining sector, which experienced a dramatic decrease during 1973–1979 due to environmental protection and energy-related developments.

Productivity analysts advance a number of possible explanations of the lagging productivity in wholesaling and retailing. First, wholesaling and retailing, as already mentioned, are labor intensive industries. Man-hours increased in these sectors at a substantially faster rate than other sectors.[25] Second, there are indications

---

*This section is based on Adel I. El-Ansary, "Distribution Productivity in the United States: Analysis and Frameworks," Proceedings of the 8th International Research Seminar in Marketing I.A.E., Aix-en-Provence, France, 1981.

[24] Philip Van Ness, *Productivity in Wholesale Distribution* (Washington, D.C.: Distribution Research and Education Foundation, 1980), p. 1.

[25] *Ibid.*, p. 5.

TABLE 11-3   Average annual increase in real output per man-hour (1968–1979)

Economic Sector	1968-1972* Percent Increase	1973-1979** Percent Increase/Decrease
Farming	4.5%	3.1%
Mining	3.9	(4.5)
Manufacturing	2.3	2.1
Wholesaling	1.7	0.0
Retailing	0.8	1.3
Total Economy	1.9%	
Total Private Sector		1.3%

Sources: *Bert C. McCammon, Jr., and William L. Hammer, "A Frame of Reference for Improving Productivity in Distribution," *Atlanta Economic Review*, Vol. 24 (September–October 1974), p. 10. **Bureau of Labor Statistics, United States Department of Labor, Washington, D.C., 1980.

that to improve productivity, the distributive trades are more dependent than manufacturing upon growth in sales volume. This issue is critical because of the possibility of persistent low growth in constant dollar retail sales.[26] Low growth in sales rates, accompanied with faster rates of increase in man-hours, guarantees lower gains in productivity. Finally, within the agricultural and manufacturing sectors of the U.S. economy, farmers, processors, and industrial firms historically have turned to innovative technology, employing capital inputs more widely. Innovations related to checkout automation, information processing, materials handling, warehouse modernization, packaging, and larger and more productive facilities were adopted in the distributive trades on a large scale only in the 1970s. Furthermore, the adoption of new technology in the distributive trades faces a number of constraints. For example, in retail supermarkets

> . . . numerous constraints to adoption (of new technology) have been noted. Major factors were:
> 1. The sharp reduction in demand and, concomitantly, the number of new stores opened.
> 2. The rising energy cost and diversion of resources from labor-saving purposes.
> 3. Consumer and labor resistance to new technologies.
> 4. High capital cost of implementation.
> 5. The necessity for complex interindustry cooperation for the achievement of savings.[27]

A more encouraging perspective of productivity in the distribution sector of the economy is revealed when one examines productivity increases for different

[26] Louis P. Bucklin, "Growth and Productivity Change in Retailing," Theory in Retailing Seminar, The American Marketing Association and the Institute for Retail Management, New York University, 1980, p. 1.

[27] Louis P. Bucklin, "Technological Change and Store Operations: The Supermarket Case," *Journal of Retailing* (Spring 1980), p. 13.

wholesale and retail types of institutions. For example, among merchant whole-salers

> . . . for the 34 individual commodity groups in the four-digit wholesale-distribution categories covered for the census years 1948 through 1972, average rates of change in sales per man-hour ranged from a 5.8% growth rate for Poultry & Poultry Products down to a negative growth rate of -1.3% for Industrial Machinery & Equipment. The second highest growth rate was that of Electrical Appliances, TVs and Radio Sets, which had 5.7%. The next-to-lowest rate was a negative -0.8% shown by Hardware.[28]

Similar variations are found in retailing, as shown in Table 11-4. Although beyond our present purposes, it should, therefore, be recognized that a complete assessment of productivity requires an examination of the subsectors, i.e., wholesaling industry groups and retail institutional types. A number of studies examining subsectors are cited below for further reference by interested readers.[29]

While productivity studies in the subsectors vary in methodology and in the number and nature of factors that determine productivity in different industries

TABLE 11-4   Relative productivity performance of five retailer types 1959–1976

Retail Type	Output		Productivity	
	Rank	Rate	Rank	Rate
New car dealers	1	3.40[a]	2	2.15[a]
Service stations	2	3.03	1	3.43
Restaurants	3	2.86	5	0.74
Department stores	4	2.20	4	1.61
Food stores	5	2.15	3	1.71

[a] Annual rate of growth, in percent.

Source: Louis P. Bucklin, "Growth and Productivity Change in Retailing," The Theory in Retailing Seminar, The American Marketing Association and the Institute for Retail Management, New York University, 1980, p. 18.

[28] Van Ness, *op. cit.,* p. 7.

[29] U.S. Bureau of Labor Statistics, "Output per Unit of Labor Input in the Retail Food Store Industry," *Monthly Labor Review* (January 1977), pp. 42–47; U.S. Bureau of Labor Statistics (b), "Report on Productivity Gains in Selected Industries." *Monthly Labor Review* (January 1977), pp. 80–83; U.S. Bureau of Labor Statistics, "Productivity and New Technology in Eating and Drinking Places," *Monthly Labor Review* (September 1977), pp. 9–15; William R. Sherrard, "Labor Productivity for the Firm: A Case Study," *Quarterly Review of Economics and Business* (Spring 1967), pp. 49–61; Marvin E. Gantz, Jr., "Productivity Measurement in Alcoa," in U.S. National Center for Productivity and Quality of Working Life, *Improving Productivity Through Industry and Company Measurement, Series 2* (Washington, D.C.: U.S. Government Printing Office, October, 1976); U.S. National Center for Productivity and Quality of Working Life, *Improving Productivity: A Description of Selected Company Programs (Series I)* (Washington, D.C.: U.S. Government Printing Office, October 1976), and Hirotaka Takeuchi, "Productivity Analysis as Resource Management Tool in the Retail Trade," unpublished Ph.D. dissertation, University of California, Berkeley, 1977.

and institutional types, all analysis points out clearly that productivity is a complex phenomenon resulting from the interaction of a number of variables. For example, one study conducted by Takeuchi reveals that the state of technology, scale of operation, capacity utilization, integration of processing facilities, level of consumer service, product assortment, quality of management, and quality of labor are the critical variables influencing productivity in the supermarket industry.[30]

Some researchers indicate that unless total factor productivity, i.e., impact of labor, capital, and land, is considered, one cannot reach sound conclusions about productivity.[31] This can be particularly true as accelerated adoption of new technology results in massive infusions of capital. Others warn that in many wholesale industries and in retailing, leasing of buildings, vehicles, fixtures, and point-of-sale terminals is commonplace. Therefore, until reliable data on leased property and equipment can be developed and analyzed, it will be difficult to assess the true impact of fixed assets on productivity in the distribution sector of the economy.[32] In another vein, some researchers documented that productivity is not only dependent on the conduct or performance of distributive institutions, but also on the structure of the markets in which they compete.[33] In its turn, structure, for example, in department store retailing, is determined by income per capita, automobile ownership, scale of operation, size of transactions, average wages, density of population, and growth/decline of population in markets studied.[34]

Setting aside the complexity of productivity analysis and the lack of systematic data on value added and gross margins as alternative measures of output, historic and landmark studies of distribution cost (a surrogate variable for inputs) and value added (a measure of output) do exist. From a distribution cost standpoint, wholesale and retail institutions account for only a portion of total marketing charges that are incurred in bringing a product from its origin to ultimate consumption. Although their share is the dominant one, accounting for perhaps as much as 75 percent of the total,[35] other institutions (manufacturers, facilitating agencies, and consumers themselves) also contribute significantly to total marketing expenditures.

From a macroperspective, it is obvious to even the most casual onlooker that the cost of distribution in industrialized societies is relatively high. In such societies, progressions in economic development and consumer affluence are accompanied by a shift toward the sales of luxury-type goods, some of which carry extremely heavy

[30] Takeuchi, *ibid.*

[31] Van Ness, *op. cit.,* pp. 15–16.

[32] *Ibid.,* p. 17.

[33] Louis P. Bucklin, "Structure, Conduct, and Productivity in Distribution," and Johan Arndt, "Exploring Relationships between Market Structure and Performance in Retailing," in Hans B. Thorelli (ed.), *Strategy Plus Structure Equals Performance* (Bloomington, Ind.: Indiana University Press, 1977), pp. 219–246.

[34] Hirotaka Takeuchi and Louis P. Bucklin, "Productivity in Retailing: Retail Structure and Public Policy," *Journal of Retailing,* Vol. 53, Number 1 (Spring 1977), pp. 35–46.

[35] Louis P. Bucklin, *Competition and Evolution in the Distributive Trades* (Englewood Cliffs, N.J.: Prentice-Hall, 1972), p. 296.

marketing costs. The evolution of industrial goods markets also adds new marketing costs to the system, concomitant with economic growth.[36]

Suspicions about the relatively high cost of distribution have been confirmed by the statistics developed in a number of studies on the subject. For example, in a thorough investigation three decades ago, Harold Barger noted that the combined gross margins of retailers and wholesalers were 37.4 percent.[37] Wholesalers' gross margins were 7.7 percent, while retailers' were 29.7 percent.[38] More recent studies on distributive costs have focused on "value added" rather than gross margins. The former excludes from gross margins the costs middlemen pay for services rendered by institutions in other sectors of the economy, such as their expenditures for fuel, electric energy, and transportation. Thus, what remains in the distributive sector are the middleman's own costs, the charges on his capital, his expenditure on labor, and his profits. "Value added" may constitute as much as 70 to 85 percent of the distributive gross margin.[39]

From a theoretical perspective, "value added" supposedly indicates the unique contribution of middlemen to the final dollar value of products or services yielded by their managerial skills in combining labor, capital, and land in various ways.[40] For the 1964–1965 time period, the value added by wholesalers and retailers combined was approximately 23 percent; for the retail sector alone, it was about 14½ percent and for wholesaling, it was 8½ percent.[41] Since 1949, the percentages have been quite stable.

In a highly innovative study, Bucklin computed the value added in the performance of marketing activities in six sectors of the U.S. economy—transportation,

---

[36] For a thorough analysis of the productivity and performance of retailing and wholesaling in the United Kingdom, see T. S. Ward, *The Distribution of Consumer Goods: Structure and Performance* (London: Cambridge University Press, 1973).

[37] Harold Barger, *Distribution's Place in the American Economy since 1869* (Princeton, N.J.: Princeton University Press, 1955), p. 60. Gross margin is always stated in terms of sales; the combined figure for retailers and wholesalers as a proportion of cost of goods sold would run over 50 percent.

[38] Stanley C. Hollander has provided some appropriate warnings about interpreting cost figures such as these in "Measuring the Cost and Value of Marketing" in William G. Moller, Jr. and David L. Wilemon (eds.), *Marketing Channels: A Systems Viewpoint* (Homewood, Ill.: Richard D. Irwin, 1971), pp. 373–383.

[39] Bucklin, *Competition and Evolution . . . , op. cit.,* p. 298.

[40] The concept of "value added" is truly meaningful only if there is sufficient competition in a market. Otherwise, prices in that market include monopoly or oligopoly profits that are of doubtful "value" to consumers. This weakness in the concept prompted Sturdivant to observe that "the emergence of the value added concept doubtless retarded objective and critical analysis of socially significant questions related to distribution. With . . . a prevailing attitude that marketing costs must equal value or else goods and services would not be purchased, it is little wonder that consumer behavior emerged as the dominant area of interest for marketing scholars." Frederick D. Sturdivant, "Distribution in American Society: Some Questions of Efficiency and Relevance," in Louis P. Bucklin (ed.), *Vertical Marketing Systems* (Glenview, Ill.: Scott, Foresman and Co., 1970), p. 98.

[41] Bucklin, *Competiton and Evolution . . . , op. cit.,* p. 300. While Bucklin's computations were called, in his study, distributive trade-cost ratios, they are very similar in nature to value-added computations. Furthermore, Bucklin's findings are similar to those presented in a thorough study by Reavis Cox, Charles S. Goodman, and Thomas C. Fichandler entitled *Distribution in a High-Level Economy* (Englewood Cliffs, N.J.: Prentice-Hall, 1965).

retailing, wholesaling, manufacturing, minerals, and advertising.[42] Although his findings are tentative and subject to error because of the way in which the data were derived, they provide some interesting comparisons, as shown in Table 11-5. Thus, in 1967, the value added in the marketing of commodities by the six sectors totaled $163.5 billion. Approximately 72 percent of the total was contributed by retailing and wholesaling, while another 14 percent was contributed by the logistical institutions comprising the transportation sector. The large share accumulated by the former two sectors indicates that any advances in their performance and productivity will have a marked effect on performance and productivity in marketing generally.[43]

CHANNEL SYSTEM PROFITABILITY*

No single measure of performance fully reflects the financial well-being of the firm. The financial performance of wholesalers and retailers is multidimensional, requiring an examination of (1) profitability or return on investment, (2) liquidity or the ability of the firm to meet its financial liabilities within a time frame, (3) capital structure or leverage ratio, (4) growth pattern of sales and profits,

TABLE 11-5   Value added in marketing of commodities in six sectors of the economy, 1948, 1958, 1963, and 1967

Sector	Millions of Dollars 1948	%	Millions of Dollars 1958	%	Millions of Dollars 1963	%	Millions of Dollars 1967	%
Transportation	$11,560	19.7	$16,070	16.1	$ 17,582	14.3	$ 23,110	14.1
Retailing	26,440	45.1	44,419	44.5	55,708	45.3	75,214	46.0
Wholesaling	12,949	22.1	24,587	24.7	32,740	26.6	43,051	26.3
Manufacturing	6,934	11.8	13,709	13.7	15,227	12.4	20,103	12.3
Minerals	270	0.5	397	0.4	412	0.3	477	0.3
Advertising	439	0.7	685	0.7	1,185	1.0	1,594	1.0
Total	58,592	100.0	99,867	100.0	122,854	100.0	163,549	100.0

Source: Louis P. Bucklin, "A Synthetic Index of Marketing Productivity," a paper presented to the 58th International Marketing Conference of the American Marketing Association, April 14-17, 1975, in Chicago, p. 7.

* This section is based on Adel I. El-Ansary, "Distribution Productivity in the United States: Analysis and Frameworks," Proceedings of the 8th International Research Seminar in Marketing, I.A.E., Aix-en-Provence, France, 1981.

[42] Louis P. Bucklin, "A Synthetic Index of Marketing Productivity," a paper presented to the 58th International Marketing Conference of the American Marketing Association, Chicago, April 14–17, 1975, pp. 4–8.

[43] For an excellent treatment of productivity in marketing, see Louis P. Bucklin, *Productivity in Marketing* (Chicago: The American Marketing Association, 1978).

and (5) growth potential of sales and profits.[44] Dun and Bradstreet's Key Business Ratios for Retailing and Wholesaling, a sample of which is shown in Tables 11-6 and 11-7, are illustrative of the types of financial ratios of interest to performance analysts. However, return on investment is accepted as an aggregate performance measure in the retail and wholesale trades.

The strategic profit model has been developed by managerial accountants to evaluate and diagnose profitability problems such as those that confront retailers and wholesalers. Because of the importance of such a model in formulating effective interorganizational strategies as well as in assessing performance in distribution, it is explained in some detail below.

The strategic profit model (SPM) is portrayed in Fig. 11-2. The SPM is basically a product of the insights into financial management generated by the DuPont Company. DuPont was one of the first to explore, in detail, the interrelationship of various financial ratios. In its planning activities, it developed and used DuPont charts (see Fig. 11-3) which illustrated the fact that, for example, asset turnover and net profit as a percentage of sales are related, since the elements contained in them lead to net profits on assets.[45]

The SPM involves multiplying a company's profit margin by its rate of asset

---

FIGURE 11-2
The Strategic Profit Model (SPM)

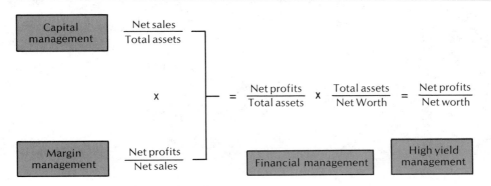

Source: Bert C. McCammon, Jr., "Perspectives for Distribution Programming," in Louis P. Bucklin (ed.), *Marketing Systems.* © 1970 by Scott, Foresman and Company. Reprinted by permission of the publisher.

---

[44] Robert F. Lusch and James M. Kenderdine, "Financial and Strategic Trends of Chain Store Retailers; 1974–1975," *Review of Regional Economics and Business* (April 1977), pp. 11–17.

[45] Erich A. Helfert, *Techniques of Financial Analysis,* 3rd ed. (Homewood, Ill.: Richard D. Irwin, 1972), p. 71. For further elaboration on profitability analysis see Frank H. Mossman, Paul M. Fischer, and W. J. E. Crissy, "New Approaches to Analyzing Marketing Profitability," *Journal of Marketing* (April 1974), pp. 43–48; and Leland L. Beik and Stephen L. Buzby, "Profitability Analysis by Market Segment," *Journal of Marketing* (July 1973), pp. 48–53.

TABLE 11-6   Key business ratios: retailing

Line of Business (and number of concerns reporting)	Current Assets to Current Debt	Net Profits on Net Sales	Net Profits on Tangible Net Worth	Net Profits on Net Working Capital	Net Sales to Tangible Net Worth
	Times	Percent	Percent	Percent	Times
5211	4.51	6.00	34.28	37.93	8.07
Lumber & Other Bldg.	2.49	3.46	17.73	19.14	4.59
Mtls. Dealers (3,699)	1.60	1.74	8.66	8.74	2.64
5411	6.36	4.27	39.68	68.37	17.39
Grocery Stores (4,197)	2.70	1.79	20.17	33.21	9.18
	1.43	.74	9.32	11.89	4.52
5511	1.76	2.27	30.51	37.65	21.28
Motor Vehicle	1.42	1.24	17.28	20.70	13.81
Doniers (7,162)	1.24	.57	8.12	8.57	8.64
5531	4.66	8.26	41.56	48.63	8.60
Auto & Home	2.33	4.26	21.64	24.03	4.85
Supply Stores (3,041)	1.45	1.86	10.37	8.51	2.58
5541	6.90	6.00	59.23	100.68	10.89
Gasoline Service	2.79	2.95	25.05	39.53	8.44
Stations (3,062)	1.42	.93	9.26	10.30	3.62
5611	5.89	9.11	34.70	38.50	6.21
Clothing & Furnishings,	2.91	4.05	16.60	18.04	3.53
Men's & Boys' (5,652)	1.81	1.48	6.19	6.00	2.16
5621	7.08	10.71	40.62	45.64	6.11
Women's Ready-to-	3.32	5.00	18.77	21.73	3.42
Wear Stores (9,558)	1.88	1.68	6.22	6.96	1.95
5712	6.18	9.02	34.95	38.57	6.59
Furniture Stores (6,941)	2.98	4.42	16.16	17.45	3.48
	1.74	1.73	6.76	6.17	1.81
5732	4.28	10.00	50.01	73.85	9.36
Radio & Television	2.09	4.01	22.20	29.72	4.71
Stores (2,396)	1.36	1.36	7.84	8.03	2.23

turnover and its leverage ratio to derive its rate of return on net worth. Let us look briefly at each of the components of the model.

NET PROFITS/NET SALES (PROFIT MARGIN).   The relationship of reported net profit to sales indicates a management's ability to recover the cost of merchandise or services, the expenses of operating the business (including depreciation) and the cost of borrowed funds from revenues generated during a given time period, as well as their adeptness in leaving a margin of reasonable compensation to

TABLE 11-6   Key business ratios: retailing (CONT.)

Net Sales to Net Working Capital	Collection Period	Net Sales to Inventory	Fixed Assets to Tangible Net Worth	Current Debt to Tangible Net Worth	Total Debt to Tangible Net Worth	Inventory to Net Working Capital	Current Debt to Inventory	Funded Debts to Net Working Capital
Times	Days	Times	Percent	Percent	Percent	Percent	Percent	Percent
8.64	53	10.0	56.8	123.7	185.2	115.2	137.1	94.1
5.01	37	6.2	25.5	55.6	80.0	78.4	78.3	49.4
3.00	23	4.1	11.3	20.9	30.8	50.8	41.6	15.2
24.88	6	22.0	92.2	92.0	166.3	129.0	104.6	197.2
13.07	2	15.4	45.6	35.9	64.5	89.4	55.3	87.4
6.37	0	10.4	20.8	11.5	19.6	59.5	22.2	28.0
24.62	10	8.6	46.8	313.9	364.4	363.7	102.3	86.1
15.80	5	6.6	23.3	191.4	217.4	234.9	89.3	41.5
9.46	3	4.9	11.1	108.3	120.9	140.3	75.3	16.1
9.79	41	8.0	63.0	147.3	214.4	145.0	121.3	106.0
5.05	22	5.1	27.2	61.8	94.1	94.5	73.3	53.5
2.82	10	3.5	12.5	20.5	33.2	62.5	33.7	19.5
28.57	18	39.3	81.4	83.5	132.4	100.4	151.5	207.2
12.54	7	22.2	44.5	29.6	50.2	67.5	71.6	75.1
5.00	2	11.4	19.4	9.3	16.2	36.8	27.2	20.1
6.26	33	5.3	38.7	104.2	153.8	149.1	81.1	90.2
3.75	15	3.6	16.4	45.3	62.4	101.7	49.8	46.6
2.38	5	2.6	6.5	16.7	22.8	70.9	25.1	48.6
6.49	34	6.9	43.1	84.6	131.7	124.3	89.8	108.1
3.86	15	4.5	19.8	34.0	52.0	87.8	50.0	56.6
2.33	5	3.0	7.6	12.0	17.5	57.8	23.0	21.8
7.02	72	6.9	39.2	108.1	161.0	130.7	102.7	90.4
3.76	32	4.4	15.1	41.9	65.7	83.2	61.7	44.3
2.04	13	3.1	5.6	15.5	24.6	45.6	31.2	16.7
12.05	20	7.5	55.5	52.2	207.8	191.3	105.6	122.6
5.99	9	4.9	26.1	60.1	84.2	106.8	72.6	54.2
3.14	4	3.3	11.7	17.5	30.4	67.4	37.0	13.9

Source: "The Ratios," *Dun's Review* (October 1979), p. 143. The center figure is the median and the figures above and below the median are, respectively, the upper and lower quartiles.

the owners for providing their capital at a risk. The ratio of net profit to sales essentially expresses the cost/price effectiveness of the operation.[46]

Although the net profit margin shows how well the firm performs given a particular level of sales, it does not show how well the firm uses the resources at its

[46] *Ibid.,* p. 53.

TABLE 11-7   Key business ratios: wholesaling

Line of Business (and number of concerns reporting)	Current Assets to Current Debt	Net Profits on Net Sales	Net Profits on Tangible Net Worth	Net Profits on Net Working Capital	Net Sales to Tangible Net Worth
	Times	Percent	Percent	Percent	Times
5013 Automotive Parts & Supplies (3,261)	5.00	6.32	34.54	37.48	8.20
	2.90	3.31	17.73	18.61	4.83
	1.72	1.55	8.47	8.29	2.89
5031 Commercial Machines & Equipment (1,563)	4.30	8.88	57.76	62.87	10.67
	2.17	4.20	27.09	26.10	5.91
	1.43	1.83	12.14	10.30	3.52
5063 Electrical Apparatus and Equipment (1,484)	3.71	6.45	40.04	45.20	10.87
	2.20	3.12	19.06	20.87	6.14
	1.54	1.30	9.80	9.34	3.53
5083 Farm Machinery & Equipment (3,214)	2.29	5.37	33.09	37.81	9.39
	1.58	2.89	17.17	19.46	5.63
	1.29	1.33	8.47	8.24	3.36
5161 Chemicals and Allied Products (587)	4.00	7.27	48.78	70.37	12.82
	2.08	3.39	22.18	28.03	6.30
	1.32	1.11	9.74	6.44	3.36
5137 Clothing & Accessories, Women's and Children's (618)	3.96	7.36	43.71	48.38	12.39
	2.07	3.07	18.96	20.69	6.70
	1.41	1.13	7.98	7.84	3.08
5136 Clothing and Furnishings, Men's & Boys' (506)	4.08	6.90	43.22	46.29	11.32
	2.01	2.92	22.45	20.41	6.28
	1.39	1.16	6.70	6.17	3.25

command.[47] The amount of net profit may be entirely satisfactory from the point of view of the sales volume; however, the sales volume may be insufficient in relation to capacity, i.e., the amount of capital invested in assets used in obtaining sales.[48]

In addition, the ratio of net profits to net sales should also be considered in connection with the turnover of inventory and accounts receivable. Rapid turnovers of inventory and receivables may be a result of reduced sales prices and relatively high rates of cash discounts. When not accompanied by reduced costs and operating expenses, the smaller sales income would result in a lower net profit. A low net profit may be a result of excessive selling and general administrative expenses.[49]

[47] For an insightful analysis, see Eugene M. Lerner, *Managerial Finance* (New York: Harcourt Brace Jovanovich, 1971), p. 46ff.

[48] Ralph D. Kennedy and Stewart Y. McMullen, *Financial Statements* (Homewood, Ill.: Richard D. Irwin, 1973), p. 390.

[49] *Ibid.*, p. 390.

TABLE 11-7   Key business ratios: wholesaling (CONT.)

Net Sales to Net Working Capital	Collection Period	Net Sales to Inventory	Fixed Assets to Tangible Net Worth	Current Debt to Tangible Net Worth	Total Debt to Tangible Net Worth	Inventory to Net Working Capital	Current Debt to Inventory	Funded Debts to Net Working Capital
Times	Days	Times	Percent	Percent	Percent	Percent	Percent	Percent
8.25	41	7.5	40.9	124.8	175.8	125.3	102.2	75.9
4.93	29	5.0	18.0	51.8	75.0	91.4	59.3	38.5
3.18	20	3.5	8.2	22.4	28.2	67.5	33.3	13.6
12.28	52	14.4	51.2	178.4	232.3	116.5	187.5	93.5
6.43	36	8.2	21.9	70.4	94.9	73.7	101.8	43.3
3.81	23	5.1	8.7	23.9	33.4	40.6	50.9	14.9
11.74	52	12.2	42.0	159.3	205.4	122.5	168.2	72.3
6.40	39	7.2	17.9	74.4	98.3	83.2	98.6	35.7
3.75	28	4.6	7.6	29.0	40.7	50.6	55.2	11.9
10.33	50	5.1	49.4	285.6	333.7	303.8	102.2	83.6
6.29	18	3.1	25.4	145.9	167.4	179.3	83.5	41.5
3.74	10	2.2	12.3	58.0	71.5	90.9	62.9	14.0
15.19	58	26.9	65.1	184.4	243.3	99.1	294.8	97.2
7.35	41	12.6	27.5	72.6	95.9	59.5	150.6	45.5
3.77	24	8.1	10.5	23.8	30.3	26.0	72.1	11.9
13.52	58	15.0	34.3	200.1	228.5	137.1	185.7	76.9
6.56	34	7.4	12.0	87.0	103.4	85.0	101.8	34.7
3.02	15	4.1	4.5	26.3	32.2	46.2	54.6	9.1
12.08	60	10.2	23.8	208.8	234.4	159.0	154.9	69.1
5.81	33	6.4	10.0	83.4	98.6	92.4	93.7	27.7
3.29	16	3.4	4.0	26.1	38.6	53.8	53.0	8.2

Source: "The Ratios," *Dun's Review* (October 1979), p. 144. The center figure is the median and the figures above and below the median are, respectively, the upper and lower quartiles.

NET SALES/TOTAL ASSETS (ASSET TURNOVER).   The ratio of net sales to total assets is a measure of the effectiveness of management's employment of capital and may show whether there is a tendency toward overinvestment in assets, especially in inventory and receivables in the case of wholesalers and retailers. This ratio (sometimes referred to as the "turnover" ratio) provides a clue as to the size of asset commitment required for a given level of sales or, conversely, the sales dollars generated for each dollar of investment.[50]

NET PROFITS/TOTAL ASSETS (RETURN ON ASSETS).   Neither the net profit margin (net profits/net sales) nor the turnover ratio (net sales/total assets) by

---

[50] It should be noted that, while simple to calculate, the overall asset turnover is a crude measure at best, since the balance sheets of most well-established companies contain a variety of assets recorded at widely different cost levels of past periods. Helfert, *op. cit.*, p. 55.

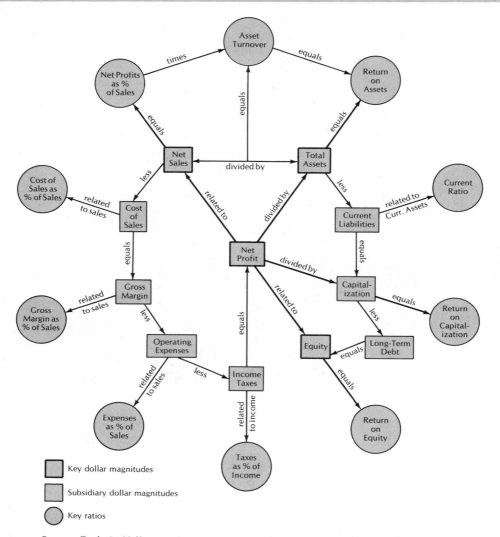

Source: Erich A. Helfert, *Techniques of Financial Analysis*, 3rd ed. (Homewood, Ill.: Richard D. Irwin, 1972), p. 71.

itself provides an adequate measure of operating efficiency. The net profit margin ignores the utilization of assets, whereas the turnover ratio ignores profitability on sales. The return on assets ratio (ROA), or earning power, resolves these shortcomings. As pointed out by Van Horne, an improvement in the earning power of a firm will result if there is an increase in turnover on existing assets, an increase in the net profit margin, or both.[51] The interrelation of these ratios is shown in the SPM (Fig. 11-2). Two firms with different asset turnovers and net profit margins may have the same earning power. For example, if wholesaler A has an asset turnover of 4:1 and a net profit margin of 3 percent and wholesaler B has an asset turnover of 1.5:1 and a net profit margin of 8 percent, both have the same earning power—12 percent—despite the vast differences in operating modes. Thus, earning power can be improved by increasing sales revenue through higher prices (and probably lower volume) or higher volume (at probably lower prices). This may increase both profit margin and turnover. Costs can be reduced up to the point where they do not affect quality, and profit margin can be widened through improved control. The amount of capital employed can be reduced by increasing the turnover of inventory and accounts receivable, and by utilizing the fixed assets more efficiently.[52]

TOTAL ASSETS/NET WORTH (LEVERAGE RATIO).   The ratio of total assets to net worth provides an indication of how reliant a firm is on borrowed funds for both short- and long-term purposes. The lower the ratio, the more the firm is being financially supported by owners' equity as opposed to debt capital. Although a low ratio indicates a high degree of solvency as well as a desire on the part of management to rely on ownership or equity capital for financing purposes, it also indicates that management is probably highly conservative and risk-averse. Debt capital requires fixed interest payments on specific dates and eventual repayment, as well as the threat of legal action by creditors relative to overdue payments. On the other hand, dividends on ownership capital are paid at the discretion of the directors, and there is no provision for repayment of capital to stockholders.

Furthermore, equity capital is typically more costly than debt capital. Thus, by retaining an excessive amount of ownership capital relative to debt capital, the company may be foregoing opportunities to trade on its equity (so-called *leveraging operations*) by refusing to borrow funds at relatively low interest rates and using these funds to earn greater rates of returns. Consequently, aggressive management will often rely heavily on debt capital, because if there is a difference between these two rates on a large investment base, management can increase earnings per share without having to increase the number of common shares outstanding.

NET PROFITS/NET WORTH (RETURN ON INVESTMENT OR RETURN ON NET WORTH).   The main interest of the owners of an enterprise will be the returns achieved by management effort on their share of the invested funds. An effective measure of the return on owners' investment (ROI) is the relationship of net profit to net worth (equity). The ratio reflects the extent to which the objective of realizing a satisfactory net income is being achieved. A low ratio of net profits to

---

[51] James C. Van Horne, *Fundamentals of Financial Management,* 2nd ed. (Englewood Cliffs, N.J.: Prentice-Hall, 1974), p. 39.

[52] Donald H. Schuckett and Edward J. Mock, *Decision Strategies in Financial Management* (New York: AMACOM, 1973), p. 122.

net worth may indicate that the business is not very successful because of several possible reasons: inefficient and ineffective production, distribution, financial, or general management; unfavorable general business conditions; or overinvestment in assets. A high ratio may be a result of efficient management throughout the company's organization, favorable general business conditions, and trading on the equity (effective leveraging).[53]

As McCammon has explained, the SPM has four important managerial purposes:

1. The model specifies that a firm's principal financial objective is to earn an adequate or target rate of return on net worth.

2. The model identifies the three "profit paths" available to an enterprise. That is, a firm with an inadequate rate of return on net worth can improve its performance by accelerating its rate of asset turnover, by increasing its profit margin, or by leveraging its operations more highly.

3. The model dramatizes the principal areas of decisionmaking within the firm, namely, capital management, margin management, and financial management. Furthermore, firms interrelating their capital, margin, and financial plans may be described effectively as engaged in the practice of high-yield management.

4. The model provides a useful perspective for appraising the financial strategies used by different organizations to achieve target rates of return on net worth.[54]

Given the significance of SPM from a managerial standpoint, we will turn our attention to the question of the past performance of wholesalers and retailers in terms of high-yield management. The answer is provided in Fig. 11-4 and 11-5. Despite the apparent improvement of return on net worth in 1979 over 1974, analysts are hardly enthusiastic about these improvements. They point out a number of reasons for their dampened enthusiasm.[55]

[53] Kennedy and McMullen, *op. cit.,* pp. 353–354.

[54] Bert C. McCammon, Jr., "Perspectives for Distribution Programming," in Louis P. Bucklin (ed.), *Vertical Marketing Systems, op. cit.,* p. 38.

[55] The following analysis is based on a number of sources including September 1980 communications with Robert F. Lusch, Distribution Research Program, The University of Oklahoma; Bert C. McCammon, Jr., Jack J. Kasulis, and Jack A. Lesser, "The New Parameters of Retail Competition: The Intensified Struggle for Market Share," in Ronald W. Stampfl and Elizabeth Hirschman (eds.), *Competitive Structure in Retailing: The Department Store Perspective* (Chicago: The American Marketing Association, 1980), pp. 108–118; Charles Ingene and Robert F. Lusch, "The Declining Rate of Return on Capital in U.S. Retailing," *International Journal of Physical Distribution,* forthcoming; and Bert C. McCammon, Jr., and William L. Hammer, "A Frame of Reference for Improving Productivity in Distribution," *Atlanta Economic Review* (September–October 1974), pp. 9–13.; Albert D. Bates and Bert C. McCammon, Jr., "Resellers' Strategies and Financial Performance of the Firm," in Hans B. Thorelli (ed.), *Strategy Plus Structure Equals Performance* (Bloomington, Ind.: Indiana University Press, 1977), pp. 146–178; Bert C. McCammon, Jr., "The Changing Economics of Wholesaling: A Strategic Analysis," in Barnett A. Greenberg (ed.), *Proceedings of the 1974 Southern Marketing Association* (Atlanta, Ga.: Georgia State University, 1975); Bert C. McCammon, Jr., et al., "Strategic Issues in Retailing: A Managerial Analysis" (Norman, Ok.: Distribution Research Program, The University of Oklahoma, 1977); and Bert C. McCammon, Jr., "Strategic Issues and Options in Wholesaling," a paper presented before the American Marketing Association Doctoral Consortium, 1979.

FIGURE 11-4
Composite Strategic Profit Model for Retailing Corporations (1968–1974–1979)

(1968–1974–1979)

$$\frac{\text{Net Profits}}{\text{Net Sales}} \times \frac{\text{Net Sales}}{\text{Total Assets}} \times \frac{\text{Total Assets}}{\text{Net Worth}} = \frac{\text{Net Profits}}{\text{Net Worth}}$$

	Percent	Times	Times	Percent
1968	1.4	2.6	2.3	8.8
1974	1.0	2.6	2.7	7.0
1979	1.7	2.9	2.5	12.3

Source: Distribution Research Program, University of Oklahoma.

First, given the double-digit inflation in 1979, these improvements can quickly disappear if return figures are inflation-adjusted to reflect real returns. Given current inflationary pressures and the strong prospects of their continuing presence in the 1980s, analysts recommend (unadjusted for inflation) target return on net worth (after taxes) around 20 percent. The reported 1979 return on net worth figures of 12.3 percent for retailing and 14.2 percent for wholesaling are well below these target returns.

FIGURE 11-5
Composite Strategic Profit Model for Wholesaling Corporations (1968–1974–1979)

(1968–1974–1979)

$$\frac{\text{Net Profits}}{\text{Net Sales}} \times \frac{\text{Net Sales}}{\text{Total Assets}} \times \frac{\text{Total Assets}}{\text{Net Worth}} = \frac{\text{Net Profits}}{\text{Net Worth}}$$

	Percent	Times	Times	Percent
1968	1.2	2.9	2.4	8.6
1974	1.1	2.6	2.6	7.5
1979	1.5	3.2	2.9	14.2

Source: Distribution Research Program, University of Oklahoma.

Second, the retail and wholesale corporations rely heavily on financial leverage to improve their financial performance. Indeed, wholesale corporations increased their leverage ratio from 2.6 in 1974 to 2.9 in 1979. Heavy reliance on leverage is not without its perils. Liquidity is an area of grave concern among financial analysts. Financial leverage reduces liquidity ratios. Analysts recommend that in the 1980s, retail and wholesale corporations should strive to improve the quality of their balance sheets by cutting back on financial leverage and improving liquidity. Recommended leverage ratios range from 2.0 to 2.2 times, in contrast to the reported 1979 figures of 2.5 times for retailing and 2.9 times for wholesaling.

Third, there is no noticeable increase in asset productivity in wholesale and retail trade, despite attempts to improve space and inventory productivity through the deployment of a number of alternative strategies, as previously discussed in Chapters 2 and 3.[56] Analysts point out that while these strategies may increase sales volume for one corporation, such gains may be achieved at the expense of other retailers or wholesalers. The net impact is shifting patronage from one retailer to another. These shifts, however modest, have major impact on the retail or wholesale operator, as amply illustrated by the following comment:

> . . . most retailers operate fairly close to their break-even points. Supermarkets, for example, with their unusually tight margins, have a break-even point that ranges between 94 and 96 percent of their current sales. General merchandise retailers, with more margin latitude, *still* have a break-even point that approaches 85 to 92 percent of the current sales, with the precise relationship depending on the firm's cost structure, managerial style, gross margin, current profitability, and other factors. Because they operate so close to their break-even points, general merchandise retailers, like others, are *unusually* vulnerable to any downturn in sales and market share, i.e., even a modest contraction in volume can convert a profitable store into a break-even or loss operation.[57]

Furthermore, improving space and inventory productivity often requires large capital investments. For example, increasing inventory turnover requires comprehensive, accurate, and timely information. This translates into the need for massive investments in point-of-sale data entry terminals and a whole complement of data processing equipment necessary to generate timely inventory management and other reports. Indeed, these large capital investments by retailers result in an increase in total assets. In summary, intensified competition results in nominal increases in sales volume, and capital requirements to improve space and inventory productivity result in increasing total assets. This combination of intensified com-

---

[56] These strategies for retailers include supermarket retailing, store positioning, market intensification, secondary market expansion, and nonstore retailing. Innovative strategies for wholesalers include system selling, multilevel merchandising, inventory and service diversification, total capability supplying, and super specialization.

[57] Bert C. McCammon, Jr., Jack J. Kasalis, and Jack A. Lesser, "The New Parameters of Retail Competition: The Intensified Struggle for Market Share," in Ronald Stampfl and Elizabeth Hirschman (eds.), *Competitive Structure in Retailing: The Department Store Perspective* (Chicago: The American Marketing Association, 1980), p. 110.

petition and increase in total assets explains the modest improvements in asset turnover in retailing from 2.6 times in 1974 to 3.2 times in 1979.

Finally, profit margins in retailing and wholesaling have not increased enough, given the impact of inflation. Indeed, the increase of profit margins for retailing from 1.0 percent in 1974 to 1.7 percent in 1979 is hardly adequate in view of the fact that the profit margin for retail corporations was 1.4 percent in 1968. Similarly, profit margins for wholesaling increased from 1.1 percent in 1974 to 1.5 percent in 1979 in contrast with 1.2 percent in 1968. What worries analysts even more is that profit margins in distributive trades have traditionally experienced a secular decline. This decline was due, primarily, to declining gross margins, rising payroll expenses, and increased occupancy cost. Given the continued intensified competition, inflationary labor wages, and ever-increasing construction costs, there is no relief in sight to rid the distributive trade of the prospects of further margin erosions.

From a microperspective, then, it is difficult to be laudatory about the aggregate performance of retailing and wholesaling institutions. There is, however, a curious contradiction in this area between macro- and microviewpoints. While businessmen view low profits as evidence of weak performance, economists and antitrust enforcement agencies often take an opposite position.[58] The latter would tend to attribute low profits to a high degree of competition in the marketplace which has served to force prices down to levels close to average and marginal costs. Although there is some evidence that competition has had some real effect on profits, as pointed out in previous chapters, it would be wrong to make the global assumption that the financial conditions in the distributive trades are solely or even primarily the result of competitive forces. In fact, it would be more logical to assume that lack of innovative, effective, and aggressive management has been as much the cause as any other factor. Organizations such as Target Stores (low margin retailers), Familian (plumbing wholesalers), W. W. Grainger (electrical distributors), Federated (department store chain), and McDonald's (fast-food restaurants) are uniquely and skillfully managed from an *inter-* as well as an *intra*organizational perspective, and, therefore, their profitability reflects this. But such organizations are obviously the exception, not the rule, in distribution.[59]

---

[58] For a discussion of these points, see Louis W. Stern and John R. Grabner, Jr., *Competition in the Marketplace* (Glenview, Ill.: Scott, Foresman and Co., 1970).

[59] For a financial analysis of some highly successful retailers and wholesalers, see Bates and McCammon, *op. cit.,* pp. 27ff; and Bert C. McCammon, Jr., and James M. Kenderdine, "High Performance Wholesaling," *Hardlines Wholesaling* (September 1975), pp. 17–51. The performance of retail, wholesale, and manufacturing institutions by line of business using SPM ratios is reported annually in *Key Business Ratios,* Dun and Bradstreet. Some trade associations report SPM ratios for classifications of their members and leading member institutions. See for example, Bert C. McCammon, Jr., and Robert F. Lusch, "The New Economics of Hardware/Home Center Retailing: A Financial Profile of 17 leading Hardware/Home Center Companies," *Hardware Retailing* (October 1976). Management consulting firms provide similar information for subscribers and clients. See, for example, Reports of Management Horizons, Inc., of Columbus, Ohio. Also, The Distribution Research Program, College of Business Administration, the University of Oklahoma under the direction of Bert C. McCammon, Jr., maintains SPM data banks and produces a number of reports annually for lecture series and conferences.

OTHER PERFORMANCE VARIABLES

There are a host of other variables that would be meaningful to evaluate in order to arrive at an overall judgment about performance in distribution.[60] From a macroperspective, it would be useful to know whether channels and channel institutions have been progressive over time, that is, whether they have been innovative and adaptive, especially with regard to changes in technology. From a social perspective, the effect of various distributive practices on energy consumption, hard-core unemployment, and the quality of the environment should be

TABLE 11-8   Quantitative measures of channel performance

1. Total distribution cost per unit
2. Transportation cost per unit
3. Warehousing cost per unit
4. Production cost per unit
5. Costs associated with avoiding stockouts
6. Percent of stockout units
7. Percent of obsolete inventories
8. Percent of bad debts
9. Customer service level by product, by market segment
10. Accuracy of sales forecasts
11. Number of errors in order filling
12. Number of new markets entered
13. Percent sales volume in new markets entered
14. Percent of markdown volume
15. Number and percent of discontinued channel intermediaries (distribution turnover)
16. Number and percent of new distributors
17. Percent of damaged merchandise
18. Percent of astray shipments
19. Size of orders
20. Ability to keep up with new technology—data transmission
21. Percent of shipments—less than truckload (LTL) vs. truckload (TL) —less than carload (LCL-used with rail shipments) vs. carload (CL)
22. Energy costs
23. Number of customer complaints

Source: Adel I. El-Ansary, "A Model for Evaluating Channel Performance," unpublished paper, Louisiana State University, 1975, pp. 10-11; reported in Douglas M. Lambert, *The Distribution Channel Decision* (New York: National Association of Accountants, 1978), p. 40.

[60] For a discussion of a number of performance variables, see Robert D. Buzzell, "Marketing and Economic Performance: Meaning and Measurement," and John R. Grabner, Jr. and Roger A. Layton, "Problems and Challenges in Market Performance Measurement," in Fred C. Allvine (ed.), *Public Policy and Marketing Practices* (Chicago: American Marketing Association, 1973), pp. 143–182. See also Steven H. Sosnick, "A Critique of the Concepts of Workable Competition," *Quarterly Journal of Economics,* Vol. 72 (August 1958).

**TABLE 11-9   Qualitative measures
of channel performance**

1. Degree of channel coordination
2. Degree of cooperation
3. Degree of conflict
4. Degree of domain concensus (role prescription and variation)
5. Recognition of superordinate goals
6. Degree of development of channel leadership
7. Degree of functional duplication
8. Degree of commitment to channel
9. Degree of power locus development
10. Degree of flexibility in functional shiftability
11. Availability of information about:
    a. Physical inventory
    b. Product characteristics
    c. Pricing structure
    d. Promotional data
        i) Personal selling assistance
        ii) Advertising
        iii) Point of purchase displays
        iv) Special promotions
    e. Market conditions
    f. Services available
    g. Organizational changes
12. Assimilation of new technology
13. Innovation in distribution generated within the channel
14. Extent of intrabrand competiton
15. Extent of routinization of channel tasks
16. Extent of use of optimal inventory standards
17. Relations with trade associations
18. Relations with consumer groups

Source. Adel I. El-Ansary, "A Model for Evaluating Channel Performance," unpublished paper, Louisiana State University, 1975, pp. 10-11; reported in Douglas M. Lambert, *The Distribution Channel Decision* (New York: National Association of Accountants, 1978), p. 41.

assessed. On the "micro" side, an evaluation of the number of stockouts, obsolete inventories, damaged shipments, and markdowns over time, among other operating variables, as listed in Tables 11-8 and 11-9, would provide a closer approximation to actual performance.

Unfortunately, aggregate measures for these macro and micro performance variables are generally unavailable or are restricted to narrow lines of trade. It is necessary, therefore, at this time to rely basically upon the information pertaining to system output, cost, efficiency, profitability, and equity provided above in arriving at a judgment about the performance of the distributive trades.

Nonetheless, a recent landmark study by the National Council for Physical Distribution Management provides comprehensive lists of productivity measures of physical distribution activities, e.g., transportation, warehousing, order processing, and inventory management.[61] Although the scope of the study does not cover empirical analysis of productivity in physical distribution, the availability of comprehensive lists and frameworks for productivity measurement should encourage their application in the future.[62]

MECHANISMS FOR AUDITING DISTRIBUTION CHANNELS

Channel members who desire to evaluate the performance of their individual firms can and do use a number of auditing mechanisms including the following: matrix analysis for auditing channel flows; channel environment, structure and policy audit; and distribution cost analysis.

Matrix Analysis for Auditing Channel Flows

The notion that the compensation of a channel member should be based on the extent to which he participates in channel flows has been emphasized previously. Gross margins and functional discounts in most lines of trade are traditionally established, however. Therefore, actual compensation may be at variance from compensation that a channel member is entitled to.

What is needed in these situations where role relationships have not been delineated in an effective and meaningful way, is an audit of the flows in the channel in order to determine the extent of participation of the members in each. An audit of this nature will not only permit an adjustment of the compensation structure within the channel, but should also lead to the elimination of cost duplication and thereby result in the lowering of prices to end-users.

The beginning point of a channel audit may involve the construction of a matrix of system relationships. Such a matrix describes the channel, permitting precise comparisons of the operations of the various channel components as well as comparisons of one channel system with others. In such a matrix, the institutions and agencies included in any given channel can be portrayed as components of the system. Important elements of the task environment (i.e., the portion of the environment upon which the system depends) can also be shown. Thus, by employing a matrix, it is possible to represent the structure of various relationships within the channel system and between system components and the task environment.

A complete matrix would encompass all firms in the channel. However, a channel might contain 500 firms, which would require 250,000 cells—a matrix too complex to portray here. Thus, levels within the channel rather than individual firms are presented in Fig. 11–6. Likewise, it is not feasible to include all com-

[61] Kearney Management Consultants, *Measuring Productivity in Physical Distribution* (Chicago: National Council for Physical Distribution Management, 1978).

[62] The extent to which many of the proposed measures are utilized by a cross section of channel members in a number of industries can be found in Douglas M. Lambert, *The Distribution Channel Decision* (New York: National Association of Accountants, 1978), pp. 82–86.

FIGURE 11–6

Matrix Analysis of Marketing Flows in a Marketing Channel for Automobiles: A Manufacturer's Perspective

		Commercial Channel				Task Environment			
		Mfr.	Dlr.	Sfc.	Ad. Ag.	Cons.	F.T.C.	N.A.D.A.	Competi-tors' Channels
		1	2	3	4	5	6	7	
Manufacturer	1		A B C D F	F D	C D		D	D	
Dealer	2	D G F		D H F		A B C D F	D	D	
Sales Finance Company	3	D E F H	D E F H			D E F	D	D	D E F H
Advertising Agency	4	D				C			D
Consumer	5		D G F	D F H					D F G H
Federal Trade Commission	6	D	D					D	D
Nat'l. Auto. Dlrs. Assn.	7	D	D				D		D
Competitors' Channels				D F H	C D	A B C D E F	D	D	

Flow: Direction: Code:
Mfr.   Cons.

Flow	Direction	Code
Ownership	→	A
Phys. Poss.	→	B
Promotion	→	C
Negotiation	← →	D
Financing	← →	E
Risking	← →	F
Ordering	←	G
Payment	←	H

Source: Adapted from Louis W. Stern and Jay W. Brown, "Distribution Channels: A Social Systems Approach," in Louis W. Stern (ed.), *Distribution Channels: Behavioral Dimensions* (Boston: Houghton Mifflin, 1969), p. 10.

ponents of the task environment, since the components are too numerous and not always identifiable. Nevertheless, the important components can be easily recognized and are portrayed here, also.

The system matrix in Fig. 11-6 uses the commercial channel for a manufacturer's new automobiles as a relatively uncomplicated example.[63] The channel consists of the manufacturer, his dealers, an advertising agency, and an independent sales finance company that finances both dealers' purchases from the manufacturer and consumers' purchases from dealers. Competitors' channels and consumers represent the most important elements of the task environment. In the history of new car distribution, additional and important task environment elements, among others, have been the Federal Trade Commission and the dealer trade organization, the National Automobile Dealers Association (NADA).

The meaning of each cell can be demonstrated by cell (row 1, column 2). This cell shows the nature of the relationship between the manufacturer and the dealer when the manufacturer initiates the interaction. The manufacturer promotes cars to dealers (C), negotiates the terms of sales (D), passes the automobile and its title to dealers (A and B), and, at the same time, accepts certain business risks (F) in his relationship with dealers. The backward flows for the dealer-manufacturer relationship are contained in cell (2, 1). The dealers order from the manufacturer (G), negotiate the terms of sales (D), and accept risk (F). All other cells are analyzed in the same way. The relationships involving the NADA and the FTC are not marketing flow relationships. Since these relationships have been characterized by bargaining, the marketing flow "negotiation" has been used to typify the nature of relationships involving these organizations. Thus, the matrix, as a starting point for an audit of channel relationships and roles, depicts the variety of channel interactions. These include *intra*organizational interactions (within a channel member's firm, e.g., cell 1, 1), *inter*organizational interactions (between channel members, e.g., cell 1, 2), and extrachannel or environmental interactions (between the channel members and the task environment elements, e.g., cell 1, 6).

Channel Environment, Structure, and Policy Audit

A channel member's performance is contingent upon the market environments in which it operates, the behavior and performance of other members in the channel system, and the marketing policies adopted throughout the channel. These relationships are illustrated in Fig. 11-7. It should be understood that the independent variables that impact on channel member performance are dynamic in nature. Therefore, a periodic audit of channel environment, structure, and policy is necessary to ensure delivery of performance according to the role specifications and expectations of all members of the marketing channel. A channel audit of this nature is best illustrated by the case study presented in the appendix to this chapter.

---

[63] For an application of the system matrix to the pharmaceutical industry, see Mickey C. Smith, Kenneth B. Roberts, and Darego Maclayton, "The Pharmaceutical Industry I: Distribution Channels and Relationships," *M M & M Journal* (January 1976), pp. 32–34.

FIGURE 11–7

An Environmental Framework for Channel System Performance

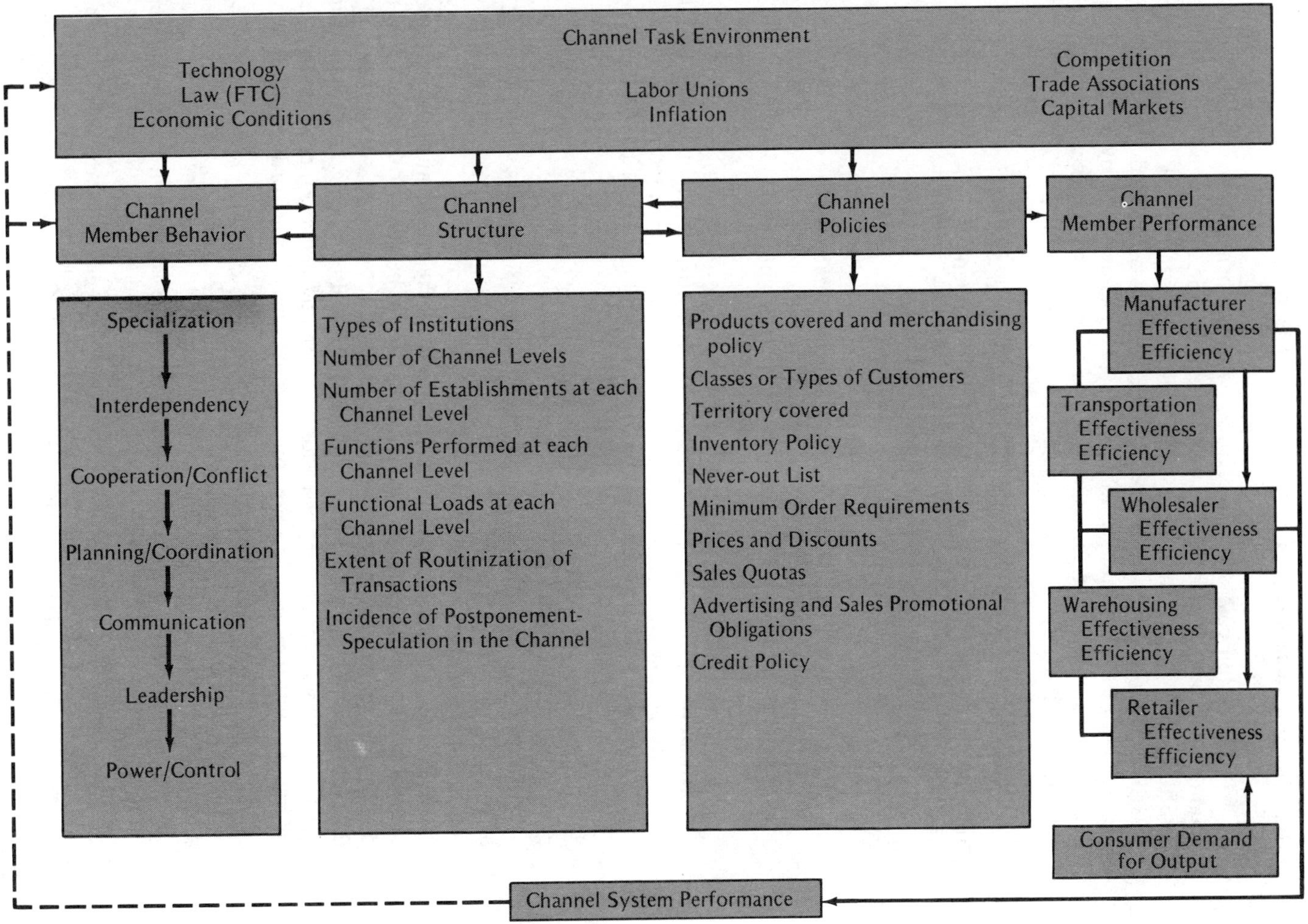

Source: Adel I. El-Ansary, "Perspectives on Channel System Performance," in Robert F. Lusch and Paul H. Zinszer (eds.), *Contemporary Issues in Marketing Channels* (Norman, Ok.: The University of Oklahoma Printing Services, 1979), p. 51.

Distribution Cost Analysis

Distribution cost analysis is a tool which, when properly employed, can aid channel members in determining whether the channels in which they participate are profitable or whether alterations and modifications in existing channels are needed based on a knowledge of the revenues and costs associated with serving them. Generally, a distribution cost analysis would be undertaken by a manufacturer or the original supplier of a particular good or service, because these channel members tend to have the greatest vested interest with respect to the performance of the good or service throughout the channel.

The use of the method rests on the adequacy of accounting data which can be manipulated to provide an assessment of various channels. The benefits of distribution cost analysis can be far-reaching. For example,

- One manufacturer allocated marketing costs to his four different channels of distribution, and on the basis of the results, one entire channel was eliminated and a number of small customers in another channel were discontinued. In addition, marketing efforts were increased on the remaining profitable channels. In one year, net profits doubled from approximately $150,000 to $300,000.
- Another manufacturer found through a distribution cost analysis that two-thirds of all customers sold direct were responsible for losses ranging from 26 to 86 percent of sales. By transferring unprofitable small accounts to wholesalers, the company has achieved a 40 to 50 percent net reduction in marketing costs and a 25 percent increase in the percentage of net profits.[64]

Thus, there appears to be considerable opportunity to reduce costs and increase profits through analyses of relative costs by channels.

In order to perform a distribution cost analysis, the accounting data typically available to a firm on its profit and loss statement must first be reorganized and reclassified into marketing function or flow categories.[65]

Assume, for example, that Table 11–10 is the profit and loss statement of Harrison Manufacturing Company, a hypothetical producer of plastic towel racks, dish drains, soap dishes, and other kitchen and bathroom accessories. Assume, also, that the expenses listed in Table 11–8 have been limited to those associated with the marketing flows of physical possession (storage and delivery), promotion (personal selling, advertising, sales promotion, and publicity), and ordering and payment

---

[64] These examples were drawn from Charles H. Sevin, *How Manufacturers Reduce Their Distribution Costs,* Economic Series No. 72, U.S. Department of Commerce (Washington, D.C.: U.S. Government Printing Office, 1948), p. 4.

[65] Complete and thorough explanations of distribution cost accounting methods and procedures can be found in J. Brooks Heckert and Robert B. Miner, *Distribution Costs,* 2nd ed. (New York: The Ronald Press Co., 1953); and Donald R. Longman and Michael Schiff, *Practical Distribution Cost Analysis* (Homewood, Ill.: Richard D. Irwin, 1955). The discussion of distribution cost analysis here is based largely on Martin Zober, *Marketing Management* (New York: John Wiley & Sons, 1964), pp. 241–267 and Philip Kotler, *Marketing Management: Analysis, Planning, and Control.* 4th ed. (Englewood Cliffs, N.J.: Prentice-Hall, 1980), pp. 639–644. Patrick M. Dunne and Harry I. Wolk, "Marketing Approach," *Journal of Marketing* (July 1977), pp. 83–94.

**TABLE 11-10   Harrison Manufacturing Company
profit and loss statement (in thousands of dollars)**

Sales		$35,000
Cost of goods sold		20,000
Gross margin		15,000
Expenses		
Salaries	$ 3,000	
Advertising	2,500	
Trucking	500	
Rent	3,500	
Insurance	1,400	
Supplies	1,000	
	11,900	
Net profit		$ 3,100

(billing and collecting). The first step in distribution cost analysis is to show how each of the natural expense items shown in Table 11–10 was incurred through Harrison's participation in each of the flows. A hypothetical breakdown is presented in Table 11–11. For example, it has been determined that most of the salaries went to salesmen and the rest went to an advertising manager, a sales promotion manager, a traffic manager, and an accountant, along with various support personnel in each area.

The simplistic example used belies the difficulty involved in splitting natural expenses into functional cost groups. Generally, careful study is required, along with considerable research, before the costs can be allocated equitably. An example of the various means by which natural expense categories may be assigned to various functional categories is provided in Table 11–12. Also, it has been assumed that all of the natural expenses listed in Table 11–10 were directly allocable to the

**TABLE 11-11   Functional (flow) expense
breakdown (in thousands of dollars)**

Natural Expenses	Total	Physical Possession		Promotion			Ordering and Payment
		Storage	Delivery	Personal Selling	Advertising	Sales Promotion	Billing and Collecting
Salaries	$ 3,000	$ 150	$ 100	$2,000	$ 500	$ 200	$ 50
Advertising	2,500				1,500	1,000	
Trucking	500		500				
Rent	3,500	2,500	50	500	200	100	150
Insurance	1,400	1,000	350				50
Supplies	1,000		500	100	150	150	100
Total	$11,900	$3,650	$1,500	$2,600	$2,350	$1,450	$350

TABLE 11-12   **Classification of natural expense
items into function—(Flow)—cost groups**

Expense Items	Means by which Natural-expense Items Are Assigned to Functional-cost Groups	Function-cost Groups to which Natural-expense Items Are Assigned
Sales salaries and expense	Time study	Order routine and promotion
Truck expense	Direct (to cost group)	Handling (or delivery)
Truck wages	Direct (to cost group)	Handling (or delivery)
Truck depreciation	Direct (to cost group)	Handling (or delivery)
Outside trucking	Direct (to cost group)	Handling (or delivery)
Warehouse wages	Time study (or direct to cost group)	Handling, storage, and investment
Office wages	Time study (or direct to cost group)	Order routine, reimbursement, or other functions
Executive salaries	Managerial estimate	All functional groups
Rent	Space measurement	All functional groups
Storage (outside)	Direct (to cost group)	Storage
Warehouse repairs	Managerial estimate	Storage and handling
Warehouse supplies	Managerial estimate	Storage and handling
Insurance:		
Property and equipment	Managerial estimate	All functional groups
Inventory	Direct (to cost group)	Investment
Personnel	Wages	All functional groups
Office expense	Direct (to cost groups and managerial estimate)	Order routine, reimbursement, promotion, or other functions
Utilities	Some direct (to cost groups), others to cost groups via space measurement	All functional groups
Professional services	Managerial estimate	Functions benefited
Taxes, inventory	Direct (to cost group)	Investment
Social Security	Add to wages	All functional groups
Bad debts	Direct (to cost group)	Reimbursement

Source: U.S. Department of Commerce, *Distribution Cost Analysis,* Economic Series No. 50 (Washington, D.C.: U.S. Government Printing Office), p. 17.

functional (flow) groupings. Clearly, this is an oversimplification, because many of the expenses incurred by a firm do not relate directly to the performance of marketing functions.

The second step in distribution cost analysis as it applies directly to marketing channel decisions involves determining how much of each activity has gone into serving the various channels used by the firm. This step calls for allocating the various costs associated with each functional (flow) category to each channel. Some of the bases available for allocating selected costs associated with various functional categories to different channel or customer groupings are shown in Table 11-13.

Assume, in the case of Harrison Manufacturing Company, that the firm sells directly to department stores, discount houses, and supermarket chains. Using allocation bases similar to those shown in Table 11-13 and applying the results to the Harrison example give the data in Table 11-14. Thus, it costs Harrison $3.65

TABLE 11-13   Selected bases of manufacturer's allocation of functional—(Flow)—cost groups to channels or customer groupings

Functional-Cost Groups	Bases of Allocation to Channels or Customer Groupings
Storage of finished goods	Floor space occupied
Order assembly (handling)	Number of invoice lines
Packing and shipping	Weight or number of shipping units
Transportation	Weight or number of shipping units
Selling	Number of sales calls
Advertising	Cost of space, etc., of specific customer advertising
Sales promotion	Cost of promotions
Order entry	Number of orders
Billing	Number of invoice lines
Credit extension	Average amount outstanding
Accounts receivable	Number of invoices posted

Source: Adapted from Martin Zober, *Marketing Management* (New York: John Wiley & Sons, 1964), p. 246.

per cubic foot of warehouse space to store the merchandise it sells, $0.65 to deliver each case of its merchandise to its retail customers, $47.00 for every sales call made to each of the stores in the various retail chains, and $35.00 for billing and collecting per order. The advertising and sales promotion figures (1.57 × and 1.45 ×)

TABLE 11-14   Allocating functional-group costs to marketing channels

Function (Flow) Group	Physical Possession		Promotion			Ordering and Payment
	Storage	Delivery	Personal Selling	Advertising	Sales Promotion	Billing and Collecting
Allocation Bases	Floor Space Occupied in Own Warehouse (000 cu ft)	Number of Shipping Units (000 cases)	Number of Sales Calls (000)	Cost of Advertising Space (000)	Cost of Promotions (000)	Number of Orders (000)
Channel types						
Department stores	200	500	5	$ 150	$ 100	1
Discount houses	450	1000	20	700	400	5
Supermarket chains	350	800	30	650	500	4
Total	1000	2300	55	$1500	$1000	10
Functional-group Cost (000)	$3650	$1500	$2600	$2350	$1450	$350
Number of units	1000	2300	55	$1500	1000	10
Average cost	$3.65	$.65	$47	1.57 ×	1.45 ×	$35

reflect the multipliers that must be applied to each advertising and sales promotion dollar expended by Harrison in each channel. These multipliers permit inclusion of the cost of the support (personnel, rent, and supplies) that has been given to each of these functional areas.

The third step in distribution cost analysis is the preparation of a profit and loss statement for each channel. In Table 11-15, cost of goods sold has been allocated to each channel in proportion to the revenues that the channel delivers to Harrison. The expense figures are derived from the information in Table 11-14. Although it is clear from Harrison's distribution cost analysis that all channels are returning a net profit (in reality, a contribution to profit, since not all cost figures have been included in this hypothetical example), the return from serving super-market chains is very low relative to the return from the other two channels. In addition, the return from the department store channel is surprisingly high. Thus, Harrison might consider increasing his business to department stores and/or de-emphasizing sales to supermarket chains.

It must be understood that the results of a distribution cost analysis *do not* constitute an adequate informational basis for making explicit moves of the type suggested. Before a decision is made to emphasize or deemphasize a particular channel or to take *any* corrective action, answers to the following kinds of questions must be generated by management.[66]

- To what extent do buyers buy on the basis of the type of retail outlet versus the brand? Would they seek out the brand in those channels that are to be emphasized?
- What are the future market trends with respect to the importance of these three channels?
- Have marketing efforts and policies directed at the three channels been optimal?

It would also be imperative to generate an analysis by product line and to study the interaction effects between channel and product profitability. In isolation, a distribution cost analysis can only indicate symptoms; coupled with a product line analysis, a channel audit, some knowledge of channel members' perceptions of marketing programs, and a strategic profit model analysis, it may lead directly to causes.

Furthermore, the decision to eliminate or deemphasize a channel is far-reaching, affecting every aspect of the business. For example, such a decision would need to be reviewed in light of the fact that smaller production runs and a reduced scale of production with the same amount of fixed costs might increase the unit manufacturing costs. In addition, a forecast of just what will happen to sales volume over a period of time is needed in order to assess the possible change in distribution policy.[67] It is also necessary to estimate the decrease in total expense

---

[66] Kotler, *op. cit.*, p. 642.

[67] Sevin, *op. cit.*, p. 11.

TABLE 11-15   **Profit and loss statement for Harrison's channels (in thousands of dollars)**

	Department Stores	Discount Houses	Supermarket Chains	Total
Sales	$7,500	$15,500	$12,000	$35,000
Cost of goods sold	4,400	8,800	6,800	20,000
Gross margin	3,100	6,700	5,200	15,000
Expenses				
Storage ($3.65 per cu ft)	$ 730	$ 1,643	$ 1,277	$ 3,650
Delivery ($0.65 per case)	325	650	525	1,500
Personal selling ($47 per call)	245	940	1,414	2,600
Advertising (1.57 ×)	235	1,095	1,020	2,350
Sales promotion (1.45 ×)	145	580	725	1,450
Billing and collecting ($35 per order)	35	175	140	350
Total expenses	$1,715	$ 5,083	$ 5,102	$11,900
Net profit (or loss)	$1,385	$ 1,617	$ 98	$ 3,100
Profit-to-sales ratio	18.5%	10.4%	0.8%	8.9%

that would result from the action. In performing such an analysis, it is important to separate the nonsaveable (fixed) costs from the saveable costs, because, even when decisions to eliminate or deemphasize a channel are made, some of the costs associated with the deemphasized channel are likely to continue.

Besides the decision-making dilemma, there is considerable controversy surrounding the allocation methods to be used in distribution cost analysis. This controversy generally revolves around whether to allocate all costs or only direct and traceable costs. If the latter is the case, as it was in the hypothetical example presented above, then the analyst must be satisfied in dealing with a contribution-to-profit figure as his final output, rather than a net profit figure. For marketing channel problems, this approach is acceptable, because it is extremely difficult, if not impossible, to find reasonable ways of allocating indirect, nontraceable common costs (e.g., general management salaries, taxes, interest, and other types of overhead) to alternate channels.[68]

Even with these accounting questions, distribution cost analysis, performed in only a rudimentary fashion, can form the beginning step in the development of a channelwide information system, for in the process of going through the exercise, the manager is forced to consider all of the critical variables making for profitable channel relations. He will, in turn, begin to ask for appropriate information from other departments within his own firm and from other channel members. This proc-

[68] Those readers interested in pursuing this controversy, as well as a deeper understanding of the details and difficulties associated with distribution cost analysis, are urged to consult Sevin, *op. cit.*, Heckert and Miner, *op. cit.*, and Longman and Schiff, *op. cit.*

ess, in and of itself, should lead to more effective communication of common problems and, it is to be hoped, more successful interorganization management.[69]

SUMMARY AND CONCLUSION   The focus of this chapter has been on assessing the performance of the distributive trades—particularly retailing and wholesaling—in terms of system effectiveness, equity, productivity, and profitability.

System effectiveness was evaluated in terms of the service outputs (lot size, delivery time, market decentralization, and assortment breadth) that the commercial channel provides to ultimate household consumers and to business and industrial users. Historically, there has been an increase in the size of retail transactions, which has generated more direct buying on the part of retailing institutions. As a result, the need for wholesalers' services in the form of large-lot buying has been reduced. On the other hand, there appears to be no slackening in the desire of customers for rapid delivery, although it is possible that such demands may soften somewhat as periods of shortages are experienced both in the United States and abroad.

Market decentralization requirements have been reduced relative to convenience goods due to the development of greater mobility in personal transportation. But decentralization has been increased relative to shopping goods with the emergence of planned regional shopping centers. In addition, the requirements on the part of customers for broader assortments have spurred the movement toward larger retail stores and have, concomitantly, created an increased need for wholesaler services in gathering together diverse merchandise for retail display. A similar development has been witnessed in certain industrial goods markets (e.g., machinery, equipment, and supplies) that have sustained relatively rapid growth and have traditionally relied on a full range of services from wholesalers. On the other hand, the incidence of "double wholesaling" has been declining as manufacturers have become more sophisticated in managing promotional flows for their industrial products.

While there is undoubtedly a great deal of flexibility and choice provided by the variety of available retailing and wholesaling institutions, from both a macro and a micro perspective, inequities in distribution do, in fact, exist, particularly with regard to the servicing of ghetto and rural communities. Although racial, economic, and social discrimination accounts for some of the inequity, the predominant reason for the problem appears to be structural inadequacies, especially in the ghetto marketplace. The atomistic retail market structures present there

---

[69] In fact, Warshaw has argued that manufacturers *must* assume responsibility for introducing wholesalers to the use of distribution cost analysis if they wish to escape wholesalers' blanket condemnations for inadequate margins. See Martin R. Warshaw, "Pricing to Gain Wholesalers' Selling Support," in William G. Moller, Jr., and David L. Wilemon (eds.), *Marketing Channels: A Systems Viewpoint* (Homewood, Ill.: Richard D. Irwin, 1971), p. 247.

are not performing as well as industrial organization economists would lead us to expect they should. Incentives on the supply side and improvements on the demand side are required if the inequity is ever to be eliminated.

System productivity, measured primarily by the percentage increases in sales per man-hour, lag in distribution behind other sectors in the economy, e.g., manufacturing and agriculture. Lagging productivity in wholesaling and retailing have been ascribed to a number of reasons. First, man-hours increased in these sectors at a substantially faster rate than other sectors. Indeed, retailing and wholesaling are labor intensive industries. Second, the distributive trades are more dependent than manufacturing upon growth in sales volume. Wholesaling and retailing have experienced low growth in constant dollar sales. Finally, the distributive trades did not turn to capital intensive technological innovations on a large scale until the late 1960s and the 1970s. Meanwhile, farmers, processors, and industrial firms turned to innovative capital-intensive technology much earlier. The gloomy picture of lagging productivity improves somewhat when the productivity of different wholesaling industry groups and retail institutional types is examined. Indeed, analysts point out that this subsector analysis is more indicative of productivity in distribution.

Productivity and profitability are different, however related, measures of the efficiency of distributive institutions. While productivity deals with physical efficiency, profitability deals with financial efficiency. Research results confirm that there is a positive relationship between profitability and productivity.[70] The strategic profit model has been employed in this chapter to assess financial efficiency in the distributive trades. Despite the apparent improvement of return on net worth (net profit/net worth), analysts are not enthusiastic about financial performance results in retailing and wholesaling. Given the double-digit inflation in the late 1970s, the 1979 return on net worth of 12.3 percent in retailing and 14.2 percent in wholesaling are hardly adequate if compared with the 20 percent target returns and more prescribed by financial analysts.

Additionally, wholesale and retail corporations rely heavily on financial leverage (total assets/net worth) to generate higher return on net worth. Recommended leverage ratios range from 2 to 2.2 times in contrast to the reported 1979 figures of 2.5 times for retailing and 2.9 for wholesaling. Therefore, retail and wholesale corporations may be compromising on their liquidity. Such compromise is perilous in view of the intensified competition and lower growth in sales volume. Analysts are also unhappy about the marginal improvements in asset productivity (net sales/total assets) in retailing and wholesaling. Despite attempts to improve space and inventory productivity, marginal results materialized as a consequence of the large required increases in fixed assets as well as the limited gains in sales volume. Finally, profit margins (net profit/net sales) in retailing and wholesaling

---

[70] Takeuchi, *Productivity Analysis as a Resource Management Tool in Retail Trade, op. cit.,* pp. 235–245.

have not increased enough, given the impact of inflation. Analysts are not comforted either by the fact that profit margins in the distributive trades have experienced secular decline. Given the prevalent inflationary pressures, there seems to be no relief in sight to detect margin erosion. In short, it is difficult to be laudatory about the aggregate financial performance of retailing and wholesaling institutions.

In general, there is a lack of data available to assess other key performance variables, such as progressiveness, ecological and environmental considerations, and operational efficiencies. Thus, it is necessary to rely on the present data in evaluating aggregate performance. On this basis alone, the conclusion must be that the overall picture is not very impressive, although it must be recognized that the standards applied are very high relative to those that might be employed in other parts of the world.

From both a macro and micro viewpoint, what appears to be needed is more coordination in distributive systems. Suboptimization is likely to occur in the absence of effective coordination. From a management perspective, improved results for retailers and wholesalers are more likely to be achieved when, working in concert with other commercial channel members, profit margins and rates of asset turnover can simultaneously be increased, especially in light of the fact that retailing and wholesaling organizations are already highly leveraged. On the macro side, it is likely that increased intrachannel coordination will lead to less duplication of efforts within the system and thus greater output at lower or at least stable costs. Furthermore, a resolution of inequities in distribution will, obviously, demand a synergistic effort on the part of government and commercial channel members. The coordination required can be accomplished through effective interorganization management combined with enlightened government policies and actions.

DISCUSSION QUESTIONS

1. What criteria should be used to evaluate the performance of the distributive trades, other than those addressed directly in this chapter, from a macro (societal) perspective? From a micro (firm) perspective? How would the distributive trades rate on the additional criteria relative to manufacturing?

2. What criteria of performance should be used to assess the work of logistical institutions, from both a macro- and a microperspective? How would logistical institutions rate relative to the distributive trades on the criteria specified?

3. Should different criteria of performance be applied to channels comprised of nonprofit or publicly financed organizations? If yes, what criteria would you suggest? If no, explain how the various criteria would have to be modified to fit nonprofit situations.

4. What steps might be taken to increase productivity (output per manhour) in wholesaling? In retailing?

5. Debate the pros and cons of using value added as a measure of performance of marketing channels.

6. Explain how capital, margin, and financial management are interrelated. What problems pose the largest hurdles to the practice of high yield management within marketing channels?

7. Describe what you perceive to be the strategic profit models (or the strategies for achieving a high return on investment) for such firms as Neiman-Marcus (a department store catering to middle class and above consumers), A & P, Levitz (a furniture warehouse-showroom chain), Graybar Electric (a wholesaler of major appliances), and McKesson (a drug wholesaling firm).

8. What alternatives are open to retailers who face declining gross margin percentages, rising payroll expense ratios, and increased occupancy costs?

9. According to industrial organization economists, one would predict that when low seller and buyer concentration, little product differentiation, and easy entry exist simultaneously in a market, the chances for good economic performance, from a social welfare perspective, are higher than in a reversed situation. How, then, could they (or you) explain the performance of the ghetto marketplace?

10. What are some likely solutions to the distribution problems in the ghetto marketplace?

11. Overall, how would you characterize the performance of the distributive trades? Is it poor, improving, or strong from a macroperspective? From a microperspective? If poor, what needs to be done in order to improve it?

12. Prepare a systems matrix for a candy manufacturer who distributes through rack jobbers to supermarkets.

APPENDIX 11A

A case study of channel environment, structure, and policy audit: Simpson Timber's Columbia Door Division

Market Environment

Simpson Timber's Columbia Door Division, a manufacturing facility for wood flush doors used in home and building construction, is located in Southwest Washington. While the major markets for this plant were in California, Oregon, and Washington, it had also penetrated the western areas of the Midwest markets (mostly Mountain States), where no flush door manufacturers existed.

Simpson was realizing major successes in the Midwest market by selling doors to major wholesalers, who supplied many of the retail units and major contractors scattered throughout an eleven-state area. While the wood flush door market was treated by most wholesalers and manufacturers in this area as a commodity market, the wholesalers, given equal treatment by the manufacturers, tended to prefer specific manufacturers like Simpson. This preference presumably arose through "personal" contacts made during the introduction of the products and the contacts made with the wholesalers by the Simpson representatives selling other lines of Simpson specialty products.

Having traditionally treated the flush door market as a commodity market, Simpson had given it minimal attention except for price and delivery. An agent served as the Midwest middleman, providing information to Simpson on competitors' prices and delivery schedules. The agent also took orders from the wholesalers. The agent provided no services to customers other than information processing. The distance between the wholesale centers in the Midwest market and the manufacturing facility made direct visits to these middlemen by Columbia Door

Source: William G. Browne and E. D. (Pat) Reiten, "Auditing Distribution Channels," *Journal of Marketing* (July 1978), pp. 38-42.

marketing personnel an infrequent event. This was deemed unnecessary because the company's share of the product's wholesale market in the region had been substantial, stable, and growing slightly.

The Problem

However, a new class of middlemen was entering the market in strong enough force to demand direct negotiations with the competitive manufacturers. Previously Simpson's Columbia Door Division had chosen to ignore other types of middlemen and protect the industry's normal channel relationship (manufacturer → wholesaler → retailer, contractor and industrial builder). This policy probably was appropriate earlier in the company's marketing efforts, when only the wholesaler had order sizes large enough to fill complete carloads (the normal lot size delivered from most building supply manufacturers).

With the advent of major industrialized home builders, major component builders and sizeable chain retail lumber yards, there were increasing pressures for the manufacturers to sell directly to these new middlemen.

Simpson Timber, with little information coming from the agent, was having a difficult time tracking the market activities of their competition and potential customers. After a gross picture of the situation was obtained by using many approximations and substantial secondary data sources, management decided to obtain a closer view of the trends and events or conditions that were supporting the trends. Accordingly, a survey was conducted in the market, covering most of the high-volume users.

The Channel Environment, Structure, and Policy Audit

Initially the Columbia Door Division's records were reviewed to develop a list of their customers for the past three years. Volume trends for each of the customers (all of them wholesalers) were established.

Building statistics were obtained from R. C. Mean's Forecasts for home-starts. From these statistics, using standardized conversion multipliers, the number of wood flush doors consumed or to be consumed in the market could be estimated. When these figures were compared with estimates of the number of units handled by wholesalers, they were noticeably larger; and the trend indicated that the gap could become even larger.

Personnel in the door division were concerned as to the accuracy of the secondary sources used in these calculations and wanted confirmation of their initial observations. It became evident that a survey would be necessary to obtain more accurate figures concerning the market impact of the new middlemen purchasing directly from manufacturers. Figures were also needed to obtain better understanding of the impact of new specialty flush doors on the middlemen's purchase intentions. Thus, the survey questionnaire was designed in part to identify the elements of the market most responsive to the specialty type doors.

To identify wholesalers, retailers, major contractors, industrialized home builders, and large component builders who might purchase wood flush doors in sizeable quantities, raw lists were developed from the *Directory of Forest Products Industry; The Bluebook of Major Homebuilders; Dun and Bradstreet, Middle Market Directory; The Yellow Pages* of local phone directories; *Lumberman's Redbook;* and Simpson's own accounting records. Best estimates were that these lists included every possible carload lot purchaser in the market. (It was recognized that a number of entries on the lists did not qualify for carload lot purchases so one of the survey's leading questions focused on purchase sizes.) The lists were consolidated into a master list with duplicate entries eliminated.

The questionnaire was developed with the major goals of obtaining information on:

- Annual wood flush door volume.
- The volume of major door sub-groups, such as unfinished and prefinished.
- The year-to-year increase in purchases of each such group.
- The number of suppliers, volume from each supplier, and breakdown of sales per customer type.
- Major competitors.
- Any major channel and product volume trends that were occurring, including trends for specialty-type subgroups.

Telephone interviews were utilized. Responses from the middlemen (wholesalers, retailers, industrial component, and home builders) verified that the historical channel arrangement (until the late 1960s) had been through the wholesaler (see Chart 1).

The data also indicated that there had been a substantial shift in the channel arrangement (see Chart 2). In particular, further expansion of direct purchases from the industrial sector was to be expected.

It was also revealed that the specialty product introduced by Masonite was being accepted readily and uniformly throughout the market. No single class of middlemen was providing for the majority of specialty product distribution. Also most of the middlemen, and especially the larger ones, expected to see substantial growth in the specialty market and were looking for new supplier competition in this part of the market.

Changes Instituted

The first change to be considered and instituted was for the company to replace the agent. Simpson feared that the substantial "goodwill" the agent may have created with the company's traditional flush door customers would be endangered.

CHART 1
Historical Channel Arrangement: Wood Flush Door Suppliers

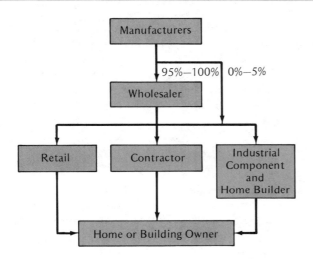

CHART 2
Current Channel Arrangement: Wood Flush Door Suppliers

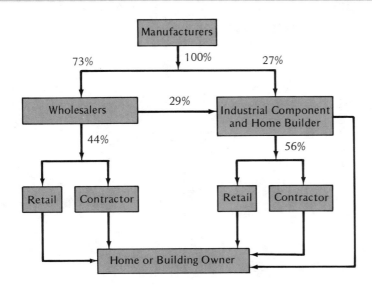

Also there was concern that the agent's product lines from other manufacturers complemented, in some way, his door offering from Simpson. However, the responses indicated that there was no direct physical connection between the agent's other products and the flush doors. Also, conversations with some of the middlemen who had been cooperative during the questionnaire stages of the project provided data to suggest that these fears should not be of great concern.

Once the decision was made to find a replacement for the agent, it was concluded that the position should be filled internally by opening a sales office in the market. This would mean that there would be a sales position in the region responsible for both the commodity door and the introduction of the new specialty substitute.

Results

Missionary work with larger retailers and contractors improved sales to the wholesalers who were serving these markets. There appeared to be an upsurge in demand, primarily to fill inventory in the retail locations where the salesman had substantial influence because of his previous experiences.

The salesman also opened direct negotiations with selected members of the industrial and retail sectors. These visits were limited to industrial and retail customers who had small, if any, flush door purchases from the company's current wholesale customers. Responses from these negotiations were favorable, with a number of initial orders. Visible concern by the current wholesale customers was not evident.

PART FOUR

CHANNEL MANAGEMENT IN OTHER CONTEXTS

The need for management in marketing channels has been amply documented in previous parts of this text. Measures of interorganization management may be deployed to varying degrees depending upon an assessment of the specific channel's ability to deliver and efficiency in delivering desired outputs to users and ultimate consumers. The validity and reliability of channel management methods, procedures, and techniques are determined by the extent to which they are applicable in a variety of situations and a multitude of contexts.

This part of the text is devoted to an examination of management of marketing channels in the international and services contexts. We believe that while marketing channels in other countries and marketing channels for services may be structurally different from marketing channels for goods in the United States, they are technically the same. For example, they are composed of interdependent institutions engaged in the performance of marketing functions in a context of interrelated flows. Successful channel management in these contexts requires the identification of special problems of these channels and the adaptation of channel management methods, procedures, and techniques, learned so far, to deal with these problems. Chapter 12 is devoted to an examination of channel management in the international arena. Similarly, Chapter 13 is devoted to a discussion of channel management in the service sector.

TWELVE

International Marketing Channels

Except for the smallest marketers of goods and services, it is doubtful whether any commercial institution can avoid contact with the international marketplace in one form or another, even if such avoidance were somewhat desirable. The opportunities to be gained from trading with foreign companies, serving foreign consumers, or offering assortments comprised of merchandise selected from the world's production are simply too great to pass by. In fact, U.S. multinational corporations' shares in the earnings of foreign affiliates were in excess of 25 billion dollars in 1978 and reached 37.8 billion dollars in 1979.[1] An increasing number of American companies receive more than half of their net income from overseas operations. Table 12–1 provides data for a few of the numerous U.S. corporations that are finding foreign markets extremely attractive. Foreign operations accounted for a very high proportion of the net earnings, percentage of sales, and percentage of assets of large U.S. multinationals, as demonstrated in Table 12–1.

Meanwhile, the volume of foreign goods carried by U.S. wholesaling and retailing firms has risen significantly over the past 25 years. Major retailing firms are expanding their operations abroad. Multinational retailers constitute a long list that includes Federated Department Stores in Madrid; Sears in Mexico, South America, and Spain; J. C. Penney in Belgium and Italy; Kresge in Australia; Walgreen in Mexico; Safeway in Great Britain, Germany and Australia; and Jewel in Belgium, Italy, Mexico, and Spain.[2] These are joined by scores of multinational franchisors exemplified by McDonald's, Kentucky Fried Chicken, Weight Watch-

---

[1] *United States Department of Commerce News* (August 26, 1980).
[2] Stanley C. Hollander, "The International Store-Keepers," *MSU Business Topics* (Spring 1969), pp. 13–22.

TABLE 12-1   Percentage of earnings, sales, and assets from foreign operations by selected U.S. multinationals in 1977

	Percentage of Net Earnings	Percentage of Sales	Percentage of Assets
American Standard	43.7	45.8	39.7
IBM	55.0	50.0	35.8
NCR	49.9	49.0	46.8
Coca-Cola	55.0	44.0	37.0
H. J. Heinz	34.2	40.7	36.3
Johnson & Johnson	47.7	30.8	33.0
Scholl, Inc.	49.3	47.5	48.0
American Cyanamid	41.0	35.0	36.9
Dow	41.8	45.6	36.4
Standard Oil of California	47.6	59.1	43.3
Black & Decker	63.0	55.1	38.6
International Systems & Controls	112.0	63.1	63.1
ITT	39.0	49.0	36.0
J. W. Thompson	58.7	43.8	33.8
F. W. Woolworth	58.9	34.7	37.6
Avon	30.6	38.3	27.9
Gillette	43.0	51.2	60.6
Mattel	45.1	19.7	41.3

Profit performance of multinational firms shows conclusively the benefits of international trading to the individual firm. Consider for example, the above figures showing the non-U.S. earnings, sales, and assets of leading U.S. firms in 1977.

Source: Philip R. Cateora and John M. Hess, *International Marketing,* 4th ed. (Homewood, Ill: Richard D. Irwin, 1979), p. 48.

ers, Avis, Hertz, and Holiday Inn, to name only a few.[3] The internationalization of retailing is not limited to U.S. retailers, however. For example, Prisunic, Monsprix, and SCOA Trading Company of France; Ahlen & Holm and EPA of Sweden; and Booker McConnell, John Holt & Company, and Hudson's Bay of Britain have tapped worldwide markets, as have certain European franchisors such as Wimpy and Carrier Cook Shops.[4] In the U.S., Gimbles Saks is owned by a British firm, and A & P and Aldi by German firms.

It is possible to postulate that unless a firm is somehow actively participating in the international marketplace—either through support of buying offices, in the

---

[3] Bruce Walker and Michael Etzel, "The Internationalization of U.S. Franchise Systems: Progress and Procedures," *Journal of Marketing,* Vol. 37 (April 1973), pp. 38–46.

[4] Stanley C. Hollander, *Multinational Retailing* (East Lansing, Mich.: Michigan State University, 1970), pp. 27–41 and 62–70. See also "Inflation and Recession Dampen Profits Worldwide," *Business Week* (July 14, 1975), pp. 71–75.

FIGURE 12-1
Marketing Channels in Selected Countries

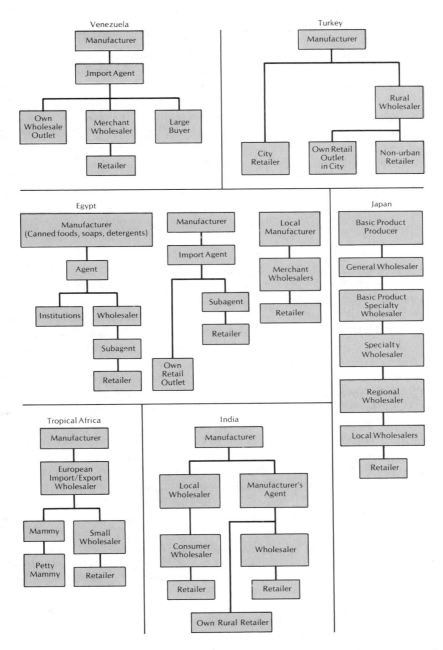

Source: George Wadinambiaratchi, "Channels of Distribution in Developing Economics," *The Business Quarterly,* Vol. 30 (Winter 1965), pp. 74-82.

case of retailers and wholesalers, or through attempts to sell abroad, in the case of manufacturers, it will suffer a severe competitive disadvantage to those that are.

The purpose of this chapter is to examine the channels of distribution available to organizations that wish to tap foreign markets and to enumerate some of the myriad interorganizational problems associated with trying to use them. Attention is also directed to describing institutional responses and possible alternatives for overcoming these problems. It is, however, very important to note at the outset that generalizations about international marketing channels are frequently deceptive because of the vast environmental differences from country to country. Indeed, the marketing channel has been described as one of the most differentiated aspects of national marketing systems. To a large extent, as was pointed out in Chapter 1, channels are shaped by their environments, and, therefore, to equate retailing in India, for example, with retailing in Egypt or to make inferences about retailing in the two countries combined would be misleading and erroneous. Although there exists in all countries some semblance of a wholesaling and a retailing structure, the variations within each structure are vast, indeed, as indicated in Fig. 12–1.[5]

INTERORGANIZATIONAL PERSPECTIVE OF ALTERNATIVE FORMS OF INTERNATIONAL EXPANSION

The perspective taken in this chapter is basically that of a U.S. manufacturer considering expansion abroad. In this respect, there appear to be four basic routes to expansion, although clearly there are numerous possible variations. The simplest form of expansion is through the *exportation* of a company's products to other nations with a demand for the products. Exportation can be achieved directly through the use of foreign distributors or agents, or by establishing overseas marketing subsidiaries. Alternatively, exportations can be achieved through the use of trading companies, domestic export management companies, or piggybacking, using marketing channels of an allied company. For example, Borg-Warner markets Hamilton Beach Co.'s small appliances, McGraw Edison Co.'s Toastmaster products, and In-Sink-Erator Co.'s garbage disposals through its established channels in Europe.[6] The advantage of exportation to foreign markets is that it involves minimal investment, and thus, the risk of failure will not usually affect the overall activities of the firm. The disadvantage of relying mainly on export agencies, however, is that the company will usually have *little control* over the marketing of its products in foreign markets.

Another form of expansion is *licensing,* whereby the company forges a contractual agreement with a foreign organization to manufacture and/or sell its products abroad with the understanding that a certain percentage of the profits will ac-

[5] Readers interested in descriptions of distribution channels in different countries may refer to overseas business reports published by the U.S. Department of Commerce.
[6] Vern Terpstra, *International Marketing,* 2nd ed. (Hinsdale, Ill.: Dryden Press, 1978), p. 318.

crue to each of the parties.[7] The ''home'' company generally is expected to furnish technical assistance to the foreign firm. The main advantages of this route are the low investment required by the home company and the assurance that at least some form of purposive marketing strategy will be adopted for the firm's products. However, as in the case of simple exportation, there may be *little real control* over the licensee's operation. It is even possible that the licensee will eventually acquire the technical expertise of the home firm, thereby altering the dependency relationship. Thus, *power*, in such situations may *rapidly shift* to the foreign firm.

A third and more involved route to expansion is via the establishment of *joint ventures* whereby, through a collaborative arrangement, two or more firms share the investment and risk of the expansionary effort. If the joint venture is forged with a foreign firm, the home firm obviously gains the commitment of the foreign firm to share its skills and its market access. Again, there are problems of control, but they appear to be less than in situations where mutual investment is not involved.

Joint ventures enable U.S. companies to penetrate difficult markets such as Japan. For example:

- Baxter Travenol Laboratories, Inc. of Deerfield, Illinois, a leading manufacturer of medical-care products, has a successful joint venture with Sumitomo Chemical Co. Sales of the joint venture are reported as increasing at a faster rate than the parent firm's 23 percent annual growth rate.[8]
- Sears Roebuck & Co. has a joint venture with Seibu Stores, Inc. in Japan. The venture operates 80 stores, and significant annual sales increases are reported in appliances and apparel.[9]
- Kentucky Fried Chicken Japan is a joint venture between Heublein, Inc. and Mitsubishi Corp. KFC opened its first ten restaurants in 1970. By 1977 the number of stores grew to 150 with 15.3 million dollars in sales.[10]

Similarly, Japanese companies cracked the U.S. market via joint ventures such as the one formed between TRW and Fujutsu.

If the home company wishes to achieve a high degree of control over the marketing of its products abroad, it will probably undertake to follow a fourth route—*direct investment*—by establishing a wholly owned subsidiary in a foreign country. If it does this, it must commit itself to learning the mores and nuances of each foreign market that it enters. The dollar amount of the investment—both in terms of capital expenditure and management time—is likely to be substantial, and

---

[7] In consumer goods marketing, soft drink companies (PepsiCo, Coca-Cola) have long been engaged in international franchising. More recently, fast-food firms, such as McDonald's, have expanded, using licensing arrangements. See ''Europe: A Wolfish Hunter for U.S. Fast Foods,'' *Business Week* (October 21, 1972), p. 34. Also see Walker and Etzel, *op. cit.*

[8] Mike Thorp, ''Drive to Bolster Dollar By Increasing Exports Encounters Obstacles,'' *Wall Street Journal,* September 20, 1978, p. 20.

[9] *Ibid.*

[10] Mike Thorp, ''Marketing in Japan Takes Twisty Turns, Foreign Firms Find,'' *Wall Street Journal,* March 9, 1977, p. 19.

there is always the risk of expropriation and nationalization, particularly in politically unstable countries.[11]

Direct investment has been encouraged by the fact that foreign trade restrictions have frequently made it difficult or impossible for a U.S. company to compete in a foreign market without having a plant or subsidiary located abroad. In addition, Robert Solomon, the Federal Reserve Board's chief adviser on international finance has observed that:

> An overvalued dollar made it cheap to acquire assets abroad. It also made it unattractive to convert foreign earnings back into dollars and thus tended to encourage reinvestment of profits abroad. In the late 1950's and the early 1960's, the profitability of investment simply was higher abroad than in the U.S.[12]

Thus, by 1979 U.S. direct investment abroad reached $192.6 billion compared with $52.2 billion of foreign direct investment in the U.S.[13] It is interesting to note that U.S. direct investment abroad continued to increase despite the contention of some experts that the gap between the profitability of investment in the United States and the investment abroad has been narrowing ever since the early 1960s. Also, the reduction of trade barriers during the late 1960s and early 1970s has made such restrictions less of a problem for exports and thus less of an incentive for direct overseas investment. Finally, unit labor costs during the 1970s rose more slowly in the United States than in other major industrial countries. This trend increased the competitiveness of U.S. exports and made production in the United States relatively more attractive, compared with production overseas.[14]

Direct investment is not without its difficulties and risks. For example, after a three-and-a-half year accumulated loss of $433,000, the European operation of the Wickes Corporation in Holland entered the black in 1975, producing $348,000 of operating income on sales of $10.9 million. Consumer resistance, inventory losses, resistance among manufacturers' cartels to supply Wickes, and charges of illegal marketing practices are among the many problems that plagued Wickes' market entry in Holland.[15]

Similarly, Tandy Corporation's Radio Shack experienced difficulties in the European markets despite its phenomenal success in the U.S. Tandy Corporation entered the market without enough knowledge of European distribution practices, customs, and regulations. First, Radio Shack stores blanketed the European market

---

[11] For a complete discussion of these and other expansionary routes, see Philip R. Cateora and John M. Hess, *International Marketing,* 4th ed. (Homewood, Ill.: Richard D. Irwin, 1979), Chapter 17. For data on some of the political difficulties encountered in direct investment, see "Multinationals Find the Going Rougher," *Business Week* (July 14, 1975), pp. 64–69.

[12] Lindley H. Clark, Jr., "Global Crossroads: Multinational Firms Under Fire All Over, Face a Changed Future," *Wall Street Journal,* December 3, 1975, p. 21.

[13] *United States Department of Commerce News* (August 26, 1980).

[14] *Ibid.*

[15] John Quirt, "Wickes Corp's Retailing Triumph in Europe," *Fortune* (August 13, 1979), pp. 178–184.

with hundreds of stores, many in poor locations. Second, Tandy Corporation did not know or overlooked host-country laws.[16]

- In Belgium it overlooked a law requiring government tax stamps on window signs.
- In Germany it violated sales laws by using heavy giveaway promotions.
- In Holland it geared its first Christmas sales promotion to December 25 instead of St. Nicholas Day, usually celebrated on December 6.
- In Britain, Belgium, and Holland, the sale of citizens band radio is prohibited. Radio Shack was at an immediate disadvantage, not able to sell its best selling item, which accounted for 22 percent of its sales volume at the time.

In selecting among foreign market entry methods, decision criteria related to the firm, its industry, the foreign market, and the entry method have to be established. Key decision criteria are summarized in Exhibit 12-1.

DESIGNING INTERNATIONAL DISTRIBUTION STRATEGY

Regardless of the expansionary route followed, the international marketer will be faced with the problem of designing and implementing a distribution strategy. The channel system for international marketing, especially for those firms not undertaking direct investment, almost always involves two channel segments, one domestic and the other foreign, as shown in Fig. 12-2. Compared to marketing within one's home country, the international marketing channel is, of necessity, longer, because it generally involves using a large number of intermediaries, which play a major role in facilitating the flow of products from domestic production to foreign consumption. Obviously, this results in increasing the complexity of managing the channel, from an interorganization perspective, because of the idiosyncracies of international intermediaries, the environments in which they operate, and the lack of effective and economically feasible control over their operations.

In designing international distribution channels and in developing distribution strategy, international marketers focus on common goals including:

1. Achieving adequate market coverage.
2. Maintaining control over goods in the channel.
3. Holding distribution costs to reasonable levels.
4. Insuring the continuity of channel relationships and, consequently, continuous presence in the market.
5. Achieving marketing goals expressed in terms of volume, market share, margin requirements, and return on investment.

---

[16] "Radio Shack's Rough Trip," *Business Week* (May 30, 1977), p. 55.

EXHIBIT 12-1

Decison Criteria for Selecting Foreign Market Entry

Number of Markets

Different entry methods offer different coverage of international markets. For example, wholly owned foreign operations are not permitted in some countries; the licensing approach may be impossible in other markets because the firm cannot find qualified licensees; or a trading company might cover certain markets very well but have no representation in other markets wanted by the producer. To get the kind of international market coverage it wants, the firm will probably have to combine different market entry methods. In some markets, it may have wholly owned operations; in others, marketing subsidiaries; in yet others, local distributors.

Penetration within Markets

Related to the number of markets covered is the quality of that coverage. An export management company, for example, might claim to give the producer access to sixty countries. The producer must probe further to find out if this "access" is to the whole national market or if it is limited to the capital or a few large cities. Having a small catalog sales office in the capital city is very different from having a sales force to cover the whole national market.

Market Feedback

If it is important or desirable that the firm know what is going on in its foreign markets, it must choose an entry method that will provide this feedback. Although in general the more direct methods of entry offer better possibilities of market information, feedback opportunities will depend in part on how the firm manages a particular form of market entry.

Learning by Experience

Experience is still the best teacher, and the firm will get more international marketing experience the more directly it is involved in foreign markets. The firm with international marketing ambitions should choose an entry method to help it gain some experience and realize these ambitions. The firm cannot "learn by doing" if others are doing the international marketing.

Control

Management control over foreign marketing ranges from none at all—for example, selling through a trading company—to complete control coupled with complete responsibility. The firm may want a strong voice in several aspects of its foreign marketing, for instance, pricing and credit terms, promotion, product quality, and servicing of its products. The extent to which such control is critical to the firm will bear heavily on its choice of entry method.

Incremental Marketing Costs

There are costs associated with international marketing, no matter who does it. However, the producer's incremental marketing outlays and working capital requirements will vary with the directness of the international marketing channel. For example, with indirect exporting there would be practically no additional outlays by the producer.

Profit Possibilities

Presumably, profit is a major goal of the company. In evaluating the profit potential of different entry methods, the long-run sales volume and costs associated with each entry method must be estimated. Costs and profit margins are less important than total profit possibilities. For example, one entry method may offer a 25 percent profit margin on a sales volume of $2 million, but another may offer a 17 percent profit margin on a sales volume of $10 million. The latter entry method probably would be more attractive, even though it has lower profit margins, because the total profit available is greater ($1.7 million as opposed to $500,000).

Investment Requirements

Investment requirements are obviously highest in wholly owned foreign operations. Plant investment, however, is not the only consideration; capital also may be required to finance inventories and to extend credit. Since the amount of capital required varies greatly by method of market entry, this financial need will be an important determinant for most firms.

Administrative Requirements

The administrative burdens and costs of international marketing vary by entry method. These include documentation and red tape, and also the amount of management and legal time required.

Personnel Requirements

Not only capital requirements vary by method of entry; so do personnel needs. Generally, the more direct and more complicated kinds of involvement require a larger number of skilled international business personnel. If the firm is short of "internationalists," it will be constrained in its alternatives.

Exposure to Foreign Problems

The more directly the firm is involved in foreign markets, the more management will have to deal directly with new kinds of legislation, regulation, taxes, labor problems, and other foreign market peculiarities.

Flexibility

If the firm expects to be in foreign markets for the long run, some flexibility in its method of entry is important. Any entry method optimal at one point in time may be less than optimal five years later. Not only do the environment and the market change, so too do the company situation and goals. The firm therefore wants flexibility—the ability to change to meet new conditions. It may wish either to expand its involvement to take advantage of rapidly growing markets, or to contract its operations because of adverse developments.

Although not easy to achieve, this flexibility will be much greater where the firm has planned for it in choosing its method of entry. For this reason, firms sometimes gain experience with limited forms of involvement before committing themselves heavily to a market. However, using distributors and licensees may not always offer the desired flexibility, even though they are limited forms of foreign market involvement.

Risk

Foreign markets are usually perceived as riskier than the domestic market. The amount of risk the firm faces is not only a function of the market itself but also of its method of involvement there. In addition to its investment, the firm risks inventories, receivables, and—perhaps—even the market itself. When planning its method of entry, the firm must do a risk analysis both of the market itself and of its method of entry. Exchange rate risk is another variable in a world of floating rates.

Risks are not only commercial; in foreign markets the firm is also faced with political risks. The firm's political vulnerability may differ from market to market for various reasons, but the firm's level of involvement will be a factor. Generally, the heavier, the more direct, the more visible the entry of the international firm in the foreign market, the more vulnerable it is politically.

Source: Vern Terpstra, *International Marketing*, 2nd ed. (Hinsdale, Ill.: Dryden Press, 1978), pp. 307-309.

FIGURE 12–2
Selected International Marketing Channels

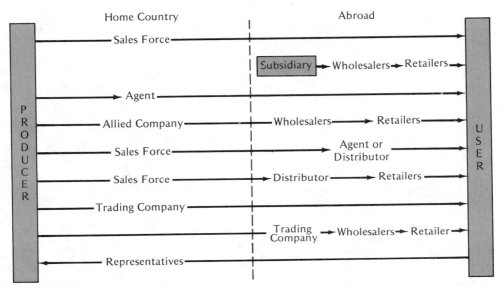

Source: Ruel Kahler and Roland Kramer, *International Marketing,* 4th ed. (Cincinnati, Ohio: Southwestern Publishing Company, 1979), p. 169.

More likely than not, international marketers find these goals illusory or difficult to achieve because of the idiosyncracies of international channels, as will become evident as we proceed to a discussion of wholesale and retail linkages and patterns in international markets.

WHOLESALE LINKAGES TO FOREIGN MARKETS[17]

Figure 12–2 provides some idea of the international channel alternatives available to a domestic producer. Domestic middlemen are located in the producer's home country and provide marketing services from the domestic base. As Cateora and Hess point out, they are convenient to use, but are removed from their foreign markets and, therefore, may not be able to provide the kind of market information and representation available from foreign-based middlemen.[18] Table 12–2 summarizes the primary functions performed by the major kinds of domestic middlemen selling

---

[17] The discussion in this section is based largely on the excellent descriptions provided in Cateora and Hess, *op. cit.,* Chapter 18.

[18] *Ibid.,* pp. 556.

TABLE 12-2   Characteristics of domestic middlemen serving international markets

Types of Duties	Agents				
	CEM	MEA	Broker	Buying[a] Offices	Other Manufacturers[b]
Take title	No	No	No	No	No
Take possession	Yes	Yes	No	Yes	Yes
Continuing relationship	Yes	Yes	No	Yes	Yes
Share of foreign output	All	All	Any	Small	All
Degree of control by principal	Fair	Fair	Nil	Nil	Good
Price authority	Advisory	Advisory	Yes (at market level)	Yes (to buy)	Advisory
Represent buyer or seller	Seller	Seller	Either	Buyer	Seller
Number of principals	Few-Many	Few-Many	Many	Small	Few
Arrange shipping	Yes	Yes	Not usually	Yes	Yes
Type of goods	Manufactured goods and commodities	Staples and commodities	Staples and commodities	Staples and commodities	Complementary to their own lines
Breadth of line	Specialty-wide	All types of staples	All types of staples	Retail goods	Narrow
Handle competitive lines	No	No	Yes	Yes-utilizes many sources	No
Extent of promotion and selling effort	Good	Good	One shot	N.A.	Good
Extends credit to principal	Occasionally	Occasionally	Seldom	Seldom	Seldom
Market information	Fair	Fair	Price and market conditions	For principal not for manufacturer	Good

[a] Commissionaire operates like a resident buyer but works on commission only.
[b] A manufacturer may take on complementary products to sell overseas. This spreads overhead and may strengthen the market position of both firms by providing a more complete line.

to foreign markets. A brief description of a few of the various types of agents is given below, based on Cateora and Hess' classification scheme.[19]

- *CEM (combination export manager):* An agent middleman who generally serves a number of principals, each of which has a relatively small international volume, and acts as the international marketing department for the firms he represents. He will usually do business under principal's name (e.g.,

[19] *Ibid.,* pp. 557–558 and 561–562.

			Merchants			
Inter-merchant[c]	Norazi	Export Merchant[d]	Export jobber[e]	Buyers for Export	Importers and Trading Companies	Complementary Marketers
No	No	Yes	Yes	Yes	Yes	Yes
No	Yes	Yes	No	Yes	Yes	Yes
No	No	No	Yes	No	Yes	Yes
Small	Small	Any	Small	Small	Any	Most
Nil	Nil	None	None	None	Nil	Fair
Some	Yes	Yes	Yes	Yes	No	Some
Both at once	Both	Self	Self	Self	Self	Self
Several per transaction	Several per transaction	Many sources	Many sources	Many sources	Many sources	One per product
No	Yes	Yes	Yes	Yes	Yes	Yes
Any	Contraband	Manufactured goods	Bulky and raw materials	All types	Manufactured goods	Complementary to line
	N.A.	Broad	Broad	Broad	Broad	Narrow
Yes	Yes	Yes	Yes	Yes	Yes	No
Nil	Nil	Nil	Nil	Nil	Good	Good
No	No	Occasionally	Seldom	Seldom	Seldom	Seldom
No	No	Nil	Nil	Nil	Fair	Good

[c] Intermerchants are export brokers who arrange switch trades or triangular trading involving several principals from different countries who need to arrange trades in order to overcome soft currency or exchange restriction problems.

[d] Also known as cable merchant.

[e] Also known as export speculator.

Source: Philip Cateora and John M. Hess, *International Marketing*, 4th ed. (Homewood, Ill.: Richard D. Irwin, 1979), pp. 560-561.

using the principal's letterhead), and thus foreign customers seldom know that they are not dealing directly with the export deparment of the principal. He operates mainly on commission but may also receive fees.

- *MEA (manufacturer's export agent):* An agent middleman similar to the CEM, except that the former does business in his own name rather than in the name of his principals.

- *Norazi:* An agent who specializes in shady or difficult transactions, such as those involving contraband materials (e.g., radioactive products, war materials), black market currency operations, untaxed liquor, and narcotics.

The "Merchants" category in Table 12–3 refers primarily to merchant wholesale operations. Their functions are almost identical to the merchant middlemen described in Chapter 3 except that they sell in foreign countries. In fact, most international merchant middlemen both import and export.[20]

Among the most important merchant middlemen dealing in international commerce are trading companies. The origin, functions, and scope of operations of trading companies are discussed in Exhibit 12–2.

Rather than dealing with the home country agents or merchant middlemen, a manufacturer may choose to deal directly with the middlemen located in foreign markets. Although such a decision will bring the manufacturer closer to these markets and shorten his channel considerably, it will also involve him with problems of language, physical distribution, communications, and financing.[21] Table 12–3 summarizes the primary functions of foreign-based middlemen. While the functions of the various agent middlemen generally follow the description of U.S. agent middlemen found in Chapter 3, it should be emphasized, once again, that in foreign commerce there seem to be very few "pure" types. In other words, the functions performed and marketing flows participated in may vary from situation to situation and are generally subject to negotiations. For example, one unique form of agent middleman is the *comprador* or *del credere* agent.

> The comprador functions in Far Eastern countries and has historically been particularly important in trade with China. He is essentially a general manager who acts as the representative of a foreign merchant in his operations in a given Oriental country. A comprador is used because of his intimate knowledge of the obscure and enigmatic customs and languages of the importing country.[22]

In many respects, foreign merchant middlemen are also not significantly different, in terms of functions performed, from the U.S. merchant middlemen. However, because of the absence of antitrust laws similar to those found in the United States, it is often possible for a U.S.-based producer to exercise greater coercive, reward, and legitimate power with regard to foreign intermediaries. Thus, many foreign distributors have been granted exclusive territorial rights by their suppliers, and relationships with suppliers are frequently formalized through tight franchise or ownership arrangements that might be challengeable in the United States.[23] Another difference is found in the fact that foreign retailers frequently engage directly in importing for both retailing *and* wholesaling purposes.

---

[20] *Ibid.,* pp. 566–567.

[21] *Ibid.,* pp. 567–568.

[22] *Ibid.,* p. 570.

[23] See "Using Foreign Distributors Without Fearing Antitrust," *Business Abroad* (March 8, 1965), p. 28.

TABLE 12–3 Characteristics of middlemen located in foreign countries

Type of Duties	Agents					Merchants			
	Broker	Factor	Manufacturer's Representative[a]	Import Commission	Comprador	Distributor	Dealer	Import Jobber[b]	Retailer
Take title	No	No	No	No	No	Yes	Yes	Yes	Yes
Take possession	No	No	Seldom	Seldom	Yes	Yes	Yes	Yes	Yes
Continuing relationship	No	Sometimes	Often	With buyer, not seller	Yes	Yes	Yes	No	Usually not
Share of foreign output	Small	Small	All or part for one area	N.A.	All one area	All, for certain countries	Assignment area	Small	Very small
Degree of control by principal	Low	Low	Fair	None	Fair	High	High	Low	Nil
Price authority	Nil	Nil	Nil	Nil	Partial	Partial	Partial	Full	Full
Represent buyer or seller	Either	Either	Seller	Buyer	Seller	Seller	Seller	Self	Self
Number of principals	Many	Many	Few	Many	Few	Small	Few major	Many	Many
Arrange shipping	No	No	No	No	No	No	No	No	No
Type of goods	Commodity and food	Commodity and food	Manufactured goods	All types manufactured goods	Manufactured goods	Manufactured goods	Manufactured goods	Manufactured goods	Manufactured consumer
Breadth of line	Broad	Broad (often specialized)	Allied lines	Broad		Narrow to broad	Narrow	Narrow to broad	Narrow to broad
Handle competitive lines	Yes	Yes	No	Yes	No	No	No	Yes	Yes
Extent of promotion and selling effort	Nil	Nil	Fair	Nil	Fair	Fair	Good	Nil	Nil usually
Extends credit to principal	No	Yes	No	No	Sometimes	Sometimes	No	No	No
Market information	Nil	Fair	Good	Nil	Good	Fair	Good	Nil	Nil

[a] Also known as sales agent, residual agent, exclusive agent, commission agent, or indent agent. (The indent agent's title is derived from his use of indent orders—those which must be confirmed and accepted before they serve as contracts.)
[b] Also known as Import house, Import merchant.

Source: Philip R. Cateora and John M. Hess, *International Marketing*, 4th ed. (Homewood, Ill.: Richard D. Irwin, 1979), pp. 568–569.

EXHIBIT 12–2

Trading Companies

The primary functions of trading companies located within a given country include accumulation, transportation, and distribution of goods imported from other countries. To supplement these activities, other services are frequently offered as well. For example, Japanese companies, in addition to operating in the traditional manner, may provide their clients with services such as market information-gathering, development and implementation of marketing plans, and facilities for merchandise handling and wholesaling. Moreover, they often finance imports and exports of merchandise, and either finance or directly invest in distributors and retailers.

There are two types of trading companies. The first type is that which is located in a developed country and which is primarily engaged in selling manufactured goods to developing countries, and in return, in buying their raw materials and unprocessed goods. The second type is typified by the Japanese companies which formed initially in the 1700s for the purpose of facilitating distribution of goods within the country, and which sequentially developed import and export operations.

As one can see, trading companies are not a new phenomenon. The Hudson Bay Company and the East India Company are two prime examples of trading vehicles which date back as far as the sixteenth century. Around the turn of this century, the French founded two major trading companies, Cie Francaise de l'Afrique Occidentale and Ste. Commerciale de l'Ouest Africain. And in 1929, the United Africa Company was formed.

Trading companies continue to be important in modern trade with developing countries. The accelerated economic growth of the Middle Eastern countries, for example, combined with market complexity, cultural differences, and language difficulties attests to the immense usefulness of these mechanisms in reaching local markets. Many companies local to this region have been built around families who have been merchants for generations. Names such as Alireza, Bugshan, Jomaih, Zahid, Al-Gosaibi, Jameel, Rajhi, and Sharbatly-Soliman are examples of powerful merchant companies which control the import trade in Saudi Arabia. These merchants also own construction companies, hotels, residential properties, transportation companies, supermarkets, and a few light industries. They provide clients with the kind of market access, adequate coverage, and political accessibility and acceptability which are vital to successful operations. Even the large U.S. industrial companies such as Union Carbide prefer to deal with these strong trading companies rather than venture into a complex market on their own.

Japanese trading companies (Sogo Shosha), on the other hand, operate on a world-wide basis. Although there are approximately 6000 trading companies currently operating in Japan, the ten largest—Mitsubishi, Mitsui, Marubeni, Itoh,

Sumitomo, Nisso-Iwai, Toymenka, Kanematsu-Gosho, Ataka, and Michimen—account for more than half of all Japanese imports and exports, one-fifth of Japan's domestic wholesale trade, one-third of Japan's GNP, and over 5 percent of the world's export trade. Although the original purpose of Sogo Shosha was to serve Japanese companies only, nowadays a substantial part of their activities consists of imports and exports of goods on behalf of manufacturers and commodity buyers in other countries. They derive their business philosophy from the Confucian cultural tradition, which emphasizes harmony and community. Rather than quick profits on single deals, they prefer to build long-lasting relationships with their business counterparts. Needless to say, this strategy has met with much success.

In Brazil, trading companies are highly favored by the government because they are efficient in international trade and they often encourage small producers to enter international markets. In the early 1970s, the Brazilian Government passed legislation giving trading companies a variety of tax advantages. Additionally, the government provides loans to the companies for the purchase of goods from local producers, which are, in turn, marketed abroad. It appears that this kind of government encouragement has shown favorable results. By 1978, there were 40 Brazilian trading companies in operation.

Sources: Based on Philip R. Cateora and John M. Hess, *International Marketing,* 4th ed. (Homewood, Ill.: Richard D. Irwin, 1979), pp. 564–566; Ruel Kahler and Roland Kramer, *International Marketing,* 4th ed. (Cincinnati, Ohio: Southwestern Publishing, 1977), pp. 175–176; Alexander K. Young, *The Sogo Shosha: Japan's Multinational Trading Companies* (Boulder, Col.: Westview Press, 1979); Don T. Dunn, Jr., "Agents and Distributors in the Middle East," *Business Horizons* (October 1979), pp. 71–72; and Mike Thorp, "Marketing in Japan Takes Twisty Turns, Foreign Firms Find," *Wall Street Journal,* March 9, 1977, p. 1 and 19. See also Masayoushi Kanabayashi, "Japan's Big and Evolving Trading Firms: Can the U.S. Use Something Like Them?" *Wall Street Journal,* December 17, 1980, p. 48.

The combination retailer-wholesaler is more important in foreign countries than in the United States. It is not at all uncommon to find most of the larger retailers in any city wholesaling their goods to local shops and dealers.[24]

From the perspective of interorganization management, control over the activities and operations of marketing channels is generally more difficult to accomplish than it is within the boundaries of the United States, even though antitrust laws may be more lenient in foreign countries. Despite the commonality in functions performed, wholesaling patterns are not as well developed as they are in the United States. It is not unusual to find that manufacturers based in such highly developed economies as Italy[25] are forced to undertake direct shipments to small retailing establishments on a daily or very frequent basis. This kind of distribution obviously eliminates any of the cost advantages of shipping merchandise in large lots as well as prohibits the obtaining of advantages accruing to an efficient division of labor within the channel. Furthermore, a recurring pattern in foreign countries is

[24] Cateora and Hess, *op. cit.,* p. 571.
[25] Pietro Gennaro, "Wholesaling in Italy," in Robert Bartels (ed.), *Comparative Marketing: Wholesaling in Fifteen Countries* (Homewood, Ill.: Richard D. Irwin, 1963), pp. 37–46.

that huge middlemen and tiny middlemen predominate.[26] This means that the supplier seeking to tap international markets must either give over control to economically and often politically powerful distributors or must develop his own system. For example,

> In Malaya, . . . fewer than a dozen merchant houses (European) handle over half of the import trade, while hundreds of local trading companies handle the balance. In Israel, there are some 1,500 wholesalers, most of whom are small. Contrast these with Hamashbir Hamerkazi, a giant wholesaler who handles all kinds of products and has full or partial ownership in 12 major industrial firms. In the early 1960's they reportedly handled approximately 1/5th of all the wholesaling volume of that country. . . . In India, . . . outside companies may have a hard time gaining distribution because the large wholesalers have such an entrenched position that by providing the package of financial and marketing services, they are able to obtain monopsonistic power. Japan's zaibatsu (trading and financial combines) finance subwholesalers, retailers, and manufacturers as well, making a completely integrated link centering around the strongest middlemen.[27]

The emergence of huge wholesaling operations in foreign countries is due, in part, to the fact that foreign manufacturers have traditionally been production-oriented and, therefore, have avoided concerning themselves deeply with marketing and distribution problems. Such a situation may change somewhat as more and more U.S. fully integrated and semi-integrated marketers become involved in international marketing. However, any changes are likely to come slowly, because wholesalers, especially importers and exporters in developing nations,[28] have such a high degree of political influence. Through such influence, they can (and do) effectively forestall improvements in distribution methods. The polarity of wholesale trade is, therefore, likely to be an integral part of international business operations for some time to come.

Perhaps one of the most fascinating examples associated with the problems of achieving effective wholesale distribution abroad is the story of Levi Strauss' efforts to gain a large market share for its clothing products (jeans, pants, and shirts) in Europe in the late 1960s and early 1970s.[29] According to a *Fortune* report on its problems, the company made "a fast grab for the European market without sufficient control on inventory and distribution."[30] The upshot of its experience was that the debacle cost Levi Strauss at least $12 million and left the company with a deficit of over $7 million in the fourth quarter of 1973. Some of the relevant facts of the debacle are detailed below.[31]

[26] For a thorough description of wholesaling in a variety of countries, see Robert Bartels (ed.), *op. cit.*

[27] Cateora and Hess, *op. cit.*, p. 588 and previous revised edition (1971), p. 826.

[28] See Reed Moyer, "The Structure of Markets in Developing Countries," in William G. Miller, Jr., and David L. Wilemon (eds.), *Marketing Channels: A Systems Viewpoint* (Homewood, Ill.: Richard D. Irwin, Inc., 1971), pp. 76–78.

[29] Peter Vanderwicken, "When Levi Strauss Burst Its Britches," *Fortune* (April 1974), pp. 131–138.

[30] *Ibid.*, p. 131.

[31] These details were reported in Vanderwicken, *op. cit.*, pp. 133–135.

Because demand in Europe was far outrunning supply, there seemed, from management's perspective, to be no pressing need for inventory controls. In 1970, Levi Strauss Europe (L.S.E)'s inventory turned over seven times (about four is normal for apparel), and the main warehouse in Antwerp had to be fully replenished an incredible 19 times. Independent distributors were buying L. S. E's merchandise without any careful planning as to future demand. Learning that a shipment was arriving, distributors would send trucks to Antwerp and buy anything they saw.

To improve Levi's distribution within Europe as quickly as possible, L. S. E. acquired the firms that had been its national distributors in 10 countries and turned them into sales subsidiaries. This move was made rather than bringing in Levi Strauss salesmen, who were experienced in domestic apparel markets but unfamiliar with marketing in Europe. Close relationships between manufacturers and retailers are vital in the apparel business, and management believed that L. S. E.'s distributors and their salesmen would provide that tie, enabling the company to keep attuned to changes in each national market. However, meshing the acquired firms with L. S. E. proved to be unexpectedly difficult. Their presidents were long-established businessmen in their own countries, and they resisted changing their methods. In Britain, one former owner resisted proposals for warehouse consolidation and other managerial changes so strongly that the company shifted him into another job.

In keeping with well-established Levi Strauss policy, each national manager retained full autonomy and profit responsibility. At first, L. S. E. received only quarterly balance sheets—outdated information. Moreover, each new subsidiary operated differently, with its own accounting and inventory-control systems. Only in Switzerland was the operation computerized, but its system did not fit with L. S. E.'s. Furthermore, several of the firms did not have accurate information about their inventories. Their reports were often so lacking in details (about sizes and styles, for example) as to be meaningless.

Almost three-quarters of the pants the company sold in Europe were imported from plants located outside the continent. Once the goods did reach Europe, L. S. E. could not keep track of where they were. Moreover, the ever-increasing volume of pants overwhelmed the efforts of clerks to keep adequate records of the movements. As a result, warehouse workers often did not know where to find goods stacked in the bins. Incredible as it seems, if a retailer returned a shipment, L. S. E.'s warehouse had no means of reentering the goods into inventory.

On top of all this, fashion changes swept Europe and compounded what already was a major catastrophe in the making. Further evidence of L. S. E.'s lack of control was found when one distributor who had not been acquired requested a particular style, which L. S. E. declined to produce. Rather than accepting L. S. E.'s decision, the distributor flew to Hong Kong and ordered two million pairs of the style he wanted directly from the Levi Strauss manufacturing subsidiary there.

Although one might argue that even with the lack of control, L. S. E. was able to accomplish its objective because it eventually captured the largest share of the

European market for jeans,[32] there can be little doubt that the European experience was, for Levi Strauss, a traumatic experience that the corporation would not like to repeat. The fact remains that the European wholesalers were, to a very large extent, the root cause of L. S. E.'s major problems and that even vertical integration was ineffective in securing the needed control over their operations. One lesson is, therefore, abundantly clear—if adequate distribution and effective interorganization management were so difficult for a sophisticated U. S. manufacturer and marketer to secure in a developed, highly industrialized market like Europe, it is likely to be even more difficult to secure in less developed economies. In international marketing channels, nothing can be taken for granted.

As is so clearly evident in the Levi Strauss case, the need to develop functioning and meaningful information systems is absolutely crucial. Above anything else, this facet of international marketing may be the most arduous problem, given the current state of foreign distribution and the power held by the middlemen in those markets. As Fayerweather has observed:

> Secretiveness is one of the prominent characteristics of the independent trader in any society. The ability to outbargain and outmaneuver competitors in the marketplace often depends upon keeping your own counsel and playing a lone wolf game. So the . . . merchant . . . is thoroughly imbued with a philosophy quite at odds with the concept of transmitting information to producers. It is rank heresy by his standards, for example, to tell a manufacturer how much inventory he has, one of the key pieces of information that can help the producer. . . .
>
> Individualistic peoples are more inclined (than group-oriented societies) to look on others as antagonists and to think, especially, in work relations, in terms of competing and outmaneuvering those around them rather than cooperating. The cultures of Latin America, the Middle East, and Far East generally lean in this direction. Clearly, group-oriented attitudes (such as exist in the U.S.) facilitate the transmission of information, while merchants in an individualistic culture find their natural disinclination to communicate reinforced.[33]

RETAILING IN INTERNATIONAL MARKETS[34]

As frustrating as it must sound to someone looking for information about international distribution channels, the structure of retailing in foreign markets is even more diverse than the structure of wholesaling. This diversity is demonstrated, for example, in Table 12–4, which documents size differences in European retailing, and Table 12–5, which demonstrates variations in European distribution channels by product and country.

[32] It has been shown that companies that have achieved the highest market shares in various industries also have the highest returns on their investments. See Robert D. Buzzell, Bradley T. Gale, and Ralph G. M. Sultan, "Market Share—A Key to Profitability,"*Harvard Business Review,* Vol. 53 (January-February 1975), pp. 97–106.

[33] John Fayerweather, *International Marketing,* 2nd ed. (Englewood Cliffs, N.J.: Prentice-Hall, 1970), pp. 71–72.

[34] The discussion in this section is based largely on John Fayerweather, *op. cit.,* pp. 60–79. See also Vern Terpstra, *International Marketing,* 2nd ed. (Hinsdale, Ill.: Dryden Press, 1978), pp. 361–368.

**TABLE 12-4   Size differences by country
in European retailing in 1971**

Country	Share of Small Independent Retailers	Number of Inhabitants per Retail Outlet	Average Employment per Retail Outlet	Average Square Feet of Selling Space
Germany	26%	115	4.8	770
Finland	28	—	—	—
Sweden	32	—	—	—
United Kingdom	40	106	5.3	705
Switzerland	44	—	—	—
Netherlands	46	87	3.9	630
Norway	47	—	—	—
France	56	97	3.6	640
Austria	56	—	—	—
Denmark	60	95	4.2	675
Ireland	65	—	—	—
Belgium	72	65	2.6	558
Italy	85	57	2.1	440

Source: Francoise Civeyrel, "Retailing Bursts Out All Over," Vision (June 1974), p. 49; and The Distributive Trade in the Common Market, Her Majesty's Stationary Office, London (1974).

It is possible to observe, however, that as industrial progress increases, retailing is, for the most part, performed by larger and larger units.[35] The retailing of food provides an example. As established in Chapter 2, food retailing in the United States is dominated by the larger supermarket. However, as Fayerweather points out:

> In Europe, supermarkets are progressing, but over 80 percent of the food trade is still in the hands of small merchants with modest stores. In India, food is still mainly sold through thousands of individual tradesmen squatting in open markets, hawking their goods from door to door, or selling from tiny hole-in-the-wall shops.[36]

The European experience appears to be paralleling the historical development of food distribution in the United States. Certain European marketers appear to have benefited markedly by the U.S. experience in the sense that as they develop new modes of food distribution, there is a high degree of concern with increased productivity. Thus, in West Germany and Switzerland, food discounting operations that provide limited assortments of merchandise have achieved remarkable performance records. These stores carry only dry groceries, are relatively small (compared to U.S. standards), lack frills, rely on bulk merchandising (as contrasted with shelf display of individual items), use a minimum number of personnel, emphasize private label merchandise at remarkable values, and are located in densely

[35] Ibid., p. 61. See also Johan Arndt, "Temporal Lags in Comparative Retailing," Journal of Marketing, Vol. 36 (October 1972), pp. 40–45.

[36] Ibid., p. 62.

TABLE 12-5 Variations in European distribution channels by product and country (percent of sales in each channel)

	Furniture		Domestic appliances		Books and Stationery		Textiles		Footwear		Clothing	
	France	UK	Germany	Netherlands	Belgium	Netherlands	Belgium	UK	Germany	UK	France	UK
Department and variety stores	8.3%	13.2%	15.6%	11.1%	25.1%	5.3%	6.2%	10.2%	23.8%	14.5%	17.4%	20.6%
Multiple chain stores	4.8	26.9	16.8	22.6	9.1	33.4	7.2	16.0	16.0	48.5	4.1	50.7
Mail order	3.1	12.8	24.9	1.5	6.3	3.9	2.5	12.0	0.7	14.0	3.2	10.3
Cooperatives	2.2	7.8	2.3	0.3	0.1	0.3	0.8	3.6	0.2	3.6	1.2	2.8
Independents and street trade	81.6	39.2	40.3	64.5	59.4	57.1	83.3	58.2	59.1	19.4	74.1	15.6

Source: Vern Terpstra, *International Marketing*, 2nd ed. (Hinsdale, Ill.: Dryden Press, 1978), p. 363. Adapted from Francoise Civeyrel, "Retailing Bursts Out All Over," *Vision* (June 1974), p. 38.

populated areas. They served as the models for the "box" stores established by Aldi, Jewel, and A&P's Plus Stores in the late 1970s in the U.S.

The diversity between Europe and India in food retailing described above is found in diverse merchandise categories in other countries as well.

> In some countries, such as Italy and Morocco, retailing is composed largely of specialty houses carrying narrow lines. In other countries, such as Finland, most retailers carry a rather general line of merchandise. Retail size is represented at one end by Japan's giant Mitsukoshi Ltd., which today continues to set an unparalleled standard of excellence of goods, fair prices, and superior service, and enjoys the patronage of more than 100,000 customers every day. The other extreme is represented in the market of Ibadan, Nigeria, which has some 3,000 one-or two-man stalls.[37]

While the size of retail establishments appears to vary with economic development, so does the service and the assortment one gains with individual establishments. Thus, in developing nations there is emphasis on personal attention, and negotiation between retailer and consumer often takes on the character of a major social event. As one moves up the development ladder, self-service begins to become the predominant service mode. Specialization is greater in lower-income economies. But, as Fayerweather has observed, there is little difference in assortment breadth between low- and middle-income countries. For example, of the 650,000 retailers in France, most are small shops specializing in one class of products.[38] It is only when one reaches the higher-income economies that one finds a proliferation of lines carried by all sorts of retailers.

The reasons for these differences in service and specialization can be explained, in part, in terms of consumer behavior. The lack of mobility, refrigeration, and other amenities, combined with the desire for social interaction, support a maintenance of the present fragmented retailing systems in many low- and middle-income countries. On the other hand, the investment required in both facilities and education to enter retailing in developing nations is extremely low.[39] For some, retailing—of one form or another—represents the only avenue open to earn a living. Thus, from both a demand and a supply side, the existing system is reinforced.

Unfortunately for such nations the cost of such a system is extremely high, both for consumers and for retailers. From the standpoint of consumption, there are no opportunities to shop at outlets where distribution economies have been achieved, and lower prices can only be gained by effective bargaining and exhaustive search. On the supply side, tradesmen have an extremely low status in their societies; in fact, shopping expeditions represent for some consumers a way of be-

[37] Cateora and Hess, *op. cit.,* p. 590.

[38] Fayerweather, *op. cit.,* p. 63.

[39] For an analytical discussion of some of these issues, with particular reference to Greece, see Lee E. Preston, "Marketing Organization and Economic Development: Structure, Products, and Management," in Louis P. Bucklin (ed.), *Vertical Marketing Systems* (Glenview, Ill.: Scott, Foresman and Co., 1970), pp. 116–133; and Arieh Goldman, "Outreach of Consumers and the Modernization of Urban Food Retailing in Developing Countries," *Journal of Marketing,* Vol. 38 (October 1974), pp. 8–16.

ing able to support their self-esteem, because during such expeditions, they can interact with someone of lower status than they. In fact, improvements in retail distribution have been seen by some as a primary means for elevating a developing country, because through lower prices, as gained through better distribution methods, the real income of the population will increase, and thus there is a greater likelihood for a long-term savings-investment cycle to commence.[40]

Retailing in many international markets has been slow to change, owing to cultural, economic, political, and managerial factors. For example, the reticence to share information and the low status accorded to merchants have had inhibiting effects. Also, in many countries, small retailers and wholesalers have, through political actions, blocked distributive innovations.[41] Also, there appears to be a natural reluctance among numerous foreign middlemen to provide adequate after-sale service and to use modern promotional methods.[42] However, there are cases where consumers and merchants have combined forces to overcome stagnation. For instance, while consumer cooperatives have had a minimal impact in the United States, they are tremendously important in most European countries. They are strongest in the Scandinavian countries, accounting for a third of retail sales in Finland and comparable portions in Norway and Sweden.[43] In Switzerland, consumer cooperatives account for one-fifth of the retail food stores and over one-fourth of retail food sales.

> The Union of Swiss Cooperative Societies (U. S. K.) and the Federation of Migros Cooperatives (Migros) account for nearly ten percent of Switzerland's total (not only food) retail sales. Each of the two leading coops boasts memberships exceeding one-third of the households in Switzerland.[44]

The existence of these and other cooperatives throughout Europe can almost always be traced to a situation in which a group of consumers felt that the private distribution system was not providing goods at fair prices or of consistent quality.

There is evidence, however, that in France, Carrefour, the supermarket chain, is winning a significant niche in its competitive arena even without enlisting the direct investment of consumers, though small food retailers and wholesalers in France appear to have a stranglehold on the issuance of supermarket licenses. Furthermore, superstores or hypermarches (hypermarkets) have made important inroads into French retailing.[45] There are, indeed, innovations in European retailing

[40] This point has been developed by Charles C. Slater, "Market Channel Coordination and Economic Development," in Louis P. Bucklin (ed.), *op. cit.,* p. 135–156.

[41] Cateora and Hess, *op. cit.,* pp. 594–595. Also see J. J. Boddewyn and Stanley C. Hollander (eds.), *Public Policy Toward Retailing* (Lexington, Mass.: Lexington Books, 1973).

[42] See Fayerweather, *op. cit.,* pp. 69–70.

[43] A. J. Alton, "Marketing in Finland," *Journal of Marketing,* Vol. 27 (July 1963), p. 49. For a detailed discussion of consumer cooperatives, see Hollander, *Multinational Retailing, op. cit.,* pp. 71–90.

[44] Cateora and Hess, *op. cit.,* p. 93.

[45] In France, hypermarchés, on average, cover an area of 268,000 sq ft, have parking space for 3000 cars, include 49 checkouts up front and 11 department registers, cost approximately $11 million to construct and generate $35 million in sales volume by retailing both general merchandise and food. Pricing averages 10 to 15 percent below normal retail, and annual sales run as high as $70 million per outlet

from which U.S. marketers could learn much.[46] But the changeover to more efficient retailing methods in foreign markets is difficult, even in the absence of political resistance, because, as Fayerweather points out, critical risk-taking assignments such as buying and the whole sensitive area of relations with customers must be turned over to hired employees.[47]

INTERNATIONAL MARKETING CHANNELS FOR BARTER TRADE

Much of the trade involving Eastern European and developing countries takes place without exchange of money. Barter or compensation agreements is a practice in which trading partners exchange unlike goods or services of equal value.[48] The following example is illustrative:

> PepsiCo, long successful in its Eastern Europe operations, is negotiating with Bulgarian officials to build about five Pizza Huts. They will be located along Bulgaria's main highways so that tourists on their way to Black Sea resorts can eat pizza washed down with Pepsi Cola if they so choose. The franchisee would be the Bulgarian government. PepsiCo would be paid for its efforts in Bulgarian products—wine, fresh fruits, machine tools—which it would sell in the West or anywhere it could find a market.[49]

Despite opposition from labor unions and industry associations in the West, barter trade is likely to become more important in East-West trade during the 1980s.[50] Because of its special nature and growing importance, marketing channels in barter trade deserves special mention. Special channels develop to handle barter trade, such as the following:

1. The selling responsibility of the goods in the barter agreement may be turned over to specialists known as barter houses, switch traders, intermerchants, or trading houses. Also, Japanese trading companies engage in non-

---

(compared with only $20 to $30 million per outlet for major U.S. discount stores). Each store stocks from 20,000 to 50,000 brand name items and sells them at an average markup of 11 to 12 percent. Since their initial appearance in France in 1963, hypermarchés have spread rapidly; there are now more than 1000 such outlets throughout Europe. See E. B. Weiss, "The Hypermarché Marches into U.S. Mass Retailing," *Advertising Age* (December 30, 1974), p. 20. See also Eric Langeard and Robert A. Peterson, "Diffusion of Large-Scale Food Retailing in France: Supermarché et Hypermarché," *Journal of Retailing,* Vol. 51 (Fall 1975), pp. 43ff; and Douglas J. Tigert, "The Changing Structure of Retailing in Europe and North America: Challenges and Opportunities," University of Toronto Retailing and Institutional Research Program Working Paper 75-02 (January 1974), pp. 17-20.

[46] See Ralph Z. Sorenson II, "U.S. Marketers Can Learn From European Innovations," *Harvard Business Review* (September-October 1972), pp. 89-99.

[47] Fayerweather, *op. cit.,* p. 68.

[48] Robert E. Weigand, "International Trade Without Money," *Harvard Business Review* (November-December 1977), pp. 28-56.

[49] Robert E. Weigand, "Barter and Buy-Backs—Problems for the Marketing Channels," in Richard P. Bagozzi (ed.), *Marketing in the 1980's: Changes and Challenges* (Chicago: American Marketing Association, 1980).

[50] "Importance of Barter in East-West Trade Seen Growing in '80's," *Wall Street Journal,* March 18, 1980, p. 17.

money trading. These specialists are located in London, Vienna, Zurich, Munich, and Hamburg, and trade virtually in anything.

2. Some multinational corporations have established in-house barter units. An example is Northrop's offset program. When Northrop sells aircraft to many countries, part of the payment is received as the transaction is concluded. The balance is paid when the offset program has successfully sold goods and services of the country that bought the aircraft to third-party countries.

3. Some multinationals look to other multinationals to help sell the products they acquire in barter trade. For example, when Pullman-Kellogg agreed to receive fertilizer in payment for designing and building a plant in Nigeria, it turned to International Mineral and Chemicals and Transcontinental Fertilizers to market the Nigerian fertilizers.[51]

4. The product received may be sold through the companies' regular marketing channels. For example:

> When the Soviet Union agreed to allow PepsiCo to ship its syrup from the United Kingdom, bottle it in the U.S.S.R., and sell it in small quantities, it was agreed that PepsiCo would take back Soviet products for its pay. Stolichnaya vodka had never sold well in the United States, partly because it must compete with American vodka and vodka coming from countries that enjoy most-favored nation treatment. Still, PepsiCo took Stolichnaya for its pay and agreed that the amount of Pepsi Cola that would be bottled would be a function of Soviet vodka sales in the United States. Fortunately for PepsiCo, the vodka fit neatly into one of Pepsi's channels. It became part of the product line of Monsieur Henri, a subsidiary of PepsiCo that imports and distributes liquor and wines for the American market.[52]

5. The product or raw material received may be used in the company's own production processes. For example, Cadbury-Schweppes (U.K.) markets its products in Eastern Europe and takes back canned fruits in payment. The fruits are shipped to England, where they are used as flavoring for Schweppes' bottled drinks.[53]

Naturally, the last two channel alternatives are the shortest and easiest. However, they are the exception rather than the rule in barter trade cases.

PROBLEMS IN ESTABLISHING AND MANAGING INTERNATIONAL MARKETING CHANNELS

Although it may appear redundant to emphasize further problems in establishing foreign distribution since numerous difficulties have already been highlighted throughout this chapter, it is essential that the marketing manager be aware of most of the major obstacles in his way prior to initiating international trade. Careful planning is crucial if a company is to obtain the lucrative benefits possible from serving foreign markets. Only through a knowledge of likely problem areas can such planning be undertaken.

---

[51] Weigand, "Barter and Buy-Backs," *op. cit.*

[52] *Ibid.*

[53] *Ibid.*

First, it is not always an easy task to find out which middlemen may be available to handle a company's merchandise. Several directories have been published that may aid in this task.[54] Other sources suggested by Cateora and Hess include foreign consulates, Chamber of Commerce groups, middlemen associations, business publications, management consultants, and carriers.[55]

Although it may be difficult to find qualified representatives and middlemen in foreign markets, rigorous selection criteria must be applied. Four selection criteria have proven to be particularly important, especially in the Middle East: (1) the representative's financial strength; (2) his connections; (3) the number and kind of other companies he represents; and (4) the quality of his local personnel, facilities, and equipment. The problem is that such information about agents and distributors may not be readily available.[56] Careful selection for foreign middlemen cannot be overemphasized. When middlemen do not perform, it may be necessary to terminate relationships. This task is formidable in many countries. Middlemen have legal protection which makes it difficult to terminate relationships. For example, in Norway a manufacturer cannot change agents without proof of negligence. Also, personal and family connections remain very important, particularly in the Middle East. Terminating a powerful middleman can result in the expulsion of the foreign firm from the country in extreme cases. Indeed, it has been observed that while international marketers may switch from local agents and distributors by developing their own marketing subsidiaries in foreign markets, in some foreign markets, particularly in the Middle East, the agent and distributor are retained permanently.[57]

Second, it is likely that a relatively larger proportion of a company's advertising budget will have to be devoted to channel communications than in the United States, because there are so many small middlemen who must be reached.[58]

Third, access to markets may be blocked by existing financial and other tie-in arrangements with middlemen often not available to companies in the United States. In Japan, for example, manufacturers are one of the primary sources of financial assistance to the middlemen with whom they deal.[59] Such assistance solidifies trade relations in that country, and, given the emphasis on the accomplishments of the group rather than the individual (e.g., Japanese manufacturers are more likely to look upon their resellers as members of their "group" than are American executives), it may be extremely difficult for an "outsider" to break into an established channel system. This is true for other countries as well; for ex-

[54] See the U.S. Department of Commerce *Trade List* and *World Trade Directory Reports* as well as the commercially published *Trade Directories of the World* and *A Guide to Foreign Business Directories,* as suggested by Cateora and Hess, *op. cit.,* pp. 597–598.

[55] Cateora and Hess, *op. cit.,* pp. 598–599.

[56] Don T. Dunn, Jr. "Agents and Distributors in the Middle East," *Business Horizons* (October 1979), p. 74.

[57] Dunn, *op. cit.*

[58] *Ibid.,* pp. 601–602. It should be noted, however, that there are even increasingly higher hurdles to overcome with respect to advertising. See "Curbs on Ads Increase Abroad as Nations Apply Standards of Fairness and Decency," *Wall Street Journal,* November 25, 1980, p. 48.

[59] Robert E. Weigand, "Aspects of Retail Pricing in Japan," in Louis W. Boone and James C. Johnson (eds.), *Marketing Channels* (Morristown, N.J.: General Learning Press, 1973), p. 320.

ample, United Fruit Company found that the only way in which it could adequately gain satisfactory distribution in Europe was to purchase distributors.[60] The seriousness of this problem is reflected in the fact that some of the largest multinational corporations maintain 80 to 90 percent of their subsidiaries abroad solely for the purpose of distribution.[61]

In fact, difficulties encountered in establishing international marketing channels account for the worldwide trend toward increased backward vertical integration into manufacturing on the part of the middlemen and forward vertical integration into wholesaling and retailing on the part of manufacturers.[62] Such a trend may provide additional barriers to new entrants to foreign markets, given the capital requirements for integration. The situation is being further aggravated by the desire of large foreign wholesalers and retailers to develop their own private branding programs.[63] Evidence of such a movement is provided by the efforts of a large voluntary chain, Spar International, which is comprised of 200 wholesalers and 36,000 retailers in 12 Western European countries, to place greater and greater emphasis on its own labels.[64]

Fourth, because middlemen in less developed countries are distinctly less venturesome than those in more advanced ones and, therefore, are less willing to accept innovation risk, companies seeking to market to such countries must assume a greater burden of demand development than they must in the United States. This is particularly true of a country like India. Furthermore, as Fayerweather observes:

> . . . the small-merchant structure is very likely to result in gaps in market coverage. At the extreme, companies selling small expendable items—toothpaste, flashlight batteries, and razor blades—find in a country like India that only 10 percent or so of the thousands of little merchants are stocking their products. The cost of inventory is one deterrent, but even discounting that, the small operator wants to limit his line to keep it within the bounds of his personal control both physically and from a management point of view.[65]

Cateora and Hess underscore this problem by stating that:

> The high cost of credit, danger of loss through inflation, lack of capital, and other concerns cause foreign middlemen in many countries to carry inadequate inventories, causing out-of-stock conditions and loss of sales to competitors. Physical

---

[60] "United Fruit Purchases Distributors to Gain Common Market Entry," *Wall Street Journal,* November 2, 1962, p. 21.

[61] C. Hederer, C. D. Hoffman, and B. Kumar, "The Internationalization of German Business," *Columbia Journal of World Business* (September-October 1972), p. 43.

[62] For examples of outright ownership of foreign wholesaling and retailing firms, see Vern Terpstra, *American Marketing in the Common Market* (New York: Frederic A. Praeger, 1967), p. 98. See also Lars-Gunnar Mattsson, *Integration and Efficiency in Marketing Systems* (Stockholm, Sweden: Economic Research Institute, 1969).

[63] Cateora and Hess, *op. cit.,* p. 585; and Terpstra, *International Marketing, op. cit.,* p. 375.

[64] Terpstra, *ibid.,* p. 367.

[65] Fayerweather, *op. cit.,* pp. 68–69.

distribution lags intensify this problem so that, in many cases, the manufacturer must provide local warehousing or extend long credit to encourage middlemen to carry large inventories.[66]

Fifth, motivating middlemen in foreign markets can be a formidable task. Agents and distributors in the Middle East are influenced by thousands of years of bazaar trading. Marketing to them means to "sit on the product" and wait for the customer to come to them. A common attitude among merchants is that they do not sell, but people buy. The "carrot and stick" philosophy of motivating agents and distributors in the U.S. and Europe fails in the Middle East. Financial incentives may not motivate them to push the product aggressively if the process is complex and long. If they are making money today, they are not particularly motivated by making more. The following comment underscores these attitudes:

> . . . We told our representatives about a special sales promotion that could increase profits by at least $50,000. Our German distributor would kill himself for that, but many of our Middle Eastern people basically yawned. They would rather go skiing in Switzerland.[67]

Finally, the myriad of problems associated with maintaining adequate distribution can be summed up in the term "control." Securing some semblance of control may be absolutely necessary if the international marketer is going to achieve any success in foreign markets. Because power may reside in the hands of large wholesalers, it may be necessary to use some form of contractual arrangement (e.g., franchising) and make broad concessions in order to convince the wholesalers to monitor the marketplace and to engage in effective marketing practices. The control gained may come to the supplier via the process of osmosis, but at least there will be some assurance (although probably not a great deal) that one's product is receiving adequate care and attention throughout the channel. (It should be noted, however, that there are also considerable obstacles in establishing franchises in foreign countries, as summarized in Table 12–6.

The above problems can be more readily understood and effectively dealt with when international marketers develop a better understanding of the traditions, customs, and evolution of the marketing channels in the countries in which they operate. Exhibit 12–3 provides a summary analysis of the Japanese philosophy and environment, and their impact on the structure and policies of the traditional Japanese marketing channel. It illustrates the type of constructive analysis that international marketers must engage in if they are to function successfully in a foreign market. The analysis underscores the fact that foreign distribution channels, structure, and practices are environmentally and culturally determined. Their roots are embedded in the basic philosophies of the culture. Therefore, environmental and cultural sensitivity is a must for successful dealing with distribution problems in international marketing.

[66] Cateora and Hess, *op. cit.*, p. 601.
[67] This example and the above discussion are from Dunn, *op. cit.*, pp. 76–77.

**TABLE 12–6   Major problems encountered
in establishing franchises in foreign countries**

Systems Encountering	Number of Responses	Percent
Governmental or legal restrictions[a]	31	60.8
Difficulty of recruiting enough qualified franchisees	23	45.1
Lack of sufficient local financing	19	37.3
Difficulty of controlling franchisees	19	37.3
Difficulty of redesigning the franchise package to make it saleable to franchisees in foreign countries	15	29.4
Trademark and/or copyright obstacles	15	29.4
Difficulty of making the products or services acceptable to foreign consumers	11	21.6
Oppressive tax structure	8	15.7
Insufficient suitable locations	6	11.8
Miscellaneous problems	10	19.6
Total	157	

[a] Read as follows: Of 31 systems specifying major problems, 60.8% designated governmental or legal restrictions as a major problem, etc.

Source: Bruce Walker and Michael Etzel, "The Internationalization of U.S. Franchise Systems: Progress and Procedures," *Journal of Marketing,* Vol. 37 (April 1973), p. 45.

INTERNATIONAL PHYSICAL DISTRIBUTION

So far our discussion has focused on the "transaction" flow in international channels. International physical distribution channels are as complex as transaction channels. The following examples are illustrative:

- Mattel owns manufacturing and distribution facilities in the U.S., Canada, Hong Kong, Taiwan, Mexico, England, West Germany, Italy, Australia, Belgium, Japan, and Venezuela.[68]
- Eaton produces in 43 countries and the U.S. Its products are exported to 100 countries through a worldwide Swiss-based marketing organization.[69]
- Texas Instruments stocks materials in 16 world market areas. These distribution facilities are hooked up with a global computer-teletype-telephone communication network.[70]

Multinationals find it beneficial to centrally plan and control physical distribution. In this manner, they can effectively maintain stable and efficient pro-

[68] Bernard J. Hale, "The Problems of Managing an International Distribution System," in James C. Johnson (ed.), *Readings in Contemporary Physical Distribution,* 2nd ed. (Tulsa, Ok.: PPC Books, 1977), p. 219.

[69] Terpstra, *op. cit.,* p. 384.

[70] *Ibid.,* p. 385.

EXHIBIT 12–3

The Anatomy of the Traditional Japanese Marketing Channel

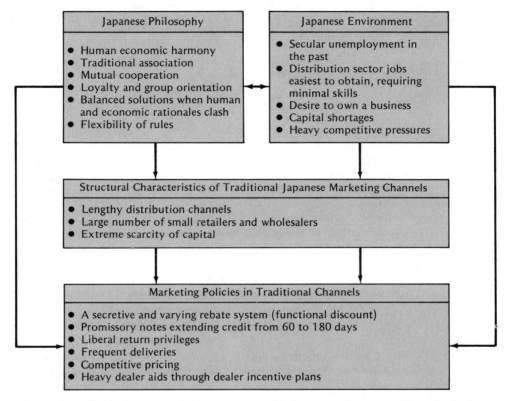

Source: Based on analysis presented in M. Shimaguchi, "Japanese Distribution Channels: Traditions, Customs, and Evolution," working paper, Keio University, Tokyo, Japan, undated; M. Shimaguchi and Larry Rosenberg, "Demystifying Japanese Distribution," *Columbia Journal of World Business* (Spring 1979), pp. 32-41; and M. Shimaguchi and William Lazer, "Japanese Distribution Channels: Invisible Barriers to Market Entry," *MSU Business Topics* (Winter 1979), pp. 49-62.

duction levels at plants in different countries, and lower distribution cost by consolidating smaller orders into larger shipments, and can provide faster customer service.[71]

International physical distribution affects the international marketer's ability to compete effectively for two reasons. First, customer service level (e.g., delivery time, availability of parts) is dependent upon the speed and efficiency of physical distribution.

Second, physical distribution cost is one of the major cost elements in interna-

[71] *Ibid.*

tional markets.[72] In addition to tariffs and customs duties, import-export license fees, and the cost of adjusting to local content, labeling, packaging, and safety laws, the cost of documentation runs very high for international distribution. International shipping documents include export declaration, ocean bill of lading, packing list, *pro forma* commercial invoice, final commercial invoice, dock receipt, delivery instructions, insurance certification, shipping instructions, delivery permit, letter of transmittal, and possibly tens of other documents, depending on the nature of goods shipped.[73] One study reported that the average export shipment requires about 36 man-hours of documentation. Similarly, import shipments require 27 man-hours. In fact, it is estimated that paperwork costs account for close to seven percent of U.S. international trade.[74] Naturally, reducing these costs means improving the profit potential of international marketing and enhancing the capability of the firm to compete.

In addition to the high cost of international distribution, the international marketer is faced with a number of other problems. These include:[75]

1. Shipping rates and charges may vary. Although water carrier conference members are not allowed to vary rates, a shipper may obtain lower rates from nonconference carriers. However, the shipper should be prepared to pay penalties on any conference-carrying shipping he might do in the same geographic area. Also, water shipping rates are determined on basis of weight and measurement. The cubic displacement of a shipment must be carefully watched. The following example is illustrative.

> One logistics department was able to save over $7 million in transportation charges for its company by using the ocean rate structure to its advantage. It was responsible for shipping 30-inch pipe and cement supplies to a foreign country that was to build a pipeline. The low weight-space ratio of pipe meant high shipping costs. Working with pipeline engineers, the logistics department was able to get the engineers to accept half of the pipe in 31-inch diameter, because it had little effect on pipeline operation. The 30-inch pipe was shipped inside the 31-inch pipe and the cavity filled with bags of cement needed for the pipeline construction. A substantial savings in freight charges resulted.[76]

2. The liability for loss and damage in international shipping is less than domestic. This means an additional burden on the shipper to provide adequate insurance coverage and extra protective packaging.

3. The physical distribution manager has to deal with a vast number of varying legal requirements and regulations imposed by governments of countries with which the company deals.

---

[72] *Ibid.,* p. 379.

[73] Ronald H. Ballou, *Basic Business Logistics* (Englewood Cliffs, N.J.: Prentice-Hall, 1978), pp. 444–445.

[74] "Reducing Paperwork," *Transportation and Distribution Management* (November 1971), p. 15.

[75] Hale, *op. cit.,* pp. 219–222.

[76] Ballou, *op. cit.,* pp. 447–448.

4. Containerization is a logical solution used by international shippers to offset expensive packaging costs and loss because of damage and pilferage. However, containerization adds its own costs, including extra loading fees and container rental fees.

Modern technology including supertankers, jumbo jets, better refrigeration, freeze-drying, and intermodal coordination, discussed in Chapter 4, can contribute to the reduction of international distribution cost and the resolution of some of the other problems referred to earlier. Also, the international marketer should avail himself of free-trade zones to overcome legal and tariff barriers, and to reduce distribution cost by taking advantage of proximity to markets and/or low-cost labor. Over forty nations have established free-trade zones where international marketers can establish manufacturing, assembly, or distribution facilities. Imported goods or materials may be left in a free-trade zone for storage, assembling, further processing, or manufacturing and later shipped out of the zone to another country without customs formalities, tariffs, and other controls imposed by the government of the foreign country where the zone is located.[77]

In this chapter, we attempted to examine channel alternatives in international markets and the myriad interorganizational problems associated with their deployment. These problems can be dealt with through effective channel management. The concepts embodied in channel management theory and analysis of domestic marketing channels are equally applicable to international channels.

SUMMARY AND CONCLUSIONS

International marketing can be very lucrative, as evidenced by the fact that an increasing number of American companies receive more than half of their net income from operations abroad. In addition, participation in the international marketplace may be a requirement if a company is to continue to survive and grow; effective distribution increasingly seems to demand a global view.

In seeking to describe channels serving foreign markets, it is essential to understand that generalizations must be treated cautiously and even with suspicion. The differences in the basic structures of distribution from country to country may not be vast, but the nuances and variations within the structures are significantly different.

The perspective taken in this chapter has basically been that of a U.S. manufacturer considering expansion abroad by either exporting, licensing, engaging in joint ventures, or direct investing. As a company moves from one expansion route to the next, the amount of control increases as does the amount of investment required on the part of the home company. In this respect, the choice and the consequences of the various routes are not far different, conceptually, from those associated with forming conventional, administered, contractual, and corporate channel systems on a domestic basis. Regardless of the expansionary route fol-

[77] Terpstra, *op. cit.,* p. 381.

lowed, the international marketer will be faced with the problem of designing and implementing a specific distribution strategy, and this problem generally involves assessing two channel segments—one domestic and the other foreign. Each segment is comprised of agent and merchant middlemen whose functions are not widely different from those performed by comparable middlemen in the United States. However, because of the mores and other environmental characteristics of international markets, the outcomes achieved by given channel arrangements may be far different from those predicted for U.S. channels. For example, control problems are more severe on an international basis because of the polarity of wholesale trade. This is true even though antitrust laws may not be as stringent as they are in the United States. Furthermore, all relationships are subject to intensive negotiations, and thus variations among and within channels abound.

In order to remain reasonably close to developments in international markets and to secure relevant and timely information, it is likely that firms seeking expansion abroad will have to rely heavily on foreign-based, as opposed to domestically-based, middlemen. Even with the market contact that such middlemen allow, difficulties can easily arise, as was evidenced in the case of Levi Strauss, which could not develop adequate distribution and inventory controls, even though it had vertically integrated a number of foreign wholesaling firms.

Retailing presents as much, if not more, diversity to the international marketer as wholesaling—and many of the frustrations. The polarity of wholesale trade is mirrored by a similar polarity on the retail level. With economic development, there is increased evidence of larger retail units, but the small shop still predominates in lower- and middle-income countries and even throughout much of Europe. Consumer cooperatives have emerged in Europe to exert a countervailing pressure on some of the inefficiencies of traditional retail distribution. In developing nations, however, the retailing systems seem uniquely suited to consumer behavior and the level of affluence and mobility, but the cost to both consumers and traders is high, especially in terms of economics for the former and in terms of status for the latter. Improvements in distribution may produce far-reaching benefits for these countries, because such improvements will probably lead to increases in real income for individual consumers.

Several problems can be highlighted relative to the establishment of international marketing channels. First, it may be difficult to determine just which middlemen are available or willing to provide adequate distribution for a particular supplier. Second, considerable intrachannel promotion will be required in order to obtain adequate attention. Third, access to particular channels may be blocked because of existing arrangements, some of which would be illegal if practiced in the United States. Fourth, middlemen, especially in developing economies, may be less prone to accepting the risks of innovation that come with the marketing of new products. In addition, they may be less willing to assume inventory burdens (as compared with U.S. middlemen), and thus may force much of the effort associated with the flow of physical possession back onto suppliers. Finally, the securing of at least some semblance of control within an international channel is likely to be critical, and, in international marketing, reliance may have to be placed on foreign middlemen as the controlling agents or channel leaders.

DISCUSSION QUESTIONS

1. Compare and contrast the routes to expansion abroad—exportation, licensing, joint ventures, and direct investment—to the conceptual foundations, institutional arrangements, strengths, and weaknesses of conventional, administered, contractual, and corporate vertical marketing systems, respectively.

2. A number of U.S. companies have been questioned by the U.S. government about improper payments overseas. Cities Service Corporation was the first large corporation to admit voluntarily that it made such payments. Specifically, according to the *Wall Street Journal* (September 14, 1975), Cities Service told the Securities and Exchange Commission that "subsidiaries abroad secretly funneled $30,000 through a Swiss Bank for 'political purposes,' paid $15,000 against a phony invoice to a foreign lobbyist and generated a $600,000 slush fund for overseas 'business purposes' funded by kickbacks from brokers and suppliers."

On the other hand, according to Adnan Khashoggi, a Saudi Arabian businessman, American companies risk losing huge sales in the Mideast unless the U.S. Government dispels the uncertainty over payments to sales agents abroad. Disclosures of large payments to foreign sales agents, as well as under-the-table payments to government officials, have made U.S. concerns wary of dealing with sales and marketing representatives. Mr. Khashoggi has been quoted as saying (*Wall Street Journal,* September 9, 1975), "If representatives can't sell American products, they'll sell someone else's," to oil-rich Mideast governments.

Do you suppose the same problem exists for foreign companies attempting to sell into the United States? Why do you suppose the problem is so acute abroad? What advice would you give to a company seeking foreign markets about such payments? What alternative does the company have, other than to make the payments?

3. In 1971, Congress, deeply concerned about the deterioration of the U.S. balance of trade, took a lesson from European competitors and established a tax incentive to increase American exports. Legislation enacted in 1971 provides that companies that form Domestic International Sales Corporations (commonly known as DISC's) may defer a portion of their income taxes on export profits, provided they plow such deferred taxes back into export development. According to Reginald H. Jones, chairman and chief executive officer of the General Electric Company, the DISC deferral of taxes is much less potent as an incentive than the tax rebates granted to exporters by the European Economic Community or the European border taxes on imports (*New York Times,* Section F, August 31, 1975). Nevertheless, the DISC tax deferrals have been remarkably successful. Since the DISC provisions were enacted, more than 7000 companies have organized DISC subsidiaries. There has, however, been a movement in Congress to repeal the DISC program. Debate the pros and cons of the DISC program and come out with a position of your own.

4. According to a *Business Week* article (July 14, 1975), governments all over the world are attempting to get for themselves a bigger share of the profits, jobs, markets, and technical and managerial skills that multinational companies create or control. To achieve this, governments are using the multinationals to promote a variety of their own objectives. For example:

- Mexico is pushing auto makers such as Ford and Volkswagenwerk to export more from their Mexican plants, requiring them eventually to sell as much abroad as in the local market.
- Colombia plans to put branches of foreign banks under majority Colombian control, thus shrinking the supply of local credit for subsidiaries of foreign companies and forcing them to bring more capital from abroad.
- Saudi Arabia is asking oil companies to set up joint venture refineries and petro-chemical plants there in return for long-term supplies of crude oil.
- France has insisted that Motorola, Inc.'s semiconductor division set up a research and development department to qualify for investment incentives.
- Canada requires foreign companies to show that they will bring "significant benefits," ranging from jobs and increased productivity to manpower training and development of depressed areas, to get approval of corporate takeovers.

What do developments such as these portend for U.S. companies desirous of doing business abroad? What impact will such governmental activity have on channel strategy? Has the government formally entered the marketing channel in such instances, or is it still in the task environment to the channel?

5. It has been stated that "from an interorganization management perspective, control over the activities and operations of international marketing channels is generally more difficult to accomplish than it is within the boundaries of the U.S. . . . " Do you agree? Why?

6. Explain Levi Strauss's European problems in behavioral (e.g., power, conflict, conflict management, roles, etc.) terms. Applying an interorganizational analysis, what solutions can you suggest so that the company can avoid similar situations?

7. Chori Company, a large wholesale trading concern specializing in textiles, averted bankruptcy in 1975 through the conclusion of a comprehensive rescue agreement with its major creditors consisting of four banks and three synthetic fiber makers. According to the *Wall Street Journal* (September 8, 1975), the seven companies decided on the move because the Japanese textile industry would be thrown into confusion should the trading company collapse. Chori, one of the "Big Three" of Japan's domestic textile wholesale trade, has dealings with about 10,000 other companies, most of them relatively vulnerable small and medium-sized concerns.

Analyze this development from an interorganization management perspective.

Is there any line of trade within the United States where wholesaling firms are likely to be accorded such support in times of crisis?

8.   What obstacles are Sears or Jewel Tea Company likely to face as they seek to continue their overseas expansion? Of the six countries described in the appendix, which two look like the best possibilities for Sears or for Jewel Tea? Which two look like poor choices? Explain your reasoning in full.

THIRTEEN

Marketing Channels for Services

Effective application of marketing channel concepts to the distribution of tangible products sold by profit-oriented organizations is obviously a necessity if the organizations responsible for those products are to remain viable competitors in their respective markets. However, it is not always immediately clear how channel concepts can be applied to contexts involving services generated by profit, non-profit, and publicly financed organizations. In fact, some have argued that their application is exceedingly nebulous. For example, in a study covering a wide variety of service industries, George and Barksdale found it difficult to develop any meaningful conclusions concerning distribution activities.[1] They stated that:

> By their very nature, services do not involve tangible products that can be directed through specific channels and about which decisions can be made in the traditional sense.[2]

While it is no doubt the case that a one-to-one correspondence between the channels for services and the channels for tangible products is often lacking, there are enough points of overlap between the two areas that the subject is very much worth pursuing. Furthermore, it is believed that any insights generated in this pursuit should lead to more careful structuring of marketing programs in the service sector.

Therefore, this chapter focuses on applying marketing channel concepts to

[1] William R. George and Hiram C. Barksdale, "Marketing Activities in the Service Industries," *Journal of Marketing,* Vol. 38 (October 1974), p. 67. Differing perspectives exist in the literature, however. See the interesting argument developed by James H. Donnelly, Jr., "Marketing Intermediaries in Channels of Distribution," *Journal of Marketing,* Vol. 40 (January 1976), pp. 55–70; and Seymour Baranoff and James H. Donnelly, Jr., "Selecting Channels of Distribution for Services," in Victor P. Buell (ed.), *Handbook of Modern Marketing* (New York: McGraw-Hill Book Co., 1970), Section 4, pp. 43–50.

[2] *Ibid.*

services of all types including those distributed by nonprofit organizations. The first section of this chapter deals with a broadened view of the concept of marketing channels and explores a key dimension in service marketing as it relates to distribution—assuring availability. It also outlines some likely channel configurations in the marketing of services, discusses the need for and character of interorganizational coordination among service organizations, and isolates the dominant features of activities in the channels for services. The second section provides five specific examples—health care, educational innovations, accident prevention, population control and family planning, and recycling—where channel concepts have been or could be readily applied by nonprofit and publicly financed agencies. The final section describes the marketing channels used by two profit-oriented service industries—lodging and insurance.

MARKETING CHANNELS: A BROADENED PERSPECTIVE

In a seminal article, Philip Kotler postulated that one of the major ways in which a marketer can seek to create value is by making the social object (product, service, idea, etc.) he is offering for consumption easier for the target market to obtain.[3] The process involved in gaining this end is the establishment of marketing channels or the securing of adequate distribution. *Broadly conceived,* distribution refers to the design, implementation, and control of institutional networks calculated to make social objects of all kinds readily *available* to the population to be served.

Achievement of availability often involves not only the reduction of the space, time, and economic cost separating consumers from the social object, but also may involve the reduction of psychic distances as well. For example, unless disadvantaged consumers feel personally at ease in using the facilities of a free or low-cost neighborhood medical clinic or day care center, it will make little difference if medical or child care services are physically decentralized. While the services may be made more readily available, they may remain inaccessible in a psychological sense. In addition, many nonprofit organizations are in direct contact with their target populations, but in order to achieve a satisfactory usage level within their budget constraints, their managements must be continuously concerned with whether improvements could be made in service level or cost.[4] Furthermore, all organizations, irrespective of orientation, must be concerned to some extent with "after-sale" services, if their managers are going to maintain and monitor the organizations' ability to deliver what they have promised.[5]

[3] Philip Kotler, "A Generic Concept of Marketing," *Journal of Marketing,* Vol. 36 (April 1972), p. 50. In fact, if a marketer is interested in dampening the demand or discouraging the use of a social object (demarketing), he may want to make the object difficult to obtain. See Philip Kotler and Sidney J. Levy, "Demarketing, Yes, Demarketing," *Harvard Business Review,* Vol. 49 (November-December 1971), pp. 78–79.

[4] Philip Kotler, *Marketing for Nonprofit Organizations* (Englewood Cliffs, N.J.: Prentice-Hall, 1975), p. 71.

[5] *Ibid.* For a cogent and provocative discussion about the consequences of not being able to deliver what has been promised, see Charles A. Reich, *The Greening of America* (New York: Random House, 1970). Particular attention should be given to Reich's description of Consciousness II.

All organizations must consider how to make their objects available, which involves decisions about the number and type of "retail" outlets to employ, the kinds of "middlemen" to use, and the extent of reliance placed on facilitating agencies. Even with regard to programs calculated to influence the acceptability of social ideas, a key element is the provision of "adequate distribution and response channels."[6] Once an individual has been motivated to adopt (or at least expose himself more fully to) an idea, he must be able to learn where the "product" can be obtained. In such situations, distribution planning means "arranging for accessible outlets which permit the translation of motivations into actions" and entails "selecting or developing appropriate outlets, deciding on their number, average size, and locations, and giving them proper motivations to perform their part of the job."[7]

From a managerial perspective, these channel decisions are often more complex for private nonprofit organizations than they are for firms in the business sector or for publicly financed agencies. The private nonprofit organization generally has two constituencies: clients to whom it provides goods and/or services, and donors from whom it receives resources.[8] Because there is frequently minimal overlap between the two groups (consider, for example, the users of and financial contributors to the Red Cross), two separate distribution systems must be established, one dealing with resource *allocation* and the other with resource *attraction*. Clearly, different marketing approaches are required to satisfy the needs of these two "markets."

Location—A Key Element in the Marketing of Services

If, in fact, one of the main goals in constructing a distribution channel is the facilitation of resource availability and accessibility, then a crucial factor determining whether that basic goal will be achieved is the location(s) chosen or the modes selected by which various relevant exchanges will take place. The process involved in the creation of time and place utilities is even more important in the marketing of services, by both profit and nonprofit organizations, than it is for the marketing of tangible commodities. As Rathmell has observed, the inability to store or ship intangibles and the need to have service facilities in existence to meet intermittent or random demand over time suggest that the price paid for many services reflects a substantial portion of these utilities in the total value of the service product.[9] This

---

[6] Philip Kotler and Gerald Zaltman, "Social Marketing: An Approach to Planned Social Change," *Journal of Marketing,* Vol. 35 (July 1971), p. 8.

[7] *Ibid.,* p. 9.

[8] Benson P. Shapiro, "Marketing for Nonprofit Organizations," *Harvard Business Review,* Vol. 51 (September-October 1973), p. 124.

[9] John M. Rathmell, *Marketing in the Service Sector* (Cambridge, Mass.: Winthrop Publishers, 1974), p. 104.

observation is clearly borne out in the marketing of telephone, emergency medical care, electrical, automobile repair, motel, and airport services, to name only a few.

Market share analysis in the car rental business underscores the importance of location for this service industry. In 1978, Hertz, Avis, National, and Budget, the four largest car rental companies, commanded 39 percent, 27.3 percent, 20.7 percent, and 9.2 percent of the airport car rental market. All other companies combined accounted for 3.7 percent market share. The success of these four companies is attributed, in major part, to the hundreds of airport locations from which they operate. For example, Avis operates in more than 800 airports, and Budget operates in 159 airports.[10]

Relative to the resource attraction functions of nonprofit organizations, location decisions are crucial, because selection of appropriate locations for both donations and services can (1) make donation easier (e.g., placement of collection tins in high-traffic outlets, or the use of direct collection by volunteers and direct mail), (2) provide a base for local fund-raising and operations, and (3) provide credibility and show an organization's interest in an area (e.g., the agency seeking a donation can point to a neighborhood facility—a health clinic, college branch campus, or a museum, for example—as evidence of the organization's commitment to a community).[11] In fact, for such organizations as well as for publicly financed agencies, location plays an even greater role in resource allocation, because location is an integral part of the service itself.[12] As Abler, Adams, and Gould have pointed out:

> Hospitals must be located in geographic space to serve the people with complete medical care, and we must build schools close to the children who have to learn. Fire stations must be located to give rapid access to potential conflagrations, and voting booths must be placed so that people can cast their ballots without expending unreasonable amounts of time, effort, or money to reach polling stations. Many of our states face the problem of locating branch campuses to serve a burgeoning and increasingly well educated population. In the cities we must create and locate playgrounds for the children. Many overpopulated countries must assign birth control clinics to reach the people with contraceptive and family planning information.[13]

Several factors underlie the importance of location in the marketing of services. First, services that are not appropriately located may not be performed at all. Compared to tangible goods, it is easier, as Rathmell has observed, to postpone the purchase of a service, except in emergencies, or discard a planned purchase of services.[14] In addition, a poorly located service facility invites a "do-it-yourself" decision. Second, there are often some constraints on the marketing of services which make location the key element of the marketing mix. For example, competition

[10] "Rent-a-Car Business Grows as Small Firms Add More Locations," *Wall Street Journal,* January 10, 1979, p. 16.
[11] Shapiro, *op. cit.,* p. 129.
[12] *Ibid.*
[13] Ronald Abler, John S. Adams, and Peter Gould, *Spatial Organization* (Englewood Cliffs, N.J.: Prentice-Hall, 1971), pp. 531–532.
[14] Rathmell, *op. cit.,* p. 108.

through either price or promotion is considered unethical in a number of service areas (e.g., medical and legal assistance). For other services, regulated monopolies or oligopolies are the dominant institutional arrangements (e.g., utilities); in such cases, the regulated service agency must concern itself with making its service available to the maximum number of potential customers.[15] With few exceptions, publicly funded or protected organizations are typically expected to serve the entire community.[16]

Although these constraints obviously force certain agencies into locations that they might not otherwise choose, the locational decision-making process for most services should not be altogether unlike that of the demarcation of trading areas and the selection of specific sites by profit-oriented retailing organizations. What is most important in this decision process, irrespective of organizational orientation, is the seller's or agent's location relative to the potential market. In fact, for all services, there has been a marked trend toward the dispersion of service locations,[17] with the increased use of consumer analysis leading to the relocation of sources of services closer to users' locations.[18]

Channel Configurations

Marketing channels for services are generally far shorter than those used in the marketing of tangible commodities. This is because there is frequently little need for reliance on physical distribution and the maintenance of inventories at various points along the channel. The dominant channel configurations in the service sector, as isolated by Rathmell, are depicted in Fig. 13–1. Direct marketing (i.e., between service creator or performer and end-users) is much more common than it is in the marketing of goods. However, intermediaries in the form of agents or brokers do appear in particular service industries.

> Their essential function is to bring performer and consumer or user together. They represent either of the primary channel components, and the longest service channel results where agents and brokers representing both seller and buyer intervene. Examples include the following. Rental agents represent the owners of rental housing and office space. Travel agents represent all types of travel services: surface and air transportation, hotels and motels, and packaged tours. Insurance agents and brokers are probably the most widely known service intermediaries. . . . Artistic performers and entertainers are represented by agents.[19]

[15] *Ibid.*

[16] Christopher H. Lovelock and Charles B. Weinberg, "Contrasting Private and Public Sector Marketing," in Ronald C. Curhan (ed.), *1974 Combined Proceedings* (Chicago: American Marketing Association, 1975), p. 246.

[17] Rathmell, *op. cit.,* p. 108.

[18] Lovelock and Weinberg, *op. cit.,* p. 243. The location factor has even become significant for dental services. Dentists are now leasing space in shopping centers and department stores. See "Moving the Dentist's Chair to Retail Stores," *Business Week* (January 19, 1981); and Kathleen Myler, "A Revolution with Teeth in It," *Chicago Tribune,* Section 4, March 10, 1981, p. 1.

[19] Rathmell, *op. cit.,* pp. 109–110. Donnelly has argued that "any extra-corporate entity between the producer of a service and prospective users that is utilized to make the service available and/or more con-

FIGURE 13-1

Dominant Channel Configurations in the Service Sector

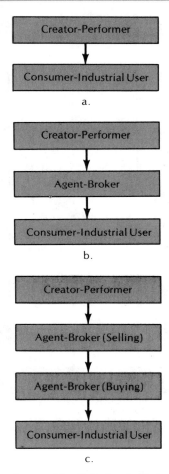

Source: John M. Rathmell, *Marketing in the Service Sector* (Cambridge, Mass.: Winthrop Publishers, Inc., 1974), p. 110. Reprinted by permission of the publisher.

The marketer of services is usually faced with a number of alternative channels, direct and indirect, as shown in Fig. 13-2, illustrating alternative marketing channels for the performing arts.

It is difficult to typify the functions performed by the various agents and

---

venient is a marketing intermediary for that service." Thus, under this definition, when an employer is authorized by his employees to deposit their pay directly into their checking accounts and when the employer agrees to participate in a bank's "direct pay deposit" plan, the employer becomes an intermediary in the distribution of the bank's service. See James H. Donnelly, Jr., *op. cit.*

FIGURE 13–2

The Marketing Channels for the Performing Arts

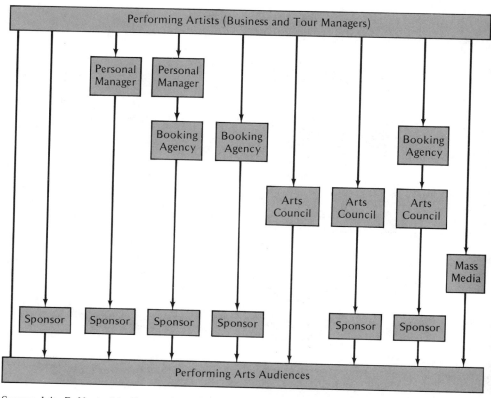

Source: John R. Nevin, "An Empirical Analysis of Marketing Channels for the Performing Arts," in Michael P. Mokwa, William M. Dawson, and E. Arthur Prieve (eds.), *Marketing the Arts* (New York: Praeger Publishers, 1980), p. 204.

brokers who appear in service channels, because the duties performed vary so widely from channel to channel. Thus, agents who represent entertainers are similar to sales agents, while rental agents are mainly processors of transactions rather than decision-makers. Clearly, however, service agents and brokers are, like their counterparts in other fields, involved primarily with the flows of promotion and negotiation. For some services, such as automobile repair and restaurants, merchant wholesalers play an important role in providing the basic supplies needed in their performance. The actual service, however, originates at the retail level. Franchising is extremely important in the marketing of a wide variety of services. In actuality, franchising, as a mode of channel organization and design, has undoubtedly become the most significant competitive force in the channels for a number of services, such as automobile rentals, carpet cleaning, dry cleaning, temporary office help, motels, and the like. In fact, any *standardized* service is an appropriate candidate for franchising.[20]

Marketing channels for services endure change in their structures and institutional practices. Usually, these changes are met with resistance. The following case example of the changing relationship in the distribution channel for air travel is illustrative:

- In early 1980, Pan Am was considering a proposed plan to sell large blocks of tickets on scheduled flights at wholesale prices to contractors or middlemen who would assume the risk and responsibility of pricing and marketing the tickets as they saw fit. Travel agents spoke out in opposition to the plan. They felt that the plan positioned them in direct competition with their own supplier, the airline. Also, they pointed out that the already bewildering fare structure could be further muddied by the diversity of prices offered by contractors, i.e., the wholesalers. Travel agents feared that the plan would allow nontravel-related merchants the possibility of retailing airline tickets at their wholesale cost as a promotional tool for their basic line of merchandise.[21]

- More than one-half of all airline tickets are sold through the 17,000 travel agencies in the U.S. Traditionally, airlines paid a fixed-rate commission of 7 percent for point-to-point domestic ticket sales. In return for creating conditions that made the travel agency profitable, airlines have always been able to write the rules governing agency competition. A Civil Aeronautics Board rule, effective May 1980, abolished the fixed-rate commission and ordered carriers to propose new plans for compensating travel agents. Officials of the agency indicated that the intent is to promote retail price competition and encourage new alternative retail outlets.

   United Airlines was the first to respond with a proposal to pay a flat $8.50 per ticket. Travel agencies reacted by diverting traffic to other airlines offering higher commissions. United suffered a 14 percent sales drop in one month as a result, in part, of the new commission. Finally, United withdrew the plan and offered an alternate sliding scale plan paying travel agents from $7.50 to $37.50, depending on distance flown. Other airlines offered different plans. For example, Eastern proposed a commission ranging from 8 to 11 percent, Frontier Airline's plan called for 10 to 11 percent, and American Airlines' plan was so complex that most agents indicated that they could not understand it.[22]

- In April 1980, the Civil Aeronautics Board was entertaining proposals from Ticketron, Inc., a computerized ticket sales company, and a group of banks to sell air transportation tickets. Ticketron already sells tickets on World Airways, Inc.'s flights through its 600 outlets in the East, West, and Midwest.

---

[20] *Ibid.*, p. 111.

[21] Josh Levine, "Pan Am Seeks Ticket Wholesaling," *Advertising Age* (January 23, 1980), pp. 1 and 84.

[22] "The Fracas Over Who Will Sell Airline Tickets," *Business Week* (April 28, 1980), p. 107; "United Air to Pay Travel Agents Flat Fee, Replacing Commissions Based on Fares," *Wall Street Journal,* February 5, 1980, p. 5; "United Air, Responding to Complaints, Alters Travel Agent Compensation Plan," *Wall Street Journal,* February 19, 1980, p. 8.

World Airways can use Ticketron because it does not belong to the Air Traffic Conference. Ticketron would like to sell tickets of all airlines at a commission lower than the travel agents' and offer the same ticket to the traveler at a lower retail price. Naturally, travel agents oppose these proposals as they pose competitive threats.[23]

The Need for Interorganizational Cooperation

Throughout this book, stress has been placed on the need for the interorganizational management of channel systems. The same stress is appropriate here, especially as services become more dispersed and decentralized. Perhaps the greatest evidence of decentralization is found in the public service area. Federal, state, and local governmental agencies are increasingly contracting with private firms to facilitate or even execute public services. In addition, as Rathmell observes:

> . . . through the revenue-sharing mechanism, the national government is turning over more and more public services to state and local government agencies. In essence, the national government *develops the social product* through legislation and compensates decentralized governmental bodies for performing the *other elements* in the social marketing mix.[24]

Furthermore, there seems to be a desperate need for interorganizational cooperation in such fields as education and health care, where redundancies, inequities, and inefficiencies exist that might be eliminated by fostering a more appropriate division of labor among the various units seeking to provide these services in a community.

Considerable attention has been given, especially by sociologists, to the subject of interorganizational relations in a wide variety of service-oriented fields.[25] However, it is important to note that most of the attention has been focused on the need for horizontal or lateral cooperation among agencies. That is, the focus has been similar to one that would urge greater collusion among manufacturers, or among wholesalers, or among retailers. Very little interorganizational research has been performed relative to vertical relationships (i.e., those among units on dif-

---

[23] "The Fracas Over Who Will Sell Airline Tickets," *op. cit.,* p. 111.

[24] Rathmell, *op. cit.,* p. 111.

[25] See, for example, with regard to health care, Sol Levine and Paul E. White, "Exchange as a Conceptual Framework for the Study of Interorganizational Relationships," *Administrative Science Quarterly,* Vol. 5 (March 1961), pp. 583–601; with regard to rehabilitation and mental health, Bertram J. Black and Harold M. Kase, "Inter-Agency Cooperation in Rehabilitation and Mental Health," *Social Science Review,* Vol. 37 (March 1963), pp. 26–32; with regard to delinquency prevention and control, William Reid, "Interagency Coordination in Delinquency Prevention and Control," *Social Science Review,* Vol. 38 (December 1964), pp. 418–428; with regard to services for the elderly, Robert Morris and Ollie A. Randall, "Planning and Organization of Community Services for the Elderly," *Social Work,* Vol. 10 (January 1965), pp. 96–102; with regard to community action, Roland L. Warren, "The Interorganizational Field as a Focus for Investigation," in Merlin B. Brinkerhoff and Phillip R. Kunz (eds.), *Complex Organizations and Their Environments* (Dubuque, Iowa: Wm. C. Brown Publishers, 1972), pp. 307–325; and with regard to government-business relations, William M. Evan, "An Organization-Set Model of Interorganizational Relations," in Matthew Tuite, Roger Chisholm, and Michael Radnor (eds.), *Interorganizational Decision Making* (Chicago: Aldine Publishing Co., 1972), pp. 181–200.

ferent distribution levels, the ultimate consumer or user being excluded.) The reason for this is relatively clear. The existence of intermediaries, while evident in some service channels, is generally not required, and, therefore, a "commercial channel" of distribution, as defined in Chapter 1, is often absent. There are certainly a large number of wholesalers with whom service organizations interact, but the primary role of the wholesalers in these situations would be to supply tangible products (e.g., auto parts, food, movies) that facilitate the performance of the basic services (e.g., auto repairs, restaurant services, screenings).[26] The service itself does not generally pass through the hands of a number of intermediaries. Health care, rehabilitation, and community action agencies, for example, deal directly with their constituencies. Although resources, in the form of consultation, funds, and program ideas, may come from other organizations (e.g., the federal government), the services provided are usually produced and consumed at the "retail" level.

Therefore, problems of managing *vertical* interorganizational relations are not as acute in the marketing of services as they are in the marketing of tangible commodities. There is, however, a much greater opportunity to concentrate on problems related to *horizontal* interorganizational relations, particularly in the absence of antitrust constraints with regard to the provision of social welfare services and concepts by nonprofit and publicly financed organizations.[27] In fact, horizontal coordination is necessary with regard to almost all social welfare concerns, and the same interorganizational principles apply to achieving such coordination as they do to situations involving vertical relations.

These observations about the character of the distribution of services is not meant, in any way, to minimize the importance of distribution questions in the service sector. Questions of availability and accessibility are absolutely crucial to the viability of any service organization. Nowhere are such questions more evident than in the marketing of public services. For example,

> A city's public library has to consider the best means of making its books available to the public. Should it establish one large library with an extensive collection of books, or several neighborhood branch libraries with duplication of books? Should it use bookmobiles that bring the books to the customers instead of relying exclusively on the customers coming to the books? Should it distribute through school libraries? Similarly the police department of a city must think through the problem of distributing

---

[26] Some producers of tangible goods and the merchant wholesalers with whom they deal are taking a more active role in facilitating the service functions of their customers. For example, in the channel for food services, increasing attention is being given to providing preportioned frozen items, broader assortments, and food portion control services to volume feeding establishments, such as airlines, cafeterias, hospitals, and government facilities and even to fine restaurants. In this case, the original suppliers and the wholesalers are, indeed, participating directly in the provision of services at the retail level. In addition, the Federal Reserve System as well as major city banks can be viewed as wholesalers in the channels for commercial banking services.

[27] Horizontal collusion is illegal, under the Sherman Act, in profit-oriented industries. Yet, collusion does take place, some of which is highly questionable from a free enterprise perspective. Fees set by lawyers, doctors, and appliance and auto repairmen are remarkably similar for certain services. The reasons for this similarity are currently under investigation by the U.S. Justice Department and the Federal Trade Commission. In addition, professional ethics apparently dictate that certain marketing practices, such as advertising of services, are not to be practiced by lawyers and doctors. The enforcement of these ethics by professional associations can also be viewed as anti-competitive.

its protective services efficiently through the community. It has to determine how much protective service to allocate to different neighborhoods; the respective merits of squad cars, motorcycles, and foot patrolmen; and the positioning of emergency phones.[28]

Similar questions exist with regard to the availability of fire and ambulance services,[29] the distribution of public welfare checks, the sale of government bonds, the provision of postal services, the establishment of public parks, and the placement of automobile license bureaus.[30] In fact, these questions are unavoidable for *every* kind of service, but are particularly important for public services. In each and every case, the dominant questions seem to relate directly to the functions and location of "retail" outlets. That is, the primary focus is on the best means available, subject to budget constraints, for permitting ultimate consumers access to specific services. Clearly, then, an appropriate combination of retailing marketing mix elements (hours of operations, facilitating services, assortments, location and facilities, expense management, promotion, etc.)[31] is critical in the service sector of the economy, irrespective of the profit orientation of the organizations providing the services or the basic nature of the service offered.

The remainder of this chapter concentrates on examples where channel concepts have been or could be applied to specific service situations. Although some attention is given to channels for commercial services (e.g., lodging and insurance), most attention is focused on services provided by nonprofit and publicly financed organizations, because the problems associated with channel organization and design in the former are very similar to those found in the marketing of commercial products, while the latter represent unique cases which demand concentrated examination.

APPLYING CHANNEL CONCEPTS TO NONPROFIT AND PUBLICLY FINANCED SERVICES

Health Care Services[32]

Four different market structures for the delivery of health care services may be isolated, although a number of others also exist. The first, called the flat nonintegrated structure (see Fig. 13-3), is the archtype of the present private prac-

---

[28] Philip Kotler and Sidney J. Levy, "Broadening the Concept of Marketing," *Journal of Marketing,* Vol. 33 (January 1969), p. 13.

[29] See Frederick E. Webster, Jr., *Social Aspects of Marketing* (Englewood Cliffs, N.J.: Prentice-Hall, 1974), p. 87.

[30] See Kotler, *Marketing for Nonprofit Organizations, op. cit.,* pp. 336–337.

[31] See Chapter 2 for a discussion of significant aspects of the retailing marketing mix.

[32] The discussion of health care services is drawn from the excellent and innovative essay by Louis P. Bucklin and James M. Carman, "Vertical Market Structure Theory and the Health Care Delivery System," in Jagdish N. Sheth and Peter L. Wright (eds.), *Marketing Analysis for Societal Problems* (Urbana, Ill.: University of Illinois Bureau of Economic and Business Research, 1974), pp. 7–39.

FIGURE 13-3

The Flat Nonintegrated Structure for the Delivery of Health Care Services

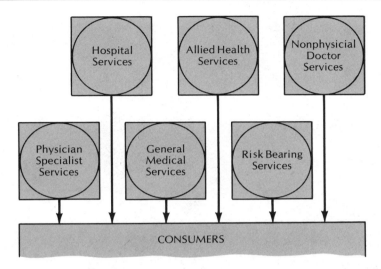

Source: Louis P. Bucklin and James M. Carman, "Vertical Market Structure Theory and the Health Care Delivery System," in Jagdish N. Sheth and Peter L. Wright (eds.), *Marketing Analysis for Societal Problems* (Urbana, Ill.: University of Illinois Bureau of Economic and Business Research, 1974), p. 23.

tice, fee-for-service system in which every hospital, each physician, and all other health care providers sell directly to consumers. The organizations involved in this system undertake no effort to coordinate their activities; any coordination that does take place comes from market pressures emanating from consumers.[33]

The second is a vertically integrated structure where coordination of the activities of all providers is shifted to a comprehensive health care institution, such as the Kaiser Health Care Foundation, which provides for all potential patient health needs within a single establishment.[34] Although there are a number of variations in existence, Fig. 13-4 is representative of a major form of these so-called health maintenance organizations (HMO's). Coordination among activities is achieved through an internal control mechanism. Payments are received from consumers on a capitation basis, and each consumer belongs to only one group.

In the third structure, coordination is achieved by means of the control exerted by one health provider or by a middleman (see Fig. 13-5). In this noninte-grated arrangement, consumers make annual capitation payments to the coor-dinator of their choice. It is then the responsibility of the central coordinator—a

[33] *Ibid.,* p. 23.

[34] *Ibid.,* p. 24. See also Patrick E. Murphy and William A. Staples, "Health Maintenance Organizations: A Marketing Perspective," a paper presented to the 1975 American Marketing Association Educators' Conference, Rochester, N.Y., August 17–20, 1975; and Michael Waldholz, "HMOs, a Hope for Keeping Medical Costs Down, Face an Uncertain Future Under Reagan's Plans," *Wall Street Journal,* April 3, 1981, p. 38.

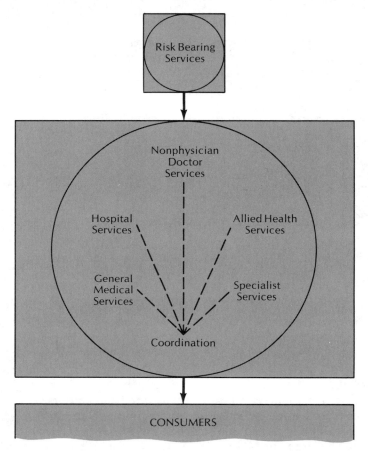

Source: Louis P. Bucklin and James M. Carman, "Vertical Market Structure Theory and the Health Care Delivery System," in Jagdish N. Sheth and Peter L. Wright (eds.), *Marketing Analysis for Societal Problems* (Urbana, Ill.: University of Illinois Bureau of Economic and Business Research, 1974), p. 25.

pure middleman, a general practitioner individual or group, a pediatric individual or group, or a general practice community clinic or hospital—to buy specialized services from other types of providers or to undertake to perform these internally.

The fourth type of arrangement is called the long, vertical nonintegrated structure (see Fig. 13-6) and is characterized by the presence of multiple modes of coordination. According to Bucklin and Carman:

> General financial support and insurance services are provided through a nonprofit foundation for a complete health package. Individual providers would similarly

FIGURE 13-5

The Vertical, Nonintegrated Structure for the Delivery of Health Care Services

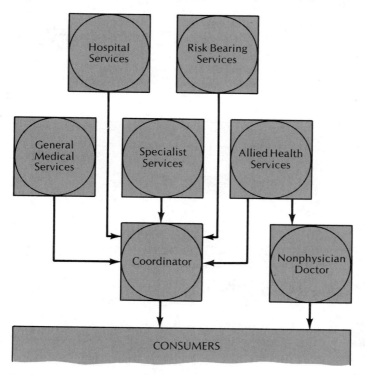

Source: Louis P. Bucklin and James M. Carman, "Vertical Marketing Structure Theory and the Health Care Delivery System," in Jagdish N. Sheth and Peter L. Wright (eds.), *Marketing Analysis for Societal Problems* (Urbana, Ill.: University of Illinois Bureau of Economic and Business Research, 1974), p. 27.

belong to the foundation which would reimburse the former on a fee-for-service basis. The foundation would develop its own techniques, such as peer review, to control the use of providers and their charges for service. All consumers within a given area, such as a county, would be members of the foundation.[35]

Under this system, as in the previous two, consumers would make an annual capitation payment, but in this case, their payment would go to the foundation.

In their analysis of these four arrangements, Bucklin and Carman have relied heavily on Bucklin's theory of channel structure, which was discussed in Chapter 1 of this book. Thus, their basic conclusions about the arrangements are couched in terms of service outputs and costs. Some of their conclusions are as follows.[36]

[35] Bucklin and Carman, *op. cit.,* pp. 26–27.
[36] *Ibid.,* pp. 29 and 35.

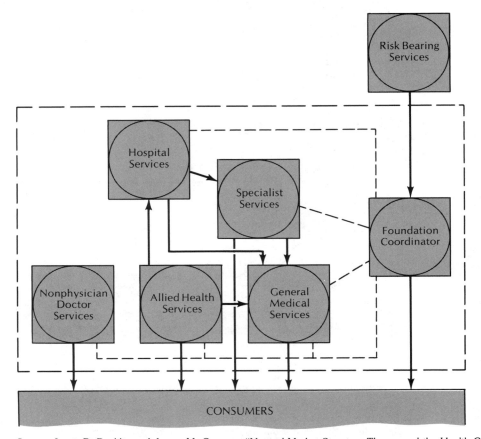

Source: Louis P. Bucklin and James M. Carman, "Vertical Market Structure Theory and the Health Care Delivery System" in Jagdish N. Sheth and Peter L. Wright (eds.), *Marketing Analysis for Societal Problems* (Urbana, Ill.: University of Illinois Bureau of Economic and Business Research, 1974), p. 28.

1. Consumer search for information and the need for seller promotion appears to be greatest in the flat, nonintegrated structure. The least seller promotion and consumer search cost is provided by the vertically integrated structure.

2. The flat, nonintegrated structure is the one that is likely to adapt best to consumer needs in terms of providing facilitating outputs. It is also the one that enables the consumer to have the greatest opportunity to select that particular health service which he perceives as best suiting his needs.

3. The flat, nonintegrated structure is likely to be the one that incurs the

greatest waste of resources, is least efficient, and provides the greatest degree of discrimination among consumer groups. Wealthy consumers may be able to cope handily with the system. Impoverished consumers may literally fail to survive.

4. The vertically integrated system (HMO) is likely to result in better use of existing health supply resources and to be more efficient. It also provides the basis for evenhanded care for all people[37] On the other hand, there is likely to be minimal adjustment of facilitating outputs to consumer needs, problems in effecting community control in the absence of competition, and a tendency over time for bureaucratic rigidities to accrue. Consumers have the least choice of specific providers.

5. The vertically nonintegrated structures provide a middle ground, involving characteristics of both ends of the spectrum. Consumer choice opportunities are improved, but the possiblities for some discrimination in resource use also appears likely. Both vertically nonintegrated systems also provide maximum opportunity for the entry of new types of structures and hence incentive for innovation.

Any analysis of health care services must recognize, implicitly or explicitly, the significance of effective interorganization managment in the organization of health care delivery systems. Each structure enumerated above varies in terms of the extent of role specification, centralization of power, and potential for conflict management that might be expected. In fact, the typology here is very similar to that developed throughout this book for conventional, administered, contractual, and corporate channels. The application of the concepts from vertical market structure theory and from interorganization management theory can, therefore, be combined to provide prescriptions for improving health care systems.[38] The following example underscores this point:

> Each year for the past five years, tiny Valley View Medical Center in Cedar City, Utah, has lost large amounts of money—up to $176,000 in 1975, when local taxpayers made up the deficit. But in 1977, Valley View ran only $800 in the red, and this year it expects to come out ahead. It has eliminated 15 jobs with salaries totaling $124,000, saved $72,000 by obtaining discounts on supplies, and avoided a disastrous jump of $12,000 to $15,000 in malpractice insurance rates.
>
> The hospital won a new lease on life and improved its service to patients because of its 1976 affiliation with Intermountain Health Care, Inc., a 21-unit hospital chain based in Salt Lake City. IHC provides management help, technical training, access to sophisticated medical expertise and equipment, and discounts on supplies by joint purchasing.

---

[37] Recent evidence indicates that HMOs have positive competitive impact in health care. They provide service at lower cost. See, for example, "FTC Staff Report Says HMOs Have Competitive Impact," *FTC News Summary* (August 1977), p. 1; "HMOs Can Hold Down Health Care Costs," *Wall Street Journal,* August 5, 1977, p. 5, and "Unhealthy Costs of Health Care," *Business Week* (September 4, 1978), pp. 58–68.

[38] For further discussion of this point, see Louis W. Stern and Frederick D. Sturdivant, "Discussion," in Jagdish N. Sheth and Peter L. Wright, *op. cit.,* pp. 39–41; and Donald E. L. Johnson, "University Hospitals Will Anchor Vertical Systems," *Modern Health Care* (December 1979), pp. 50–54.

IHC is the largest example of a new phenomenon in the financially stricken hospital field—the nonprofit hospital chain that owns, leases, or manages its affiliates. Of the 31 major chains (representing 399 hospitals with 84,000 beds), almost all began within the past decade and most within the past five years. Health care experts see in them a survival formula for many hospitals that otherwise might close their doors or raise their rates to a level prohibitive to patients, insurers, and employers, who pay much of the insurance bill.[39]

Educational Services[40]

Distribution channel concepts may be applied to the problem of disseminating educational innovations. A key agency responsible for speeding up the diffusion of worthwhile educational innovations among the nation's locally controlled 18,000 school districts is the National Institute of Education (NIE).[41] Figure 13–7 illustrates four different distribution models that might be used by NIE to achieve its ends. According to Kotler:[42]

> The first model calls for direct distribution of innovations from NIE to each of the 18,000 school districts. This is clearly an inefficient system of distribution, involving too many first-hand contacts and the absence of an appreciation of local conditions.
> The second model calls for NIE to present the innovations to *regional dissemination centers* (RDC's-perhaps major universities) which in turn would disseminate them to all the local schools in their area.
> The third model is similar to the second, with the modification that the RDCs would not deal with all the school districts in their region but mainly with those schools designated as innovator schools which are looked up to by other schools in the region. These innovator schools will "retail" the innovations and presumably be more effective because of the high esteem in which they are held by other schools.
> The fourth model adds still one more channel link to the market, in the form of designated school district change agents. Each school district would designate one person to be the school district's change agent. This person would be responsible to the school district for (1) searching for new ideas and solutions to local school district problems by going to the local RDC, the NIE, or elsewhere, and (2) bringing innovations to the right parties within their school district. The establishment of this formal position within all school districts would make it easier for NIE and RDC to determine who to contact for information and communication.

While the above example is primarily normative in nature, there are instances where marketing channels have emerged in education under circumstances not unlike the ones described by Kotler. The curriculum reform movement of the late 1950s provides an actual illustration.[43] The Physical Science Study Committee, a

---

[39] "The Chain: A Survival Formula for Hospitals," *Business Week* (January 16, 1978), p. 113.

[40] The discussion of educational services is drawn from Kotler, *Marketing for Nonprofit Organizations, op. cit.,* pp. 192–194; and Burton R. Clark, "Interorganizational Patterns in Education," in Merlin B. Brinkerhoff and Philip R. Kunz, *op. cit.,* pp. 360–362.

[41] Kotler, *ibid.,* p. 192.

[42] *Ibid.,* pp. 192 and 194.

[43] Clark, *op. cit.,* p. 360.

1. Direct Marketing Model
   (Zero-level marketing channel)

   0. NIE → all school districts

2. Regional Dissemination Center Model
   (One-level marketing channel)

   0. NIE → RDC
   1. RDC → school districts

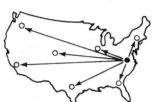

3. RDC and Innovator School Model
   (Two-level marketing channel)

   0. NIE → RDC
   1. RDC → innovator schools
   2. Innovator schools → other schools

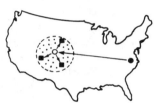

4. RDC, Innovator School, and Local
   Change Agent Model

   (Three-level marketing channel)

   0. NIE → RDC
   1. RDC → innovator schools
   2. Innovator schools → school district
      change agents
   3. Change agents → other schools

Symbols: ● NIE-National Institute of Education
              ○ RDC-Regional dissemination center
              ■ Innovator school
              □ School district change agents
              · School district

Source: Philip Kotler, *Marketing for Nonprofit Organizations* (Englewood Cliffs, N.J.: Prentice-Hall, 1975), p. 193. By permission.

563

group of professors and secondary school teachers funded by the National Science Foundation, undertook to improve the teaching of physical sciences in the nation's secondary schools. Once it had developed suitable materials, the Committee then saw to it that the materials would be actively promoted and made widely available throughout the nation by putting them into the hands of profit-oriented organizations with preformed marketing channels. Thus, during the winter of 1959–1960, the Committee gave its printed materials to a schoolbook publisher, its new scientific equipment to a manufacturer of scientific apparatus, and its films to an educational film distributor. Concurrently, the National Science Foundation also initiated and supported a program of summer institutes that were voluntary throughout—for the colleges that offered them, the professors who directed and staffed them and the teachers who came as students. The Physical Science Study Committee was, for the most part, successful in convincing institutes to use its materials.

Thus, in this channel example, a federal agency provided the funds; a private nonprofit group received the money and developed a new course; commercial organizations made the new materials available to all units of the decentralized educational system; dispersed universities and colleges used the new materials to train teachers in all regions of the country; and eventually, existing local authorities adopted the materials and allowed their teachers to reshape local courses.

Clearly, the effective dissemination of the innovation rested to a large extent on the expert power of the various actors. As Clark observes;

> The National Science Foundation was expert and prestigeful; so also were the Committee, the Institutes, the teachers trained in the new materials. The very materials themselves traveled under the same aura.[44]

In this instance, the expert power of each channel member was reinforcing and not conflictful. The absence of dysfunctional conflict can be attributed, in part, to the presence of a superordinate goal based on the recognition, at the time, that our secondary school system was far inferior to that of the Soviet Union in the teaching of the physical sciences. Interorganization management could be practiced in a supportive atmosphere, indeed. The final outcome was that, as early as 1963, 40 to 50 percent of the students taking high school physics were studying the materials generated by the Committee, even though the materials did not become available until after 1958.

Accident Prevention Services[45]

Several nonprofit organizations are involved with providing services that will serve to reduce the incidence of industrial and consumer accidents, but perhaps the most prominent of these is the National Safety Council. One of the Council's goals

---

[44] *Ibid.,* p. 362.

[45] The discussion of accident prevention services is drawn from Kotler and Zaltman, *op. cit.,* p. 11.

concerns the promotion of highway safety, and one of the services it offers to help cut down on the number of highway mishaps is a defensive driving course (DDC).

Figure 13–8 shows the various channels through which this course is marketed along with the promotional tools its uses. The National Safety Council reaches potential prospects through business firms, service organizations, schools, and the police and court system.[46] For the 1970s the National Safety Council adopted

> . . . a four-point marketing program . . . One of the first objectives is to increase the sales effectiveness of our existing 150 state and local safety council cooperating agencies . . . The second part of the program is to create 500 new training agencies in communities not now served by safety councils . . . The third part of the marketing program will be aimed at selling big industry on adopting DDC as a training course for all employees in plant-run training programs . . . The fourth part of the marketing plan deals with a nationwide promotional effort built around a series of community special-emphasis campaigns running from February 1 through Memorial Day each year of the decade.[47]

FIGURE 13–8

Marketing Channels and Promotional Tools Used by the National Safety Council: Defensive Driving Course

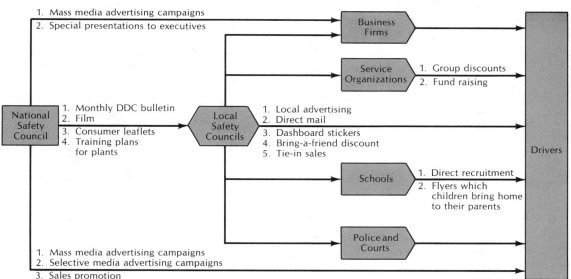

Source: Philip Kotler, *Marketing for Nonprofit Organizations* (Englewood Cliffs, N.J.: Prentice-Hall, 1975), p. 299. By permission.

[46] *Ibid.*

[47] Chris Imhoff, "DDC's Decisive Decade," *Traffic Safety Magazine,* Vol. 69 (December 1969), pp. 20 and 26.

In order for the National Safety Council to achieve its goals, it has to rely on its expert, referent, and legitimate power bases in convincing channel members to do what they might not otherwise do. And while its power may be great relative to the issue of highway safety, for example, the issue itself may not be salient enough to the other firms within its channels to induce them to action. In other words, the Council has to provide some significant inducement in order to secure the contribution of the channel members depicted in Fig. 13–8. Unless it can somehow mediate rewards of punishments for compliance, its efforts may be in vain.

Because such efforts on the part of the Council really involve the marketing of an idea—the concept of defensive driving as a deterrant to highway accidents—it is clear that there must be an effective merging of distribution and promotion in its program. The use of specific agents who can carry out the idea and enforce it must be blended with such vehicles as advertising, press releases, and other promotional tools. Clearly, no marketing program can rely on any one element of the marketing mix; each must use all elements in combination in order to achieve its goals.

Population Control and Family Planning Services[48]

The topic of population control and family planning is highly controversial. Population control refers to the *control* of births, while family planning refers to the spacing of births and the limiting of family size to some number of children *desired* by the individual couple. Population control advocates are highly critical of the family planning approach to the world's population problem.

Without engaging in this debate, it is possible to observe that the present system in the United States for distributing birth control services to the population is quite fragmented and highly decentralized. Medical birth control services (e.g., abortion, the IUD, sterilization, and birth control pills) may be distributed through private or public health practice. In addition, they may be offered through clinics established solely for this purpose and staffed by personnel possessing the required level of medical expertise. The channels for nonmedical methods (e.g., condoms, chemical preparations, and information on so-called natural methods of contraception such as the rhythm system) are largely identical to those for the medically dependent techniques, except for one important exception—the addition of traditional commercial channels, including retail drug outlets and vending machines.

If one is interested in seeking improvements in the dissemination of birth control devices and information—either for population control or family planning purposes—attention must be focused on reducing the costs of the physical, temporal, and psychic distances separating individuals from the agencies providing the services or mechanisms. Private medical practitioners have, on the whole, historically been hesitant to *initiate* the subject of birth control with their established patients.[49]

---

[48] The discussion of population control and family planning services is drawn from an unpublished term paper by Raymond Neil Maddox, "Distribution and Social Problems."

[49] Sydney S. Spivack, "Family Planning in Medical Practice," in Clyde V. Kiser (ed.), *Research in Family Planning* (Princeton, N.J.: Princeton University Press, 1962), pp. 211–230.

Presumably, they would be even more reluctant to become active agents in any channel whose sole function is the providing of such services. It is expected that if this group is to assume a more active role, two steps must be taken. First, the program must be remunerative to physicians. Second, the norms of the medical profession must be supportive of such activities.

Enrolling the physician as an active participant would definitely increase the availability of birth control services to the more affluent of the population. However, as pointed out earlier in the discussion of the present flat, nonintegrated structure in health care delivery, among the problems confronting the less fortunate is the limited availability of medical services of any type. Therefore, this suggestion would be, at best, of limited utility in raising the level of accessibility for these groups.

An innovative approach in solving the problem of accessibility has been that adopted in Louisiana. As reported by El-Ansary and Kramer, a major component of the so-called "Louisiana model" was an improvement in clinic site selection and service level determination.

> To reduce travel time, strategic locations were selected for the program's clinic satellites. Also, clinic layout was planned to reduce the time consumed in information and physical flows. The areas assigned for waiting rooms were limited to force faster customer flows. Bottlenecks in the system were identified and eliminated. It was realized that improving the service level would result not only in a higher percentage of kept appointments and active customers but also in better utilization of physical facilities and human resources.[50]

Although heavy reliance on clinics to provide birth control services may be functional in parts of the United States, it is not always the best distribution approach, especially in underdeveloped countries. As Farley and Leavitt point out,[51]

> . . . a complete reliance upon clinics as outlets is questionable, especially when one considers their high cost per client visit and the relatively poor revisit rates they achieve. Several problems contribute to this situation:
> —Medical resources, especially personnel, are expensive and generally in short supply. . .
> —Red tape may be substantial because of overly complex control systems . . .
> —Clinical systems may bias a program's emphasis to the exclusion of (nonmedical types of contraception) . . .
> —As a distribution network, clinics tend to be sparsely dispersed . . . (Also,) a visit to a clinic may involve substantial waiting time . . .
> —Clinics lack anonymity . . .

However, in both developed and underdeveloped economies, the commercial

[50] Adel I. El-Ansary and Oscar E. Kramer, Jr., "Social Marketing: The Family Planning Experience," *Journal of Marketing,* Vol. 37 (July 1973), p. 3.

[51] John U. Farley and Harold J. Leavitt, "Marketing and Population Problems," *Journal of Marketing,* Vol. 35 (July 1971), p. 31.

distribution of nonmedical means seems to offer the greatest potential for rapidly expanding the number and availability of birth control mechanisms.

> . . . most cultures have a functioning distribution structure which delivers basic commodities to even the most remote areas of the countryside. The network is intensive and provides relatively anonymous outlets which are physically close to the customer. Wholesalers and retailers know how to deliver goods to customers, and distributors know how to stimulate consumer demand. It is possible that the retail structure could be utilized to provide distribution outlets for contraceptive materials, thus helping resolve the logistical problems facing the clinic system . . . Other channels, such as mail order, could be used in some nations to supplement the clinic system's distribution of certain items.[52]

Indeed, if food and variety stores, as well as pharmacies, were engaged as distributors of point-of-purchase information, contraceptive chemicals, and contraceptive devices, the increase in the number and accessibility of outlets would be tremendous. In India, for example, the goverment engaged the distribution services of some of the largest packaged-goods companies in the country, including Hindustan Lever, ITC, and Brooke Bond, because of their reach into the remotest areas.[53] In fact, the government eventually elected to work with the following retailers: (a) health clinics, (b) barbers, (c) field workers, (d) retail stores, and (e) vending machines.

A major advantage in using traditional commercial channels for the distribution of birth control services is that they tend to help reduce psychic distance, that is, the hesitancy to seek birth control services owing to the intimate nature of the product and the modesty or shyness associated with its use. Medical channels, including public agencies no matter how available, are separated from certain segments of the population by major psychological barriers.[54] A consumer's basic familiarity with commercial retail outlets is an important means of reducing this distance factor.

There is a close correspondence between the marketing of birth control services and the marketing of "normal" products, because most contraceptive devices are tangible items. While there are numerous ancillary services (such as counseling) that attend population control and family planning, a major problem in this area is achieving the availability and accessibility of the devices themselves. Thus, thinking in terms of traditional marketing approaches seems to be a natural course. The principles of interorganization management seems as relevant here as they are to the marketing of all forms of packaged goods.

[52] *Ibid.*

[53] Kotler, *Marketing for Nonprofit Organizations, op. cit.*, p. 196.

[54] See Gerald Zaltman and Ilan Vertinsky, "Health Service Marketing: A Suggested Model," *Journal of Marketing*, Vol. 35 (July 1971), p. 26.

Recycling Services[55]

The recycling of waste products has become a subject of considerable notoriety over the past decade, as increased concern has been voiced over environmental quality.

> Municipal solid waste (residential, commercial, and institutional sources) amounted to about 130 million metric tons in 1976, enough to fill the New Orleans Superdome from floor to ceiling, twice a day, weekends and holidays included. Per capita generation amounts to 1300 pounds a year. By 1985, the yearly total is projected to increase to 180 million tons.[56]

Although the problem is primarily commercial in nature and thus directly involves the activities of profit-oriented organizations, the major forces behind the movement to improve recycling services have been nonprofit organizations (e.g., the Crusade for a Clean Environment), private citizens and legislators. For this latter reason, a discussion of the distribution issues involved in this service area has been included in this section.

Considering the low prices paid currently for waste materials (i.e., bottles, cans, paper, etc.) and the high costs involved in the collecting, sorting, and transportation of these objects to recycling plants, industry is relying heavily on civic and community groups, who use volunteer help primarily in the collection process. Normal business costs are usually absent when these groups handle the collection, because labor and vehicles are generally donated. However, one of the problems in relying on these groups is that their efforts are generally very sporadic, at best. Furthermore, the problem is growing faster than the membership of ecology-minded groups.

Traditional distribution channels have been used in some recycling efforts. During the immediate post-World War II years and before, distribution of soft drinks, for example, was specifically tied in to the use of the returnable bottle. From the bottler's point of view, the returnable bottle was desirable because its use reduced his production costs. He found it more economical to clean existing bottles and reuse them than to buy new bottles. Middlemen, such as retail food stores, cooperated because the system was the most convenient for the producer involved, and he could bring pressure to bear on the middlemen to secure their cooperation. Currently, however, returnable bottles account for less than 50 percent of the soft drink industry's business, because both retailers and consumers resisted the returning and handling of empty bottles.[57] Supermarkets directly influenced bottlers to in-

[55] The discussion of recycling services is drawn primarily from an unpublished term paper by Sam B. Dunbar, Jr., "The Recycling of Waste Products: Effects on Distribution Channels and Marketing."
[56] *Solid Waste Facts, A Statistical Handbook,* Office of Solid Waste, Environmental Protection Agency, Washington, D.C., 1978, p. 2.
[57] "Packaging Advances Promise Much But Environment Dampens Outlook," *Soft Drink Industry* (May 29, 1970), p. 1.

troduce soft drinks in one-way bottles as early as 1948.[58] While one-way containers have increased the bottler's costs, these costs have been passed on to the consumer. The response of the consumers has been demonstrated by their willingness to pay higher prices for the convenience afforded by these containers. Thus, the recycling problem in this area has multiplied.

If recycling is to be a feasible solution to waste disposal, some means must be developed to channel these wastes back to firms for further use. But traditional channel concepts must be reversed because, in the case of soft drinks especially, the consumer is the *producer* of the waste materials that are to be recycled. Thus, the consumer becomes the first link in the recycling channel of distribution rather than the last. The recycling of waste materials is, therefore, essentially a "reverse-distribution" process.[59]

The contrast between forward and reverse channels is illustrated in Fig. 13–9 and in Table 13–1. The reverse direction channel returns the reusable waste products from consumer to producer.

FIGURE 13–9
Forward and Reverse Channels of Distribution

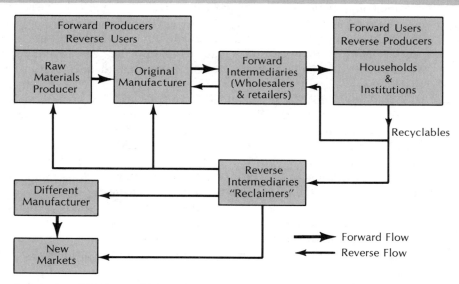

Source: Joseph Guiltinan and Nonyelu Nwokoye, "Reverse Channels for Recycling: An Analysis of Alternat and Public Policy Implications," in Ronald C. Curhan (ed.) *1974 Combined Proceedings* (Chicago: Amer Marketing Association, 1975), p. 341.

[58] William G. Zikmund and William J. Stanton, "Recycling Solid Wastes: A Channels-of-Distribution Problem," *Journal of Marketing,* Vol. 35 (July 1971), p. 36.
[59] *Ibid.,* pp. 34–35.

TABLE 13–1   Forward versus reverse channels: some key distinctions

Forward Channels	Reverse Channels
Products:	
High unit value	Low unit value
Highly differentiated	Little or no differentiation
Much product innovation	Little or no innovation
Few producers	Many originators
Markets:	
Routinized transactions established	Routinized transactions not established
Many final users	Few final users
Varied customer demands	Standardized demands
Supply often less than or equal to demand	Supply typically greater than demand
Large assortment discrepancy	Small assortment discrepancy
Key Functions:	
Assorting	Sorting
Allocation	Accumulation
Heavy promotional effort	Low promotional effort
Speculative inventories	Few speculative inventories
Packaging	Collection

Source: Joseph Guiltinan and Nonyelu Nwokoye, "Reverse Channels for Recycling: An Analysis of Alternatives and Public Policy Implications," in Ronald C. Curhan (ed.), *1974 Combined Proceedings* (Chicago, Ill.: American Marketing Association, 1975), p. 342.

Conceptually, reverse distribution is identical to the traditional channel of distribution. The consumer has a product to sell, and in essence, he assumes the same position as a manufacturer selling a new product. The consumer's (seller's) role is to distribute his waste materials to the market that demands his product.[60]

However, the consumer, in most instances, does not consider himself to be the producer of waste materials. Therefore, he is not readily concerned with planning a marketing strategy for his product, which would be reusable wastes. When the producer is unaware of or indifferent to the fact that he is the producer, then the problem becomes acute.

So far, many recycling channels eliminate the middleman, unless that middleman is a voluntary group. The fact that there are generally no established middlemen in these backward channels between the producer and the consumer of waste products is unfortunate. It causes the producer (consumer) a number of inconveniences. Foremost is the accumulation of waste materials on his part, without adequate storage facilities, as well as an absence of transportation facilities when he does accumulate a mass of waste materials.

On the other hand, in the area of trash recycling, private and municipal trash collection systems provide the collection and storage functions. The buyer of the

[60] *Ibid.*, p. 35.

571

collected wastes may be a power plant, a metals company, a fertilizer company, etc. This channel is a convenient channel for the individual household. However, trash collection by basic trash collection agencies may not be the ultimate answer to the recycling problem. Trash needs to be sorted and then routed to storage centers for ultimate transportation to recycling centers, and most municipalities are unwilling to incur the costs associated with these tasks.

If an effective reverse channel of distribution is to become a reality, the ultimate consumer must first be motivated to start the reverse flow. In addition, a greater degree of cooperation has to be achieved among channel members than presently occurs relative to this problem area. A barrier to increased cooperation and coordination is the lack of profitability. In the absence of legislation mandating recycling efforts (or taxing noncompliers), improved recycling efforts may depend on a higher order of social responsibility on the part of middlemen, given the lack of profits. Several new types of intermediaries may emerge to facilitate recycling processes. One of these is the reclamation or recycling center, a modernized "junk yard" placed in a convenient location for the customer, who would be paid an equitable amount for his waste goods. Initial processing of the waste materials, when they are collected, might be accomplished at these centers. For example, aluminum producers, can makers, and beverage distributors have set up more than 2000 recycling centers across the U.S.A. Some producers send trucks to neighborhoods to pick up cans at 23¢ a pound.[61] In addition, central processing warehouses may be developed by existing middlemen in traditional channels, where trash can be stored and where limited processing operations on waste material may be performed.[62] For example, aluminum can producers are equipping beverage distributors with can flatteners, shredders, compactors, and truck trailers to encourage them to accept empties for recycling.[63] Transportation costs would likely represent a major barrier to such recycling efforts, however. Other possibilities include such reverse channels as manufacturer-controlled recycling centers, joint-venture resource recovery centers, and secondary dealers.[64]

The development of solid waste reverse channels of distribution has been influenced by federal, state, and local legislation directed at all phases of the environment. For example, reverse channels have been given considerable impetus in states enacting "bottle bills," banning nonreturnable drink containers. Oregon, Vermont, and South Dakota, among several other states, enacted such recycling laws. In October 1972, the "Oregon Minimum Deposit Act" became effective. It is the most comprehensive recycling law, requiring retailers and distributors to accept and pay refunds on all empty cans and bottles of the kind, size, and brands sold by them. As

[61] "Recycling Ease Gives Aluminum an Edge Over Steel in Beverage-Can Market Battle," *Wall Street Journal,* January 2, 1980, p. 28.
[62] "Tomorrow's Markets: Refuse Disposal, Trash Removal, Traffic Jam," *Sales Management* (November 10, 1969), pp. 24–26.
[63] "Recycling Ease Gives Aluminum an Edge Over Steel in Beverage-Can Market Battle," *op. cit.*
[64] For a discussion of these latter channels, see Joseph Guiltinan and Nonyelu Nwokoye, "Reverse Channels for Recycling: An Analysis of Alternatives and Public Policy Implications," in Ronald C. Curhan (ed.), *op. cit.,* pp. 343–344; and Zikmund and Stanton, *op. cit.,* p. 38.

more states, counties, and localities enact similar laws, reverse distribution channels will become a permanent part of the distribution structure in the U.S.[65]

APPLYING CHANNEL CONCEPTS TO PROFIT-ORIENTED SERVICES

Lodging Services[66]

Marketing channels associated with the lodging industry (hotels, motels, motor inns, tourist courts, etc.) are becoming increasingly complex and sophisticated, even in view of the fact that, in the United States, nearly 50 percent of the people have never stayed in a hotel, journeyed more than 200 miles from home, or travelled by plane or train.[67] While hotels throughout the world tend to be small (e.g., over 40 percent of U.S. hotels and motels are too small to have even one paid employee), there is an increasing amount of economic concentration in the lodging industry that has been due, in part, to the development of interorganizational communication systems, franchised networks, and corporate vertical marketing systems. The various channels of distribution in the lodging industry are shown in Fig. 13-10. Direct channels of distribution between hotels, motels, and other lodging operations and their customers are mainly concerned with the sales function. That is, an individual hotel's salesmen concentrate on:

1. Maintaining sales contact with channel intermediaries such as tour operators, travel agents, representatives and transportation companies.
2. Maintaining sales contact with community firms and organizations in an attempt to obtain lodging and function business.
3. Following the leads furnished by other sources.[68]

Indirect channels, however, are more significant to lodging providers than are direct channels. Intermediaries in these channels include travel agents, hotel representatives, tour operators, space brokers, airlines and the centralized reservation and sales operations of franchised or chain hotels.

- *Travel agents* may contract for rooms on a customer's behalf, but they more frequently deal through other intermediaries who hold blocks of rooms or otherwise act as agents for the hotels.

[65] Peter M. Ginter and Jack M. Starling, "Reverse Distribution Channels for Recycling," *California Management Review* (Spring 1978), pp. 77 and 78.
[66] The discussion of lodging services is drawn from William H. Kaven, "Channels of Distribution in the Hotel Industry," in John M. Rathmell, *op. cit.,* pp. 114–121.
[67] *Ibid.,* p. 115.
[68] *Ibid.,* p. 116.

FIGURE 13–10

Marketing Channels for Lodging Services

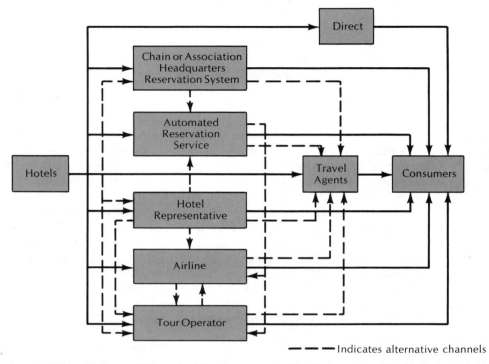

- - - Indicates alternative channels

Source: William H. Kaven, "Channels of Distribution in the Hotel Industry," in John M. Rathmell (ed.) *Marketing in the Service Sector* (Cambridge, Mass.: Winthrop Publishers, Inc., 1974), p. 118. Reprinted by permission of the publisher.

- *Hotel representatives* act as sales and reservation agents for a number of non-competing hotels, such as resorts.

- *Automated reservation services,* such as American Express Space Bank, maintain for a fee in their computers an inventory of available hotel rooms from around the world so that travel agents can buy rooms for their customers.

- *Airlines,* chiefly for overseas destinations, maintain an inventory of room availability to accommodate customers and travel agents who prefer to make complete arrangements with but one phone call for flight and room reservations.

- *Centralized reservation and sales operations* of associated, franchised, or chain hotels/motels facilitate the flow of room availability information to potential consumers and promote, sell, and accept reservations for space.[69]

[69] *Ibid.,* pp. 116–117. Interorganizational linkages between airlines and travel agents are becoming highly sophisticated. TWA and American Airlines are offering their own automated reservations and ticketing equipment to travel agents with terminals linked to each airline's computerized reservations system. See

With the increased dependence of many hotel and motel operators on these intermediaries, power has shifted in the channels for lodging services. The intermediaries can maintain a wide number of alternatives and can mediate considerable rewards for lodging providers. Thus, in part as a reaction to the changing character of the power relationships, there has been a considerable movement within the industry to the formation of vertical marketing systems initiated not only by hotel and motel owners but by organizations closely connected to the industry, such as airlines. Either through contractual or ownership arrangements, these systems permit control over all channel flows, especially those associated with information processing.

Clearly, the move to vertical marketing arrangements, such as those forged by Holiday Inns and others, has been motivated by other reasons as well. Such arrangements permit greater economies of scale in promotion, increased speed and economy in the flow of information, and an increased closeness to consumers when they are making their purchase decisions. The use of toll-free nationwide hotel reservation numbers, for example, has made the desired closeness to consumers a reality for many lodging organizations. In addition, these kinds of systems frequently lead to economies of scale in purchasing and operations. Most importantly, vertical systems that effectively employ interorganization management principles and techniques present to the public the image of a national or regional company of high standards with whom customers can deal with confidence.

Property and Casualty Insurance Services[70]

Although there are two main segments of the insurance industry—life and health insurance *and* property and casualty insurance—attention is focused here on the latter, because the channels are somewhat more complex and dramatic changes are taking place within them. Over the past thirty years, the typical fragmented pattern of marketing property and casualty insurance—the so-called American agency system—has been consistently losing ground to centrally coordinated systems—so-called direct-writing or direct-selling systems, which now control more than a quarter of the overall property and casualty market and close to half of the automobile insurance market.[71]

Under the American agency system, insurance representatives are commission-compensated "independent agents," who may and usually do represent several insurers. Independent agents sell only for insurers who are willing to permit them to retain ownership and control over policy and expiration records.[72] This means that, if an independent agent terminates his relationship with a particular insurance com-

"American Air, TWA To Offer Travel Agents Automated Systems," *Wall Street Journal,* February 2, 1976, p. 2.

[70] The discussion of property and casualty insurance services is drawn from Michael Etgar, "The Effects of Forward Vertical Integration on Service Performance of a Distributive Industry," *The Journal of Industrial Economics* (March 1978), p. 249.

[71] Etgar, *ibid.,* p. 251.

[72] Bickelhaupt, *op. cit.,* p. 128.

pany, he customarily has the legal right to retain all agency records and to receive commissions on unexpired policies with the insurer in question. The independent agent's accounts cannot be assigned to other agents, but he may sell to another agent his right to seek renewal of policies sold. The historical roots of the American agency system go back to the second half of the nineteenth century. In order to serve a widely dispersed population and, at the same time, diversify their risk portfolios, insurance companies designed a distributive system that allowed them to have representatives in many population centers.[73]

The direct writing system, on the other hand, comprises a variety of different modes of distributing property and casualty insurance. In many cases, the distributor for a direct writing company has no ownership rights in renewals and represents only one company. Compensation for the representatives of a direct writing company may be in the form of commissions, salaries with bonuses, or a combination of these methods. When commissions are paid, the representatives are usually paid reduced commissions on renewed policies. The representatives are employees of the insurance company (e.g., Allstate) and not independent contractors.

Another form of the direct writing system is found in certain companies that typically develop out of an association with farm bureau organizations. These firms are represented by exclusive representatives who are independent contractors. The most prominent insurance companies that operate this way are those that belong to the State Farm Mutual Insurance Group and the Nationwide Mutual Insurance Group. The larger exclusive agency insurers have made tremendous increases in their sales of automobile insurance in the last decade and more recently are showing substantial gains in fire, homeowners, and even life and health insurance.[74]

A few insurers solicit business directly by mail. The most prominent insurance company that operates in this manner is Government Employees Insurance Company (GEICO). Although GEICO was initially established to sell insurance to employees of the Federal government, it now sells insurance to all. The applications that are received as a result of mail promotions are handled by company employees in headquarters and branch offices.

In a sense, the three modes of direct-writing distribution represent a continuum of centralized coordination and control. On one end of the spectrum is the channel that is closest in form to the independent agency—that is, distribution of property and casualty insurance by exclusive representatives who are independent contractors. In the middle, there is the commissioned employee system, and at the far end is the mail order system. The latter two are examples of corporate vertical marketing systems.

According to Bickelhaupt, the main advantage of the direct writing system is lower cost through reduced commissions or decreased expenses due to centralization of some functions, such as policy writing, records keeping, billing, training,

[73] James L. Athearn, *General Insurance Agency Management* (Homewood, Ill.: Richard D. Irwin, 1965), p. 10.
[74] Bickelhaupt, *op. cit.*, pp. 128–129.

advertising, and sales.[75] On the other hand, the American agency system offers the advantage of having a wide variety of independent entrepreneurs who provide an assortment of options, in the form of the companies they represent, to potential consumers.

Given the threat posed by the increasing trend toward contractual and corporate direct-writing marketing systems, there has been some evidence that the American agency system has begun to incorporate some features present in the former systems. Several of the largest insurance companies using independent agents (e.g., Insurance Company of North America, Chubb Insurance Group, and Royal-Globe Group) began during the early 1970s to issue exclusive agency contracts for their regular clients.[76] In addition, billing arrangements have been routinized in a manner similar to that for direct-writing companies. On the other hand, some direct-writing insurers have granted their larger and more successful exclusive agents certain rights similar to the ownership rights that independent agents have to renewals and records. Under these agreements, the established exclusive agent, if he terminates his relationship with the insurer or retires from business, would be paid by the insurer for his book of business.[77]

In general, however, it is likely that the independent agency system is going to have to move closer to the direct-writing system (rather than vice versa) in order to remain competitive. The advantages that the latter are securing are similar to those that have been gained by vertical marketing systems in other fields.[78] There is, however, always the tradeoff between benefits of increased efficiencies in operation and the attractiveness to consumers of providing large assortments. In fact, direct-writing companies have begun to develop a wide line of "products," under different brand names, in order to serve the variety of segments in the market for insurance and thus are showing a willingness to sacrifice some of their efficiencies for even deeper market penetration.

SUMMARY AND CONCLUSIONS   In applying marketing channel concepts to the service sector, it is generally useful to adopt a broadened perspective of channel activities, because there is not always a one-to-one correspondence between the distribution of tangible products and the distribution of intangibles. Broadly conceived, distribution refers to the design, implementation, and control of institutional networks calculated to make social objects of all kinds readily *available* to the population to be served. It should be carefully noted, however, that there is often a difference between achieving availability and achieving accessiblity. While certain services may be available, they may be inaccessible because of the economic and psychic costs

---

[75] *Ibid.,* p. 129.

[76] *Ibid.,* p. 130.

[77] *Ibid.*

[78] For an empirical study of the power relationships in the channel for property and casualty insurance, see Michael Etgar, "Effects of Administrative Control on Efficiency of Vertical Marketing Systems," *Journal of Marketing Research* (February 1976), pp. 12–23; and "Channel Domination and Countervailing Power in Distributive Channels," *Journal of Marketing Research* (August 1976), pp. 254–262.

associated with obtaining them. This latter observation is especially true for many disadvantaged consumers.

Critical decisions in assuring the availability and accessibility of services are those associated with location and determining the type of "retail" outlets through which services are to be dispensed. The process involved in the creation of time and place utilities is even more important in the marketing of services than it is in the marketing of tangible products. In addition, problems in establishing marketing channels for certain services are often compounded by the need of some organizations to attract resources from groups that are different from those to whom their services are provided.

Marketing channels for services are generally very short; direct marketing (between service creator or performer and end-users) is the norm. Franchising is, however, becoming an increasingly important form of channel organization in the profit-oriented service sector.

Services are also becoming more widely dispersed and decentralized, and thus the need for interorganizational cooperation and coordination has increased. In addition, redundancies, inequities, and inefficiencies are especially prevalent in the provision of many social welfare services. These deficiencies can be reduced considerably through the application of interorganization management principles. However, for the most part, the emphasis must be placed on interorganizational coordination at the "retail" level of distribution, because many services are both produced and distributed at the local level and do not involve the kind of extensive vertical networks that are found in the marketing of tangible commodities. Services do not generally pass through the hands of intermediaries. Concentrated attention must, then, be placed on developing effective combinations of the *retailing* marketing mix elements (e.g., hours of operations, facilitating services, assortments, location and facilities, expense management, promotion, and the like).

Although there are literally hundreds of service industries to which channel concepts have been or might be applied, the bulk of this chapter has been devoted to providing only seven examples. Five of the examples have been taken from the nonprofit and publicly financed service sectors; the specific illustrations include health care services, educational services, accident prevention services, population control and family planning services, and recycling services. The remaining two—lodging services and insurance services—come from the profit-oriented service sector. Similar examples could and should be developed for other service industries as well, because the process involves a rethinking of the roles of the agencies and institutions participating in the various channels and may thereby lead to a restructuring and reappraisal of the way in which a number of services are provided.[79]

---

[79] For very useful steps along this line, see Rathmell, *op. cit.,* for discussions and descriptions of air travel, regulated industries, spectator sports, commercial banking, medical care, and business services (e.g., consulting, public accounting); and Kotler, *Marketing for Nonprofit Organizations, op. cit.,* for discussions and descriptions of health services, public services, educational services, and political candidate marketing as well as case studies on planning commissions, art museums, the U.S. Army, colleges, recreation departments, mass transit, tourism, and the model cities program, among others.

DISCUSSION QUESTIONS

1. Is it appropriate to apply interorganization management concepts developed in connection with the marketing of tangible goods to the marketing of services? What are the basic differences between the marketing of goods and the marketing of services that make a transfer of concepts difficult? What concepts from interorganization management of channels appear to be most relevant to an analysis of services?

2. What is the difference between availability and accessibility? How might a health systems manager go about making health services more available? More accessible?

3. For a religious organization (church, crusade, etc.), isolate two separate distribution systems—one dealing with resource *allocation* and the other dealing with resource *attraction*. Which interorganization management concepts, if any, appear to apply to the two systems?

4. Why is it that "the process involved in the creation of time and place utilities is even more important in the marketing of services . . . than it is for the marketing of tangible commodities"?

5. Relate the discussion in Chapter 2 relative to location decisions to the marketing of services. Which aspects of the former discussion seem to be most pertinent to the marketing of services, and which appear to be least pertinent?

6. For health care delivery systems, explain the tradeoffs between the number of available product alternatives *and* search and information costs; between spatial convenience *and* seller costs.

7. Under which of the various health system structures outlined under "Health Care Services" is the consumer likely to be better off (if there is no government payment for health insurance)? Under which will the physician be better off? Which health system is likely to be most effective, over the long run? Which most efficient?

8. Explain how interorganization concepts were operating during the curriculum reform movement of the late 1950s.

9. If you were the marketing manager for the National Safety Council, what would you do to make the channel for its defensive driving concept more effective?

10. Does one set of institutions or agencies appear to be the logical locus of channel control in the distribution of population control and family planning services? If yes, what role should this set play in the channel—in other words, how could it manage the channel more effectively to achieve the goal(s) of the channel?

11. Portray, in diagram form, the specific flows (e.g., physical possession, ownership, etc.) involved in the channels for recycling services. Which institutions or agencies within these channels are likely to participate most heavily in each of the flows?

12. Analyze the role of travel agents in the marketing channels for lodging services. How much power do they have? What are the bases of their power? What types of conflicts are they likely to be involved in? Should they assume the role of channel managers?

13.   According to a *Wall Street Journal* article of October 13, 1975, direct-writing agents of Sears Roebuck's Allstate Insurance Company have been attempting to form collective bargaining units. The movement to form such units resulted from what agents said was "an attempt by the company to alter its marketing strategy, bypassing the agent and, thereby, reducing the agent's income." Jim Barricks, an Allstate agent, has said that Allstate promised the agents that management would meet quarterly with agent representatives selected by the agents themselves to improve communications between the two groups. "Allstate had just lost sight of the fact that the agent is the mainstay of the company," according to Mr. Barricks.

Visit a number of Allstate agents in your local community and attempt to understand what the basic cause of the conflict seems to be. Then, develop a conflict management strategy for the Allstate system.

Index

AUTHOR

581

SUBJECT

587

588